TABLE OF CONTENTS

This volume contains a total of 358 pages

PREFACE

This volume completes the trilogy of my collected studies on specific themes relating to the period between the early Christian era and the eve of the Reformation. The focal point of this volume is the interrelationship between pure, mainly academic scholarship and the actuality of the political situation. The interdependence of scholarship and practical politics proved itself mutually fructifying and beneficial. Governmental measures formed the topics of lectures and books and tracts, incited academic interest and profoundly affected the development of principles. Vice-versa, as often as not the academic teachers and universities as corporations initiated and propelled certain governmental measures and in turn gave rise to political principles which were sometimes of considerable dimensions and reverberated through the subsequent ages. A case in point is the new orientation in outlook which with quite astonishing rapidity engulfed scholarship in the thirteenth century, for its Aristotelian-inspired naturalism was a well-nigh perfect *pièce justificative* for the already conspicuous naturalism in non-academic circles, pursuits and environs. The concomitant secularism and the consequential de-mundanization of a good deal that was hitherto comprehended within an ecclesiological purview, resulted in dismemberment and fragmentation of what was once considered one indivisible whole.

It was — as so often in history and especially in medieval history — the effect of challenge which acted as a driving force. Challenge of hitherto unquestioned premises and assumptions produced an ineluctable dynamic reaction in the literal meaning of the term.

On the one hand, there was the proliferation of new theses and new weapons employed which yielded a new world outlook. On the other hand, old weapons were used to combat the new themes. One such crucial new theme was the territorial sovereignty of the king. By resuscitating the ancient Roman emperor and the never obliterated Roman law, the king emerged as the properly autonomous ruler of the national State with consequences which are clearly perceptible down to this century. Unwittingly, the papal curia potently assisted by scholarship itself contributed to the dismemberment of the formerly undivided whole. The combination of personal with territorial sovereignty, paradoxically enough, opened up the avenue at the end of which stood the king as the ultimate governor of the Church within his own territory, who, moreover, could not be cited *extra territorium* before a 'foreign' court. In principle this was little more than the logical application of the idea that everyone and everything within the kingdom was subjected to the ruler. Here indeed was the concrete manifestation of the ancient Ulpian definition of the public law: *ius publicum in sacris, sacerdotibus et in magistratibus consistit.* It had stood its test in the measures of Constantine the Great and his successors down to the late fifth century when because of its deleterious effects upon the working of a Christian society Gelasius I by a dexterous manipulation of Leonine and biblical themes, made this Roman public law inoperative and inapplicable within a Christian context. In some basic respects he can be said to have been instrumental in giving Latin Europe the complexion it was eventually to assume. And as a result of scholarship this Roman *ius publicum* was very effectively revived and 'reborn' at the dawn of the modern era.

The growth of gilds, corporations and towns from the thirteenth century onwards stimulated wide-ranging discussions among the jurist scholars on the legal status of these corporate bodies and especially their delictal responsibility. This, as has been shown elsewhere, powerfully affected the subsequent constitutional complexion of the towns themselves. But it would be erroneous to think that the relationship between scholarship and politics was confined to the medieval period − in the modern age too the interpretation of the political situation in the Middle Ages was to

become an issue of heated debate that had wide, topical ramifications. The essay on the medieval empire illustrates such a
controversy.

Perhaps more so than the previous volumes the studies here
included strongly reflect my own personal penetration into the
matrix and fabric of medieval history. Its full grasp — no less than
that of modern history — presupposes a virtually constant pre-
occupation with, and immersion in, the sources. Unless one listens
to them intently, alertly, sympathetically and 'contemporaneously'
and tries to put oneself into the position of the respective author
and his intended reader, one cannot possibly get their message,
and this applies with particular force to academic writings on
jurisprudential matters. It is unfortunately true that few present-
day medievalists have much jurisprudential knowledge, and yet the
oldest and best transmitted sources belong to the juristic category.
The overriding theme of all scholarly discussion concerned the
idea of law. What indissolubly joined scholarship and politics
together was the never ending search for the right law. Over and
above this search stands the perennial problem besetting all
civilized societies — the creation of law, to use a neutral term.
For on this hinges the structure, aim and fate of the community
or the State. Who is to take part in the law-creative process?
Who is to play which part? How far did or should the principle of
co-determination extend? The fabric of the medieval historical
process was jurisprudential in its comprehensive sense — to the
connoisseur this is of course a truism, yet in view of the prevalent
unfamiliarity with jurisprudence this needs to be repeated explicitly.
The all-too-frequent concentration on, if not regurgitation of,
medieval trivia, purely peripheral or mere antiquarian points reveals
the innocent naivety of the ignoramus who, though unaware of
essential ingredients of the historical process in the Middle Ages,
certainly can no longer plead *ignorantia invincibilis*. For to read
the sources without regard to basic jurisprudential assumptions is
little more than an exercise in superficiality which is at best merely
futile and at its worst yields dangerously misleading results. In
reliability, topical earthiness, quality, contemporaneous relevance,
objectivity, the legal source material stands on a far higher level
than the narratives of chroniclers and annalists. The importance of

this vast jurisprudential reservoir also readily explains the avidity with which academic scholars seized it, interpreted it, glossed it and thereby in ample measure enriched the contemporary intellectual capacity which is far from being recognized by modern medievalists, some of whom when confronted with the relevant research display an embarrassing incomprehension that sometimes amounts to intolerance for which it is perhaps difficult to find adequate parallels. One must not forget that the oldest species of higher professional learning was (and remained for a long time) legal scholarship. The oldest universities were high-powered law schools.

Close companionship with the sources for some forty years – only partly interrupted by war service – has made it possible for me gradually to abstract a number of principles from the variegated source material of jurisprudential provenance. This kind of abstracting process is of course the ready tool for all jurists. It has potently influenced the social sciences and found a fertile soil in virtually all branches of learning which are, in the best sense of the term, interdisciplinary and integrative. Such principles or themes in actual fact obtrude themselves at every turn upon those who are alert and willing to receive the message of the sources. To name just a few, there are the principles of totality (indivisibility), unipolarity, bipolarity, division of labour, the theocratic thesis, the mediatory role, the theme of the ruler's forming an estate of his own, the concept of rebirth (both in the individual and social sense), the concession principle, the petrinological principle, the derivational principle, the functional principle, the tutorial principle, and so on and so forth. The problem of 'making' and 'giving' the law at all historic times played a crucial role – indeed, the ancient Romans expressed the difference most persuasively by the distinction between the *lex lata* and the *lex data* – because it referred to the source of authority which created the law, whence comes the ascending theme of government and law and its counterpart, the descending theme. Directly derived from the primary sources, these have proved themselves operationally useful interpretative tools and are in themselves merely classifying descriptions of lengthy thought-processes. They are convenient labels and the counterpart of the inductive and deductive methods of enquiry in other fields of intellectual pursuits, and they demonstrably show themselves fruitful in investigations which are conducted on thematic and scientific lines. But many more such axioms, themes, theses, etc. could be cited to indicate how fructifying medieval scholarship was in the service of politics.

There remains once more the agreeable duty to express my very deep gratitude to all editors and publishers for their ready permission to reprint the studies in this volume. It was, again, the flattering and gratifying encouragement of a number of most distinguished editors who spontaneously, though undeservedly, have honoured me by their generous response.

WALTER ULLMANN

Cambridge
Autumn 1977

I

The Constitutional Significance of Constantine the Great's Settlement[1]

Among the topics of Constantine's governmental measures affecting the Church there is one which has received little or no attention in modern scholarship. And yet this topic would seem at least as important as the numerous disquisitions relative to his motivations, sincerity, honesty of purpose and similar questions which have virtually suffocated modern Constantinean research. The problem which would appear to demand an exhaustive analysis, is so much conditioned by the ramifications of antecedent history as well as by the constitutional development that on this occasion I can do no more than tentatively indicate its extent and scope.

The question which obtrudes itself surely is this: by what authority did Constantine intervene in the affairs of the Christian Church, since for the greater part of his life and reign he was not formally a Christian,[2] however much he favoured Christianity and advocated its tenets, maxims and substance? By what right did he intervene in disputes and controversies which *prima facie* seemed to concern the Christian Church alone? By what title-deed did he as emperor convene synods? On what grounds can he not only successfully claim the chairmanship in what was assuredly a novelty in the empire—that is, an ecumenical synod—but also steer the synod attended as it was by several hundred bishops towards the kind of conclusion that had been his aim? After all, these governmental measures taken by an emperor were so novel that one of the most eminent modern authorities could say: 'It was altogether unheard of that a universally valid creed should be fixed merely by the authority of an emperor who

---

[1] A brief summary of this paper was read at the Seventh International Patristic Conference at Oxford on 12 September 1975.
[2] Eusebius, *Historica Ecclesiastica* (*H.E.*) x. 4. 63, i. f.; J. Vogt in *Reallexikon für Antike und Christentum* (*RAC*) iii (1957) 306 ff., at 359 f. with further literature; N. Baynes, *Constantine the Great and the Christian Church*, new ed. by H. Chadwick, Oxford 1972, 92 f. 'Nicht mehr Heide, aber noch nicht Christ' was the verdict of Th. Mommsen, *Gesammelte Schriften*, Berlin 1913, viii. 37.

was not even permitted to take part in the celebration of the Eucharist'.[1] And Eduard Schwartz goes on to say: 'Against this monstrous interference not a single bishop had dared to utter a word of disapproval or contradiction'. Numerous similar views have been expressed by lesser modern luminaries. Surely, one can hardly assume that all these bishops assembled at Nicaea were knaves so soon after the Diocletian persecutions which many of them must have experienced themselves?

I think that an analysis that promises some success must set out from the incontrovertible premiss which fully takes account of Constantine's constitutional position. He accomplished and concluded the reforms initiated by Diocletian, with the consequence that as a ruler he had absolute legislative powers, unimpeded and unhampered by any considerations of accountability for his governmental actions. After the victory over Maxentius one governmental aim of Constantine stood out clearly: revival, renewal, rebirth of the ancient splendour and glory of Rome:[2] there was to be a veritable *Renovatio Romae*. But this presupposed the co-operation of all subjects of the empire. And since all groups and sections and parts of the empire were to play a role in this gigantic task, Constantine could not be expected to side with any particular section or parties: to succeed he had to stand above all of them. Indeed, in his governmental function he assumed a curatorial or tutorial position in regard to the empire entrusted to him, as in fact his abundant legislation amply demonstrated.[3] The thread that runs through his hundreds of edicts, laws, decrees, etc., was the care for the Roman empire and its subjects. In his capacity as legislator he stood metaphorically speaking outside and above the empire: he was, so to speak, the arbiter, and the vast increase in governmental powers facilitated this imperial role. With a watchful eye he surveyed the situation and its needs in order to bring to fruition his aim, and hence the unparalleled legislative output that has an unadulterated Roman stamp.

Precisely because of his solicitude for the empire Constantine adopted a policy of toleration. That is to say, despite an undoubted predilection for Christianity and the consequential preferential treatment of

---

[1] E. Schwartz, *Kaiser Konstantin und die christliche Kirche,* Leipzig-Berlin 1913, 141 (the second edition of 1936 was not accessible to me). For a balanced assessment of Schwartz's views see H. Dörries, 'Konstantin und sein Zeitalter' in *Konstantin der Grosse,* ed. H. Kraft, Darmstadt 1974, 273 ff., at 293 n. 19 (= op. cit., below note 2, at 410 n. 1). Though useful, the bibliography of recent Constantinean literature by U. Schmidt (ibid. at 457–62) is not without inaccuracies. For additional literature see H. Chadwick, in N. Baynes, ed. cit., Preface.

[2] See the inscription on Constantine's statue: Eusebius, *Vita Constantini* (*V.C.*) i. 40; *H.E.,* ix. 11; E. Peterson, *Theologische Traktate,* Munich 1951, 88 ff.; H. Dörries, *Das Selbstzeugnis Kaiser Konstantins* (= Abhandlungen der Akademie der Wissenschaften Göttingen, philolog.-hist. Klasse, dritte Folge, no. 34, 1954), 215 f.

[3] See H. Dörries, op. cit., 16–240; special kinds of legislation at 162 ff., and 227 ff. F. Wieacker, *Vom römischen Recht,* Stuttgart 1962, remarks that imperial legislation in the early fourth century had intervened to a hitherto unknown degree 'fürsorglich und bevormundend in das tägliche Rechtsleben' (81).

Christians, he did not suppress paganism nor outlaw Judaism.[1] The basic law in regard to the Christian Church was the edict of Galerius in 311 which two years later was given sharper contours by the raising, in a formal juristic manner, of each individual church, and therefore the whole, the universal Church, to the level of a full juristic personality: this was the acknowledgement of the Church as a *corpus* in a juristic sense.[2]

The terminology of the *corpus* was sure to strike familiar chords with the Stoics and Christians alike, since the anthropomorphic and allegorical use of the *corpus* idea was highly characteristic of Pauline doctrine.[3] The Christian Church became part of the legal system of Rome and was thus far in every respect subjected to the rulings of the legislator, to wit Constantine himself. Toleration in other words meant the release of proscribed groups or congregations of people from their underground existence through their being acknowledged as corporations in the full legal sense and hence 'incorporated' into the legal order of Rome. This was a most effective measure which enabled and encouraged the Christians to take part in the public matters of the empire. In their corporate capacity the Christians became an integral element of the public order, organisation and structure, precisely because they formed legally recognised corporations.

This last consideration leads straight into the core of the topic which has received but scanty attention. Having been integrated into the public legal order by the application of the corporational principle, the Roman public law was directly applicable to them. For it is self-evident and incontrovertible that the Christian Church referred *per definitionem* to sacred things and their administration through the *sacerdotes*. The specific issues of the ancient Roman public law—to which I will turn presently—applied with singular force to the Christian Church. Now this legal-constitutional situation was quite obviously familiar to contemporary Christians, as is for example evidenced by Lactantius, who scornfully attacked the hypocrisy of those (jurists) who called themselves *iustos ac prudentes*, because they pretended to worship justice, and yet in reality were the tormentors, butchers and murderers of Christians: this passage of Lactantius—rarely noted as it is by Constantinean historians—is a commentary on the very passage which has the famous designation of jurists as *sacerdotes iustitiae* and above all contains the classic definition of the

---

[1] See J. Vogt, 'Zur Frage des christlichen Einflusses auf die Gesetzgebung Konstantins d. Gr.' in *Festschrift für Leopold Wenger*, Munich 1944, ii. 119 ff., especially 127 ff.; id., *RAC*, iii. 334. Cf. also H. Dorries, *Constantine and religious liberty*, Yale 1960.

[2] Eusebius, *H.E.*, x. 5. 2 ff.; Lactantius, *De mortibus persecutorum*, cap. 48, ed. in *CSEL*, xxvii. 228 ff.; also in C. Kirch, *Enchiridion fontium historiae ecclesiasticae antiquae*, 6th ed. by L. Ueding, Barcelona 1947, no. 352. On the importance of this see above all A. Ehrhardt, 'Das Corpus Christi und die Korporation im spätrömischen Recht' in *Zeitschr. der Savigny Stiftung für Rechtsgeschichte, Rom. Abt.*, lxx (1953) 299 ff., and ibid., lxxi (1954) 21 ff., especially 37 ff., who was the first to have fully assessed the significance of this terminology; see further id., ibid. lxxii (1955), 171 f.

[3] Cf. 1 Cor. xii. 17, 20, 27; Eph. iv. 4; Col. i. 18, 24; etc.

Roman public law.[1] There is every warrant for saying that the familiarity of the Christians with the legal situation goes a long way towards explaining the absence of any contemporary 'protest' by them against the 'intervention' by the imperial government in church matters.

Indeed, Constantine's government witnessed a most remarkable confluence of Christian monotheistic ideas and Roman-monarchic principles, and the significance of this confluence can best be assessed when seen against the backcloth of the Roman public law. Polyarchy was to yield to monarchy, just as polytheism was to give way to monotheism.[2] None of the governmental measures taken by Constantine in regard to the Christians were outside his strictly constitutional competence: they were in fact well within the framework of the Roman public law. Further, they were thoroughly conservative, in no wise different from the conservative character of his general legislation.[3] The Christians on the other hand saw in these measures the fulfilment of the very basic functions of any ruler who—they had always maintained—had received his *potestas* of government from divinity in order to bring the divine scheme of things to its fruition, a standpoint wholly shared by Constantine. Hence to express wonderment at the absence of protest by the Christians at his governmental measures, is to read history backwards.[4] His policy was alleged to have entailed an astounding reversal of the development, since his universal monarchy acknowledged the Church and thereby deprived it of its freedom in a manner which no compulsory measures could ever have achieved: it was as if the Church had been blinded and intoxicated by the

---

[1] See Lactantius, *Divinae Institutiones,* ed. *CSEL,* xix: Bk v.c. 11 f. at 436–7; further v.8, at 421, line 12. The reference to Ulpian's writings has long been noted by A. Rudorff, 'Über den Liber de officio proconsulis' in *Abhandlungen der königlichen Akademie der Wissenschaften zu Berlin,* Berlin 1866, 259 ff.; but especially by C. Ferrini in 1894: 'La cognizioni giuridiche di Lattanzio, Arnobio e Minucio Felice' in *Memorie Accademia Scienze Modena,* x (1894), 195–210, and id., 'Die juristischen Kenntnisse des Arnobius und Lactantius' in *Z.R.G., Rom. Abt.,* xv (1895), 343 ff., especially 350 ff. See C. Ferrini, *Opere,* ed. E. Albertario, Milan 1929, ii. 467 ff., and 481 ff. Cf. also F. Schulz, *History of Roman Legal Science,* new ed. Oxford 1953, 243 f., and F. Wieacker, *Textstufen klassischer Juristen* (= Abhandlungen der Akademie der Wissenschaften Göttingen, philolog.-hist. Klasse, dritte Folge, no. 45, 1960), 213. I have not seen a reference to this assuredly not unimportant point in the vast literature on the Constantinean settlement.

[2] See E. Peterson, op. cit., 45 ff., especially 87 ff.; H. Dörries, op. cit., 136, 138, 356 ff.; A. Ehrhardt, art. cit., lxxii (1955), 150. For the background see above all F. Dvornik, *Early Christian and Byzantine political philosophy,* Dumbarton Oaks 1966, 611 ff. The work of Lactantius was to set forth in the fashion of juristic Institutes the Christian theme which meant the exposition of the monotheistic ideas; see Lactantius, *Div. Inst.,* 1.1, at 4 lines 3 ff. This is rightly pointed out by H. v. Campenhausen, *The Fathers of the Latin Church,* repr. London 1972, 68, though without realising the relevance to the Constantinean settlement.

[3] H. Dörries, op. cit., no. 73, also no. 135.

[4] Cf., for instance, E. Schwartz, op. cit., 149: 'The bishops did not pay any heed to the emperor's arrogation of two rights, that is, to convoke imperial synods and to endow their decrees with legality and enforceability'. For a conspectus of similar interpretations cf. K. Baus, *Handbuch der Kirchengeschichte,* ed. H. Jedin, 3rd ed. Freiburg-Basel-Vienna 1965, i. 476 f. For penetrating observations on this topic cf. also H. Schmidinger, 'Konstantin und die "Konstantinische Ära"' in *Freiburger Zeitschrift für Philosophie und Theologie,* xvi (1969), 3 ff.

THE SIGNIFICANCE OF CONSTANTINE'S SETTLEMENT

imperial favours and had failed to realise the immense price it had to pay for the rise in its status.[1]

A proper assessment of the manipulation of the Roman public law must begin with the law-creative power of the emperor: imperial legislation was now from Constantine onwards 'die einzige Entstehungsquelle des Rechts'.[2] And in thus legislating Constantine not only showed himself conservative, but was also aware of the need to preserve historic continuity.[3] The role of public law can best be understood in the present context by recalling the definition given by Ulpian in the late second century: *'Publicum ius est, quod ad statum rei Romanae spectat . . . Publicum ius in sacris, in sacerdotibus, in magistratibus consistit'.*[4] Public law, in a word, is that law which concerns the Roman commonwealth and focuses attention upon its interests. Public law refers to the structure and constitution of the empire. Public law in essence is the legal manifestation of the concept of public interest—*utilitas publica*.[5] It is evident that by the early fourth century this Roman public law assumed wide connotations and had come to embrace all matters concerned with religion, its cult and practice as well as the personnel who administered religion, the *sacerdotes*, their organisation, function, position and activities. The judiciary or magistracy formed the third pillar of this Roman public law. There can be no doubt whatsoever that Constantine's legislation in regard to the Christians came wholly within the precincts of this ancient Roman public law, and was *ius publicum* writ large. Each and everyone of his respective governmental measures and enactments can be subsumed under the heading of the *ius publicum*. Differently expressed, it was in the public interest that measures were taken to liberate the Christians and to regulate matters relating to them. The public law enabled Constantine to integrate the Christian body into the empire and to allocate to it a decisive role in the task of the empire's revival. There is warrant for saying that the

[1] E. Schwartz, op. cit., loc. cit.
[2] L. Wenger, *Die Quellen des römischen Rechts*, Vienna 1953, 531; H. Siber, *Römisches Verfassungsrecht in geschichtlicher Entwicklung*, Lahr 1962, 382; see also id., *Römisches Recht*, Darmstadt 1968, 63 f.; W. Kunkel, *Introduction to Roman legal and constitutional history*, 2nd ed., English transl. by J. N. Kelly, Oxford 1973, 137 ff. See also A. Alföldi, *The conversion of Constantine and pagan Rome*, repr. Oxford 1970, 11 f., 56 f., 69 f.; A. Heuss, *Römische Geschichte*, 2nd ed. Braunsberg 1964, 443 ff. See also H. Kraft, *Kaiser Konstantins religiöse Entwicklung*, Tübingen 1955, 11 ff.
[3] For this see H. Dörries op. cit., especially nos. 83, 84, 103 = Codex Theodosianus (C. Th.) xv. 14. 1–3, with the significant insistence on the *ius vetus*.
[4] Ulpian in *Dig.*, 1. 1. 1. 2. About the truncated text in *Inst.*, I. 1. 4, see F. Wieacker, *Textstufen*, 206 n. 135, and 213. Cf. Gaius, *Inst.*, II. 2. For Ulpian see W. Kunkel, *Herkunft und soziale Stellung der römischen Juristen*, 2nd ed., Cologne-Graz 1967, 245 ff. and for the literature concerning this noted passage see M. Kaser, *Das römische Privatrecht*, 2nd ed. Munich 1971, i. 197 n. 34, and ii (1959), 38.
[5] Cf. A. Berger, 'L'operis novi nuntiatio e il concetto di ius publicum' in *Iura*, i (1950), 102 ff., at 111: 'Ulpiano senza dubbio avrebbe potuto dire simplicemente "ius publicum est quod ad utilitatem rei Romanae spectat" '. How far Constantine's church foundations moved within the precincts of the *status rei Romanae* has been most meritoriously shown by L. Voelkl, *Die Kirchenstiftungen des Kaisers Konstantin im Lichte des römischen Sakralrechts* (= Arbeitsgemeinschaft für Forschung des Landes Nordrhein-Westfalen, fasc. 117 (1964)), 9 ff.; here also an analysis of the wide meaning of the term *sacrum*.

Roman public law appeared as if it had been fashioned for Constantine's religious and ecclesiastical legislation.

It was the historic realisation of Constantine that the empire's rebirth could be mightily assisted if the latent talents of the Christians were harnessed to this task. For, during the recent persecutions, they had shown strength of character, resilience, conviction and steadfastness, but what may well have counted more with him was their intellectual programme: they had a cosmology, they had a theme and a plan which they alleged had divine origin. On the other hand, the Roman pagans had very little in this respect that could be of use in the reconstruction of the empire. The Christian scheme of things had an intellectual and rational substance that in contemporary conditions was attractive and appealed to a ruler of Constantine's calibre. And here the monotheistic theme of Christianity was of quite especial significance. Monotheism in different shapes, but notably in that of the *sol invictus*, had made great strides by this time and indubitably facilitated the acceptance of Christian monotheism which saw in Christ the *sol iustitiae*.[1] What, however, distinguished this Christian monotheism was that it could look back on a respectable body of literature which in depth, width and breadth by far surpassed anything that could be found in the corresponding pagan religious literature. Above all, this Christian literature had scope and range of universal, of 'catholic' dimensions, a feature of some considerable importance at that time. Its themes fell on fertile soil.

Obviously, Roman public law stood in intimate connexion with the role of the emperor as *pontifex maximus*. Significantly enough, this role had been assumed by Augustus in about 12 B.C.[2] and remained the designation of the emperors: Constantine used it[3] and so did his successors right down to Gratian in 379.[4] In the following generation the function became sometimes attached to the imperial title.[5] Considering,

---

[1] A. Ehrhardt, art. cit., 150; J. Vogt in *RAC*, cit., 335–6; K. Latte, *Römische Religionsgeschichte*, Munich 1960, 353, 359. In a different context the intellectual superiority of the churchmen is touched upon by A. Momigliano, 'Christianity and the decline of the Roman empire' in *The conflict between paganism and Christianity in the fourth century*, ed. A. Momigliano, Oxford 1963, 1 ff. at 9 ff.

[2] See *Res gestae divi Augusti*, ed. P. A. Brunt and J. M. Moore, Oxford 1967, vii. 3; x. 2, and xi, at 20, 22, 49 f., 52 f. See also E. Weber, *Augustus: meine Taten: res gestae divi Augusti nach dem Monumentum Ancyranum*, Munich 1970, 64, 68 f.

[3] See H. Dörries, op. cit., 217, 219, 220 (all from inscriptions). Cf. also the edict concerning military privileges (of 311) in which the title is 'pontifex maximus' in *Fontes iuris Romani anteiustiniani*, ed. S. Riccobono, Florence 1941, 456.

[4] For this see A. Alföldi, 'A festival of Isis in Rome under the Christian emperors of the fourth century' in *Dissertationes Pannonicae*, series iii, fasc. 8, Budapest 1937, 36 ff. (early 379); here also the proof that the characteristic *vota publica*—the vows for good health and success of the emperor which appeared on all fourth-century coins—disappeared at exactly the same time. For the *vota* cf. additional numismatic evidence by P. Bruun, 'The Christian signs on the coins of Constantine' in *Arctos: Acta Philologica Fennica*, new series, iii (1962) 1 ff., at 10 ff.

[5] W. Ullmann, *The Growth of Papal Government in the Middle Ages*, 3rd–4th ed. London 1970, 24 n.1, with some instances.

THE SIGNIFICANCE OF CONSTANTINE'S SETTLEMENT

therefore, his role as a *pontifex maximus* one can effortlessly understand why and how the Roman public law was considered directly applicable to his legislation in regard to Christians: this legislation would be difficult to explain on any other grounds. The two departments of the public law—the *sacra* and the *sacerdotes*—were so to speak the channels through which Constantine's Christian legislation passed. And by virtue of the monarchic government, the administration, interpretation, the application, modification and, if necessary, creation of public law lay exclusively in the hands of the emperor himself. It was all very Roman in the contemporary sense.

Even the most perfunctory glance at the legislative measures of Constantine will bear out the importance of public law for the understanding of what is commonly called his religious policy.[1] To begin with, the very acknowledgement of the individual churches as *corpora* within the law made it possible for them to receive benefactions, bequests, donations, to sue and be sued, and so forth. It was also on this basis that restitution of confiscated property appeared feasible, and not primarily to individual Christians, but to the whole *corpus* as such.[2] Over and above this legal aspect stands the special consideration which he consistently gave to the observation of the *publica iura*.[3] It was legislation which in the best Roman sense demonstrated the care and solicitude of the ruler for the subjects under his control and entrusted to him by divinity.[4] In the preamble to the declaration (the so-called Edict) of Milan of 313 the very term of the *securitas publica* is strikingly significant, revealing as it does the close link with the by then traditional Roman axioms.[5] Not until Justinian can an emperor be shown to have displayed that regard for the *forma publici iuris observanda* (*est*) as Constantine did[6] or for the *publica disciplina*.[7] What, therefore, deserves special emphasis in the present context is his care for the *salus hominum*,[8] and for the attainment of this *salus* the *lex christiana* was

---

[1] Here one must express some reservations about the viewpoint of F. Dvornik, op. cit., 637: 'It was the definition of Hellenistic royal competence that legally entitled him (Constantine) to interfere (scil. in Church affairs)'. The essential point is not, as far as Constantine is concerned. Hellenistic kingship, but the application of the readily available and universally understood Roman public law which was virtually tailored to suit his ecclesiastical legislation and designs.

[2] *H.E.*, x. 5. 15–17. Here, as pointed out by A. Ehrhardt, art. cit., 171 f., the corporational emphasis should be particularly noted. See further *C.Th.* XVI. 2. 4: legacies to be left to the corporate Church. Later in the Eastern provinces however individuals benefited from various relief measures: *V.C.*, ii. 24 ff., especially 30 f.

[3] Cf. *C. Th.*, I. 2. 2: 'Quod enim publica iura perscribunt, magis sequi iudices debent'.

[4] H. v. Soden, *Urkunden zur Entstehungsgeschichte des Donatismus* (in Hans Lietzmann, Kleine Texte für Vorlesungen und Übungen, no. 122) no. 14, line 70. On this letter cf. H. Kraft, op. cit., 172 ff.

[5] The *securitas Augusti* became the *securitas populi Romani* in the reigns of Galba and Otho, to emerge as *securitas publica* on the coins; see H. U. Instinsky, *Sicherheit als politisches Problem des römischen Kaisertums*, Baden-Baden 1952, 25 f., and Table 2.

[6] *C. Th.*, XII. 1. 2.

[7] *C. Justin.*, I. 40. 2.

[8] *C. Th.*, IX. 16. 3.

to be binding even in civil matters:[1] every litigant could invoke the episcopal court, the decision of which was inappellable.[2]

These premisses make it comprehensible why the (Christian) *sacerdotes* received special attention. They were given public status in regard to certain functions exercised by them. Thus their exemption from public duties, the reason being that acceptance of magistracies and public offices involved great financial burdens for the individuals concerned and, as Constantine stressed, the performance of public duties might gravely interfere with the clerics' observation of their own law. Therefore those 'who give their services to this holy religion and are commonly called clergymen, be entirely exempted from all public duties, so that they may not be taken away from the service of divinity, but may devote themselves unimpededly to their proper laws' and he concludes that by allowing the clerics to devote themselves to their vocation, 'the greatest benefits will accrue to the empire'.[3] Here, in fact, one can witness the combination of all three departments of the Roman public law: the magistracy, sacral matters and their administrators. The privileges and reliefs bear out that each and every element of public law was involved, and not merely individually but all three indissolubly linked with each other. Similar privileges had already been enjoyed by pagan priests in regard to their public duties.[4] The conferment of judicial powers on clerics in connexion with manumissions of slaves was particularly important: if released from slavery within a church by a cleric this had exactly the same effect as any ordinary manumission.[5] The churches founded by Constantine were consequently designated as *basilicae* which were public buildings.[6] It really would seem impossible to overlook in these instances the combination of the three elements constituting public law.

One can go further and say that in a very specific sense the *sacra* as conceived within the framework of the public law in the early fourth century included the external observance of the faith by the appropriate cult, rituals, ceremonies, in other words, such outward manifestations which incontrovertibly indicated harmony, concord and unity of the faith symbolically or externally expressed. It is not, therefore, without interest that in the earliest intervention of Constantine—in the Donatist troubles—he shows his anxiety very markedly about the *observantia sanctissimae legis catholicae*, a term which occurs no fewer than three times in the relevant instructions[7] and which assumes still greater significance when linked with the *debitus cultus sanctissimae religionis*.[8] The attainment of the (external)

---

[1] *C. Th.*, I. 27. 1.

[2] For some observations on this cf. J. Vogt, *Festschrift Wenger*, cit., 124.

[3] *H.E.*, x. 7. For a critical analysis of the privileges see C. Dupont, 'Les privilèges des clercs sous Constantin' in *Revue d'histoire ecclésiastique*, lxii (1967), 729–52.

[4] See also. Vogt, art. cit., 127.

[5] *C. Th.*, IV. 7. 1.

[6] See for this L. Voelkl, op. cit., 29 ff.

[7] Soden, *Urkunden*, cit., no. 14.

[8] Ibid., lines 4, 32, 35, 65, 74 f. Cf. further no. 33, lines 2 f.: 'observatores catholicae legis' = *C. Th.*, XVI. 5. 1.

observance of the law common to the whole Church was one of the main concerns of Constantine as a monarchic ruler. And the designation of an addressee (Aelafius; Ablabius?) as *Dei summi cultor* fits perfectly into this scheme of things: a Christian is a *cultor Dei*[1] who shows 'meritàm omnipotenti Deo *culturam*.'[2] Since there are evidently many other Constantinean instances of the *sacra* being invoked in this sense, these sources are in need of detailed scrutiny in regard to this feature.

Only from the point of view of public law is the convocation by an emperor who is no Christian in any formal sense, comprehensible. His presidency of a council, organisation, participation, confirmation of its decrees and conferment of legal, that is, enforceable character on them is accessible to understanding only from the standpoint of the Roman public law which manipulated (as it now was) by an absolute ruler, considers him as the custodian, the guardian, the curator or conservator of the *status rei Romanae*. To act in the interests of this *status* is the ruler's foremost duty, and especially when this so recently liberated body of Christians exhibited a degree of dissension that threatened the very programme which Constantine pursued. That he had recourse to the purely ecclesiastical institution of the synod in order to restore unity, concord and harmony of the Christian body public, shows his alertness as well as his adaptability. It should be borne in mind that the synod as a special assembly had been operative in Rome certainly since the end of the second century under pope Victor I. The model might well have been the council of the apostles.[3] In any case the synod was a properly convened assembly that was to decide in a collective or corporate capacity controversial issues of fact or of doctrine.[4] Down to the late fourth century the synod was the supreme, inappellable organ that, because inspired by the Holy Ghost, finally laid controversies to rest.

It was the employment of the instrument of the synod which can be reckoned by all accounts a real master stroke on the part of Constantine—and entirely within the framework of the public law. In order to prevent an infectious germ that already had caused dissension from spreading, Constantine realized the potentialities which the approach by an African Christian body to him presented. He asked the pope, Miltiades, to enquire together with other bishops, into the pending

---

[1] See, for example, Lactantius, *Div. Inst.*, v. 11, at 436, line 13. Cf. Kraft, op. cit., 54, 183.
[2] Soden, *Urkunden*, no. 23, line 45.
[3] Acts xv.
[4] The subject of the early synods, their development, structure, organisation, etc., is still far too little explored. For some general remarks cf. G. Lardone, 'Il diritto romano e i concilii' in *Acta congressus iuridici internationalis*, Rome 1934, ii. 101–2; W. Plöchl, *Geschichte des Kirchenrechts*, Vienna 1953, i. 55 f.; H. E. Feine, *Kirchliche Rechtsgeschichte*, 5th ed. Cologne-Graz 1973, 53 f. Tertullian is said to have been the first to use the term *concilium*, see his *De ieiunio*, 13, ed. *CSEL*, xx. 292: 'Aguntur preterea in certis locis *concilia* ex universis ecclesiis . . . et ipsa *representatio* totius ńominis christiani magna veneratione celebretur'. Dionysius of Alexandria (ob. 265) is alleged to have first employed the term *synodos*. There is ample literature for the post-Constantinean period relative to councils. For the term 'synod' see most recently A. Lumpe, 'Zur Geschichte des Wortes σύνοδος in der antiken christlichen Gräzität' in *Annuarium Historiae Conciliorum*, vi (1974), 40–53, esp. 43 f.

questions, because, he said, he could not out of reverence for the Church tolerate σχίσμα ἢ διχοστασίαν ἔν τινι τόπῳ.[1] When the desired result was not achieved in October 313 and appeal was made to him, he himself now ordered that a synod take place at Arles on 1 August 314.[2] And he was ever more anxious to obtain concord; even the imperial transport system was to be made available to the participants of this synod.[3] The specific significance of this measure of Constantine was that the eventual decision was formally to be taken by the ecclesiastics and, therefore, be synodal, although it was Constantine's will alone which brought the synod into existence and sustained it. The very fact that so soon after the liberation he was formally appealed to, and this on a point the core of which was indisputably dogmatic, reflects the Christian view that this issue came within the ambit of the public law of which the emperor was the supreme guardian. The conflict was seen to be his direct concern and he was considered the sole organ able to resolve the difficulties and to restore unity within a disunited body. The significance of this acknowledgement lies in the Christians' practical affirmation of the Pauline doctrine and resultant Christian theories that 'nulla potestas nisi a Deo'; this had, indeed, long been expressed also in liturgy as well as in doxology including the prayer *Pro salute imperatoris*.[4] What all this amounted to was the concrete assertion that here matters of such public concern were at stake which, since they were comprehended in public law, could only be effectively dealt with by the emperor. It was a most remarkable consonance of imperial and Christian viewpoints.

Arles was such a success that it served Constantine as a model ten years later when he was able to go very much further. Statesmanship means maturity of reflexion and the realistic assessment of a situation. Con-

---

[1] *H.E.*, x. 5; Soden, *Urkunden*, no. 12, line 29. There is no mention of this in the *Liber Pontificalis* in the entry of Miltiades. Whether the meeting was to be a tribunal or a synod is really a terminological question. According to B. Lohse, 'Kaiser und Papst im Donatistenstreit' in *Ecclesia und Respublica*, ed. B. Kretschmar and B. Lohse (= *Festgabe für K. D. Schmidt*), Göttingen 1961, 75 ff., at 78: 'nicht eine Synode, sondern ein Gericht'. But cf. Eusebius himself, loc. cit. For an attractive juristic interpretation of this procedure, see H. U. Instinsky, *Bischofstuhl und Kaiserthron*, Munich 1955, 59 ff. For the need to preserve peace in North Africa, the main source of corn supply, see A. Ehrhardt, loc. cit., and W. H. C. Frend, *The Donatist Church*, 2nd ed. Oxford 1971, 66 ff., 145 ff.

[2] *H.E.*, x. 5. 21 ff.; Soden, *Urkunden*, no. 15, line 44: ἐκελεύσαμεν. The decrees of the synod are in C. H. Turner, *Ecclesiae Occidentalis Monumenta Iuris Antiquissimi*, Oxford 1939, i. 381 ff. It is misleading to say that 'Vers la fin de l'année 313 il (Constantin) fut investi évêque des affaires internes': J. M. Petritakis, 'Interventions dynamiques de l'empereur de Byzance dans les affaires ecclésiastiques' in *Byzantina*, iii (1971), 141. About the letter written by the Arles synodists to the pope, see I. Mazzini, 'Lettera del concilio di Arles (314) a papa Silvestro tradita dal Codex Paris. Lat. 1711' in *Vigiliae Christianae*, xxvii (1973), 282–300.

[3] Soden, *Urkunden*, no. 14 to Aelafius (Ablabius?).

[4] It was only from this standpoint understandable that in 272 Antioch petitioned Aurelian in his function as ruler whose *power* was derived from divinity (cf. *H.E.*, vii. 30. 28). How much more reason was there now to approach, petition and appeal to the emperor, since every individual church constituted a licit *corpus* and as such was integrated into the Roman legal framework, the guardian of which the emperor was. About Aurelian and Antioch cf. H. Kraft, 'Kaiser Konstantin und das Bischofsamt' in *Saeculum*, viii (1957), 32 f.

THE SIGNIFICANCE OF CONSTANTINE'S SETTLEMENT

vocation, chairmanship, organisation, management of the proceedings at Nicaea was in imperial hands, and the decrees displayed legal validity only after he had conferred it on them and published them. Again, in a purely formal sense it was the ecclesiastical assembly which reached the fateful compromise formula and decided other points, such as the date of Easter, and so on, but materially it was the emperor's will that turned these decisions into law. And it was his management that steered the synodists towards that compromise which suited his governmental scheme. It is understandable, therefore, why the emperor did not take part in the voting[1]—the decisions had to appear to be ecclesiastical verdicts which re-emerged as a proper law solely through the *voluntas principis*. Again, it is profitable to realise why to the participants this appeared to be the correct way of going about the matter. Leaving aside less pressing issues, here was a serious problem—the Arian question—which profoundly affected the unity and harmony of the Christian body, itself now an integral element of the empire. Yet the restoration of unity within the empire could be expected from the emperor alone as the custodian of the public law. It is this consideration which not only makes understandable the co-operation of the synodists, but also why the respective decree was drafted in the imperial chancery to be executed by imperial officers the majority of whom were not Christian.[2] To see in these (and other) Constantinean legislative and governmental measures the beginning of Eastern Caesaropapism (as is frequently enough asserted) is wholly erroneous.[3] By turning the Christian Church into a body public which was clearly the most effective way of securing its liberation, Constantine integrated it into the legal framework of the empire. Thereby Christian *sacra* and *sacerdotes* necessarily became issues of the Roman public law. All the legislative potentialities of Constantine were therefore fully deployed, acting as he did in the curatorial or tutorial role of the ruler, the very role which made it possible for him to intervene in a perfectly legitimate manner in ecclesiastical matters. If ever there was a traditional Roman constitutionalist, it was Constantine: he used old bottles for new wine, and the prophetic expression was also to become true—the new wine was to burst the bottles and the bottles were to perish.

It is his function as the administrator, moderator and creator of public law in the Roman sense which may also be the clue to the understanding

---

[1] According to F. Dvornik, op. cit., 641, Constantine by not voting preserved constitutional propriety, because the emperor had no right to vote in the senate. 'This was the Senators' privilege only ... saved in principle even under the most autocratic emperors ... there is no trace in the accounts of the Council of Constantine voting with the bishops'. For the pre-Constantinean Eastern sources of the term ὁμοούσιος see A. Ehrhardt, *Politische Metaphysik von Solon bis Augustin*, Tübingen 1959, ii. 269 n. 5.

[2] Cf. A. Alföldi, op. cit., 76; also L. Voelkl, *Der Kaiser Konstantin: Annalen einer Zeitenwende*, Munich 1957, 143.

[3] For some perceptive observations thrown against a wide background see S. Mazzarino, 'Politologisches bei Jacob Burckhardt' in *Saeculum*, xxii (1971), 25 ff. (comparing the historian Burckhardt with the jurist Mommsen). Cf. also S. L. Greenslade, *Church and State from Constantine to Theodosius*, London 1954, 16, 20.

of the much debated expression he used in addressing himself to bishops at an informal gathering.[1] According to Eusebius, Constantine, when entertaining bishops, let it be known that he too was a bishop: he appeared to draw a distinction between their and his function as 'overseer' (or bishop). They were overseers τῶν εἴσω τῆς ἐκκλησίας, whereas he was the overseer τῶν ἐκτός.[2] The former referred to matters internal to the Church, such as dogmatic or doctrinal issues, and the latter concerned the external apparel, such as cult, ritual, ceremonies, which in substance manifested doctrine or dogma. If one adequately assesses the legal framework within which Constantine operated, it would seem that there are no insuperable difficulties in explaining his views. To him the term ἐπίσκοπος meant overseer, supervisor, one who watches over the interests of others and takes care of them. Indeed, ἐπίσκοπος meant not only a controller, but also guardian and not at all surprisingly a *tutor*.[3] It was in exactly the same sense that he considered himself as the divinely appointed monarchic guardian or tutor—a function not at all confined to the Christians, though expressed in terms easily comprehensible to them[4]—so that his control of external matters relating to the Church was understandable without much effort. This function brought into clear relief the view that as far as the Church was concerned, its organisation, machinery, administration, no less than the external ritual and cult, in brief the kind of *public* workship which reflects a commonly agreed doctrine and demonstrates unity and inner coherence of the body of believers in an external way, was of immediate interest to him as the guardian and pivot of the matters touching the *status rei Romanae*. After all, cult, ritual, ceremonial were at all times taken as vehicles to express an idea, doctrine, opinion by easily understood external, visible means. The instrument by which the (external) unity of the empire was to be achieved lay at hand: the (public) law which furthered the *utilitas publica*.

In this context it might be pointed out that acting as ἐπίσκοπος τῶν ἐκτός Constantine decreed Sunday as a regular weekly day of rest: clearly the fixation of a day as the *dies solis* was something without precedent in

---

[1] *V. C.*, iv. 24.

[2] The most trenchant and searching examination of this old problem is by J. Straub, 'Kaiser Konstantin als ἐπίσκοπος τῶν ἐκτός in his *Regeneratio Imperii*, Darmstadt 1972, 119 ff. Cf. also H. Kraft, op. cit., 105 f.; A. H. M. Jones, *Constantine and the conversion of Europe*, Harmondsworth 1972, 194 ff. As it will become evident, our conclusions are not in complete agreement with theirs which is now largely accepted, according to which the term meant 'bishop for *those who* are outside the Church'. For a penetrating criticism of this view see F. Vittinghoff, 'Eusebius als Verfasser der V.C.' in *Rheinisches Museum für Philologie*, new series, xcvi (1953), 330 ff. at 356 ff., whose own conclusion also seems rather unsatisfactory: Constantine appeared as 'a divinely appointed bishop for *those matters which* are outside the Church' (369) (my italics).

[3] Cf., for example, H. Liddell-R. Scott, *A Greek-English Lexicon*, repr. Oxford 1968, s.v., at 657, with relevant examples.

[4] The reference is to the κοινὸς ἐπίσκοπος as reported in *V. C.*, iv. 8; cf. also Soden, *Urkunden*, no. 23, lines 20 ff. For the whole question see J. Straub, 'Konstantin als κοινὸς ἐπίσκοπος' in op. cit., 134 ff., esp. 151 f. Are there any lines of communication with the Ciceronian terms of the *communis patria* or the *communis pater*, or even with *pater patrum*?

antiquity.[1] This was a purely external matter for which no previous 'internal' decision by bishops was necessary and which he as monarchic guardian of the *status rei Romanae* was able to decree on his own. This applies also to his legislation concerning clerical exemptions from public duties and the conferment of jurisdictional powers upon bishops. On the other hand, he refused to decide the purely dogmatic issues raised by the Donatists and declared 'meum iudicium postulant qui ipse iudicium Christi expecto!' only to continue by saying that 'it was the truth that the judgment of the priests should be respected as if the Lord Himself had given it'.[2] Similarly, because doctrines such as those propagated by Arius, were 'internal' matters, they were within the competence of the Nicaean synodists who excommunicated him, but in order to neutralise effectively the spread of Arian heresies, the imperial law had to step in. In a word, matters of doctrinal substance were 'internal'; matters of cult, organisation, administration, were 'external'.

The skill of Constantine lay in that having steered the synodists in the desired direction, he made them decide doctrinal issues, the very issues concerned with faith,[3] but within the orbit of the *status rei Romanae* doctrine alone was clearly insufficient: it was the law that preserved this *status*, and since *sacra* and *sacerdotes* were conspicuously involved, it was evidently only the public law that enabled Constantine to display all his legislative competence, which indeed in this respect amounted to omnipotence. The Roman public law with its tripartite division began a new lease of life and was the means by which the emperor's curatorial or tutorial or indeed 'episcopal' role could be realised. Whether or not Christ was 'like the Father' or 'identical with the Father'—these were for him purely 'internal' matters with which the bishops were to concern themselves and clearly a subject reserved to them. Constantine never claimed to be and never was a theologian: this severe theological problem was for him 'ein Buch mit sieben Siegeln'.[4] His religious ideas were essentially primitive and his understanding of Christianity was far from being clear.[5] What he was, was at

[1] See A. Piganiol, *L'empereur Constantin*, Paris 1932, 128 f.; J. Vogt in *RAC*, cit., 337; A. Ehrhardt, art. cit., 181 f.; H. Dörries, op. cit., 322 who also stresses that this was an issue of the cult. See especially on the point H. Chadwick, *The Early Church*, Harmondsworth 1968, 128 f. The enactment is in *C. Th.*, ii. 8. 1.

[2] Soden, *Urkunden*, no. 18, lines 39 ff.: '... Dico enim, ut se veritas habet, sacerdotum iudicium ita se debet haberi, ac si Dominus ipse residens iudicet'.

[3] Cf. *V.C.*, iii. 17, Constantine writing to the churches after Nicaea: 'I have judged it ought to be the first object of my efforts that unity of *faith*, sincerity of love and a community of feeling in regard to the *worship* of God' should predominate, and in the Council 'every question received fullest examination ... so that no room was left for further discussion or controversies in regard to the *faith*'. H. Kraft, op. cit., 224, takes for granted that this was a *Diktat* of the emperor, though he supplies no evidence for this statement.

[4] A. Heuss, op. cit., 457.

[5] A. Alföldi, op. cit., 20; H. Chadwick, op. cit., 125. About his reported reversion to the pagan ruler cult in Constantinople in 330, cf. J. Karayannopulos, 'Konstantin und der Kaiserkult' in *Historia*, v (1956), 341 ff., where the various views are neatly assembled (at 342–4); see further F. Winkelmann, 'Zur Geschichte der V.C.' in *Klio*, xl (1962), 187 ff., at 234 ff; and C. Ligota, 'Constantiniana' in *Journ. of the Warburg and Courtauld Institutes*, xxvi (1963) 178 ff. at 185. According to H. Kraft, op. cit., 153, Constantine considered himself in relation to the Church 'not a learner, but a teacher'.

all times a monarch who perceived his mission in the *Renovatio Romae* and to this task the Christians were to be harnessed. His success in steering the synodists towards a compromise formula only goes to show the realisation on their part that a 'solution' of the theological controversy was in the interests of the empire as well as of the Church. This was merely another aspect of the consonance of viewpoints already mentioned. The very fact that a compromise was reached in so delicate and difficult a matter—which assuredly did not admit of a 'compromise' as the subsequent history all too clearly proved—would indicate that the formula reflected governmental as well as ecclesiastical exigencies which required that points of conflicts and dissensions were seen to have been eliminated. The formula 'was to be an eirenicon, and not a source of further disagreements.'[1] He himself was neither equipped nor capable of grasping the real character of the dispute, and the same observation also seems to be applicable to the bishops, the bulk of whom were obviously lost in the intricacies of the debates.[2] That the ecclesiastical organisation of the Church fixed by the synodists at Nicaea was in essential points an adaptation of the imperial administrative system, is one more proof of the 'streamlining' operation conducted by Constantine as ἐπίσκοπος τῶν ἐκτός.[3]

The curatorial or tutorial function of the emperor abundantly demonstrated in his legislation, permits of the historically only justifiable conclusion that Constantine's government was firmly embedded in the Roman tradition and constitution of which the *ius publicum* was an integral part. 'Constantine lived and thought as a Roman. He was formed by Roman law'.[4] It was precisely this conjunction of the Roman constitution with the new Christian ideas which yielded an entirely new situation. The communication by Constantine to the Alexandrian community in June 325 strikes tones which may well mark the symbiosis of *Romanitas* and *Christianitas*. The former conveyed the idea that his government continued Roman imperial traditions: it is a historical element that stands in the foreground; it is historicity which showed itself most palpably in the emperor's law-creative capacity guarding the interests of the *status rei Romanae*. By subsuming the Christian *sacra* and *sacerdotes* under the umbrella of the *ius publicum, Christianitas* became inextricably woven into the fabric of the Roman constitution.

The classical Roman conception of the *ius publicum* was the instrument that created the symbiosis of *Romanitas* and *Christianitas*, as is clearly

---

[1] N. Baynes in *Cambridge Ancient History*, xii (1939), at 697.

[2] Cf. E. Schwartz, op. cit., 141 f.: 'die Mehrzahl der Synodalen nach dem Urteil eines Zeitgenossen von der theologischen Kontroverse nichts verstand'. Cf. also H. Berkhof, *Kirche und Kaiser: eine Untersuchung der byzantinischen und theokratischen Staatsauffassung im 4. Jahrhundert* (German transl. of the Dutch original) Zürich 1947, 93: everyone accepted the formula of the *Homoousios* 'obwohl niemand etwas damit anzufangen wusste'.

[3] L. Voelkl, op. cit., 142, referred in this context to a *Gleichschaltung*.

[4] Id., *Kirchenstiftungen*, 64. Cf. also H. Schmidinger, art. cit., 7.

THE SIGNIFICANCE OF CONSTANTINE'S SETTLEMENT

evidenced by the letters despatched immediately after Nicaea, such as the general epistle to which we have already invited attention. But in the just-mentioned communication to Alexandria he makes furthermore plain that the Council of Nicaea, the convening of which was inspired by God (*nutu Dei*, as the Latin translation has it), declared the divine will. For what 300 and more bishops have determined with amazing sagacity is nothing elase but a judgment of God (τοῦ Θεοῦ γνώμη = *Dei sententia*), notably as the Holy Ghost had entered the minds of so many and such highly qualified men and had made known the divine will (τὴν Θείαν βούλησιν).There is now one God and therefore one common body, schism and dissensions having been removed.[1] And another enactment shows that the divine protection of the Christians works through the mediation of the emperor—a more convincing expression of the descending theme of government within the symbiosis of *Romanitas* and *Christianitas* is hardly possible, even leaving aside the mediatory role assumed by the emperor himself.[2] There can be no doubt that a pronouncedly developed historical sense pervaded Constantine's legislation.[3] This constitutional aspect of his measures allows Constantinean historiography to be defused and the emotional, moralising but historically irrelevant assessments to be discarded, their place being taken by strictly legal and rational considerations. These, however, abundantly prove that it is misleading to ascribe to Constantine sacerdotal or quasi-sacerdotal functions, however much the ethos in the East might have suggested this ascription, for which there is no evidence in the reign of Constantine, the ruler of the late Roman stamp for whom the *ius* was still the norm and guide of his governmental actions.

It is the symbiosis of *Romanitas* and *Christianitas* which begins to set its seal upon the development in the Eastern half of the empire. This symbiosis was to sustain the Byzantine empire in the following millenium. It was a symbiosis which was not Caesaropapism or Byzantinism as it is so often erroneously labelled, because it had its deep and strong roots in the historico-legal soil: the *Romanitas*, loudly and persistently proclaimed as the focal point of all Byzantine governmental measures, was little else but the emphatic insistence on continuing the Roman imperial constitution, and no other part of this constitution was more important than the *ius publicum* of ancient and distinguished parentage. The core of the Byzan-

---

[1] H.-G. Opitz (ed.), *Urkunden zur Geschichte des arianischen Streites* (= *Athanasius Werke,* iii, 1), Berlin 1935, no. 25.
[2] See the *Constitutio* in H. Dörries, no. 138, who comments: 'Eigenartig, aber Konstantin zuzutrauen ist der Gedanke, dass der Christ durch Gott geschützt werden wird, aber unter Vermittlung der Staatsordnung ...'. I' do not think that there is anything 'peculiar' in this: the curatorial function of the ruler in connexion with the manipulation of the public law could hardly lead to any other view, especially when the full implications of the descending theme of government are taken into account.
[3] Rightly pointed out by H. Dörries, at no. 103: *C. Th.,* xv. 14. 1 and 2. See also ibid., xv 14. 3: 'Quae tyrannus contra ius rescribsit non valere praecipimus...'.

tine government was that it absorbed *Christianitas* effortlessly into the historically conditioned constitutional law.[1]

Yet exactly the same two notions of *Romanitas* and *Christianitas* also came to be current in the West when in the Frankish age Europe came to assume its own identity and complexion, though here an entirely different connotation was attached to them. In the medieval West *Romanitas* was—in contrast to the East—not historically but pre-eminently ecclesiologically understood. Because the West received its *Christianitas* overwhelmingly, if not exclusively, from the *ecclesia Romana*, there emerged a fusion of *Romanitas* and *Christianitas*: a Christian was a Roman, as the sources (legal, liturgical, doxological, etc.) down to the fourteenth century make abundantly clear. In the foreground in the West stood faith, religion, *Christianitas*, which indeed in many fundamental respects shaped, if it did not create, the history of Western Europe in the Middle Ages. In the East, in Constantinople, it was history and the historical continuity of the empire which was the focal point: the constitution of the empire provided a living space for *Christianitas*. The role played by history in the East was replaced in the West by faith. In the East it was *Romanitas* that primarily mattered, whereas in the West it was *Christianitas*. In the East 'Rome' and 'Roman' were historical notions, hence New Rome as a historical continuation of (Old) Rome, and the emperor, the αὐτοκράτωρ and vice-gerent of the παμβασιλεὺς καὶ παντο-κράτωρ, a successor of the Roman emperors calling himself βασιλεὺς τῶν 'Ρωμαίων, whose coronation by the patriarch was merely declaratory. In the West 'Rome' and 'Roman' were ecclesiological notions—hence the strong ecclesiological substance of the Western *Imperator Romanorum* whose coronation by his creator, the *pontifex Romanus*, was constitutive—and these notions had in themselves nothing to do with history. And in the different meanings of these notions of *Romanitas* and *Christianitas* lie some of the basic differences between Constantinople and Rome, between East and West in the Middle Ages—differences which at least partly were the bequest of Constantine the Great.[2]

[1] The question so frequently asked why in the East the Church permitted the far-reaching interventions by the government, is based on a faulty premiss. Cf., for instance, H. Berkhof, op. cit., 83, asking how the Church could tolerate becoming a 'Dienerin des Staates'. This was Byzantinism which meant 'die unkritische, gehorsame und segnende Haltung', that characterised the Church in Byzantium. The present sketch has attempted an explanation of the situation on legal-historical grounds. That later there was opposition to the scheme, however much historically explicable, has been shown by H.-G. Beck, 'Vom Staatsdenken der Byzantiner' in *Sitzungsberichte der Bayrischen Akademie*, phil.-hist. Klasse, 1970, fasc. 2, 36–8.

[2] Cf. W. Ullmann, *A Short History of the Papacy in the Middle Ages*, 2nd ed. London 1974, 23 f., 32, 85, 155, 330. It is an urgent task to subject Constantine's official and unofficial declarations to a rigorous analysis in regard to subject-matter, style, semantics, syntax, in order to trace the paternity of the ideas put forward. To say, as it is so often asserted, that he himself composed his edicts, etc. (i.e. were his own *Diktat*), is unrealistic, if not naive. The dissection of the numerous religious strains in his laws is necessary if only to discover their provenance in antecedent Christian literature. The personal composition of his chancery should long have been the object of research. A. Ehrhardt, art. cit., *Z.R.G., Rom. Abt.* lxxii (1955), 154 f., was one of the first who was aware of these needs. A detailed examination might profitably begin with an investigation of the small number of select *notarii* with whom Constantine surrounded himself, see for this F. Dölger, *Byzantinische Urkundenlehre*, Munich 1968, 59.

II

ÜBER DIE RECHTLICHE BEDEUTUNG DER SPÄTRÖMISCHEN KAISERTITULATUR FÜR DAS PAPSTTUM

Obgleich die ehrende Einladung zur Beteiligung an der Willibald Plöchl gewidmeten Festschrift mich erst zu später Stunde erreichte, will ich dennoch nicht versäumen, meinen Tribut dem verdienten Bannerträger der österreichischen Kirchenrechtswissenschaft in der Form eines Kurzbeitrags zu zollen. Ich darf bloß hoffen, daß er diese kleine Skizze als ein Zeichen aufrichtiger kollegialer Wertschätzung entgegennehmen wird. In Willibald Plöchl ehren wir den bewunderungswürdigen Vollstrecker und zielbewußten Vollender des von Rudolf Köstler erstrebten Werkes. Mit seiner glanzvollen Leistung hat er sich um die österreichische Kirchenrechtswissenschaft bleibende Verdienste erworben. Sein großartiges Schaffen und Wirken bekundet von neuem die lebendige Kraft der österreichischen Kanonistik.

In seinem Abschnitt „Das Kirchenrecht im römischen Rechts- und Kulturkreis", worüber der Jubilar im ersten Band seiner grundlegenden *Geschichte des Kirchenrechts* handelt, kommt er aus verständlichen Gründen auf die spätrömische Kaisertitulatur und die darin sich äußernde kaiserliche Funktion zu sprechen. Wie bekannt, hatte sich Gelasius in einem seiner Traktate mit dieser Frage beschäftigt, indem er ausführte, daß es seit Christus keinen Herrscher gegeben hätte, der sich *Pontifex* genannt hätte, denn Christus allein sei der wahre *Rex* und *Pontifex* gewesen[1]. Dreierlei ist zu beachten. Erstens: noch bis Gratian hatten sich die Kaiser als *Pontifices maximi* bezeichnet. Wie der Jubilar mit Recht sagt, lehnte Gratian „für sich die mit dem Kaisertum verbundene Würde eines Pontifex maximus ab"[2]. Gratians Ablehnung

---

[1] Gelasius, Tractatus IV, c. 2, hg. in A. Thiel, Epistulae Romanorum Pontificum Genuinae, Braunsberg 1868, 567f., und in Ed. Schwartz, Publizistische Sammlungen zum acacianischen Schisma, in: Abhandlungen der Bayrischen Akademie der Wissenschaften, Phil.-Hist. Abt., n. F., Heft 10 (1934) 7ff., hier 14, Z. 5ff. Die Stelle ist auch in H. Rahner, Kirche und Staat im frühen Christentum. München 1962, 262ff. (lateinischer und deutscher Text); C. Mirbt, Quellen zur Geschichte des Papsttums und des römischen Katholizismus, 6. Aufl. hg. K. Aland, Tübingen 1967, 223f.; W. Ullmann, Growth of papal government in the Middle Ages⁴. London 1970, 25 A. 1. Gratian (Dist. 96, c. 6) entnahm die Stelle vorangegangenen Kirchenrechtssammlungen.

[2] A. Alföldi, A festival of Isis in Rome under the Christian emperors of the fourth century, in: Dissertationes Pannonicae, 3. Serie, Heft 8, Budapest 1937, 36f., hat auf breitem Hintergrund die Frage geklärt. Das von A. Cameron, Gratian's repudiation

steht offenbar in Zusammenhang mit dem von ihm und seinem Mitkaiser Theodosius d. Gr. erlassenen Edikt, demgemäß die christliche Religion als die allein legitime Religion im Reich gelten sollte[3]. Schon aus diesem Grunde allein konnte sich ein christlicher Kaiser nicht mehr *Pontifex maximus* nennen: für die Funktion eines „Obersten Priesters" hatte ganz gewiß der Zeitgenosse eines Ambrosius keine Eignung. Diese Überlegung führt zum zweiten Punkt, der das Wesen und hiermit die Terminologie eines *Pontifex* in Verbindung mit einem christlichen Herrschertum betrifft und auch noch genauerer Untersuchung bedarf, denn auch hier stellt sich die Gesetzgebung von Theodosius und Gratian als eine tiefe Caesur dar, weil die petrinische Lehre vom *regale sacerdotium*[4] in gerade diesem Zusammenhang nicht außer Betracht bleiben darf. Dieser Lehre gemäß kommt ein „königliches Priestertum" allen Christen zu. Und in der Tat kommt Gelasius in genau diesem Kontext und in genau derselben Stelle (was viel zu wenig von der Forschung beachtet worden ist) auf die petrinische Äußerung zurück. Die Vermutung liegt daher sehr nahe, daß diese Lehre die Gedankenführung des Papsttums und insbesondere des Gelasius beeinflußt hatte. Um das Problem aber abzurunden, ist drittens zu beobachten, daß sich die Kaiser in eben diesem Jahrhundert und zur gleichen Zeit, als Gelasius darüber schrieb, zwar nicht *Pontifex maximus* nannten, wohl aber hin und wieder den Titel eines *Pontifex inclytus* beilegten[5]. Man kann wohl kaum annehmen, daß Gelasius diese Titulatur, von der wir sogleich das eine oder andere Beispiel geben werden, unbekannt geblieben war. Wie aber ist dann seine Aussage zu erklären? Liegt hier ein krasser Widerspruch vor? So weit mir bekannt, hat diese ganz offenbare Problematik weder die Geschichts- noch die Kirchenrechtswissenschaft beschäftigt.

Das Problem verdichtet sich noch, wenn man bedenkt, daß derselbe Gelasius in den Diensten seiner Vorgänger, der Päpste Simplicius und Felix III., stand und der geistige Urheber, wenn nicht sogar der Verfasser (Dictator) einer Anzahl von wichtigen päpstlichen Schreiben war[6]. Um nur eines heraus-

---

of the pontifical robe, in: Journal of Roman Studies 58 (1968) 96ff. vorgeschlagene Jahr der Ablehnung des Titels (383 anstatt 379, worüber vgl. schon die Literatur zitiert bei Alföldi, A. 44) bedarf doch noch genauerer Untersuchung und neuer Beweisstücke, um zu überzeugen.

[3] In dem gemeinsamen Erlaß der Kaiser *(Cunctos populos)*, der im Cod. Theod., XVI. 1.2 und Cod. Just. I. 1.1 ist.

[4] Siehe I Pet. 2. 9: βασίλειον ἱεράτευμα = *regale sacerdotium*. Darüber vgl. J. Blinzler Hierateuma, in: Episcopus. Festschrift für Kardinal Michael Faulhaber. München 1949, 58—62; und H. Schelkle, Die Petrusbriefe, in: Herders Theologischer Kommentar, XIII. 2, Freiburg-Basel-Wien 1961, 64ff. (hier auch weitere Literatur).

[5] Darauf habe ich schon kurz hingewiesen in op. cit. (A. 1), 24, A. 1.

[6] Dazu vgl. H. Koch, Gelasius im kirchenpolitischen Dienst seiner Vorgänger Simplicius und Felix III., in: Sitzungsberichte der Bayrischen Akademie der Wissenschaften, Phil.-Hist. Kl., Heft 6 (1935); N. Ertl, Dictatoren frühmittelalterlicher Papstbriefe, in: Archiv f. Urkundenforschung 15 (1937), hier 61—66.

zugreifen, preist im Jahre 479 Simplicius Kaiser Zeno als den Verteidiger des Glaubens und gibt seiner Genugtuung Ausdruck über die kaiserliche Intervention in Antiocheia:

Venerandos mihi semper vestrae pietatis apices gavisus accepi, quibus ingenito vobis studio catholicae religionis post *defensionem fidei*, quae vos servata custodit ... exultantes vobis inesse *animum* fidelissimi *sacerdotis* et *principis*, ut imperialis auctoritas iuncta christianae devotioni acceptabilior Deo fieret ... [7]

Es kann vernünftigerweise kein Zweifel darüber bestehen, daß der Papst hier dem Kaiser einen „animus sacerdotis" sowie „principis" zuschrieb. In der Tat kann man diese Zuschreibung auch bei Leo I. lesen, der von seinem kaiserlichen Zeitgenossen Leon I. behauptet, er hätte „non solum regiam set et sacerdotalem mentem"[8]. Diese leicht zu vermehrenden Beispiele mögen gegenwärtig genügen, um das Problem voll erfassen zu können. Auf der einen Seite steht die kräftige gelasianische Behauptung, daß kein Kaiser pontifikale Gewalt beansprucht hätte, und auf der anderen Seite unterstreicht die päpstliche Kanzlei die priesterliche Gesinnung des Kaisers.

Die dem Kaiser zugeschriebene Funktion läßt sich zum Teil aus seiner amtlichen Intitulation, zum Teil aus Anreden und zum Teil aus amtlichen Schreiben deutlich erkennen. In ihrem gemeinsamen Edikt, das Ausführungsbestimmungen des Konzils von Chalcedon enthielt und im Jahre 452 erlassen wurde, trugen Valentinian III. und Marcian die folgende Titulatur:

Imperatores Caesares Flavius Valentinianus *pontifex inclitus* Germanicus inclitus Alamannicus inclitus ... et Flavius Marcianus *pontifex inclitus* Germanicus inclitus Sarmaticus inclitus Alamannicus inclitus Francicus inclitus ... [9]

Das Konzil selbst wurde eröffnet

secundum praeceptionem sacratissimi et piissimi domini nostri Marciani ... [10]

---

[7] Collectio Avellana, nr. 66, hg. in: Corpus scriptorum ecclesiasticorum latinorum (CSEL) 35.147, Z. 3—9: 22. Juni 479.

[8] Leo I. an Theodosius II. (18. Februar 449) in Ed. Schwartz, Acta Conciliorum Oecumenicorum (ACO). Berlin 1932, II. 4 (Leonis Papae I epistularum collectiones) nr. 2, S. 3 (= J. P. Migne, Patrologia Latina 54, Ep. 24), Z. 13ff.: „... litteris, quas ad me misistis, ostenditur, ut vobis non solum regium, sed etiam sacerdotalem inesse animum gaudeamus". Im Brief des Papstes Simplicius an den Kaiser Zeno sprach Gelasius (vgl. oben A. 6) von dem Kaiser als *fidei imitator* (Avellana nr. 60, S. 137, Z. 8f.). In der noch immer vorbildlichen Studie von O. Treitinger, Die oströmische Kaiser- und Reichsidee (Nachdruck Darmstadt 1956) hat sich der Verfasser etwas vergriffen, als er schrieb (S. 125 A. O), daß solche und ähnliche Ausdrücke bloße Phrasen gewesen wären, die den Kaiser beeinflussen sollten, und mit denen die päpstliche Kanzlei spielte. Diese Ausdrücke sind biblischer Herkunft.

[9] ACO II. 3, S. 346, Z. 38. Eine frühere und ähnliche Intitulation ist möglicherweise in jener Aussage enthalten, die Servius am Anfang des 5. Jahrhunderts machte, indem er erklärte: „Hodieque imperatores *pontifices* dicimus", zit. nach A. Cameron, art. cit. (oben A. 2), S. 101, der freilich nicht zwischen *pontifex* und *pontifex maximus* zu unterscheiden scheint. Ein Teil des Ediktes der beiden Kaiser ist im Cod. Just. I. 1. 4.

[10] ACO II. 3, S. 27, Z. 7.

In seinem Schreiben an den römischen Senat vom 28. Juli 516 lautet der Amtstitel des Kaisers Anastasius I. wie folgt:

Imperator Caesar Flavius Anastasius *pontifex inclitus* Germanicus inclitus Alamannicus inclitus Francicus inclitus ...[11]

Amtliche Schreiben sowie Ergebenheitsadressen von Bischöfen, Synodalen und anderen lassen keinen Zweifel aufkommen an der dem Kaiser zugedachten Funktion eines *Pontifex.* Darüber hinaus schrieb z. B. der Bischof Sebastian an den Kaiser Leon I. bald nach dem Konzil von Chalcedon unter gleichzeitiger Hervorhebung der kaiserlichen allumfassenden monarchischen Herrschaftsmacht:

Post Deum domino totius orbis piissimo et christianissimo nostro principi Leoni in Domino salutem ...[12]

Auch der skytische Bischof Theotinus äußert sich in der gleichen Weise, indem er den Kaiser Leon I. mit *sacratissime et venerabilis imperator* apostrophiert, wie es eben auch schon sein Amtsgenosse Sebastian getan hatte[13].

Im modernen Schrifttum hat dieses Problem wenig Widerhall gefunden. So hat z. B. Wilhelm Ensslin in seiner überaus verdienstvollen Studie über Gottkaiser und Kaiser von Gottes Gnaden nirgends, wie es scheinen möchte, dieses zentrale Problem berührt[14]. Weder Otto Treitinger noch Franz Dölger haben sich mit der Frage der Kaisertitulatur beschäftigt[15]. Louis Bréhier hat in schürfenden Untersuchungen zwar den Kaisertitel untersucht, setzte aber seine Forschungen erst viel später an[16]. Auch in seiner wertvollen Byzantini-

---

[11] Avellana nr. 113, S. 506. Nach C. Capizzi, L'imperatore Anastasio I (491—518) (= Orientalia Christiana Analecta 184 [1969]), S. 242, soll diese Intitulation eine „sopravvivenza pagana esplicite" sein.

[12] ACO II. 5, nr. 17, S. 30.

[13] Ebda, nr. 18, S. 31; auch nr. 17, S. 30 Z. 16 usw. „A Deo coronato", nr. 23, S. 40 Z. 8.

[14] W. Ensslin, in Sitzungsberichte der Bayrischen Akademie d. Wissenschaften, Phil.-Hist. Abt., Heft 6 (1943). Neudruck in: Das byzantinische Herrscherbild, hrsg. v. H. Hunger (Wege der Foschung CCCXLI, Darmstadt 1975) S. 54—85. Vgl. Ensslin, Der Kaiser in der Spätantike, in: Hist. Z. 177 (1954) 449ff.,, wo er den Kaisertitel nicht erwähnt und auch keine Verfassungsfragen berührt. K. Voigt, Staat und Kirche von Konstantin d. Gr. bis zum Ende der Karolingerzeit. Stuttgart 1936, 76 A. 11 kommt nicht an die Problematik heran und weiß mit der von ihm zitierten Akklamation (unten A. 32) nichts anzufangen. Sie wird auch erwähnt von A. Michel, Die Kaisermacht in der Ostkirche. Darmstadt 1959, 5, der sie nicht erklärt und den Päpsten vorwirft, sie hätten sich in der Sprache „vergriffen" (A. 30, 31), wo er den petrinischen Gehalt der Papstaussagen nicht erkannte (oben bei und in A. 8).

[15] O. Treitinger, op. cit. (oben A. 8). F. Dölger, Byzantinische Diplomatik. Ettal 1956, 130—51, behandelt eine spätere Zeit.

[16] L. Bréhier, L'origine des titres impériaux à Byzance, in: Byzantinische Z. 15 (1906) 161ff. Auch seine Skizze ΙΕΡΕΥΣ ΚΑΙ ΒΑΣΙΛΕΥΣ, in: Archives de l'orient chrétien 1 (1948) (= Mémorial Louis Petit), S. 41ff. setzt zu spät ein. P. Batiffol, L'église et les survivances du culte impérial (Paris 1920) ging auf diese Eigenheiten nicht ein. J. Deininger, Von der Republik zur Monarchie: Die Ursprünge der Herrschertitulatur des Prinzipats, in: Aufstieg und Niedergang der römischen Welt, hg. H. Tempo-

schen Urkundenlehre kam der umsichtige und hellhörige Verfasser auf dieses
Problem nicht zu sprechen[17]. Nichtsdestoweniger ist aber mit Sicherheit anzunehmen, daß hier — wie auch sonst bei der Abfassung von Urkunden[18] — auf
die Titulatur viel Gedankenarbeit verwendet wurde. Und genau dasselbe läßt
sich wohl von den zahlreichen Ergebenheitsadressen und amtlichen Schreiben
aussagen. Titel usw. sind wichtigste Erkenntnismittel, die dem Forscher Einblick gewähren in lange, komplizierte und verwickelte Denkprozesse, und in
kurzschriftlicher Form Aufschluß geben über Herrschaftsgrundsätze und
deshalb ganz besonders für die Staatslehre von Bedeutung sind. Daß sie
das Ergebnis vieler und grundlegender Überlegungen waren, kann füglich
nicht bezweifelt werden. Titel und „Formeln" sind zweckdienliche und -ent-
sprechende sprachlich gedrängte und erklärende Feststellungen, die klar,
einfach und unzweideutig herrschaftliche Grundsätze verkünden[19].

    Überblickt man die Quellen und die für den Kaiser gemünzten Titulaturen,
dann scheint sich um die Mitte des 5. Jahrhunderts ein zeitweiliger und zeit-
bedingter Wandel vollzogen zu haben, der in engem Zusammenhang mit den
die Primatialrechte des Papsttums berührenden Fragen steht. Diese Fragen
waren, wie allseits bekannt, besonders aktuell zur Zeit des Konzils von Chalcedon. Bei der Auseinandersetzung um diesen Problemkreis ging es hart auf
hart. Nichts steht der Annahme entgegen, daß z. B. die Wiederaufnahme des
Pontifex-Titels durch die kaiserliche Kanzlei (wenngleich auch ohne den
Maximus-Zusatz) das Wesen und die Funktion des Kaisers eindeutig zum
Ausdruck bringen sollte. Die Erinnerung an den *Pontifex maximus* war ganz
gewiß noch lebendig, freilich war dessen Wesen und Funktion unmöglich auf
den christlichen Kaiser anwendbar.

    Strukturell hatte sich jedoch an der Funktion und rechtlichen Stellung des
Kaisers innerhalb der Ökumene sehr wenig geändert — im Gegenteil, die
kaiserliche Verfügung, daß das Christentum die römische Staatsreligion werden
sollte, die Verlagerung der das Reich tragenden ideellen und religiösen Kräfte
von der heidnischen auf die christliche Ebene, das Bekenntnis der Kaiser
selbst zum Christentum einerseits, und die innerhalb der Christenheit bald
in Erscheinung tretende Zerrissenheit und Zerklüftung, die zahlreichen dogmatischen Streitigkeiten, die die erwünschte Einheit des Reiches nicht nur
nicht herbeiführten, sondern das Reichsgefüge sogar ernstlich bedrohten

rini, I. 1 (1972) 982ff. reicht nur bis Augustus, und D. Mannsperger, ebda, Die Selbst-
darstellung des Kaisertums in der römischen Reichsprägung, II. 1 (1974) 919—89, reicht
nur bis Konstantin.

    [17] F. Dölger, Byzantinische Urkundenlehre. München 1968.

    [18] Dieser Punkt wird von H. Fichtenau mit Recht stark betont: Arenga, Spät-
antike und Mittelalter im Spiegel von Urkundenformeln (MIÖG Erg. Bd. XVIII [1957]).

    [19] Auf den heuristischen Wert der Urkundensprache versuchte ich hinzuweisen in:
The Church & the Law in the early Middle Ages (Collected Studies I: London 1975)
Kap. XIX. Vgl. noch The future of medieval history. Cambridge 1973, 15f.

andererseits, ermöglichte nicht nur die kaiserliche Machtentfaltung im Interesse der römisch-christlichen Ökumene, sondern forderte sie geradezu heraus, um die Einheit, den Zusammenhalt und die Unversehrtheit dieser Ökumene herzustellen und zu gewährleisten. Und hier wird die Brücke vom spätrömischen Kaisertum zum alten noch wesentlich republikanischen Verfassungsrecht sichtbar. Die durch die religiösen Wirren in Gefahr gebrachte Einheit des Reiches rief nach fester Führung und Intervention, die verfassungsmäßig ausschließlich beim Kaiser lag. Die auf republikanischen Grundlagen ruhende kaiserliche Stellung innerhalb des Verfassungsrechts ließ sich unschwer für die Rettung der Reichseinheit dienstbar machen. Die klassische römische Jurisprudenz hatte klar die Funktion des öffentlichen Rechts erfaßt und seit der Dominatszeit, insbesondere der spätrömischen Kaiserzeit lag dessen Schöpfung, Anwendung, Änderung und Aufhebung ausschließlich in den Händen des Kaisers. Nach der klassischen Definition Ulpians umfaßte das öffentliche Recht aber alles, was den *Status rei Romanae* anging, und im einzelnen erstreckte sich das öffentliche Recht auf die *Sacra*, die *Sacerdotes* und die Magistratur[20]. Hier sei daran erinnert, daß das römische öffentliche Recht die Grundlage für Konstantins d. Gr. Religionspolitik und für die durch sie ausgelösten Maßnahmen bildete[21]. Die Anwendung des öffentlichen Rechts durch Konstantin wurde auch ohne Einschränkung von den kirchlicherseits Berufenen voll anerkannt[22].

Die eben erwähnten innerkirchlichen Querelen und religiösen Streitigkeiten, die das Gefüge des Reichs erschütterten und es auch in seinem friedlichen Bestand bedrohten, drängten, wie erwähnt, auf die Anwendung der im öffentlichen Recht verankerten und griffbereiten kaiserlichen Befugnisse, um dem

---

[20] Dig. 1. 1. 1. 2. Dazu M. Kaser, Zur Methodologie der römischen Rechtsquellenforschung, in: Sitzungsberichte der österreichischen Akademie der Wissenschaften, Phil.-Hist. Kl. 227 (1972), bes. S. 44 A. 75 und S. 56; vgl. ders., Römisches Privatrecht, II². München 1975, 53 A. 7. Siehe ferner G. Crifò, Ulpiano, in: Aufstieg (oben A. 16) II. 15 (1976) S. 708—89. Besonders beachtenswert ist seine Ansicht vom Princeps, der die „cura et tutela reipublicae universa" innehat, s. unten bei A. 33. . . . Siehe im allgemeinen noch G. Dulckeit - F. Schwartz, Römische Rechtsgeschichte, 6. Aufl. bearb. W. Waldstein, München 1975, 258ff.

[21] Vgl. W. Ullmann, The constitutional significance of Constantine's settlement, in: Journal of Ecclesiastical History 27 (1976) 1ff.

[22] Vgl. art. cit. (vorige A.) S. 4. Es war gerade dieses Mittel, das die Christen veranlaßte, Konstantins Politik wärmstens anzuerkennen, denn auch nach der stets vertretenen christlichen Lehre stammte die Herrschergewalt auch des heidnischen Kaisers von Gott (unter Berufung auf Röm. 13. 1ff.), was aber nicht die *divinitas* des Kaisers selbst miteinschloß. Daraus erklären sich die Verfolgungen und der gegen die Christen erhobene Vorwurf des Atheismus, s. A. Harnack, Der Vorwurf des Atheismus in den ersten drei Jahrhunderten, in: Texte und Untersuchungen zur Gesch. der altchristl. Lit. 28 (1905) Heft 4; Th. Mommsen, Römisches Strafrecht. Leipzig 1899, 575ff.; W. Ullmann, Law and Politics in the Middle Ages. London 1975, 35f.

Reich die notwendig gewordene Ordnung und Ruhe auf geistigem und religiösem Gebiet zu geben. Die von Caspar einmal so treffend genannte ,,Politik der Zwangsunion"[23] war juristisch gesehen die praktische Verwirklichung der im alten römischen öffentlichen Recht verwurzelten Pflichten und Befugnisse: die Verfestigung der öffentlichen Ordnung im römischen Gemeinwesen und die Herstellung der Eintracht, eben weil es um den *Status rei Romanae* ging. Und nur aus dieser Sicht läßt sich erklären, wie und warum die Kaiser, beginnend mit Konstantin (der nicht einmal Christ war, oder wie Mommsen es einmal ausdrückte: ,,nicht mehr Heide, aber noch nicht Christ"[24]), allgemeine Konzilien einzuberufen sich für berechtigt hielten[25], sie leiteten und deren Dekreten Rechtskraft verliehen und auch sonstige Verwaltungsmaßnahmen innerhalb der kirchlichen Organisation ergriffen, wie etwa Ernennung oder Bestätigung der Wahl von kirchlichen Amtsträgern, Übertragung weitgehender Amtshandlungen an Geistliche, vornehmlich Bischöfe, etwa Fürsorge- und Armenwesen, auch Aufsicht über Gefängnisse usw. Kurzum, die Faktizität des religiösen und kirchlichen Lebens im 5. Jahrhundert gab dem Kaiser die Möglichkeit, die im öffentlichen Recht ruhende Vollgewalt zum Besten des Reichs auszunützen.

Stellt man nun in Rechnung, daß insbesondere seit dem Pontifikat des Damasus und Innozenz das Papsttum seine Rechte innerhalb des kirchlichen Gemeinwesens anmeldete und ihnen mit steigender Beharrlichkeit kräftigen Ausdruck verlieh, begann sich am nicht zu fernen Horizont eine erhebliche Verschiedenheit der Denkvoraussetzungen im kaiserlichen und päpstlichen Lager abzuzeichnen. Die vom Papsttum angemeldeten Rechte leiteten sich mitnichten aus menschlichen Rechtssatzungen, Verfügungen und Anordnungen ab, sondern, wie die Päpste im 5. Jahrhundert schärfstens betonten, gingen ausschließlich auf göttliche Verheißung zurück. Menschliche Satzung stand göttlicher Anordnung gegenüber. Sowohl die kaiserliche als auch die päpstliche Seite wollte ihre Befugnisse in adäquater Weise zur Darstellung bringen und begründen. Das Kaisertum berief sich auf das überkommene, alte römische öffentliche Recht — das Papsttum auf göttliche Verordnung, denn nach Matt. 16. 18f. gründete Christus *uno ictu* eine Gesellschaft und die Herrschaftsform, die in dieser Gesellschaft, der Kirche, obwalten sollte. Anders ausgedrückt, das Kaisertum berief sich auf eine geschichtlich unanfechtbare Verfassungsgrundlage, die ihm breit genug erschien, auch christliche Bereiche

---

[23] E. Caspar, Geschichte des Papsttums, I (Tübingen 1930) S. 167ff.

[24] Th. Mommsen, Gesammelte Schriften VIII (1913) S. 37.

[25] Vgl. J. Hefele - H. Leclercq, Histoire des conciles, I. Paris 1907, 14ff.; J. Gaudemet, L'église dans l'empire romain. Paris 1958, 461f.; T.-P. Camelot, Les conciles oecumeniques du IV et V siècles, in: Le concile et les conciles, hg. B. Botte et al. (Paris 1960) S. 49f.; vgl. noch A. M. Ritter, Das Konzil von Konstantinopel und sein Symbol. Göttingen 1965, 232f., 236.

miteinzubeziehen, und kurzschriftlich in dem rehabilitierten *Pontifex* ausgedrückt war. Das Papsttum stützte sich auf den *Principatus Romanae ecclesiae*, der seinerseits in verkürzter, aber zeitgenössisch prägnanter Form herausstellte, daß die Lenkung der (neuen) Gesellschaft, der Kirche, dem Papst als Nachfolger Petri und daher, wie Leo d. Gr. klassisch dargelegt hatte, als dessen „unwürdigen Erben" *(indignus haeres*[26]*)* anvertraut war. Es standen sich hier geschichtlich gewordenes Recht und ein auf Glauben gegründetes Recht gegenüber[27].

Von diesem Gesichtswinkel aus betrachtet, ist die Titulatur des Kaisers als *Pontifex* verständlich. Es gibt zu bedenken, daß weder Gelasius noch seine Vorgänger Protest eingelegt hatten gegen des Kaisers Einberufung von Konzilien oder gegen die Leitung derselben durch kaiserlich bestellte Kommissionen oder gegen die Bestätigung der Konzilsschlüsse, gegen kaiserliche Maßnahmen, die die Tagesordnung bei den Konzilien regelten, die die Vertagung der Sitzungen zum Gegenstand hatten usw. Auch hatten sich weder Gelasius als Dictator der amtlichen Schreiben von Simplicius und Felix noch deren Vorgänger gegen die Verwendung des *Pontifex*-Titels der Kaiser gewandt. Die Möglichkeit, daß dessen Verwendung den Päpsten unbekannt geblieben war, ist so gut wie auszuschließen, insbesondere bei Gelasius, der so lange in päpstlichen Diensten gestanden hatte und ständig mit der kaiserlichen Kanzlei in Verbindung war. Man wird in der Annahme nicht fehlgehen, daß Titulatur und kaiserliche Maßnahmen auf kirchlichem Gebiete, einschließlich der Konzilsberufungen, Ernennungen usw., aus ein und derselben Quelle entstammten, und diese war das öffentliche Recht altrömischer Prägung. Dieses allein erklärt auch die immer wieder von den Kaisern hervorgekehrte Schützerrolle gegenüber der Kirche. Es sei betont, daß sich die Sprache der kaiserlichen und päpstlichen Kanzlei rücksichtlich der Funktion des Kaisers als Hüters, Bewahrers und Verteidigers des Glaubens und der Kirche so ähnelten, daß kaiserliche und päpstliche Äußerungen leicht auswechselbar waren. Eines der vornehmsten Hauptanliegen der Kaiser im 5. Jahrhundert war die Erhaltung des unverfälschten Glaubens und der rechten Ordnung, worin sich seine Funktion im Sinne des öffentlichen Rechts als Wahrers der das Reich betreffenden Interessen ganz vorzüglich ausdrückte[28]. War doch

---

[26] Siehe W. Ullmann, op. cit. (oben A. 19), Kap. IV. Über die Bedeutung des *Principatus Romanae ecclesiae* in gerade diesem Zusammenhang vgl. die noch immer klassische Darstellung bei P. Batiffol, *Cathedra Petri:* Études d'histoire ancienne de l'église. Paris 1938, 83ff. Daß sich vor dem Renaissance-Zeitalter kein Papst *Pontifex maximus* nannte, wurde nachgewiesen von R. Schieffer, Der Papst als Pontifex Maximus, in: Zeitschrift der Savigny-Stiftung f. Rechtsgesch., Kan. Abt. 68 (1971) 300ff.

[27] Über diese gegensätzliche Fundierung des Rechts vgl. W. Ullmann, A short history of the papacy in the Middle Ages². London 1974, 17f., 23, 31f., 66, 85, 330.

[28] Vgl. etwa Leo d. Gr. an Kaiser Leon I. (1. Dezember 457), ACO II. 4, nr. 96, S. 102 bis 103 Z. 1 (= Patr. Lat. 54, Ep. 154): der Kaiser solle beachten (da er durch Gott so

der Kaiser von Gott berufen zu herrschen *in fidei defensione*, wie sich Leo d. Gr. in einem hochoffiziellen Schreiben an den Kaiser ausließ, womit der Herrschaft eines christlichen Kaisers — hier auch mit *pietas vestra* apostrophiert — ihre besondere Note erhalten sollte[29]. Aus päpstlicher Sicht war der Kaiser *defensor fidei*, eben weil ihm die oberste Gewalt von Gott — das *praesidium ecclesiae*[30] — überantwortet worden war: die ideelle Grundlage der (römischen) Welt war aber der christliche Glaube. Die Ableitung der kaiserlichen Schutzpflicht aus dem weitgerahmten öffentlichen Recht liegt so klar zu Tage, daß sich jede weitere Ausführung erübrigt[31]. Der Kaiser war der *custos fidei*, wie ihn die in Ephesus und Chalcedon versammelten Bischöfe akklamierten[32].

In der Bezeichnung des Kaisers als *Pontifex inclitus* kann man nicht umhin, die Funktion des konstantinischen ἐπίσκοπος τῶν ἐκτός wiederzuerkennen. Diese Funktion erschöpfte sich in den schon erwähnten Maßnahmen der spätrömischen Kaiser. Sie alle betrafen die *Externa* der Verwaltung. Soweit die Kirche und die Religion in Frage kamen, war der Kaiser das Organ, dem die Obhut der äußeren Struktur und Ordnung der Kirche anvertraut worden war. Die sogenannten *Interna* gingen ihn nichts an: Dogma, Doktrin, Auslegung der Bibel, Festlegung von Glaubenssätzen u. dgl. waren nicht in der Funktion eines ἐπίσκοπος τῶν ἐκτός inbegriffen[33]. Recht und Pflicht des

---

viel Erleuchtung über die Mysterien erhalten habe), daß ihm nicht nur die Gewalt über die Welt, sondern und vor allem der Schutz über die Kirche obliegt: „... debes incunctanter advertere regiam potestatem tibi non solum mundi regimen, sed maxime ad *ecclesiae praesidium* esse collatam." In demselben Sinne auch ACO II. 4, nr. 103, S. 110 Z. 27 ff. = Patr. Lat. 54, Ep. 164, Kol. 551. In genau dem gleichen Sinne äußerte sich Kaiser Valentinian III. i. J. 445 in der Arenga zu seiner Verfügung über die Jurisdiktionsgewalt der römischen Kirche (zit. unten A. 41): „in imperio nostro *unicum* esse *praesidium* in supernae divinitatis favore ..."

[29] Avellana nr. 51, S. 117, vom 17. Juni 460. Siehe auch Leo d. Gr. an Theodosius II. am 18. Februar 449, in ACO II. 4, nr. 2, S. 3, Z. 16: dem Kaiser obliegt die *sollicitudo christianae religionis*. Ferner Simplicius an Zeno in Avellana nr. 66, S. 147 Z. 5: der Kaiser als *defensor fidei*.

[30] Siehe oben A. 28.

[31] Vgl. etwa Kaiser Honorius in Avellana nr. 35, S. 81: „Inter omnes curas nec illa nos minus sollicitant, quae pertinere ad sacerdotium iudicamus. Cum enim de confirmando episcopo urbis aeternae controversia tractaretur atque ... episcopi de tanto negocio paucos se aestimarent ad sententiam proferendam, placuerat ..." Ferner Valentinian III. an Theodosius II. (22. Februar 450) über die Gründe, ein Konzil einzuberufen (ACO II. 3, S. 14 Z. 6 ff.): weil die *fides* „perturbata, quam nos a nostris maioribus traditam debemus cum omni competenti devotione *defendere* et ... *conservare* ... domine sacratissime pater et venerabilis imperator ..."

[32] Siehe die Akklamation im Konzil von Ephesus (449) in ACO II. 1. 1, S. 138 Z. 28; II. 3, S. 121 Z. 5f. (in der lateinischen Übersetzung): „Multos annos imperatori ... fidei custodibus multos annos, multos annos pontifici imperatori (τῶι ἀρχιερεῖ βασιλεῖ)." Die Akklamation in Chalcedon in ACO II. 1. 2, nr. 20, S. 157 Z. 29 (τῶι ἱερεῖ, τῶι βασιλεῖ = sacerdoti imperatori).

[33] Zu diesem Problemkreis vgl. J. Straub, Kaiser Konstantin als ἐπίσκοπος τῶν

Kaisers, allgemeine Konzilien einzuberufen, um strittige Glaubensfragen entscheiden zu lassen, erklärt sich unschwer und überzeugend aus der Trennung der *Externa* von den *Interna:* jene standen dem Kaiser zu, diese nur denen, die die entsprechende Qualifikation hatten, über Glaubenssachen autoritative Auskunft erteilen zu können. Als ἐπίσκοπος τῶν ἐκτός war er, wie erwähnt, *curator*, *tutor*, Aufseher über das römische Gemeinwesen, und seine Hauptaufgabe in dieser Funktion war eben die Aufrechterhaltung der Ordnung in der *res Romana*, denn ihm war die „cura et tutela rei publicae universa" übertragen. Schließlich bedeutete ἐπίσκοπος nichts anderes als Aufseher, Beschützer u. dgl. (auch *speculator* oder *curator*[34]) und rücksichtlich kirchlicher oder kultischer oder religiöser Interessen wird der ἐπίσκοπος staatsrechtlich zum *Pontifex*, der Hüter der sakralen Ordnung, Wahrer des göttlichen Rechts ist und im Kaiser als dem obersten *Pontifex* zum rechtssetzenden Organ in kultischer, sakraler Hinsicht wird. Besonders zu beachten ist, daß der *Pontifex* keiner Inauguratio bedurfte. Da aber das römische Reich seit Ende des 4. Jahrhunderts auf den Grundsätzen des Christentums aufgebaut war, bezog sich die Tutor- oder Curatorpflicht des Kaisers auf die Erhaltung des christlichen Glaubens und daher auch auf die Wahrung der kirchlichen Interessen im Reich. Das, und nichts anderes, sollte die Bezeichnung des Kaisers als *Pontifex* zum Ausdruck bringen. Gegen den Hintergrund des römischen Verfassungsrechts zerrinnt der ohnehin sehr vage Priesterkönig *(Rex-Sacerdos)* in nichts. Dagegen gewinnt der Kaiser ein scharfes Profil, weil er historisch und juristisch vollauf verständlich wird. Diese neue Erkenntnis drängt sich auf, sobald man an die Funktion des spätrömischen Kaisers historische und juristische Maßstäbe anlegt. Der „Priesterkönig" ist eine bloße Hilfskonstruktion, die ein Schattendasein am Rande der Geschichte und des Rechts führt.

Insoweit allerdings scheint alles ohne Schwierigkeit einer Lösung zugänglich zu sein. Die Schwierigkeit beginnt, die, soweit ich zu sehen vermag, auch noch nicht erkannt worden ist, sobald man sich vergegenwärtigt, daß weder sprachlich noch sachlich dem römisch-lateinischen *Pontifex* ein griechischer Begriff oder Terminus entspricht. Die gängige Übersetzung des Pontifex in ἱερεύς (oder ἀρχιερεύς) wird sicherlich dem dem römischen Verfassungsrecht angehörenden *Pontifex* nicht gerecht, denn in der Rückübersetzung kommt dabei

---

ἐκτός, in: J. Straub, Regeneratio imperii. Darmstadt 1972, 119ff.; F. Vittinghoff, Eusebius als Verfasser der Vita Constantini, in: Rheinische Vierteljahrschrift 96 (1953) 330ff., bes. 356ff.; W. Ullmann, art. cit. (oben A. 21) S. 11ff. Die hier vorgetragene Auffassung deckt sich vollends mit der von Ambrosius in seinem Brief an Valentinian II. schwungvoll vertretenen: Ep. 21, in Patr. Lat. 16. 1145—49.

[34] Dazu W. Pape, Griechisch-deutsches Handwörterbuch[3] (Nachdruck Graz 1954), S. 979f. Die Leiter der von Athen unterworfenen Städte hatten dieselbe Bezeichnung, ebda. S. 980.

der *sacerdos* heraus, der gewiß nicht mit dem altrömischen *sacerdos* identisch
war. Daß diese sprachliche Eigentümlichkeit Verzerrungen zur Folge hatte,
ist klar, und daß sie auch zu schwerwiegenden Mißverständnissen und Ver-
wicklungen verleitete, bedarf keiner großen Vorstellungskraft. Aber es war
gerade dieser Umstand, der in Rechnung gestellt werden muß, will man den
päpstlichen Standpunkt, und vor allem jenen des Gelasius, verstehen. Denn
bei ihm hat, wie wir sogleich sehen werden, der Begriff des *Pontifex* eine neue
und ausschließliche, im christlichen Sinne fest umrissene Bedeutung erhalten
— eines durch besondere Gnade und Charisma ausgezeichneten Priesters,
vor allem eines Bischofs, der mit dem alten heidnischen bloß den Namen,
aber sonst nichts gemein hatte. Dies war seine Ausgangsstellung, und insoferne
war sein Protest vollends begründet, denn seine zeitgenössischen Kaiser waren
jedenfalls keine Priester. Hier tut sich in der Tat eine tiefe Kluft auf: der
Priester (Bischof) ist Träger eines Charisma, das göttlichen Ursprungs ist.
Es wird im Rahmen der Weihe oder der Konsekration erworben durch Vermittlung einer besonderen göttlichen Gnade. Der hier interessierende altrömische *Pontifex* ist Nur-Träger eines Amtes, er ist ein kultisches Organ,
dessen Grundlage das öffentliche Recht ist und deshalb an sich nichts mit
Gnade oder Charisma usw. zu tun hat[35]. Man betritt hier den schillernden,
zwielichtigen Untergrund der sprachlichen Zweideutigkeiten. Die schon erwähnte Akklamation im Konzil von Ephesus und Chalcedon besagt an sich
bloß, daß die Synodalen mit dem griechischen Ausdruck den *Pontifex* altrömischer Herkunft (d. h. den ἐπίσκοπος τῶν ἐκτός konstantinischer Prägung)
akklamierten. Die Akklamation bedeutete also nicht, daß die Synodalen im
Kaiser auch einen konsekrierten Bischof (oder geweihten Priester) erblickten.
Das zur Verfügung stehende Sprachmittel war einfach unzulänglich. Nebenbei
sei bemerkt, daß auch dem lateinischen *imperator* auf griechisch nichts Gleich-
wertiges entsprach — daher auch die unzähligen Mißverständnisse und Kon-
flikte, die sich daraus im Mittelalter ergaben: dem βασιλεύς entsprach in der
lateinischen Übersetzung der *rex*, der sich freilich wesenhaft vom *imperator*
abhob. Es ist gewiß interessant zu beobachten, daß bei den höchsten Ämtern
in der Spätantike und im Mittelalter die Sprache versagte.

---

[35] Siehe Th. Mommsen, Römisches Staatsrecht³, II. 1. Leipzig 1887, 18f., 42f., 51f.;
F. de Zulueta, in: Cambridge Ancient History IX (1933) 845ff.; A. D. Nock, ebda. XII
(1939) 412; K. Latte, Römische Religionsgeschichte. München 1960, 400ff.; H. de
Bonniec, in: Lexikon der alten Welt. München-Zürich 1965, Sp. 2409f.; auch Sp. 1378.
Es gibt keinen Anhaltspunkt für die Annahme, daß der römische *sacerdos* = *pontifex*
eine Mittlerrolle eingenommen hätte, wie P. Stockmeier, Leo I. des Großen Beurteilung
der kaiserlichen Religionspolitik. München 1959, 131 meint. Ganz klarerweise handelt
es sich hier um Opferhandlungen. Was sollte ein heidnischer Priester vermitteln? Dazu
s. G. Wissowa, Religion und Kultus der Römer². München 1912, 479f.: Die Priester
sind „nicht Vermittler zwischen Gottheit und Mensch . . ., sie sind vielmehr wie der ganze
Staatskult ein Zweig der Staatsverwaltung" und deshalb Organe derselben.

Wir können hier etwas weiter ausholen und auf eine ergänzende Parallele im Bereich der Sprache verweisen. Auch diese sprachliche Eigenheit war durchaus von keiner untergeordneten Bedeutung in unserem Zusammenhang, hat aber ebenfalls bisher noch keine Aufmerksamkeit auf sich gelenkt. Es handelt sich um die sprachlich wie wesenhaft unterschiedliche Bedeutung, die dem Begriff des *sacer* und dem des *sanctus* zukommt. Innerhalb des hier interessierenden Zeitraumes dürfte *sacer* (und also auch *sacratus* und *sacratissimus*) eine Eigenschaft bedeuten, die einer Sache an sich, einem Begriff oder einer Person als solcher zukommt. Die Eigenschaft haftet der Sache, der Person oder dem Begriff an und wird vor allem nicht erworben. Opferhandlungen und Kultverrichtungen gehören hierher, weil sie das sakrale Moment in sich selbst tragen — sie werden zu keinen *sacra*, weil sie schon solche sind. Und das die Opferhandlungen ausführende Organ ist ein *sacerdos*, nicht weil er selbst *sacer* ist, sondern weil er Opfer- und Kulthandlungen vollzieht[36]. Es dürften sich aber beachtliche Schwierigkeiten einer Austauschmöglichkeit der Begriffe *sacer* und *sanctus* entgegenstellen. Denn der *sanctus*-Charakter wird in unserem Zeitraum vorwiegend erworben und haftet nicht einer Sache oder einer Person an. Der Erwerb erfolgt durch göttlichen Auftrag oder Gnade oder besonderes Verhalten, durch Äußerungen, Erklärungen, Erläuterungen, die von wesentlicher Bedeutung für das Christentum oder die Christenheit sind und für die Entwicklung der christlichen Grundgedanken besonders wichtig erscheinen[37]. Man sprach (und spricht) von der *sancta Romana ecclesia*, jedoch kaum von der *sacra Romana ecclesia*, wie man umgekehrt auch vom *sacrum imperium* (und nicht vom *sanctum imperium*) sprach.

Gewiß, eine klare und scharfe Trennungslinie zwischen *sacer* und *sanctus* wird sich wohl schwer festlegen lassen, aber es verdient doch hervorgehoben zu werden, daß die Kaiser in unserer Zeitspanne (genau wie in der vorkonstantinischen Zeit) das Epitheton *sacer* ohne christlichen Einwand trugen und auch von kirchlichen Würdenträgern so apostrophiert wurden, wie umgekehrt und in genau demselben Ausmaße der Begriff des *sanctus* auf den Papst oder andere hochgestellte kirchliche Organe Anwendung fand. Die Anrede *Sanctitas vestra* war nahezu ein Monopol der Päpste, Patriarchen oder anderer hoher geistlicher Würdenträger geworden. So sprach z. B. Kaiser Honorius den hl. Augustinus mit *Sanctitas tua* an[38] und genau ein Jahrhundert später verwendete Kaiser Anastasius an Hormisdas dieselbe Terminologie[39]. Auf der

---

[36] Damit stimmen überein A. Ernout - A. Meillert, Dict. étymologique de la langue latine: Histoire des mots⁴. Paris 1959, 586 b: „Sacerdos: celui qui accomplit les cérémonies sacrées."

[37] Ebda, S. 587 a: der *sanctus* sei „*rendu* sacré ou inviolable". Wesentlich ist, daß "l'état de sanctus est *obtenu* par un rite de caractère religieux: sacre indique un *état*, sanctus le *résultat* d'un acte". (Hervorhebung von mir.)

[38] Avellana nr. 26, S. 72; nr. 27, S. 73.

[39] Avellana nr. 125, S. 537 Z. 16.

anderen Seite ist es häufig genug der Fall, daß der Kaiser in direkter Rede mit *Sacratissime et invictissime principum* angesprochen wurde[40]. Eine unleugbar bedeutsame Anwendung desselben Gedankens ist die offenbare Identität von *sacratissimus* und *divinissimus*, worüber die Akten des Chalcedonense zahlreiche Beispiele bringen. Dem entspricht auch die Anrede des Kaisers mit *Divinitas vestra*[41] oder als *Christianitas vestra*[42], Anreden, die man vergeblich beim Papst sucht. Schon im konstantinischen Zeitalter liest man, die christliche Religion sei eine *sanctissima religio*, doch nirgends liest man von einer *sacratissima religio*[43].

Die Trennungslinie zwischen den *Externa* und den *Interna* war freilich dünn und fließend. Wie erwähnt, oblag es dem Kaiser in Verfolg seiner Stellung als ἐπίσκοπος τῶν ἐκτός, allgemeine Konzilien zur Beilegung von dogmatischen Schwierigkeiten zu berufen, doch war er es auch, der entschied, wo, warum und wie darüber abgehandelt werden sollte. Gleichwohl muß betont werden, daß er sich formell einer Intervention in *Interna* enthielt. Daß sich aber auf dem Umweg über organisatorische Maßnahmen (die alle formell im Bereich der *Externa* verblieben) ein machtvoller Einfluß des Kaisers auf die Gestaltung der Lösung der Probleme im Bereiche der *Interna* bemerkbar machen konnte, hatten alle vier allgemeinen Konzilien bewiesen. Darüber hinaus war schon vermöge der für das Wohl des Reiches — der (Ulpianischen) *res Romana* — sehr bedeutsam gewordenen Stellung der Priester (im weitesten Sinne, einschließlich der Bischöfe, Metropoliten und Patriarchen) die Ausübung der kaiserlichen Kontrolle und Disziplinargewalt über sie im öffentlichen Recht miteinbegriffen. Und eng verwandt damit waren die kaiserlichen Maßnahmen, die sich auf die Festlegung von Diözesan- und Provinzgrenzen bezogen, ganz zu schweigen von seinem Einfluß in Besetzungsfragen, vor allem durch sein Bestätigungsrecht usw. Gewiß, alle diese Maßnahmen und Befugnisse konnten sich durch das Wesen des öffentlichen Rechts begründen lassen. Nichtsdestoweniger drängte doch die Frage zur Beantwortung, ob denn überhaupt die *sacerdotes* des *ius publicum* Ulpianischer Prägung identisch waren mit den *sacerdotes* christlicher Herkunft. Ferner schlummerte noch eine weitere heikle und bei näherem Zusehen grundlegende Frage im Hintergrund, ob denn das alte römische öffentliche Recht auch seine volle Wirkkraft innerhalb eines christlichen Gemeinwesens weiterhin entfalten konnte. Ließ sich mit anderen

---

[40] Vgl. etwa ACO II. 5, S. 63f.
[41] ACO II. 3, S. 14, Z. 18f. und öfter. Daher auch die Bezeichnung der Kaiser als *divi principes* oder *divi parentes* u. ä., worüber P. Batiffol, Survivances (oben A. 16) geistvoll abhandelte. Bisher unbeachtet geblieben ist, daß Valentinian III. seinen Erlaß vom J. 445, der die Jurisdiktionsgewalt der römischen Kirche festlegte, zeichnete: *Manu divina* ... (G. Haenel, Corpus iuris Romani anteiustininiani [Bonn 1944], Teil 6, Sp. 173). Vgl. dieselbe Eigenheit in seiner Novelle vom selben Jahre, Sp. 188.
[42] Vgl. etwa ACO II. 5, S. 28 Z. 19; S. 29 Z. 14; S. 95 Z. 18 usw.
[43] Vgl. art. cit. (oben A. 21), S. 8.

36

Worten Begriff und Bedeutung der *sacra* und *sacerdotes* überhaupt auf den christlichen Bereich übertragen? Was die obwaltende Verfassung angeht, gab das alte römische *ius publicum* zweifellos auch dem christlichen Kaiser Mittel in die Hand, die auf das Gefüge der Kirche einen entscheidenden Einfluß auszuüben geeignet waren. Aber die Frage erhob sich damals, vielleicht zum ersten Male, ob das auch das richtige Recht war[44]. Wie die weitere Entwicklung im 5. Jahrhundert zeigen sollte, lag in der weit gespannten Anwendungsmöglichkeit des *ius publicum* der Keim einer Ausdehnung und Ausweitung kaiserlicher Funktionen, insbesondere wenn man die Faktizität der kirchlichen Verhältnisse in der zweiten Hälfte des Jahrhunderts in Anschlag bringt. Es waren diese Verhältnisse, die geradezu eine Überschreitung der bisher (man wäre versucht zu sagen: kaiserlicherseits peinlich) eingehaltenen Trennungslinie, die die Interna von den Externa schied, postulierten, sollte die Einheit des Glaubens und damit des Reiches gewährleistet werden. Aus dem rechtlichen, verfassungsmäßigen Organ des Pontifex, dem die oberste Verwaltung, Disziplinargewalt und Organisation des auf christlicher Grundlage ruhenden Gemeinwesens oblag, konnte sich unschwer unter Berücksichtigung der zeitgenössischen Umstände ein Pontifex entfalten, der diese Rechts- und Verfassungsgrundlage verließ und sich zum Verkünder dogmatischer Lehrsätze entwickelte. Das aber war Kompetenzüberschreitung, und das war der Schritt, den Kaiser Zeno in seinem *Henotikon* getan hatte. Sehr zutreffend hat Caspar diesen Erlaß als ein einseitiges kaiserliches Glaubensedikt gekennzeichnet[44a]. Damit hatte der Kaiser als *Pontifex* jenen verfassungsmäßig und auch gewohnheitsmäßig verankerten Kompetenzbereich überschritten und sich auf das schlüpfrige Gebiet der Dogmen und Glaubenssätze begeben. Als Pontifex war er oberster Treuhänder und Verwalter aller Externa, die sich auf die Erhaltung des orthodoxen Glaubens und der äußeren Ruhe des kirchlichen Gemeinwesens bezogen, hatte aber

---

[44] Es war genau dieselbe Fragestellung, die im hochmittelalterlichen Investiturstreit zur entscheidenden wurde. Darüber vgl. W. Ullmann, Von Canossa nach Pavia: Zum Strukturwandel der Herrschaftsgrundlagen im salischen und staufischen Zeitalter, in: Hist. Jahrb. 93 (1973) 265ff.; jetzt in: The papacy and political ideas in the Middle Ages (Collected Studies II: London 1976) Kap. II.

[44a] E. Caspar, op. cit. (oben A. 23), II. 35. Zum *Henotikon* und acacianischen Schisma s. H.-G. Beck, Die frühbyzantinische Kirche, in: H. Jedin, Handbuch der Kirchengeschichte, II. 2, Freiburg-Basel-Wien 1975, 3ff., der freilich im *Henotikon* eine bloße *explicatio fidei* erblicken will. Nach H. Rahner, op. cit. (oben A. 1) ist es „ein typisches cäsaropapistisches Flickwerk" (S. 224). Sein Verfasser war Acacius. Für J. Haller war es „an sich ein Meisterwerk" (Das Papsttum: Idee und Wirklichkeit, neue Aufl. [Rowohlt Reinbeck 1965] I. 163). Gegen die Ansicht Caspars und anderer, damit hätte der Cäsaropapismus seinen Anfang genommen, muß man doch gewisse Bedenken anmelden, denn die Kompetenzerweiterung fand im Rahmen des *ius publicum* statt. Die kaiserlich verfügte Kompromißlösung sollte die religiöse Einheit wiederherstellen, die unabdingbar war für das Wohlergehen des Reiches.

trotzdem keinerlei Befugnis, lehrmäßig aufzutreten. Es fehlte ihm dazu das
erforderliche Charisma, der Einbau in den priesterlichen Ordo und daher dessen
Mitgliedschaft. Er ermangelte mit einem Wort der dafür notwendigen Qualifikation. Er hatte den rechtlich und gewohnheitsmäßig fixierten „Pontifikalbereich" auf Glaubenssachen ausgedehnt (wozu möglicherweise die
griechische Übersetzung in ἱερεύς Vorschub geleistet haben mag[45]). Zum
ersten Male erließ nunmehr ein Kaiser aus eigener „Machtvollkommenheit"
ein Edikt, das grundsätzliche Glaubensfragen zum Inhalt hatte: nicht im
entferntesten hatte er daran gedacht, ein Konzil damit zu befassen. Der
kaiserliche Leitgedanke war gewiß die Erhaltung des religiösen, d. h. öffentlichen Friedens im Reich, wozu ihn seine Funktion als Pontifex verpflichtete,
und diese ließ sich aus dem öffentlichen Recht ableiten.

Jetzt, wo wir uns den Blick auf die Rolle des Kaisers als *Pontifex* geschärft
haben, wird es nicht schwer fallen, die eingangs erwähnte Aussage des Papstes
Gelasius zu klären. Diese Aussage kann nur gegen den zeitgenössischen Hintergrund und die voraufgegangene Entwicklung verstanden werden. Im Hintergrund standen die schweren Krisen auf christologischem Gebiet, die ja in der
Tat die Einheit des Reiches gefährdeten. In der kaiserlichen Maßnahme,
die Einheit des Glaubens durch das *Henotikon* wiederherzustellen, erblickte
Gelasius eine Anmaßung von Rechten, die einem Kaiser nie zustanden, weil
sie ganz offenbar zu den christlichen Interna gehörten. Die Rolle, die sich
nunmehr der Kaiser zulegte, widersprach der seit Ambrosius über Leo d. Gr.
vertretenen Lehre des Priestertums, dessen Wesen in der Verkündigung von
Offenbarungswahrheiten und der göttlichen Lehre bestand. Die Voraussetzung
war Weihe, die zur Mitteilung der göttlichen Gnadengaben und der besonderen
göttlichen Geheimnisse an die anderen Gläubigen ermächtigte[46]. Das traf aber
nur auf den Beruf des *sacerdos* zu — gerade jene Eignung, die der Kaiser nicht
besaß. Gelasius vertrat die Ansicht, daß Zeno durch seine Kompetenzüberschreitung tatsächlich die Rolle des Priesters zu spielen begonnen hatte. Der
Traktat, in dem der Pontifex-Titel dem Kaiser abgesprochen wird, richtete
sich doch nicht an den Westen, sondern ausschließlich an den Osten. Er
war kein amtliches Schriftstück, sondern eine private gelehrte Auseinandersetzung, die denselben Zweck verfolgte wie ein amtliches Schriftstück: daß

---

[45] Eine erste Spur der Einbeziehung von Glaubenssachen in den kaiserlichen Bereich
enthält möglicherweise die Akklamation in Chalcedon, wo die Synodalen, ohne ersichtlichen Anlaß, den Kaiser akklamierten: διδάσκαλε πίστεως (ACO II. 1. 2, S. 157
Z. 30). Es fragt sich aber, ob „Lehrer des Glaubens" den Sinn richtig wiedergibt oder ob
nicht der Kaiser als die Verkörperung des rechten Glaubens und der Treue zu Gott angesprochen wurde, der dadurch als Lehrer oder Vorbild wirkte, etwa im Sinne eines
Wahrers, Treuhänders oder Kenners des Glaubens. Vgl. oben A. 8: der Kaiser als *fidei
imitator* (Simplicius).

[46] Einen Hinweis gab schon Leo d. Gr. in ACO II. 4, nr. 103, S. 111 Z. 18f. (= Patr.
Lat. 54, Ep. 164 c. 2): „Verae fidei sufficit scire, *quis* doceat."

sich Gelasius dieses Mittels bediente, wird aus der Situation heraus erklärbar — er wollte den Kaiser nicht unnötig reizen. Der Papst war doch schließlich verfassungsmäßig Untertan des Kaisers. Umso höher ist das schriftstellerische Geschick Gelasius' zu bewerten, der in eben demselben Traktat und in genau derselben Stelle die petrinische Aussage zur Stützung seines Standpunktes heranzog. Obwohl wir alle als Christen ein königliches Priestertum innehaben, gibt diese Eigenschaft an sich keinen Rechtstitel ab, auch über christliche Lehrprobleme zu entscheiden. Dazu hat der nicht-ordinierte Christ nicht das entsprechende Rüstzeug, weder in persönlicher noch in sachlicher Hinsicht.

Was Gelasius in seinem Traktat und in der damals erhitzten und gespannten Atmosphäre als „Privatmann" sagte, war sachlich bloß ein Kommentar zu den Schreiben des Papstes Felix III. (deren Verfasser mit an Gewißheit grenzender Wahrscheinlichkeit Gelasius selbst war), aber vor allem zu seinen ersten amtlichen Schreiben als Papst[47]. Darin wird die aus dem öffentlichen Recht abgeleitete Befugnis des Kaisers scharf abgelehnt. Die auf das öffentliche Recht gegründeten Disziplinarmaßnahmen in der Form von Einsetzungs- und Absetzungssentenzen wurden als unzulässige Erweiterungen des kaiserlichen Kompetenzbereichs *tout court* zurückgewiesen. Mit aller wünschenswerten Deutlichkeit spricht Gelasius den Grundsatz aus, daß das öffentliche Recht altrömischer Herkunft für eine christliche Gemeinschaft keine Geltung besitze. Die dem Grundsatz innewohnende Tiefe hat gewiß Ambrosius zum geistigen Vater, aber die Schärfe der Formulierung stammt von Gelasius. Will der Kaiser als Katholik gelten, dann ist er ein Sohn der Kirche, und nicht deren Leiter.

Quod si dixeris (sagt Gelasius), „Sed imperator catholicus est": salva pace ipsius dixerimus, filius est, non praesul ecclesiae,

und deshalb hat er nicht nur keine Befugnis zu Verwaltungs- und Disziplinarmaßnahmen gegen Kleriker[48], sondern auch, und vor allem, kein Recht, in Sachen des Glaubens gesetzgeberisch aufzutreten:

Quod ad religionem competit, discere ei convenit, non docere[49].

Obwohl das scharf geprägte Gegensatzpaar von *discere-docere* schon längst

---

[47] A. Thiel, ed. cit. (oben A. 1), S. 292f. (Ep. 1 c. 10); Ed. Schwartz, Sammlungen (oben A. 1), nr. 11, S. 35. Gelasius als Verfasser der Briefe seiner Vorgänger, oben A. 6.

[48] Der vielschichtige Hintergrund bezieht sich auf die Ein- und Absetzung von Bischöfen und Patriarchen im Osten des Reiches. In der Verwerfung des römischrechtlichen *ius publicum* liegt der Keim des späteren *privilegium fori* (vgl. Growth, oben A. 1, S. 27).

[49] Ep. cit. (oben A. 47); ferner Ep. 10, c. 9, Thiel, S. 347; Ed. Schwartz, Publizistische Sammlungen (oben A. 1), S. 19 Z. 1ff. Es handelt sich um die Übertragung der Matthäus-Stelle auf die Ebene der öffentlichen Gewalt: „Der Schüler steht nicht über den Meister noch der Knecht über seinen Herrn" (Matt. 10. 24). Gelasius zitiert die Stelle ausdrücklich (Thiel, S. 291; Schwartz, S. 18, Z. 38f., wo das biblische Zitat nicht ausgewiesen wird).

beobachtet wurde[50], ist der juristische Hintergrund ungenügend berücksichtigt worden. Die Absage an das traditionsgeschwängerte römische öffentliche Recht hätte kaum treffsicherer gestaltet werden können als in diesen amtlichen Papstäußerungen.

Der Begriff des *Pontifex* wurde von Gelasius umgedeutet. Aus dem kultischen Organ, das über das Ritual bis zum Totenkult wachte, wurde ein durch göttliche Gnade ausgezeichneter Träger eines besonderen Charisma. Gelasius verstand den *Pontifex* in diesem letzteren Sinne. Sowohl der *sacerdos* (in der Ulpianischen Formulierung des *ius publicum*) als auch der verfassungsmäßig verstandene altrömische *Pontifex* haben nach Gelasius in einem christlich orientierten, ekklesiologisch begriffenen Gemeinwesen keine Daseinsfunktion. Hier — wie so oft — darf Identität des sprachlichen Ausdrucks nicht mit Bedeutungsidentität gleichgesetzt werden: ein und derselbe Ausdruck mag völlig andere Bedeutungen in veränderten Umständen und Verhältnissen annehmen. Die Schlußfolgerung des Gelasius, daß sich der Kaiser durch seine Kompetenzüberschreitung auf ein ihm fremdes, nicht zustehendes Gebiet begeben hätte, ergab sich zwingend. Es ist nicht leicht, der profunden Bedeutung der gelasianischen Formulierung voll gerecht zu werden. Mit einer an Kürze kaum zu überbietenden Schärfe und Prägnanz wird vom Standpunkt der (neuen) römisch-christlichen Doktrin das (alte) römische öffentliche Recht seiner Wirksamkeit im ekklesiologischen und damit im universal-kirchlichen Bereich entkleidet.

Damit ist aber die volle Bedeutung des gelasianischen Gesichtspunktes bei weitem nicht erschöpft. Es wird nämlich nicht nur die Anwendbarkeit des (alten) römischen öffentlichen Rechts auf das christliche Gemeinwesen bestritten und damit auch gleichzeitig die *Pontifex*-Funktion des Kaisers geleugnet, sondern, was vielleicht noch bedeutsamer ist, aus dieser Negierung erwächst zugleich der bisher viel zu wenig beachtete neue Grundsatz der Arbeitsteilung[51]. Dieser Grundsatz besagt, daß sich in einer geordneten Gesellschaft jedermann auf die ihm zugewiesene Funktion beschränken soll, um Unordnung und soziales Chaos zu vermeiden. Vor allem in einem christlichen Gemeinwesen, der Kirche, solle diese Funktionsbeschränkung der

---

[50] Vgl. E. Caspar, op. cit., II. 33, 63. An sich war dieses Gegensatzpaar nicht ganz neu, weil Papst Caelestinus schon den gewichtigen Satz geprägt hatte: *Populus docendus, non sequendus est* (Patr. Lat. 50.437, zit. in meinen Principles of government and politics in the Middle Ages³. London 1974, 134. Der Satz wurde sehr häufig wiederholt, insbesondere im karolingischen Zeitalter.

[51] Auf die Bedeutung dieses neuen Grundsatzes habe ich schon mehrmals hingewiesen. Vgl. etwa Growth (oben A. 1), S. 25, 41, 212, 278f., 433ff., 442ff.; Principles (vorige A.), S. 66f., 135, 194; Papst und König. Salzburg-München 1966, 28ff.; Law and Politics (oben A. 22), S. 123, 178, 230, 239f., 250, 255. Den Zusammenhang mit dem öffentlichen Recht hatte ich allerdings nicht erkannt. Die großartige Leistung Gelasius' rückt erst durch die Erkenntnis dieses Zusammenhangs vollends ins Licht. Vgl. Text.

einzelnen Amtsträger ein feststehendes Prinzip sein, weil nur dadurch die (paulinisch geforderte) Integration aller den Gesamtorganismus konstituierenden Teile erreicht und gewährleistet werden kann[52]. Es versteht sich, daß dieser Arbeitsteilungsgrundsatz Ausfluß des Funktionsgrundsatzes ist, worin die tiefgründige teleologische Idee ihre Verkörperung findet. Denn die Teile und Glieder eines Organismus verfolgen genau programmierte und formulierte Zwecke — wie Paulus erklärte, sind zum Funktionieren des Leibes Christi alle Teile notwendig. „Es gibt verschiedene Ämter, aber es ist nur ein Herr ..." Jeder Leib, sagt er, habe viele Glieder, die aber trotz ihrer Vielfalt nur einen Leib ausmachen, denn auch der menschliche Leib bestehe nicht aus einem Glied, sondern aus vielen: das Ohr ist genau so wichtig wie das Auge, die Hand wie der Fuß usw.[53]. Mit dieser anthropomorphischen Grundlegung wollte Paulus nichts anderes als den Arbeitsteilungsgrundsatz illustrieren. „Nun hat aber Gott den einzelnen Gliedern am Leibe ihre Stelle (d. h. ihre Funktion) zugewiesen ... es sind viele Glieder, aber doch nur ein Leib"[54].

Der Fortschritt der gelasianischen Lehre lag in der Verlagerung und Anwendung dieser paulinischen Grundsätze auf die Ebene der Kirchenleitung. Damit wahrte er den Einheitsgrundsatz der obersten Gewalt[55], den er im Anschluß an Leo d. G. in dem juristischen Nachfolger Petri personifiziert sah, und vermochte auf dieser Grundlage die autonome päpstliche *auctoritas* innerhalb der kirchlichen Gemeinschaft zu beanspruchen: die einzelnen Glieder der Kirche blieben auf die ihnen zugewiesenen „Stellen" (d. h. Funktionen) beschränkt. Hierin erblickte Gelasius — in voller Übereinstimmung mit der voraufgehenden Lehre — die Gewähr für die Verwirklichung der monokratischen Lenkung der christlichen Gemeinschaft, der Kirche[56]. Die maßgeblichen Richtlinien, die für die Rechtsgestaltung bestimmend sein sollen, können nur von jenen abgegeben werden, die dazu befähigt sind. Mit anderen Worten, was christlich und was nicht christlich ist, kann zuletzt nur vom Nachfolger Petri verkündet werden, weil Christus auf ihn die Kirche

---

[52] Siehe bes. I Kor. 12. 4; Eph. 1. 23; 4. 10; 5. 22—24; auch Röm. 12. 4 usw.

[53] I Kor. 12. 4 und 12ff.

[54] Ebda, 19—23.

[55] Ebda, 12. 5.

[56] Es ist gewiß keine Zufälligkeit, daß in genau diesen Jahren (den siebziger und achtziger Jahren) des 5. Jahrhunderts Ps. Dionysius mit seinen beiden Schriften über die *Hierarchia coelestis* und die *Hierarchia ecclesiastica* hervortrat. Der hierarchische Grundsatz wurde hier zum ersten Male von einem angeblichen Schüler des hl. Paulus vorgetragen. Er war es auch, der den Begriff der Hierarchie münzte, der dem klassischen Griechisch unbekannt war. Die Deszendenzthese von Herrschaft und Recht fand hier ihre klassische Formulierung. Dazu Principles (oben A. 50), S. 46f., 306, 317. Zur Begriffsbildung vgl. J. Stiglmayr, in: Zeitschrift f. katholische Theologie, 22 (1898) 180ff.; zur Verfasserfrage siehe U. Riedinger, in: Z. f. Kirchengeschichte 75 (1964) 146ff.

aufzubauen verheißen hatte[57]. Obwohl, wie er in dem Brief an die östlichen Bischöfe unterstrich, es um den Bestand, um gedeihliche Entwicklung oder Untergang des Reichs ginge, stünde nicht dem Kaiser die Befugnis zu, die die innere Ordnung des Reichs gefährdenden Streitigkeiten zu entscheiden. Mit dem geübten Griff des Juristen legt Gelasius dar, daß, soweit die ideellen Grundfesten des Reichs in Betracht kamen, es sich in der Tat um den *status rei Romanae* handelte, ihm als Petri Nachfolger aber allein das Recht zustünde, autoritativ Lehrstreitigkeiten zu entscheiden. Damit wurde das alte *ius publicum* aus dem römisch-christlichen Wirkungsfeld gebannt, wenn es sich um grundlegende religiöse Interessen handelte. Dies war im wesentlichen der Inhalt seines großen offiziellen Schreibens an die Orientalen. In verschiedenen Fassungen wird der Arbeitsteilungsgrundsatz von Gelasius vorgetragen, von denen die folgende vielleicht eine der besten ist:

Ad sacerdotes enim Deus voluit, quae ecclesiae disponenda sunt, pertinere, non ad saeculi potestates, quae, si fideles sunt, ecclesiae suae et sacerdotibus voluit esse subiectas. Non sibi *vindicet alienum ius* et ministerium, quod alteri deputatum est, ne contra eum tendat abrupte, a quo omnia constituta sunt, et contra illius *beneficia* pugnare videatur, a quo propriam consecutus est potestatem. *Non legibus publicis* ... sed a pontificibus ... Deus christianae religionis dominos et sacerdotes voluit *ordinari* ... *imperatores christiani subdere* debent executiones suas ecclesiasticis praesulibus, non praeferre[58].

Damit ist zugleich auch der Begriff des rechten Ordo festgelegt, in dem es für einen Pontifex, wenn auch „bloß" im römischrechtlichen Sinne, innerhalb eines christlichen Gemeinwesens keinen Raum mehr gab. Für das alte römische *ius publicum* sollte es in diesem Rahmen keine Entfaltungsmöglichkeit mehr geben.

Mit der Verwerfung des hergebrachten Verfassungsgrundsatzes errichtete Gelasius zugleich den aus paulinischen Quellen gewonnenen neuen Grundsatz der Arbeitsteilung, auf dem seine berühmte Epistola 12 an den Kaiser Anastasius I. aufgebaut ist[59]. Der Grundton dieser Erklärungen lag, jedenfalls was die *congregatio fidelium* betraf, in der Betonung des reibungslosen Ineinandergreifens aller Teile, damit das Ganze richtig funktionieren könne. Richtige Funktion setzt richtiges Recht voraus — und das einer christlichen Gesell-

---

[57] Vgl. etwa Gelasius, Ep. 10, c. 9, Thiel, S. 347; Schwartz, nr. 7, S. 19: „A pontificibus et praecipue a B. Petri vicario debet cognoscere (scil. potestas saecularis), quae divina sunt, non eadem ipsa iudicare. Nec sibi quisquam potentissimus saeculi, qui tamen Christianus est, vindicare praesumit, nisi religionem forsitan persequentes." Die Bedeutung eines solchen Satzes erhellt sofort, wenn man überlegt, daß die Grundlage des Reiches die christliche Religion sein sollte, daher auch „nulla tamen maior est necessitas quam divino cultui et religioni, unde omnia prosperantur ..." (Ep. 1, c. 23, Thiel, S. 299; Schwartz, nr. 11, S. 40 Z. 22).

[58] Thiel, S. 293; Schwartz, S. 35. Vgl. ferner Tract. IV, cap. 11, wo der Arbeitsteilungsgrundsatz verdeutlicht wird: Thiel, S. 567f.; Schwartz, S. 14f.

[59] Ep. 12, Thiel, S. 350f.; Schwartz, nr. 8, S. 20f. Über den Begriff der Verantwortlichkeit des Papstes für das Handeln der weltlichen Herrscher — hier klar ausgedrückt in der berühmten *Duo quippe* Stelle — vgl. meine Schüler J. L. Nelson, Gela-

schaft entsprechende richtige Recht konnte nur auf jenen (christlichen) Maximen beruhen, deren Inhalt und Wesen ausschließlich von den dazu Befähigten festgesetzt werden konnte[60]. Was uns hier entgegentritt, ist vom juristischen Standpunkt aus gesehen höchst beachtenswert — handelt es sich doch um nichts Geringeres als um die Ersetzung einer geschichtlich fundierten Rechtsidee durch eine, die aus religiösen Quellen gespeist wird. Damit wurde Gelasius der Vollender der leoninischen Gedankengänge: die Errichtung der Kirche (das *aedificare* i. S. der Matthäus Stelle) auf dem Felsen wurde hier in bündigster und kraftvollster Form juristisch vorgetragen.

Hiermit wurde vor allem der Rechtsidee selbst eine bisher unbekannte Bedeutung verliehen. In der Kirche, der *congregatio fidelium*, kann richtiges Recht nur ein christlich durchtränktes Recht sein. Damit erhielt die alte hellenistische Diastase von der *anima* und dem *corpus* völlig neues Leben. Das Recht wurde zu seiner höchsten Potenz erhoben: es verleiht dem *Corpus Christi* das ihm adäquate Leben und wird zu dessen Seele. Wie das einzelne corpus sein Leben aus der anima empfängt, genau so empfängt das Kollektiv des corpus aller Christen aus dem Recht als seiner anima seine Lebenskraft. Im buchstäblichen Sinne beseelt das Recht die Körperschaft der Gläubigen, die Kirche: es haucht Atem in die Gemeinschaft[61]. Die von Christus in der Verheißung (Matt. 16. 18f.) verkündete Sempiternität der Kirche findet ihren eindrucksvollsten Widerhall in der Sempiternität der christlich verstandenen Rechtsidee selbst, weil das Recht unzertrennlich mit dem „Bau der Kirche" verknüpft ist[62]. Genau so wie Unsterblichkeit der Kirche zugeschrieben wurde — und wie oft liest man nicht in juristischen Schriften des Mittelalters: *ecclesia mori non potest*, oder abgewandelt: *regnum mori non potest*, u. dgl. — in ebendemselben Sinne wurde der Rechtsidee als der *anima* des *corpus* der Christen Sempiternität zuerkannt. Diese Gedanken erhielten ihre erste Formulierung durch Gelasius, jenen Papst, der symbolhaft an der schicksalhaften Wende Europas auf Petri Stuhl saß. Mit dem faktischen Zusammenbruch des (weströmischen) Reichs stürzte gleichzeitig auch ideell und juristisch einer der bedeutendsten römischen Rechtsgrundsätze ein: das *ius publicum* alter römisch-heidnischer Abkunft[63]. Zugleich hinterließ Gelasius ein konstruktives,

---

sius' doctrine of responsibility, in: Journal of Theological Studies, n. F. 18 (1968) 154ff. (möglicherweise war die Noxalklage das Modell) und M. H. Hoeflich, Gelasius I and the Roman Law, ebda, 26 (1975) 114ff., der wahrscheinlich macht, daß die römische Tutel als Vorbild diente.

[60] Vgl. dazu oben A. 58. Viele andere gleichartige Aussagen ließen sich zitieren.

[61] Hier sei an den Satz im westgotischen Recht erinnert: „*Lex* est *anima* totius *corporis* popularis" (MG. Leges Visigothorum, I. 2. 2).

[62] Einige Bemerkungen darüber in Papst und König (oben A. 51), S. 36—40.

[63] Das gleichzeitige acacianische Schisma (484—517; Literatur oben A. 44a; vgl. neuestens W. C. H. Frend, Eastern attitudes to Rome during the Acacian schism, in: Studies in Church History XIII [1976] 69—81) läßt sich geradezu als Symbol der Tren-

positives Vermächtnis, das Europas Antlitz auf Jahrhunderte hinaus gestalten sollte. Er war Zeuge des Unterganges der antiken Welt, wurde aber selbst, trotz seines kurzen Pontifikats von nur vier Jahren, zu einem der hervorragendsten Architekten der neuen, anbrechenden, abendländischen Welt. Vom rechtshistorischen Blickwinkel gesehen hat im Kampf des geschichtlich gewordenen Rechts mit dem religiös verankerten Recht dieses obsiegt, wie die Entwicklung des mittelalterlichen christlichen Abendlandes erweisen sollte. Erst im rechtlichen und herrscherlichen Bereich wurde die volle Wucht der christlichen Weltanschauung erkennbar, weil sich in ihr das Zeitliche mit dem Ewigen zu einer festgefügten Einheit zusammenschloß.

---

nung von Ost und West erfassen. Im Osten unbeschränkte weitere Geltung des alten römischen öffentlichen Rechts, im Westen dessen Unanwendbarkeit. Man denke nur an die profilierten Äußerungen Justinians knapp eine Generation nach Gelasius: ,,ex *nostro divino* ore" stamme sein Recht (Cod. I. 17. 1. 6); sein Rechtssatz sei ein *divinum praeceptum* (Nov. 13, Epil.) usw. Über die rechtshistorische Bedeutung solcher und anderer Sätze vgl. Law and Politics (oben A. 22) S. 60 ff. Hierher gehört auch die Schlußansprache des Vorsitzenden, des Patriarchen Menas, in der Synode von 536: Gesta synodi de Anthimo, hg. E. Schwartz in ACO III (1940) nr. 130, S. 181 Z. 35 f. Solche Aussagen lassen sich im Westen nicht nachweisen, weil dort das alte römische *ius publicum* im Mittelalter nicht zur Anwendung kam. Die seit dem 12. Jahrhundert geförderte Kenntnis des römischen Rechts und die darauf fußende hochentwickelte Jurisprudenz zivilistischer Prägung waren Voraussetzungen, die die Eingliederung dieses römischen *ius publicum* in die Rechtsstrukturen des Westens bedeutend erleichterten, wenn nicht sogar in Gang setzten. Als Beispiel mag die Kurzformel *Rex in regno est imperator* dienen, worin die Übernahme der spätrömischen kaiserlichen Funktion durch den Landesherrn zum Ausdruck kommen sollte. Diese Formel drückte im säkularen Sprachgebrauch genau das aus, was die dem ekklesiologischen Bereich entstammende Formel vom *Princeps in ecclesia* zum Inhalt hatte: der ursprüngliche ambrosianische Gedanke — ,,*imperator intra ecclesiam*, non supra ecclesiam est" (Rede gegen Auxentius, in Patr. Lat. 16. 1061 B (cap. 36)) — wurde dadurch geradezu auf den Kopf gestellt. In der Rezeption des römischen *ius publicum* liegt eine der noch viel zu wenig beachteten Wurzeln des späteren Landeskirchentums und schließlich auch der landesherrlich befürworteten Reformation. Das Verständnis des Gallikanismus und des Anglikanismus, insbesondere in der Form, die ihm Heinrich VIII. gegeben hatte, wird durch diese rechtshistorischen Erkenntnisse erheblich vertieft.

III

REFLECTIONS ON THE MEDIEVAL EMPIRE

IF it is true that any worth-while historiographical analysis aims at a better understanding of past events or institutions, the present subject is in no need of justification. For it is admitted on all sides that the medieval empire constituted within the central medieval period a historic entity which to a very large extent shaped and influenced the destiny of many parts of Central, Eastern and Southern, and to a lesser extent also of Western, Europe. No particular effort is required to visualize what great attraction the vast extent of the medieval empire, whose core was thoroughly German, can easily exercise upon minds which are susceptible to the view that the present should continue the past. Amongst German historians there has been for exactly a century an almost morbid obsession with the medieval empire, not, however, in its purely historical setting, but in its bearing upon modern Germany. Why was it that German historians have debated the question so hotly whether or not medieval imperial policy was justified? After all, to all intents and purposes the medieval empire has been dead for more than 600 years: why should it then provoke so much excitement, so much heart-searching, so much emotional historiography? Nothing even faintly resembling this phenomenon do we find in English or French historiography.

It is certainly not without some interest to note the time and the occasion which witnessed the emergence of the problem of the medieval empire. We must try to put our mind back to the mid-nineteenth century when there still was no Germany as a political unit. We are in the fortunate position to fix the beginning of the fierce conflict amongst German historians to the year 1855 in which appeared the first volume of Wilhelm Giesebrecht's *Geschichte der deutschen Kaiserzeit*. The work, that has gone through numerous editions, was addressed to the Germans in whom a historical sense was to be awakened and for whom the great imperial time was to be the *leitmotif* in their quest for German unity. The subject of the book, the preface tells us, is the period in which the will, the word and the sword of the German emperors decided the fate of the Occident; they assured for the German nation a centuries-lasting world-dominating influence. The medieval empire was to be the guide as well as the aim of the German nation.

Four years later Heinrich von Sybel, the pupil of Ranke, severely challenged the assumptions of Giesebrecht. Sybel's thesis was that the disunity of Germany was precisely the consequence of the medieval empire: the policy pursued by the emperors was disastrous for the German nation, because they dissipated the nation's energies in their campaigns in Italy and squandered their wealth in colonizing attempts in Eastern Europe; they pursued a phantom which had no tangible basis in the German nation itself. In so far Germany was left far behind by both England and France which had long been united and, constitutionally, fully-developed countries. To take the *Kaiserzeit* as a guide was to invite the Germans to resurrect and perpetuate a disastrous past.

Julius Ficker, the great legal historian and diplomatist at Innsbruck, attacked Sybel's standpoint. The controversy between him and his Munich colleague, Sybel, though clad in historical terms, but fought with hardly surpassable acerbity and animosity, assumed an overwhelmingly political flavour.[1] The Sybel party could indeed be gratified by the events of 1870–71, and it is noteworthy that from now on the Ficker standpoint was very much in the background. But from the end of the first war onwards the fronts in historiography began visibly to change— from the 1920's down to the collapse of Germany in 1945 the dominant theme was that of justification, if not glorification, of the medieval empire as the political expression of the German nation which had created and dominated Europe. What was once Europe hegemonially led by the empire could well become the

[1] The numerous writings of Sybel and Ficker are edited by F. Schneider, *Universalstaat oder Nationalstaat: Macht und Ende des Ersten Deutschen Reiches: Die Streitschriften von Heinrich von Sybel und Julius Ficker* (Innsbruck, 1941). For Giesebrecht (Ordinarius at Königsberg and from 1861 at Munich), see *Allg. Deutsche Biographie*, xlix (Leipzig, 1908), pp. 341–49; for Sybel (Ordinarius at Munich until 1861, then at Bonn), *ibid.*, liv, pp. 645–67; for Ficker (the founder of the historical seminar), see *Oesterr. Biograph. Lexikon*, i (Graz-Cologne, 1957), pp. 309–10.

modern Europe hegemonially ruled by modern Germany. The Italian and Eastern policies of the emperors were no longer objects of vituperation, but objects of commendable statesmanship. The Second Empire, founded by Bismarck, appeared as a stage towards the Third Empire.[1] Karl Brandi paid special tribute to Ficker for having recognized the fateful North–South axis in the Middle Ages as a European necessity.[2]

Scores of German historians can be cited to show how much the adulation of the medieval empire had captured historiography. Names with a very great reputation can be garnered: Johannes Haller, Heinrich von Srbik, Fritz Hartung, Philipp Hiltebrandt, Hermann Oncken, Albert Brackmann, Otto Westphal, and many others, by no means all followers of the régime. For Haller the subjection of Italy and the founding of the Germanic–Roman empire was a 'political deed which has remained the most splendid of our nation to this day.'[3] For Srbik the imperial task consisted in the emperor's mission for world peace: the German faith in the empire is eternal.[4] 'With immeasurable pride can our nation look back to its great imperial past and look forward into the future confidently,' Albert Brackmann confessed.[5] Hermann Oncken, the nestor of German historians, declared that the empire constituted the first stage of the world-historic vocation (*Berufung*) of the Germans, who because they embraced universalism had

[1] See also Heinrich Ritter von Srbik, 'Die Reichsidee und das Werden deutscher Einheit', *Hist[orische] Zeitsch[rift]*, clxiv (1941), p. 470.

[2] *Cf.* F. Schneider, *Die neueren Anschauungen der deutschen Historiker über die deutsche Kaiserpolitik des Mittelalters*, 6th edn (Weimar, 1943), pp. 51 ff.

[3] J. Haller, *Die Epochen der deutschen Geschichte* (Stuttgart, 1927), p. 53.

[4] *Hist. Zeitsch.*, clxiv, p. 460. Professional historian as he was, he was bound to emphasize the Christian and Roman elements of the empire. This emphasis earned him severe censures by G. Krüger, 'Um den Reichsgedanken', *ibid.*, clxv (1942), pp. 457–58.

[5] A. Brackmann, 'Der Streit um die deutsche Kaiserpolitik', *Velhagen und Klasings Monatshefte*, xliii (1929), pp. 443–44. For Brackmann (Ordinarius in Berlin to 1929, then Director of the Prussian State Archives), see *Neue Deutsche Biographie*, ii, pp. 504 ff. He received special commendation for his zeal to have kept alive historical scholarship during the German impotency in the inter-war period: he kept alive the historic idea of the German mission to the East; see L. Bittner in his review (*Hist. Zeitsch.*, clxii (1940), p. 618) of Brackmann's *Krisis und Aufbau in Osteuropa* (Ahnenerbe-Stiftung, 1939). He expressed his views unmistakably after the defeat of Poland in 1939; see Schneider, *op. cit.*, p. 95.

become the leaders of Europe which ought to be indebted to them.[1]
A. O. Meyer held that the empire ideology had been the uniting
bond of the German nation and it was this which had awakened
in the Germans the awareness of being a *Herrenvolk*.[2]

It is impossible to evade the suspicion that a large part of
German historiography had harnessed history to a definite political programme,[3] that history had become the handmaid of
politics and that history was applied with a pronounced political
bias. The problem whether the empire, considered as a historical
institution, operating in space and time, could or should serve as
a yardstick, is not one that properly belongs to the historian.
What is necessary is that the link between history and politics
be cut by attempting to look at the empire in its historic setting.
This procedure would also do away with all the vices of moral
judgments which open the gates to a purely subjective—or
national—evaluation, which serious historiography had long
hoped to see relegated to the museum of antiquities. What appears
to be required is an explanation, an answer to the question, why,
given the historic premisses, the medieval emperors pursued the
policies which they did? What is not required is justification or
condemnation, that is, judgments based on hindsight and therefore not within the historian's terms of reference.

The attempt to explain the empire and the policy of the emperors makes imperative an analysis of how this entity and its
rulers actually came about. In all the din of the voluminous German literature we shall find remarkably few attempts to go back

[1] H. Oncken, *Nation und Geschichte* (Berlin, 1935), pp. 25, 45.

[2] *Cf.* Schneider, *op. cit.*, p. 90. See also P. Kirn, 'Die Verdienste der
staufischen Kaiser . . .', *Hist. Zeitsch.*, clxiv (1941), p. 261: the Staufen species
is characterized by a strong *Herrenbewusstsein*. These views are faithfully
reflected by A. Rosenberg, who with singular directness declared that today
(March 1940) the task is to raise Germany again to that position which is her
due since the days of the great Saxon and Staufen emperors; the medieval
monarchy made Europe into one single state, and now there is a grandiose
re-birth of this idea (*Tradition und Geschichte* (Munich, 1943), pp. 364, 368;
see also p. 273).

[3] For a juxtaposition of the First and Third *Reich*, see H. Aubin, 'Vom
Aufbau des mittelalterlichen deutschen Reiches', *Hist. Zeitsch.*, clxii (1940),
p. 480, and G. Krüger, *ibid.*, clxv, p. 460. For a more recent nostalgic view
on the medieval *imperium mundi*, see A. Bergstraesser, 'Deutsche Einheit',
Vierteljahrshefte für Zeitgeschichte, iii (1955), p. 336; see also H. J. Kirfel,
Weltherrschaftsidee und Bündnispolitik (Bonn, 1959), pp. 16, 28.

to the roots of the empire itself. It is as if divinity had pre-
ordained that the empire was to be in German hands. There can
have been few other institutions which exhibited such tenuous
links with the ancient period as the Roman empire in the Middle
Ages, but which was nevertheless proclaimed on all sides to be
the direct descendant of the ancient Roman empire, that thus became its involuntary begetter. Are there any objective and historical links between the ancient and medieval empire? Was there,
on the basis of objective reality, any indication that the one continued the other?[1]

How and why, then, did such an institution as the medieval
empire come about? To ask this question forces the enquirer to
focus his attention on the historically available material, and here
the obvious fact stares him in the face that there was indeed a
direct continuation of the ancient Roman empire in the shape of
the Byzantine empire, which had never lost its historic and genetic
continuity with ancient Rome throughout the millenium of its
existence. To state this truism, however, is merely to state the
problem of the Western empire in a much more accentuated
form: although the Byzantine empire was the true descendant of
Rome, how and why could there come about in the West another
entity that not only claimed precisely the same Roman roots, but
also, by virtue of this claim, considered itself the only true Roman
empire, with the consequence that Byzantium was derogatively
devalued as a kingdom of the Greeks or at best as an empire of
the Greeks?

Indeed, the Byzantine empire furnishes the clue to a better
appreciation of the problem of the medieval empire. In the Byzantine empire the ancient Roman conception of a universal
empire had absorbed the Christian universalist conception. Hel-
lenism, Romanism and Christianity coalesced into one indivisible
whole. The emperor, the *autokrator*, on whom divinity had conferred the government of the Roman and Christian *orbis*, was
internally and externally the one autonomous monarch. Internally, whatever affected the empire was the emperor's concern,
which meant, because Christianity had become an integral part

---

[1] Even F. Dölger, *Byzanz und die europäische Staatenwelt* (Ettal, 1953),
p. 289, can do no better than say: 'Von Seite des fränkischen Hofes ist die
Schöpfung des westlichen Kaisertums der Ausdruck eines ererbten dynam-
isch-politischen Sinnes'.

of the governmental organism, that ecclesiastical questions were
to be finally settled by the emperor himself; externally, because
the empire was world-wide, universal in any respect, there could
be no other ruler who could legitimately raise the same claim to be
the *dominus mundi*. Both these aspects are vital for an understanding of the Western empire.

The internal autonomy expressed itself and above all in providing the subjects with suitable ecclesiastical officers and with
supplying orthodox doctrine. Because dogma and the mechanics
of the ecclesiastical organism came within the emperor's sole
jurisdiction, there arose against him his great opponent in the
West: the pope in Rome. By virtue of his petrinological function,
he denied the very function of the imperial vice-gerent of God
on earth, whose task was to learn, not to teach. The first papal
challenge to Byzantium in the second half of the fifth century
resulted also in the first schism. Because the popes were subjects
of the emperor, their denial of the emperor's right to legislate on
matters of the pope's concern was tantamount to high treason, to
a *laesio divinae majestatis* in the person of the emperor. On the
other hand, the popes would have been oblivious of their function had they not pushed their petrinological claim towards the
East: a pope who willingly accepted the doctrinal and organizational rulings of the emperor would have forfeited his claim to be
a successor of St Peter.

It was the cute realization of Gregory I that it was not only
dangerous but also useless to push papal claims against the East.
It might be regrettable, but it was unalterable that the Byzantine
government was impervious to the true state of affairs. Hence his
opening up of the fallow Western soil to the very idea which
found in Byzantium an impenetrable barrier, that is, the primatial
idea of the Roman Church. What the Roman Church could not
achieve in the East, nay, what exposed the popes to a charge of
treason, could in the West be pushed to the farthest possible
extent. Statesmanship of a quite extraordinary kind enabled
Gregory to pursue a policy of bi-furcation—one fork to the West
where all the resounding chords of the Leonine–Gelasian theme
could be struck up, one fork to the East where this very same
theme was skilfully played down. As long as Rome remained part
of the empire, there was no possibility of deploying the Roman
primacy in all its potentialities. Hence two ways stood open to

achieve this: either the popes removed themselves physically from Rome, or the city of Rome itself was removed from the framework of the empire. The first alternative was, for a very brief period, indulged in by Gregory II, but discarded. The adoption of the second alternative meant carving out of the empire a territory that stood on its own feet, eventually becoming the papal state.

The handle by which this excision of a part of the body of the Roman empire was accomplished was provided by the *Constitutum Constantini*, according to which the establishment of the government in Constantinople, and its rise to the position of the capital, was due to the acquiescence and volition of the popes. Because Silvester did not wish to wear the crown offered to him by Constantine, the latter took it to Constantinople, but if the pope had so wished, he could have worn the crown himself: the crown, the readily-understood symbol of true Roman imperial power, was in Constantinople so long as the popes acquiesced in this. The erection of the papal state in 754–56 was, however, only a step towards the full extrication of the papacy from Byzantium, which led to the second step, transferring the crown from Constantinople to Rome and culminating in the coronation of Charlemagne: this, the final act in the story, was primarily, if not exclusively, directed against Byzantium.

It is important to keep this point in mind, because this original design provides one of the constant factors in the history of the Western empire. The second constant factor concerns the creative role of the pope: without active papal participation there was never to be a Roman emperor in the West, who, moreover, was charged with specific tasks by his creator. An autonomous emperorship there never was in the West: the intervention of the pope was vital and indispensable. Roman emperorship in the West presupposed the acceptance of the papal function and rôle. The third constant factor—and here papal and Byzantine conceptions were identical—concerns the universality of the Roman emperor's rule. It is in regard to this third factor that the Western empire assumed its proper complexion vis-à-vis Byzantium and the papacy.

We should do well to bear in mind that the idea of a Roman empire in the West was exclusively the intellectual offspring of the papacy: it was a constructive device to free it from the fetters

of the true Roman empire and prepare the way for the establishment of Roman primacy in the East, by making an emperor of
its own who could be none other but a Roman emperor. The
artificial creation of this one Roman emperor who had no roots
in history, but all the stronger ones in papal ideas, was an act of
statesmanship, the like of which cannot easily be found. Although
Charlemagne stood aloof from all these speculations, the dynamic initiative of the papacy secured the eventual victory of the
papal idea of a Roman empire. There is no need here to depict in
detail the stages of how this idea won its success through the
events of 816, 823, 850 and 875. The coronation of Otto I in 962
continued what can already be called a tradition of fact and of
idea. The undisputed fact was—in the West—that only the pope
was the lawful dispenser of the imperial crown, a view eloquently
expressed in Louis II's communication to Byzantium;[1] the idea
consisted in that this imperial function papally conferred was the
same as that which was embodied in the ancient Roman emperor,
i.e. universality of rule, and to this Roman universality was
added the Christian-papal idea of universality. From 962 the
empire was both Roman and Christian, Roman in a double sense.
For the West, the empire in Byzantium had therefore sunk to a
mere kingdom of the Greeks, which, because it did not accept the
tenet of papal primacy, was not Roman and therefore really
heretical.[2]

The anatomical dissection of the medieval empire should

[1] For details, see W. Ullmann, *Growth of Papal Government in the Middle
Ages*, 2nd edn (London, 1962), pp. 216 ff. For Otto I as '*Imperator Romanorum et Francorum*' see *M[onumenta] G[ermaniae] H[istorica], Diplomata*,
i, pp. 318, 322, 324, 326, 329; *Romanorum imperator, ibid.*, p. 346 (*Die
Urkunden der deutschen Könige und Kaiser*, ed. Th. Sickel, i (Hanover, 1884),
pp. 432, 436, 439, 441, 443, 473).

[2] See the texts cited in Ullmann, *op. cit.*, pp. 199 (n. 2), 202 (n. 5), 215,
217, 218 (n. 3); see also John VIII in *M.G.H., Ep[istolae]*, vii, p. 291. This
theme is later also clearly expressed by canonists, *e.g.* by Huguccio: 'Quid
ergo de *graeculo*? Abusive (!) et *sola usurpatione* dicitur imperator . . .'
(S. Mochi Onory, *La crisi del sacro Romano imperio* (Milan, 1951), p. 170).
The same argument in [Ansbert], *Hist. de expeditione Frederici Imperatoris*,
ed. A. Chroust (*M.G.H., S[criptores] R[erum] G[ermanicarum]* (1928), pp.
49–50): 'Denique solito fastu idem *Graeculus* se *mendose* imperatorem
Romanorum, ipsum vero nostrum serenissimum Augustum non imperatorem Romanorum, sed regem tantum Alemanniae nuncupavit'; the Byzantine designation was an 'usurpatum vocabulum'.

enable us to see the emperor in the light in which he was seen by his creator, the pope. As a result of the rivalry with the East, there were continued attempts to assert the universality in a practical manner, and the most convincing way of so doing was to widen the frontiers of a purely Germanic kingdom: after all, there were the Capetians, there were the Northern kings, later also the Anglo-Norman kings, who, from a royal point of view, were the equals of the German kings. But universality demanded expansion of the kingdom, so as to dominate other nations[1]—hence the so-called Eastern colonization and the subjection of the Slavs. In attempting to translate the universal idea of government into reality, the imperial government acted as a catalyst of the papacy.

Moreover, as a presupposition for his emperorship, an emperor of the Romans had to have control over the Romans. What sort of Roman emperor is this who exercises no power over those whose emperor he calls himself? Hence the continued campaigns into Italy to assert themselves as rulers, and hence also the somewhat weird designation of the future emperor as the *Rex Romanorum*, for which no historical precedent can be cited, but which was to designate actual physical control.[2] On the other hand, the exercise of some royal control in Italy over the Romans was also a handle against Byzantium, because the Eastern emperors had precisely not that control, and yet had, according to the Westerners, the temerity of calling themselves Βασιλεῖς τῶν 'Ρωμαίων.

Did the imperial crown add any powers to those he had in any case as king? This question is usually denied, and not without reason. But it would appear that some re-thinking is advisable. Of course, it is true that emperorship added nothing to actual royal powers, and yet at once the question arises why then the Germans from Otto I throughout the medieval period were so

---

[1] This was the current ninth-century view of the substance of an emperor; see Notker in Ullmann, *op. cit.*, p. 102, n. 3; *Annales Fuldenses*, ed. F. Kurze (*M.G.H., S.R.G.*, 1891), pp. 70, 86: Charles the Bald 'omnem consuetudinem regum Francorum contemnens Graecas glorias optimas arbitrabatur . . . ablato regis nomine se imperatorem et augustum omnium regum cis mare consistentium appellare praecepit'; Regino of Prüm, *Chronicon*, ed. F. Kurze (*M.G.H., S.R.G.*, 1890), p. 116.

[2] For this, see Ullmann, *op. cit.*, pp. 163–64. For the significance of this concept *cf.* Ullmann, '*Dies ortus imperii*', in the forthcoming commemoration essays for Accursius.

anxious to receive the crown? Merely for the sake of some dignity? Should one really assume that this constituted such a lure that every one of them embarked on costly Italian campaigns, which involved years of absence from Germany, which made the establishment of orderly government in Germany an excruciatingly difficult task, which entailed so much loss in men and material—and all this just for the sake of an imperial dignity? I feel that the medieval German kings were by no means so romantic and so unrealistic as to be credited with such chimerical motives.

The answer to this question will be easier if we recall the twin roots of the emperor's universality—Roman in the ancient and ecclesiastical sense. The emperor's function as *dominus mundi* was derived from the fact that he was crowned by the pope: the pope's universality of rule was reflected in that of the emperor. (This, incidentally, is the source of the sun-moon allegory.) This claim to universality is the one feature which distinguishes the emperor from any other medieval king. But universality of rule was not quite as meaningless as you might perhaps think. As king of the Germans, no Saxon, Salian or Staufen could claim universality, but in his function as emperor this claim to universality actually became a duty: what pitiable rôle would he have played vis-à-vis Byzantium, if the Western emperor had not asserted and at least attempted to translate into reality this claim? He would have been no more than a ludicrous puppet on the historical stage.

This duty of asserting his universal rule was given considerable endorsement by the ancient ideas of the purpose of the Roman empire in the Christian setting. There is the famous Good-Friday prayer text from the fifth century which stated:[1]

'Oremus pro christianissimo imperatore nostro, ut Deus et Dominus noster *subditas* illi faciat *omnes barbaras nationes*, ad nostram perpetuam pacem.'

There is also the prayer text during the imperial coronation mass, dating from just before the coronation of Otto I:[2]

'Deus, qui ad praedicandum aeterni regis evangelium Romanum imperium praeparasti',

[1] H. A. Wilson, *The Gelasian Sacramentary* (Oxford, 1894), p. 76.
[2] *Ordines Coronationis Imperialis*, ed. R. Elze (*Fontes Iuris Germanici Antiqui*, 1960), Ordo II.9, p. 6.

which was employed throughout the medieval period down to Charles V in 1530. Both these texts imposed a duty on the emperor to spread Christianity in the shape of missionary activity. We note that these (and other relevant) texts exhibit Roman Christianity and are conspicuously absent in the Eastern ceremonial. What needs emphasizing is that the missions of the German emperors to the East, understandably approved by the papacy, had also as their by-product the establishment of imperial rule in regions which had nothing to do with Germany. For a purely German kingdom there would have been no justification for the extension of power.[1]

It is the wide expanses inhabited by the Slavs in the East-European space which continued to attract the attention of the emperors. What we witness from Saxon times onwards is the extension of imperial rule by either incorporating Slav territories or making them vassal dependencies under the cover of a mission. By the late tenth century the territories annexed were far larger in extent than the territory of any single German component part.[2] These territorial acquisitions can hardly be disguised under the cloak of a mission, for, as it is admitted on all sides, extremely little was done to spread Christianity amongst the Slavs.[3] The treatment meted out to them would reveal little regard for Christian principles, even measured by the standards of the time.[4] What had started, at least in name, as a missionary enterprise became by the twelfth century nothing but exploitation and Germanization (*Eindeutschung*) under the innocuous

---

[1] For this, see J. Kirchberg, *Kaiseridee und Mission* (Berlin, 1934), pp. 132–33. For the development of the crusading idea and the subsequent wars against the Eastern pagans, cf. now the instructive essays in *Heidenmission und Kreuzzugsgedanke in der deutschen Ostpolitik des Mittelalters*, ed. H. Beumann (Darmstadt, 1963).

[2] See A. Hauck, *Kirchengeschichte Deutschlands*, iii (Leipzig, 1924), pp. 77 ff.

[3] *Ibid.*, iii, pp. 628 ff. According to H. Aubin (*Hist. Zeitsch.*, clxii, pp. 489 ff.), Eastern policy was dictated by the Slav threats, whilst, however, according to K. Kasiske ('Das Wesen der ostdeutschen Kolonisation', *Hist. Zeitsch.*, clxiv (1941), pp. 286 ff.), German Eastern colonization was the result of Slav invitations issued to the Germans as the leading Europeans, who eagerly accepted the call out of a sense of duty and mission.

[4] See, for instance, Thietmar, *Chronicon*, ed. R. Holtzmann (*M.G.H.*, *S.R.G.*, 1935), iii. 17, p. 118, and p. 119, line 26; vi. 25 ff., pp. 304–5; Ruotger, *Vita Brunonis*, ed. Irene Ott (*M.G.H.*, *S.R.G.*, 1951), p. 4:

name of colonization. One must here ask whether there was any need for colonization: the German kingdom was in any case the largest on the Continent; it was still thinly populated and there were wide stretches which, though perfectly accessible to cultivation, remained uninhabited.[1] Why then colonize Slav districts in the East and assimilate the Slavs?[2] The German settlers brought their own men, their own laws, their own customs, and the acceleration of this policy led to the virtual absorption of the Slav population in formerly purely Slav regions. The importance which Otto I attached to the erection of Magdeburg as an archbishopric can easily be appreciated.

The 'missionary' efforts must, however, be seen also against the background of Eastern–Byzantine missions. The rivalry between East and West greatly stimulated missionary efforts on both sides.[3] Germany's eyes began to be directed towards Russia when quite unexpectedly ambassadors from the government at Kiev arrived at Otto's court with the request for missionaries. That the reason behind this was purely internal Russian policy may not have been known to Otto, who evidently viewed the matter from a different angle. That Kiev had been for some time the target of Byzantine missions can surely not have been

---

'centifida Sclavorum rabies barbarorum frendens'; Helmold, *Chron. Slavorum*, ed. B. Schmeidler (*M.G.H., S.R.G.*, 1909), p. 34, lines 34 ff.: ' . . . iam canes, non homines iudicemur'. Some examples of atrocities in Widukind, *Rerum Gestarum Saxonicarum Libri Tres*, ed. P. Hirsch (*M.G.H., S.R.G.*, 1935), ii. 20, p. 84; iii. 55, pp. 134–35.

[1] H. Dannenbauer, cited in Schneider, *op. cit.*, pp. 74 ff., calculates that (within the corners of Magdeburg, Bolzano, Cambrai and Hamburg) Germany had in the eleventh century an extent of some 300,000 square miles with about 5 million inhabitants. The problem of Eastern colonization has now once again assumed topical political flavour; see W. Schlesinger, *Mitteldeutsche Beiträge zur deutschen Verfassungsgesch. des Mittelalters* (Göttingen, 1961), especially pp. 447 ff.

[2] F. Dvornik, *The Slavs, their Early History and Civilization* (Boston, 1956), p. 107, without any regard to the imperial theme, considers the Eastern expansion of Germany as the *Drang nach Osten* which, according to him, came to a halt 1,000 years later on the Volga in 1942.

[3] This is rightly pointed out by Kirchberg, *op. cit.*, p. 65. For the lively missionary activity carried out from Byzantium, though rarely by the government, amongst the Slavs, see F. Dölger, *op. cit.*, pp. 341 ff. Byzantine missionaries did not attempt to incorporate missionized regions or to colonize them by sending settlers; see Dölger, *op. cit.*, pp. 263, 339–40.

unknown to him. With both hands, so to speak, he took the opportunity which led, however, to no result. The continued interest which imperial Germany showed for Russia and Kiev is explicable also by geography. Before the second half of the twelfth century the Western empire had no foothold in the Mediterranean and the only way open to the East was that provided by the land route.

The union of the kingdom of Sicily with the empire can be understood only if the ever-active imperial motivation of the Western emperors is properly assessed. Under Barbarossa's son, Henry VI, imperial rule stretched also to the farthest Southern province of Europe which happened to be most advantageously placed on the Mediterranean seaboard. Rivalry between East and West had been translated into open conflict and warfare. Manuel Comnenos made determined efforts to reconquer Italy to realize the Byzantine plan of world-dominion. The plan was by no means as unrealistic as it is often presented. Although it was eventually thwarted, it touched the nerve-centre of Barbarossa's own Roman universal policy, and hardly had he come to terms with the papacy in the Peace of Venice than he went into the attack against Byzantium. Nothing illustrates better the aim of this emperor than the peremptory demand he made to Manuel in high-sounding, bombastic and sonorous Roman terms. Divinity, he said, had transmitted to him the *monarchia*, so that not only the Roman empire was his, but also that the Greek kingdom should be ruled by him:

> 'Ut non solum Romanum imperium nostro moderamine disponatur, verum etiam regnum Graeciae ad nutum nostrum regi et sub nostro imperio gubernari debeat'.[1]

This was the opening barrage of Barbarossa's planned military operation to take Constantinople with his German army by a

---

[1] First edited by H. von Kap-Herr, *Die abendländische Politik Kaiser Manuels* (Strasbourg, 1881), Appendix V, pp. 155-56. The sonorous beginning of the letter is also in the *Annales Stadenses* (*M.G.H.*, S., xvi, p. 349, lines 24 ff.): 'Fredericus . . . Romanorum imperator a Deo coronatus . . . Graecorum moderator (!) . . .' He operated here with his own two-sword theory, which on closer inspection seems to be dependent on the views expressed by John II, the Byzantine emperor, in his letter to Honorius II; see A. Theiner and F. Miklosich, *Monumenta spectantia ad unionem ecclesiae Graecae et Romanae* (Vienna, 1872), pp. 5-6. See also Frederick's

frontal assault—the treaty of Adrianople (1190) made him abandon the plan.[1]

But Barbarossa also adopted more peaceful means to assure the success of the plan: the marriage of his son Henry to the Sicilian heiress Constanza was not only to prevent a recurrence of a Byzantine threat to the Western empire, but also to give German power a firm footing in the sea, which alone was then of any consequence. Not only were now, in pursuit of this universalism, islands, notably Sardinia, claimed to be imperial territory, but the vassalage of Richard I brought also England into the imperial orbit, with the result that Richard was to be one of the organs that were to render effective assistance in the imperial subjugation of France.[2]

The conquest of Sicily by Henry VI made the plan of true Roman-imperial world-dominion a matter of practical politics. After the conquest he realized the potentialities of marrying Irene, the daughter of Isaac, to his brother Philip of Swabia, for Irene was legitimate heir to the Byzantine throne. The marriage was to provide the handle by which the unity of the one Roman empire could be demonstrated: we are reminded of a similar plan in the late eighth century. But this was only the beginning of Henry's Eastern engagements. Shortly afterwards an embassy of Henry appeared in Constantinople demanding the cession of all Byzantine provinces between Dyrrhachion and Thessalonika, which was a large part of the Greek peninsula. He also demanded parts

---

reply to the Byzantine legation in 1189: 'Omnibus qui sanae mentis essent, constat quia *unus* est *monarchos*, imperator Romanorum, sicut et unus est pater universalis, pontifex Romanus' (*Hist. de expeditione* . . . , p. 50).

[1] For details, see W. Norden, *Das Papsttum und Byzanz* (Berlin, 1903), pp. 117 ff.; G. Ostrogorsky, *Geschichte des byzantinischen Staates* (Munich, 1940), pp. 289–90; A. Waas, *Geschichte der Kreuzzüge*, i (Freiburg, 1956), pp. 192 ff.

[2] See the report of Roger de Hoveden, cited in Ullmann, *op. cit.*, p. 235, last note; *cf.* also Roger's statement (*op. cit.*, p. 300): Henry VI 'mandans ei [*i.e.* Richard I] in fide, quam illi debebat, quod ipse terram regis Franciae hostiliter invaderet . . .' Independent testimony comes from Innocent III in his letter to Philip II (*R[egestum Innocentii iii Papae super] N[egotio Romani] I[mperii]*, ed. F. Kempf (*Misc. Hist. Pontif.*, xii, Rome, 1947), no. 64): ' . . . Henricus affirmans quod te de cetero ad fidelitatem sibi compelleret exhibendam'.

of the Byzantine fleet under his command for the fight against the infidels.[1] When once again as a result of a palace revolution a change of government was made in 1195, German troops were ready to land on Byzantine territory: the new régime gave Henry the excuse to insist on the title-deed of his sister-in-law. Nothing less was now demanded than the cession of the Byzantine empire. Skilful Byzantine policy, however, managed to delay the deadly blow by offering enormous sums. Henry on his part thought of only postponing, and not of abandoning, his plan.[2] He was just then also engaged in military preparations for the conquest of the North-African coast.[3] His plans were well laid; now that both the king of Cyprus, Amalric, and the king of Armenia, Leo, had become his vassals, the fearful encirclement of the Byzantine empire, weakened as it was internally and drained of so much of its wealth, very nearly became a fact. The death of the near-world ruler and imitator of Justinian, Henry VI, in September 1197 prevented the execution of the plan.[4]

Henry VI's reign shows the full maturity of the empire ideology culminating in the attempt at a conquest of Byzantium. That this pre-occupation with establishing the *dominium mundi* over-shadowed, if it did not make impossible, every governmental activity in Germany proper cannot be doubted. Both Eastern and Southern imperial policy were in fact dictated by the concept of Roman emperorship. One cannot, however, resist the temptation to think that this whole complex of imperial aims and ambitions, and of the European problems created by them, breathed an air of artificiality and unreality which is only heightened by

[1] For the Byzantine reaction, see Norden, *op. cit.*, p. 126.

[2] Ostrogorsky, *op. cit.*, p. 293.

[3] For details, see H. Töche, *Jahrbücher des deutschen Reiches unter Heinrich VI.* (Leipzig, 1867), pp. 366 ff.

[4] E. and L. Schönbauer, 'Die Imperiumspolitik Kaiser Friedrichs II.', *Festschrift K. G. Hugelmann* (Aalen, 1959), p. 554, n. 5: 'Zum Unglück für das deutsche Reich starb er viel zu früh'. According to Kirfel, *op. cit.*, the thesis that the Staufen aimed at world dominion is maintained by the *Ausland*, notably by Roger de Hoveden and Niketas (p. 144). For a correct assessment of Henry VI's policy, see J. Rousset de Pina, *Histoire de l'église*, ed. A. Fliche and V. Martin, ix (Paris, 1953), p. 221: 'Reprendre la lutte contre l'empire byzantin . . . reconstituer à ses dépens la monarchie universelle, telles étaient alors les ambitions de Henri VI. Déjà l'encerclement de Byzance se dessinait'. See also S. Runciman, *Hist. of the Crusades*, iii (Cambridge, 1954), pp. 108–9.

the continued efforts and equally artificial devices to emphasize the Roman character of the empire.

Into this category fall the numerous devices and measures of imitating, if not copying, a number of institutions, nomenclatures, offices, emblems, rites, and so on, which could be observed 'over there' in Byzantium. This process of imitation and borrowing—space does not allow details[1]—was in the beginning a conscious process to harness to the otherwise bare Roman emperor the external trappings which he so conspicuously lacked. This imitative rivalry was in fact the tacit admission that true Roman emperorship could be found only in the East—otherwise why borrow? But, as it so often happens, in course of time and through usage the original manner of acquisition fades out of sight and the borrowed article acquires its own status in its right: it becomes property. This is exactly what happened with the 'borrowed articles'. They all came to be viewed by the twelfth century as the original belongings of the Western emperor, who acted as if he had always been the original owner.[2] A quite unparalleled accentuation of Roman elements, legal, political, constitutional, was bolstered up by scholarship and littérateurs. Even the laws of the medieval emperors were incorporated into the Roman law, because the Germans were the successors of the Roman Caesars. And since there was only one *dominus mundi*, other kings were demoted to mere *reguli* or mere *reges provinciarum*.[3] But, however loudly proclaimed the Roman character of the emperor was, nothing could hide the inconvenient fact that between him and the one whom he claimed to succeed was an unbridgeable gulf: the real Roman emperor was indeed autonomous, and it was precisely this feature of autonomy which the medieval emperor conspicuously lacked. Let us not be deceived by appearances: the medieval emperor was made by the pope for special purposes; he could also be unmade by the pope.

It is this—the assertion of autonomous emperorship—which is at the bottom of the conflicts between popes and emperors.

[1] For details, see W. Ohnsorge, *Abendland und Byzanz* (Darmstadt, 1958), pp. 1–49, 261–87. See also J. Déer, 'Byzanz und die Herrschaftszeichen des Abendlandes', *Byzantinische Zeitsch.*, l (1957), pp. 405 ff.

[2] 'Er rezipierte alles, was sich rezipieren liess' (W. Sickel, 'Das byzantinische Krönungsrecht', *Byzantinische Zeitsch.*, vii (1898), p. 529).

[3] As far as I can see, the term *regulus* was first used by Gregory VII; see his *Register* (ii. 70).

There is discernible a remarkable double thinking: in order to become emperor, the king had to supplicate the *favor apostolicus*, had to be in receipt of papal favours, for he had no *right* to the imperial crown. His emperorship was a *divinum beneficium* transmitted by the pope;[1] he knew that in the traditional papal view he was to become an officer charged with specific tasks; he also knew that he had to undergo an examination in the form of question and answer (*scrutinium*) and to take a *juramentum subditi*. There was not even an enthronement when he received the imperial crown, for why should an officer be enthroned? Anyone acquainted with the symbolic meaning of a throne will realize the significance of the absence of any kind of enthronement: of course, an officer never sat on a throne.[2] In the very fact of the German king supplicating for the imperial crown lies the implicit acknowledgment and acceptance of the papal standpoint that only the pope was the legitimate organ through which the Roman-imperial crown could be had. The coronation by the pope was constitutive. And yet, as soon as the pope had conferred the crown on him, had given him the sword, the symbol of physical power, had been given the promise that he would be an obedient *filius* of the Roman Church, as soon as the coronation festivities were over, he asserted with all the greater insistence that he was the real Roman emperor to whom all the appurtenances of his supposed ancestor belonged. The inconvenient factor that in all this the pope was the fulcrum, that without him there would not have arisen in the first instance a Roman emperor in the West, and that without him the Germans could not have held the Roman empire,[3] was suppressed by loud assertions of autonomy, accompanied by the trappings of hegemonial power. All this was a

[1] For this, see W. Ullmann, 'Cardinal Roland and Besançon', *Misc. Hist. Pont.*, xviii (1954), pp. 106 ff.; 'The Pontificate of Adrian IV', *Cambridge Historical Journal*, xi (1955), pp. 242 ff.; 'Ueber eine kanonistische Vorlage Friedrichs I.', *Zeitsch. der Savigny Stiftung für Rechtsgeschichte, Kan. Abteilung*, xlvi (1960), pp. 430 ff. For the general meaning of *beneficium*, see Ullmann, *Principles of Government and Politics in the Middle Ages* (London, 1961), pp. 57 ff.

[2] For the throne in the Byzantine ritual, see Constantine VII's *Liber de Ceremoniis*, ed. A. Vogt (Paris, 1939), ii. 47, p. 2, lines 14–15. Further, O. Treitinger, *Die oströmische Kaiser- und Reichsidee*, 2nd edn (Darmstadt, 1956), pp. 20 ff., 56 ff.

[3] Frederick I's reply to the Byzantine legates at Philippopolis in Oct. 1189

device to create an *alibi* and to escape the consequences which the popes drew from their function as dispensers of the imperial office. The Staufen view that the coronation was a mere formality, that even before the coronation the king held an *imperatura*—a significant coinage—and that the election of the king of the Romans gave a right to the crown, should not deceive anyone: if the coronation was a formality, why then all the exhibition of submission to the pope and the latter's examination and confirmation before the coronation? Or were the actual and threatened depositions also mere formalities? Deposition lost him not only his emperorship, but his kingship as well.[1] Despite their severe conflicts with the popes, the emperors never intended to abolish the institution of the papacy: they needed it.

As far, however, as practical politics were concerned, the obstacle to the full deployment of universal Roman emperorship as well as to the deployment of papal universality was the same—Byzantium. Never had Constantinople given up the claim to universality of its rule. The final break in 1054 made only obvious in the ecclesiastical sphere what in any case had already been a fact. But the important implication of this was the emergence of the crusading idea less that twenty years afterwards. Gregory VII appealed for the crusade to liberate the oppressed brethren in the holy places, but at the same time also declared that Constantinople was the aim: what moved him to the military measures, he said, was to bring about the union between East and West. And when eventually Constantinople did fall to the crusaders in 1204, Innocent III exclaimed that by the grace of God the church of Constantinople had now returned to her mother, the Roman

---

illustrates the imperial attitude. He gave four reasons why he, and not the Byzantine, was the true Roman emperor; see *Hist. de expeditione . . .* , pp. 49–50. Adopting the papal reasoning, he had no qualms in saying to the legates that their master had used 'indebitum vocabulum et glorietur stulte alieno sibi prorsus honore, cum liquido noverit me et nomine dici et re Fridericum Romanorum imperatorem semper augustum' (*ibid.*, p. 50, lines 12 ff.; *cf.* also Bishop Dietpold's report in *M.G.H., S.*, xvii, p. 510, lines 37 ff.).

[1] All this, including the paraphernalia before the coronation, should be compared with the situation in Byzantium in order to obtain a clear view of the fundamental differences between the two Roman emperors. In Byzantium there was no *scrutinium*, no coronation oath, and the coronation by the patriarch had no constitutive effects; etc.

Church, so that there was now *unum ovile, unus pastor*.[1] What appeared denied to the emperors fell into the lap of the papacy, though the discerning historian will be inclined to see in the result of the fourth crusade the culmination of a long development. The history of the medieval empire prompts reflexions which in their bearing go far beyond the purpose of this paper. The conclusion inescapably emerges, however, that the empire was rooted in a pure idea, and that it itself became and remained an idea. The idea, simple in itself, however far-reaching its impact, was that by virtue of his plenitude of power the pope was entitled to create the universal Roman emperor in the West by transferring the crown from Byzantium to Rome, so as to escape his subjection to Byzantium. From the late eighth century to the extinction of the empire the pope was the fulcrum, however inconvenient the fact was for the Germans, who managed to convince themselves (and a good deal of posterity) that the Roman empire was theirs by right. Purely fictive notions profoundly affected the history of Western Europe, over which towered the phantom of the artificial creation of the Holy Roman Emperor. His creation by the pope was the papal answer to Byzantine aims: it was the pope who supplied the frame, the substance and the contents of emperorship in the West. But this universalist papal element acted—and this is the crucial point—as a stimulating catalyst and in course of time assumed with the Germans a complexion of its own.

The medieval empire with all its glittering external apparel could not fail to impress itself upon the Germans in the nineteenth century when their historical sense was to be awakened. A romantic historicity, conditioned by political problems of the time, conveniently disregarded the shadowiness of the *incredibile monstrum*, the medieval empire, 'the most memorable imitation in history'.[2] Here is a classic instance of the great social responsibility

[1] *R.N.I.*, no. 113, of 29 Oct. 1204, and repeated several times; see *Register* of Innocent III (Migne, *Patrologia Latina*, ccxiv–ccxv), vii. 203; viii. 19, 24, 153; in viii. 26, he speaks of the Church of Constantinople as having been reborn into a new youth: 'in novam . . . infantiam'. About his dealings with Philip of Swabia in 1203 (*cf. M.G.H., Const.*, ii, p. 9, no. 8, §7: 'Si omnipotens Dominus regnum Grecorum michi vel leviro meo subdiderit, ecclesiam Constantinopolitanam Romanae ecclesiae . . . faciam fore subiectam'), see now A. Frolow, *Recherches sur la déviation de la IVe croisade vers Constantinople* (Paris, 1955).

[2] Sickel, *art. cit.*, p. 529.

of professional historiography, the effects of which radiate into the least historically trained sections of the populace, always ready to extract a political programme from an alleged historical fact. Does not the medieval past bear heavily on the Germans? Is not the politically arrested development of Germany a legacy of the medieval past? Is not the typically German concept of the *Obrigkeitsstaat* a persuasive demonstration of at least some effects of the regrettable symbiosis of history and politics? Can the more discerning spectator suppress the thought that German historiography had a share in shaping German politics? Large questions indeed, but questions which obtrude themselves upon those who reflectingly distinguish between the empire and the romantic aureole with which historians have enveloped it.

Trinity College, Cambridge.

IV

A SCOTTISH CHARTER AND ITS PLACE IN MEDIEVAL CANON LAW

I

MEDIEVAL scribes and copyists were not renowned for a profound knowledge of geographical facts. The scribes in the papal chancery who were employed to make out the numerous rescripts, bulls, decrees, constitutions, and so forth, cared little whether the paleographically and therefore much contractedly written name of a locality would be intelligible to a copyist who had not the fortune to have access to the official papal Registers. Papal decrees, usually laying down a rule of law to be observed until superseded by a later papal pronouncement, were copied wherever the word of a medieval pope held sway. But in these copies the scribes frequently gave full rein to their imaginations by writing quite unintelligible, and, in a number of cases, non-existent and fictitious addresses at the head of a particular papal decree. To the copyist, indeed, it made no difference at all whether the decretal was directed to London, Lyons, Limoges or Lund, to York or Evreux, to Lincoln or Langres. As Maitland once observed, the proper names of decretals, especially place names, had often been defaced beyond hope of recognition.[1] Dealing with one particular decretal (II.xiii.4) in which the lawsuit between two English parsons was decided, Maitland referred to the eighteen variants of the one village—" Pelen, Pele, Petel, Ploren., Pelin., Peleren., Pelerenen., Positione, Positioni, Pon., Porni, Peieren., Poinone, Portione, Pone, Portino, Porten, Potton "—and to a mere ten variants of the other

---

[1] Frederic William Maitland, *Roman Canon Law in the Church of England*, pp. 122–23.

place : "Sander, Santer, Santen, Sandeia, Sandria, Sandinia, Sandeta, Sandaia, Sand., Sandola ". " Anyone who for his sins has endured the railway journey between Oxford and Cambridge will guess that the one village is Sandy, and the other Potton; but to the decretist the whereabouts of these places was less than nothing. They might be in Spain, they might be in Hungary, they might be nowhere ".

It is this distortion and defacing of place names, often amounting to a mere caricature, which makes it extremely difficult, if not impossible, to identify the right address. This difficulty is enhanced by the medieval custom not to write the recipient's name in full, but only his initial. Thus R. might well stand for Richard, Robert, Roger, Ralph, Rupert, Rodolphus, Raymundus, Rainaldus, Ranulphus, and so forth. In a great many cases the original papal communication has been lost, and all that has come down to us is a copy which may well be the copy of another copy, itself a mere replica—and in this way the distortion of the name and place of the recipient may have grown exuberantly and luxuriously. This occurred especially frequently if the place name concerned some outlandish locality of which the scribe or copyist may never have heard. Naturally, the paleographical contractions themselves greatly assisted this process of defacing place and proper names, since the brachigraphical signs used by the scribes were not uniform throughout Western Europe; and a slight modification (or a mis-reading) may change London into Lyons, and the like. Verification in these cases, then, meets with considerable difficulties.

The collection of decretals issued by Pope Gregory IX, the so-called *Gregoriana* (*Liber Extra*) and published on September 5, 1234, was the work of the Dominican Raymundus de Pennaforte. This compilation was the first official canon law book and was based upon five previously published compilations, three of which were private works.[2]

---

[2] See the words of Gregory IX in his bull of publication: " Sane diversas constitutiones et decretales epistolas prædecessorum nostrorum, in diversa dispersas

Raymundus did not embody in his collection all the decretals
which he had found in the previous five compilations, but,
for reasons which are not relevant to the present enquiry,
he rejected a number of decretals which until then had
formed the common law of the medieval Church.[3] Amongst
the decretals which the Dominican incorporated in the
Gregoriana was also one which was the sixth chapter of the
title " De Donationibus " in the third book (*Extra* : III.
xxiv.6). This decretal was originally issued by Innocent III,
and the *Gregoriana* gives us the following address : " Idem
(*scil.* Innocent III) R. de Burg. et G. Berburg. abbatibus" ;
the decretal begins with the words : " Cum dilecti filii ".
Now this address would naturally assist us very little in
tracing the whereabouts of these abbots. When we enquire
into the genesis of this chapter, we shall find that Raymundus took it from the *Compilatio Tertia*, that is to say, from
the compilation of decretals which had the official sanction
of Innocent III and was made upon his explicit order
by the papal notary, Petrus Collivaccinus Beneventanus,
between 1208 and 1210.[4] It was promulgated, probably,
about the turn of the years 1209 and 1210, and contained a
pontifically approved selection of decretals which were
issued during the first twelve years of Innocent's reign.
The preamble addressed to the masters and scholars at
Bologna notifies them that they may use this compilation
" tam in judiciis quam in scholis ".

The immediate predecessor of Innocent's *Compilatio
Tertia* was the so-called *Compilatio Romana*, the work of

volumina, quarum aliquæ propter nimiam similitudinem, et quædam propter
contrarietatem, nonnullæ etiam propter sui prolixitatem, confusionem inducere
videbantur; aliquæ vero vagabantur extra volumina supradicta, quæ tamquam
incertæ frequenter in judiciis vacillabant, Ad communem et maxime studentium
utilitatem, per dilectum filium fratrem Raymundum capellanum et pœnitentiarium
nostrum, illas in unum volumen (resecatis superfluis) providimus redigendas,
adjicientes constitutiones nostras et decretales epistolas, per quas nonnulla, quæ in
prioribus erant dubia, declarantur. Volentes igitur. . .".
3 A useful conspectus of the chapters which the Church did not " receive ", will be
found in Friedberg's *Quinque Compilationes Antiquæ*, pp. vii, xxiv, xxvii, xxxiii,
xxxiv.
4 For the exact date of its publication, see now Kuttner in *Miscellanea Mercati*,
1946, Vol. 5, p. 621, and *idem*, " Liber Canonicus: A Note on ' Dictatus Papæ ',
c. 17 " in *Studi Gregoriani*, 1947, Vol. 2, p. 387.

Master Bernardus Compostellanus Antiquus.[5] But although
Bernard relied exclusively on the official Registers of
Innocent III and hence could not be charged with incorporating apocryphal or spurious decretals, his papal master
did not approve his work for use in the schools : Innocent's
reason was that a number of decretals was included which
were, in his opinion, unsuitable for juristic and legislative
treatment.[6] Hence, Innocent ordered his notary to compile
the official collection.   Nevertheless, in Bernard's *Compilatio Romana* we also find the above-mentioned decretal
" Cum dilecti ", which is here the third chapter of the title
" De Donationibus " in the third book.[7]

But this compilation of Master Bernard was not the first
effort to gather together and bring under appropriate title
headings decretals issued by this extremely busy pope.   The
first effort to make a collection, on the basis of a selection,
of his decretals came from the pen of a Benedictine monk,
Rainerius de Pomposa, who published his work in the
autumn of 1201.[8] The collection of the Benedictine was
soon superseded by the compilation of the English canonist,
Gilbert.   His collection consists of Innocentian as well as
pre-Innocentian decretals[9] and was published in the early
summer of 1202.   Another English canonist, Alan, published his compilation in 1206.   Alan's compilation is on a

---

[5] First MS. (B.M., Royal 9 B XI) discovered and described by A. Theiner, *Dis-
quisitiones Criticæ in Præcipuas Canonum et Decretalium Canones*, Rome, 1836,
pp. 129–36 (disquis. II, cap. iv). Further MSS. (B.M. Harl. 3834; Paris, Bibl. Nat.
Lat. 18223) described by H. Singer, " Die Dekretalensammlung des Bernardus
Compostellanus Antiquus " in *Sitzungsberichte der kaiserlichen Akademie der
Wissenschaften*, Vienna, phil.hist.Kl., Vol. 171, part 2, 1914, pp. 9, 12; cf. also
Ourliac, in *Dictionnaire de Droit Canonique*, Vol. 2, p. 775, and Kuttner, *Repertorium*, p. 319, *idem*, " Bernardus Compostellanus Antiquus " in *Traditio*, Vol. 1,
1944, p. 327 and notes, who identified a fourth copy of Bernard's compilation in
Modena, Bibl. Estense (*Repertorium*, p. 317, and *art. cit.*, p. 328).
[6] See the prologue of Tancred to the *Apparatus* on the *Compilatio Tertia*, *infra*
note 11, Hostiensis, *Summa Aurea*, proem., and the observations of Singer,
loc. cit., pp. 29–31.
[7] According to the analysis of Bernard's compilation by Singer, p. 79.
[8] See F. Heyer in *Zeitschrift der Savigny Stiftung für Rechtsgeschichte*,
Kanonistische Abt., Vol. 4, 1914, p. 596.
[9] 290 chapters made out of 258 decretals; ninety-six chapters (compiled out of
ninety decretals) belong to Innocent III, see R. v. Heckel, " Die Dekretalensammlungen des Gilbertus und Alanus " in *Zeitschrift der Savigny Stiftung, Kanonist.
Abt.*, Vol. 29, 1940, pp. 116–357, at p. 144.

far greater scale than Gilbert's.[10] These two collections
formed the backbone of the later so-called *Compilatio
Secunda*, which was the work of the Welshman, Johannes
Galensis, and which was published between 1210 and 1215.
Although John's collection followed Innocent's *Compilatio
Tertia*, it still kept the name of " Secunda " for chrono-
logical reasons.[11]

Now to return to the decretal of the *Gregoriana* which
has that enigmatic address. As we said before, this decretal
will be re-discovered in the *Compilatio Tertia*, where it also
appears under the title " De Donationibus " (ch. 3), but
with a heading which is again different : " Idem R. Cede-
burgen. et G. Briburgen. abbatibus et mag. I rectori
ecclesiæ de Bilchiale ". That is the address which Friedberg's edition of the *Compilatio Tertia* gives us. But when
we turn to one of the numerous MSS. of the *Compilatio
Tertia*, we shall find still another discrepancy, for instead

---

10 It contains 484 chapters, of which 139 come from popes prior to Innocent III,
whilst the latter's amount to 345, see Heckel, *art. cit.*, p. 147. Because of the
enormous activity of this pope and the increase in rules of law laid down by him
in his numerous decrees, the compiling of his letters, etc., became almost inevitable, if the schools and courts were to have up-to-date guidance.

11 It may be advisable to transcribe in full the chief source of our knowledge concerning the so-called *compilationes antiquæ*, that is the prologue of Tancred, the
Bolognese professor of canon law, to his great *Apparatus* on the *Compilatio Tertia*.
The prologue is here transcribed from MS. C III 4 of Durham Cathedral Chapter
Library, fol. 95ra : " Post compilationem factam a Gratiano multæ a Romana
curia epistolæ emanaverunt, quas magister B(ernardus), tunc præpositus, post-
modum episcopus Papiensis, ad studentium utilitatem sub competentibus titulis
collocavit, quædam antiquiora interserendo, et vocatur Compilatio Prima. Et
post illam compilationem aliæ quædam decretales a diversis apostolicis emanaverunt, quas magister Gilbertus ad instar primæ compilationis sub titulis collocavit. Post illum vero magister Alanus suam similiter compilationem effecit,
tandem magister Bernardus Compostellanus, archidiaconus in Romana curia, in
qua curia moram faciens aliquantum, de regestis domini Innocentii papæ unam
fecit decretalium compilationem, quam Bononiæ studentes Romanam compilationem aliquanto vocaverunt. Verum, quia in ipsa compilatione quædam reperie-
bantur decretales, quas Romana curia refutabat, sicut hodie quædam sunt
in secundis, quas curia ipsa non recipit, idcirco felicis recordationis dominus papa Innocentius III, suas decretales usque ad annum XII editas per
magistrum P(etrum) Beneventanum notarium suum in præsenti opere com-
pilatas Bononiæ studentes compilavit. Post illarum receptionem magister
Johannes Galensis decretales omnium apostolorum, qui præcesserant Innocentium
de dictis compilationibus Gilberti et Alani extrahens quandam compilationem
ordinavit, quæ hodie mediæ sive secundæ decretales dicuntur ". There is also a
transcription of this prologue in A. Friedberg, *op. cit.*, p. xxiii, and J. F. v. Schulte,
Geschichte der Quellen und Literatur des Canonischen Rechts, Vol. 1, p. 224, and
parts of it by Singer, *loc. cit.*, p. 3, note 2.

230   A SCOTTISH CHARTER

of the "ecclesia de Bilchiale" we have an "ecclesia de barch".[12] Moreover, the text in the *Gregoriana* begins : "Cum dilecti filii abbas et monachi de Melios", whilst the text in the Royal MS. reads : "Cum dilecti filius [*sic*] abbas et monachi de Mellitis . . .". It seems almost impossible to discover where the monks of "Melios" or "Mellitis" were located.

As far as can be established, the decretal "Cum dilecti" made its first appearance as a legislative and generally applicable measure in the collection of the Englishman, Alan, who brought it under the heading "De Fide Instrumentorum", where it formed the third chapter. But the location of the monks appears to meet with insuperable difficulties, since another discrepancy here arises ; the address reads in Alan's collection : "Innocentius III R. de Sede Wrege et G. de Riburg. abbatibus et magistro I. rectori ecclesiæ de Lilen" : *Compilatio Alani* : II.xii.3,[13] whilst still another MS. copy of Alan's work has "ecclesiæ de Lien".[14] It is still a matter of conjecture rather than of scientific certainty where Alan obtained the wording and matter of the decretals which he had incorporated in his collection. If the copyist of the Fulda MSS., from which the above transcriptions are taken, was reliable, then the possibility that Alan had relied on the official Registers of Innocent III must be dismissed, since this decretal will also be found in them, but with still another discrepancy, for we have here the following address : "R. de Geclewerds, G. de Driburg, et T. (instead of I.) rectori ecclesiæ de Lilleschæ".[15] It seems that Potthast in his *Regesta* relied on the official Register of Innocent III as transcribed by Migne.[15a] The confusion now seems complete : the rector of the church is sometimes situated in "Lilen", sometimes in "Lien", and sometimes in "Lilleschæ" ; the abbots change their places from "Sedes

---

12 MS. B.M., Royal 11 C VII, fol. 174va.
13 See Heckel, *art. cit.*, p. 251, transcribing from MS. Fulda, Landes Bibliothek, D.14.
14 Heckel, *loc. cit.*, MS. Fulda, D.5.
15 Migne, *Patr. Lat.*, Vol. 215, *Registrum Innocentii III*, cols. 309–10.
15a See Potthast, *Regesta Pontificum Romanorum*, No. 2151.

Wrege " and " Riburg " to " Geclewerds " and " Driburg " as well as to the truncated " Burg." and "Berburg."
Furthermore, the monks sometimes live at " Melios ",
sometimes at " Mellitis " and, according to the Register,
at " Melros ". Looking at the contents of the decretal
itself the confusion, if possible, is still heightened by the
variants of the names : whilst in the *Gregoriana* we read of
a " nobilis vir Alanus " who had molested the monks,
situated in some undefined place, we find in the Registers
that it was a " nobilis vir Albanus " who had behaved thus
wickedly. The pious father of this culprit is not named in
the *Gregoriana*, whilst the Registers pretend to know that
his name was " Willelmus ". How can order be brought
into this utter confusion of names and places?

II

The already mentioned MSS. at Fulda—D.5, D.14—
were first made known and described by the late J. F. v.
Schulte.[16] He correctly identified the collections contained
in these two MSS. as Alan's compilations, although he went
very much astray in determining the relationship between
the two. It has recently been established by R. v. Heckel
that—in contrast to the view held by Schulte—the one
Fulda MS., D.14, is a copy of an older Alan MS. which
embodies his compilation in a less developed state than
D.14.[17] Where the archetype of Alan's compilation is, in
what state it may be, and how much it differs from the final
Compilatio Alani—no attempt has been made to ascertain.
When working on his " Prodromus Corporis Glossarum ",
Professor St. Kuttner found a compilation of decretals in
Durham Cathedral Chapter Library, which he was unable
to identify.[18]

---

[16] See J. F. v. Schulte, " Die Compilationen Gilberts und Alanus " in *Sitzungsberichte der kaiserl. Akademie der Wissenschaften*, phil.hist.Kl., Vol. 65, 1870,
pp. 595–698.

[17] This MS., D.14, according to Heckel, pp. 130, 138, formed the basis of D.5, so
that there are at least three stages of the MS. tradition : MS. (x), D.14, D.5.

[18] Kuttner, *Repertorium*, pp. 319–20. I desire to express my thanks to the Dean
and Chapter of Durham Cathedral for the loan of their MS. C III 3. This collection

A close study of this Durham MS. reveals a compilation
of decretals which shows a considerable affinity with Alan's
own compilation. Without anticipating the detailed
results of a thorough analysis of this compilation [19] we
venture to say that it may well present Alan's compilation
in a preparatory state : it has as yet no title headings, the
chapters do not yet seem to follow an arranged pattern,
they are almost invariably given in full together with the
pars decisa, and the work was certainly that of an English
canonist, as is evidenced by the almost always correct way
of spelling proper names, such as Kenilworth, Wenlock,
Bridlington, Ramsay, Dorchester, Colchester, and so forth,
names which had been so much corrupted by non-English
scribes and copyists.[20]   Furthermore, a quite dispropor-
tionate part of the decretals deals with English persons and
places, and a number of decretals will be found in this
Compilatio Dunelmensis which were not embodied in any
later collection and which were concerned with some English
bishopric or abbacy : the compiler must therefore have had
some personal interest in inserting these decretals into his
collection.[21]   As so often when studying a canonical collection, the student is confronted with a whole set of new
problems, and not infrequently he is faced with material
that sheds new light on events hitherto regarded as unimpeachable.

In the presently discussed collection, too, we come upon
an entry that is at first sight puzzling.   For on fol. 154rb

---

has 188 chapters (fol. 123ra to fol. 158ra) according to my computation, but
in the bottom margins many Innocentian decretals had been added. Glosses are
found only occasionally, none of them bearing any siglum.

[19] We hope to publish a detailed analysis of this interesting compilation in a subsequent article.

[20] Other English place names occurring in our *Compilatio Dunelmensis* are, for
instance, Evesham, Coventry, Menevia and Bangor, St. Albans, Richmond,
Chichester, Bath, quite apart from the ever recurring Canterbury, York, Durham,
London, Norwich, Worcester, Winchester, Leicester, Exeter, and so forth.
Even the less well-known names are invariably correctly spelt.

[21] From this point of view there is some resemblance between the *Compilatio Dunelmensis* and the *Collectio Sangermanensis* which is also almost certainly an
English product, see H. Singer, " Neue Beiträge über die Dekretalensammlungen
vor und nach Bernard von Pavia " in *Sitzungsberichte der kaiserl. Akad. d. Wiss.*,
Vol. 171, part 1, 1914, pp. 113–14.

we unexpectedly find the 143rd chapter which is headed :
" Omnibus sanctæ matris ecclesiæ filiis tam præsentibus
quam futuris Walter filius Alani dapifer regis salutem ".
It is certainly startling to find in a compilation designed to
follow the usual demands of canonical collections, a chapter
headed in the traditional charter way and to all intents and
purposes appearing as part and parcel of the collection—in
midst of all the papal rescripts, bulls, etc., addressed to
archiepiscopal, episcopal, abbatial and other clerical recipi-
ents. This " chapter ", a canonically irrelevant element
in a collection, contains a charter of Walter the Steward,
in which he made certain grants to the monks of the convent
at Melrose, a Cistercian settlement. But when we look at
the 144th chapter on the same folio and in the same column,
we shall discover that the foregoing entry, however unusual,
was well justified.

   This 144th chapter bears the heading in our *Compilatio
Dunelmensis* : " Idem (*scil.* Innocent III) dilectis filiis R.
de jedewit et G. de derburg et magistro I. rectori ecclesiæ
de lilesclive ", and turns out to be a mandatory letter of
Innocent III to the clerics named in the address. They
are instructed to rectify some alleged wrong which the
grantor's son, Alan, had inflicted on the monks in violation
of his father's promises as set forth in the charter (chapter
143). The charter was obviously included by the compiler
in order to facilitate the understanding of Innocent's injunctions. However unusual this procedure is, it is of great
help in assessing the worth of Innocent's juristic arguments,
and also in appraising the juristic value of the charter itself.
The very fact of its insertion in this collection strongly
suggests that the compiler must have been well acquainted
with the genesis of Innocent's mandate and that he must
have had access to the original of the charter ; in view of its
merely local importance one would not presume that it was
available in copies. How little this charter and the resultant
dispute were taken note of can be gauged by the silence of
the Chronicle of Melrose to which we will presently turn.

Moreover, it may be tentatively suggested that the compiler, if not a Northerner, at least must have worked on his compilation in the North of England,[22] perhaps in the border district.[23]

This charter was printed, as far as could be established, only once, namely, in the *Liber de Melrose*, published in 1837.[24] Since no date is given in the charter, we can but fix the grant within a certain period. The *terminus a quo* must be 1164, the year in which King William began his reign; he is named as the ruling Scottish King. For its *terminus ad quem* no other clue is available but the year in which the death of Walter occurred, that is, 1177.[25] This Walter was a " familiaris noster " of the convent, as the Chronicle called him, that is to say, a lay associate of the monastery.[26] He had previously founded Paisley priory between 1161 and 1164.[27] The charter makes it clear that his official title was still only " dapifer " (butler) of the King, and not yet the more dignified Seneschall. He had been the first High Steward of Scotland, having been appointed by King David.[28] Our collection transcribes only the juristically relevant parts of the charter, omitting the actual geographical boundaries of the grant in land and the usual closing words with the names of the witnesses present.

---

22 Melrose was a daughter foundation of Riveaulx in Yorkshire: there was much intercourse between them, see Sir M. Powicke, " Ailred of Riveaulx " in *Bulletin of the John Rylands Library*, Vol. 6, 1921–22, pp. 336, 341, 344, 460–66, 480.

23 I was unable to trace the origin of this MS. According to the *Catalogi Veteres Librorum Ecclesiæ Cathedralis Dunelmensis*, ed. Beriah Botfield, Surtees Society Publications, Vol. 7, p. 35, this MS (C III 3) was in Durham Cathedral Chapter Library in the year 1390. The hand is almost certainly an early thirteenth-century English hand; the marginal glosses are definitely of English provenance. The spelling of " Makelin " should also be borne in mind. I am much indebted to my colleague, Dr. D. E. Easson, for helping me with the verification of Scottish names.

24 *Liber Sanctæ Mariæ de Melrose*, Monumenta vetustiora monasterii cisterciensis de Melrose, Bannatyne publication, Edinburgh, 1837, Vol. 1, No. 66, pp. 55–56.

25 See *Chronica de Mailros*, in *Rerum Anglicarum Scriptorum Veterum tomus primus*, Oxoniæ, 1684, p. 174, and A. O. Anderson, *Early Sources of Scottish History*, Vol. 2, p. 297.

26 "Walterus filius Alani dapifer regis Scotiæ, familiaris noster, diem obiit, cuius beata anima vivat in gloria ", Chronicle of Melrose, *loc. cit.*

27 Anderson, *op. cit.*, p. 251, note 2.

28 See *Scots Peerage*, ed. by J. B. Paul and others, Vol. 1, pp. 11–12; and Anderson, *op. cit.*, Vol. 2, p. 362, note 1.

If for no other reason, the importance of this charter for the medieval canon law warrants its transcription in the appendix.

There is no reason to doubt the correctness of the date of Innocent III's mandate as given in the Register: II Nonas Martii (March 6) of the seventh year of Innocent's pontificate, that is, 1204.[29] This, incidentally, was the same year in which Alan, Walter Steward's son and the alleged culprit, died.[30] The names of persons and places mentioned in the papal rescript can easily be verified, thanks to the geographical knowledge of compiler and scribe of our collection. " Jedewit " is Jedburgh, " Derburg " is Dryburgh, and the last name, Lilesclive is almost correctly spelt (Lilliesleaf). R. certainly stands for Ralph, the abbot of Jedburgh,[31] who died in 1205, whilst G. is the initial of abbot Geoffrey of Dryburgh,[32] a Premonstratensian monastery. It was not possible to establish the identity of the rector I.[33] It may also be profitable to transcribe this mandate and to show the variants.

III

There are three stipulations in the juristically certainly not satisfactory charter of Walter Steward. In the first place he granted in alms certain lands, mainly in Roxburghshire, to the church of the monks at Mauchline. Walter therefore expressed the wish that the monks should use these lands unencumbered by secular interference ; in particular they should be freed from the duty of paying taxes for the lands granted. In the second place Walter granted the monks the right of pasture in his forest within the specified boundaries (between Douglas, Lesmahagow, Glengivel and the River Ayr) as well as certain other privileges (*asiamenta*,

---

[29] Potthast, No. 2151, also registers the letter under this date, also *Calendar of Papal Registers, Letters*, ed. W. H. Bliss, Vol. 1, p. 16.

[30] Chronicle of Melrose, *ed. cit.*, p. 181.

[31] Chronicle of Melrose, *ed. cit.*, p. 179.

[32] See Anderson, *op. cit.*, Vol. 2, p. 362, note 8.

[33] *Cal. Pap. Reg., Letters*, Vol. 1, p. 16, Migne, *loc. cit.*, as well as Anderson give his initial as T, but in view of the variant in our MS. as well as in the Royal MS. (*supra*, note 12) the correctness of T is open to doubt.

carucata). In the third place Walter stipulated an annual payment of five silver marks for the last-named grants and he prohibited the monks from hunting in his forest for beasts and birds.

It was this last-mentioned proviso of the charter that gave rise to a dispute between the monks of Melrose and Walter Steward's son, Alan (not Albanus, as in the Registers).[34] Alan, according to Innocent's mandate to the clerics, tried to turn those lands which his father Walter had given to the monks in alms, into a forest, so that the second and third stipulations of the charter were now also to refer to the first stipulation, or in other words, that he attempted to regain the lands given away by Walter, in which the monks were now to have only certain specified rights, but not the exclusive property (which Walter obviously meant them to have). The wording of the charter was most unfortunate and left ample room for almost any kind of interpretation.

We gather from the papal rescript that the case had been brought to the notice of the pope the year before, *i.e.*, 1203. For in the mandatory letter referred to in this decretal the pope instructed the three clerics (Ralph, Geoffrey, and Rector I or T) to order Alan to abstain, on pain of ecclesiastical censures, from further molestation of the monks in the lands given by Walter Steward, to examine witnesses on the disputed points, and to arrive at a decision as to the rights and wrongs of the case. But the three delegated judges were unable to come to any decision, despite their careful examination of witnesses and documents. They therefore submitted all the files and the whole material to Rome requesting the pope to decide the case. In view of the loose wording of the charter the helplessness of the three judges cannot occasion surprise. Although a term was fixed for both parties to appear in Rome, only the abbot cared to come, whilst Alan did not trouble to send proctors. The pope, consequently, examined the evidence submitted,

---

[34] This Alan should not, of course, be confused with his grandfather Alan.

and recognized that on its basis judgment should be rendered in favour of the monks. He therefore returned all the material to the three judges instructing them to proceed to the afore-mentioned judgment and to compel Alan and his party under the threat of ecclesiastical censures to refrain from turning the lands into a forest. In the opinion of Innocent III the clause concerning the forest could not be extended to the previous donation of the lands which were given to the monks without any reservation. This apparently was the intention of the donor, as Innocent argued, and in the realm of gifts (" beneficia ") the greatest latitude in interpreting the donor's intentions must be allowed.

To recapitulate. Apart from our collection, the *Compilatio Dunelmensis*, this Innocentian letter was also incorporated in the compilation of Alan, but he had excised a good deal of it. From Alan's collection the decretal went into the so-called *Compilatio Romana* (1208) of Bernardus Compostellanus Antiquus (III.xix.2) and from here it made its way into the Innocentian compilation, the *Compilatio Tertia* (1209–1210). It was finally taken into the *Gregoriana* (III.xxiv.6) in a still more truncated form and then remained the " jus commune " of the medieval Church until the promulgation of the new *Codex Juris Canonici* in 1918. Nevertheless, the decretal, especially in its considerably abbreviated form, cannot be properly understood, unless the original charter (out of which the dispute arose) is taken into account. It is not, therefore, surprising to find that the *glossa ordinaria* on this decretal in the *Compilatio Tertia* contains only one gloss which helps little in interpreting the text : the gloss is on the word " foreste " and merely says : " Foresta est locus ubi includuntur feræ et ubi jus venandi non habetur ".[35] This paucity of glossatorial activity in respect of this decretal is quite understandable, since by the time the *Compilatio Tertia* came to be glossed (*i.e.*, after 1210) hardly anyone outside the

---

[35] This gloss, fol. 174va, MS. Royal 11 C VII, though unsigned, seems to come from the pen of Tancred himself.

immediate neighbourhood of this Scottish district knew what the case was really about.   Here in the *Compilatio Dunelmensis* we are provided with the key to this decretal, since the compiler, though grossly violating the canonical tradition of not including in a collection of papal decrees any nonpapal material, obviously foresaw the interpretative difficulties which future canonists would have without the original charter.   An otherwise negligible and quite unimportant donation of mere local Scottish interest has thus helped to shape the common law of the medieval Church.

WALTER ULLMANN.

APPENDIX

A

The Charter of Walter, son of Alan *

Omnibus sanctæ matris ecclesiæ filiis tam præsentibus quam futuris, Walter filius Alani dapifer regis scottorum salutem.

Sciant omnes tam præsentes quam futuri me dedisse et hac carta mea [1] confirmasse deo et ecclesiæ sanctæ mariæ de melrose et monachis ibidem [2] servientibus pro animabus davidis et malcolmi regis dominorum meorum et comitis henrici et patris mei et matris meæ et omnium antecessorum meorum [3] et successorum meorum et pro salute willelmi regis scotiæ [4] et davidis fratris eius et pro salute mea et omnium hæredum meorum in liberam et puram et perpetuam elemosinam totam terram de makelin per divisas tales etc.[5] hanc [6] elemosinam volo ut prædicti monachi de melrose ita libere et quiete et honorifice perpetuo tenore ab omnibus servitiis et placitis asisis quoque et auxiliis et omni exactione sæculari et consuetudine in perpetuum teneant et possideant, sicut liberius et quietius et honorificentius aliqua elemosina teneri potest et possideri.   Prætereæ dedi eis [7] et concessi eis

---

* Abbreviation used: L : *Liber de Melrose, ed. cit.,* pp. 55–56, No. 66.
[1] L: mea carta.
[2] L: inserts deo.
[3] L: om.meorum.
[4] L: scottorum.
[5] L gives here the geographical boundaries.
[6] MS. has between "hanc" and "elemosinam" a "p" with the corrector's dot under the "p" (p). This "p" obviously is a scribal mistake.
[7] L: om.eis.

totam pasturam forestæ meæ usque ad divisas de diveglas et de
lesmahagu et de glenegevel a parte aquionali fluminis ar cum
omnibus asiamentis in nemore et in omnibus eis necessariis et
unam carrucatam terræ ad excolendam in illis locis ubi provi-
derint melius et utilius esse ad opus suum libere et quiete de
me et hæredibus meis ab omnibus servitiis perpetuo tenore
possidendam, excepto quod V m argenti mihi et hæredibus meis
annuatim persolvent, salva tamen foresta mea tantum in bestiis
et avibus.[8]

B

The letter of Innocent III †

Innocentius dilectio filio [1] R. de jedewit [2] et G. de derburg [3]
et magistro I.[4] rectori ecclesiæ de lilesclive.[5]

Cum dilecti filii abbas et conventus [6] de melrose [7] proposuerint
coram nobis quod nobilis vir Alanus [8] quasdam terras a W.
quondam patre [9] ipsius eorum ecclesiæ de makelin [10] in elemosinam assignatas violenter redigere cupiens [11] in forestam [12] eos
super ipsis [13] indebite molestaret, vobis dedisse recolimus in
mandatis, ut ipsum A. ab ipsorum super [14] terris indebita
molestatione desistere per censuram ecclesiasticam appellatione
postposita cogeretis. Verum, ut [15] super causa ipsa mandatum
apostolicum impleretis, diligentius procedentes in causam [16]
partibus in vestra præsentia [17] constitutis, testes recepistis

---

[8] In L follow the signatures of the witnesses.

† The decretal (Potthast, No. 2151) is contained: Register (Migne, *Patr. Lat.*, *loc.
cit.*, cols. 309–10); *Compilatio Romana*: III.xix.3; *Compilatio Tertia*: III.xviii.3;
Extra: III.xxiv.6. First incorporated by Alan: *Compilatio Alani*: II.xii.3.
Abbreviations used: G: *Gregoriana* (*Extra*); R: Register.

[1] GR: om. dilecto filio.
[2] R: Geclewerds.
[3] R: Driburg.
[4] R: T.
[5] R: Lilleschæ. G has this address: Idem R. de Burg. et G. Berburg. abbatibus.
[6] GR: monachi.
[7] G: melios. R: melros.
[8] R: Albanus.
[9] G: om. W. quondam; R: reads Willelmo.
[10] R: machelin.
[11] G: cupiat.
[12] G begins here the *pars decisa* down to mandamus.
[13] G: his for ipsis.
[14] GR: insert illis between super and terris.
[15] G: reads cum instead of ut.
[16] G: causa.
[17] G: præsentia nostra.

hincinde ac [18] super attestationibus eorum [19] et [20] in [20a] instrumentis, diu [21] disputationibus ac disceptationibus [22] habitis, in causa ipsa usque ad sententiæ calculum processistis et [23] causam ipsam sufficienter instructam, ad nostram audientiam remittentes, octavas [24] sancti andreæ [25] proximo præteritas pro termino partibus assignastis. Parte igitur abbatis et monachorum [26] ad ipsum terminum veniente, tandem, quia pars adversa diutius exspectata non venit, super instrumentis jam dictis, depositionibus [27] testium et partis allegationibus utriusque, cum fratribus nostris tractatum habuimus diligentem et, inquisita veritate diligentius, et discussa, evidenter agnovimus, super ipsa causa sententiam [28] jam dicto monasterio esse dandam. Ut autem per diligentiam vestram [29] finis causæ imponatur eidem, instrumentorum tenorem, depositiones testium et [30] allegationes et,[31] prout ea receperatis [32] sigillorum nostrorum [33] munimine consignata,[34] vobis sub bulla nostra [35] remittimus interclusa, per apostolica scripta vobis mandamus,[36] quod,[37] auctoritate nostra suffulti, ad sententiam pro ipso monasterio proferendam non obstante contradictione vel appellatione cuiuslibet, procedatis contradictores censura ecclesiastica [38] compescentes, et facientes, quod judicaveritis auctoritate nostra firmiter observari,[39] cum ex tenore instrumenti evidenter [40] appareat, quod hæc [41] fuit

---

[18] G: et instead of ac.
[19] G: illorum instead of eorum.
[20] R: ut instead of et.
[20a] R: etiam for in.
[21] G: om. diu.
[22] G: discrepationibus.
[23] G: om. et.
[24] G: om. from octavas down to dandam.
[25] MS.: andrei.
[26] MS.: monachi.
[27] MS.: disputationibus.
[28] R: inserts pro before jam.
[29] G: nostram (for vestram).
[30] R: om. et.
[31] GR: etiam for et.
[32] MS.: receperam. R: receperamus.
[33] G: vestrorum (for nostrorum).
[34] G: roborata vel consignata.
[35] G: sigillo nostro.
[36] R: præcipiendo mandantes.
[37] GR: quatenus.
[38] R: per cens. eccl.
[39] G has this reading: Mandamus, quatenus ad sententiam pro ipso monasterio proferendam appellatione postposita procedatis, cum ex tenore. . . .
[40] G: vehementer.
[41] MS.: hoc.

mens et intentio donatoris, ut clausula [42] de foresta, quæ in fine
ponitur instrumenti, non ad superiorem donationem, quæ tam
pura et libera fuit, ut immunis esset ab omni [43] exactione et
consuetudine sæculari, sed ad inferiorem concessionem, quæ
pensionem et determinationem habet insertam, juxta sanum
referri debet intellectum, quia in contractibus [44] plena, in testa-
mentis plenior est, in beneficiis quoque plenissima interpretatio [45]
adhibenda.

---

[42] MS.: clausa.
[43] G: om. ab omni.
[44] MS.: actibus.
[45] MS.: interceptio.

V
SOME REFLECTIONS ON THE OPPOSITION
OF FREDERIK II TO THE PAPACY

I

The present occasion may perhaps be a suitable opportunity to ask the question, how far the charges of Frederick II against his contemporary papacy were justified on general ideological grounds. That is to say, did the reasons of Frederick for not accepting the papal verdicts, attack the fundamental position of the pope? Were in other words the arguments advanced by him apt to deliver the intended decisive blow against the ideological position of the papacy? Did his arguments attack the papal doctrine on its own ground? To ask these questions appears all the more important as the conflict between him and the papacy stood virtually at the end of a long line of distinguished battles between the two contestants. The papacy under Gregory IX and Innocent IV produced no new arguments; no novel or hitherto unheard-of views were expressed; although the arguments were presented with greater force and were more sharply formulated, the ideological line of the papacy kept entirely within the framework which tradition had marked out. The assumption is warranted that the Frederician arguments against the exercise of true papal monarchical powers in fact — and not only in theory — were not *ad hoc* prepared or rashly put together, but presented themselves as the mature and deliberate answer on the part of the imperial chancery. Challenged as he was by an extremely well-equipped opponent, how did Frederick counteract? His reasons may well be taken as the considerate reply on the part of the whole Staufen ideology.

More than that: no other king or emperor before him had such long « experience » with the papal curia and its ideological set-up as Frederick II had: in his youth he was, so to speak, nurtured at the bosom of Innocent III to whose own reasonings he owed so much; he had imbibed the very air of papal ideology and had acted in its very spirit, as his earlier legislation showed; he had faced Gregory IX in the first duel in 1227, and through the protracted negotiations and vicissitudes of the thirties he had gained an invaluable experience. It is no exaggeration to say that there was hardly any other ruler in medieval Europe who virtue of his very long reign could have accumulated such vast experience, full grasp and intimate knowledge of his opponent's ways of thinking as Frederick had. It is therefore clear that this asset is of inestimable value in a contest which is almost exclusively based upon the ideological standpoint. When we now take into account that the papacy of Frederick's time produced no new material, sprang no surprises and moved wholly within the precincts of its own — and ancient — programme, we may well be entitled to expect an equally ripe and considered reply on the part of its opponent.

There is a further consideration which is applicable to Frederick alone. Though it would be hard to deny that his predecessors, notably his grandfather — as also the Salians — had able advisers, Frederick could call upon a whole reservoir of first-class counsellors and experts in preciseley this ideological field. Like him, they too had been witnesses and actors for a considerable time; they were the alert, open-minded and keen students of law producing that mixture of diplomatic statesman and juristic expert; they enjoyed the confidence of their master to an unparallelled degree. They were, in a word, the best experienced, best trained and ablest advisers who could well be the envy of any ruler in the thirteenth century, or for that matter in any century: which European court had such a gallaxy of talent at its disposal? Smooth, flexible, versatile, perfect masters of the written and spoken word, adaptable and quickly sensing an opponent's flaw of thought in the argument, in short capable men Frederick was fortunate enough in relying upon, men who were almost born for the position they occupied.

Moreover, although independent of the specific conditions prevailing in the Frederician court, the attitude in the other European courts was by no means one of obsequiousness to the papal court or cause. If at any time there was an atmosphere which prima facie was inclined to favour the cause of the emperor, it was then. The practical advances which the Innocentian papacy had made in the beginning of the century, did not by any means endear the papal-hierocratic programme to those who still mattered, and this quite apart from the — one might almost be tempted to say — natural antagonism of the episcopacy to the papacy. The soil, no doubt, was fertile for the acceptance of the imperial arguments: as Frederick himself on more than one occasion pointed out, his cause was the cause of all secular rulers. The receptivity of the soil for the « secular reasoning » must be taken into account, if one wishes to assess the Zeitgeist and to evaluate the strenght and efficacy of Frederick's arguments.

In sum, then, the setting was by no means unfavourable for the Staufen emperor in the decisive years of 1239-1240 and 1245. The question therefore is: how effectively did he deal, equipped as he was, advised as he was, and favoured as his cause was by the temper of the time, with the shattering onslaught delivered by the papacy against him? That the papacy based itself upon its traditional application of the *plenitudo potestatis* with all its attendant consequences; that the papacy acted within the framework of its hierocratically conceived monarchic status; that the popes invoked the all-comprehensive binding and loosing powers as the legal basis for their juristically conceived sentences; that above all the imperial position itself — the ideological offspring of the papal mind — offered the papacy an easy target — all this is so well known that no further comment is called for. As the papacy acted on these premisses the Frederician reply, one reasonably expects, was to concentrate on these premisses: it is useless to attack an opponent on his flanks or on his periphery; a worth while attack must be directed against the core, against the substance, that is, on the premisses themselves. For if they are correct, the consequences too must be correct. The only way that therefore promised hope of success was to demolish the bases upon which the papacy worked. And these were, as I have pointed out, not new at all.

The perusal of the Frederician manifestoes, encyclicals, protests, and so forth, in these decisive years of 1239 and 1245 yields however some strange results. In the first place, they reveal a very real paucity of ideological arguments and reasons. However ably conceived and drafted they were, and however much they were tuned to achieving propagandistic effects, they contain, in comparison with the wealth of factual detail, extraordinary little which could be classed as ideological or fundamental in its conception. And what there is, is almost tucked away inmidst the din of vituperations and charges. In the second place, they do not go, when they deal with the substance of the papal position, into an argumentative exposition — and this surely was required if the basic essence of the papal standpoint was to be decisively attacked — but they content themselves with mere assertions, without the attempt to reason them out or to buttress them with easily available material. Nevertheless, even in their paucity the Frederician arguments allow us a glimpse into his conceptions, however little constructive they may be considered or however little new they were. And this seems to me the most significant feature of the Frederican standpoint, namely that the papal attack did not provoke a reply within the precincts of the papal programme itself, did not, in other words, attack the hierocratic theme on its own ground, although the anti-papal side had on the one hand at least two centuries in which an effective reply could have been formulated and on the other hand had specifically in Frederick II and his advisers the best guarantors of an effective all-out attack. When even under these presuppositions, in these gruelling situations in which Frederick was to find himself, no worth while counter-attack could be delivered, the question appears indeed legitimate: was there, in the mid-thirteenth century, a possibility of delivering this all-out blow? We may postpone the answer to this crucial question — which seems to me the really significant facet of this *Letzten Waffengang* between the papacy and the Swabian house — until we have gone through some of the more pertinent statements made by Frederick II.

I I

Two lines of argumentation can be detected in the public protests of Frederick and both converged into the same channel. The one line of attack consists or Frederick's exposing the moral depravity of the popes: breach of faith, ingratitude for the services he had rendered to them, corruption and intrigues, incitement to perjury, deception and fraud, allying themselves with heretics, sowing dissension and civil strife, and so forth. This moral turpitude on the part of the popes makes them unfitted to fill the post which they occupy: they are therefore unsuitable to act as popes (1) and cannot claim that their judgments are the judgments of a *judex competens* or *judex justus*. How should he be a fair judge who

> per inhumanitatis opera non solum a divinitate sepossitus, set humanitate discretus... et non prout sancti per fidem regna vicerunt, set perfidiam et perjuria predicans universis? (2).

---

(1) It was on this conclusion that Frederick's appeal to the cardinals for a general council was based. Cf. *MGH. Const*, II, 290, n. 214.

(2) Ibid., p. 292. Cf. p. 296: « Per talem, quem merito judicem non habemus, nullam posse fieri reputamus injuriam, utpote cum se prius inimicum capitalem quam judicem nostrum et opere fuerit professus et verbo, rebelles nostros et hostes imperii publice confovendo ».

Hence it is that the popes had forfeited the right to issue orders and to command respect for their verdicts. It is the personal defect of the popes — seen entirely on a moral level — which precludes them from demanding obedience. Therefore, Frederick is anxious to stress his adherence to the orthodox faith and to protest his fullest respect for the papal office as such. He consequently distinguishes between the papal office and the individual pope:

> Illum habere preterea Christi vicarium et successorem Petri ac dispensatorem animarum fidelium indigne fatemur non ob dignitatis injuriam, sed ob *persone deffectum,*

and shortly afterwards he declares:

> Deffectum et prevaricationem ipsius in illo dolemus... itaque non miretur universalis ecclesia nec populus Christianus, si nos tales sentencias judicis non veremur, non in contemptu *papalis officii* vel apostolice dignitatis, cui omnes ortodosse fidei professores et nos specialius ceteris subesse fatemur, sed *persone prevaricationem* arguimus, qui se solio tanti regiminis monstravit indignum (3).

This line of argument is as characteristic of the 1239 protest as it is of the manifesto of 16 March 1240. Here too the main point in-midst a good deal of factual detail, is the moral depravity of Gregory IX. After declaring that,

> Nos autem, quia processum huiusmodi temeritate plenum et justitia vacuum habebamus, ad confratres suos litteras et legatos transmisimus generale petentes convocari concilium, in quo judicis corrupti nequitiam ac imperii nostri justitiam et innocentiam nostram argumentis arguere luce clarioribus spondebamus,

he exclaims:

> Attendite igitur et videte, si sunt ista facta papalia, si sunt hec opera sanctitatis, mundum exponere, nostram conculcare justitiam et secundum Mediolanensium faciem judicare! (4).

---

(3) Ibid., p. 297, lines 22 ff.
(4) Ibid., p. 310.

The tenor of this attack was therefore the personal unworthiness of Gregory IX, a defect which robs his governmental actions of legitimate value.

Whilst consequently the mode of argumentation in 1239-1240 confined itself to the personal unsuitability of Gregory IX, in 1245 we witness a notable shifting of Frederick's ground. True, the rumblings and growlings about the depravity of the papacy are still audible (5), but they take up a rather subordinate position. What stands in the foreground here is the concentration upon the papal office. This second line of attack culminates in the assertion that the papacy had transgressed the functions proper to the papal office and had therefore acted *ultra vires*. He declares that he would be prepared to accept papal verdicts, if the vicar of Christ had implemented the *vices Christi* and imitated the example of his predecessor, St. Peter (6). And what were the *vices Christi*? Frederick gives a perfectly clear answer: they consist of the *potestas in spiritualibus plenaria*, so that, even if the pope should be a sinner, his judgments within these terms of his competent functions produce automatic effects on earth and in heaven — but neither the divine nor the human law even faintly suggests that the pope could take away empires or could issue judgments *temporaliter*. In other words, the grievance of Frederick is that the pope has assumed the *potestas in temporalibus*, for which assumption no warrant anywhere can be ascertained. Let us quote this significant passage:

> Nam etsi nos nostre catholice fidei debito suggerente manifestissime fateamur, collatam a Domino sacrosancte Romane sedis antistiti plenariam potestatem in spiritualibus, quantumcumque quod absit sit ipse peccator, ut quod in terra ligaverit sit ligatum in celis, et quod solverit sit solutum, nusquam tamen legitur divina sibi vel humana lege concessum, quod transferre pro libito possit imperia aut de

---

(5) Cf., for instance, the manifesto of late 1245, in which this grievance is now extended to all clerics: « Porro qui clerici nunc censentur, patrum elemosinis inpinguati filios opprimunt ipsique nostrorum filii subditorum patrie condicionis obliti nec imperatorem nec regem aliqua veneratione dignantur, quociens in patres apostolicos ordinantur » (E. WINKELMANN, *Acta Imperii inedita* (Innsbruck 1885), II, 50 n. 46).

(6) *MGH., Const.* II, 362, n. 262, lines 7 ff.: « Si denique Christi vicarius Christi vices impleverit et si predecessoris Petri successor eiusdem imitetur exemplum... ».

puniendis temporaliter in privacione regnorum regibus aut terre principibus judicare (7).

Nor can on this presupposition the papal claim have any validity to deprive him of his emperorship. Admittedly, the imperial « consecration » belongs by right to the pope, but this does not entail the further right to depose the emperor (8). Moreover, even supposing, not admitting, that the pope has this right, it cannot be within the terms of the *plenitudo potestatis* to proceed « nullo prorsus ordine juris » against those, « quos asserit sue jurisdictioni subjectos ».

Now anyone acquainted with papal reasonings and papal doctrines will at once see that these objections and arguments of Frederick were weak, so weak in fact they not only could not produce any of the desired propagandistic effects, but also did not touch the essence of the papal ideology. For, to begin with the first line of attack, the moral depravity of a pope at no time of reflective papal thinking was considered to affect the papal function or to deprive his actions of validity. In actual fact, the objection had been implicitly anticipated as early as Leo I who by designating the pope as the *indignus heres* of Peter made with all desirable clarity that very distinction between the office and the person of the office holder which Frederick considered his strategic line of attack in 1239-1240. According to the — by then indubitably — traditional view the personal merits and demerits of the pope counted nothing: his governmental acts were as legitimate as they were valid, be they issued by a Saint or by a villain. The history of the medieval papacy would in fact bear out that this leonine distinction was at all times operative — witness a John XII in the tenth century or the popes in the mid-eleventh century (9). Perfectly clearly this view was also

---

(7) Ibid., lines 11 ff. Cf., furthermore, p. 365, lines 12 ff.: « Spirituales autem penas per sacerdotales nobis penitentias indicendas, tam pro contemptu clavium quam pro aliis transgressionis humane peccatis, nedum a summo pontifice, quem in spiritualibus patrem nostrum et dominum profitemur, si tamen ipse nos filium debita ratione cognoscat, sed per quemlibet sacerdotem reverenter accipimus et devote servamus ».

(8) Ibid., p. 362, lines 17 ff.: « Nam licet ad eum de jure et more majorum consecracio nostra pertineat, non magis ad ipsum privacio seu remocio pertinet quam ad quoslibet regnorum prelatos, qui reges suos, prout assolet, consecrant et inungunt ».

(9) The one or other instance should be given and I choose them on purpose from the eleventh century. Cf., for example, Leo IX writing to the patriarch of Constantinople (*P.L.*, CXLIII, 766 cap. 35): « Profecto sumus qualis Petrus, et non sumus qualis Petrus, quia *idem sumus officio,* et non idem

expressed — and later became the law — by Humbert who declared that only for heresy could the pope be judged, but for no other conceivable crime (10). And in the canonistic literature of the twelfth and thirteenth centuries there is plenty of discussion concerning the individual, personal failings of the pope on the one hand and his unaccountability on the other hand. This distinction between office and person belonged to the *eisernen Bestand* of papal reasoning.

Consequently, by emphasizing the distinction between office and person Frederick in actual fact used one of the papacy's most cherished arguments and adopted the very manner of papal argumentation. The pope inherits the petrine *office* — and not the personal sanctity or the personal merits of St Peter — and actions performed within the terms of his office are conceptually the actions of Peter who himself had been given the *vices Christi*. Considerations concerning the personal worth of the office holder did not enter. The binding and loosing by the pope produces automatic effects on earth and in heaven, and this quite irrespective of whether the binding and loosing concerns spiritual or temporal things, as we shall presently see : it is the objective, de-personalized action flowing from the office which, according to papal raisonnement, demands attention, and this quite irrespective of the excellence or turpitude of him who had inherited these powers. In brief, the exercise of powers was independent of the person. The judgment, sentence, verdict, order, command, decree, etc., of the pope was considered, so papal reasoning ran, entirely on the objective plane : once issued, it ceased to have any con-

---

merito... Ac si meritum Petri non habentes, *officium* autem *Petri* exsequentes, *officio nostro* debitos reposcimus honores... ita quod male vivimus, nostrum est. Quod vero bona dicimus, *cathedrae,* cuius occasione necesse habemus recta predicare... *non propter nos* in loco Petri despiciat, quia ex cathedra eius, cui auctore Deo, *qualescumque* praesidemus, debita sibi jura nostrum officium reclamat ». (The term *qualiscumque* denoting the personal demerits of the individual office holder was already used by Gelasius I, in his *Ep.* 26, cap. 11, in A. Thiel, *Epistolae Romanorum Pontificum genuinae* (Braunschweig 1862), p. 407 (= *Avellana,* Ep. 95, cap. 58, in *C.S.E.L.,* xxxv, 390): Qualescumque pontifices, etsi errore humanitus accedente... »). Peter Damian in his *Liber gratissimus (MGH., Lib. de lite,* I, 31, lines 9 ff.), says : « Licet *persona* prorsus *indigna* inveniatur, officium tamen, quod utique bonum est, competens aliquando gratia concedatur ». In fact Leo IX had with unambiguous clarity stigmatized some of his recent predecessors in the office by likening them to « mercinariis et non pastoribus, a quibus sua, non quae sunt Jesu Christi quaerentibus, devastata (Romana ecclesia) jacebat miserabiliter hactenus » (*Ep.* cit., col. 779).

(10) On this cf. W. Ullmann *in Studi Gregoriani,* iv (1952), pp. 111 ff.

nexion with the subjective personality of the office holder. The judgment, etc., was an effluence of the office, and not of the person.

Frederick's exclamation — « Attendite et videte, si sunt ista facta papalia, si sunt hec opera sanctitatis » (11) — consequently would indicate a somewhat serious misconception of the papal function altogether. That is to say, his view is that the actions of the pope must be in consonance with the « moral sanctity » of the pope. Indeed, here Frederick touches upon one of the most important points, namely the alleged sanctity of the pope: *opera sanctitatis.* The thesis that the pope was a sanctus, that he was addressed as *sanctus pater* or as *sanctitas vestra* and the like, was old papal *Ge-dankengut.* Gregory VII had given it a prominent place in his *Dictatus Papae* (no. 23), and it had a distinguished pedigree reaching back as far as the late fifth century. Although Frederick moved, as we shall see in a moment, in good company by emphasizing the personal sanctity of the pope, this view nevertheless would show some serious misunderstanding of what the papacy attributed to the pope's *sanctus* character. This *sanctus* qualification of the pope has nothing to do with the liturgical meaning of the term: the *sanctitas* of the pope is once again of an objective kind and can be understood only from the effects which papal rulings produce. This designation classically expresses the automatic effects of the exercise of binding and loosing powers: whatever the pope in his capacity as heir of petrine powers binds on earth, will automatically be bound in heaven, hence produces automatic effects in heaven. In so far the pope *qua* pope stands with one leg in heaven and with the other on earth: he is indeed the *Schnittpunkt* between heaven and earth. It is, in other words, the office and the functions contained in the office which make the pope a *sanctus,* because his rulings affect (or were said to affect) the heavenly order itself. All this belonged to the traditional papal thinking (12), and that is why we read in numerous papal statements, long before Innocent IV

---

(11) See supra n. 4. Cf. also his address to the cardinals: « Verum si obicit, nos, quod absit, minus de fide recte sentire, possumus et nos replicare, apostolicum contra fidem venire, qui cum sit illius vicarius, qui cum maledicebat, cum pateretur, non comminabatur, non debuit ex abrupto nos maledicionum jaculis propulsare. Sic cum Deo non sentit, qui cum Deo non facit » (WINKELMANN, *Acta,* cit., I, 314, lines 37 ff.)

(12) Cf. W. ULLMANN, « Romanus Pontifex indubitanter efficitur sanctus: D. P. 23 in retrospect and prospect » in the forthcoming volume vi of the *Studi Gregoriani,* pp. 229-64.

that the pope has the « jus apostolicum, quod et coelis imperat et terris » (13). The test of this *sanctus* qualification of the pope lies in the sole papal right to canonization, that is, his right to enlarge the number of those who were co-regents of Christ in heaven, were objects of particular veneration and had a special place in the liturgy of the mass (14). But what needs emphasizing is that this *sanctus* character has an exclusively juristic connotation referring as it does to the automatic effects of the judicial papal binding and loosing. That the pope was a *sanctus* in this sense, followed from his entering into the inheritance of Peter, from his assuming those very petrine powers which display these automatic effects in heaven. It is this character of the office, that is, the petrinity of the office, which bestows *sanctitas* — so at least the papal argument ran.

What Frederick did, however, was to consider this *sanctitas* not on the ground on which the papacy gave the term its peculiar complexion, but on the level of a moral sanctity, hence exposing the concept to a purely subjective evaluation. Although he misunderstood the essence of this character, he — or his draftsman — had assuredly as his model Gratian of the preceding century. In introducing his *Dist.* 40 of the *Decretum* which deals with the responsibility (or its absence) of the pope — « papa a nemine judicatur » — the Bolognese monk declared, virtually in direct opposition to papal doctrine that

> Non enim loca, sed *vita et mores sanctum faciunt* sacerdotem. Unde ex suscepto officio non licentiam peccandi, sed necessitatem *bene vivendi* se noverint asseoutos (15).

----

(13) See, for instance, 200 years before the time under discussion Clement II in his *Ep.* 8, *P. L.*, CXLII, 589.

(14) For the correct point of view see E. W. KEMP, *Canonization and authority in the Western Church* (Oxford 1948), pp. 64 ff., esp. pp. 70-1, 79-81. Cf. furthermore R. KLAUSER, *Zur Entwicklung des Heiligsprechungsverfahrens*, in Savigny Zeitschrift, Kan. Abt. xl (1954), pp. 85 ff., at 99 ff., and M. SCHWARZ, « *Heiligsprechungen im 12. Jahrhundert* », in Archiv f. Kulturgesch., xxxix (1957), pp. 43 ff., at 58 ff. The untenable view of S. KUTTNER (*La réserve papale du droit de canonisation*, in Revue historique de droit français et étranger, xvii (1938), 172 f.) is the result of giving inadequate attention to the binding and loosing powers of the pope which is after all the crux materiae. On this misinterpretation by Kuttner cf. KEMP, op. cit., p. 102-4 and KLAUSER, art. cit., p. 100 n. 35.

(15) Gratian, Dict. a.c.1, *Dist.* 40. K. HOFMANN, *Der Dictatus Papae Gregors VII* (Paderborn 1933), p. 72, has already drawn attention to this oblique view of Gratian.

This view is as far removed from a correct appreciation of the papal standpoint as Frederick's or, for that matter, of the later papal opponents (16). It is virtually the contrary of what the popes had expounded on this theme. For it is the subjective view which is the hallmark of this a-papal thesis (becoming in fact an anti-papal argument in course of time), the view that the moral bearing of the office holder, his *vita et mores,* confer the *sanctus* character on him: that the judgments on what constitutes sanctity in this sense may widely differ, needs no emphasis. But on the other hand, it was precisely the strength of the papal thesis that it kept the *sanctitas* free from the *vita et mores*: on the contrary, it was the effluence of the objective fact of the pope's having inherited petrine powers, no more and no less. Behind Frederick's assertions — and those of the later anti-papalists — there is always detectable the personal-subjective view of either Peter or Christ or God: it is the projection of the individual's view on them which determines the answer to the question of whether or not their earthly representatives act in accordance with this (pre-conceived) pattern. « Sic cum Deo non sentit (papa), qui cum Deo non facit » as Frederick himself had declared (17). The subjectively conceived concord of the *sentire* is the criterion within this framework, and not the objective functions of the office. Of course, from Frederick's standpoint the grievance made perfect sense, only it did not touch the core of the papal argument (17a). Nevertheless, he brought, as we shall see, an

---

(16) Such as John Hus in the fifteenth century: « Nemo gerit vicem Christi vel Petri nisi sequatur eum in moribus » or « papa non est verus manifestus successor Petri, si vivit moribus contrariis Petro » (J. D. Mansi, *Concil. coll.* xxvii, 1210).

(17) See supra n. 11.

(17a) It is possible that by *sanctitas* Frederick may also have understood the antithesis to legal rulings, to issuing legal judgments, to the pope operating with the law. Cf., for instance, the passage cited supra n. 2: «non prout sancti *per fidem* regna vicerunt». But he did not drive home this view. With most of the anti-hierocrats the juristic nature of papal rulings, the law, was the *pièce de résistance*. The implicit denial of jurisdictional powers would confine the pope's functions to mere persuasion, to preaching the *verbum Dei,* but this view did not take account of the nature of the papacy as primarily a governmental institution, and every governmental institution must needs operate with the enforceable law, the *preceptum coactivum,* and cannot confine itself to merely persuasive efforts. And why should,, within this juristic framework, excommunication or for that matter deposition, be a matter of « temporal » jurisdiction? Only when the concept of the Church itself had undergone some change, could the anti-papal view progress; cf.

important point to the fore, a point with an infinite variety of applications.

Certainly in 1239-1240 Frederick's aim was the removal of the pope by the machinery of a general council. I am not here concerned with the legal question which received some answer in the early fifteenth century, as to whether a general council convoked without the participation of the pope, had any validity. What I am concerned with is the purpose of this general council suggested by Frederick, that is, to give him a chance to expose « judicis corrupti nequitiam ». Although past history may have lent some support to this demand, it could not be squared with the existing canon law nor with the traditional view of the pope's immunity from conciliar judgment. And what did Frederick really expect this general council to do, once it had exposed the iniquity of the pope? Could a council depose him? Could a council proceed to a new election? This argument persuasively put to the cardinals was far too inchoate and inarticulate to command much respect. But quite apart from this technical consideration there is also another consideration which may well appear to indicate a certain incoherence in Frederick's mind.

It is this. In the manifesto protesting against the sentence of deposition and excommunication there occurs a statement which would seem to shed some light on Frederick's inconsistent ways of thinking. The sentence of deposition, he says, violates a fundamental principle, for by vitrue of this papal sentence

> Imperator Romanus, imperialis rector et dominus majestatis, lese majestatis dicitur crimine condempnatus, per quam (scil. sententiam) ridiculose subicitur legi, qui *legibus omnibus est imperialiter solutus,* de quo temporales pene sumende, cum temporalem hominem superiorem non habeat, *non sunt in homine, sed in Deo* (18).

The significance of this passage lies in his claiming that very same immunity from judgment which he has denied to the pope. Differently expressed: he would not submit to any human judgment, because he is *legibus solutus* which is precisely the reverse of what

---

also infra at n. 35. It is, I think, not without reason that Frederick did not touch upon the fundamental theme of law as a vital ingredient of the papal institution.

(18) *MGH. Const.,* II, 365, lines 6 ff.

he had demanded the general council should do, namely to give him an opportunity to unmask the pope's corruption and depravity, so as to judge the pope as unfit. Even on the presupposition of his dualism, this refusal to submit the emperor to human judgment and the demand to put the pope before the bar of a general council, seems rather incoherent (19).

This inconsistency is difficult to explain. Frederick had no equal in the understanding of the proper theocratic point of view, according to which all power comes from above — the descending theory of government and law, as I have termed it somewhere else — and according to which power is conferred by God on the ruler: the community under the ruler's care, be it a kingdom or the universal Church, is entrusted to the ruler. The *populus tibi commissus,* as we read in the royal coronation orders since the ninth century (Benedictional of Freising), or the *ecclesia nobis commissa,* as we read in the thousands of papal communications since the fourth century, express very succinctly the thesis that the community under the ruler's care has no power of conferring the office of rulership — election merely designating a particular person to the divinely created office — and therefore no power of withdrawing the office from him. In fact, the community entrusted to the ruler is not, within the theocratic framework, endowed with any autonomous powers. Seen against this background the pauline « nulla potestas nisi a Deo » assumes very practical significance. According to the descending thesis the pope forms an estate of his own — he has his own *status* — and no juristic lines of communications beween the community and the pope exist: the former had nothing to do with the conferment of papal power, on the contrary, it is entrusted to the pope's care. The consideration of the community's interests, not of its wishes, is the focal point of the theocratic ruler. Or as Innocent III had classically expressed it, he is « *medius* constitutus inter hominem et Deum », an expression which brings into clear relief the view that the pope occupies an estate of his own. Frederick could have had no doubt on this score — he himself was without a parallel in understanding this theme — and his appeal for a general council, however vaguely conceived it was as regards its actual competency, is a serious defect

---

(19) About the double vicariate of Christ, one in the pope, and one in the emperor, cf. my *Growth of Papal Government in the Middle Ages* (London 1955), p. 343 and note 3; also *Miscellanea Hist. Pontificiae,* xviii (1954), at pp. 118 ff.

in his attack. For to maintain this point of view would in fact amount to subscribing to the ascending thesis, according to which original power resided with the people acting through their own (elected or appointed) agencies and organs, such as a general council. And this seems to me to reveal the real inconsistency of Frederick: the adherence to the descending standpoint, as far as he himself is concerned, and the adherence to the ascending standpoint, as far as the pope is concerned (20). In other words, his own functions as an emperor are not subjected to human judgment, whilst the functions of the pope are to be subjected to the judgment of a general council.

Closely allied to these considerations are those arguments which are contained in what we have termed the second line of attack. Here again, although pointing up the one or the other element, the argumentation follows rather closely the Staufen ideology of a dualism of government. This Frederick expresses in the statement already referred to, concerning the pope's *potestas in spiritualibus plenaria* standing next to the imperial *potestas in temporalibus plenaria*. Now this nomenclature of the temporal (secular) and the spiritual is of pauline origin who in the very same passage (i Cor. vi. 3) had given here as in so many other respects — the medieval papacy a perfectly well constructed theme of the teleological order. The teleological and christo-centric standpoint quite understandably forbade to attribute to the so-called « temporal » any autonomous or independent value, to ascribe to it *Eigenwert* or *Eigenständigkeit*: the pauline-papal viewpoint was that the « temporal » had no life of its own, but in order to be useful must be harnessed to a telos, to an end, to a finis. It is simply a means to an end; only in so far it assumes decisive value. Hence from the papal point of view there was no notional distinction between the « temporal » and the « spiritual ». Frederick's standpoint, however, can be epitomized in the view (which later with Dante was to become of fundamental importance) that Man was in need of a twofold direction, being composed of body and soul, of matter and mind.

> Eterna provisio in firmamento terre duo voluit preesse re-
> gimina, sacerdocium et imperium, unum ad tutelam, reli-
> quum ad cautelam, ut homo, qui erat duobus componentibus
> dissolutus, duobus retinaculis frenaretur (21).

---

(20) In her excellent work, *Vom Imperium zum nationalen Königtum* (Berlin-Munich 1933), H. WIERUSZOWSKI (pp. 179 ff.) has not seen this fundamental dichotomy in Frederick's argumentation nor the basis upon which the Frederician standpoint rested.

(21) E. WINKELMANN, *Acta,* cit., I, 314, no. 355, lines 21 ff.

This statement leaves nothing to be desired, either in regard to its clarity or its underlying theme which is the very reverse of the pauline-papal thesis. The latter operated — and it could not operate on any other basis, considering the *Gesamtanspruch* of medieval Christian norms which claimed the whole of Man — with one end of man's life, namely his eventual salvation, whilst the imperial point of view denied this oneness of man and his one end by postulating two principles (21a): the body (temporal) had its own life, and so had the soul (spiritual), and each was autonomous, and for their government *duo regimina* were instituted *in firmamento terre*. It goes without saying that this fundamental dichotomy could not possibly be squared with the traditional medieval outlook, and the weakness of this view, if not fallacy of a non-existing distinction, emerges perhaps best in the same statement: how are the two regiments to work? Moreover, this view implicitly rests on the possibility of a tidy, neat and notional distinction between the « spiritual » and the « temporal », but in the long and weary discussion on this theme we shall search in vain for any criterion that would enable one to draw a dividing line. And who was to draw it? It is no exaggeration to say that within a wholly christo-centric society the attempt to find that criterion is bound to be a fruitless exercise in mental gymnastics. The dualism of the anti-papal ideology was built on the shifty foundations of a fictitious and chimeric distinction: the Staufen dualism was merely a postulate (22).

(21a) It is of course well known that on the basis of this dualism Luther was to postulate « die zwey Regiment » which should « von einander gesondert und geschieden bleiben, sol man anders das rechte Evangelium und den rechten Glauben erhalten » (Weimar ed., vol. XLVI, 734). Cf. also the passage ibid., vol. LI 239, with its emphatic insistence on the « Scheidung der beiden Gewalten »; also Augsburg Confession, art. 28.

(22) From this point of view the often repeated papal statement « Duo principia ponere haereticum est » assumes very practical significance. The postulate of the two principles — ineffective it is true it was because from the standpoint of medieval Christianity it indubitably did violence to the traditional ways of thinking — nevertheless had a very great future, especially when on the one hand the Aristotelian distinction between « the good man » and « the good citizen » came to be fully understood (for this distinction in itself presupposes two entirely different sets of norms and criteria) and on the other hand when the same Aristotelian-inspired theme of naturalism (and the consequential complement, supra-naturalism) came to be made a principle of theoretical speculation since Thomas Aquinas.

The Frederician argument had been answered before by the papacy, though most likely Frederick was not aware of these papal statements (23). Furthermore, where was the biblical or doctrinal proof that the pope had been given only a *potestas in spiritualibus?* This assertion is a logical consequence of the figment of a distinction. It seems that Frederick's grandfather — or Rainald of Dassel — was the inventor of the hair-raising theme of a double vicariate of Christ. To his great credit be it remarked that Frederick II did not operate with this theme, in itself once again a necessary consequence of the dualistic aspect, but in essence there seems little difference betwen him and the older Staufen ideology. Again, on a higher level the papacy had anticipated the objections of the imperial side before there was any Western emperor at all (24). In a word, the petrine power was conceived as monarchy in the literal meaning of the term, exercised over the whole body of Christians. Frederick's objection in reality therefore concerned the function of the pope as a monarch, a function which was wholly defensible on doctrinal grounds and which notionally excluded any other monarch; hence his recourse to a dualism, that is, the splitting up of functions to be exercised over the « temporal » on the

---

(23) Cf., for instance, Gregory VII: « Cui ergo aperiendi claudendique coeli data est potestas, de terra judicare non licet? Absit » (*Reg.*, viii, 21, ed. E. Caspar, p. 550) or: « Si enim coelestia et spiritualia sedes beati Petri solvit et judicat, quanto magis terrena et saecularia » (ibid., iv, 24, p. 338); Celestine III: « Non solum corporum, sed etiam animarum judiciariam accepit (Romana ecclesia) potestatem » (*Ep.* 235, in *P.L.*, ccvi, 1127); Innocent III: « Hac igitur ratione sacrosancta Romana ecclesia, quae super omnes alias coelesti privilegio obtinet principatum, quaeque non solum terrena sed coelestia quoque dijudicat... » (*Suppl. Reg.*, cap. 89 *bis,* in *P.L.*, ccvii, 131); according to Gregory IX the pope has not only « animarum imperium » but also « in universo mundo rerum et corporum principatum » (*Epp. sell. XIII saec.*, I, 604, n. 703). These statements could be easily multiplied.

(24) Cf., for example, Leo I: « *Nihil* erit ligatum, *nihil* solutum nisi quod beatus Petrus aut solverit aut ligaverit » (*P.L.*, LIV. 151); Gelasius I: « Sicut his verbis (scil. Quodcumque ligaveris...) nihil constat exceptum, sic per apostolicae dispensationis officium et *totum* possit generaliter alligari et *totum* consequenter absolvi » (*Ep.* 30, cap. 12, in A. THIEL, cit., p. 445); Nicholas I: «In quibuscumque *omnia* sunt, quantacumque et qualiacumque sint (*Ep.* 4, in *MGH., Epp.*, VI, 701); the same view was expressed by John VIII, ibid., VII, 187, *Ep.* 210; Gregory VII: « *Nullum* excipit, *nichil* ab eius potestate subtraxit » (*Reg.*, IV, 2); Innocent III: « *Nihil* excipiens qui dixit 'Quodcumque ligaveris...' » (X: I. 33. 6) Again these examples could easily be multiplied.

one hand, and the « spiritual » on the other. Here as elsewhere Frederick II moved within the precincts of the earlier royalist argumentation. From the fifth century onwards the possibilities inherent in the all-comprehensive « *Quodcumque* ligaveris » of the Matthean verses were increasingly recognized — it was the totality of human actions which was the object of the petrine-papal binding and loosing, and from this papal standpoint the alleged distinction between « temporal » and « spiritual » could indeed have no meaning: the papal charge that Frederick had acted *in contemptu clavium*, was, seen from this angle, fully justified. Did not he himself stigmatize the papal exercise of the comprehensive binding and loosing powers as an *abusio sacerdotalis potestatis?* (25) In actual ract, Frederick made it only worse by protesting his acceptance of papal rulings in « spiritual » affairs and by refusing to accept any « temporal » infliction, for the latter was a necessary consequence of the former, if due recognition is given to the nature of the petrine commission. Innocent IV, on the other hand, had no doctrinal difficulties stating that « Vicario conditoris omnis creatura subdita est » (26). It was not, as Frederick seems to have believed, that Innocent IV had raised the claim of tansferring empires and kingdoms, because Gregory VII, nearly two centuries before, had explicitly laid this petrine-papal right down, and Innocent IV on his part merely moved within the precincts delineated by the earlier papacy (27). And when Frederick admitted the papal right to his imperial « consecratio » but at the same time denied the papal claim to deprive him of the imperial office, he again seems to have beeen the victim of incoherent reasonings: it was an old legal ma-

---

(25) E. WINKELMANN, *Acta*, cit., p. 50, n. 46.

(26) Comm. ad X: ed. Frankfort, fol. 2v. It was perhaps no more than a stratagem of Frederick to put these questions: « In quo enim apostolice sedis auctoritas leditur, si superbam et recalcitrantem Liguriam cesarea ultione plectamus? si honorem imperii ampliamus? » (*Acta*, I, 314, lines 29-30).

(27) There is a vociferous group of writers nowadays who either in culpable ignorance of historical facts or in wilful ignorance of the constant papal theme would like to ascribe to the papacy a dualistic programme, the very programme which was so tenaciously fought by the papacy. This sort of « historiography » motivated as it is by entirely un-historical considerations is nothing else but the attempt at falsifying history itself for rather mundane purposes, and all this under the fig-leaf of « pure » scholarship. The simple truth, however, looks quite different.

xim that he who conferred something could also take it away (28). Apart from this, like any other public office, emperorship was considered a *divinum beneficium* which could be mediated only through the pope; the conferment of the imperial office was an *apostolicus favor,* something to which the recipient had no right (29). It is no doubt interesting to see that Frederick avoids the very term « coronatio », in other words, the one act that made the king of the Romans an emperor, for without papal imposition of the crown there was no possibility of becoming an emperor. What Frederick had most likely in mind was that the coronation was a mere liturgical formality without constitutive effects — hence his emphasis of the « consecratio » — which is nothing else but the translation of the notion of *imperatura* into hard facts (30). But the mere choice of words cannot do away with the indisputable fact that, in the mid-thirteenth century, the coronation of the king of the Romans by the pope had constitutive effects.

III

What, then, in sum was the target of the argumentative efforts of Frederick II? Behind all the vituperations and arguments there is, I think, detectable one common element, and that is that the

---

(28) Just a century before, John of Salisbury with reference to this point, had stated this: « Porro de ratione juris eius est nolle, cuius est velle, et eius est aufferre, qui de jure conferre potest » (*Policraticus,* IV, 3). Similarly Hugh of St Victor, cf. the passages cited in *Growth of Papal Government,* cit., pp. 439 ff.

(29) For this cf. *Misc. Hist. Pont.,* cit., pp. 107-26; also « *The Pontificate of Adrian IV* » in Cambridge Hist. Journal, XI (1955), pp. 233-253.

(30) Wheter the intitulation of Frederick as « Divina favente clementia Romanorum imperator, semper augustus, et rex Siciliae » in July 1220, was merely premature or had greater significance, remains to be seen. See HUILLARD-BRÉHOLLES, *Historia Diplomatica Federici II* (Paris 1852), I, 800; in this confirmation of monastic privileges the dating is also according to imperial years, although he was not crowned emperor until 22 November 1220. A point of view similar to that expressed in *imperatura* is also in the election decree of February 1237: »... firmavimus, quod prefatum Conradum a nobis in regem electum post mortem prenominati patris sui dominum et *imperatorem nostrum habebimus,* eidem in omnibus, quae ad imperium et jus imperii pertinent, intendentes... » (*MGH., Const.,* II, 441, n. 329, lines 23 ff.) Similarly the view expressed in the *Annales Stadenses* (*MGH. SS.,* XVI. 369).

present state of affairs was caused by the lack of any constitutional machinery which would have prevented the — in Frederick's eyes — unwarranted actions of the papacy. The target of his opposition was the *plenitudo potestatis,* or positively expressed, the establishment of what might nowadays be called constitional monarchy. It is this, I think, which formed the constant element in Frederick's attacks. If this is so, he had indeed taken upon himself a herculean task, and undertaken it with inadequate means. But at once the question obtrudes itself: what means should Frederick have employed to achieve what he — and not a few of his contemporaries — would have wished to see realized? In the background to this question there looms a much more fundamental one: were there any means by which the pope could become a constitutional monarch, so that be could be deprived of his monarchic status and of this *plenitudo potestatis,* so that he could be made to govern with the binding advice and counsel of some organs? Or seen from yet another angle, this question resolves itself into: What is one to do with an unsuitable pope, that is one who is incapable of fulfilling his petrine functions, such as an insane pope? What I think Frederick was groping for was to find a constitutional machinery which keeps a check on the pope, which can, if necessary, take action against him and, if further warranted, depose him.

However ineffective Frederick's opposition was, succeeding generations were indebted to him for bringing this particular problem with all desirable clarity into the open: no king or emperor before him in his official protests and writings had so clearly put his finger on that vital problem as Frederick did when he appealed to the college of cardinals to convoke a general council: dum credat (papa) *sibi licere quod libeat* (31). Clearly, the actions and judgments of the pope did appear to Frederick as nothing but sheer arbitrariness — « voluntatis sue arbitrio plus debito laxatis habenis » (32), — convinced as he was of the *justitia nostri imperii* (33), but the crucial question was, how to prevent this state of affairs? If Frederick and his able advisers could not find the answer, one may be forgiven for asking whether any answer was possible at all.

The general problem emerging in all its sombre and stark reality in the last decade of Frederick's reign was far more significant

---

(31) *MGH., Const.,* II, 290, n. 214.
(32) Ibid.
(33) Ibid., p. 310, line 23.

than the concrete questions which provoked the conflict. It was Frederick II who was destined to concentrate and to epitomize in himself the age-old problem of a secular monarchy within a theocentric and christocentric setting. Even though he lost the battle, both in actual fact and in pure theory, the historic significance of his stand must not be minimised. True, an all-out frontal attack on the very foundations of the papal monarchy, that is, the petrinity of papal powers and all its attendant consequences, his opposition did not reveal. In so far, then, he moved on the paths trodden by his predecessors. But there is one element in his opposition to which I have already drawn attention, namely the ideologically indefensible distinction between the pope answerable to a general council and the emperor standing above the law — an element which contains ingredients of an entirely different make, with pregnant implications.

Logical argumentation apparently made Frederick apply the ascending point of view the papacy. For as long as the unadulterated theocratic-descending standpoint was adhered to, no possibility in the realm of thought existed to deprive the ruler of his peculiar status, to rob him of his theocratically conceived plenitude of power (34). The seat of power is God, and whatever power is found « down below » is derived from this source through appropriate intermediaries: but this power is not autonomous, it is at best delegated and is an indubitably derived power. Hence it contradicts the laws of reasoning to say that those to whom power was delegated, who derived it from a superior organ, should then control that superior organ. Within the framework of the theocratic government no control of the papal monarch was possible. Consequently, when Frederick suggested the general council as a tribunal and a forum before which the iniquities of the pope were to be exposed, this forum quite obviously had the function of judging, which is nothing else but the practical exercise of controls and checks — a tenet that clearly violates the most fundamental principles of any theocratic rulership. Therefore, the underlying presupposition of this suggestion is the (at least implicit) denial of theo-

---

(34) The whole magnitude of the problem emerges if the function of the pope as *vicarius Dei* is properly appreciated. Even though this function has only juristic connotations, it was precisely because of the juristic contents that the exercise of this function displayed, or claimed to display, effects in this as well as in the other world.

cratic-monarchic premisses and the (again at least implicit) assertion of a residual possession of power with the general council,
independent of the pope himself. Correctly understood, this is the
ascending theme, according to which power originally resides « down
below » and ascends upwards through various agencies and organs.
The suggested general council was merely « representative » of the
whole Church. In brief, this Frederician proposal of a general council was the expression of the view — not new, but hardly before
him propounded in this practical manner — that the universal
Church was the bearer of all power and rights, and the pope consequently answerable to it. The pope, in this scheme of things, was
an organ of the universal Church. It is evident that the problem
concerned nothing more nor less than the concept of Church: was
it founded on Peter (the papal standpoint) or was Peter founded
on the Church (the imperial standpoint, and, with the adoption of
the ascending conception, also the standpoint of the conciliarists
in the following century). Differently expressed: is the Church, the
whole *congregatio fidelium,* endowed with original power or are
its power derivative? The answer to this question hinges on the
crucial Matthean verses, and Frederick opened the public discussion on this crucial dilemma in a very practical and concrete manner. Veiled under the threat of damaging the whole Church, this
view may have given rise to the statement:

> Vos igitur, dillecti principes, non nobis solum set *ecclesie,*
> *que congregatio est omnium Christi fidelium,* condolete,
> cuius capud languidum... *vir eius infidelis,* sacerdos eius
> polluens sanctum, *injuste faciens contra legem* (35),

as well as to the exclamation:

> Dolemus tamen et ex corde dolemus propter verecundiam
> universalis ecclesie matris nostre, quam Dominus Jesus Chri-
> stus sub specie virginis gloriosse in passionis testamento dis-
> cipulis commendavit (36).

The fundamental point in this ascending view of Frederick is
that it alone seemed to offer a possibility of bringing a pope to book:
of course, it meant the overthrow of the theocratic-hierocratic pat-

---

(35) Ibid., p. 298, lines 7 ff.
(36) Ibid., p. 296, lines 34 ff.

tern altogether, and this attempt to fix the seat of power in the universal Church, that is, the *populus christianus,* is the tacit admission that on the theocratic-hierocratic level no machinery could be devised to achieve the reduction of the papal-petrine *plenitudo potestatis,* to put fetters on the goverment of the pope or to subject him to a supervisory control. This is not the place to depict the further fate of this Frederician stratagem, suffice it to say that the idea of the *populus christianus* being the bearer of power, made astonishingly rapid progress: the policy of Philip IV of France towards Boniface VIII is one example (37), and the conciliar movement is another instance of the appeal which the ascending-populist ideology was to make in the purely ecclesiological field.

It would, however, be futile to overlook the inevitable consequences which this ascending-populist theme entailed for the theocratically conceived secular monarchy. We have already noticed the dichotomy in Frederick's thinking between the pope's and the emperor's position: the latter, as we have seen, was for the so-called « temporal » matters unaccountable to anyone. Why should the theocratic standpoint be valid for the emperor, but not for the pope? No plausible anwer can be given and I fear does not exist. But this is not an aspect which concerns Frederick only: in his great imitator, Philip IV, we witness exactly the same feature, this time only much more accentuated. The time was not so far off — and in literature certainly was propagated by men like Thomas Aquinas (with whom a very similar dichotomy is detectable) (38) and notably by John of Paris and Marsiglio of Padua — which applied to the king the same consideration which Frederick had in mind in regard to the pope. The impossibility of his finding an adequate answer to

---

(37) For the way in which Philip's government relied on the models provided by Frederick, see H. WIERUSZOWSKI, op. cit., esp. pp. 42 ff. and 89 ff.

(38) It was no more than an ideological device to construct the theme of the natural origin of organised human society, the State, and the supranatural origin of the Church. This was merely a figleaf for hiding the dichotomy. In parenthesis it may be remarked that this device made matters only worse (for the hierocrats), because the supra-natural idea lent considerable support to the purely mystical-sacramental conception of the Church, for which indeed no law, no tribunal, no organisation, no government, were necessary. And Marsiglio was not slow to make the most use of this conception. Behind all this stands the Thomist principle of a *duplex ordo in rebus* which in both Dante and Marsiglio became a fundamental principle of operation.

the papal-hierocratic scheme led him to propose that very theme which was to redound to the detriment of all theocratic rulership. The significance of this last papal-imperial conflict lies in that the door was opened, paradoxically enough by the emperor, for the influx of those themes which were to prove the undoing of both empire and papacy.

Seen from a wider vista, however, the Frederician attack on the personal failings, on the moral turpitude of his contemporary popes, had perhaps an even greater importance. Indubitably, the strength of the papal point of view lay precisely in withdrawing the person of the office holder from judgment: it was, as we have termed it, the de-personalized view which focused attention on the institution of the papacy, on the office of the pope, to the exclusion of the person of the office holder. It is as somewhat rarefied view, conceived entirely in the realms of doctrine and dogma, and in this lay its strength which Frederick was unable to shake. But its very strength was also its weakness: whilst it derived the former from the programme, impersonal and unalterable as it was, the theme took little account of the — from the human point of view — very understandable natural human element: is it a realistic approach, considering the natural laws propelling human inclinations and proclivities, to divorce so sharply the (objective) office from the (subjective) person? Could it not be said that this distinction and still more the practical consequences drawn from it, were a convenient cloak for justifying each and every action, however much it was inspired by motives far removed from all the precincts of the office itself, provided that the action somehow bore the stamp of the *officium?* Has it not been at all times the very human experience, the very natural « law » to judge the person executing the office rather than the de-personalized office? Is, in other words, the papal standpoint, consistent and logically flawless as it is, conformable to the natural laws of humanity? Did not in fact, though not in theory, Frederick II propound a view that was more conformable to the natural-human experience? Or for that matter, did not Gratian's misunderstanding reveal that he took account of the natural-human element? And is it really a mere coincidence that as the thirteenth century wears on, this natural-human outlook was to gain ascendancy, so much so that Philip IV and a distinguished gallaxy of writers were to make this the focal point in their attack against the popes? Did not this natural-unsophisticated human outlook contribute so powerfully to the decline of the papacy's standing, because the subjective evaluation of the pope as man became more and more the measure and criterion? The laws of logical reasoning can find no fault in the imposing papal-hierocratic edifice culminating in the office, de-personalized and objective, but are the laws of logical reasoning always compatible with the laws of natural reasoning? However inadequate the means were which he employed, Frederick's opposition brought this very natural and human facet to the fore, a facet that was, so soon after him, brought into the clearest possible relief by the introduction of a scientific (Aristotelian-Thomist) naturalism which with all the available means directed attention onto Man himself and away from the impersonal office. Then the field was opened up to tackling this complex problem by no longer shielding the pope as man behind the office, but by forcing him into the foreground and making him absorb the office. And the further significance of Frederick's attack lay in preparing the soil for the receptivity of this natural-human point of view. The fruits were not gathered by him, but by succeeding generations: it was they who resolved the antinomy between logical reasoning and natural reasoning in the latter's favour.

VI

DIE BULLE UNAM SANCTAM: RÜCKBLICK UND AUSBLICK

Trotz der vielseitigen Beachtung, die die Bulle *Unam sanctam* gefunden hat, möchte es scheinen, daß noch manche wesentliche Frage keine oder nur eine unbefriedigende Antwort erhalten hat*). Die Bulle gibt keinerlei Aufschluß über den Anlaß, auch wird keine Tatsache erwähnt, aus der sich Schlüsse über den Anlaß ziehen ließen; sie richtet sich an keinen Adressaten; sie nimmt keinen Bezug auf irgendeine Begebenheit oder Persönlichkeit; niemand wird einer Glaubensunwahrheit geziehen; sie enthält keinen Angriff auf irgendein Land, einen Herrscher oder eine Gruppe von Personen — kurzum, aus dem Inhalt der Urkunde, so wie sie überliefert ist, läßt sich nichts über diese doch immerhin zentralen Punkte erfahren. Darüber hinaus erhebt sich die m. E. nicht unwesentliche Frage, ob denn *Unam sanctam* überhaupt förmlich publiziert worden ist. Wie bekannt, hat sich bis heute keine Originalausfertigung finden lassen[1]. Der Text steht zwar als Bulle — *Ad perpetuam rei memoriam* — im amtlichen Register der *Litterae curiales*, ist aber zeitlich ganz und gar unerwartet eingereiht. Sie steht nämlich erst nach Eintragungen aus dem Juli des Jahres 1303[2], obwohl sie selbst das Datum 18. November 1302 trägt. Dieser Umstand mag vielleicht weniger ins Gewicht fallen als die Tatsache, daß sie keinerlei Schlußformel hat. Bei der Bedeutung der in ihr niedergelegten Grundsätze und Folgerungen hätte man wohl eine förmliche Schlußformel erwarten dürfen, oder zumindest eine Sanktion der üblichen Art. Aber nichts von alledem.

Obwohl dies Fragen sind, die schon längst hätten beantwortet werden sollen, gibt es keinen Rest eines Zweifels an dem äußerst konservativen Charakter des Inhalts. Seit langem steht fest, daß darin kein einziger neuer Gesichtspunkt vorgetragen wird. Jede der in ihr aufgegriffenen Stellen konnte

---

*) Vorliegende Ausführungen lagen einem Vortrage zugrunde, der am 4. April 1974 am Österreichischen Kulturinstitut in Rom gehalten wurde (Red.).
[1] Siehe Henricus Denifle, Specimina palaeographica ex Vaticani tabularii Romanorum Pontificum registris selecta (Romae 1888) 44 zu Taf. XLVI.
[2] Les Registres de Boniface VIII, ed. Georges Digard u. a. (= Bibliothèque des Écoles françaises d'Athènes et de Rome, Paris 1921) 888—890 nr. 5382. Die Bulle ist auch in den Extravagantes communes: V. 9.1; ferner bei Odoricus Raynaldus, Annales ecclesiastici, ed. Augustinus Theiner, XXIII (Barri-Ducis 1871) 303—305; Henricus Denzinger, Enchiridion symbolorum (Barcinone, Friburgi—Brisgoviae, Romae, Neo-Eboraci ³⁴1967) 279—281 nr. 468; Carl Mirbt, Quellen zur Geschichte des Papsttums und des römischen Katholizismus (Tübingen ⁶1967) 458f. nr. 746).

man seit der Mitte des 13. Jahrhunderts in der einschlägigen Traktatenliteratur oder in den zünftigen kanonistischen Erzeugnissen lesen. Selbst der in so feierlicher Weise ausklingende Schlußakkord war durchaus nicht neu, wenn er auch in dieser scharfen, geschliffenen und pointierten Form vielleicht noch nicht so vertraut war wie die voraufgehenden Grundsätze. Im ganzen hätte diese Bulle ebensogut ein halbes Jahrhundert vorher von jedem anderen Papst erlassen werden können. Sie wurde aber nicht erlassen — und umso dringlicher erscheint die Frage: warum wurde sie gerade damals erlassen? Was war der Zweck?

Der Zweck dürfte nicht gewesen sein, ein Herrschaftsprogramm oder gar einen Weltherrschaftsanspruch des Papsttums anzumelden oder zu verkünden, obwohl dies immer wieder behauptet wird. In der Papstsprache kann man nur sagen *Miramur plurimum*, wenn erklärt wird, diese Bulle sei der beredteste und schroffste Ausdruck eines unerbittlichen Papalsystems gewesen. Solche Behauptungen enthalten aber noch keine Antwort auf die Frage, warum das Papsttum um die Wende des 13. und 14. Jahrhunderts es für notwendig befunden haben sollte, eine solche scholastisch aufgebaute überspitzte Erklärung zu verfassen. Bonifaz VIII. war ein gewiegter Jurist mit großer praktischer Erfahrung und einem stark ausgeprägten Wirklichkeitssinn, der genau wußte, welche konkrete Sprache zu führen und welche konkreten Mittel im gegebenen Fall anzuwenden sind[3]). Man bedenke doch, daß, um nicht weiter zurückzugehen, weder *Clericis laicos* noch *Salvator mundi* noch *Ausculta fili* etwas an Deutlichkeit und Prägnanz der Fassung zu wünschen übrig ließen. Die in allen bisherigen päpstlichen Erlassen enthaltenen Drohungen gegen weltliche Fürsten, den französischen König einbeschlossen, fußten in allzu handgreiflicher Form gerade auf jenen monarchischen Gedanken, die sich hier in der Bulle wieder finden[4]). Warum also sollte der Papst eine Bulle verfassen, die sattsam bekannte, abgegriffene Sätze enthielt, rein sachlicher Natur ist und nicht die geringste persönliche Spitze hat? Daß sie mit der Tagespolitik in Verbindung steht, dafür ergibt sich kein Anhaltspunkt.

---

[3]) Vgl. etwa Iohannis Iperii abbatis Chronicon monasterii S. Bertini, ed. Edmundus Martène et Ursinus Durand, Thesaurus novus anecdotorum III (Lutetiae Parisiorum 1717) 774: (Celestinus) *virum subtilem et industrium, et unum de maioribus clericis iuristis totius orbis secum retinuit.* Ferner Petri abbatis Aulae Regiae tertii Chronicon Aulae Regiae, ed. Gelasius Dobner, Monumenta historica Boemiae V (Pragae 1784) 107: *Utriusque iuris scientia preditus ac in omni temporali negotio mirabiliter eruditus . . . vir magnanimus.* Auch die zuerst genannte Quelle nennt ihn: *Bonifacius iste iurista permaximus.*

[4]) Über die päpstliche Vollgewalt ließ sich Bonifaz unzweideutig im Konsistorium am 24. Juni 1302 aus, vgl. Pierre Dupuy, Histoire du différend d'entre le pape Boniface VIII et Philippe le Bel Roy de France (Paris 1655, Neudruck: Tucson [Ariz.] 1963) 77—79. Die kritische Einstellung bei Denzinger a. a. O. zur Bulle ist irreführend. Die Stelle aus der Konsistorialansprache des Papstes bezieht sich überhaupt nicht auf die Bulle, weil diese erst fünf Monate später „erlassen" wurde. Diese Angabe wird unkritisch wiederholt von Hans Wolter, Die Krise des Papsttums und der Kirche im Ausgang des 13. Jahrhunderts (1274—1303), in: Handbuch der Kirchengeschichte, hrsg. von Hubert Jedin III/2 (Freiburg, Basel, Wien 1968) 352

Ich glaube, es ist an der Zeit, den Versuch aufzugeben, die Bulle vordergründig erklären zu können. Eine sehr frühe Glosse des berühmten Kanonisten und Kardinals Johannes Monachus leistet uns gute Dienste. Nach unbestrittener Meinung war diese Glosse schon geschrieben, als die Bulle selbst in Umlauf gesetzt wurde, d. h. vor dem Sommer 1303[5]). Daß dieser Kurienkardinal von der Entstehung und den mit ihr verbundenen Zwecken Kenntnis hatte, darf man wohl als gesichert annehmen. Die ersten Worte seiner Glosse enthalten, wie mir scheinen möchte, einen sehr gewichtigen Fingerzeig, wenn nicht einen Schlüssel zum Verständnis und zur Erklärung. Hier kommt er auf den Casus zu sprechen und sagt, daß es gewisse Leute gibt, die zweifeln oder glauben oder sogar behaupten, es sei nicht heilsnotwendig, dem Papst zu unterstehen[6]). Es verdient Beachtung, daß der Casus durchaus nicht hypothetisch gefaßt wurde, sondern als Tatsache wiedergegeben wird. Der Kardinal fährt fort, daß der Papst diese Dekretale herausgegeben hat, um dieser pestartigen Krankheit zu begegnen: *Huic autem morbo pestifero obviare volens sanctissimus pater et dominus Bonifacius papa hanc decretalem edidit.* Diese Aussage kann doch wohl nur als eine unmißverständliche Anspielung auf

---

Anm. 3, der noch dazu ein „quod" in ein „quasi" verändert und den für Bonifaz wesentlichen Zusatz, daß jeder König und jeder Gläubige *sit nobis subiectus ratione peccati* nicht abdruckt. Einige Erlässe Bonifaz', welche die Jurisdiktionsgewalt in den Vordergrund stellen, seien hier in Auswahl angezeigt: Augustus Potthast, Regesta Pontificum Romanorum, II (Berolini 1874/75) nr. 14020; 24096; 24131; 24291; 24398; 24468; 24549; 24607; 24772; 24833; 24898; 25071; 25096; 25097; 25159; 25230; 25236; 25256; 25262; 25276. Vgl. auch des Papstes Ansprache anläßlich der Bestätigung Albrechts I. als König in: M. G. H. Legum sectio IV: Constitutiones et acta publica imperatorum et regum 4/1 (Hannoverae 1904—1906) 139 Z. 36ff. nr. 17 (Berufung auf die Untertaneneigenschaft des französischen Königtums unter das Kaisertum, und zwar unter ausdrücklicher Betonung der päpstlichen Primatialgewalt): *Non insurgat hic superbia Gallicana, quae dicit quod non recognoscit superiorem. Mentiuntur, quia de iure sunt et esse debent sub rege Romano et imperatore ... constat, quod christiani subditi fuerunt monarchis ecclesiae Romanae et esse debent.*

[5]) Die Bulle mit der Glosse abgedruckt in den meisten Ausgaben der Extravagantes communes unter dem Titel: „De maioritate et obedientia". Ich zitiere nach der Ausgabe: Lyon 1553. Zur Glosse vgl. auch Heinrich Finke, Aus den Tagen Bonifaz' VIII. Funde und Forschungen (= Vorreformationsgeschichtliche Forschungen II, Münster 1902) 177ff. Die Vermutung von Johannes Haller, Das Papsttum. Idee und Wirklichkeit, V (Stuttgart 1953) 381, wonach die Bulle erst zur Zeit ihrer Registrierung veröffentlicht wurde, hat viel für sich. Der Kommentar des Guido Vernani (ed. Martin Grabmann, Die Aristotelesverwertung im hierokratischen System. Sitzungsberichte der Bayerischen Akademie der Wissenschaften, phil.-hist. Klasse 1934, Heft 2, 144—157) lehnt sich so stark an die Glosse an, daß man von einer direkten Entlehnung sprechen könnte, brächte sie nicht an ganz unerwarteten Stellen selbständige Gedanken.

[6]) Iohannes Monachus beginnt: *Erant quidam dubitantes et forte credentes vel etiam asserentes non esse de necessitate salutis subesse summo pontifici, quod quidem vel verbo fieri poterat, quia forte sic dicebantur, vel facto, quia talia agebant et operabantur ac si non esset de necessitate salutis.* Ganz ähnlich Vernani in seinem zuvor angeführten Kommentar (Anm. 5).

geistige Strömungen verstanden werden, die jedenfalls so bedeutsam, weitverbreitet und einflußreich gewesen sein mußten, daß sie den Papst veranlaßten, eine nicht mißzuverstehende und unzweideutige Erklärung abzugeben. Die Ausführungen eines so berufenen Kenners wie die des Johannes Monachus machten auch deutlich, daß der Schlußsatz der Bulle als die notwendige Folgerung aus den voraufgegangenen Argumenten aufgefaßt werden sollte.

Jede Lehre von Herrschaft ruht auf außer-herrscherlichen Grundsätzen, hier auf rein religiösen oder ekklesiologischen Voraussetzungen, denn das Wesen des mittelalterlichen Papsttums selbst ist eine, historisch gesehen, einzigartige Verquickung und Verknüpfung von religiösen und juristischen Grundlagen. In sehr vieler Hinsicht ist das Papsttum eine Institution sui generis. Denn sowohl der Primat als Herrschaftsgrundsatz wie auch die Gesellschaft, über die der Primat ausgeübt werden sollte, wurden *uno ictu* von Christus selbst in durchaus unmißverständlicher Art niedergelegt. Das heißt, sowohl die Gesellschaft, die Kirche, wie die Herrschaft über sie und das Herrschaftsmittel, gingen auf göttliche Anordnung zurück. Das jedenfalls war die Exegese der matthäischen und johanneischen Stellen, die im 5. Jahrhundert ihre feste Form erhalten hatte[7]). Daher kann das mittelalterliche Papsttum als Herrschaftsorgan nur aus dieser religiösen, biblischen Sicht verstanden werden — das Fundament der Gesellschaft, der Kirche, war die *fides*[8]). Wenn sich nun der Schlußsatz auf die primatiale Gewalt des Papstes beruft, so drückt er in präziser Form eine alte Wahrheit aus. Jede Gesellschaft bedarf einer Herrschaft. Diese Überlegung hilft uns aber noch nicht, die Frage nach dem Zweck der Bulle zu beantworten. Um einer Antwort näherzukommen, dürfte es ratsam sein, die Bulle gegen den weitgespannten Hintergrund des zeitgenössischen Denkens zu sehen, womit auch zugleich der Tagespolitik die ihr entsprechende untergeordnete Rolle zugewiesen wird. Die Bulle stellt sich als eine sehr eindringliche, lehramtliche Äußerung des Papsttums dar, die Abwehrstellung und programmatische Zusammenfassung zugleich sein sollte — einerseits Abwehrstellung gegen Lehren und deren Manifestation im praktischen Bereich, wie sie von wachsamen und hellhörigen Zeitgenossen schon seit einiger Zeit wahrgenommen wurden, und andererseits programmatischbündige Zusammenfassung der für eine christliche Gesellschaft und Herrschaft geltenden Maxime, verstanden aus der Perspektive des ausgehenden 13. Jahrhunderts. Die Bulle nimmt Stellung gegen jene Lehrmeinungen, die

---

[7]) Darüber vgl. Walter Ullmann, Leo I and the theme of papal primacy. Journal of Theological Studies N. S. 11 (1960) 25—51. Über das Recht in diesem Rahmen als Herrschaftsmittel: ders., Papst und König. Grundlagen des Papsttums und der englischen Verfassung im Mittelalter (= Salzburger Universitätsschriften 3, Salzburg und München 1966) 39f.

[8]) Das hebt Vernani in seinem Kommentar besonders hervor: *Fides est in ecclesia tamquam fundamentum* (a. a. O., 145). Die ganze Stelle ist lehrreich; sie findet sich nicht bei Iohannes Monachus in der von mir benutzten Ausgabe. Unterstrichen sei die „*fides*", weil in dieser Gemeinschaft gewohnheitsmäßige Bindungen, sprachliche, geographische, ethnische, biologische etc. Beziehungen nicht entscheidend waren.

nach Auffassung des Papsttums die Grundfesten der bestehenden christlichen
Weltanschauung und damit der Gesellschaft unterwanderten und aushöhlten.
Dazu gehören vor allem — ich versuche, das Geschichtsbild mit den Augen
eines bonifazianischen Zeitgenossen zu sehen — die Überflutung fast des ge-
samten intellektuellen Lebens mit aristotelischen Gedankengängen, eine Überflutung, die manchem Zeitgenossen und ganz gewiß Bonifaz VIII. und seinen
Ratgebern als eine Verseuchung und Verpestung einer bisher klaren und un-
verdorbenen Luft vorgekommen sein mag. Es war die aristotelische Grundkonzeption, an der konservativ orientierte Geister Anstoß nahmen[9]). Diese
Grundkonzeption erschien vornehmlich im sog. lateinischen Averroismus, die
der eine oder der andere Zeitgenosse auch in verschiedenen thomistischen
Äußerungen wiederzuerkennen geglaubt haben konnte. Über die radikale
Änderung, die die Rezeption des aristotelischen Naturalismus in der Weltanschauung des 13. Jahrhunderts zur Folge hatte, dürfte wohl kein Zweifel
mehr bestehen. Kein Geringerer als Heinrich Mitteis hat einmal gesagt, daß
wir heute noch gar nicht in der Lage seien, den ganzen Umfang der durch das
Eindringen aristotelischer Gedanken verursachten Änderung des Weltbildes
zu ermessen[10]). Auch im praktischen Rechtsleben fand diese aristotelische
Lehre eine Bestätigung, und zwar anfänglich ganz und gar unabhängig davon,
in der rechtlich unterbauten nationalstaatlichen Souveränität, die sich dann
am Anfang des 14. Jahrhunderts in der Tat auf aristotelische Grundsätze zu
stützen vermochte[11]). In diesen geistigen und rechtlichen Manifestationen sah
man an der Kurie die untrüglichen Symptome von Bewegungen, die, wenn
nicht zum Stehen gebracht, nicht bloß zu einer Krise, sondern zur Zerstörung
des traditionellen christlichen Weltbildes führen mußten. Das Fundament
schien erschüttert und ins Wanken gekommen zu sein. Ein Zeichen dieser
Bewegung war, daß sie trotz ihrer philosophischen Grundlegung immer wei-

---

[9]) Vgl. die einführenden Beobachtungen von Georges de Lagarde, La naissance de
l'esprit laique au déclin du moyen âge: secteur social de la scolastique (Louvain—
Paris ²1958) 28ff. Über die an der Kurie seit den frühen sechziger Jahren zu beob-
achtende Unruhe hinsichtlich der Orientierung der Pariser Professoren, insbesondere
der aristotelischen Richtung ihrer Lehren, unterrichtet ausgezeichnet André Callebaut, Jean Pecham et l'augustinisme. Archivum Franciscanum Historicum 18
(1925) 441—472; hier auch die Anklagen der Päpste Johannes XXI. (459f.) und
Martin IV. gegen die Pariser Fakultät. Schon Gregor IX. äußerte schwere Bedenken über die aristotelischen Wirkungen in seinem Schreiben an die Pariser Theo-
logen vom 7. Juli 1228: Potthast nr. 8231.

[10]) Siehe Heinrich Mitteis, in: Historische Zeitschrift 163 (1941) 281: „... eine Änderung des Weltbildes durch das Eindringen aristotelischer und nacharistotelischer
Gedanken, deren ganzen Umfang zu ermessen wir heute noch gar nicht in der Lage
sind".

[11]) Über den Hintergrund vgl. Jean Rivière, Le problème de l'église et de l'état au
temps de Philippe le Bel (Louvain—Paris 1926) 423ff.; Otto Brunner, Land und
Herrschaft. Grundfragen der territorialen Verfassungsgeschichte Österreichs im späten Mittelalter (Wien, Wiesbaden ⁴1959). Jetzt siehe Bruno Paradisi, Il pensiero
politico dei giuristi medievali, in: Storia delle idee politiche, economiche e sociali,
hrsg. von Luigi Firpo (Torino 1973) 57ff. und 149f.

tere Kreise in ihre Einflußzone zog und eine Kettenreaktion auszulösen vermochte.

Ein Zeitgenosse konnte unschwer die ernsten Gefahren für die damalige
christliche Kosmologie erkennen. Ihm blieben freilich die tieferen und auch
die subtilen Unterschiede zwischen dem radikalen Averroismus und der kristall-
klaren, dem christlichen Weltbild konformen, thomistischen Synthese verborgen, und er konnte wohl auch die Neigung empfinden, beide gleicherweise zu
verwerfen, eben weil in ihnen in geradezu revolutionärer Weise eine neue
Begriffswelt ihm entgegentrat. Denn es handelte sich hier nicht um einen
üblichen Schulenstreit, sondern um tiefgreifende weltanschauliche Kämpfe[12]).
Das der neuen Richtung gemeinsame Element war die Betonung der Idee der
Natur als einer eigenständigen und selbständigen Kraft und Wirkursache.
Der Bereich, auf dem sich Averroismus und Thomismus grundsätzlich schie-
den, betraf die Stellung und Funktion der Natur innerhalb der christlichen
Kosmologie, wie sie der Aquinate in meisterhafter Weise dargestellt hatte.
Freilich konnten bei grober und oberflächlicher Betrachtung einige thomisti-
sche Thesen ein Opfer der averroistischen Verurteilungssentenz durch den
Pariser Bischof Étienne Tempier in den Jahren 1270 und 1277 werden[13]).

Ich kann mir eine eingehende Darstellung jener averroistischen Thesen
ersparen, die allgemein als gefährlich für die damalige christliche Weltanschauung erkannt wurden (und auch zum Teil noch werden). Zum Beispiel
die These von der Doppelwahrheit, die, ob nun tatsächlich von den Aver-
roisten vertreten oder auf Mißverständnis beruhend, als Bestandteil ihrer
Lehren angesehen wurde. Andere Meinungen, die dem Averroismus entweder
unterschoben oder von ihm tatsächlich befürwortet wurden, betrafen die
Leugnung der *virtutes infusae* oder des sündhaften Charakters der *fornicatio*

---

[12]) Das hob schon Martin Grabmann, Der lateinische Averroismus des 13. Jahrhunderts und seine Stellung zur christlichen Weltanschauung. Sitzungsberichte der
Bayerischen Akademie der Wissenschaften, phil.-hist. Klasse 1931, Heft 2, 76 hervor. Beste Einführung in Sigers Lehren ist Fernand Van Steenberghen, Les
oeuvres et la doctrine de Siger de Brabant (= Mémoires de l'Académie Royale de
Belgique 39, 1938); kurzer populärwissenschaftlicher Abriß bei David Knowles,
The evolution of medieval thought (London 1962) 291f., wo die neuere Literatur
etwas zu kurz kommt. Vgl. Van Steenberghen (wie Anm. 13) 386.

[13]) Am 10. Dezember 1270: siehe Henricus Denifle—Aemilius Chatelain, Chartularium Universitatis Parisiensis I (Paris 1889) 486f. nr. 432; 7. März 1277, ibid.,
543ff. nr. 473. Vgl. auch Paul Mandonnet, Siger de Brabant et l'averroisme latin
au XIIIe siècle (= Philosophes Belges VI—VII, Louvain 1908—1911), II, 441ff.,
hier 458ff. Über Siger und Thomas besonders instruktiv: Fernand Van Steenberghen, La philosophie au XIIIe siècle (Louvain—Paris 1966) 393f., 397ff., 430ff.,
und über die beiden Pariser Verurteilungen, ibid., 472ff., 483ff. Über die Oxforder
Verurteilungen (einschließlich thomistischer Thesen) durch Richard Kilwardby und
John Pecham: ibid., 488ff. (Bibliographie Anm. 163f.). Über Kilwardby und Pecham
in diesem Zusammenhang noch Callebaut (wie Anm. 9) mit vielen Einzelheiten.
Über die thomistische Verurteilung im besonderen vgl. noch Fernand Van Steenberghen, Siger dans l'histoire de l'Aristotélisme (= Philosophes Belges: Textes et
Études XIII, Louvain 1942) II, 728ff.

oder die Ablehnung des Postulats der geschlechtlichen Enthaltsamkeit, usw.[14]).

Aber von den Thesen, die für das Verständnis des Hintergrundes unserer Bulle von unmittelbarem Interesse sind, kommt in erster Linie die auch von Thomas vertretene Idee von der Natur in Betracht, die nach seiner Auffassung dem Menschen als Vernunftwesen eignet und dessen Verhalten in seinen gesellschaftlichen Beziehungen bestimmt[15]). Diese gründeten sich nicht auf Dogma, auf kirchliche Lehren, auf die Erkenntnis von der göttlichen Lenkung des Kosmos, sondern auf die Erfahrung, auf die rein menschliche natürliche Vernunft und das daraus fließende Urteil, das von besonderer Sachkenntnis häufig unbeschwert und von theologischen oder religiösen Erkenntnissen oft unbeeinflußt war. Um eine thomistische Äußerung zu zitieren, kam hier zum Zuge der *instinctus naturae*, der zum sozialen Zusammenleben drängt und vor allem zum Begriff des Staates leitete.

Das war in der Tat der Begriff, der nunmehr zum ehernen Gerüst der neuen Gesellschaftslehre wurde. Es war gerade im Zusammenhang mit dem Begriff des Staates, daß Thomas den *instinctus naturae* einführte. Er behauptete, daß der Staat ins Leben gerufen werde *per instinctum naturae inditum a summo regente, qui est auctor naturae*[16]). An einer anderen Stelle führte er aus, daß es der *impetus naturalis* sei, der als Triebkraft die *communitas civitatis* im Gefolge hätte. Der Rechtsbegriff des Staates wurde in der thomistischen Lehre nach aristotelischem Vorbild als natürliche Wesenheit dargestellt, wobei der grundsätzliche Standpunkt bei Thomas zu beobachten ist[17]), daß der *auctor naturae* stets Gott selbst ist und bleibt. Daher die thomistische Schlußfolgerung, daß der Staat eine autonome, selbständige, eigenständige Einheit ist, die ihren eigenen innewohnenden Normen folgt, ihr natürlich-eigenes Ziel anstrebt und sich nach ihren eigenen Gesetzen richtet. Der Staat ist Ausfluß des *naturale iudicatorium humanae rationis*, um den Aquinaten nochmals zu zitieren[18]). Der Staat ist, wie gesagt, die *communitas perfectissima*[19]), eben weil die Natur selbst nichts unvollständig läßt[20]). Als Rechtsinstitution hat der Staat nach dem Thomismus nichts mit irgendeiner anderen

---

[14]) Siehe Denifle—Chatelain, Chartularium, I 486f. und Mandonnet (wie Anm. 13) II, 463; Grabmann (wie Anm. 12) 6—10. Gute Übersicht bei de Lagarde (wie Anm. 9) 35ff.

[15]) Thomas, De regimine principum, I. 1: *Est autem unicuique hominum naturaliter insitum rationis lumen, quo in suis actibus dirigatur ad finem.* Ähnlich an vielen anderen Stellen. Das innerste Wesen einer Sache versteht er als deren Natur: *Essentia speciei vocatur etiam natura* (Summa theologiae, III qu. 2, art. 1c) oder *natura nihil aliud est quam ratio . . . indita rebus* (Commentaria ad Libros Phys., II 14f.).

[16]) Einzelnachweise bei Walter Ullmann, Principles of Government and Politics in the Middle Ages (London [3]1974) 249.

[17]) In diesem Zusammenhang vgl. vor allem Martin Grabmann, Die mittelalterlichen Kommentare zur Politik des Aristoteles. Sitzungsberichte der Bayerischen Akademie der Wissenschaften, phil.-hist. Klasse, 1941, Heft 10, hier 12ff.

[18]) Thomas, Summa theologiae, I—II qu. 76, art. 6 ad 4.

[19]) Thomas, Kommentar zur Politik, I lectio 1.

[20]) Vgl. etwa seinen Kommentar In tres libros De anima III, 14. 1; Summa theologiae, I—II qu. 91, art. 2, obj. 1.

Institution zu tun. Er ist keine menschliche Erfindung oder Einrichtung, keine gekünstelte Gestaltung, und hat entstehungsmäßig und wirkungsmäßig weder mit der Kirche noch dem Papsttum oder göttlicher Gnade etwas zu tun. Er ist autonom. Der natürlich-menschliche Trieb hat ihn erzeugt. Diese Vorstellung vom Wesen des Staates involviert den mit ihm unzertrennlich verbundenen Begriff des *civis*. Der Staat setzt sich aus den *cives* zusammen. Nun hier stoßen wir auf einen sehr bedeutsamen Begriff, denn der aristotelisch-thomistische *civis* ist nichts anderes als der natürliche Mensch, den Paulus als einen *homo animalis* bezeichnet hatte und der sehr richtig mit „natürlichem Menschen" übersetzt wird. Wir betreten damit das von Mediävisten so sehr vernachlässigte Rechtsgebiet der Taufe. Denn die Wirkung der Taufe bestand darin, daß das natürliche Wesen des Menschen sich in eine *nova creatura* verwandelte, die als *homo novus* auftrat, für den nunmehr die Normen der *novitas vitae* gelten sollten. Die *nova creatura* war der *fidelis christianus*, der an die Gebote der göttlich bestellten Amtsträger gebunden war. Rechtlich bedeutete die Taufe den Eintritt in die Kirche, die als göttliche Heilsanstalt die ihr immanenten Ziele verfolgte. Als *fidelis* war der Einzelne der (christlichen) Obrigkeit untertan. Es handelte sich, wie Paulus betont hatte, um eine *regeneratio hominis*, eine Wiedererstehung des natürlichen Menschen in der Gestalt des Christen. Wohlgemerkt, die natürliche *generatio* wich einer *regeneratio*, weil er wiedergeboren wurde *per lavacrum regenerationis et renovationis*[21]). Die Idee der Wiedergeburt fand ihren einprägsamsten Ausdruck in der Antwort Christi auf die Frage des Nikodemus: „Wie kann ein Mensch geboren werden, wenn er schon alt ist? Kann er etwa in den Schoß seiner Mutter zurückkehren und aufs neue geboren werden?"[22]).

Gedanklich erlebte jetzt in der neuen Lehre des 13. Jahrhunderts der natürliche Mensch eine Wiedergeburt, und zwar eine Wiedergeburt, die der

---

[21]) Tit. 3, 5; ferner I Kor. 2, 14f.; II Kor. 5, 17; Gal. 6, 15; Eph. 4, 23. Die Novitas vitae in Röm. 6, 4. Der Homo novus in Eph. 2, 15 und 4, 24. Ganz in Übereinstimmung damit lautete das Gebet des Papstes bei der Ostertaufe: ... *ut omnis homo hoc sacramentum regenerationis ingressus in vera innocentia nova infantia renascatur* (Liber sacramentorum Romanae ecclesiae ordinis anni circuli [Sacramentarium Gelasianum], ed. L. C. Mohlberg [Romae 1960] 73f. nr. 448). Das Gebet war bis in die jüngste Zeit noch in Gebrauch. Genau diesen Wiedergeburtsgedanken verwendete Papst Innocenz III. nach der Eroberung Konstantinopels durch die Kreuzfahrer 1204: *Cum ecclesia Constantinopolitana in novam quodammodo infantiam renascatur* (Reg. VIII, 26 = PL 215, 579).

[22]) Ioh. 3, 4f. Zu dieser Stelle vgl. Rudolf Schnackenburg, Das Johannes-Evangelium (Freiburg—Basel—Wien 1965) 380ff., der hervorhebt, daß jeder christliche Hörer oder Leser sofort an die Taufe denken mußte (383). Zum Hintergrund der Wiedergeburtsidee vgl. aus der reichen Literatur: Adolf von Harnack, Die Terminologie der Wiedergeburt und verwandter Erlebnisse in der ältesten Kirche. In: Texte und Untersuchungen zur altchristlichen Literatur 42 (1918) 97—143; Othmar Heggelbacher, Die christliche Taufe als Rechtsakt nach dem Zeugnis der frühen Christenheit (Freiburg/Schweiz 1953; grundlegend); H. D. Betz, Der Apostel Paulus und die sokratische Tradition (Tübingen 1972) 138ff. Vgl. noch Karl Baus, in: Handbuch der Kirchengeschichte (wie Anm. 4) I, 128ff.

durch die Taufe erwirkten Wiedergeburt analog war. Bildlich gesprochen, hatte sich der natürliche Mensch bis ins 13. Jahrhundert hinein in einem Winterschlaf befunden, denn was zählte, war ja nicht er, sondern der *homo renatus*[23]), d. h. der *fidelis christianus*. Was man im Anschluß an die aristotelische Rezeption beobachtet, ist die Wiedergeburt, die Renaissance oder Wiederkehr dieses verdrängten natürlichen Menschen, der sich im öffentlich-rechtlichen Bereich zum *civis* verwandelte. Und wir erinnern uns, daß Thomas Aristoteles erweiternd von dem *animal politicum et sociale* sprach[24]). Die Erinnerung an den *homo animalis* war gewiß nicht nur nicht verblaßt, sondern erleichterte seine Wiedererstehung in sehr erheblichem Maße. Was ferner die Wiedergeburt des Rechtsbegriffs des *civis* förderte, war auch hier der Sprachgebrauch, denn von den *cives* handelten doch unzählige Diplomata usw., aber funktionell waren sie nichts anderes als *subditi*. Jetzt beginnen sie rechtlich bedeutsame Gestalt anzunehmen, weil sie als *cives* konstituierende und integrierende Bestandteile des Staates waren. Man könnte hier wohl von einer *regeneratio civis* sprechen. Betont soll werden, daß — im Gegensatz zum Eintritt in die Kirche — es keiner besonderen Rechtshandlung bedurfte, um Mitglied des Staates zu werden. Vermöge seines natürlichen Ursprungs war er Bürger: Staat und Bürger ergänzten sich notwendigerweise und beide gehörten dem Bereich der Natur an, wie die aristotelisch-thomistische Lehre hervorhob. Daher konnte der Einzelne nunmehr einer zweifachen Betrachtungsweise unterliegen — einer natürlichen im öffentlichen Bereich in seiner Eigenschaft als *civis* und einer übernatürlichen im ekklesiologischen als *fidelis christianus*. In jener Funktion war er autonom, in dieser untertan der Obrigkeit[25]). Der natürliche Mensch wurde nicht mehr verdrängt, sondern voll verwertet. Seine in ihm schlummernden Kräfte und Fähigkeiten sollten ihre Entfaltung und Erfüllung erfahren, und zwar im privat-moralischen Bereich als Mensch schlechthin und im öffentlichen Leben als Bürger[26]).

Da die Bürger sich hinsichtlich ihres eigenen Zusammenlebens irgendwie ins Benehmen setzen, das Zusammenleben in ihrem Staate irgendwie regeln und entsprechende Gesetze schaffen müssen, entwickelten sie eine Tätigkeit, die Aristoteles mit dem dem mittelalterlichen Westen völlig neuen Ausdruck des *politeuein* bezeichnete. Wilhelm von Moerbeke münzte wohl zutreffend den neuen Terminus *politizare*, d. h. Handeln als Bürger innerhalb des Rahmens der natürlichen Gemeinschaft des Staates[27]), das die Bedeutung des

---

23) Ioh. 3, 3 und I Petr. 1, 23.

24) De regimine principum I, 1: *Naturale autem est homini, ut sit animal sociale et politicum.*

25) Einzelheiten bei Louis Lachance, L'humanisme politique de s. Thomas d'Aquin (Paris—Montreal 1965) 203 ff.; vgl. noch Walter Ullmann, The Individual and Society in the Middle Ages (London 1967) 121 ff.

26) Diese Unterscheidung geht auf Aristoteles zurück: Politik III, 5, 10 (1278 b). Darüber siehe besonders Thomas in seinem Kommentar zur Politik III, 3.

27) S. F. Susemihl, Aristotelis Libri Octo Politicorum (Lipsiae 1872) 307 Z. 12 (Pol. VII. 14 [15], 1333 b).

Herrschens im weiteren Sinne haben sollte. Damit begegnen wir dem dritten hier wesentlichen Begriff. Neben dem Staat und dem Bürger jetzt noch die Politik, gerade jene Tätigkeit, die die *cives* in dieser Eigenschaft entfalten, wenn es um die Ordnung ihres eigenen Gemeinwesens geht. Wie der Staat begrifflich autonom ist, so ist auch die Politik seiner Bürger: sie weist dem Staat die Richtung. Sie setzt sich ihre eigenen Kriterien, sie ruht auf ihren von ihr selbst bestimmten Normen, und die Wissenschaft von der Politik ist verständlicherweise eine der *scientiae humanae*, um den Aquinaten nochmals zu bemühen, aber vor allem ist sie eine *scientia architectonica*, weil sie *ultimum et perfectum bonum in rebus humanis* als Zweck verfolgt[28]). Darüber hinaus ist die *scientia politica* selbst eine neue Wort- und Begriffsbildung, die den Inhalt ziemlich genau umschreibt. Sie ist eine jener Wissenschaften, die *operativae secundum imitationem naturae* sind[29]). Daher nennt Thomas auch ganz folgerichtig die *doctrina politica* eine *scientia civilis*[30]). Daß in dieser neuen Begriffswelt auch eine neue Weltanschauung enthalten war, dürfte unschwer zu erkennen sein. Der Staat, die Bürger, die Politik und ihre Wissenschaft, sie alle ließen sich ohne Schwierigkeit dem Oberbegriff der *humanitas* unterordnen[31]). Das Zeitalter des Humanismus rückt in greifbare Nähe.

Diese neue Begriffswelt begann nun ihren Siegeszug anzutreten. Da wäre z. B. zu nennen die thomistische Neuprägung vom *regimen politicum* oder von der *communitas politica*, wovon man bisher noch nichts gehört hatte. Daneben gab es nach dem Thomismus einen *status popularis*, charakterisiert dadurch, daß *ex popularibus possunt eligi principes, et ad populum pertinet electio principum.* Dem entspricht es, wenn der Herrscher verstanden wurde als *persona populi,* d. h. daß er in seiner Person das Volk repräsentiert. Damit wurde die schon fast verschollene Aszendenzthese von Herrschaft und Recht wiederbelebt[32]).

Der Thomismus fügte die aristotelische Lehre nahtlos in den christlichen Gesamtbau ein, so daß man von einem umfassenden System zu sprechen befugt ist. Das sollen zwei Beispiele klarstellen. Erstens, die thomistische Doktrin beseitigte nicht die bisherige Tugendlehre, sondern vervollständigte sie. Wie bekannt, konnten Handlungen, die auf eine der vier sog. Kardinaltugenden (*iustitia, prudentia, temperantia* und *fortitudo*)[33]) zurückgingen, erst dann vollen sittlichen Wert beanspruchen, wenn sie auch von einer der drei sog. theologischen Tugenden getragen wurden (Glaube, Hoffnung und Liebe). Auch hier im Bereich der Tugendlehre half der Sprachgebrauch, der der neuen Lehre den Zutritt erleichterte, denn nach makrobischem Muster hießen diese

---

[28]) Kommentar zur Politik, I lectio 1.
[29]) Belege bei Ullmann, Principles (wie Anm. 16) 251—253.
[30]) Kommentar zur Politik, I lectio 1.
[31]) Dazu Lachance (wie Anm. 25) 349ff.
[32]) Vgl. Ullmann, Principles (wie Anm. 16) 252ff.
[33]) Über sie vgl. Sibylle Mähl, Quadriga Virtutum (Köln—Wien 1969), bes. für das karolingische Zeitalter.

Tugenden auch *virtutes politicae*[34]). Nun Thomas hat hier wiederum den Weg gewiesen und den Kardinaltugenden vollen Tugendwert zuerkannt, indem er Handlungen, die sich auf sie stützten, als sittlich „gut" anerkannte, zugleich aber betonte, daß sie verdienstvoll wären, wenn sie von einer der theologischen Tugenden inspiriert wurden: *Actus virtutis politicae non est indifferens, sed est de se bonus, et si gratia informatus, erit meritorius*[35]). Hier wird mit aller wünschenswerten Klarheit die Autonomie der Kardinaltugenden unterstrichen, deren Wirkkraft durch die theologischen so sehr erhöht wird, daß sie sich erst dann vollkommen entfalten können, mit dem Ergebnis, daß das menschliche Verhalten verdienstvoll wird.

Eine Parallelthese findet sich in der thomistischen Lehre von dem Verhältnis zwischen Natur und Gnade, denn *gratia non tollit naturam, sed perficit*. Auch hier sieht man, wie die beiden Pole sich in ein fugenloses System einordnen lassen und aufeinander abgestimmt werden können. Welch tiefe Einbrüche in die überkommene Gesellschafts- und Herrschaftlehre sich dabei auftaten, bedarf wohl keiner Betonung. Das Natürliche und das Übernatürliche bildeten die beiden Grundpfeiler der neuen Kosmologie[36]). Gewiß waren sie nicht von gleichem Rang, aber das Entscheidende war, daß jedem der beiden Pole Eigenständigkeit und Eigenwert zukam. Innerhalb dieser kosmologischen Einheit konnte man von einer Rang- und Stufenordnung sprechen. Und es war eben dieses Merkmal, das den Thomismus vom Averroismus grundsätzlich unterschied, denn im letzteren standen sich Natur und Gnade unversöhnlich gegenüber.

Die dem natürlichen Bereich angehörenden Begriffe des Staates, des Bürgers und der Politik sollten von nun ab nicht mehr aus dem Blickfeld verschwinden. Bisher, d. h. bis zur aristotelischen Rezeption, existierten sie nicht als Begriffselemente einer Gesellschafts- und Herrschaftslehre. Nunmehr aber, wie der Aquinate vollends gezeigt hatte, und wie seine Schüler und Nachfolger dartun sollten, dienten gerade diese Begriffe als vorzügliche Mittel, mit denen sich ein bipolares Gesellschafts- und Herrschaftssystem errichten ließ, d. h. ein System, das nicht auf den unipolaren ekklesiologischen Grundfesten ruhte, sondern auf dem Naturgebilde des Staates und der Heilsanstalt der Kirche. Eine neue Welt begann sich vor den Zeitgenossen aufzutun, die ohnehin für dieses neue Weltbild empfänglich waren. Die Voraussetzungen waren gegeben, denn völlig unabhängig von Aristoteles hatte sich seit dem Ende des 12. Jahrhunderts eine Entwicklung auf fast allen geistigen Bereichen angebahnt, die dann seit der Mitte des 13. Jahrhunderts feste Formen annahm und den Boden für die Aufnahme aristotelischer Ideen befruchtete. Gewiß, der Naturalismus in besonders krasser Art mit seinen für die christliche Kosmologie gefährden-

---

[34]) Macrobius, Commentaria in Somnium Scipionis (ed. Lipsiae 1774) I. 8, 50f.

[35]) Darüber im besonderen Odon Lottin, Les vertus morales acquises, sont-elles de vraies vertus? Recherches de théologie ancienne et médiévale 20 (1953) 34—36, welcher erst war, der auf die grundlegende Bedeutung dieser thomistischen Aussage hingewiesen hat.

[36]) Zum Ganzen vgl. Lachance (wie Anm. 25) 54ff., 353ff.

den Folgerungen war in den letzten Dezennien an der Pariser Universität in ein akutes Stadium getreten, was auch an anderen Lehranstalten zu beobachten war. Man braucht bloß auf Siger von Brabant oder Heinrich von Gent zu verweisen, um zu sehen, wie weit die naturalistische Auffassung zu gehen bereit war [37]). Aber dieser krasse Naturalismus war doch nur eine Teilerscheinung. Er bildete nur einen markanten Ausschnitt aus dem Gesamtbild. Und dieses Gesamtbild wies Züge und Merkmale auf, die durchaus unbeeinflußt von Aristoteles und vom Averroismus das Landschaftsbild seit der Mitte des 13. Jahrhunderts verändert hatten.

Auf allen Gebieten des schöpferischen Geistes zeigt sich nämlich ein spürbarer Wandel und eine unmißverständliche Neigung zur naturalistischen Betrachtung, so vor allem im künstlerischen Schaffen, in der Architektur, in der Malerei und besonders in der Skulptur [38]), aber nicht weniger im neuesten Wissenszweig, in der *scientia naturalis* — der Ausdruck ist genauso eine Neuprägung wie die *scientia politica* (Albert der Große münzte ihn [39]) — und in der durch sie befruchteten Medizin, aber ebenso auch in der Geschichtsschreibung läßt sich eine auffallende Neigung zur rein menschlichen Erklärung geschichtlicher Ereignisse wahrnehmen [40]), und Poesie und Prosa und sogar Rechtsbücher bedienen sich jetzt in wachsendem Maße der Volkssprache. Diese vermochte das natürlich-menschliche Element viel kräftiger zum Ausdruck zu bringen als das etwas steife, ungelenke, fremde Latein. Damit steht in Einklang, daß sich im Laufe des 13. Jahrhunderts das Laienelement immer menr nach vorne schiebt — man braucht nur an die Universitäten zu denken, an die Gerichtsbarkeit und herrscherlichen Organe, besonders dort, wo das Lehnsrecht ausgeprägt war, etwa in England, oder an das kommunale Verfassungswesen, wie man es durchwegs in Oberitalien entwickelt sah, um sich ein ungefähres Bild von der Veränderung zu machen, die das Zeitalter aufzeigte [41]). Zusätzlich ist erwähnenswert, und zwar vornehmlich im herrscherlichen Bereich, die dem Naturalismus verwandte Säkularisierungstendenz, die im staufischen Zeitalter die Herrschaftsstruktur ganz wesentlich verändert hatte. Diese Säkularisierung zog einen dicken Strich unter die bisherige ekklesiologisch-theokratisch ausgerichteten Herrschaftsgrundlagen [42]). Nur auf dem

---

[37]) Vgl. die oben unter Anm. 13 zitierte Literatur.

[38]) Zur Orientierung vgl. etwa Richard Hamann, Geschichte der Kunst (Berlin 1933) 295 ff., der vom Zeitalter des Naturalismus, Humanismus und Renaissance spricht (310).

[39]) Albert der Große, De Mineralibus (ed. Venedig 1517) III, 1, 1, S. 139: *Scientiae naturalis enim non est simpliciter narrata accipere, sed in rebus naturalibus inquirere causas*. Sein Zeitgenosse Roger Bacon in Oxford sprach von den *scientiae experimentales*. Siehe E. J. Dijksterhuis, The mechanization of the world picture (Oxford 1961) 138 f.

[40]) Einzelheiten in Ullmann, Individual and Society (wie Anm. 25) 110 ff.

[41]) Über den Hintergrund vgl. noch immer wertvoll de Lagarde (wie Anm. 9) I, 159 ff. und II (1958) 28 ff., 51 ff. und 106 ff.

[42]) Dazu vgl. die Beobachtungen von Walter Ullmann, Von Canossa nach Pavia: Zum Strukturwandel der Herrschaftsgrundlagen im salischen und staufischen Zeitalter. Historisches Jahrbuch 93 (1973) 265—300.

Weg einer Zusammenschau läßt sich die volle Bedeutung der aristotelischen Rezeption erkennen. Man beginnt zu verstehen, wie und warum dieser Einfluß so rasche und weitreichende Fortschritte gerade in der Gesellschafts- und Herrschaftslehre machen konnte. Solche gewaltige geistige Strömungen lassen sich doch nur im Zusammenhang mit der historischen Faktizität erklären. Erst dann werden Aktion und Reaktion verständlich, erst dann Ursache und Wirkung begreiflich, Spiel und Gegenspiel faßlich.

Indem die neuen Begriffe um die Jahrhundertwende zu Werkzeugen der Gesellschafts- und Herrschaftslehre wurden, übten sie eine bisher nur unvollkommen erkannte Wirkung aus, eben weil sie die Eigenständigkeit der Sachverhalte voraussetzten. An die Stelle der Unipolarität trat immer häufiger die Bipolarität. Man könnte auch sagen, daß die *humanitas* als die abstrakte Manifestation des natürlich Menschlichen in ihrem vollen Licht in Erscheinung trat und neben der *christianitas* stand. Weite Perspektiven begannen sich abzuzeichnen, jetzt, wo der *homo animalis* in seiner öffentlich-rechtlichen Funktion seinen Platz einnahm[43]). Gedanklich und begrifflich sind die Gemeinschaft der Bürger, der Staat, von der Gemeinschaft der Gläubigen, der Kirche, zu scheiden. Staat, Bürger, Politik standen juristisch und begrifflich in keinem Verhältnis zur Kirche und zum Kirchenrecht, denn sie entstammten dem natürlichen Bereich und waren aus diesem Grund eigenständig. Füglich bedeutete die neue Gesellschafts- und Herrschaftslehre eine erhebliche Beschränkung der Jurisdiktionsgewalt der ekklesiologisch bedingten Amtswalter, weil das juristische Bindeglied fehlte. Auch kam weder dem Staat noch dem Bürger noch der Politik irgendein sakramentaler Charakter zu. Es ist deshalb klar, warum jetzt wenigstens in manchen literarischen Erzeugnissen für den Bereich der natürlich gewordenen Gemeinschaft der Bürger die aszendente These von Herrschaft und Recht zur Anwendung kam und die deszendente These auf den Bereich der von Christus gestifteten Heilsanstalt der Kirche beschränkt blieb[44]). Damit aber ergaben sich tiefgreifende Probleme, an denen die Zeitgenossen der Jahrhundertwende nicht vorübergehen konnten.

Diese neuen Thesen führten kein erträumtes Dasein über den Wolken, sondern waren recht erdverbunden und wirklichkeitsbezogen. Vor allem, sie waren mit einem geradezu brisanten Applikationspotential versehen. Man stelle sich bloß vor, daß in diesem Rahmen keine Rechte von der Obrigkeit konzediert oder überantwortet wurden, sie auch nicht zurückgefordert werden konnten. In diesem Rahmen tritt der theokratische Herrschaftsgedanke in demselben Verhältnis in den Hintergrund, in dem der säkularisierte Herrscher in den Vordergrund rückt. Die Tiefe der Kluft, die die alten von den neuen Thesen

---

[43]) Einzelheiten bei de Lagarde (wie Anm. 9) II, 80ff.

[44]) Über diese beiden Thesen vgl. die Buchrezension von Walter Ullmann in Revue d'histoire du droit 26 (1958) 360ff. sowie ders., Principles (wie Anm. 16) 20ff. Das auf natürlichen Gesetzen beruhende Wachstum des Staates und seine natürliche Entwicklung im Vergleich zur gestifteten Kirche soll hervorgehoben werden.

58

trennte, läßt sich einleuchtend erkennen beim *Rex Dei gratia*. Im bisherigen praktisch unangefochtenen Herrschaftssystem war der Herrscher das, was er war, durch die Gnade Gottes[45]), aber im Rahmen der neuen nun wirklich einmal politischen Theorien kam eine solche Grundlegung der herrscherlichen Macht nicht mehr zum Zug. Allein von diesem Gesichtswinkel aus gesehen, läßt sich die Beschneidung der kirchlichen Jurisdiktionsgewalt vollends ermessen[46]). Auf weitere Erscheinungsformen der neuen volksbezogenen Gesellschaftslehre brauche ich nicht einzugehen. Als bloße Beispiele seien erwähnt der sich jetzt kräftig entwickelnde Repräsentationsgedanke an Stelle des Delegationsgrundsatzes, die These von der im Volk ruhenden Rechtssetzungsgewalt, die Entwicklung der Volksvertretung und des Parlamentarismus[47]), die Bestellung der öffentlichen Organe und deren Verantwortlichkeit dem Volk gegenüber, die Absetzungsmöglichkeit von Herrschern durch das Volk, usw.[48]). Was man allenthalben beobachtet, ist die Neugeburt einer Kosmologie, die, und das soll betont werden, durchaus nicht dem Christentum gegenüberstand — Thomas hatte die meisterhafte Symbiose geschaffen —, sondern neben ihm stehen sollte.

Die Reaktion im päpstlichen Lager ließ sich vernünftigerweise voraussehen. Dem bisher als *plenitudo potestatis* verstandenen monarchischen Herrschaftsanspruch des Papstes wurden scharf umrissene Grenzen gesetzt. Diese Einengung ging nach päpstlicher Auffassung auf eine Begriffswelt zurück, die mit der vom Papsttum seit Jahrhunderten vertretenen christlichen Gesellschaftslehre nicht nur nichts gemein hatte, sondern ihr auch in wesentlichen

---

45) Vgl. etwa Boso, König von Burgund: *Ego Boso, Dei gratia id quod sum* (nach Ullmann, Individual and Society [wie Anm. 25] 19 Anm. 39). Aus späterer Zeit wäre Heinrich V. zu nennen: *Heinricus Dei gratia sum id quod sum* (Codex Udalrici n. 94, ed. Philippus Jaffé, Bibliotheca rerum Germanicarum 5, Berolini 1869; Neudruck 1965, 182). Auch bei Bischöfen findet sich diese ausdrückliche Bezugnahme auf Paulus.

46) Ein untrügliches Symptom dafür ist auch die fast gleichzeitige Änderung in der Zählung der Regierungsjahre bei den englischen und französischen Königen. Sowohl Eduard I. als auch Philipp III. begannen, ihre Regierungsjahre nicht vom Tage der Krönung bzw. Salbung, sondern vom tatsächlichen Herrschaftsantritt an zu zählen. Bemerkt sei in diesem Zusammenhang, daß der Staufer Philipp von Schwaben offenbar aus denselben Gründen seine Herrschaft vom Wahltag an rechnete (8. März 1198), und nicht erst von seinem Krönungstag an (8. September 1198): M. G. H. Legum sectio IV: Constitutiones et acta publica imperatorum et regum 2 (Hannoverae 1896) 2 nr. 1 (vom 29. Juni 1198); ferner 18 nr. 15. Diesem Umstand wird viel zuwenig Beachtung geschenkt.

47) Die ständischen Versammlungen hatten den Boden dafür schon vorbereitet. Im weiteren Sinne lassen sich hier hinsichtlich des Lehenswesens dieselben Beobachtungen machen wie bei der Emanzipation des Einzelnen, worüber Ullmann, Individual and Society (wie Anm. 25) Kap. II zu vergleichen ist. Diese befruchtende Funktion des Lehenswesens, das ohne Übertreibung als ein Vorstadium zur populistischen These und zur humanistischen Renaissance verstanden werden kann, ist noch nicht voll erkannt.

48) All dies sind bloße Erscheinungsformen der aszendenten oder populistischen These von Herrschaft und Recht.

Punkten entgegengesetzt war. Die unipolare Gesellschafts- und Herrschaftsordnung begann heftig umstritten zu werden. Das alles wurde aber über-
schattet von der drohenden Gefahr einer Durchlöcherung der ganzheitlichen
christlichen Weltanschauung. Dem aufmerksam beobachtenden Zeitgenossen
konnte diese Bedrohung nicht entgehen. Der ganzheitlichen Grundauffassung
entsprechend war das irdische Leben bloß ein Vorbereitungsstadium und
besaß deshalb auch keinen Selbstwert, sondern empfing erst seinen Wert aus
der Relation zum Seelenheil, die für jeden Christen als selbstverständlich ver-
pflichtend angesehen wurde. Jetzt jedoch wurde dem natürlich-irdischen
Leben offenbar voller autonomer Wert zugesprochen. Demgemäß schienen
sich die alten Bindungen und Ordnungen zu lockern, wenn nicht gar aufzu-
lösen, weil die Maßstäbe, Rangordnungen und Wertungen nicht mehr wie
ehedem unwidersprochen galten. Der nagende Zweifel hatte eingesetzt. Diese
geistige Entwicklung wurde vom Papsttum als ein schwerer, harter Schlag
gegen fundamentale christliche Grundsätze und -wahrheiten empfunden. Und
der Schlag mußte pariert und der Herausforderung eine geeignete Abwehr
entgegengesetzt werden, um die Christenheit vor Siechtum, Zerfall, Zerbrök-
kelung und Zersplitterung zu bewahren. Das Selbstverständnis des Papsttums,
das sich stets als Schutzhort der reinen christlichen Lebens-, Gesellschafts-
und Herrschaftsordnung betrachtete, legte ihm die Verpflichtung auf, eine
Abwehrfront gegen die neuen und mit geradezu alarmierender Schnelligkeit
um sich greifenden Thesen zu errichten, eben weil sie nach päpstlicher Ansicht
die Zersetzung und Zerklüftung der abendländischen Christenheit zur Folge
haben würden. Das innerste Wesen der ekklesiologischen universalen Einheit
mochte wohl durch die zeitgenössischen geistigen Wirrnisse angegriffen erscheinen.

Für diese auf praktischer Ebene vollzogene Verbreitung der neuen Thesen
kann wohl die französische Situation als Beispiel dienen. Daß sich die Potentialität der neuen Thematik in eine für das Papsttum höchst gefährliche
Realität ohne sonderliche Schwierigkeit umwandeln ließ, sollte der französische König zeigen, der den taktisch raffinierten Plan verfolgte, mit der praktischen Verwirklichung der aszendenten-populistischen These Ernst zu machen,
um die Kurie entsprechend zu beeindrucken, wenn nicht einzuschüchtern.
Und daß sowohl der Papst als auch die Kardinäle in der Tat bestürzt waren,
wird durch die erregten Reden bezeugt, die man im Konsistorium im Juni
1302 hören konnte. Die gerissene Art, mit der sich Philipp IV. der neumodi-
schen populistischen These im Kampf mit dem Papsttum bediente, ist höchst
aufschlußreich. Zum 10. April 1302 berief er eine Versammlung ein, an der
das französische Volk durch alle drei Stände vertreten war. Es war das erste
Mal, daß der dritte Stand — die Bürgerschaft — zu einer hochwichtigen
öffentlichen Transaktion geladen wurde. Und als dann der Adel seine Erklärung und der soeben emanzipierte dritte Stand — die *universitas civitatum
et villarum regni Franciae* — ein versiegeltes Schreiben an die Kurie absandten,
wurde die vom König berechnete und vorausgesehene Wirkung auch erzielt.
Der Kurie bemächtigte sich Unruhe, Erregung und Bestürzung. Die Kalku-

60

lation des Königs, daß die Kurie durch diese praktische Manifestation der populistischen These in Schrecken versetzt werde, erwies sich als durchaus richtig: er handelte — das war der zu erweckende Eindruck — bloß im Namen des französischen Volkes. Träger politischer Willensbildung wäre nicht er, sondern das Volk. Gerade an diesem Beispiel zeigte sich, wie weit zum Teil schon durch Rechtsgewohnheit vorbereitet, aszendente Thesen in die Tat umgesetzt werden konnten, denn was hier wesentlich war, war der Repräsentationsgedanke, die Politik, der Bürger und schließlich der Staatsgedanke[49]). Damit eröffnete sich aber eine sehr gefährliche Front für das Papsttum. Dieses hatte bisher nur mit Einzelherrschern zu tun gehabt, an deren Stelle nunmehr die amorphe Masse treten sollte. Und dafür hatte man noch kein Mittel parat.

Der Mann, der sich die Verteidigung der überlieferten juristischen Theologie schon früher sehr angelegen sein ließ, befand sich seit einiger Zeit an der bonifazianischen Kurie. Als Benedetto Caetani im Jahre 1290 päpstlicher Gesandter in Frankreich war, bestellte er den *venerabilis magister* des Augustinerordens, Aegidius Romanus[50]), zu seinem Exekutivorgan, um den berühmten Heinrich von Gent wegen der von ihm vertretenen Ansichten, die nach gängiger kurialer Auffassung mit der christlichen Lebensordnung nicht in Einklang zu bringen waren, aus dem Lehramt an der Pariser Universität zu entfernen. In seiner Ansprache vor dem Pariser Nationalkonzil machte sich Caetani über die Rechtgläubigkeit der Pariser Professoren mit beißender Ironie lustig[51]). Er hob hervor die *fatuitas* der Pariser Magister, die ihren Hochmut fahrenlassen sollten, denn an der römischen Kurie hätten sie den Ruf, dümmer als die dümmsten zu sein: *quia non solum se, set etiam totum orbem sua doctrina pestifera repleverunt*[52]). Obwohl diese scharfen Worte das aktuelle Problem der Minoritenprivilegien betrafen, mindern sie durchaus

---

[49]) Das versiegelte Schreiben ist nicht mehr erhalten, wohl aber das Schreiben des Adels. Für dieses und die Konsistorialansprachen siehe Dupuy (wie Anm. 4) 60ff. Daß diese ,,Volksversammlung" — wie auch jene des nächsten Jahres — ausgezeichnet gesteuert war, steht fest. Einzelheiten bei Helene Wieruszowski, Vom Imperium zum nationalen Königtum (Beiheft 30 der Historischen Zeitschrift, München 1933) 132ff.; T. S. R. Boase, Boniface VIII (London 1933) 305f.; Georges Digard, Philippe le Bel et le Saint-Siège de 1285—1304, II (Paris 1936) 101f.; neuerdings Thomas M. Bisson, The general assemblies of Philip the Fair: their character reconsidered. Studia Gratiana 15 (1972) 537—564, bes. 558ff. In anderem Zusammenhang verwies ich auf die Bedeutung dieser Versammlungen: Ullmann, Principles (wie Anm. 16) 107f. Bedauerlicherweise enthält der sonst so wertvolle Band 8 der Miscellanea Mediaevalia (,,Der Begriff der Repraesentatio im Mittelalter", hrsg. von Albert Zimmermann, Berlin 1971) keinen Beitrag zu diesem wichtigen Thema.

[50]) Zusammen mit dem anderen Lehrer an der Pariser Universität, Johannes de Muro: Denifle—Chatelain, Chartularium (wie Anm. 13) II, 12 nr. 542. Zum Ganzen vgl. Finke (wie Anm. 5) 17f.; Digard (wie Anm. 49) II, 117ff. Über Aegidius: Van Steenberghen (wie Anm. 13) 503f. (mit Bibliographie).

[51]) Über ihn als kurialen Ratgeber hinsichtlich früherer theologischer Probleme in Paris ist sehr aufschlußreich Callebaut (wie Anm. 9) 453f., 466f.

[52]) Siehe Finke (wie Anm. 5), Quellen, S. V nr. I.

nicht den symptomatischen Aussagewert — ganz im Gegenteil, die beißende
Zurückweisung der Pariser Professoren läßt zwingend auf deren Verachtung
durch den damaligen Kardinallegaten schließen.

Der seitdem das kuriale Vertrauen genießende Aegidius Romanus war wohl
einer der gewandtesten, belesensten und tiefsten Denker, der ebenso im Thomismus zu Hause war wie in dem von ihm bekämpften Averroismus[53]), der
aber stets selbständig seine Gedanken formte. Seine Lehre war eine Mischung
aus Augustinismus und Thomismus, wobei Aristoteles nur eine bescheidene
Rolle zuteil wurde[54]). Es wird zuwenig beachtet, daß er in seiner an der
Kurie verfaßten Schrift „De ecclesiastica potestate" der Taufe als rechtlich
erheblicher Tatsache allerhöchste und entscheidende Bedeutung zuschrieb[55]).
Jedenfalls schenkte der *regeneratio* kein hochmittelalterlicher Schriftsteller
soviel Aufmerksamkeit wie Aegidius. Da sich *Unam sanctam* so stark an diese
Schrift anlehnt, muß dieser Gesichtspunkt besonders unterstrichen werden[56]).
Die *regeneratio*, die der Mensch vermöge der Taufe an sich erfährt, ist Unter-
bau und Gerüst dieser Schrift. Damit befand er sich in vollstem Einklang mit
der paulinischen Lehre und der vorausgehenden Dogmatik. Nachdrücklich
faßte er die Taufe als rechtliche Wiedergeburt auf und nahm von der gerade
damals hoch im Kurs stehenden Wiedergeburt des natürlichen Menschen keine
Kenntnis. Die Folge war, daß der *homo animalis* wieder in die untergeordnete
Rolle zurückgedrängt wurde, die er in der überlieferten christlichen Kosmologie hatte. Zugleich wurde die frühere überragende Rolle des *homo renatus*
kräftigst hervorgehoben[57]). Die Beobachtung der kirchlichen Normen wurde
in diesem aegidianischen System zu einer Voraussetzung für das Seelenheil
des Christen: *Nullus possit consequi salutem nisi subiectus ecclesiae et nisi sit
eius filius* führt er im Zusammenhang mit der Taufe aus[58]).

Zuvörderst ergibt sich für ihn die ekklesiologische Grundthese, der entsprechend alles weltliche Recht und alle weltliche Herrschaft auf das kanonische

---

[53]) Darüber Van Steenberghen (wie Anm. 13) 447, 476f. und 481.

[54]) Über seine Auffassungen unterrichtet noch immer am besten Richard Scholz, Die
Publizistik zur Zeit Philipps des Schönen und Bonifaz' VIII. (Stuttgart 1903) 33ff.

[55]) Er nennt die Taufe das *sacramentum universale* in seiner Schrift De ecclesiastica
potestate, ed. Richard Scholz (Weimar 1929), II. 7, S. 72; an anderer Stelle nennt er
sie die *ianua* (II. 1, S. 98f.). Die Rechtsstellung innerhalb der christlichen Gemeinschaft bezieht die *nova creatura* aus der Mitgliedschaft der Kirche. Seine Grundauffassung stimmt völlig mit Augustinus überein. Vgl. dessen Sermo 121 in Migne,
PL 38, 679f. (*Prima nativitas ex masculo et femina, secunda nativitas ex Deo et ecclesia*);
Expos. in Ep. ad Romanos, ibid. 35, 2102 (*Renovatio in baptismo est*). Siehe ferner
De Genesi ad Litteram, ibid., 34, 353f. und Gratian, De cons., Dist. 4, c. 3f.

[56]) Es ist auffallend, daß ein so ausgezeichneter Kenner wie Yves Congar, L'église de
s. Augustin à l'époque moderne (Paris 1970) 272f. dieses entscheidende Element bei
Aegidius nicht erkannte. Auch Wilhelm Kölmel, Regimen christianum (Berlin 1970)
300f., 325, 349f. scheint die Bedeutung entgangen zu sein, obzwar er eine sehr markante Stelle zitiert, ohne jedoch deren Aussagewert zu ermessen (301). Auch Rivière
(wie Anm. 11) 191ff. und de Lagarde (wie Anm. 9) I, 194 entging die Bedeutung
der *regeneratio*.

[57]) A. a. O., II. 7 p. t. und III. 1, S. 149; III. 11, S. 202 usw.

[58]) Ibid., II. 7, S. 72f.

62

Recht auszurichten sei: *Omnes leges imperiales et terrenae potestates sunt ad ecclesiasticos canones ordinandae, ut sumant robur*[59]). Daher wurde von ihm das teleologische Element und der damit verknüpfte ganzheitliche Zusammenhang schärfstens in den Vordergrund gerückt[60]). Es ist deshalb einleuchtend, warum die schon fast vergessene These vom Eigentum und Besitz als Ausfluß göttlicher Gnade wieder ihre Auferstehung feierte. Wie erinnerlich, hat Gregor VII. in eindrucksvoller Weise Eigentum als Objekt der Binde- und Lösegewalt erklärt[61]). Hier bei Aegidius wird der Eigentumsbegriff zu einem wesentlichen Strukturelement der Ekklesiologie, nicht weniger aber auch der Herrschaftsbegriff selbst. Immer wieder kehrt er zu diesen wesentlichen Bestandteilen seiner Ekklesiologie zurück, so wenn er behauptet, daß die Taufe allein über die rechtmäßige Ausübung von Herrschaft und den rechtmäßigen Besitz entscheide: *Non sufficit, quod quicumque sit generatus carnaliter, nisi sit per ecclesiam regeneratus, quod possit cum iustitia rei alicui dominari nec rem aliquam possidere*[62]). Nun ist diese Ansicht gewiß nicht als epochemachend zu bezeichnen[63]), denn in dem Kulturkreis, in dem und für den Aegidius schrieb, gab es doch nur *homines regenerati*, die Besitz hatten und Herrschaft ausübten. Die Bedeutung, die er seiner These beilegt, kann wohl nur darin liegen, daß er den bestehenden Rechtszustand als Beweis für die Richtigkeit seiner Ekklesiologie heranzieht. Denn nach der implicite angegriffenen Lehre war der Empfang der Taufe keineswegs Voraussetzung für rechtmäßige Herrschaft oder für Eigentumserwerb. Nach Aegidius aber begründet die Taufe die Verpflichtung, ekklesiologische Normen zu beobachten, sofern — und das muß wohl unterstellt werden — man noch von einer christlichen Gesellschaft

---

[59]) Ibid., II. 10, S. 92.

[60]) Ibid., III. 4, S. 162: *Temporalia, ut temporalia sunt, ecclesiae sunt subiecta, quod non est intelligendum, quod ipsa temporalia per se et primo ecclesiae sunt subiecta, sed intelligendum est, quod sunt subiecta per se, sed non primo ... ipsa enim temporalia in se ipsis habent causam, ut subiciantur spiritualibus et ut ordinentur ad illa.* Damit hängt zusammen die teleologische Betrachtung der Funktion des weltlichen Herrschers: ibid., II. 6, S. 68: *Officium ergo terrenae potestatis est materiam preparare, ne princeps ecclesiasticus in spiritualibus impediatur.* Ferner die Ausführungen in II. 4, S. 49f., wo die Zweckgebundenheit besonders der *temporalia* in den Vordergrund tritt.

[61]) Reg. VII. 14a, ed. Erich C a s p a r (Weimar 1920) 487. Vgl. schon Gregor I. bei M i g n e, PL 76, 1200.

[62]) Aegidius, a. a. O., II. 7, S. 70. Damit im Zusammenhang vgl. noch die augustinische *prima* und *secunda nativitas* (oben Anm. 55). In seiner „Reportatio errorum" betitelten Schrift bringt Guilielmus Amidani de Cremona, der Nachfolger des Aegidius als Augustinergeneral, genau den gleichen Gedanken: *Ad iuste et legitime possidendi res temporales plus facit regeneratio per ecclesiam, quae spiritualis est, quam generatio paterna, quae fuit carnalis* (ed. Richard S c h o l z, Unbekannte kirchenpolitische Streitschriften, II [Rom 1914] 18). Die Schrift wurde von Papst Johannes XXII. veranlaßt, und die *errores* waren jene im „Defensor Pacis" des Marsilius von Padua enthaltenen Aussagen. Derselbe Regenerationsgedanke wurde auch scharf von einem Zeitgenossen, dem an der Oxforder und Cambridge Universität lehrenden Johann Baconthorpe, in seinem Sentenzenkommentar unterstrichen: In Sententias (Neudruck: 1969) IV. 11, qu. 1, art. 4, S. 386; vgl. auch IV. 5, qu. 3, art. 1, S. 339.

[63]) Vgl. noch Augustinus, De civitate Dei, II. 22.

und Lebensordnung sprechen kann [64]). Und daraus erklärt sich seine Sicht und Emphase, daß man nur unter der Herrschaft Christi Rechte ausüben kann. Diese Befugnis erwirbt man nach Aegidius aber nur durch Unterwerfung unter das Gesetz Christi, was durch die Taufe geschieht: *per quam regeneracionem collocatur sub domino Christo suo* [65]).

Mit dieser Grundthese ist unzertrennlich verbunden die These von der monarchischen Herrschaft des Papstes, denn, und hier stimmt er wiederum vollauf mit der frühchristlichen und hochmittelalterlichen Lehre überein, mit der Gründung der Kirche hat Christus auch zugleich die monarchische Herrschaft des Papstes als Nachfolgers Petri gestiftet. Für ihn ergibt sich daraus die wesentlich ekklesiologische Bezogenheit aller öffentlichen Gewalt [66]). Umgekehrt muß betont werden, daß nirgends in diesem Traktat die Idee oder der Begriff des Staates, des Bürgers, der Politik und anderer Elemente der neuen Thematik aufscheint. Ganz offenbar vermeidet der Traktat diese neuen Begriffsbildungen [67]). Daß das nicht auf Versehen oder Unwissenheit beruht, ist klar, weil derselbe Aegidius wenige Jahre vorher einen stark mit aristotelisch-thomistischen Elementen und Ideen durchtränkten Fürstenspiegel geschrieben hatte [68]). Man könnte sehr wohl in dem Traktat eine Kampfschrift erblicken gegen die Politik als selbständigen Normenkreis und eigenständige Wissenschaft, als eine unabhängig von den überkommenen Lehrsätzen existierende Erkenntnisquelle und Verhaltensgrundlage.

Ob nun Aegidius zur Abfassung des Traktats oder der *Unam sanctam* aufgefordert wurde, läßt sich nicht mehr mit Sicherheit feststellen, ist aber auch weniger wesentlich als Aufbau und Inhalt und Struktur der Bulle selbst. Sie ist nichts anderes als eine sehr gewandte Zusammenfassung und Raffung der

---

[64]) Seine Betonung, daß *omnes reges* usw. seine von ihm niedergelegten Grundsätze zu beachten hätten, *si velint esse fideles* (II. 5, S. 59), ist daher wesentlich für das Verständnis seiner Lehre. Von hier aus läßt sich auch seine ekklesiologisch gefaßte Herrschergewalt besser verstehen: *Terrena potestas est per ecclesiasticam et ab ecclesiastica et in opus ecclesiastice constituta* (ibid.). Vgl. auch II. 5, S. 55: *In hoc tractatu hominibus fidelibus loquimur, quia nihil ad nos de hiis, qui foris sunt.*

[65]) II. 7, S. 74: *Si enim miles nollet esse sub rege, dignum esset, ut subditi eius non deberent esse sub milite . . . Dignum est, quod privetur omni dominio suo iste, qui est carnaliter a patre generatus: per quam . . .* (wie Text). Vgl. noch den erwähnten Guilielmus de Cremona (oben Anm. 62), der diesen Gedanken noch schärfer formuliert: *Qui enim non vult esse sub Christi dominio, nullius rei dominus esse possit iuste . . . magis debes recognoscere ab ecclesia et per ecclesiam, quia es filius ecclesiae quam a patre tuo carnali et per ipsum, quia tu es filius eius.*

[66]) Vgl. oben bei und in Anm. 64.

[67]) Auch dies wurde weder von Rivière (wie Anm. 11) 214ff. noch von Congar (wie Anm. 56) 273 bzw. Kölmel (wie Anm. 56) 401ff. erkannt. Der Erstgenannte sprach sogar von einem „problème de l'église et de l'état" (215).

[68]) Siehe seinen Fürstenspiegel „De regimine principium", geschrieben für den jungen Philipp IV. Ich benutze die Ausgabe: Venedig 1502. Dieses Werk wurde in viele Sprachen übersetzt. Vgl. Wilhelm Berges, Die Fürstenspiegel des hohen Mittelalters (= Schriften des Reichsinstituts für ältere deutsche Geschichtskunde 2, Stuttgart 1938) 320—322. Zur Charakterisierung auch Kölmel (wie Anm. 56) 292—294.

in diesem Traktat niedergelegten Thesen. Sie gibt sich aus als eine fugenlose und geschickt konstruierte Zusammenstellung von Grundsätzen, die das Papsttum als Pfeiler und Garanten einer christlich verstandenen Lebensordnung auswiesen. Und wie Aegidius setzte das Papsttum an der Stelle ein, an der die neue Thematik eingesetzt hatte, d. h. am Wiedergeburtsgedanken, an der *regeneratio (hominis)*. Damit wurde die Taufe als Rechtsakt und die dadurch bewirkte Kirchgliedschaft zum Mittelpunkt der kurialen Opposition gegen die neuen Thesen[69]). Die Bulle ist kein Dekret im herkömmlichen Sinne, sondern eine förmliche Proklamation von Grundsätzen in einem Zeitalter, das durch Verwirrung, Widersprüchlichkeiten, Zerfahrenheit und geistige Unruhe gekennzeichnet war. Sie skizzierte, gestützt auf als unumstößlich vom Papsttum angesehene Grundsätze, eindeutige Richtlinien, sollte die überlieferte Gesellschafts- und Rechtsauffassung weiter bestehen können. Sie hat gar nichts zu tun mit der Formulierung eines päpstlichen Weltherrschaftsanspruchs oder den vielen Attributen, die ihr von den Anhängern beider Konfessionen im Laufe der Jahrhunderte beigelegt wurden, sondern war gedacht als verpflichtende, lehrmäßige Erklärung von Fundamentalthesen, die eine Gemeinschaft, die sich christlich nennen wollte, beobachten sollte. Man kann die Bulle nur vom zeitgenössischen Hintergrund aus verstehen. Wie bei vielen mittelalterlichen Quellen sieht man auch hier, daß das Unausgesprochene das wirklich Wesentliche war. Denn genau gesehen, ist jede der sorgsam ausgewählten Thesen eine kräftige Erwiderung auf die neue Thematik, die nach der Papstauffassung unvereinbar war mit einer christlichen Lebensordnung. Aus diesem Gesichtswinkel läßt sich auch die innere Struktur der Bulle gut verstehen. Sie hat festen, sachlichen, geschlossenen Zusammenhalt und strengsten logischen Aufbau. Was sie auszeichnet, ist eine straffe Folgerichtigkeit.

Sie hebt an mit einem machtvollen Bekenntnis zum ekklesiologischen Substrat, der einen universalen, all-umfassenden Kirchenidee, die alle Gläubigen miteinschließt[70]). Dieser Grundton durchzieht die ganze Bulle. Dementsprechend konnte es keine irdische Gemeinschaft geben, die neben der all-umfassenden Gemeinschaft rechtlichen Anspruch auf Eigenständigkeit erheben konnte. Darum ist in der Bulle das Wesen der universalen Gemeinschaft mit dem Wesen der Herrschaft unzertrennlich verwoben. Und da die Gesellschaft eine einzige ekklesiologische Einheit ist, kann Herrschaft über sie nur im Sinne der monarchischen Papstgewalt ausgeübt werden. Dieses Wesen der

---

[69]) Die Bulle steht, was den Anspruch auf monarchische Herrschaft des Papstes betrifft, den grundsätzlichen Äußerungen etwa Gregors IX. sehr nahe (M. G. H. Epistolae saec. XIII e regestis pontificum Romanorum selectae, I [Berolini 1883] 604 nr. 703). Der Rechtsgrund bei Gregor IX. ist allerdings das Constitutum Constantini, während Bonifaz VIII. mit ekklesiologischen Begriffen operiert.

[70]) Die offenbare Grundlage war Cyprians Ep. 55, c. 24 (ed. Corpus scriptorum ecclesiasticorum Latinorum III [Vindobonae — Lipsiae 1868—1871] 642): *Cum sit a Christo una ecclesia per totum mundum in multa membra divisa . . .* — Für den naheliegenden Begriff der *christianitas* siehe Cyprian in: De singularitate clericorum, ed. ibid., Appendix, 181 Z. 1.

Gesellschaft erklärt aber auch, warum die Bulle den konstituierenden Anteil des Papsttums an der Kreierung des weltlichen Organs[71]) in einer christlichen Gemeinschaft unterstreicht[72]). Das war eine unzweideutige Bestreitung der von den neuen Lehren behaupteten Autonomie jener öffentlichen Körperschaften oder Gemeinschaften, die sich vermöge ihrer Eigenständigkeit ihre Herrscher selbst erwählen und damit ihnen Herrschermacht verleihen konnten. Vor allem aber betont die Bulle — was doch wirklich damals überflüssig erscheinen mochte — die Idee und den Begriff der *regeneratio*, genau jene *regeneratio*, die das Rückgrat der aegidianischen Schrift war[73]). Der Zweck war, den natürlichen Menschen auf die frühere untergeordnete Rolle zurückzudrängen. Es versteht sich, warum die der päpstlichen Herrschaftsidee als ganz besonders gefährlich erscheinenden neuen Ideen von der Eigenständigkeit des Staates, des Bürgers und der Politik in diesem rein ekklesiologischen

---

[71]) Der Begriff des *instituere*, den die Bulle verwendet (s. auch Anm. 72) wird meist mißverständlich ausgelegt. Bei näherer geschichtlicher Analyse erkennt man freilich, daß er zusammenfassend ausdrückt, was schon längst aus der Doxologie der Krönungsordines bekannt war. Man vgl. etwa die bei Kaiser- und mehr noch bei Königskrönungen gebrauchten liturgischen Texte, wie etwa die Krönungsformel oder die Schwertformel etc., die keinen Zweifel zulassen an dem konstituierenden Anteil des Coronators, sei dieser nun Papst oder Metropolit. Dazu kommt noch, daß Bonifaz selbst bei der Krönung König Karls II. von Anjou durch Papst Nikolaus IV. am Pfingstsonntag (= 29. Mai) 1289 als Kardinal zugegen war, wo er genau den Sinn dieser Gebete und Formeln wahrnehmen konnte. Über diese Krönung vgl. Raynaldus (wie Anm. 2) 42 und jetzt Bernhard Schimmelpfennig, Die Zeremonienbücher der römischen Kirche im Mittelalter (= Bibliothek des Deutschen Historischen Instituts in Rom 40, Tübingen 1973) Ordo XIVb und XV, S. 174ff. Zur ganzen Frage noch Walter Ullmann, Der Souveränitätsgedanke in den mittelalterlichen Krönungsordines. In: Festschrift für Percy Ernst Schramm (Wiesbaden 1964) 71—89; ders., A History of political ideas in the Middle Ages (London ²1970) 85ff.; 93ff. Mit dieser konstituierenden Bedeutung der Königskrönung hing auch zusammen die ihr vorausgegangene „Wahl", die rechtlich eine bloße Designation war; der rechtlich bedeutsame Wahlakt wurde innerhalb des Krönungsritus vollzogen, wie das Gebet *Omnipotens, sempiterne Deus, creator omnium* ... zum Ausdruck bringt: ... *hunc famulum, quem supplici devotione in regem eligimus* ... Darüber vor allem Heinrich Mitteis, Die deutsche Königswahl (Brünn ²1944); vgl. auch meine Einleitung zur Ausgabe des „Liber regie capelle" (Cambridge, Henry Bradshaw Society 91, 1961) 40f. Bemerkt sei, daß das von Benedikt XIV. herausgegebene Pontificale Romanum (ich benutze die Ausgabe: Venedig 1836), das bis in die jüngste Zeit gültig war, genau dieselbe Formulierung bei der Königskrönung hatte (142).

[72]) Die Vorlage der Bulle, die Lehre des Hugo von St. Viktor (darüber Walter Ullmann, The Growth of Papal Government in the Middle Ages [London ³⁻⁴1970] 439f.) hatte: *instituere ut sit.* An diese Stelle des *ut sit* trat in der Bulle *veritate testante.* Auch dies entging Congar (wie Anm. 56) 276f. Diente vielleicht Gregors VII. Schreiben an Wilhelm den Eroberer als Muster, wo *divina testatur scriptura* als Quelle einer Aussage gemacht wurde, die in Wirklichkeit von Gelasius I. stammte? Vgl. Gregors VII. Reg. VII. 25, S. 506; darüber Ullmann, Growth, 282 mit Anm. 2.

[73]) Umso erstaunlicher ist es, wenn Marie-Dominique Chenu, Dogme et théologie dans la Bulle Unam Sanctam. Recherches de science religieuse 40 (1952) 307ff. mit keiner Silbe den die Bulle tragenden Pfeiler der baptismalen Wiedergeburt erwähnt.

Rahmen keinen Platz finden konnten. Da sie Fremdkörper waren, fehlt jede Bezugnahme auf sie[74]). Man tat, als ob die neuen Begriffsinhalte nicht existierten. Gestützt auf die baptismale Wiedergeburt in Verbindung mit Matth. 16, 18f. und Röm. 13, 1f. erreicht die Bulle den Schluß- und Höhepunkt, daß um des Seelenheils willen jedermann dem Papst untertan sein müsse[75]).

Innerhalb der ekklesiologischen Einheit, all-umfassend, wie sie einmal ist, kam ausschließlich die unipolare, ganzheitliche These zum Zug[76]), und für Bipolarität (oder gar Multipolarität) blieb kein Raum. Den Begriffen Staat, Bürger, Politik wurden die ekklesiologisch ausgerichteten Begriffe der ganzheitlichen Universalität, der baptismalen Wiedergeburt und der päpstlichen Monarchie gegenübergestellt. Es erschien der Kurie einfach unvorstellbar, daß die Unipolarität durch eine Bipolarität ersetzt werden könnte, denn das hieße *duo capita*, also *quasi monstrum* postulieren und *duo principia* anerkennen, was, wie die Bulle ebenfalls hervorhebt, dem Manichäismus ähneln würde und deshalb *falsum et haereticum* ist[77]).

Restauration und Sicherstellung des gefährdeten Gedankengutes war das Anliegen der Bulle. An dem vom Papsttum seit dem 5. Jahrhundert festgehaltenen Grundsatz der Arbeitsteilung rührte die Bulle nirgends und in der Tat sprach sich der nämliche Bonifaz völlig unzweideutig darüber aus. Weder er noch seine Vorgänger haben den paulinischen Grundsatz mißachtet oder in

---

74) Chenu in: Lexikon für Theologie und Kirche 10 (Freiburg ²1965) 462 kommt der hier vorgetragenen Ansicht nahe: „Weder auf politischer (?) noch allgemein moralischer Ebene respektiert sie (= die Bulle) die Eigenständigkeit der Natur, der Vernunft und der irdischen Wirklichkeiten".

75) In seinem Opusculum contra errores Graecorum ad Urbanum IV (ed. Venetiis 1593) fol. 9b erklärte der Aquinate: *Ostenditur, quod subesse Romano pontifici sit de necessitate salutis.* Zur Sache vgl. Ullmann, Growth (wie Anm. 72), 444 Anm. 1. Auch hier hatte Cyprian den Weg gewiesen: *salus extra ecclesiam non est* (Ep. 73, c. 21 [wie in Anm. 70] III, 795, auch hier unter Bezugnahme auf Ioh. 3, 5). Ferner Gregor VII. in seinem D. P. 26 und die von Caspar 207 angegebenen Bezugstellen. Auch Innocenz III. ließ sich in ganz demselben Sinne im 4. Laterankonzil aus: vgl. Extra I. 1. 1 und vollständig in Conciliorum oecumenicorum decreta, ed. Iosephus Alberigo u. a. (Bologna ³1973) 230: *Una vero est fidelium universalis ecclesia, extra quam nullus omnino salvatur.*

76) Diese ganzheitliche Betonung scharf bei Johannes Monachus in seiner Glosse: *Illud est perfectum quod totum est.* Auch Guido Vernani in seinem (wie Anm. 5) Kommentar 146: *Totum dicitur quod omnia habet. Universale autem totum quoddam est, catholicum autem universale seu generale dicitur.* Konrad von Megenberg in seinem Traktat De translatione Romani imperii, cap. 12 (ed. Richard Scholz, Unbekannte kirchenpolitische Streitschriften [wie Anm. 62] II, 292) drückte den Ganzheitsgrundsatz besonders gut aus: *Liquidum est religionem christianam quoddam totum esse et iurisdictionem temporalem et spiritualem quasdam partes ipsius regitivas.*

77) Offenbar diente als Vorbild Gratian XXIV. 3. 39 (Aufzählung der ketzerischen Sekten). Denselben Gedanken trug Bonifaz schon vor Erlaß der Bulle in einem Schreiben an den französischen Episkopat und die Doktoren beider Rechte im Juni 1302 vor: *Nonne duo principia nituntur ponere, qui dicunt temporalia spiritualibus non subesse?* (Potthast nr. 25184; Dupuy [wie Anm. 4] 66).

Frage gestellt: *Nulla potestas nisi a Deo*[78]). Darüber hinaus wurde die ebenso alte grundsätzliche Unterscheidung von Amt (*officium — status*) und der Person des Amtsträgers so zugespitzt, daß das Amt des Papstes in dem Begriff des *spiritualis homo* aufging und die darauf bezügliche paulinische Aussage unmittelbar auf den Papst Anwendung fand. Nur so läßt sich eine befriedigende Erklärung für die Anwendung dieses paulinischen Ausspruchs auf den Papst allein in der Bulle geben: *Spiritualis homo iudicat omnia, ipse autem a nemine iudicatur* (I Kor. 2, 14 f.)[79]). Hier wird also der Wiedergeburtsgedanke in den Dienst der Herrschaftsidee selbst gestellt, denn dieser paulinische Ausspruch entnimmt seinen Sinn der Gegenüberstellung des *homo animalis* mit dem *homo spiritualis*.

Nicht darin liegt der tiefere Sinn der Bulle, daß sie ein Ausdrucksmittel unersättlicher Machtgelüste und Herrschsucht des Papsttums und in Sonderheit Bonifaz' VIII. war, sondern in der Negation der neuen, alarmierend alle Gebiete des öffentlichen Lebens ergreifenden und beeinflussenden Denkschemata. Indem die Kurie einen Leitfaden von durchaus bekannten und vertrauten christlichen Grundsätzen — christlich aus der Sicht des späten 13. Jahrhunderts — sozusagen edierte, negierte sie schärfstens die ihnen entgegenstehenden Axiome. Daraus erklärt sich der äußerst konservative Charakter der Bulle, aber auch das höchst bemerkenswerte und bezeichnende Verschweigen gerade jener Begriffe, die zum unabdingbaren Rüstzeug der neuen Grundsätzlichkeiten gehörten. Die Schwierigkeit, vor die sich die Kurie gestellt sah, konnte nicht mehr mit jenen leicht zugänglichen und griffbereiten Mitteln, wie etwa dem Constitutum Constantini oder der sog. Translatio imperii[80]),

---

[78]) Vgl. den gereizten Ton Bonifaz' selbst: *Quadraginta anni sunt quod nos sumus experti in iure et scimus quod duae potestates ordinatae a Deo: quis ergo debet credere quod tanta fatuitas, tanta insipientia fuerit in capite nostro? Dicimus quod in nullo volumus usurpare iurisdictionem regis . . . non potest negare rex seu quicumque alter fidelis, quin sit subiectus ratione peccati* (Dupuy 77). Die Betonung der weltlichen Jurisdiktionsgewalt *quantum ad usum* und *actus* durch Kardinal Aquasparta, auf dessen Rede im selben Konsistorium sich Bonifaz zustimmend beruft, ist gerade in diesem Zusammenhang wichtig (ibid., 76). Zum Arbeitsteilungsgrundsatz, der übrigens eine mächtige paulinische Grundlage hatte, vgl. Ullmann, Growth (wie Anm. 72) 25, 41 und 442ff.; ders., Principles (wie Anm. 16) 66f., 135; ders., A Short History of the Papacy in the Middle Ages (London 1972) 32f., 44 und 183. Aegidius vertrat denselben Grundsatz: II. 5, S. 54ff.

[79]) Siehe dazu auch die Glosse des Johannes Monachus: *Personaliter ergo possunt esse et forte sunt multi sanctiores papa et spirituales, sed secundum statum nullus est adeo spiritualis nec ita sanctus* (gl. ad v. Ergo si); siehe auch Guido Vernani (wie Anm. 5) 156: *Possunt ergo summi pontifices non esse spirituales personaliter et tamen spirituales secundum statum, et ex hoc debet quilibet eum nominare sanctissimum.* Über die auf Leo I. zurückgehende begriffliche Unterscheidung von Amt und Person des Amtsträgers vgl. Ullmann, Leo I (wie Anm. 5) 25ff. und ders., Pontifex romanus indubitanter efficitur sanctus: D. P. 23 in retrospect and prospect. Studi Gregoriani 6 (1959) 229—264.

[80]) Vgl. oben Anm. 69 für Gregor IX.; Innocenz III. in seinem Regestum super negotio Romani imperii (ed. Friedrich Kempf, Miscellanea Historiae Pontificiae 12 [Roma

gemeistert werden, sondern verlangte eine amtliche Erklärung, die auf vorwiegend christlichen und ekklesiologischen Prämissen aufgebaut war. Deshalb
steht diese Bulle, vom rein sachlichen Standpunkt aus gesehen, auf unvergleichlich höherer Ebene als früher ergangene Papsterklärungen, die zur
Stützung der monarchischen Papstherrschaft Zuflucht nehmen mußten zu
Hilfskonstruktionen und Scheinargumenten[81]).

Darin erschöpfte sich die Bedeutung der Bulle und ihres Schlußsatzes bei
weitem nicht[82]). Die päpstliche Forderung nach Freiheit der kirchlichen Amtsträger von Laienbeherrschung und ihrer Kontrolle durch das Papsttum sollte
stets die Einheit und Freiheit der Kirche garantieren. Nun ist aber wohl
bekannt, daß sich im Laufe des 13. Jahrhunderts aus Gründen, auf die ich
hier nicht einzugehen brauche, die aber starke Berührungspunkte mit den
neuen Thesen aufwiesen, die Autonomie der weltlichen Herrscher im öffentlich-rechtlichen Bereich kräftig entwickelt hatte, vor allem in England und
Frankreich. Mit immer größerem Nachdruck findet man im Anschluß an bis
ins frühe 13. Jahrhundert zurückreichende Aussagen den Satz *Rex in regno
suo imperator est*[83]).

Im modernen Schrifttum hat der Satz vielfache Beachtung gefunden, doch
scheint mir seine volle Bedeutung noch nicht ganz erkannt zu sein. In diesem
Zusammenhang wird der Rolle des Kaisers in der altrömischen Verfassung
zuwenig gedacht. Das aber ist notwendig, will man die Substanz und das
Potential des Satzes erfassen. Der spätrömische Kaiser und natürlich der
byzantinische hatten eine in der Verfassung verankerte starke Stellung gegen-

---

1947] nr. 18, 29, 62 usw.). Bonifaz war ein viel zu erfahrener Jurist, um sich auf
Argumente zu stützen, die bei diesen und anderen Papsterklärungen herangezogen
wurden, in der Absicht, die monarchische Herrschaftsgewalt des Papstes zu erweisen.
Er sah Herrschaft wesentlich gesellschaftsbezogen an. Das war ein Akzent, der bei
anderen nicht sogleich sichtbar wurde.

[81]) Chenu (wie Anm. 74) stellt die nicht leicht verständliche Behauptung auf, man könne
zu dem Schluß kommen, „hier habe der Papst als ein kleiner, auf den geschichtlich
kontingenten Rechten einer verfallenden Christenheit bestehender Feudalfürst (sic)
nicht begriffen, wie sich in der Entwicklung der Gesellschaft und im Bewußtsein der
Nationalstaaten (wofür der König von Frankreich ein Beispiel war) berechtigt und
heilsam der Wert der politischen Realitäten entsprechend der Schöpfungsordnung
zur Geltung brachte". Ähnlich auch in dem Anm. 73 zitierten Artikel: „Baron romain
imbu des principes féodaux" (312).

[82]) Daß der Schlußsatz eine irreformable dogmatische Aussage enthält, unterstreicht
Chenu a. a. O.; so bereits Denifle (wie Anm. 1) 44. Vgl. auch den Neuerlaß der
Bulle, insbesondere den Schlußsatz im 5. Laterankonzil, in: Conciliorum oecumeni-
corum decreta (wie Anm. 75) 643 (Bulle *Pastor Aeternus*).

[83]) Reiche Literaturangaben jetzt bei Paradisi (wie Anm. 11) 57 ff. und 149 ff. Hinzu-
zufügen wäre: André Bossuat, La formule „Le roi est empereur en son royaume".
Revue historique de droit français et étranger 39 (1961) 371—381; Pierre Chaplais,
La souveraineté du roi de France et le pouvoir législatif en Guyenne au début du
XIVe siècle. Moyen Age 69 (1963) 449—469; Robert Feenstra, Jean de Blanot et
la formule „Rex Franciae in regno suo princeps est". In: Études dédiées à Gabriel
Le Bras 2 (Paris 1965) 885—895; Frederic L. Cheyette, The Sovereign and the
Pirates, 1332. Speculum 45 (1970) 40—68.

über dem kirchlichen Organismus, denn kirchliche Angelegenheiten, etwa Organisation, Verwaltung, Disziplin, einschließlich der Kirchenversammlungen, die Ökumenizität beanspruchten, gehörten in den Bereich des *ius publicum*. Nach Ulpians Definition bestand es aus dem *ius in sacris, sacerdotibus et magistratibus*[84]). Da aber der Kaiser die Quelle allen öffentlichen Rechts war, besaß er auch Jurisdiktionsgewalt über kirchliche Dinge. Die altrömische Funktion des Kaisers als *pontifex maximus* hatte daher verfassungsmäßige Bedeutung, auch als er zum bloßen *pontifex inclytus* seit dem späten 4. Jahrhundert abgesunken war. Und gerade aus dem öffentlichen Recht floß seine Befugnis, in kirchliche Dinge einzugreifen, so etwa Synoden einzuberufen, kirchlich-disziplinäre sowie organisatorische Maßnahmen zu ergreifen und sich manchmal auch in dogmatischen Fragen zu versuchen. Diese genuin römische Stellung des Kaisers hat, nachdem das römische Recht durch die Wissenschaft voll erschlossen worden war, sehr zum Werden und Erstarken des Säkularisierungsgedankens seit der Stauferzeit beigetragen[85]).

Wenn sich nun der Landesherr, wie etwa der englische oder französische König, die Funktion des Kaisers aneignete, so wollte er ganz gewiß damit keine universal-herrscherlichen Absichten ausdrücken. Im Gegenteil, jeder Landesherr wurde in Ausübung dieser kaiserlichen Funktion zum Werkzeug der Dekomposition, das zur schließlichen Zersplitterung, Zerbröckelung und Durchlöcherung der als universal und einheitlich verstandenen ekklesiologisch gefaßten Menschheit zu führen geeignet war. Darin liegt der tiefere Sinn der territorialen Souveränität gegründet, deren handgreifliche Begleiterscheinung der rasch emporwachsende Nationalismus war[86]). Damit steht in Zusammenhang, daß gerade im späten 13. Jahrhundert konkrete Anzeichen einer national-

---

[84]) Ulpian in Dig. 1. 1. 1 (2).

[85]) Über die praktische Anwendung des Grundsatzes am Anfang der Stauferzeit, vgl. Ullmann, Von Canossa nach Pavia (wie Anm. 42), bes. 289—296.

[86]) Nur auf das eine oder andere Beispiel sei kurz verwiesen. Im 2. Konzil von Lyon wurde nach Nationen abgestimmt, nachdem an den Universitäten diese als stimmberechtigte Gruppen sich eingebürgert hatten. Damals erschienen auch Schriften, die das Prinzip der Nationalität zum aufbauenden Element einer neuen Weltordnung machen wollten, wie beispielsweise der Kanonikus Alexander von Roes (sein Memoriale, ed. Heinrich Grundmann—Hermann Heimpel [Weimar 1949]; andere seiner Schriften in M. G. H. Staatsschriften des späteren Mittelalters I/1 [Stuttgart 1958]), der die Deutschen, Franzosen und Italiener zu tragenden Pfeilern seiner Gesellschaftsordnung machte (darüber Ullmann, History of Political Ideas in the Middle Ages [wie Anm. 71] 187ff.). Oder unmittelbar nach der Jahrhundertwende schlug der gerissene Laie im Königslager, Pierre Dubois, in seiner Schrift De recuperatione terrae sanctae (ed. C.-V. Langlois [Paris 1891]) einen scharfen, geradezu chauvinistischen Ton an und befürwortete die territoriale Souveränität des Königs auf Kosten des Universalismus. Hier seien auch die anonymen Schriften der Pariser Gelehrten angeführt, die einem nationalen Königtume huldigten, wie etwa die Disputatio inter clericum et militem (darüber jetzt unergiebig: Th. J. Renna, Kingship in the Disputatio. Speculum 48 [1973] 675—693) oder die mit Rex pacificus beginnende Schrift Quaestio de potestate papae (ed. Dupuy [wie Anm. 4] 663ff.). Noch immer lehrreich ist Rivière (wie Anm. 11) 274ff.

kirchlichen Bewegung in Erscheinung traten[87]). Die Verbindungslinien zwischen König und Hierarchie waren unzweideutige Symptome des (späteren) Gallikanismus, und diese gegenseitige Annäherung konnte nicht umhin, einerseits die Bande zum Papsttum zu schwächen und andererseits die Bindung der Hierarchie an den König zu stärken und dessen Macht zu vergrößern. Von hier führt eine gerade Linie von der *appellatio tamquam ab abusu*[88]) über die Reichsversammlung von Vincennes[89]) zur verfassungsmäßigen Verankerung des Gallikanismus, um nur die französischen Meilensteine der Entwicklung anzuführen[90]).

Historisch betrachtet, kommt dem so häufig verrufenen Schlußsatz der Bulle eine viel größere Bedeutung zu als die übliche billige Interpretation wahrhaben möchte. Der Sinn ist klar: die letzte Instanz innerhalb des ekklesiologisch verstandenen Menschheitsverbandes ist der Papst, der demgemäß seine im Interesse des Seelenheils ausgeübte Jurisdiktionsgewalt auf universaler Ebene beansprucht[91]). Die Spitze richtete sich gegen die landesherrlichen Autonomiebestrebungen, gegen die kräftig anhebende Territorialsouveränität und nationalkirchliche Aspirationen. Auch in diesem Sinne ist die Bulle konservativ. Sie versucht, die Idee der Universalität zu retten, indem sie auf dem Hintergrund der Ekklesiologie den universalen Jurisdiktionsprimat zum krönenden Abschluß der Erklärung erhebt[92]). Hervorgehoben sei, daß der im Schlußsatz aus I Petr. 2, 13 entlehnte Begriff der *omnis humana creatura* nicht „Geschöpf" bedeutet, sondern „Schöpfung", „Ordnung" und sich damit unschwer in den ekklesiologisch-universalen Rahmen einfügt.

---

[87]) Darauf spielte Johannes Monachus in seiner Glosse deutlich an: *Si ergo fides quam tenet ecclesia esset particularis, continens unam gentem vel unum populum, sicut sunt multi populi sive multae gentes sic forte essent multae ecclesiae et multa capita. Sed cum sit catholica . . .*

[88]) Darüber vgl. Robert Généstal, Les origines de l'appel comme d'abus (Paris 1950).

[89]) Die Verhandlungen in Melchior Goldast, Monarchia (ed. Frankfurt 1661) II, 1361ff.

[90]) Die Gesetzgebung — insbesondere unter den englischen Königen Eduard I. und Eduard III. — verfolgte dieselbe Richtung.

[91]) Die flandrischen Gesandten, die Ende 1298 in Rom weilten, richteten an den Papst eine Gedenkschrift, die mit guter juristischer Begründung die Notwendigkeit eines päpstlichen Universalitätsanspruchs in einer christlichen Gemeinschaft zu erweisen sucht. Dadurch würde ein über Fürsten und Könige stehendes rechtsprechendes Organ gewährleistet werden, das der immanenten Idee des Rechts dient. Diese Eingabe verdient mehr Beachtung als sie bisher erfahren hat (ed. v. Joseph Kervin de Lettenhove, Études sur l'histoire du XIIIe siècle. Mémoires de l'Académie Royale des Sciences, des Lettres et des Beaux-Arts de Belgique 28 [1854] 74—78). Zum Grundgedanken vgl. noch die Beobachtungen bei Walter Ullmann, The medieval papal court as an international tribunal. Virginia Journal of International Law (= Essays in honour of Hardy Cross Dillard) 11 (1971) 356—381.

[92]) Da die Bulle gegen niemand gerichtet war, konnte Klemens V. in dem Dekret *Meruit* die gewünschte Erklärung abgeben, ohne die Bedeutung der Bulle im geringsten zu schmälern. Daß sich die Kurie mit dieser Erklärung nichts vergeben hatte, betont mit Recht Kölmel (wie Anm. 56) 407.

Von außerordentlicher Bedeutung ist, daß die Bulle geradezu den Auftakt für die reiche Traktatenliteratur zu geben scheint, die die Idee der Universalität im ekklesiologischen wie auch im säkularisierten Sinne scharf betont. Diese neue Literaturrichtung zeigt, wie hellhörig und weitsichtig eine Anzahl von Gelehrten des frühen 14. Jahrhunderts war. Je stärker die landesherrliche Souveränität in den Vordergrund trat, mit umso größerem Eifer wurde der Universalitätsgedanke literarisch befürwortet. Sollte der Zerbröckelung und Zerstückelung Einhalt geboten werden, konnte man nur mit der Idee der Ganzheit auf vornehmlich traditioneller Grundlage operieren. Dem autonomen Einzelstaatswesen wurde wenigstens auf literarischer Ebene die universale all-umfassende Einheit gegenübergestellt. Diese universalistische Orientierung ist so auffallend, daß man sich bloß wundern kann, warum sie bisher nicht zum Gegenstand gesonderter Analysen gemacht wurde [93]). Klänge es nicht bizarr, könnte man wohl die ersten Dezennien des 14. Jahrhunderts als das Zeitalter des wenigstens literarisch vertretenen Universalismus bezeichnen [94]). *Unam sanctam* wie auch die ihr folgende Literatur wollten dem Zersetzungsprozeß auf kirchlichem, ideellem und kulturellem Gebiet durch einen äußersten Konservativismus vorbeugen. Ob das nun das richtige Mittel war, kann man wohl bezweifeln. Was man nicht bezweifeln kann und darf, ist der tiefe sittliche Ernst, der diese Literatur kennzeichnet.

Aber nicht bloß im literarischen Rahmen läßt sich der Einfluß der Bulle wahrnehmen. Wenigstens anmerkungsweise sollte hier der gesetzgeberischen Verfügung Kaiser Heinrichs VII. aus dem Jahre 1312, also genau zehn Jahre nach der *Unam sanctam*, gedacht werden. In dem Reichsgesetz *Ad reprimendum* erklärt er mit der einem römischen Kaiser geziemenden volltönenden Sonorität die Oberhoheit des römischen Monarchen über jede Seele. Göttliches und menschliches Recht schreiben vor, behauptet er in dem Gesetz, *quod omnis anima Romanorum principi subiecta sit* [95]). Daß er damit die päpstliche Äußerung Bonifaz' zum Muster nahm, kann wohl nicht ernstlich bezweifelt werden, wenn auch, im Gegensatz zu ihrem Vorbild, diese kaiserliche Maßnahme ohne jede Einschränkung die Jurisdiktionsgewalt des Kaisers postuliert.

---

[93]) Auch Richard Scholz in seiner geistvollen Studie: Weltstaat und Staatenwelt in der Anschauung des Mittelalters. Zeitschrift für deutsche Geisteswissenschaft 4 (1941) 81 ff. ist die Bedeutung entgangen. In seiner fleißigen Arbeit: Papal plenitudo potestatis and the source of temporal authority in late medieval papal hierocratic thought. Speculum 48 (1973) 654—674 bemerkt W. D. McCready zwar den universalistischen Zug in den besprochenen Schriften nicht, macht dafür aber richtig auf die Bedeutung des baptismalen Wiedergeburtsgedankens aufmerksam (663).

[94]) Einem so ausgezeichneten Kenner des päpstlichen Symbolismus und Zeremonienwesens wie Schimmelpfennig (wie Anm. 71) 4 fiel auf, daß der Begriff der (universal verstandenen) *christianitas* in den Zeremonienbüchern des 14. Jahrhunderts zu Avignon einen viel breiteren Raum einnahm als bisher, obwohl diese Bücher vorwiegend für den internen Gebrauch bestimmt waren.

[95]) M. G. H. Legum sectio IV: Constitutiones et acta publica imperatorum et regum 4/2 (Hannoverae 1909—1911) nr. 929 und 930 in französischer Übersetzung; auch als Collatio IX dem Corpus Iuris Civilis einverleibt.

Mißachtung der kaiserlichen Obrigkeit begründe das Verbrechen des Hoch-verrates[96]).

Auf bloß einige markante Beispiele aus der Literatur sei mir gestattet zu verweisen. Ihnen allen ist gemeinsam, daß für sie, genau wie für die Bulle, die Begriffe Staat, Bürger, Politik nicht existierten. Sie setzen sich auch nicht mit diesen neuen Ideen auseinander. In unmittelbar zeitlicher Nähe steht der Traktat des Jakob von Viterbo ,,De regimine christiano". Wie der Herausgeber im Titel seiner Ausgabe richtig hervorhob, war dies der älteste Traktat, dessen Thema der Kirchenbegriff selbst war[97]). Das Hauptanliegen des Verfassers entsprach vollends jenem der *Unam sanctam*. Er war sich der Aushöhlung und Unterwanderung der überkommenen christlichen Gesellschafts- und Herr-schaftslehre durch die neuen Denkschemata vollkommen im klaren. Ein wis-senschaftlich ansprechendes Gegenstück sollte diesen neuen Lehren entgegen-gestellt werden. Seine Schrift war die deutliche Absage an die immer stärker hervortretende atomisierende und zerklüftende These von der Bipolarität und gipfelte in dem Postulat der souveränen all-umfassenden Einheit der Kirche, die er wesensmäßig als *regnum* verstand. Die innerste Substanz dieses *regnum* war aber nicht, wie dies bei anderen Königreichen der Fall war, eine natürlich bedingte Entwicklung und ein historisch erklärbares Wachstum, wenn auch Jakob formale Anleihen bei Aristoteles machte, um den stufenweisen gedank-lichen Aufbau von der Familie über die Gemeinde zur Völkerschaft und schließlich zur universal-kirchlichen Gesellschaft darzutun. Vielmehr handelte es sich hier, wie Jakob unterstreicht, um eine *regeneratio* dieser natürlichen Einheiten und Gruppen durch die Gnade[98]), die bei ihm im Verhältnis zur Natur eine über den Aquinaten hinausgehende Funktion ausübt[99]). Als allein souveränes Königreich und als juristischer, organischer und sichtbarer Verband beinhaltet die Kirche alle (christlichen) Verbände und Nationen. Die Be-zeichnung *regnum* sollte die innere Wesenheit der Kirche in der jedermann leicht zugänglichen und verständlichen Terminologie ausdrücken. Dieser Ge-meinschaft der *fideles* — von den natürlichen Menschen nimmt er keine Kennt-nis — entspricht auch die Herrschaftsform, d. h. die Monarchie, verwirklicht

---

[96]) Es war gewiß bittere Ironie des Geschickes, daß gerade dieses Reichsgesetz und der davon unmittelbar betroffene König Robert von Sizilien zum Anlaß werden sollten, die territoriale Souveränität auf Grund rein formaljuristischer Erwägungen in der Dekretale *Pastoralis cura* zu fixieren. Dazu vgl. auch Walter Ullmann, Zur Ent-wicklung des Souveränitätsbegriffs im Spätmittelalter (demnächst in Festschrift für Nikolaus Grass). Konrad von Megenberg traf mit seiner Behauptung, daß das Reichs-gesetz durch *iura canonica* aufgehoben worden sei, den Nagel auf den Kopf (wie Anm. 76, 382).

[97]) Jakobus von Viterbo, Le plus ancien traité de l'église: De regimine christiano, ed. François X. Arquillière (Paris 1926). Neben der Einleitung durch den Heraus-geber vgl. noch Scholz, Publizistik (wie Anm. 54) 129 ff. und Rivière (wie Anm. 11) 228 ff., der aber diesen Traktat zu sehr am tagespolitischen Geschehen orientiert sieht.

[98]) Obzwar die Kirche ein *regnum* ist, sagt Jakob, *non sit communitas nature, sed gratie, ut ipsum nomen insinuat* (94).

[99]) Ibid., 176: *Gratia non tollit naturam, sed format et perficit.*

im Papst. Auch hier sind, sehr verständlich, Herrschaft und Gesellschaft aufeinander abgestimmt. Die Herausforderung durch die neue Thematik trug sehr erheblich bei zur Erkenntnis und gedanklichen Klärung des juristischen Wesens der Kirche und ihrer organischen Strukturelemente und befruchtete das adäquate Verständnis der ekklesiologisch bedingten Begriffe, die nichts gemein hatten mit jenen des Staates, des Bürgers und der Politik. Der Traktat beweist, welch mächtige Impulse am Werk gewesen sein mußten, um zur analytischen Erkenntnis der Kirche als universales Königreich vorzustoßen[100]).

Trotz fundamentaler Verschiedenheit der Ausgangsstellung ist der Gedankengang Dantes gar nicht so unähnlich jenem, den wir bisher kennengelernt haben. Während bei Jakob der universale christliche Verband zum *regnum* wird, wird bei Dante der gesamte Menschheitsverband zum universalen *imperium*[101]). Dantes Grundton lag fürwahr nicht auf religiös-ekklesiologischer Ebene. Das religiöse Element spielte in seiner *civilitas* gar keine konstituierende Rolle, weil diese sich als eine natürlich-universale Einheit aller *cives*, d. h. ohne Rücksicht auf Glauben, Religion, Kult, Nation, ethnische Zugehörigkeit, Stamm, usw., darstellte. Die Dominante Dantes war daher nicht die Unipolarität, sondern eine sehr energisch vorgetragene Bipolarität der *beatitudo huius vitae* und der *beatitudo vitae aeternae*. Wie bekannt, wurde er gerade wegen seines bipolaren Standpunktes von Guido Vernani so heftig angegriffen[102]). Das Ziel Dantes war genau dasselbe, das Jakob, Bonifaz und Aegidius verfolgt hatten. Und das war die Absage an die landesherrliche Autonomie, die Abkehr von der einzelstaatlichen Autonomie und die Leugnung herrscherlicher Selbständigkeit. Nur auf dieser weitest gefaßten natürlich-politischen Grundlage glaubte Dante der Zersplitterung und Atomisierung Europas Herr werden zu können. Ihm durchaus nicht unähnlich in Absicht, Zweck und Gedankenführung war der gleichzeitige Traktat des Abtes Engelbert von Admont, der ebenfalls, um widerchristlichen Lehren einen Riegel vorzuschieben, die Wiedererrichtung des Römischen Reiches empfahl[103]). Nur wenige Jahre später schrieb Alvarus Pelagius seinen umfänglichen, vielgelesenen und

---

[100]) Daher erfreute sich diese Schrift großer Popularität im 14. Jahrhundert. Vgl. etwa Alexander de S. Elpidio und Alvarus Pelagius, worauf Michael J. Wilks, The Problem of Sovereignty in the later Middle Ages (Cambridge 1963) 553 verwies (so etwa 304 bei und in Anm. 1).

[101]) Beste, neueste Ausgabe von P. G. Ricci, Dante Alighieri: Monarchia (Milano 1965).

[102]) Über die *duo fines* siehe Monarchia III. 15. 7 (S. 273); hier die beiden Glückseligkeiten: Z. 26—28. Vernanis Reprobatio Monarchiae, ed. Thomas Käppeli, Der Dantegegner Guido Vernani O. P. von Rimini. Quellen und Forschungen aus italienischen Archiven und Bibliotheken 28 (1938) 123—146, hier 125f.: alle Menschen *appetunt unum ultimum finem, scilicet beatitudinem*. Der Gedanke klang schon an bei Friedrich II. Vgl. das Zitat bei Walter Ullmann, Reflexions on the opposition to Frederick II to the papacy. Archivio storico Pugliese 13 (1960) 3—27, hier 16.

[103]) De ortu et fine Romani imperii, ed. Melchior Goldast, Politica imperialia sive discursus politici (Francofurti 1614) pars 18 (754ff.).

stark von Jakob von Viterbo abhängigen Traktat „De planctu ecclesiae"[104]). Obwohl er ein scharfer Kritiker des avignonesischen Papsttums war, versuchte auch er, in straffer Gedankenführung die Gesamtheit der *fideles* zur einzigen autonomen Körperschaft zu erheben. Aber da eine Gesellschaftsordnung ohne Herrschaftsordnung undenkbar ist, verfolgte auch er die monarchische Herrschaftsform, die ihm als die allein adäquate erschien[105]). Hier entsprach der unipolaren Gesellschaft die monarchische Herrschaft. Auf ganz ähnlichen Grundlagen baute der Deutsche Konrad von Megenberg seinen „Planctus ecclesiae in Germaniam"[106]) auf — das Papsttum sollte das Organ werden, das den universalen Staat kreieren werde[107]).

Überblickt man diese literarischen Beispiele aus der ersten Hälfte des 14. Jahrhunderts, so ergibt sich ein Bild, in dem die Fronten klar abgezeichnet sind. Aegidius und Bonifaz begannen den Versuch der ideologischen Restauration, indem sie auf gesichertem Hintergrund die ganzheitliche christliche Gesellschafts- und Herrschaftsordnung von neuem und mit besonderem Nachdruck proklamierten. Die Bulle selbst war durchaus kein Manifest päpstlicher Herrschaftsansprüche, sondern enthielt in einprägsamer, anschaulicher und allgemein verständlicher Form eine Skizze von Fundamentalsätzen, die in einer sich christlich heißenden Gesellschaft obwalten sollten — christlich im Sinne des 13. Jahrhunderts verstanden. Zweitens, in Verfolg der unipolaren These, bestritt sie die Eigenständigkeit der politischen Denkkategorien und damit den autonomen Staat. Die Bulle operierte ausschließlich auf ekklesiologischer und juristischer Ebene. In diesem Rahmen gab es keinen Raum für den *civis*, sondern nur für den *homo renatus*, den *fidelis*. Es sei nochmals betont, daß die Bulle nur aus der zeitgenössischen Perspektive verstanden und beurteilt werden kann. Es ist unhistorisch und unwissenschaftlich zugleich, in ihr

---

[104]) Ed. Venedig 1580. Einzelheiten bei Nicolas Iung, Alvaro Pelayo (Paris 1931); vgl. auch Wilks (wie Anm. 100) 65, 318 ff., 387 f., 402 ff., 502 und 510 Anm. 3.

[105]) Dieses Argument wurde im 14. Jahrhundert oftmals wiederholt, vgl. etwa Egidius Spiritalis de Perusio in seiner Schrift Contra infideles et inobedientes (ed. Scholz [wie Anm. 62] II, 105 ff., hier 112 f.): ... *unum debet habere caput, ne in uno corpore sint plura capita quasi monstrum. Unum est corpus scilicet tocius humani generis congregatio, quod quidem corpus sive universitas unum rectorem habere debet tanquam caput.*

[106]) Ed. Richard Scholz, Die Werke des Konrad von Megenberg. 1. Stück: Planctus Ecclesiae in Germaniam. M. G. H. Staatsschriften des späteren Mittelalters 2/1 (Stuttgart 1941); auch Horst Kusch, Leipziger Übersetzungen und Abhandlungen zum Mittelalter (Leipzig 1956).

[107]) Aus dieser Sicht erklärt sich auch, warum dann Schriftsteller, die den Standpunkt der Bulle teilten, das teleologische Element stark in den Vordergrund rückten. Vgl. etwa den eben erwähnten Egidius de Perusio (wie Anm. 105) 126: *Temporalia omnia sunt propter spiritualia sicut propter finem* ... oder Hermann de Schilditz in seinem Traktat Contra haereticos (wie Anm. 62) 130 ff., hier 135 f.: *Bona fortune sunt organa quedam et instrumenta ad finem ultimum ordinata* ... *qui finem suum ponit in temporalibus sive sint bona utilia sive delectabilia sive honor temporalis, numquam attinget felicitatem.* Damit steht in Einklang, daß nach diesem Schriftsteller die *felicitas politica* bloß *huic vite transitorie* entspricht (cap. XIV, S. 152).

die Proklamation der päpstlichen Weltherrschaft zu erblicken. Ob sie Weisheit, Voraussicht und kühle Beurteilung der Gegebenheiten und der neuen Ideen beweist, mag dahingestellt und kann auch mit Recht bezweifelt werden. Es bedarf nur der Erwähnung der Schriften des Dominikaners Johannes Quidort[108]) oder des Marsilius von Padua[109], um die dynamische Durchschlagskraft, den Schwung und das geistige Anregungsvermögen der neuen Denkschemata auch nur annähernd ermessen zu können. Insbesondere der letztgenannte entwickelte eine Gesellschaftslehre, die die Folgerungen aus den naturalistischen Prämissen zog, indem sie den *legislator humanus* und die *universitas civium*, den Staat, zum alleinigen Gegenstand der politischen Wissenschaft erhob, die jeden Zusammenhang mit übernatürlichen Grundsätzen bestritt. Marsilius vollzog den Bruch mit der überlieferten Lehre, weil bei ihm ein auf Glauben ruhendes Recht keinen Anspruch auf Erzwingbarkeit hatte, sondern nur ein solches, das der aszendenten These entsprechend auf dem Volkswillen fußte — das aber war der Inbegriff der Volkssouveränität. Marsilius vollzog aber auch den Bruch mit der thomistischen Lehre — er durchschnitt die wesentliche thomistische Verbindung zwischen Natur und Gott. Seine Lehre war ein System, das im Spätmittelalter am vollkommensten den diesseitigen Ausschließlichkeitscharakter des Staates, des Bürgers und der Politik darstellte[110]).

Die kuriale Einstellung und die ihr folgende literarische Strömung in den ersten Jahren des 14. Jahrhunderts waren gekennzeichnet durch das zähe Festhalten an den überlieferten gesellschaftlichen und herrscherlichen Grundlagen, in denen man eine Manifestation von der untrennbaren Verknüpfung von Glaube, Recht und Geschichte zu erblicken geneigt war. Und gerade in diesem Zusammenhang tut sich eine gewisse historische Tragik kund. Man sah offenbar keine Möglichkeit, dieser Verklammerung zu entkommen. Es schien zu fehlen an der Einsicht in die Potentialität, Anziehungskraft und Wucht der neuen Thematik und an der Erkenntnis der Aufnahmsbereitschaft des Bodens für das neue bipolare Weltbild. Kurie und die ihr zur Seite stehende Wissenschaft ließen Elastizität und das entsprechende Anpassungsvermögen vermissen, also genau jene Merkmale, die so viel zum geschichtlichen Werden

---

108) Siehe die neueste Ausgabe mit deutscher Übersetzung von Fritz Bleienstein, Über königliche und päpstliche Gewalt: De regia potestate et papali (Stuttgart 1969). Zur Sache: Ullmann, Principles (wie Anm. 16) 263 ff.

109) Ed. Richard Scholz, Marsilii de Padua Defensor Pacis. M. G. H. Fontes iuris Germanici antiqui, 2 Bde. (Hannoverae 1932/33). Zur Sache vgl. Georges de Lagarde, Le Defensor Pacis (Paris 1970); Jeannine Quillet, La philosophie politique de Marsile de Padoue (Paris 1970) (mit ausgezeichneten Analysen und Literaturangaben); Ullmann, Principles (wie Anm. 16) 269 ff. und neuerdings Michael Wilks, Corporation and representation in the Defensor Pacis. Studia Gratiana 15 (1972) 253—292.

110) Treffend bemerkt D. W. Maurer, Luthers Lehre von den drei Hierarchien und ihr mittelalterlicher Hintergrund. Sitzungsberichte der Bayerischen Akademie der Wissenschaften, phil.-hist. Klasse 1970, 94: „Der Areopagite entmachtet; eine Entwicklung von beinahe 600 Jahren aufgehoben; Aristoteles triumphiert". Der Hierarch wurde ersetzt durch den *yconomus* sowie den Bürger.

des Papsttums beigetragen hatten. An der Kurie hat man nicht erkannt, wie stark wirklichkeitsbezogen und besonders entwicklungsverbunden die neuen Denkschemata waren. Vor allem hat man die Beziehung des aus dieser Thematik fließenden Rechts zur zeitgenössischen Gesellschaft nicht oder nur unzulänglich erfaßt. In dieser gesellschaftsbezogenen Rechtsidee verbarg sich aber das wahre Energiepotential der neuen Ideologie und Kosmologie[111]).

Das kuriale Unverständnis gegenüber der zeitgenössischen faktischen und geistigen Situation ist umso bemerkenswerter, als die Kurie bisher die Initiative und Führung in gerade den hier berührten Fragen fest in der Hand gehabt hatte. Es möchte scheinen, daß der Zusammenklang von faktischer und geistiger Entwicklung während des 13. Jahrhunderts von der Kurie nicht vernommen wurde. Die Initiative und die Dynamik, die in so offenbarer Weise die europäische Vormachtstellung des Papsttums erwirkt hatten, waren ihm verlorengegangen, und die Kurie sah sich in die Defensive gedrängt. Die Erkenntnis von den Dimensionen, die die neue Richtung erreicht hatten, erwuchs der Kurie gleichzeitig mit der Erkenntnis von der Schwächung der als unantastbar und unanfechtbar gehaltenen Grundlagen von Herrschaft und Gesellschaft. Und es sind diese Erkenntnisse der Kurie, von denen die Bulle ein so eindrucksvolles, wenn nicht sogar erschütterndes Bild entwirft. Sie kamen zu einer Zeit, in der die neue Thematik bereits recht kräftige Wurzeln geschlagen und sich Eingang in viele Bereiche des geistigen, kulturellen und sozialen, und zum Teil auch schon des religiös-kirchlichen Lebens zu verschaffen gewußt hatte.

Die Zukunft gehörte der neuen Orientierung und Thematik, denn die Entwicklung zur nationalstaatlichen Souveränität mit all den voraussehbaren und auch teilweise vorausgesehenen Begleiterscheinungen wurde durch die Bulle nicht aufgehalten. Aber noch viel schwerwiegender und unvergleichlich ernster war, daß der territorialen Zersplitterung alsbald die religiöse Zerklüftung folgen sollte. Auch der Neuerlaß der Bulle durch das 5. Laterankonzil, buchstäblich am Vorabend der Reformation, konnte die kirchlich-religiöse Einheit vor dem Einsturz nicht bewahren. Die dadurch bedingte Gestaltung Europas löste Wirkungen aus, die bis zum heutigen Tage spürbar sind. Bonifaz konnte diese Sturmflut nicht voraussehen, aber wer möchte wagen, zu bestreiten, daß er die Gefahren für den friedlichen Fortbestand der einen römisch-orientierten *universitas fidelium* erkannt hatte, wenn ihm auch der Ablauf der zukünftigen Dekomposition verborgen bleiben mußte? Eine dringende Aufgabe der Forschung ist eine gründliche Analyse jener strukturell reich verästelten, ideologisch komplizierten Bewegungen, die die Umwälzung der Kosmologie ver-

---

[111]) Man vgl. etwa Johannes Quidort (Iohannes Parisiensis) (wie Anm. 108) cap. 25, S. 209 Z. 10f.: *Sicut per consensum hominum iurisdictio datur, ita per consensum contrarium tollitur.* Vor allem gründete Marsilius von Padua die Erzwingbarkeit des Rechts — das ein *praeceptum coactivum* war — ausschließlich auf den Konsens der Bürger, weshalb für ihn das Gesetz treffend zum *oculus ex multis oculis* wurde: Defensor Pacis (wie Anm. 109) I. 11, S. 57 Z. 4f.

ursachten und damit das Wesen der universalen Kirche nachhaltig beein-
flußten. Am Beginn der Zeitspanne, in der diese Veränderungen unaufhaltsam
vorwärtsschritten, stand Bonifaz VIII. und seine Bulle *Unam sanctam*, die
die päpstliche Reaktion auf die Anfangsstadien jener Entwicklung wider-
spiegelt, an deren Ende ein in sich zerrissenes, zerspaltenes und zerrüttetes
Europa erstehen sollte. Die griechische Kirche im Osten war eben gefesselt,
wenn nicht erdrosselt worden, und die einmal in sich fest gefügte Einheit der
lateinischen im Westen löste sich in mehrere feindliche sich verbissen be-
kämpfende Lager auf. Erst in der historischen Zusammenschau und Perspektive läßt sich die Bedeutung der *Unam sanctam* erkennen. Mit ihrem Postulat
nach kirchlicher Einheit richtete sie den Blick gleicherweise auf die Vergangen-
heit und auf die Zukunft.

VII

BONIFACE VIII AND HIS CONTEMPORARY SCHOLARSHIP

TO say that the pontificate of Boniface VIII marked a cesura in papal history is to state a truism. What however would seem to be in need of detailed investigation is the relationship of this pontificate to contemporary scholarship, for, to anticipate one of my points, it assumes its special significance in relation to the new learning that could be witnessed in virtually all academic institutions, but in none more so than at Paris. Within the limits of a short *exposé* it is not, however, possible to shed light on all the virtually hidden lines of communication between the papacy and the universities during the last decades of the thirteenth century. I will therefore concentrate on one particular aspect of the new scholarship, and that is the one that concerns the social ordering, the government of Christian society and, above all, the premisses, axioms and maxims, in short the cosmology upon which the social order rested. A brief outline sketch of the intellectual developments and trends in the thirteenth century and their impact upon the papacy seems to me a necessary presupposition for a historically correct assessment of Boniface's reactions. For far too often this pontificate has been seen in isolation whereas in actual fact it is merely the conclusion of a very long, involved and complex evolution. Although overwhelmingly confined to the lecture hall and academic debate, in reality this development profoundly affected the very substance of the social manifestation of medieval Christianity and therefore also its nerve centre, the papacy, as a governmental institution.

Let me begin by saying that the pontificate of Boniface VIII continued the traditional educational policy of its predecessors. Boniface possibly paid a higher degree of attention to advanced academic studies than some of his immediate predecessors. He was the founder of the university of the city of Rome which like other universities at the time was intended for all faculties though in actual fact the only subjects studied there were law and jurisprudence.[1] He gave strong support to the university of Salamanca, and as a sign of his appreciation of this university's standing he chose it in the same way in which he chose Bologna, Paris, Oxford, etc., as a suitable place of publishing the new

[1] See H. Rashdall, *The Universities of Europe in the Middle Ages*, ed. F. M. Powicke and A. B. Emden, ii (Oxford, 1936), p. 38.

law-book, the *Liber Sextus*.[1] He authorized upon request by James II
of Aragon this king's foundation of the university of Lérida in 1301.[2]
He licensed the erection of a *studium generale* at Avignon on 1 July
1303.[3] That the university of Pamiers never became operational was
not Boniface's fault: he had granted the necessary licence to erect a
studium generale in this city in 1295, but its implementation was impeded
by a number of circumstances beyond his control.[4] If we add to these
measures the substantial help which he gave to individual scholars,
such as to Matthew of Aquasparta[5] or possibly to Master Eckhart,[6] the
assumption is justified that this comparatively short pontificate can be
regarded as not altogether ineffective in educational respects.

Where, however, a reassessment of this pontificate is called for is its
relationship with the newly orientated learning and scholarship that had
gained rapid ascendancy in recent decades. In practical and theoretical
respects the papacy claimed to apply concretely Christian cosmology
or *Weltanschauung* embodied as this was in the readily available papal
doctrine relative to society, government, and law. And this cosmological
pattern entirely corresponded to the universally accepted one, at any
rate in the Latin West. In its essential features this was ecclesiology in
theory that was applied in practice on a mundane level. What the observer witnesses here—and what, I may add, is far too little appreciated
by medievalists—is the most conspicuous reliance of a governmental
institution on a programmatic blueprint which it distilled—or attempted
to distil—into the concise language of the law.[7] Among governments on
a historical plane the papacy was one of the very few which avowedly
based its governmental actions on a scholarly elaborated theme.

[1] Ibid., pp. 82, 88. See A. Potthast, *Regesta pontificum Romanorum* (repr.
Graz, 1957), no. 24726 (23 September 1298).

[2] Rashdall, ii, p. 92.

[3] Potthast, no. 25269. See further *Les Régistres de Boniface VIII*, ed. C.
Digard *et al.* (Bibliothèque des écoles françaises d'Athènes et de Rome, 1921),
no. 5256; Rashdall, ii, p. 175.

[4] *Reg.* (as above, n. 3), no. 658. For Oxford University and Merton College
cf. T. S. R. Boase, *Boniface VIII* (London, 1933), p. 343 (a fair assessment of
Boniface's interest in higher studies).

[5] P. Glorieux, *La Littérature quodlibétique*, ii (Paris, 1935), pp. 194–8.

[6] The statement by J. Quetif–J. Echard, *Scriptores Ordinis Praedicatorum*, i
(Lutetiae–Paris, 1719), p. 507 ('sententias legebat [at Paris] sed exorto tum
graviori illo inter Bonifacium VIII et Philippum regem Franciae dissidio
Aicardum . . . Romam evocavit Bonifacius et doctorem ipse inauguravit' (anno
1302) is invalidated by J. Koch, 'Kritische Studien zum Leben Meister Eck-
harts' in *Archivum Fratrum Praedicatorum*, xxix (1959), pp. 5 ff., at 17.

[7] About the implementation of the idea of the rule of law by the papacy cf.
W. Ullmann, *A Short History of the Papacy in the Middle Ages*, 2nd ed. (London, 1974), pp. 11, 16, 43, 69; id., *Law and Politics in the Middle Ages* (London,
1975), pp. 29, 47 f., 71, 92, 120, 153 f., 209, 285.

60

This cosmology was highly intellectualized, if not sophisticated. As far as the papacy was concerned, the thought-pattern operated on a plane that had little in common with what could be termed natural insight, natural assessment, natural appraisal and judgement, natural outlook, or the natural laws relating to evolutionary growth or tradition. Medieval Christian social (and governmental) theory was not based on intuition, but on a severely rational programme eventually derived from the Bible. This programme rested on the realization of the Pauline thesis of baptismal rebirth and the consequential emergence of the *homo novus* or *renatus*[1] or the *nova creatura*[2] who as a result of the rebirth had lost his naturalness and was no longer a natural being,[3] but was incorporated in the society of Christians and became its member. As such he was subjected to this society's norms, in the making of which he had evidently had no share, so that, to use one more Pauline expression, the reborn man adopted a *novitas vitae*,[4] that engulfed all his being and directed his life. Hence the wholeness point of view with its attendant unipolarity—the one aim that mattered: salvation—and the strict hierarchical system that expressed itself in the theme of obedience of the lower to higher authority, the very ingredient of the descending theme of government and law[5] classically manifested as it was in the medieval papacy. In brief, the core of this programme that was held to have been entrusted to the papacy, was conceived to be biblically anchored—the society and its government were said to have been founded *uno ictu* by Christ Himself.[6]

The transformation of the programme into the social fabric necessitated the deployment of the law as one of the chief vehicles. There can be no legitimate doubt that the physiognomy of Western Europe

---

[1] 1 Cor. ii. 14; Ephes. ii. 15; iv. 24; Joh. iii. 3–5; 1 Pet. i. 23.

[2] 2 Cor. v. 17; Gal. vi. 15. On baptismal rebirth as a juristic phenomenon see, for instance, J. Dey, 'Palingenesia' in *Neutestamentliche Abhandlungen*, xvii. 5 (1937), esp. pp. 8 ff.; O. Heggelbacher, *Die christliche Taufe als Rechtsakt nach dem Zeugnis der frühen Christenheit* (Fribourg, 1953); W. Ullmann, 'Der Wiedergeburtsgedanke in der Staatslehre des Mittelalters' in *Aufstieg und Niedergang der römischen Welt*, ed. H. Temporini, vol. iii (forthcoming).

[3] That is *homo animalis* (the Greek has *anthropos psychikos*). This was common doctrine. Cf., among numerous writers in the twelfth century, Richard of St. Victor, *De superexcellenti baptismo Christi*, in *Patr. Lat.* cxcviii. 1017: 'Incipimus non esse quod fuimus.' Or as Thomas Aquinas expressed it: 'Homo spiritualis ex habitu caritatis habet inclinationem *ad recte iudicandum de omnibus secundum regulas divinas*' (*Summa theol.* ii–2, qu. 60, art. 1 ad 2).

[4] Rom. vi. 4. It should be borne in mind that all these conceptions had a very long history reaching back to the Hellenistic age.

[5] About this (and the ascending counterpart) cf. W. Ullmann, *Principles of Government and Politics in the Middle Ages*, 3rd ed. (London, 1974), pp. 19 ff.

[6] Matt. xvi. 18 f.

was profoundly shaped by this legalized ecclesiology universally accepted as it was. Overwhelmingly the organ which transformed pure doctrine into the enforceable law was the papacy.[1] This resilient cosmology, that had strong roots in the antecedent development, and the papacy complemented each other very well—there was mutual interdependence and fructification. Both spoke the same language, the one in the abstract, the other in the concrete as an institution of government. There was indeed a *communité des matières*, as de Ghellinck once felicitously expressed it,[2] between theologians, jurists, and the papal government. This feature explains the intimate, if not cordial, contact which the papacy had with Bologna and the other law universities. For the jurist—here it is the canonist who primarily matters—was the technician who translated the abstract cosmology into concrete terms in order to shape and define the path of society.[3]

In the present context it is of particular interest to note that from the early thirteenth century onwards the relations between the papacy and the law universities on the one hand and Paris university on the other began to show some considerable differences. That the papal contact with the former remained on an even keel is easily explicable: the jurists interpreted papal law, refined it, and provided further legal arguments for papal enactments—in a word, they continued to move intellectually speaking on the same level as the papacy. Their scholarship unquestioningly rested upon the traditional cosmology. But at Paris not only had jurisprudence in any case been at an infinitely lower level than, say, at Bologna, and this especially after Honorius III had prohibited the study of Roman law in 1219,[4] but there also was the intellectual unrest prompted by the infiltration and dissemination of Aristotle in the early decades of the thirteenth century. In Paris there had always been a noticeable trend towards the philosophical, that is, ante-juristic inquiry. The jurist began his analyses at the point where the philosopher or theologian had left off.[5]

It was a sign of the intellectual unrest at Paris that a provincial council held at Paris under the chairmanship of the archbishop of Sens,

---

[1] About this feature cf. *Short History* (above, p. 2, n. 7), pp. 17, 99, 128, 140, 143, 208, 244, 268.

[2] J. de Ghellinck, *Le Mouvement théologique du xiie siècle*, 2nd ed. (Paris, 1949), pp. 422–65.

[3] For some details cf. W. Ullmann, *The Growth of Papal Government in the Middle Ages*, 4th ed. (London, 1970), pp. 359 ff.

[4] For this cf. *Principles* (as above, p. 3, n. 5), p. 199, n. 4, with further literature.

[5] For some observations on the differences between juristic scholarship and philosophical studies cf. ibid., pp. 289 ff.

62

Peter of Corbeil, forbade the teaching of Aristotle's natural philosophy publicly and privately,[1] and this prohibition was confirmed and endorsed by the papal legate Robert Courson in 1215.[2] The significance of these steps is that the ecclesiastical authorities obviously began to realize that Aristotelian assumptions touched highly sensitive nerves and areas in Christian cosmology and could arguably lead to undesirable, if not inflammable, situations. For let us recall the essential, nay, vital foundation stone of Christian cosmology—that is, the idea of baptismal rebirth by which natural man was transformed into a new creature which, seen from another point of view, was nothing else but the conquest of nature by (divine) grace. But among Aristotelian doctrines the effective role attributed to the concept of nature was profound, prominent, and vital in the literal meaning of the term, and if pursued logically and philosophically could indeed play havoc with hitherto unquestioned Christian tenets.

It was this latter reflection which brought the papacy itself into the arena. In 1228 Gregory IX who fully grasped the potential dangers to Christian doctrine by the new teachings, issued a sternly worded letter to the Paris theologians in which he took them to task for their deviations from the traditional views: the focal point of his grievance was precisely this, that the Paris theologians attributed to nature what properly belonged to grace, for nature cannot by itself lead to salvation.[3] Quite clearly this *was* the crux of the problem. According to this letter, philosophy should be the *ancilla theologiae*, and not the latter's mistress.[4] The papal anxiety about the corrosive and destructive character of the new naturalist themes emerges here with all desirable clarity: the document is in fact a clarion call to halt the advance of the new

[1] See H. Denifle–A. Chatelain, *Chartularium Universitatis Parisiensis* i (Paris, 1889), p. 70, no. 11: 'Nec libri Aristotelis de naturali philosophia nec commenta legantur Parisius publice vel secreto, et hoc sub poena excommunicationis inhibemus.'

[2] Ibid., pp. 78–9, no. 20: 'Non legantur libri Aristotelis de metafisica et de naturali philosophia nec summae eiusdem.'

[3] Ibid., pp. 114 ff., no. 59; also in O. Raynaldus, *Annales ecclesiastici*, ed. A. Theiner, xx (Bar-le-Duc, 1870), pp. 555–6; H. Denzinger, *Enchiridion symbolorum*, 34th ed. (Barcelona–Fribourg–Vienna, 1968), no. 442. The importance of this letter is not apprehended by L. Thorndyke, *University Records and Life in the Middle Ages* (repr. New York, 1949) who does not include it in his collection, though he has the synodal prohibition and its endorsement (pp. 26, 27). Nor is its great significance realized by D. Knowles, *The evolution of medieval thought* (London, 1962), who does not mention it.

[4] 'Ipsi doctrinis variis et peregrinis abducti redigunt caput in caudam et *ancille cogunt famulari reginam* videlicet documentis terrenis celeste quod est gratie tribuendo nature. Profecto scientie naturalium plus debito insistentes ad infirma et egena elementa mundi, quibus dum essent parvuli, servierunt reversi, et eis denuo servientes tamquam imbecilles in Christo . . .'

ideological forces.[1] This letter reflects the first papal misgivings about the emerging new cosmology broadcast through the medium of pure scholarship. It set the tone of the papacy's reaction towards the new Aristotelian influences, the most sensitive topic of which was the autonomous role attached to nature and natural forces—it was this which within the next generation led to the rebirth of the concept of the citizen and of the State.[2] At any rate, the famous letter by the same Gregory IX to Paris university in 1231, *Parens scientiarum*, must be seen in this context and was a sequel to the one issued three years earlier.[3] Clearly, this letter shows that Aristotelian natural philosophy had already proved itself rather attractive which is furthermore demonstrated by the propagandistic advertisement issued by the just-founded university of Toulouse—founded in fact by the same Gregory IX in 1229—which the Masters of Toulouse towards the end of the same year 1229 had addressed to other seats of learning. Without the advance of natural philosophy this propaganda piece would be incomprehensible. It makes a special point about 'scholastic freedom' by stressing that 'the natural books' prohibited at Paris formed the subject of teaching at Toulouse:

> Libros naturales, qui fuerant parisius prohibiti, poterunt
> illic audire, qui volunt nature sinum medullitus perscrutari.
> Quid deerit vobis igitur? Libertas scholastica? Nequaquam,
> quia nullius habenis dediti propria gaudebitis libertati.[4]

Too much importance should not be attached to this Tolosan claim which could hardly mirror an actual state of affairs: the schools had, literally speaking, only just been opened, and of the teachers only one had taken up residence there—John Garland—who was probably the

---

[1] 'Et dum fidem conantur plus debito ratione adstruere naturali, nonne illam reddunt quomodo inutilem et inanem? . . . dicunt huiusmodi naturalium sectatores, ante quorum oculos gratia videtur proscripta, quod verbum erat . . . (John i.1) . . . *estne gratie an nature?*' For a masterly exposition of the relationship of philosophy and theology see M. Grabmann, *I divieti ecclesiastici di Aristotele sotto Innocenzo III e Gregorio IX* (= *Misc. Hist. Pont.* v. 7 (1941)) with numerous examples of the earlier development reaching back to Clement of Alexandria (pp. 71 ff.).

[2] For the antecedent background cf. W. Ullmann, 'Juristic obstacles to the emergence of the concept of the state in the Middle Ages' in *Annali di storia del diritto*, xiii (1970) (=Memorial volume for Francesco Calasso), pp. 41 ff.

[3] See Denifle–Chatelain, *Chartularium*, pp. 136 ff., no. 79: '. . . libris naturalibus, qui in concilio provinciali ex certa causa prohibiti fuere, Parisius non utantur quousque examinati fuerint et ab omni errorum suspitione purgati.'

[4] Ibid., pp. 129 ff., at p. 131, no. 72, also translated by L. Thorndyke, pp. 33 ff. Part of the background of the Tolosan foundation was the suppression of heresy in Languedoc and partly the exodus of the Paris Masters in 1229 after the troubles within the university. On this cf. H. Rashdall, op. cit., i, pp. 334 ff.

64

author of this glowing advertisement:[1] it should be borne in mind that
the papacy had not yet formally decreed the prohibition of Aristotle's
natural books at Paris or, for that matter, anywhere else. And as a
university Toulouse virtually withered away in the thirties, until
Innocent IV in 1245 conferred upon it ample privileges and, of immediate interest in the present context, literally copied Gregory's
Parens scientiarum, and thereby also enacted in regard to Toulouse the
prohibition concerning the teaching of Aristotelian natural philosophy.[2]
This Innocentian decree constitutes the real start of the university of
Toulouse.[3]

There is neither space nor need to go into details concerning the
attitude of the papacy towards the new learning in the thirteenth
century. It must suffice to say that the prohibition of the Aristotelian
books was not only extended to Toulouse, but was also re-enacted in
regard to Paris by Urban IV in 1263 (19 January 1263)[4] although the
Arts Faculty had in fact prescribed the *Physics* and *Metaphysics* and
the *De animalibus* as books to be lectured on.[5] Furthermore, John XXI,
himself a luminary in scholarship, addressed a letter to the bishop of
Paris on 18 January 1277 which breathes an air of profound distress
about Parisian trends.[6] It was this papal inquiry which two months later
led to the second condemnation of the 219 (Averroist) propositions by
the bishop of Paris, Stephen Tempier.[7] And on 28 April 1277 the latter
was once more addressed by the pope in very earnest terms on the same
topic concerning the substance of theological teaching in the Faculty.[8]
But by that time intellectual inquiries had long left behind the

---

[1] H. Rashdall, ii, pp. 163 f.

[2] Cf. Denifle–Chatelain, *Chartularium*, no. 20, p. 79.

[3] Potthast, no. 11903. See Cl. Devic and J. Vaissete, *Histoire générale de
Languedoc*, viii (Toulouse, 1879), pp. 1184 ff., esp. 1187, no. 388. The provincial
council was that held in 1210.

[4] Potthast, no. 18470; Denifle–Chatelain, *Chartularium*, no. 384, pp. 427 ff.

[5] Statute of 19 March 1255: Denifle–Chatelain, *Chartularium*, no. 246, p. 278.

[6] Potthast, no. 21215 of 18 January 1277; *Chartularium*, no. 471, p. 541:
perturbing information had reached him 'quod Parisius ubi fons vivus sapientie
salutaris habundanter hucusque scaturiit suos rivos limpidissimos fidem pate-
facientes catholicam usque ad terminos orbis terre diffundens, quidam errores
in preiudicium eiusdem fidei de novo pullulasse dicuntur . . . diligenter facias
inspici vel inquiri, a quibus personis et in quibus locis errores huiusmodi dicti
sunt sive scripti . . .'

[7] *Chartularium*, no. 473, p. 543; the earlier condemnation, ibid., no. 432.
At one time Stephen Tempier was a Master of Theology at Paris, cf. P. Glorieux,
Répertoire des maîtres en théologie de Paris au xiiie siècle, i (Paris, 1933), no. 177,
pp. 362 f.

[8] See the letter ed. by A. Callebaut, art. cit. (below, p. 65, n. 4), at
pp. 459–60.

cosmology upon which the papacy as an institution rested and operated.[1] To make the picture complete, it should be mentioned that throughout these critical decades the papacy, for understandable reasons, showed some predilection for those scholars who adhered to the traditional Augustinian cosmology or, still better, used Augustine for an attack on the new Aristotle, whether in the shape of Averroists or in that of Thomists. Such was assuredly the case with Matthew of Aquasparta.[2] Another instance is Giles of Rome who fiercely defended Thomas Aquinas' theses at Paris after the second condemnation in 1277 and was similarly censured for his adherence and defence. It was only after renouncing these views and after the bishop's death that Honorius IV was able to secure for him the Mastership in theology at Paris in 1285.[3] That in general the papacy favoured the Franciscans in matters of scholarship would seem understandable—they at any rate looked askance at the infiltration of Aristotelian theses into the traditional philosophical and theological framework.[4]

By the sixties and seventies all knowledge of Aristotle was easily available in competent translations which opened up a new world to man in the second half of the thirteenth century.[5] For he appeared to provide a full explanation of nature as a material and formal cause on purely rational, philosophical grounds: the age-old diastasis of nature and grace which was nothing else but the theological expression of the idea of baptismal rebirth manifesting itself in the dichotomy of *generatio carnalis* and *regeneratio spiritualis*, began to look fundamentally dif-

[1] Urban IV's re-enactment of *Parens scientiarum* seems to have been a mere routine matter handled by the chancery which was quite a common feature: when reissuing a decree it simply dispatched a copy of the original with little regard to actuality or change of circumstances.

[2] F. Ueberweg–B. Geyer, *Grundriss der Geschichte der Philosophie*, 12th ed. (Basel, 1951), pp. 481, 483.

[3] Potthast, no. 22239 of 1 June 1285; *Chartularium*, no. 522, p. 633.

[4] In this context cf. A. Callebaut, 'Jean Pecham et l'augustinisme' in *Archivum Franciscanum Historicum*, xviii (1925), pp. 441 ff. For Nicholas III (Cardinal Simon de Brion: 'ne fut jamais sympathique à l'Aristotélisme') and Martin IV as well as the cardinals who displayed the same attitude cf. ibid., pp. 447, 453 f., 461, 467. For the relations of the Franciscans to Thomism cf. F. van Steenberghen, *The philosophic movement in the thirteenth century* (Edinburgh, 1955), pp. 102 f.: 'The innovations introduced by Thomas Aquinas seemed to them gravely suspect on account of their undeniable kinship with Siger's Aristotelism.' The Franciscan Masters at Paris tried 'to keep Thomism and radical Aristotelism at bay'.

[5] See esp. H. Mitteis in *Hist. Zeitschr.* clxiii (1941), p. 281: ' . . . eine Änderung des Weltbildes durch das Eindringen aristotelischer und nacharistotelischer Gedanken, deren ganzen Umfang zu ermessen wir heute noch gar nicht in der Lage sind.'

66

ferent from this new angle.[1] To conservative and less radically inclined contemporaries a number of the new theses appeared to undermine all traditional assumptions with serious repercussions on social structures, social relations, social norms, and on government itself.[2] The thesis, for instance, that the same proposition may be true philosophically but false theologically was bound to create uneasiness and cause perturbing effects. This so-called double truth was considered, rightly or wrongly, an essential part of the Aristotelian teachings as set forth in the contemporary writings of some Paris Masters. Thomas Aquinas was their exact contemporary and colleague, and in his system there too can be detected a thesis that may have shown, at least superficially, considerable kinship with the Averroists' thesis: there was, Thomas said, a *duplex ordo in rebus*.[3] Other themes propounded by the radical Averroists concerned the extent of divine omnipotence and the rejection of the religious values of human actions. If permissiveness appears fairly new to us today, it had nevertheless a distinguished ancestry in the teachings of some of the Averroists: fornication was not necessarily evil; chastity not absolutely virtuous, nor humility nor sexual continence.[4] In the all-important doctrine of virtues the so-called *virtutes infusae* were relegated to an inferior place, if not rejected, and the four cardinal virtues given prominence.[5] What however was important from the point of view of society was the role accorded to nature. Natural reason, natural experience, natural judgement and insight were to be the cornerstones of the new cosmological pattern. And in this Averroists and Thomists were not all that dissimilar.

[1] Cf. E. Gilson, *History of Christian Philosophy in the Middle Ages* (London, 1955), pp. 244 f.: 'The Latin world was then discovering the universe of Greek science. For the first time and at one fell swoop the men of the Middle Ages found themselves face to face with a purely philosophical explanation of nature. The fundamental principles of this explanation they found in many treatises of astronomy, physics and biology . . .'. See also F. van Steenberghen, *La philosophie au xiiie siècle* (Louvain–Paris, 1966), pp. 393 ff., 397 ff., 430 ff.

[2] Cf. F. van Steenberghen, op. cit., pp. 472 ff., 488 ff. (with bibliography, notes 163 and 164); id., *Siger dans l'histoire de l'Aristotélisme*, ii (Louvain–Paris, 1942), pp. 728 ff.

[3] Thomas Aquinas, *Summa theol.*, I, qu. 21, art. 1 ad 3; cf. also his commentary on the *Ethics*, lecture 1.

[4] Details in M. Grabmann, 'Der lateinische Averroismus des 13. Jahrhunderts und seine Stellung zur christlichen Weltanschauung' in *Sitzungsberichte der Bayrischen Akademie, phil. hist. Kl.* (Munich, 1931), fasc. 2. Further F. van Steenberghen, *Les œuvres et la doctrine de Siger de Brabant* (= *Mémoires de l'Académie royale de Belgique*, xxxix (1938)); id., *Aristotle in the West* (Louvain, 1970), pp. 205 ff., esp. p. 220.

[5] Cf. *Principles* (above, p. 60, n. 5), pp. 245 ff.; cf. O. Lottin, 'Les vertus morales acquises, sont-elles de vraies vertus?' in *Recherches de théologie ancienne et médiévale*, xx (1953), at pp. 34–6.

According to both natural reasoning was the distinguishing mark of man, because it determined the social relations which thus did not rest on ecclesiological premisses or ecclesiastical dogma or the acknowledgement of the divine government of the world. Social relations rested upon purely human–natural assessments of human contingencies unencumbered by religious or theological doctrines. What did demand attention, was, to quote Thomas, the *instinctus naturae*[1] which impelled social living together and engendered social harmony.

It should be stressed, however, that despite indubitable identity of certain basic themes there was nevertheless an unbridgeable gulf between Thomism and contemporary Averroism, and that concerned the very concept I have just mentioned: nature. For the Averroists nature was wholly independent and autonomous, whereas for Thomas nature was an essential part of the divine ordering of things. In accommodating the notion of nature to Christian cosmology Thomas performed the gigantic task of reconciling disparate elements: the synthesis may well have seemed brittle, but was none the less intellectually plausible. On the other hand, for the Averroists there was what has recently been called a naturalistic ethics,[2] that applied purely natural criteria to judge the goodness or badness of a cause. Yet, the less subtle and perceptive contemporaries were only impressed by the superficial identity or similarity of Averroism and Thomism; they were obviously incapable of discerning the fundamental gulf that separated the two systems, although Thomas had in fact written a special tract against the Averroists. That therefore the official condemnations of 1270 and 1277, though primarily concerned with Averroistic theses, gravely affected Thomism, stands to reason. 'Both Siger and Thomas were to the conservative theologians tarred with the same Averroistic brush.'[3] Moreover, Peckham's condemnation at Oxford in 1284 renewing that of Kilwardby seven years earlier, was directed against Thomism itself. What is of immediate interest is that these later condemnations were merely sequels to the papal steps taken in 1277. 'In 1277,' it has rightly been observed, 'Latin Aristotelianism was condemned in its two most vigorous forms—that of Siger of Brabant and that of Thomas Aquinas.'[4]

It needs little imagination to visualize the effect which the cosmological and ideological changes wrought by scholarship had upon the papacy

---

[1] For detailed references cf. *Principles*, pp. 249 f.
[2] G. Leff, *Paris and Oxford Universities in the thirteenth and fourteenth centuries* (New York, 1968), p. 237.
[3] Ibid., p. 228. For the background see I. Brady, 'Background to the condemnation of 1270: Master William of Baglione' in *Franciscan Studies*, xxx (1970), pp. 5–48.
[4] F. van Steenberghen, *Aristotle* (above, p. 66, n. 4), p. 238.

68

as an institution. They struck at the roots of hitherto unquestioned premisses underlying society and its government. Bipolarity of thought and action replaced unipolarity—there was a natural and a supra-natural end—whereas the citizen corresponded to the former and the subject to the latter. Hand in hand with this went the notional emergence of the concept of the State as a product of nature, autonomous, self-sufficient, and independent of any other agency and organ, brought into being by what Thomas called the *instinctus naturae*,[1] and that concept was nothing else but the collectivized, resuscitated or revivified, reborn natural man. By virtue of his restoration he had now come, so to speak, of age, autonomous and independent, after his centuries-long veritable hibernation. The State as a product of nature incorporates by definition only citizens, and since they have to arrange and fix their relations within society in some orderly way, they can do this, as Aristotle had pointed out,[2] by *politizare*, that is, by discussing and acting and creating the law as fully autonomous members of the *polis*, the State. Neither the term *politicum* nor *politizare* had been familiar to governments, jurists, and writers on public governmental matters, because the mental category did not exist: it was the *ganzheitliche* unipolarity that mattered. There was only conceptualized indivisibility of human motivations and actions. Hence there was no need for this term, and it is of some considerable interest that William of Moerbeke, the translator of Aristotle, had to coin a new Latin word for the Greek *politeuein*.[3]

What the much censored Averroist and Thomist schools of thought propounded was a triad that was seen as a destructive agent of the accustomed thought-system resulting in the collapse of the prevailing social structure. This triad consisted of the State, its component part, the citizen, and the citizens' public activity, politics. Its potentially dangerous character was attributed to the Thomist accommodation of Aristotelian and Christian thought which was clearly considered to lead to a dilution of the purity of the traditional Christian principles. The Thomist synthesis was perhaps best expressed in the statement *Gratia non tollit naturam, sed perficit*.[4] Thereby a reconciliation of what was hitherto held irreconcilable, was achieved: within the natural order the ascending theme of government and law

[1] See also *Summa theol.* i–2, qu. 76, art. 6 ad 4.
[2] Aristotle, *Politics*, vii. 14. 15 (1333^b).
[3] S. F. Susemihl (ed.), *Aristotelis libri octo politicorum* (Leipzig, 1872), p. 307, line 12.
[4] Cf. on the whole cluster of problems L. Lachance, *L'humanisme politique de s. Thomas d'Aquin* (Paris–Montreal, 1965), pp. 54 ff., 353 ff., 374 f.

prevailed,[1] whereas in the supra-natural counterpart the descending theme operated.[2]

To these considerations must be adjoined a further reflection. Every theory is somehow or other linked with its environs and surrounding reality, and can be appreciated only in the historical context. This truism applies with particular force to the present topic. The time was extraordinarily favourable for the reception of the Thomist system, and this particularly in two respects. First, there had been noticeable throughout the thirteenth century a very strong and unmistakable disposition towards the naturalist orientation in virtually all segments of artistic creation, in painting, in architecture, in sculpture, no less than in the emergence of the new *scientia naturalis*[3]—the very counterpart of the similarly new *scientia politica*[4]—and in the great strides which vernacular poetry and prose had made from the mid thirteenth century onwards. Historiography, too, began to assume a complexion which substantially differed from the stereotyped, annalistic chronicles of the earlier periods.[5] Not least important in the present context was the strong infiltration, if not influx of the lay element into the universities whose scholarly contributions grew in quantity as well as in quality, especially in matters which were of concern to society and government. The law had always been one of the prominent disciplines of academic pursuit,[6] but law merely distilled the ante-legal, ante-juristic ideology relevant to a particular society. And this society was ecclesiologically orientated and ecclesiological in substance. Hence also the attentive care and tender attention which the papacy as supreme governing organ of this Christian society lavished on the law, and for this reason was supremely concerned with the orthodoxy of theological teachings and

---

[1] Cf., for example, Thomas: '*Politicum* autem regimen est, quando ille, qui praeest, habet potestatem coarctatam secundum aliquas leges civitatis' (I *Politics*, lectura 1). For the *status popularis*, cf. III *Pol.* lecturae 5 and 6. See further his *Summa theol.* i-2, qu. 105, art. 1: 'Ex popularibus possunt eligi principes et *ad populum* pertinet electio principum, et hoc fuit institutum secundum legem divinam.'

[2] Hence also the still heavy reliance on Ps. Denys as the source of the hierarchical theme.

[3] Cf. Gregory IX (above, p. 62, n. 4): 'Scientia naturalium.'

[4] The term was apparently coined by Thomas: I *Pol.* lect. 1: 'Si igitur principaliter scientia est, quae est de nobiliori et perfectiori, necesse est *politicam* inter omnes scientias practicas *principalissimam* et *architectonicam* omnium aliarum, utpote considerans ultimum bonum in rebus *humanis*.'

[5] For some details on these manifestations cf. W. Ullmann, *Individual and Society in the Middle Ages* (London, 1967), pp. 104 ff., with supplementary literature in the Italian translation (Bari–Rome, 1974), pp. 89 ff. and in the German edition (Göttingen, 1974), pp. 77 ff., 128 ff.

[6] Cf. *Law and Politics* (above, p. 59, n. 7), chs. 2, 4, and 7.

70

doctrines. After all, it was these ideological axioms and theological premisses which formed the foundation of Christian society. The concern of the papacy for the new teachings is comprehensible.[1]

On the plane of governmental reality there was a development that went parallel to that observable in scholarship, in the arts, in vernacular literature, and so forth. This is the second contemporary aspect which requires attention. It concerned the national Ruler's function and position which showed the advance that the idea of secularization had made since the mid twelfth century.[2] As a consequence of this secularization the foundations of government had perceptibly shifted from the theocratic to the mundane-historical level, with the result that structurally the ancient Roman law became an integral part of the governmental machinery. In practical terms the public law was the Ruler's own law, but according to the classical Roman law this public law related to *sacra, sacerdotes et magistratus*.[3] The essential point is that in these matters—in modern parlance: religious affairs, ecclesiastical discipline, and the judiciary—the ancient Roman emperor was the source of this self-same public law. He exercised his monarchic powers without legal restraint. If this juristic feature is applied to the national king the really profound significance the *Rex in regno suo est imperator*—ever more insistently proclaimed in thirteenth-century France and in substance also in other kingdoms—becomes understandable.[4] The hit at the universality of the Western emperor may well have been there, but primarily the significance was that the king had full powers in regard to the public law which in practical terms meant exercise of his government over the ecclesiastical body in consonance with the ancient Roman *ius publicum*. Taken in conjunction with the new learning this governmental device of the king arrogating to himself the exercise of the *ius publicum* constituted indeed a very real danger to the universality of the

---

[1] For the hostility with which pure scholarship received some Thomist theses see the still most valuable work by F. Ehrle, 'Der Kampf um die Lehre des hl. Thomas in den ersten 50 Jahren nach seinem Tode' in *Z.f. kathol. Theologie*, xxxvii (1913), pp. 266–318. Cf. also for examples P. Glorieux, *Les premières polémiques thomistes*, i (1927) (= *Bibl. thomiste*, ii) and ii (1956) (ibid. ix).

[2] For the first concrete manifestation of secularism in government cf. W. Ullmann, 'Von Canossa nach Pavia: zum Strukturwandel der Herrschaftsgrundlagen im salischen und staufischen Zeitalter', in *Hist. Jahrbuch*, xciii (1973), pp. 265–300.

[3] Ulpian in *Dig.* 1. 1. 1 (2): 'Publicum ius est quod ad statum rei Romanae spectat. Publicum ius in sacris, sacerdotibus et magistratibus consistit.' Cf. also *Inst.* I. i. 4.

[4] Cf. *Law and Politics*, 102 f., 182, 222 n. 2. Full bibliography in B. Paradisi in *Storia delle idee politiche, economiche e sociali*, ed. L. Firpo (Turin, 1973), pp. 43 ff., 147 ff.

Christian body as well as of the universality of the papal government.[1] This was a formidable combination of forces which had developed entirely independently of each other and yet tended towards the same end—disintegration of the one *societas christiana* into fragments. Scholarship and governmental practice combined promoted a national governmental outlook, that is, territorial sovereignty, with a consequential diminution of the universal papal jurisdiction.[2]

No great imaginative powers are necessary to realize how gravely the papacy was affected by this unprecedented and purely coincidental alliance. Yet, there is no suggestion whatsoever that any attack on the papacy was intended: nevertheless, the powers of the institution as such were unwittingly and unintentionally exposed to drastic restrictions. The situation was not made easier for the papacy by the frequent short pontificates in the relevant decades of the thirteenth century when, moreover, a good deal of papal energy was absorbed by extraneous circumstances.[3] In other words, the academic and governmental features which by their very nature were slowly evolving and barely perceptible, did not receive the attention which they deserved, because the papacy had to concentrate on immediate needs. Between Alexander IV's death (1261) and Boniface VIII's accession (1294) there were eleven popes, of whom there were three who succeeded one another in the course of one year, and only two ruled between three and four years; there were also frequent and long vacancies on the papal throne— all factors little conducive to an adequate assessment of the intellectual situation and to enacting appropriate measures.

Appropriate measures—what was at the disposal of the papacy to deal with contingencies which were so far mostly subterranean and as yet not directly challenging the governmental powers of the papacy? True, some of the new themes had been condemned; true also that previously papal policy towards national kings had in fact, though not designedly, nourished the governmental aspirations of the kings;[4] true furthermore

[1] One of the progenitors of this governmental stance was no doubt the rising nationalism which was not confined to France. Cf., for instance, the Cologne Canon Alexander of Roes who propounded a 'world' government on nationalist lines (see his *Memoriale*, ed. H. Grundmann and H. Heimpel, Weimar, 1949). Further the emergence of the *appellatio tamquam ab abusu* is one more symptom of this governmental device, cf. R. Génestal, *Les origines de l'appel comme d'abus* (Paris, 1950). The emergence of Gallicanism and the ties between the hierarchy and the royal government should also be considered in the early years of the fourteenth century.

[2] For some details cf. W. Ullmann, 'Zur Entwicklung des Souveränitätsbegriffs im Spätmittelalter' in *Festschrift f. Nikolaus Grass* i (Innsbruck–Munich, 1975), pp. 9 ff.   [3] Cf. *Short History of the Papacy*, pp. 265 ff.

[4] Such as, for example, Innocent III's *Per Venerabilem* (X: IV. xvii. 13).

72

that the papal law still stood intact and enjoyed a measure of academic attention only rivalled by the new philosophical and theological learning. But both the new scholarship and the royal stance were as yet too elusive to be the object of papal legislation—and in any case what precise points should have been the subject of legislation? Specific legislation relative to papal power and contingent individual topics had been in the past and in Boniface's pontificate plentiful, unambiguous, expansive, exact, and also quite effective, but now the papacy was faced by a wholly new situation—a new cosmology in combination with an ancient governmental structure. So far, and this point should be kept in mind, the papacy had always dealt with specific legal points in its decretals.[1] There is no instance in which the papacy in its function as a governmental institution had propounded in its decretals a coherent, consistent, concise, well-knitted doctrinal theme or a whole programme systematically covering fundamental questions and setting forth in appropriately succinct language the guidelines and conceptual framework of a particular ideology. Indeed, was the decretal the right vehicle? It dealt *per definitionem* with a particular legally controversial point that was decided. Yet in the present context there was in actual fact not one particular point at issue but a whole cosmology. That was not a suitable topic for a decretal. There remained what is technically called a constitution, but this too dealt with juristic–constitutional, mainly disciplinary matters or law-creative problems: once more hardly the problem in the outgoing thirteenth century, for the new cosmology and the royal standpoint did not *per se* impinge upon the kind of constitutional problems which awaited a decision by the papacy. What was at stake was the traditional Christian cosmology now threatened by a symbiosis of Aristotelian and Christian elements which in its totality and in combination with actual royal claims constituted the perhaps most severe challenge which the papacy had had to face in its long history.

To meet the challenge a thorough knowledge of the old as well as of the new cosmology was needed. That Boniface VIII had the appropriate juristic equipment and also very great practical experience, is so well known that nothing more needs to be said about it.[2] But this was not

[1] The decretals, notably those addressed to Philip IV, were clear and admitted of no ambiguity, but deal with legally well circumscribed problems which in the one or the other case (for instance in *Clericis laicos* or *Ausculta fili*, and so on) served Boniface as *points d'appui* for some general observations. The same is true of his letter to the German electors on 13 March 1300, in *M.G.H. Const.* iv. 1, no. 105, p. 80.

[2] See his own testimony: 'Quadraginta anni sunt quod nos sumus experti in iure et scimus quod duae potestates ordinatae a Deo: quis ergo debet credere

sufficient because what was needed was a connected thematic exposition of the very cosmology that was—in papal eyes—seen to be threatened by the academic and scholastic avalanche and the governmental stance taken up in the just quoted adage, which indeed may have served as a factor propelling the Bonifacian papacy to act. Specifically, it was the rising tide of bipolarity, the rapidly gaining ascendancy of the concept of the State, the rebirth of the citizen and not least the very idea of politics, the underlying assumption being the *right* of the citizen to *politizare* and thereby to take part in the law-creative process itself. All these elements of the new learning were utterly opposed to the pattern to which Christianity and the papacy had hitherto unquestioningly adhered. Boniface gave his answer in *Unam sanctam*. *Unam sanctam* constitutes the end of the development which began with the letter of Gregory IX some eighty years earlier addressed to the Masters at Paris. Papal policy was constant and consistent—Gregory IX no less than Innocent III before him or Innocent IV and others after him would have endorsed the theme and substance of *Unam sanctam*. It should be kept in mind that apart from two exegetical points not a single new topic emerged in it. Gregory IX stood at the beginning of the era which witnessed the new development of thought and Boniface VIII at the end when its fundamental theses had been hammered out in precisely the fashion which Gregory IX had feared: he had grasped the significance of the themes when as yet they were in an embryonic stage.[1] By the time of Boniface VIII they had become an all-pervading and mature system.

Unam sanctam presents some considerable problems, not indeed in regard to its contents but in regard to its character. But none of these problems has as yet been the subject of any worthwhile investigation or analysis—despite the acres of paper that have been devoted to its general assessment and evaluation. To begin with, there is no certainty at all that it was ever formally published, though it is in the official papal Register in the section of the *Litterae curiales* and could technically be called a bull which was the new kind of papal document since

---

quod tanta fatuitas, tanta insipientia fuerit in capite nostro?' (ed. in P. Dupuy, *Histoire du differend entre le pape Boniface VIII et Phillippe le Bel* (repr. Tucson, 1963): *Preuves*, p. 77). Cf. also the independent testimony in *Iperii chronicon s. Bertini*, ed. E. Martène–U. Durand, *Thesaurus novus anecdotorum*, iii (Paris, 1717), p. 774: 'iurista permaximus.' Cf. further *Chronicon aulae regiae*, ed. F. J. Dobner, *Monumenta historiae Boemiae*, v (Prag, 1784), p. 107: 'Utriusque iuris scientia preditus . . . mirabiliter eruditus.'

[1] For some details, mainly philosophical, see M. Grabmann, *I divieti* (above, p. 63, n. 1), pp. 75–86.

74

Innocent IV.[1] But as no original has ever been discovered,[2] one must rely on the text which the Register has, and there at once a whole crop of questions arises: no papal name, no *intitulatio*, no address, no salutation, no sanction, the barest kind of dating (which indeed is open to serious doubt)[3]—in brief, there is a great deal that needs to be explained. In view of the importance commonly attached to this document one would have expected that great care would have been taken to attend to these details. Moreover, although it has a minimal dating, it is enregistered in the wrong place.[4] These are strange omissions and irregularities, as far as the formal side is concerned. In substance similarly there are questions: no answer is possible about the occasion which prompted its issue, if indeed a formal issue had taken place;[5] there is no reference to a king, or any person or event which would give a clue to its purpose; no single individual or group of persons is charged with any deviation from orthodox faith. This together with the absence of any novel point of view makes this indubitably official papal document still more interesting or attractive or enigmatic, whatever standpoint one takes up. What was it?

[1] For this new species of papal chancery products see H. Bresslau, *Handbuch der Urkundenlehre*, 3rd ed. (Berlin, 1954), p. 83; A. Giry, *Manuel de diplomatique* (Paris, 1925), p. 695.

[2] See H. Denifle, *Specimina palaeographica ex Vaticani tabularii Romanorum pontificum registris selecta* (Rome, 1888), p. 44 and Table XLVI which is a facsimile of the official Register entry.

[3] The day—18 November—was a Roman feast day (dedication of SS. Peter and Paul) and no consistory or other meeting could have taken place on this or the preceding day. See Cardinal Jacobus Stephaneschi in *Ordo Romanus*, XIV (ed. *Patr. Lat.* lxxvi. 1230). Cf. also B. Schimmelpfennig, *Die Zeremonienbücher der römischen Kirche im Mittelalter* (Tübingen, 1973), esp. pp. 72 f.; text ibid., p. 213: xxxiii. 10 which goes back to the twelfth century (*Liber censuum*).

[4] Dated: 18 November 1302, but in the Register (no. 5382) it is entered after the documents issued in July 1303.

[5] The only source known to me which claims that it was formulated in consistory, was the indictment drawn up by William Playsian (and others) against Boniface, ed. in P. Dupuy (above, p. 72, n. 2), *Preuves* at p. 335: 'Frequenter dixit (scil. Bonifacius) quod rex et regnum Franciae et Gallici omnes erant haeretici et impingebant in articulum unam sanctam catholicam, etc., et super hoc voluit edere constitutionem, quam in consistorio legi fecit, quae incipiebat Unam sanctam, et concludebat, quod omnes, qui dicerent se Romano pontifici non esse temporaliter etiam et in temporalibus subiectos, iudicat haereticos.' It was in this lengthy charge sheet that the pope was accused of virtually any conceivable crime, including disbelief in the immortality of the soul, approval of fornication, embezzlement of moneys, murder of Celestine V in a cruel manner, execution of clerics in the presence of other clerics, compelling clerics to violate the secrecy of the confessional, oppression of cardinals, monks, and friars, unlawful dissolution of marriages, etc.

The one thing that is certain is that it is an abstract, scholastic and learned, even if slightly arid, declaration concerning the ecclesiological structure of society and its government. At no time could society exist without government. In substance it is intended to be the papal answer to the new cosmology with its threat to the unity and universality of Christian society. The answer is given by way of a summary or epitome of ancient and biblically based religious and ecclesiastical themes, none of which was in the past controversial or even queried. In short it was a scholarly declaration which meant to be a scholarly refutation of fashionable, current avant-gardist learned theses, precisely those which in their aggregate were seen by the papacy to be a peril to contemporary society.[1] Thrown against the contemporary background of scholarship *Unam sanctam* is more interesting and more significant for what it does not say.

The *spiritus rector* of this declaration was the Augustinian General Giles of Rome, who for a number of years had taken up residence in the curia. He was one of the most fertile and also versatile brains, having been a pupil of Thomas Aquinas and also thoroughly familiar with Siger's and Henry of Ghent's doctrines.[2] One might well say that Boniface called upon scholarship in the person of Giles to combat scholarship, and he could not have chosen an abler 'ghost writer' if so modern a term is permitted. His services in the curia may well mark a new trend, for hitherto the curia had always and with a certain predilection surrounded itself with eminent jurists. Of theologians of note or eminence we hear very little. Now, however, the papacy apparently began to call upon theologians to assist it in the task of formulating a social and governmental theory that was germane and relevant to the papacy as an institution of government, and above all one that was derived from Christian principles which had stood the test of time. The significance of this step was that the papacy had become aware of the change which contemporary scholarship had wrought in cosmology and its attendant consequences in regard to society and government. Academic learning for the first time had assumed the magnitude of a force with which the papacy now had to reckon. This indeed was a new feature altogether.[3]

[1] For some details of what follows cf. W. Ullmann, 'Die Bulle Unam sanctam: Rückblick und Ausblick' in *Römische Hist. Mitteilungen*, xvi (1974), pp. 45 ff.

[2] For his main works and bibliography see E. Gilson, op. cit., p. 735, n. 87; P. Glorieux (above, p. 64, n. 7), pp. 293–308, no. 400; id., *La Faculté des Arts et ses maîtres* (Paris, 1971), pp. 148 ff., no. 126. For Siger, ibid., pp. 351 ff., no. 427.

[3] This subject is virtually virgin soil, that is, the reaction of the papacy to the new learning and the various measures of intervention in the academic field. The duty of intervention was eventually based on the decree of the Roman council of 826, cap. 34: *M.G.H. Concilia*, ii. 581.

76

And in Giles of Rome there was a man with an exceptional command of the difficult theological and ideological material which formed the backbone of academic learning. As a former Master at the university of Paris he knew, so to speak, both sides of the controversy equally well —the ancient Augustinian and the new Thomist cosmology. In fact, the *Doctor fundatissimus*[1] was the learned adviser of the papacy in precisely the topical questions which exercised and divided men's minds at the time. Among these topics none was more important than the triad of State, citizen, and politics.

In the very first year of the fourteenth century Giles, while residing in the curia, wrote the tract *De ecclesiastica potestate*,[2] clearly intended as a repudiation of the new cosmology and notably of its implications and ramifications in the social and governmental spheres. The design and structure of the tract is clear and so is its message. The absence of any reference to the fundamental Thomist triad is conspicuous and explicable by the paramount importance he attaches to the idea of baptismal rebirth as the basic element in Christian social and governmental doctrines. By concentrating upon this idea as a legal notion he attempted to stem the tide of a resuscitated naturalism, so fulsomely exhibited in contemporary scholarship. Baptismal *regeneratio* (or *renovatio*) had been the focal point in antecedent scholarship and its re-emphasis by Giles was to stress its social and governmental link and to recall one of the vital ingredients of Christian cosmology within which there were only *homines renati* following the norms of the *novitas vitae* laid down by divinely instituted authority. The natural or human element played no role in it. Baptism was the *sacramentum universale*[3] or the *ianua*.[4] What quite obviously was the author's intention was to relegate natural man to the subordinate role in which he had always moved within Christian cosmology, because only thereby could the

[1] Both pope and Augustinian General had known each other for a very long time. When Benedict Caetani was cardinal-legate in France, he spotted the talents of Giles. In fact, it was the frequent exercise of legatine functions in France and especially in Paris which familiarized the later pope with the academic situation. On the whole he had very little respect for the Paris theologians and artists. Cf., for instance, the report about the French national council of 1290 and the characterizations by Benedict, ed. by H. Finke, *Aus den Tagen Bonifaz' VIII* (Münster, 1902): *Quellen*, no. i. 1, p. V.

[2] Ed. R. Scholz, *Aegidius Romanus: De ecclesiastica potestate* (Leipzig, 1929).

[3] Ed. cit., ii. 7, p. 72.

[4] Ibid., ii. 1, pp. 98, 99: 'A flumine igitur, id est a baptismo, qui est ianua omnium sacramentorum, habet ecclesia, quod dominatur a mari usque ad mare sive ad terminos orbis terrarum . . . consequens est, quod omnes possessiones nostras et omnia temporalia nostra recognoscamus ab ecclesia, per quam *baptizati* et spiritualiter *regenerati* ac per alia sacramenta a peccatis liberati fimus bonorum nostrorum iusti et debiti possessores.'

determinative role of reborn man be brought into clearest possible relief. In other words, the biblically based wholeness point of view must be revivified, be renewed, if Christian society in the hitherto accepted sense was to continue and survive. The full implications of baptismal rebirth had hardly ever before been drawn so trenchantly as in this tract.

From this basic presupposition of baptismal rebirth follow some very important conclusions which were by no means new, but for precisely this reason at the time and in context significant, because they starkly contrasted with the new Aristotelian–Thomist outlook and in this way were held to reinforce the traditional ecclesiology. Hence the emphasis on the ecclesiological theme with its corporational appendix—the incorporation into the Christian body through which salvation was to be secured. This presupposed, however, subjection to the laws of this body:

> Nullus possit consequi salutem nisi sit subiectus
> ecclesie et nisi sit eius filius.[1]

The wholeness point of view with its salvific and teleological unipolarity was consequential on this premiss. Further, the concepts of property and rulership were not only embedded in this ecclesiological unipolarity but also directly orientated by it. Either could legitimately be exercised within a Christian framework only by the *renati*. This point of view might well have seemed too obvious to have needed specific mentioning, let alone detailed examination—after all, the society within and for which Giles wrote was wholly Christian and in any case consisted of *renati* only. Here is the point which most clearly reveals the real target of this tract. For within the Aristotelian–Thomist thesis there was no need at all to have undergone baptismal rebirth and to obey the commands of legitimate ecclesiastical authority: and natural man was entitled to have property and to exercise rulership, and this on no other ground than that he was natural man. Above all, property, inheritance, and rulership were outside the precincts of divine grace altogether[2]— they were issues which had nothing at all to do with grace. The invocation therefore of the ancient theme of grace by Giles in respect of these issues is doubly significant. On the one hand, the existing state of affairs

---

[1] Ibid., ii. 7, pp. 72–3.
[2] Precisely the theme in the classical medieval period: property no less than rulership were considered issues of divine grace, hence a *beneficium divinum* which also explains Gregory VII's prayer to the two apostles on the occasion of Henry IV's final excommunication and deposition: *Reg.* vii. 14a (ed. E. Caspar, p. 487). Hence the great significance of the (mediatory) role of the ordained clerics in mediating divine grace by which property, rulership, etc., were acquired.

78

was considered by Giles to be sufficient proof of the correctness of his own thesis that baptismal rebirth was the right and proper means to qualify for ownership and rulership. On the other hand, the new theories were to be shown incompatible with fundamental Christian principles which required the acceptance of, and obedience to, the norms constituting the *novitas vitae*, in other words, subjection of reborn man to ecclesiastical authority. Perhaps nothing demonstrates the thought-process of Giles better than his simple statement:

> Non sufficit quod quicumque sit *generatus* carnaliter
> nisi sit per ecclesiam *regeneratus* quod possit cum
> iustitia rei alicui dominari nec rem aliquam possidere.[1]

Only through and under ecclesiastical authority can one be a 'dignus dominator' or 'dignus princeps' or 'possessor rerum'.[2]

These were the premisses which led Giles effortlessly to restate in sharply accentuated form the ancient principles of government relative to Christian society, and above all the principle of monarchy exercised by the pope. The universality of the Christian body demanded universality of its government which was the late thirteenth-century expression of the petrinological standpoint, according to which Christ had *uno ictu* founded a new society and established its government. And these premisses excluded *ab initio* any room for the new concept of the State, of the citizen, and of politics (as an autonomous intellectual activity).[3] It is therefore comprehensible not only why there was no reference at all to these concepts in Giles's tract but also why in a society that claimed to be built on Christian foundations, these concepts were considered alien intruders. This tract at once was a thinly disguised attack on the new cosmology that had with alarming rapidity gained adherents

---

[1] *Aegidius*, p. 70. Although Giles operated with the idea of baptismal rebirth so prominently, virtually all modern authors have inadequately assessed it or not noticed it at all. Cf., for example, Y. Congar, *L'Église de s. Augustine à l'époque moderne* (Paris, 1970), pp. 272 ff.; W. Kölmel, *Regimen christianum* (Berlin, 1970), pp. 300 f., 325, 349 f.; see also G. de Lagarde, *La Naissance de l'ésprit laïque au déclin du moyen âge*, 2nd ed., i (Paris–Louvain, 1958), p. 194.

[2] Ed. cit., ii. 8, p. 79. He continues: 'Clare igitur vides, quod reges regnorum, principes principatuum et alii fideles possessionum suarum sunt magis digni possessores per suam matrem ecclesiam, per quam sunt spiritualiter *regenerati* quam per suos patres et per haereditatem paternam, a quibus *patribus carnalibus* et per quos *nascuntur* in peccato originali, *nascuntur non subiecti Deo*, sed pocius aversi ab eo.'

[3] That he was in fact thoroughly familiar with the triad is clear from his tract *De regimine principum* written for the young Philip IV. This was wholly Aristotelian–Thomist in conception and execution. Details in W. Berges, *Die Fürstenspiegel des hohen Mittelalters* (Stuttgart, 1938), pp. 320 ff.; it was translated into many languages.

in academic and non-academic circles as well as a scholarly exposition of some fundamental Christian points of view on a coherent, systematic manner. Considering therefore the time and place of the composition of the tract, it would not be too much to claim that it constituted, in modern parlance, a white or a green paper or a report by a committee appointed by the government of the day in which future legislative or governmental measures are proposed and argued in great detail. There can be no doubt that the tract was attuned to, if it did not actually reflect, Boniface's own points of view. Nor can be doubted the intellectual harmony that had not only brought Giles and Boniface together, but also resulted in something approaching personal friendship. What is, however, of immediate concern is that the curia had at its disposal a scholar of renown, capability, profundity of knowledge, and the required versatility, and I cannot refrain from repeating that this was one of the earliest instances in which the curia used the expertise of non-juristic scholarship for governmental purposes.[1] Hardly ever before had academic intelligence been of such direct value to a governmental institution as in this instance. And not the least significance of this teamwork was that the papacy was revealed as an institution that at any rate by implication admitted its utter dependence upon an abstract programme that, by that time, could be successfully handled only by experienced philosophical and theological scholars. Giles' tract set forth with great economy and verve precisely the themes that mattered from the contemporary papal point of view—unity, universality, unipolarity, and monarchy. It is therefore understandable why the diastasis of *generatio carnalis* and *regeneratio spiritualis* formed the backbone of the book.[2]

Boniface's *Unam sanctam* is a well-structured, logically composed summary of the points made in this treatise by Giles. It is one of the

[1] To judge by the letter written to the Oxford Chancellor, John de Lutterworth, by Stephen de Kettelbergh from Avignon some 20 years later, John XXII had made a determined attempt to attract theologians in preference to jurists to the curia at Avignon; he also promised handsome rewards, including bishoprics, see *Snappe's Formulary*, ed. H. E. Salter (Oxford Hist. Soc., lxxx (1924)), pp. 304 ff. The Chancellor is told 'quod dominus noster summus pontifex magnam et specialem affectionem, quam pre hiis temporibus pretextu sapiencie civilis erga iuristas conceperat, modo de novo ad theologos et maxime ad magistros in sacra pagina transtulit integre et perfecte, adeo quod quiscumque magister expertus re et nomine in theologia dignus habere nomen magisterie dignitatis, hic ad sedem apostolicam veniens, a curia non recedit. In primis dominus papa de dignitatibus magnis et prebendis eis libenter providet et secundum varias condiciones personarum quosdam ad culmen episcopalis dignitatis et alios ad sedes archiepiscopales transfert . . .'

[2] Cf., apart from the passages already referred to, ii. 7, p. 71; iii. 1, p. 149; iii. 11, p. 202.

first, if not the first, official papal document that sets forth the substance of a social and governmental doctrine in a methodical, systematic and comprehensive manner, and it does this by proceeding from one stage of the argument to the next, beginning with a powerful—and, let me add, rhythmically well structured—affirmation of the unity of the Christian body and leading to the climax of the unity of its government.[1] All this is—I should not need to mention this specifically—conceived in contemporary thirteenth-century terms. Some topics, however, need emphasis. It contains nothing that is in any technical or formal sense juristic and is conceived entirely on the level of doctrine. It must be stressed that neither a juristic nor a papal statement is invoked to support its conclusions or interpretations.[2] It is precisely in this context that the absence of a sanction assumes its proper significance: the only explanation can be that the document was to be viewed as a purely doctrinal or magisterial systematic exposition of some fundamental principles which the papacy considered on the one hand vital for the continuance and survival of Christian society and on the other hand was to censure, by implication at least, if not outright explication, the new scholarship, as far as it bore on social and governmental questions. The piece is an official declaration *sui generis*—neither a decree nor a decretal nor a constitution nor really a bull despite its heading *Ad perpetuam rei memoriam* in the Register. It is the papacy acting entirely within the terms of its *magisterium* that in stark contrast to contemporary scholarship postulates rigid adherence to fundamental axioms, if contemporary society were still to be called Christian. Like its *pièce justificative*, *Unam sanctam* does not and cannot know of the State, the citizen, and politics. By issuing this document the papacy was apparently aware of the novelty of its step—hence the various irregularities already mentioned.[3] There is no warrant for saying that it played a part in the conflict between the pope and Philip IV.

Although the new Thomist system moved in close proximity to the

---

[1] Although setting out from his 'political' Augustinianism H. X. Arquillière put his finger on the vital point: 'Il y a dans ce document pontifical, si ramassé et si plein, la substance d'un traité de l'église' (*Dict. de droit canonique*, ii. 945).

[2] The crucial statements in *Unam sanctam* are either biblical quotations or their (monopolistic) interpretations and applications or expressions by non-juristic writers, such as St. Bernard, Hugh of St. Victor, Ps. Denys, etc., though none is mentioned by name, except Denys who was believed to be St. Paul's pupil. There is above all no reference to jurisdiction *ratione peccati* as formulated by Innocent III in *Novit ille* (X: II. i. 13) following the lead given by St. Bernard (cf. *Growth*, p. 434). R. Scholz in his introduction to his edition (p. ix) rightly said: 'Aegidius ist durchaus Theologe, nicht Kanonist.'

[3] See above, p. 73 f.

so-called Latin Averroism, it did not intend to supplant the old cosmology, but to complement and supplement it. Yet whatever the intention or design, the papacy viewed this new trend with great suspicion
and as a challenge to accepted ways of thinking and governing. It would
not have been wise, even if it had been possible, to condemn Thomism
tout court, as it indubitably was conceived within a Christian framework,
however much it deviated from its traditional form. There should be
no longer any doubt that Boniface intended to issue a very stern warning
against any kind of revisionism.

Precisely because it was a new departure, *Unam sanctam* suffered from
many deficiencies which were, one is inclined to say, unavoidable: as
a chancery product it was most unusual; its 'publication' similarly, and
its contents no less so. It was a formal, solemn, official pronouncement
that focused attention on potentially undesirable conclusions of the
new learning in so far as it affected social and governmental theory
and practice. As a classic anti-revisionist product it was a forerunner of
papal declarations that dealt with similar questions at a much later age,
for which the encyclical letter was to become the appropriate vehicle of
dissemination. But in the late thirteenth century this was a wholly
unknown instrument for the kind of declaration that was intended—what
other means were at the papacy's disposal to make known its opposition
to current fashions? For the first time the papacy was virtually forced
to enter the arena of scholarship. The impulse had come from the
academics, and the papacy had no choice but to meet them on their
own terms. The new standpoint could not be called heretical *per se*
and yet the papacy foresaw the potential dangers, since some assumptions of the traditional ecclesiology were no longer immune from doubt,
or believed to be unchallengeable and inaccessible to external influences.
For Boniface there was to be no tampering, no modification, no accommodation to, and no revision of, what the papacy as the custodian of
basic Christian axioms held to be true. The accepted fabric and matrix
of the Christian social order were believed to be in jeopardy. From the
point of view of the thirteenth-century observer, the deep apprehension
of the papacy is easily comprehensible.

This background explains why the themes set forth in *Unam sanctam*
adduced only unquestioned and unquestionable premises which had
served medieval Christianity well: unity and unipolarity as the corner-
stone of the ecclesiologically conceived society in which operated the
hierarchical principle and its sequel, division of labour. The ecclesiological character of society makes intelligible the importance which
Unam sanctam attaches to the creation and function of the secular
Ruler, because only in this way could the ancient Pauline principle of

82

division of labour be adequately implemented.[1] Thereby the autonomy
of secular rulership was implicitly denied. And seen from a wider angle,
this was precisely one of the topics which affected the whole traditional
social and governmental edifice, that is, the ascription of autonomy to
communities, societies, corporations, which, because they were natural
products, were able to elect their own officers, including the Ruler, who
remained responsible to them.[2] This ascending theme of government
and law was ideologically as well as governmentally the very opposite
of what the papacy on its own ground held to be the 'right order',[3]
in which prevailed the wholeness point of view and unipolarity. How
could the State, the citizen, and politics be fitted into this framework?

What has always caused apprehension, if not misgivings, was the last
sentence of the document, but this too was not new[4] and in actual fact
followed from the premises just mentioned. The sentence—*Porro
subesse Romano pontifici omni humanae creaturae declaramus, dicimus,
definimus et pronuntiamus omnino esse de necessitate salutis*—must be
thrown against the exclusively ecclesiological background which alone
gives meaning to it.[5] In order to comprehend the sentence in its historical context it should be kept in mind that the idea of rebirth is
here made to serve a purpose which, because it rests on an extensive

[1] The source was Hugh of St. Victor's *De sacramentis* which had 'instituere
ut sit' (*Growth*, pp. 439–40). The place of *ut sit* was taken in *Unam sanctam* by
veritate testante, a replacement that has escaped all commentators. The possibility should not be excluded that Gregory VII's letter to the Conqueror might
have served as a model for this device: here 'divina testante scriptura' was
applied to a statement made by Gelasius I (cf. *Reg.* vii. 25, ed. cit., p. 506; for
Gelasius' statement cf. *Growth*, p. 282, n. 2). Similarly, *Unam sanctam* referred
to the *lex divinitatis* which was nothing else but the hierarchical ordering propounded by Ps. Denys. The explanation may be that the 'divinization' or
'canonization' of certain statements was intended to increase their weight and
authority.

[2] This was, as it may be recalled, the very theme which conciliarism adopted,
according to which the pope remained responsible to the whole Church where
the totality of power resided. Cf. *Short History of the Papacy*, pp. 298 ff.

[3] For this terminology cf. W. Ullmann in *Revue d'histoire du droit*, xxvi
(1958), pp. 360 ff. (book review); cf. John xix. 11; St. Augustine in Gratian,
Dist. viii. 1, and the formulations chosen by Ps. Denys in his tracts, *Principles*,
pp. 46 ff., 306, 317.

[4] See Thomas in his *Opusculum contra errores Graecorum ad Urbanum IV*
(1263) (ed. Venice, 1593, fol. 9b): 'Ostenditur quod subesse Romano pontifici
sit de necessitate salutis.' About Thomas's development at this time, see
E. Gilson, op. cit. (above, p. 66, n. 1), pp. 387 ff., also 403 ff.

[5] This background makes understandable the strong condemnation of bipolarity in *Unam sanctam* by positing that this amounts to postulating *duo
principia* 'quod falsum et haereticum iudicamus'. As an ecclesiological body
(the 'una sancta ecclesia') could not have two heads ('duo capita') each representing different, though not necessarily opposed ends.

interpretation, may possibly be called novel. Whereas in Pauline doctrine baptismal rebirth confers immunity on regenerated or reborn man—the *homo spiritualis*[1]—for Boniface and his draftsman[2] the concept of *homo spiritualis* reappeared as a hierarchical concept in the shape of *suprema potestas*: baptismal rebirth was pressed into the hierarchical order.[3] Seen differently, the age-old distinction between office and person[4] was here put to a new use by combining it with the equally old immunity of the pope *qua* pope from any kind of judgement (*papa a nemine iudicatur*)[5] so that the Pauline statement of the *spiritualis homo* who *a nemine iudicatur*, re-emerged within an hierarchical framework and referred solely to the pope in his capacity as office holder which indeed was the unambiguous meaning of the *suprema potestas*. Evidently, the substance had a distinguished pedigree and was also acted upon ever since the formulation of *prima sedes a nemine iudicatur*.[6] In brief, the concept of baptismal rebirth was monopolized to construct a theory of papal sovereignty.

This construction served as a springboard upon which *Unam sanctam* reaches the climax in the claim to universal papal monarchy. Once more, this claim can make sense only in an ecclesiological context. The continued existence of this ecclesiological society was threatened on the

[1] 1 Cor. ii. 15: 'Spiritualis (homo) autem iudicat omnia et ipse a nemine iudicatur.' His antipode was the *homo animalis*, ibid., ii. 14. The Greek counterpart to the *anthropos psychikos* was the *pneumatikos*.

[2] See Giles, ed. cit., i. 2, pp. 6 ff., with the juxtaposition of the *homo animalis* and *spiritualis* (esp. p. 7).

[3] The statement in *Unam sanctam* is: 'Ergo si deviat terrena potestas iudicabitur a potestate spirituali, sed si deviat spiritualis minor a superiore, si vero suprema a solo Deo, non ab homine poterit iudicari, testante apostolo . . .' (follows 1 Cor. ii. 15). In substance this is Hugh of St. Victor (cf. *Growth*, pp. 440 f.) and a similar view could be read in Gratian, *Dist.* xxi. 4 (Nicholas I). On the official papal level the idea of baptismal rebirth had never been so clearly and pointedly applied in a hierarchical sense as in this piece.

[4] On this cf. W. Ullmann, 'Leo I and the theme of papal primacy' in *J.T.S.* N.S. xi (1960), pp. 25 ff.; id., 'Pontifex Romanus indubitanter efficitur sanctus: D.P. 23 in retrospect and prospect' in *Studi Gregoriani*, vi (1962), pp. 129 ff. See further Giles, ed. cit., p. 7 ('secundum statum') who admits that 'multi sunt laici, qui sunt sancciores et spiritualiores quam multi clerici, et multi subditi quam prelati', but what matters here is the *status* or the office.

[5] For this see *Constitutum Silvestri*, cc. 3, 20 (early sixth century) in J. D. Mansi, *Conciliorum collectio amplissima*, ii (Venice, 1769), 631, 632. Although this *Constitutum* was spurious, its kernel was perfectly genuine, see Pope Zosimus (anno 418) in *Patr. Lat.* xx. 677.

[6] It may be recalled that in pursuit of the principle of papal non-justiciability Charlemagne refused to sit in judgement over Leo III, cf. *Growth*, pp. 117 f. with sources and literature. First application of this principle was under Boniface II in 530, see *Liber Pontificalis*, ed. L. Duchesne (repr. Paris, 1955), i, p. 281, lines 12 ff.

84

one hand by the new learning and on the other by the royal assertions of territorial sovereignty which in practice meant royal control of the ecclesiastical body in disciplinary, administrative, organizational, and possibly other respects.[1] The alarming spectre of the collapse of what constituted a universal and united body monarchically governed, was a contingency that had to be taken note of by any pope in the late thirteenth century.[2] The reassertion of universal papal monarchy was an implicit refutation of the new theses which proclaimed the autonomous standing of kingdoms, etc., and the explicit attempt to save, if not to restore, the universality of the Christian body which was one and indivisible. This was, Boniface declared, the intrinsic meaning of *Pasce oves meas*: 'meas, inquit, et generaliter, non singulariter has vel illas; per quod commisisse sibi intelligitur universas.'

The emphatic assertion of the *necessitas salutis* underlines the ecclesiological context and at the same time serves as a justification for the frequently overlooked invocation of another biblical passage, that is, the quotation of the *omnis humana creatura* from 1 Pet. ii. 13. Here as well as in *Unam sanctam* this does not mean 'creature' but rather *res creata* or a humanly created thing.[3] This explanation has at least the merit that it moves within the ancient framework; the focal point of the statement is the depersonalized measure which receives its objective meaning and relevance from the end—salvation.[4] The novelty lies in that *Unam*

[1] Clement V's *Meruit* changed nothing in all this, because *Unam sanctam* was in any case not directed against Philip IV.

[2] This point was stressed by Cardinal Johannes Monachus in his gloss on *Unam sanctam* (which he wrote early in 1303): 'Si ergo fides quam tenet ecclesia esset particularis continens unam gentem vel unum populum, sicut sunt multi populi sive multae gentes, sic forte essent multae ecclesiae et multa capita. Sed cum sit catholica . . .' The gloss is in all early editions of the *Extravagantes communes* which embody *Unam sanctam*.

[3] Which is in consonance with most of the adequate translations of the biblical text: 'every ordinance of man' (authorized version); 'jede menschliche Ordnung' (German Catholic); 'alle menschliche Ordnung' (Luther Bible); 'authority of every social institution' (Jerusalem Bible, 1970); 'every human institution' (Oxford–Cambridge Bible, 1970); 'toute autorité établie' (La sainte Bible, transl. L. Segond, 1969); 'toute institution humaine' (La Bible: nouvelle version catholique, 1969). For commentary see F. Hauck, *Die Briefe des Jakobus, Petrus, Judas und Johannes*, 7th ed. (Göttingen, 1954), pp. 56–9 ('menschliche Ordnung'); K. H. Schelkle, *Die Petrusbriefe* (= Herder's Theolog. Kommentar zum Neuen Testament, xiii–2, Freiburg, 1962), pp. 72 f. ('(göttliche) Schöpfung unter den Menschen').

[4] For the depersonalized, objective thesis, characteristic of early and medieval Christianity, cf. *Principles*, pp. 102 ff. It was the objective office (the *potestas*, the *dignitas*, the *status*, the *officium*) that mattered, and not the person or his personal merits or demerits, hence also in early Christianity the refusal to accept the divinity of the emperor which was accompanied by the exaltation of his office, because 'nulla *potestas* nisi a Deo'. It is well known that this attitude led to the

sanctam here paraphrastically combines a Petrine with a Pauline passage (Rom. xiii. 1–3) and applies the result to the pope.[1] This is one more instance of monopolizing the Bible in the service of the papal government, a feature with which the historian of the papacy is not unfamiliar.[2] It is high time that the modern rendering of the final clause in *Unam sanctam* be accordingly adjusted. Its usual translation is open to grave objections, because it blurs the issue and expresses something for which the text furnishes no warrant.[3]

To sum up. As an anti-revisionist document *Unam sanctam* constitutes a new departure in official papal output, because it is essentially a scholastic–doctrinal *exposé*. It contained no juristic elements and did

persecutions of the Christians who incurred the charge of the *crimen laesae maiestatis*: they had refused tò swear by the emperor's genius (on this see Tertullian, *Apologeticus*, xxiv. 1, ed. Loeb Classical Library, 1931, p. 130); hence also the charge of atheism against the Christians, on which see A. Harnack, 'Der Vorwurf des Atheismus in den ersten drei Jahrhunderten' in *Texte & Untersuchungen zur Geschichte der altchristl. Literatur*, xxviii (1905), fasc. 4; cf. also Th. Mommsen, *Römisches Strafrecht* (Leipzig, 1899), pp. 575 ff.

[1] The two passages were frequently combined, cf., for instance, in the ninth century, Haimo of Auxerre, *Expositio in Epistolas s. Pauli*, cap. 8, in *Patr. Lat.* cxvii. 478–9, but he considered *creatura* to mean 'man' ('hoc est omnibus hominibus'), just as the Douai and Jansenist translations of the Bible do. For Giles himself cf. ed. cit., i. 5, p. 14.

[2] Boniface supplies another instance, cf. above, p. 72, n. 1, where he makes Ps. lxi. 2 (Rom. xiii. 1) ('Deo subiecta erit anima mea') applicable to the papacy alone ('apostolica sedes . . . cui omnis anima . . . debet esse subiecta'). The non-justiciability of the pope (above, p. 83, n. 5) is another old instance of monopolization. When Gregory II in 729 in his memorable letter to the emperor in Constantinople referred to 'Christi sensum nos habemus' (cf. *Growth*, p. 46), he monopolized 1 Cor. ii. 16 for the papacy. This subject of monopolization is in need of *ex professo* treatment.

[3] In his *Pastor aeternus* Leo X re-enacted on 19 December 1516 *Unam sanctam*, but replaced *omnis humana creatura* (of 1 Pet. ii. 13) by *omnes christifideles*. Although the change was clearly intended to eliminate a misunderstanding and to restrict papal jurisdiction to Christians only, it had far wider significance which is not recognized at all. For thereby the original objective notion— the institution, order, or measure—was now subjectivized or personalized which not inconsiderably changed the tenor of *Unam sanctam*. Here in parenthesis it should be mentioned that from yet another angle the scope and extent of papal monarchy was tackled by Innocent IV in his Commentary on the *Liber Extra*. He operated here with what may be termed the creational principle, according to which the pope as vicar of Christ had inherited Christ's powers through his being the successor of Peter: 'Credimus quod papa qui est vicarius Jesu Christi potestatem habet non tantum super christianos, sed etiam super omnes infideles, cum enim Christus habuit potestatem super omnes . . . omnes autem tam infideles quam fideles oves sunt Christi *per creationem*, licet non sint de ovili ecclesiae et sic per predicta apparet quod papa super omnes habet potestatem et iurisdictionem de iure, sed non de facto' (*Commentaria in quinque libros decretalium*, ed. Frankfurt, 1570, ad X: III. xxxiv. 8). I have checked this text with that in MS. 188 of Pembroke College, Cambridge, which is identical.

86

not invoke a single papal statement in its support. The heading in the Register—*Ad perpetuam rei memoriam*—can in itself hardly confer legal character upon it. Apart from the citations of biblical texts, all other statements come from writers who were not jurists. It was intended to be restorative and raises no claim that had not been made by the papacy before. All the castigations, vituperations, and aspersions in which both Catholics and Protestants vied with each other in condemning *Unam sanctam*[1] seem to me quite pointless, because they disregard the fundamental canon which is to consider a document in its historical context. Historical scholarship postulates that this papal declaration be seen in its general and particular environs. The customary denigration of *Unam sanctam* should be replaced by comprehension of the spirit in which it was conceived—as a magisterial answer to contemporary challenges.

Seen from this angle, there is warrant for saying that it begins the long line of distinguished literary and publicistic tracts in which the basic themes of *Unam sanctam* are treated at great length, though most certainly not always from the specific papal standpoint. On the one hand there are scholars of the persuasion of James of Viterbo, Alvarus Pelagius, Augustinus Triumphus, and a host of others; on the other hand there is Dante, Engelbert of Admont *et eorum sequaces* who represent a different persuasion.[2] What unites them all is resistance to the process of disintegration and decomposition, so painfully obvious at the time. In a word, however paradoxical it may sound, the universalist theme now begins to be treated professionally as a special topic of scholarship partly with the old, and partly with the new weapons. But despite the solemnity of the formal papal declaration and the many tracts, scholarly expositions and *Summae* which it inspired—leaving aside altogether such blatant imitations as the Emperor Henry VII's pronouncement that *Omnis anima Romanorum principi subiecta sit*[3]—the future belonged to the new orientation in scholarship which was already producing at this very time publicistic works developing the concepts of bipolarity, territorial State sovereignty, and politics, with panache, elegance, verve, and dynamic potency—witness John of Paris, Marsilius of Padua, and

[1] M. D. Chenu, 'Dogme et théologie dans la bulle Unam sanctam' in *Recherches de science religieuse*, xl (1952), pp. 307 ff., is wholly unaware of the vital point of baptismal rebirth, so conspicuously displayed in the document itself.

[2] For some details cf. art. cit. (above, p. 75, n. 1), at pp. 72 ff.

[3] *M.G.H. Const.*, iv. 2, no. 929, also incorporated as *Collatio* XI in the *Corpus Iuris Civilis*. The possibility of an imperial attempt to imitate the papal monopolization of the Bible (Ps. lxi. 2; Rom. xiii. 1) should not be dismissed. This would clearly be in line with the earlier imitative rivalry of the two institutions.

many others—and which came to emerge in the ecclesiastical field proper as the conciliar movement.

From a wider historical perspective *Unam sanctam* assumes additional significance. As indicated, it was a product of scholarship issued by the papacy in order to counteract certain contemporary trends in scholarship. Even though the immediate practical effect of *Unam sanctam* was minimal, it assumed all the greater significance in the very field in which it was composed, that is, in that of scholarship: it opened up the long and distinctive line of papal pronouncements on vital questions relative to society which were (and are) treated with all the paraphernalia of true scholarship. Precisely because it held itself to be the custodian of orthodox doctrine, the papacy began in the fourteenth century to expand the magisterial dimension, scope, and extent of its statements on contingent religious issues in a methodical, systematic, and scholarly way. This pontificate thus marks the beginning of a new phase in papal history that seems to have reached its apex in the modern age providing an abundance of magisterial–papal pronouncements on topical problems of the day.

VIII

DANTE'S "MONARCHIA" AS AN ILLUSTRATION OF A POLITICO-RELIGIOUS "RENOVATIO"*

To honour Winfried Zeller by a contribution to his Festschrift provides a welcome and suitable occasion of repaying a great debt to him and of indicating in a modest way a sense of gratitude for the manysided stimulus he has provided in his supremely perceptive and original writings: directly or indirectly they concern themselves with the central theme of crisis and its conquest through re-form or *renovatio*. May the jubiland accept this short essay as a token of profound esteem and respect.

Experience proves that banishment and exile not only sharpen political awareness, but also stimulate creative thinking to an extent as perhaps nothing else does. It was this heightened political perception that made Dante turn his attention to a critical, rational and partly also historical analysis of the factors which gave rise to a state of crisis, characterized by the decomposition and disintegration of what was once a more or less well integrated whole. Although they had a distinguished ancestry, the foundations of his contemporary Europe seemed to have been severely corroded by extraneous influences which robbed them of their inner strength and resilience. In particular to the discerning eye the Christian cosmology had by the second half of the 13th century no longer the dynamic force and impetus which it previously had. As universal institution the papacy was also gravely affected by the ever increasing demands resulting from purely regional policies pursued with singular zeal and vigour by the countries in the West.

This factual situation must be seen against the background of the intellectual movements in the 13th century which exhibited restlessness, disquiet and uncertainty where formerly there had been rocklike certainty. And the focal point of these movements and their influences was the crucial element of the faith upon which the Church as an universal body rested, transgressing as it did ethnic, linguistic, regional differences and welding them into a coherent whole. It was precisely this universalist cosmology which was detrimentally affected by the combined effects of practice and theory. By the end of the century one could indeed speak of a virtual eclipse of the universalist outlook. Not only did the traditional pillars of the social fabric show signs of decay, but what must also have caused perceptive contemporaries even greater apprehension was that the institutions of government appeared to countenance the decline of the universalist standpoint.

---

* In view of the restricted space footnotes and references have been kept to an irreducible minimum.

Additionally, sentiments of nationhood became crystallized and were increasingly turned into instruments of politics during the closing years of the century. This was assuredly detectable throughout Western Europe. The sentiment manifested itself furthermore in the rapid advance which vernacular language had made in poetry, prose, even in legal collections, with the result that the universal language, Latin, began to lose its monopolistic position in all branches of learning. Linguistic differences acted as forces of national identification. As long as nationalism was confined to the organisation of universities and to the voting in ecclesiastical councils, it was quite harmless, but when once it became operational in the public-legal field, it could, as indeed it did, become a destructive element. It is therefore noteworthy that there were some littérateurs who in order to defuse the disintegrating force of nationalism, attempted to harness it to the preservation of the old universal order by advocating a structure in which the three leading European nations, the French, the Germans and the Italians were to be the foundations[1]. On the other hand, the nationality principle was emphatically propagated by writers, such as Pierre Dubois, in the very first years of the 14th century. A pupil of Thomas Aquinas and Siger of Brabant, he adopted in his tract *De recuperatione sanctae terrae* a veritably chauvinistic French tone and eloquently pleaded for national sovereignty by rejecting any kind of universalism[2].

Indeed, this kind of literature merely reflected a state of affairs that was discernible both in the doctrine and practice of government. The concept of territorial sovereignty was epitomized in the adage *Rex in regno suo est imperator*[3]. The significant (and hardly ever noticed) substance of this concept consisted in that it transferred the functions of the Ruler of the late Roman empire to the sphere of late medieval royalty: the king was said to be equipped with the same rights within his territory which the emperor had, including ecclesiastical functions[4]. Since the Roman emperor was held to embody the fullest possible sovereignty, the application of this idea to regional kingdoms in conjunction with the already strongly devel-

---

[1] The scheme was proposed by the Cologne canon Alexander of Roes, *Memoriale,* ed. H. Grundmann – H. Heimpel, Weimar 1949; further critical edition in *Staatsschriften des späteren Mittelalters,* Stuttgart 1958. For some details cf. W. Ullmann, *History of Political Thought in the Middle Ages,* rev. ed. London 1970, 187 ff.

[2] *De recuperatione s. terrae,* ed. C.-V. Langlois, Paris 1891. The tract was composed about 1305–1306; important observations by L. Boyle in: Medieval Studies 34 (1972) 468 ff. Details in R. Scholz, *Die Publizistik zur Zeit Philipps d. Schönen,* Leipzig 1903, 391 ff; also M. J. Wilks, *The Problem of Sovereignty in the later Middle Ages,* Cambridge 1963, 36, 445 ff. In a special memorandum to Philip IV (1308) he craftily suggested that the king should propose to Clement V his (the king's) creation as an emperor by depriving the German electors of their papally (!) granted electoral rights, because they had misused this right by electing papal opponents. Even the amount of the bribe was fixed by him. See E. Boutaric (ed.) in: Notices et extraits 20 (1865), part 2, no. 30, 186 ff.

[3] For some details cf. W. Ullmann, *The development of the medieval idea of sovereignty* in EHR 64 (1949) 1 ff. Rich literature in B. Paradisi, *Il pensiero politico dei giuristi medievali,* in: *Storia delle idee politiche, economiche e sociali,* ed. L. Firpo, Turin 1973, 57 ff, 149 f.

[4] The essential point is that the late Roman emperor was the source of all law, hence also of public law. He had "inherited" the previous constitutional position of the emperor as *pontifex maximus.* "Ius publicum in sacris, in sacerdotibus, in magistratibus consistit" (Dig. 1.1.1.3 [Ulpian]), and it was administered by the emperor. The *ius in sacris* applied to organisational, administrative, disciplinary ecclesiastical matters and also to the convocation of general councils. About the implications cf. W. Ullmann, *Short History of the Papacy in the Middle Ages,* London ²1974, 7, 11, 23.

oped national sentiments clearly constituted a grave danger to the very idea of a universal entity embodied as it had been in the concept of the universal Church. The adage just cited was merely a symptom of the extent which the religious crisis had already assumed.

An adequate understanding of the intellectual background of Dante's *Monarchia*[5] presupposes an appropriate assessment of the intellectual forces prevalent in his time. They had a veritably revolutionary character, as they potently affected hitherto unquestioned assumptions relative to Christian cosmology. For the latter's dominant theme was its wholeness point of view or the principle of indivisibility[6], according to which Christianity seized the whole of man. This precluded the atomisation of the *Ganzheit* into different categories, such as religious, moral, political, etc. The absorption of Aristotelian axioms was of immediate concern to this standpoint with its concomitant theme of unipolarity, according to which all actions were directed to one end – salvation. „Omnes actiones ordinatae sunt ad consequendam vitam aeternam"[7]. This unipolarity came to be replaced by bipolarity. The *aut-aut* gave way to an *et-et*.

The foundation of this Christian unipolarity standpoint was the rebirth effected through baptism. This was conceived to be a *regeneratio* or a *renovatio*: it resulted in the change of the *homo animalis* into a *nova creatura*, to use Pauline terminology[8]. To this cardinal feature of medieval Christian cosmology far too little attention is paid by ecclesiastical historians, and hence the dimensions of the intellectual revolution in the 13th century as well as of its reactions are hardly appreciated. Conceptually, this rebirth amounted to a fundamental transformation of the individual, for the baptismal waters had washed away – or were said to have washed away – the *naturalness* of man. It was this naturalness that had hitherto directed man's path in accordance with his purely natural insights and judgments which were lost and replaced by an entirely different set of norms. Man acquired a *novitas vitae*, the bases of which were no longer natural insights and evaluations, and the like, but the laws of that society into which he had gained entry *per lavacrum regenerationis et renovationis*[9]. And that society was the divinely founded Church. Through baptism man became a *homo renatus*[10], a *homo novus*, in short a *fidelis*. As such he was to follow the norms laid down by the Church into which he was

[5] All references are to the edition by P. G. Ricci, Milan 1965. In my opinion it was written in stages and without reference to actual events, probably circa 1316–18. Cf. I. 12. 6, p. 158, line 26f.: "sicut in Paradiso Comedie iam dixi" which is an important clue. On the question of dating cf. F. Baethgen, *Die Entstehungszeit von Dantes Monarchia*, SAM 1967, fasc. 5, esp. 22ff. See also H. Löwe, *Von Cassiodor zu Dante*, Berlin 1973, 307 n. 38 who rightly criticises the artificial explanation by A. P. d'Entrèves, *Dante as a political thinker*, Oxford 1952.

[6] About this cf. W. Ullmann, *Principles of Government and Politics in the Middle Ages* (abbrev. *PGP.*), London ³1974, 33f, 74, 97f, 234, 264, 305.

[7] Still in the 14th cent. this *ganzheitliche* standpoint was advocated, for instance by the German Conrad of Megenberg, *De translatione Romani imperii*, cap. 12 (ed. R. Scholz, *Unbekannte kirchenpolitische Streitschriften* II, Rome 1914, 292): "Liquidum est religionem christianam quoddam *totum* esse..."

[8] The main passages are: Tit. 3. 5; I Cor. 2. 14f; II Cor. 5. 17; Gal. 6. 15; the *homo novus* in Ephes. 2. 15 and 4. 24; *novitas vitae*: Rom. 6. 4.

[9] See preceding note. In some respects the homiletic commentary by John Chrysostom on John 3. 5f is a classic statement: *Hom.* 25 in: PG 59, 149–50.

[10] John 3. 3 and 5; I Pet. 1. 23.

104

incorporated[11] and which alone provided the means of achieving the aim: salvation. This unipolarity was an unquestioned premiss and theme. It permeated all public, private and social life. With it went hand in hand the essential ecclesiological standpoint according to which on a mundane level the Church was the sole autonomous public body comprising as it did both laity and clergy. The crucial point of this unipolarity was the elimination of any consideration which belonged to the sphere of unregenerated, natural man[12]. What was determinative was the sum-total of all the norms which constituted the fabric of the Church, and, so it was held, these were *per definitionem* of a divine and not human provenance.

The core of the new doctrines in the 13th century was the (re)introduction of the concept of nature as an operational instrument[13]. Thereby "natural" man came to be re-instituted in his pristine function. He came to be re-born in every sense and thus re-integrated into the cosmological thought-pattern from which he had been banished for so long. It was a *renovatio* or resuscitation of natural man. The effect of this rebirth was that the naturalness of man was set free, so that he could exercise his own judgment in an autonomous manner. In itself this was a severe breach in the fortifications of the prevailing system of unipolarity: next to the supra-natural end of man there was now also conceived a perfectly legitimate natural end. This consideration powerfully paved the way for the theme of bipolarity which, on closer analysis, was merely an extension of the Aristotelian differentiation between morals and politics (which in an ideal society should nevertheless be identical)[14]. In the natural order of things man's *humanitas (homo)* became determinative, whereas in the supra-natural order where divine grace dominated, the norms of *christianitas* set the tone[15]. In the political field there emerged the citizen as a fully autonomous being who replaced the *subditus*. To the *renovatio hominis* in the ethical sphere corresponded the *renovatio civis* in the political[16]. Both the reborn *homo* and the *civis* stood conceptually apart from the *fidelis*. Thereby new perspectives and new orientations opened themselves up. The facet that can clearly be discerned on the intellectual horizon of the 13th century constituted the opening bars of the humanist symphony: humanism properly understood is not primarily a cultural or educational or idealistic movement, but one that arose out of the *renovatio hominis*, out of the re-instatement of natural man into his full autonomous stature[17].

In essence this was the Thomist synthesis. And precisely because he was perfectly familiar with it[18], Dante also realized the undesirable by-products this new outlook

---

[11] For this see esp. O. Heggelbacher, *Die christliche Taufe als Rechtsakt nach dem Zeugnis der frühen Christenheit*, Freiburg/Schw. 1953; cf. also H.D.Betz, *Der Apostel Paulus und die sokratische Tradition*, Tübingen 1973.

[12] The theme of nature as opposed to grace is perhaps best brought out by John Chrysostom in *Hom.* cit. (above n. 9) when he made Christ say to Nicodemus in order to drive the point home: τί τῇ τῆς φύσεως ἀνάγκῃ τὸ πρᾶγμα ὑποβάλλεις; (cur *naturae* necessitati rem illam subiicis?).

[13] For this cf. W. Ullmann, *Individual & Society in the Middle Ages*, London 1967, ch. 3.

[14] Aristotle, *Politics* III. 4. 4 (= 1276b).

[15] *PGP*. 245, 246f.   [16] Ibid.

[17] For this cf. *Individual* (as cit. n. 13), 143ff.

[18] On this cf. E. Gilson, *Dante the Philosopher*, London 1947; cf. also P. Mandonnet, *Dante le théologien*, Paris 1935; further B. Nardi, *Dante e la cultura medievale*, Bari ²1949,

was capable of generating. Among these was certainly the ideological furtherance of the already existing trend towards national sovereignty[19] of which none was more aware than he himself. It was the threat of fragmentation inherent in the thesis of national sovereignty which prompted him to use the Thomist framework constructively to prevent a disintegration otherwise unavoidable and to indicate how unity embracing all men can be achieved, and not merely the unity of the Christians.

Within the present context only two points of Dante's philosophy can be dealt with. First, he extended the concept of the individual citizen and collectivised it on the largest possible scale. The result was the Dantesque *humana civilitas*. Second, he utilized the historical notion of the Roman empire (and hence of the Roman emperor) as an operational instrument with the help of which universal peace and justice were to be achieved. His programmatic declarations rested on the ideological rebirth of the Roman empire and the humanistic, above all the basically religious idea and the theological concept of the *renovatio hominis*. In the application of these religious topics to the solution of the contemporary crisis of mundane society and government lies the profound contribution of Dante.

Dante's concept of *humana civilitas* was the core of his political philosophy embedded as it was in the antecedent theological development. It designated the universality of mankind, a universalist idea hitherto monopolised by the Church[20]. Dante's concept de-mundanised the Church and transferred it to the supra-natural order. By this de-mundanisation Dante began a process that in some respects may be seen as the purification of the Church, in others its veritable rebirth, and yet in others as the faint heraldings of the Reformation. His *humana civilitas* embraced not only Christians, but also Jews, pagans, heretics, infidels, in a word, it was the *homo* writ large. From this angle alone his tract is a first-rate document which throws light on one of the most critical phases in the intellectual and religious evolution of Europe, the dimensions of which are as yet hardly realized.

In pursuit of the theme of bipolarity Dante evidently was bound to reject ecclesiologically or theologically grounded claims of the papacy which considered axiomatic the inseparability of a Christian's life in this and the next world, the former appearing merely as preparatory to the latter. What had been before in governmental and social doctrine and practice dualism in the shape of functionalism manifesting itself as the principle of division of labour[21], underwent now a radical transformation: the dualism applicable only within the unipolarity of Christian ife gave way to an a-Christian bipolarity. What was before one *totum*, came now

and id., *Saggi e note di critica Dantesca*, Milan–Naples 1966; K.Foster, in: *The Mind of Dante*, ed. U.Limentani, Cambridge 1965, 47ff, also further literature ibid.

[19] Cf., for instance, Thomas, *Summa theologiae*, II–II, qu. 85, art. 1 ("nationes hominum"). He holds that *natio*, like *natura*, stems etymologically from *nasci*. Cf. further John of Paris, Dante's exact contemporary, in *PGP*. 262f, 270.

[20] The idea of universal mankind was not Aristotelian. He knew only of the *polis*, but of no comprehensive unit. Cf. F.Kern, *Humana civilitas*, Leipzig 1913, 138, who also emphasized the organic and political character of this Dantesque unit (138–139). The most appropriate German equivalent would seem to be *Gesamtbürgerschaft*, and in English "universal citizenship". It is not always realised that John of Salisbury had used this term, though in the sense of "civility" (*Policraticus* VIII. 9).

[21] On this cf. *PGP*. 66f. The background is I Cor. 12. 4ff; Ephes. 1. 23; 4. 10f, 16; Rom. 12. 4.

to be seen as two entities, each with its own telos and functions[22] characterized by the operation of the principle of division of labour[23]. Thereby the totality point of view evaporated and with it the papal jurisdictional claims[24]. As Dante put it: „Man was in need of a twofold directive power according to his twofold goal"[25]. The principle of bipolarity could hardly be better expressed, for there was a *beatitudo huius vitae*[26] as well as one *vitae aeternae*[27]. In short, there is a *duplex ordo in rebus*[28]. This Dantesque idea was the former ecclesiological theme writ large.

In no wise did Dante deny that the Church (or the papacy) had on its own premisses, that is, within the supra-natural sphere, autonomous standing. What he did deny was that the vocation of the Church as a body divinely founded specifically for the salvation of man, constituted it as a mundane body on a universal scale. He utilized the ancient ecclesiological framework in order to overcome the crisis of his age and thereby renovated the idea of the Church itself. Next to the Christians forming the Church there were others who were constituent members of the larger entity of universal mankind. Dante based his political philosophy on the thesis of the "renovated" or resuscitated man as a purely natural being who was autonomous and responsible, precisely because he was a rational *human* creature and pursued his naturally reasonable goal. This was evidently in entire agreement with the Thomist thesis[29]. Dante, however, went further by identifying the collectivised *homo* with the *universitas hominum* which was *humanitas*[30] writ large or the *humanum genus* as such[31]. According to him it was a viable unit because only that which has intellect and reasoning powers may claim to belong to it. The Church on the other hand as the congregation of the faithful, was based on faith[32]. Dante

---

[22] Hence it is that the teleological theme was so strongly marked in Dante: I. 3. 3, p. 140.

[23] Cf. I. 14. 2, p. 163, lines 9 ff.

[24] The totality of the papal jurisdiction (based on Matt. 16. 18f) was claimed in the 5th cent., cf. Gelasius I in his *Tractatus* IV, c. 5, ed. A. Thiel, *Epistolae pontificum Romanorum genuinae*, Braunsberg 1862, 562; Felix III before him, ibid., Ep. 2, c. 7, p. 237, also Gelasius in another Ep., p. 445. In the high Middle Ages this appeared as the *universale regimen* (Gregory VII) or as used by Innocent III in *Lib. Extra:* I. 33. 6. Dante's opposition to this unipolarity and totality standpoint forms part of the third book. Cf. M. Maccarrone, *Il terzo libro della Monarchia,* Studi Danteschi 33 (1955) 3–142; but cf. also B. Nardi, *Dal Convivio alla Commedia,* Rome 1960, 152ff; G. Vinay, *Interpretazione della Monarchia di Dante,* Florence 1962.

[25] III. 15. 7, p. 273.

[26] To this bipolarity corresponded wholly different locations of original power. Within natural society the ascending theme of government was operative: all power was located in the people, whence it "ascends". In the supra-natural society (in the Church) original power was located in the supreme being whence it "descends". About these concepts cf. *PGP.* 20ff.

[27] This bipolarity of Dante's was the target of a special attack by Guido Vernani in the *Reprobatio Monarchiae,* ed. Th. Käppeli, *Der Dantegegner Guido Vernani,* QFIAB 26 (1938) 107ff, at 125, 126–128, 145f. It has rightly been remarked that Dante pressed the theme of bipolarity "so far as almost to identify life on earth with *human* life proper (italics original) and to seem almost to leave in abeyance ... any connexion with life after death", K. Foster, loc. cit. (above n. 18) 68.

[28] I. 6. 2, p. 147, line 6. The concept of *duplex ordo in rebus* is in Thomas, *S. Theologiae,* I, qu. 21, art. 1, ad 3 ("Est autem considerandus duplex ordo in rebus"). Cf. also his *Eth.,* lectura 1.

[29] Cf. *PGP.* 252ff.   [30] I. 3. 4–5, p. 140.

[31] I. 2. 8, p. 139, and in other places.

[32] In his commentary on Boniface's *Unam sanctam* the Dante opponent, Guido Vernani, made this one of his basic themes: "Fides est in ecclesia tamquam fundamentum", ed. M. Grabmann in SAM 1934, fasc. 2, 145.

therefore released man's pure and natural humanity from its Christian restrictions and encrustations and set it free: he "naturalised" and mundanised the Christian by liberating him from the bondage in which as a subject to higher authority he was held[33]. The effect of this rebirth or restoration of man was his acquisition of liberty which was the hallmark of man as a citizen. "Liberty is the greatest gift conferred by God on human nature"[34]. Wherefrom Dante's postulate arose that liberty was a necessary prerequisite for the full deployment of the faculties inherent in mankind[35]. Here too the two different cosmologies can be discerned, for to the freedom within the natural society of the *humana civilitas* corresponded obedience within the supra-natural society of the Church. Within the former man was a *civis*, within the latter a *subditus*, because ecclesiologically incorporated.

What Dante's thesis showed was the highly important but barely noticed effect of the intellectual process which put the idea of baptismal rebirth into reverse, a process that was clearly the underlying theme of the immediately preceding humanist development. The vacuum left by the working of the system of unipolarity was now filled by the effect of the reversal that resuscitated the individual as man and as citizen without in any way impinging upon his status as a *fidelis*[36]. Thrown against this background his plea for a monarchic government of the universally conceived citizenhood can be more easily understood. In substance both the government and the governed were merely contemporary linguistic expressions of concepts which were both new and old: they were regenerated or renovated concepts of a distinguished parentage. They were shorthand devices with the help of which Dante tried to ward off disintegration and decomposition. The religious crisis that produced the danger of disintegration was to be overcome by the similarly religious belief in the universality of mankind, conceived not as a body held together by the bond of Christian faith, but bound together by the faith in the efficacy of nature as a cementing element.

Dante's monarch was not a Ruler of the usual stamp, not a governor who issued laws and decrees, not one who was crowned and anointed. Monarchy to him designated the pure and abstract idea of Rulership. Being a divine emanation, in no wise different from nature itself[37], this Ruler stood outside and above ordinary mankind and functioned as the guarantor of liberty and peace by means of exercising justice. This Dantesque Ruler did not belong to one nation, but to all[38] and was unappealable authority, set over mankind and above the cities, kingdoms,

---

[33] For this see Rom. 13. 1ff, and for the background and views down to Dante's age W. Affeldt, *Die weltliche Gewalt in der Paulusexegese: Römer 13. 1–7 in den Römerbriefkommentaren der lateinischen Kirche bis zum Ende des 13. Jahrhunderts*, Göttingen 1969.
[34] I. 12. 6, p. 158: "Maximum donum humanae naturae a Deo collatum quia per ipsum hic *felicitamur ut homines*".
[35] Ibid.
[36] This explains the final plea in III. 15. 17f, p. 275 which is in entire correspondence with the Thomist doctrine. The view of A.P. d'Entrèves, op. cit. (above n. 5) 58, is astonishingly naive: the sentence was supposed to be a "last-minute correction" and nothing really changed. U. Limentani, op. cit. (above n. 18) 126 is rightly critical.
[37] Cf. *PGP*. 245f.
[38] The tract in no wise warrants the view that only the German kings were rightful claimants to the imperial crown, nor is Henry VII mentioned anywhere. Cf. B. Nardi, *Dal Convivio alla Commedia* (above n. 24) 175f, also 257ff. Further U. Limentani, 119–20.

national states[39]. "His jurisdiction is bounded by the ocean alone"[40] and he is "the purest subject of justice among mortals"[41]. This monarch was nothing more than the personification of the idea of law and justice[42], for the law is to him the directive of life[43]. He was, so to speak, fetched down from the heavens to preside over mankind[44] by delineating and pronouncing upon the permanent and unchangeable ideas of law and justice[45]. He was the *curator orbis*[46]. Dante's thesis of emperorship represented a typology of Rulership, one more concept that was modelled on ecclesiastical prototypes. His Rulership constituted the *Alleinherrschaft des Rechts*.

But Dante's conceptualized Rulership was only one half of his thesis. The other concerned the society that was to be governed. For society and government were (and are) complementary to each other. Again, he used contemporary terminology to show in concrete ways the meaning of the *humana civilitas*. The essential point is again that a traditional nomenclature served Dante to express his novel design: the concept of the Roman empire was as much purely conceptualized as was the universal monarch.

Dante would not have been a follower of Thomas Aquinas, had he omitted to employ the teleological argument in its specific form of the priority principle. Accordingly, since the state was prior to the individual and therefore the whole necessarily prior to the part, Dante conceived the universal state in its Roman shape on this Aristotelian-Thomist premiss. That is to say, nations, kingdoms, regional entities were to him emanations of the universal empire that was to him preportrayed in the ancient Roman empire, but now understood in a global context. Precisely because individual states and nations were conceptually derived from the all-embracing universal unit, could they prosper and flourish. The universal union of mankind was not the sum-total of all the nations and states comprised in it, but rather their source and "cause"[47]. In other words, just as the individual citizen is orientated towards the state, in the same way kingdoms, and so on, derive their sustenance from, and are orientated towards, the universal unit which is the totality of all[48]. The parallelism between the integral parts of the world state and the reborn or resuscitated citizen is indeed noteworthy. Since the latter was a political and social animal, he was able to deploy his faculties only within the state[49], and so could the kingdoms, nations, regional communities realize their full potentiality only within the universal state, the end of which was the pursuit of liberty and peace[50]. To him this universal state was prefigured in the ancient Roman empire, because within its confines there was no sovereign entity apart from the empire itself[51]. And it was this which in his vision secured peace and tranquillity in the

---

[39] I. 14. 5, p. 169.   [40] I. 11. 12, p. 155.
[41] I. 11. 12–13, p. 155, lines 55 ff.
[42] For the concept of *lex animata* see A. Steinwenter in: Anzeiger d. Akad. d. Wissenschaften, Vienna 1946, 250 ff (with a wealth of material).
[43] "Est enim lex regula directiva vitae" (I. 14. 5, p. 164, line 26).
[44] III. 15. 13, p. 274–5.
[45] I. 14. 7, p. 165, lines 35 f; also I. 11. 7, p. 154 (the Digest definition of justice).
[46] Obviously an allusion to the usual designation of the pope as *speculator omnium*: III. 15. 11, p. 274: "curator orbis qui dicitur romanus princeps".
[47] I. 6, p. 147 f. and 7, p. 148 f.   [48] Ibid.
[49] *PGP.* 261. The context is rightly recognized by H. Löwe, op. cit. 306–307.
[50] I. 3–4, p. 139.   [51] II. 1. 3–6, p. 172 f.

empire of the Romans. For at no other time had there been so much peace as under Augustus: "Non inveniemus nisi sub divo Augusto monarcha existente monarchia perfecta, mundum undique fuisse quietem"[52]. And to this tranquillity all witnesses testify, pagans no less than the evangelist and St. Paul who called this very age the "plenitudo temporis"[53].

Since this ancient Roman empire provided the pattern for Dante's universal monarchy, its legitimacy and justness had to be proved. What other institution could boast of a more resilient and enduring tradition than the Roman empire and evoke more powerful echoes in contemporaries' minds? It was precisely part of Dante's design to utilise this very marked tradition and echo in the service of his *renovatio*. Here he linked history with a religious interpretation and adopted what might be called teleological historicism[54]. While previously the Roman empire was said to have assisted the spread of Christianity and of the Church, it was now to serve, at least conceptually, as a means to overcome the contemporary crisis. Although the ancient Romans were in no wise connected with the Church and were "mere men" and not yet "new creatures", their empire had for Dante nonetheless the prototypical attributes of a world-state, because it had been distinguished by divinity in a singularly convincing way. The introduction of divine volition and sanction as a decisive element in the historical process is a noteworthy device of Dante to underpin his argumentation. For Providence accorded to the Romans – themselves pagans – a crucial role in the spiritual evolution of mankind. Christ was born within their empire; Christ vouchsafed to suffer the supreme penalty under the Romans' authority, and Christianity began to spread within the confines of the empire[55]. Indeed this was the climax of his argumentation in the second book of the tract, for which the other arguments, especially the literary testimonies were merely preliminaries[56]. In parenthesis it may be remarked that Dante faced here a difficulty that was similar to the one which confronted the jurists when they came to answer the question concerning the source of the emperor's universal jurisdiction. Their answer was that in the *lex regia* the Roman people had transferred their power to him[57]. This was as much a constructive device intended to soothe troubled juristic consciences as were the "pièces justificatives" adduced by Dante to prove the justness of the Roman empire. His conclusion was that "Christ gave assurance by deed that the edict of Augustus who exercised the authority of the Romans was just"[58] – in brief, "the Romans prevailed by divine judgment"[59]. It was entirely in line with this historico-religious thesis that Dante operated with the old theory of the four empires, itself based on the Daniel prophesy[60], in which the Roman appeared to complete what had been begun by its precursors[61].

---

[52] I. 16. 1, p. 168f.   [53] Luke 2. 1ff; Gal. 4. 4; Ephes. 1. 10.
[54] Cf. C.T. Davis, *Dante and the idea of Rome*, Oxford 1957, 40f., esp. 55. In dealing with these arguments Guido Vernani said: "Hic iste homo copiosissime deliravit" (ed. cit., 137).
[55] II. 10. 11, p. 212ff. The influence of Orosius and his teleology of history is evident.
[56] The comment by J. Rivière, *Le problème de l'église et de l'état au temps de Philippe le Bel*, Paris–Louvain 1926, 331, seems inappropriate.
[57] Dig. 1. 4. 1. Cf. *PGP*. 101, 223, 281, 296f.
[58] II. 10. 8, p. 214, lines 35–36.   [59] II. 8. 15, p. 203f.
[60] Dan. 7. 14 and 23. The source was clearly Orosius' *Hist. adversus paganos.*
[61] II. 8. 2, p. 200, lines 10–12.

But Dante's universal state is certainly not the Roman-Christian empire reborn by Charlemagne[62] which the Ottonians continued, but primarily the secularised universal state which was to be revived after centuries of hibernation[63]. Quite in keeping with the concept of the citizen who as a result of his rebirth was released from Christian restrictions, Dante released the medieval empire from the ecclesiological embrace which had been one of its central features[64]. The medieval Western empire as depicted in papal decretals and in canonistic writings, was conceived on a purely functional level. Its function was expressed in pregnant concrete symbolism, in rich doxology and in abundant literary expositions. The emperor was to be the extended strong arm of the papacy, its *brachium saeculare* on a universal scale – as universal as the papacy's own writ ran – and was originally in the Frankish age intended as a papal instrument against Byzantium[65]. The auxiliary function of the emperor was amply demonstrated by the absence of a throne and of any kind of enthronement. Evidently, a mere officer needed (and needs) no throne[66]. That the complexion of the medieval Roman emperor was strongly ecclesiological, is therefore comprehensible. Imperial power was derivative and contingent upon the papal *favor apostolicus*[67].

Now this conception of the medieval Roman emperor corresponded in more than one respect to that of the *nova creatura*[68]. Before becoming emperor of the Romans this Ruler was a mere king, paradoxically enough even "king of the Romans", and raised to the pinnacle of supreme power by the papacy but entirely *within* the ecclesiastical framework[69]. Emperorship – like any other Rulership – was the result of the working of divine *gratia* or *favor*[70], was in short a favour, a *beneficium*, as it had already been held in the 5th century[71], and was mediated by the pope, as medieval doctrine and practice had it. No autonomous character attached itself to it. Hence this emperor was made and also unmade by the pope. And when deposed as emperor he was unable to revert to his former kingship. For through his imperial rebirth he had shed his kingly character and was treated on a level different from that which was accorded to him in this royal function. Consequently, a deposed emperor could not regain his kingship of which he had divested himself on becoming emperor.

It is not indeed difficult to see here a very close parallel with the Christian who came into existence through baptismal rebirth. This, it will be recalled, washed

---

[62] On this cf. W. Ullmann, *The Carolingian Renaissance*, London 1969, 138, 169 ff.

[63] Cf. id., *Von Canossa nach Pavia*, HJ 93 (1973) 265 ff.

[64] The imperial coronation ordines are first-rate witnesses. See R. Elze (ed.), *Ordines coronationis imperialis*, Hannover 1960.

[65] For some details W. Ullmann, *Reflexions on the medieval empire*, Transactions Royal Hist. Society, n. s. 14 (1964) 118 ff.

[66] On this see *Short History of the Papacy* (above n. 4) 84 ff, 116 ff, 187.

[67] Allegorically expressed in the sun-moon metaphor to show that the emperor merely reflected papal universal authority, hence Dante's fierce attack on the axiom underlying this allegory.

[68] The papacy always treated the Byzantine emperor as "unregenerated" and the empire as "natural", because it was not "baptized" and not integrated in the ecclesiological framework devised by the papacy. The "renovated" empire was in the West.

[69] Thus the need for a *scrutinium* in some coronation orders.

[70] Cf. *PGP*, 60 n. 2.

away the naturalness of his being and made him a *novus homo*[72]. What Dante quite clearly intended – and both his nomenclature and argumentation bear this out abundantly – was the de-clericalisation of emperor and empire and their rebirth or restoration in the shape of a wholly secular universal Ruler and state. Here again a process of reversal took place: the medieval Roman empire was to revert to, and regain its original character and meaning as the divinely destined entity which had provided the global basis for the deployment of an unadulterated Christianity[73]. This view of Dante's throws significant light on his attempt to master the contemporary crisis by a return to pristine Christianity. This indeed seems to be one of the major themes of Dante unrecognized by modern writers.

Further, on the plane of government, the Ruler was the exact parallel to the individual citizen. Like he, the emperor was now to be autonomous, and his government also. That is why Dante coined the new term of *imperiatus*[74] – a coinage not at all appreciated in its profundity by modern scholarship – which in its juxtaposition with the *papatus* brought the bipolarity into the clearest possible relief. And this *imperiatus* was the abstract expression of monarchy: it *was* the idea of the rule of law which was as autonomous as the citizen was. The Dantesque idea of law was free from ecclesiastical tutelage and encumbrances, and yet was intended by him to serve the cause of Christianity better than the ecclesiastical or canon law which he castigated so severely. And the frequent recourse to the element of nature in his argumentation becomes wholly comprehensible. His universal state was the secularized and mundanised medieval empire – hence its "global" and inclusive character. It was the *humana civilitas* institutionalised and a veritable *renovatio imperii romani*[75], within which Christianity was to reach its purified form to overcome its crisis.

Dante's rebirth of the Ruler and of the idea of law brought in its train a further manifestation of rebirth or *renovatio*. In accordance with his Aristotelian-Thomist basis and the consequential ascending theme of government and law Dante adhered to the point of view that government existed for the sake of the citizens and that government was service to the people. Transposed to public government this thesis meant that the monarch as the governing organ was a *minister omnium*, the servant of all[76]. Now in this personified conception of the rule of law can be found the rebirth or *renovatio* of the Pauline and traditional medieval conception of the Ruler as a *minister Dei* who in the natural order of things reveals himself as the *minister omnium*. In short, government, law and public administration were there for the benefit of man, taking account of his exigencies[77]. Whereas the *minister Dei* was

[71] See Gelasius in the 5th cent., above n. 24, Ep. 12, c. 2, p. 349; also p. 292.
[72] See above n. 8.
[73] In this context cf. Dante's views on Constantine's gifts, *Inferno* 19. 115 ff.
[74] III. 12. 6.
[75] It need hardly be said that this Dantesque idea of *renovatio* signified the process of reversing the baptismal rebirth and had nothing in common with the inscription on Charlemagne's seal.
[76] I. 12. 12, p. 160, lines 34 f.
[77] Thus his emphasis on the specialities and needs of nations, kingdoms, etc. regulated by their own detailed laws: I. 14. 5, p. 164, lines 24 ff. His plea for the vernacular (in *De vulgari eloquentia*) is understandable, because in it the individuality has an adequate outlet.

evidently ecclesiologically as well as theologically conceived and fitted perfectly the descending theme of government and law, the *minister omnium* whether taken in the concrete or abstract sense was the exact counterpart of the reborn citizen: mundane, autonomous, without ecclesiastical accessories.

Furthermore, and also entirely in keeping with the tenor of the tract and its design, the very concept of "Roman" underwent a similar rebirth. Hitherto for governmental purposes the term denoted the adherents of the Church of Rome and was to mark off the contrast to the Greeks who since the 9th century were labelled heretics because of their refusal to acknowledge the primatial function of the papacy. In other words, the term bore for the greater part of the Middle Ages a markedly ecclesiological complexion[78]. In Dante's thought-pattern this concept too shed its traditional connotation, and he was careful enough not to attach the term to the local Romans about whom he kept a significant silence. To him the term "Roman" or Romanity expressed the idea of universality of the rule of law, for which ancient Rome had always been the model. Dante's "Roman" was in short a citizen-member of the conceptually understood world-state that was not composed of Christians only, but of all the *genus humanum*.

In some respects Dante's tract may well be considered, and was certainly intended by him, as a reply to Boniface VIII's *Unam sanctam*, issued a little more than a decade earlier. Yet, the underlying aim of both these products was identical. Their identity of purpose is far from being recognized by modern scholarship. What united them was the rejection of particularism and the aim to find measures by which the fragmentation and disintegration of what was once an integrated whole were to be neutralised. In brief, they both intended to overcome a profoundly religious crisis. What separated them was the means to achieve this end[79].

The means differed fundamentally. These products may well be viewed as classic examples of two opposing schools of thought. *Unam sanctam* realized the dangerous inroads which the fashionable new theses might make into the fabric of the traditional and until recently unquestioned ecclesiological substance characterizing society and government. In order to stem this tide Boniface issued his bull which was constructed on ancient and wholly traditional themes and was intended to present some guidelines for what the papacy held – in the terms of the late 13th century – to be essential axioms if the crisis besetting Christian society and government was to be conquered. Hence once more the emphasis on baptismal rebirth with its attendant consequences for society and government. The theme was the old ecclesiological universalism transgressing all linguistic, ethnic, regional peculiarities. Within this universalist scheme there was no room for a territorial sovereignty, but – and this is the really relevant point – there was also no room for precisely those new concepts which were largely responsible for the decomposition and atomisation, in short were held responsible for bringing about the contemporary religious crisis. And these concepts were the state, the citizen, politics resulting in nationally

[78] For the background cf. W. Ullmann, *On the use of the term Romani in the sources of the early Middle Ages*, Studia Patristica II (1957) 155 ff; G. Tellenbach, *Christlicher und römischer Reichsgedanke*, SAH 1934–35.

[79] For some details of the points here raised cf. W. Ullmann, *Die Bulle Unam Sanctam: Rückblick und Ausblick*, Röm. Hist. Mitt. 16 (1974) 32–60.

inspired churches. The theme underlying these new concepts was the rebirth or *renovatio* of the hitherto forgotten natural man. Their substance was a *duplex ordo*, was bipolarity. It is one of the most fascinating features of the literature of the early 14th century that for the first time in the Middle Ages tracts came to be written which *ex professo* dealt with the old and now seriously threatened universalism. The literary products which followed the lead given by *Unam sanctam* provided no space and could not provide any for the accomodation of the citizen, the state and politics either as a science or as the public activity of the citizens. The system of unipolarity militated against any such accomodation or incorporation of these inherently antagonistic concepts.

Dante on the other hand although pursuing these same aims in order to master the contemporary crisis, operated almost exclusively with the new concepts in constructing his philosophy, that is, the *humana civilitas*, the *materia politica* and above all the citizen and his main public occupation which was *politizare*[80]. In this civic activity of *politizare* which eventually means government, lies the hallmark of the citizen. The subject has the duty to obey the law given by superior authority and cannot within this descending theme of government argue or discuss or *politizare* in the Aristotelian or Dantesque sense[81]. It is indeed rare that within a decade two tracts appeared which pursued identical aims, and yet set out from entirely different standpoints. The identity of their interests centred in the deeply religious crisis that had largely arisen from the critical stage through which contemporary theology was passing. The intellectual and religious crisis of the early 14th century was epitomized in Dante and Boniface. The former postulated consent based on freedom of choice: the pursuit of eternal beatitude was in no wise thereby affected – it was facilitated. The latter represented the traditional view for whom salvation resulting from faith alone mattered. His unipolarity looked backwards, whereas Dante's bipolarity looked forward.

---

[80] I. 12. 9, p. 159f. Shortly afterwards Marsilius of Padua was also to use this term: *Defensor Pacis* I. 13. 2. The term itself was a new coinage and a Latin form of the Greek *politeuein*.

[81] P. G. Ricci, ed. cit., ad loc. p. 160 says "il verbo *politizare* indice sempre (?) il governo secondo il rispetto delle leggi a vantaggio del bene comune". The term has not attracted the attention which is its due.

IX

ZUR ENTWICKLUNG DES SOUVERÄNITÄTSBEGRIFFES IM SPÄTMITTELALTER

Der bescheidene Beitrag, mit dem ich mich an der Nikolaus Grass gewidmeten Festschrift beteilige, berührt sich in manchen Punkten mit den vielschichtigen Arbeitsthemen des Jubilars. Die bewunderungswürdige Spannweite seiner Arbeiten auf rechtshistorischem, liturgischem, lokalhistorischem, kirchengeschichtlichem und politisch-historischem Gebiete hat die Wahl eines ihn vielleicht ansprechenden Themas insofern erleichtert, als es sich mit einer Problematik beschäftigt, die innig mit der allgemeinen Rechtsgeschichte, dem nie versiegenden Einfluß des römischen Rechts und der auf das moderne staatsrechtliche Denken nachhaltig einwirkenden päpstlichen Dekretalengesetzgebung verzahnt ist. Möge der Aufsatz von dem verehrten Jubilar im Geiste landsmannschaftlicher Verbundenheit und kollegialer Freundschaft entgegengenommen werden. Wir beide sind dankbare Söhne der Alma Mater Oenipontana, deren Lehrer unserer Generation immer Vorbilder selbstloser, der reinen Wissenschaft allein ergebenen Forscher gewesen sind.

I.

In den zahlreichen Untersuchungen über den Hintergrund und die Entwicklung des Begriffes der Souveränität (oder der Hoheit) wird, so will es scheinen, zu wenig Beachtung einer grundsätzlichen Unterscheidung geschenkt. Es handelt sich um die Unterteilung des Begriffes in eine persönliche und eine unpersönliche Komponente. Die erstere ließe sich auch mit innerer, die letztere mit äußerer Souveränität wiedergeben.

Soweit sich feststellen läßt, hat bisher die persönliche oder innere Souveränität das Interesse der Forschung erweckt. Das hat ganz gewiß seinen guten Grund, denn historisch hat sich diese Komponente — wie so vieles andere im Niemandsland, das zwischen Recht und Politik liegt — aus dem römisch-rechtlichen Begriff der Jurisdiktion entwickelt[1]. Nur hätte diese persönliche Seite der Souveränität nicht zum ausschließlichen Gegenstand der Forschung gemacht werden sollen. Die Frage, die um diese persönlich bezogene Souveränität kreist, ließe sich vulgärsprachlich aber in immerhin anschaulicher Art in die Worte kleiden: „Wer ist der Herr im Hause?" Es dürfte daher verständlich sein, wenn man die Behauptung aufstellt, daß der Urgrund der staats-

---

[1] Zu diesem Begriff vgl. zuletzt P. Costa, Iurisdictio: Semantica del potere politico nella pubblicistica medioevale (Mailand 1969) (= Pubblicazioni della Facoltà di Giurisprudenza; Università di Firenze, Bd. 1), bes. S. 94ff.; vgl. auch W. Ullmann, Law and the Medieval Historian, Rapports du XIe Congrès international des sciences historiques (Stockholm 1960), Bd. 3, S. 34ff.

rechtlichen Souveränität, d. h. der inneren Komponente, in der Gesetzgebungsgewalt liegt, was so viel heißt, daß die endgültige und oberste Entscheidung
sich in der Formulierung und Festlegung eines bindenden Rechtssatzes äußert.
Im Vordergrund steht die richterliche Funktion desjenigen, der die Macht hat
ius dicere. Innerhalb dieses gedanklichen Rahmens der „Jurisdiktion" entspricht die Fixierung des bindenden Rechtssatzes einem Urteil, das von der
obersten Gerichtsinstanz erlassen ist. Die in allen frühen Rechtsordnungen
anzutreffende oberstrichterliche Befugnis des Herrschers wird begreiflicherweise zum Vorstadium der Rechtsetzungsbefugnis. Erst damit erhält der
Gedanke der Souveränität greifbare Gestalt. Deren ursprüngliches Wesen
bestand in der Unanfechtbarkeit der erlassenen Entscheidung.

Geschichtlich und im Rahmen der westeuropäischen mittelalterlichen
Entwicklung hat sich diese Komponente des Souveränitätsbegriffes geäußert
in dem Sprachbild von dem Herrscher, der *supra populum* stand. Das Volk
wurde als dem Herrscher überantwortet aufgefaßt — *populus sibi commissus* —
und dieser Gedanke kehrt in einer Anzahl von Redewendungen wieder, von
denen die meisten sich auf kirchenrechtliche Vorstellungen und theologische
Vorbilder zurückführen lassen[2]. Die Voraussetzung für diese Begriffsentwicklung war die Scheidung — wenigstens gedanklich — zwischen Herrscher und
Volk. Jener setzte sich von diesem ab, womit sehr deutlich zum Ausdruck kam,
daß das Volk dem Herrscher keine Macht verliehen hatte. Grundlage und
Ausgangspunkt war der theokratische Gedanke, der sich im *Rex Dei gratia*
manifestierte. Die rechtstheoretische Folge war, daß das Volk diese Macht
weder einschränken noch erweitern noch entziehen konnte. Die Gleichsetzung
des Volkes mit einem Minderjährigen in der Staatslehre des Mittelalters findet
daher ihre zwanglose Erklärung[3].

Der wesentliche Bestandteil dieser persönlichen Komponente war der
Herrscher und seine Person, und nicht eine abstrakte Wesenheit, die sich als
Mittelpunkt des Begriffs erwies. Diesem persönlich verstandenen Souveränitätsbegriff ist es zuzuschreiben, daß das Verbrechen des *crimen laesae maiestatis*
zwingend als die Kehrseite des Begriffs angesehen werden mußte. Das heißt,
weil der Herrscher über dem Volk steht, weil das Volk ihm anvertraut ist,

---

[2] Vgl. darüber W. Ullmann, Principles of Government and Politics in the Middle Ages,
2. Aufl. (London 1966), S. 121 ff.; ders., Der Souveränitätsgedanke in den mittelalterlichen
Krönungsordines, in: Festschrift für P. E. Schramm, Bd. 1 (Wiesbaden 1964), S. 72 ff.

[3] Verwiesen sei auf meinen Aufsatz, Juristic obstacles to the emergence of the concept of the
state in the Middle Ages, in: Annali di storia del diritto, 12—13 (1968—69) (= Gedächtnisschrift für F. Calasso), S. 40 ff., bes., 52 ff., sowie The Carolingian Renaissance and the Idea
of kingship (London 1969), S. 178 ff. Gaines Post, Studies in medieval legal thought (Princeton 1964), versucht oftmals über den Souveränitätsbegriff abzuhandeln, bringt uns aber trotz
seines großen Fleißes nicht weiter, weil er sich über grundsätzliche Dinge nicht klar geworden
ist. Er verwässert die Begriffe, die dabei zerfließen. Vorstellungen wie Patriotismus, Nationalismus, u. ä. mehr, wenn sie ins 13. oder 14. Jh. hineingetragen werden, können nur Unheil
anrichten. Vgl. auch unten A. 16.

steht er bildlich gesprochen „höher" *(magis)* als das Volk, was einerseits zum Rechtsbegriff der Hoheit *(Magestas = Maiestas)* sowie zur personifizierten Hoheit, Altezza, Majestät usw. führt, und anderseits, vom staatsrechtlichen Standpunkt aus gesehen, ein Angriff auf die Hoheit als Verletzung dieser selbigen Majestät notwendigerweise verstanden werden mußte, was dann strafrechtlich wiederum zum *Hoch*verrat (dem Majestätsverbrechen) wurde. Und mit dieser persönlich gefaßten Souveränitätskomponente steht in innigstem Zusammenhang die Rechtssymbolik des Throns und die damit rechtssymbolisch wie auch rechtstheoretisch bedeutsame Thronsetzung, denn wer „magis" („maius") ist, muß auch in entsprechender Weise äußerlich als „höher stehend" in Erscheinung treten, was am eindrucksvollsten durch den erhöhten Sitz ausgedrückt werden konnte[4]. Daß die Weihe des Herrschers die Bedeutung des persönlichen Elements der Souveränität nachdrücklichst und schärfstens betonte, ist so einleuchtend, daß ich mir weitere Einzelheiten ersparen darf[5]. Die Weihe des Herrschers stellte sich — dies sei en passant vermerkt — als ein sehr erhebliches Hindernis für die gedankliche Erfassung des Staates im abstrakten Sinne dar, denn es war der Herrscher selbst (und nicht ein fingiertes oder abstraktes Rechtsgebilde), der von Gott in einzigartiger Weise ausgezeichnet worden war. Er allein empfing die Weihe zum König; er allein wurde König durch den Empfang der göttlichen Gnade (d. h. *Rex Dei gratia*), die ihm das *beneficium* der Herrschergewalt verlieh, was schließlich nichts anderes als die konkretisierte mittelalterliche Auslegung und Anwendung der paulinischen Lehre war (Röm. 13. 1 ff.).

Eben weil der Herrscher über dem Volk stand, hatte er die Superiorität *(Superioritas = Soveranitas)*, die sich begrifflich als Souveränität im vollen Umfang erweist, und zwar innerhalb der rein persönlichen Komponente[6]. Der Herrscher verkörpert alle dem Hoheitsbegriff eigentümlichen Rechte — daher die (rechtliche) Unmöglichkeit, ihn vor die Schranken eines Gerichtes zu ziehen; daher besitzt er auch Vollgewalt (die *plenitudo potestatis*) der Rechtssetzung, eine Idee, die sowohl im römischen als auch im kanonischen Recht grundsätzliche Bedeutung erlangt hatte und sich in dem Satz widerspiegelte, daß der *Princeps omnia iura in suo pectore habet*[7]; daher auch der als unum-

---

[4] Es sei nebenbei bemerkt, daß der Thron in Westeuropa sehr wahrscheinlich auf bischöfliches Vorbild zurückgeht. Vgl. H. U. Instinsky, Bischofsstuhl und Kaiserthron (München 1955); vor allem P. E. Schramm, Herrschaftszeichen, Bd. 2 (Stuttgart 1958).

[5] Die Königsweihe blieb ein Sakrament bis tief ins 13. Jh. Vgl. etwa Robert Grosseteste, den Bischof von Lincoln, zit. bei L. Wickham-Legg, English Coronation Records (London 1901), S. 67; oder auch Papst Alexander IV. in 1257, zit. bei P. E. Schramm, Der König von Navarra, in: ZRG Germ. Abt. 68 (1951), S. 147.

[6] Reiche Angaben über die Etymologie bei F. Calasso, I Glossatori e la teoria della sovranità: studio di diritto comune pubblico, 3. Aufl. (Mailand 1957), S. 44, A. 11.

[7] Römisches Recht: C. VI. 23. 19; Kirchenrecht: VI: I. 2. 1. Vgl. in diesem Zusammenhang die Anwendung auf den französischen König: "Cum rex Francie omne imperium habet in regno suo, quod imperator habet in imperio ... et de potest dici (sicut de imperatore dicitur)

stößlich geltende Grundsatz, daß der Herrscher kein Unrecht setzen kann
(The king can do no wrong) und er rechtlich ungebunden war — *legibus solutus*[8] — was der Stellung des Herrschers als einer *Lex animata* gleichkommt[9];
daher auch die rechtliche Unmöglichkeit, seine Entscheidungen, seien sie
rechtssetzender, rechtsfindender oder urteilender Art, einer höheren Instanz
zur Prüfung vorzulegen, wie es schon im frühen 5. Jh. für den Papst beansprucht wurde[10] oder wie Innozenz III. i. J. 1203 für den französischen König
postulierte: „Cum Rex (Francorum) superiorem in temporalibus minime
recognoscat"[11]. Das Gegenstück zur *Superioritas* war die Stellung des Einzelnen
als *inferior*, als Unter/tan, als *sub/ditus*, als *sub/ject*[12]. Der Herrscher bildete,
sozusagen, seinen eigenen Stand, den er mit niemand teilen konnte noch auch
zu teilen gewillt war. Die scharfe Profilierung der persönlichen Souveränitätskomponente erfuhr durch den Untertaneneid noch eine sehr beachtliche
Verstärkung. Denn der Eid, den der *inferior* (der Untertan) dem *Superior*
(dem Herrscher) leistete, brachte die Souveränität des letzteren gegenüber dem
Untertanen durch seine feierliche religiöse Form umso überzeugender zum
Ausdruck.

Die Entwicklung des monarchisch verstandenen Souveränitätsgedankens
im Bereich der Staatslehre wurde mächtig gefördert durch das Eindringen und
die Verbreitung weiterer römisch-rechtlicher Grundsätze, wie sie in der
Justinianischen Kodifikation dem Hochmittelalter vermittelt wurden. Unter
diesen Grundsätzen nimmt einen hervorragenden Platz der Rechtssatz ein:
Quod principi placuit, habet legis vigorem[13]. Diese eine weite Verbreitung
findenden Rechtsgrundsätze in Verbindung mit der deutschrechtlichen Munt
formten das staatsrechtliche Antlitz des Herrschers nachhaltig[14]. Was insbe-

---

videlicet quod omnia iura, precipue iura competentia regno suo, in eius pectore sunt inclusa,
et ideo de eo et de eius actibus et conscientia sic debet presumi, ut scriptum est de imperatore . . .
Rex Francie . . ." (wie Text): französische Denkschrift verfaßt etwa 1296, hsg. F. Kern, Acta
Imperii Angliae et Franciae (Tübingen, 1911), S. 200, nr. 271, Z. 9ff. Ähnliche Gedankengänge
auch in der Denkschrift der französischen Regierung selbst, ebd., S. 201—206, nr. 274.

[8] Diese Maxime haben zum Gegenstand nicht so sehr das materielle Recht, sondern die
Rechtsdurchsetzung. Der Herrscher kann nicht zum Gegenstand von Anklagen gemacht
werden, obwohl (sachlich und materiell-rechtlich gesprochen) sein Verhalten Unrecht darstellt.
Vgl. dazu meine Ausführungen in Principles (wie oben A. 2), S. 176ff. und die sehr lehrreichen
Beobachtungen bei P. Costa (oben A. 1), S. 186—191.

[9] Über die *Lex animata* siehe die vorbildliche Untersuchung von A. Steinwenter, Νόμος
ἔμψυχος: Zur Geschichte einer politischen Theorie, Anzeiger der Akademie der Wissenschaften
Wien, phil. hist. Kl. 83 (1946).

[10] Siehe Migne, P. L. 20. 676 (auch in der Avellana, S. 115—16) und Kol. 777f.; vgl. ebenfalls Coelestin I., ebd. 50.437.

[11] Innozenz III. in X: IV. 13. 17.

[12] Für die Einzelheiten darf ich verweisen auf Individual and Society in the Middle Ages
(Baltimore/London 1966), bes. S. 13ff. (deutsch (Göttingen 1974) S. 15ff.).

[13] Dig. 1. 4. 1 (Ulpian). Siehe auch E. Cortese, Il problema della sovranità nel pensiero
giuridico medioevale (Rom, 1966), S. 93ff.

[14] Vgl. meine Beobachtungen in meiner Carolingian Renaissance, cit. (oben A. 3), S. 175ff.

sondere festzuhalten gilt, ist erstens die Betonung der *voluntas principis* als des Elements, das dem Rechtssatz bindende Wirkung verleiht, und zweitens die Übertragung dieser im wesentlichen durch die Rechtslehre verbreiteten Anschauungen vom römischen Princeps auf den mittelalterlichen König. Das Ergebnis war die klare Formulierung des Grundsatzes, der das staatsrechtliche Bild auf Generationen hinaus beeinflußte, daß der König in seinem Königreich dem Kaiser gleichzustellen sei: *Rex in regno suo est imperator*[15]. Das bedeutete natürlich nicht, daß auch der ideelle universalistische Grundgedanke des Kaisertums übernommen wurde. Im Laufe des 13. Jhs. fand dieses trächtige Schlagwort reichen Widerhall, sowohl in der Literatur als auch in den Urkunden der Könige[16].

Diese höchst einprägsame Formel drückte im gängigen Sprachgebrauch des 13. Jhs. die Idee der Souveränität aus, wodurch gleichzeitig die Lehre der Souveränität auf praktischer Ebene einen gewaltigen Antrieb erhielt. Zweierlei soll allerdings dabei beachtet werden.

Erstens die Rechts- und Staatslehre des 13. Jhs., insbesondere in Frankreich[17], begann den persönlich gefaßten Souveränitätsbegriff viel schärfer zu fassen als dies bisher der Fall gewesen war. Das ist auch leicht verständlich, wenn man bedenkt, daß die reale Machtbasis eines Königs es erleichterte, eine der Rechtswirklichkeit adäquate Lehre zu gestalten. Die Formel des *Rex-Imperator* hatte eine zweifache Spitze. Die eine richtete sich gegen den auf universaler Ebene

---

[15] Ob und welche Verbindungslinien zwischen Innozenz III. und der zeitgenössischen Kanonistik bestanden, bedarf noch genauerer Untersuchung. Jedenfalls sei auf eine Äußerung eines Zeitgenossen Innozenz' verwiesen, der behauptete, "rex eadem auctoritate, eadem consecratione et eodem crismate inungitur (wie der Kaiser, was übrigens nicht ganz richtig war), non ergo potestatis diversitas". Die Stelle habe ich zitiert in einem größeren Zusammenhang in Medieval Papalism (London 1949), S. 145 A. 2 a. E. Vgl. ferner Alanus Anglicus: "Et quod dictum est de imperatore, dictum habeatur de quolibet rege vel principe, qui nulli subest. Unusquisque enim tantum iuris habet in regno suo, quantum imperator in imperio" zit. nach J. F. Schulte in Sitz. Ber. Wien, phil. hist. Kl. 66 (1870), S. 89. Vgl. schon Huguccio in seinem Dekret Kommentar: "Rex in regno suo edidit edictum, imperator constituit constitutionem, vel idem est rex et imperator" (ad Dist. 2, c. 4, in Hs. Pembroke College, Cambridge no. 72, fol. 118ra). Über die Synthese, die Huguccio bereits erreicht hatte, s. S. Mochi Onory, Fonti canonistiche dell'idea moderna dello stato (Mailand 1951), bes. S. 165 ff. (die hier zit. Stelle S. 167).

[16] Aus der Literatur, die zahlreiche Stellen bringt, sei erwähnt S. Mochi Onory (vorige Anm.), S. 271 ff.; W. Ullmann, The development of medieval idea of sovereignty, in: Engl. Hist. Rev. 64 (1949), S. 7 ff.; F. Ercole, L'origine francese di una nota formula bartoliana, in: Archivio storico italiano, 73 (1915), S. 274 ff.; F. Calasso, I glossatori, zit. (oben A. 6), bes. S. 42 ff. (mit einer ausgezeichneten Exegese der Dekretale Innozenz' III.) und seine Entdeckung und Ausgabe von Marinus de Caramanico, ebd., S. 125 ff. (Edition der Vorrede, S. 175 ff.). Vgl. ferner G. de Vergottini, Il diritto pubblico italiano nei s. XII—XIV, 3. Aufl. (Mailand 1960), S. 203 ff. O. Brunner, Land und Herrschaft, 4. Aufl. (Wien-Wiesbaden 1959) u. 5. Aufl. (Wien 1965), S. 390 ff., die 6. Aufl. (anastatischer Nachdruck, Wiesbaden 1970) ist unverändert. Obwohl bei ihm ein Kapitel die Überschrift trägt *Rex-Imperator*, ist sich G. Post (oben A. 3) weder über die staatsrechtliche noch rechtstheoretische Bedeutung klar, trotz der vielen Stellen, die er emsig zusammengetragen hat.

[17] Darüber s. F. Ercole, op. cit.; auch F. Calasso, op. cit., bes. S. 42 ff.

verstandenen Kaiser der Römer und seine ebenso universal gedachte Jurisdiktionsgewalt, die durch die Übertragung eben derselben Hoheitsrechte auf den König beschnitten werden sollte. Man wäre fast versucht, zu sagen, das Substrat dieser Lehre gipfelte in der Parole ,,mit dem römischen Recht gegen den römischen Kaiser". Die andere Spitze hatte zum Ziel, den König mit Hilfe römisch-rechtlicher Rechtssätze gegen die kirchlichen und adeligen Mächte abzuschirmen, um so den schon etwas angeschlagenen monarchischen Gedanken zu neuem Glanz wiederherzustellen. Erst dadurch sah man die Möglichkeit, der Idee des ,,Herrn im eigenen Hause" einen konkreten Inhalt zu verleihen.

Die zweite Überlegung führt über das rein staatsrechtliche Gebiet hinaus und eröffnet Perspektiven, die den Souveränitätsgedanken erst richtig ins Blickfeld der Rechtsgeschichte rücken lassen, die aber ebenso einen Einblick in das keimhafte, wenn auch zur Geltung drängende Völkerrecht gewähren. In den bisherigen Untersuchungen wird allenthalben übersehen, daß die persönlich gefaßte Komponente der Souveränitätsidee nur einen — wenn auch wesentlichen und unabdingbaren — Bestandteil des vollen Souveränitätsbegriffs ausmacht. Zu der persönlichen Komponente tritt eine unpersönliche, und zwar eine solche, die man als die dingliche Komponente bezeichnen könnte. Diese Behauptung zwingt aber, jetzt, wo wir uns den Blick für einige strukturelle Elemente geschärft haben, zu Bemerkungen allgemein-grundsätzlicher Art.

II.

Die persönliche Komponente der Souveränität sagt ihrem ureigensten Wesen entsprechend noch nichts aus über den räumlichen Geltungsbereich des vom Herrscher erlassenen Rechts oder seiner Entscheidungen. Die Frage, die sich hier mit zwingender Notwendigkeit aufdrängt, betrifft den räumlichen Wirkungsbereich der hoheitlichen Rechtsverfügungen. Auf welches Territorium sind die Rechtsanordnungen des Herrschers, gleichgültig welcher Art, anwendbar? Für uns im 20. Jh. birgt eine solche Frage keinerlei Schwierigkeiten, aber es bedarf nur geringer historischer Vorstellungskraft, sich zu vergegenwärtigen, daß, wenn sie einmal gestellt wurde, die Frage im 13. oder 14. Jh. von durchaus keiner untergeordneten Bedeutung war. Obwohl zweifellos eine tatsächlich beobachtete Rechtsübung viel zur Klärung der Frage beigetragen hat, stand dennoch eine rechtsdogmatisch befriedigende Lösung noch aus. Als unumstößlicher Grundsatz muß festgehalten werden, daß an dem ideell verstandenen universalen Jurisdiktionsanspruch des Kaisers der Römer wenigstens theoretisch vor Ende des 13. Jhs. nicht gerüttelt worden war. Neben ihm aber bestanden gerade jene Könige, die sich selbst genau dieselben Hoheitsrechte zuschrieben wie sie der Kaiser besaß, wenn auch nicht auf universaler Ebene. Das Nebeneinander der beiden unversöhnlichen Gegensätze barg ganz gewiß ein sehr ernstes Problem in sich, das auch mit nicht zu

unterschätzenden Gefahren politischer Art verbunden war. Die Problematik
in ihrer ganzen Tragweite und Wucht erschloß sich im frühen 14. Jh., und
zwar anläßlich eines konkreten Falles, der schlagartig die tiefe Bedeutung der
Frage erkennen ließ. Es handelt sich um nichts Geringeres als um den Kern
und das Wesen des Kaisers der Römer in seiner rechtlichen Beziehung zu den
Territorialstaaten. Im modernen Sprachgebrauch: Das Problem betraf die
existentielle Berechtigung einer überstaatlichen, wenn auch rein ideellen
Macht in der Form des römisch-kaiserlichen Jurisdiktionsanspruchs.

Es leuchtet ein, daß der richtig verstandene Kaiserbegriff — der *Imperator
Romanorum* als *dominus mundi*, wie ihn die *Lex Rhodia* seit unvordenklichen
Zeiten bezeichnete[18] — an keine territorial begrenzte Jurisdiktionsgewalt
gebunden sein konnte, wenn auch in der rauhen Wirklichkeit dieser Jurisdiktionsanspruch bloße Theorie geblieben war. Aber der ideelle Anspruch war
einmal da, und als solcher verdiente er in seiner theoretischen mit dem Kaiserbegriff untrennbar verbundenen Struktur immerhin Bedeutung. Um diesem
universalen Jurisdiktionsanspruch den entsprechenden Nachdruck zu verleihen,
erließ Kaiser Heinrich VII. am 2. April 1313 ein grundlegendes Reichsgesetz.
Darin brachte er den im römischen Kaisertum gegründeten universalen Jurisdiktionsanspruch klar und unzweideutig zum Ausdruck[19]. Den Sinn dieses
Gesetzes drückte Heinrich Mitteis einmal sehr schön aus — es sei, „als wolle
der Kaiseradler noch einmal seine Schwingen entfalten, als sollten die Wunsch-
träume politischer Denker in Erfüllung gehen"[20].

In diesem kaiserlichen Verfassungsgesetz erklärte Heinrich VII., daß in dem
ungestörten Bestand des römischen Reiches die sinngemäße Ordnung des
Erdkreises ruhe — *in cuius* (scil. Romani imperii) *tranquillitate totius orbis
regularitas requiescit* — daß aber dieser Zustand durch Verschwörungen und
Aufwiegelungen ernstlich gestört sei. Er erinnert daran, daß jedermann dem
Kaiser untertan sei, was sowohl weltliche als auch geistliche Gesetze schon
lange als Recht niedergelegt hätten: *Quibus* (scil. praeceptis) *iubetur, quod
omnis anima Romano principi sit subiecta.* Der Anklang an die bonifazianische
Unam sanctam kann kaum überhört werden. Um den Frieden wiederherzustellen, sei ein rein summarisches Verfahren gegen Übeltäter und Friedens-
störer angemessen. Sollten jene, die des Verbrechens des Hochverrates ange-

---

[18] Vgl. etwa Accursius in seiner Glosse ad Dig. 2. 1. 1, s. v. Potestas. Weder hier noch an
anderen Stellen wird das territoriale Element erwähnt. Oder von den späteren vgl. etwa Cynus,
ibid. (ed. Frankfurt 1553), fol. 21va, nr. 15: "Iurisdictio est potestas publicae personae competens, officium est exercitium ipsius potestatis". Der Aufsatz von A. Cecchini, Impero,
papato e comunità nelle dottrine dei glossatori, in: Atti Accursiani, hsg. G. Rossi (Mailand
1968), I. 115—130, behandelt bloß die Abgrenzung der Jurisdiktionsgewalt der Kirche und
des Kaisers im Lichte der neueren Literatur.

[19] M. G. H. Const. IV. 2, nr. 929 und nr. 930 in französischer Übersetzung.

[20] H. Mitteis, Der Staat des hohen Mittelalters, 2. durchges. Aufl. (Weimar 1944), S. 1 u.
8. Aufl. (Weimar 1968), S. 2.

klagt seien, trotz förmlicher Vorladung nicht erscheinen, seien sie rechtmäßig nach summarischer Beweisaufnahme abzuurteilen. Schließlich wurde dieses Gesetz auch mit rückwirkender Kraft ausgestattet[21].

Auf Grund dieses Gesetzes wurde in der Tat kurz nachher Anklage gegen König Robert von Neapel wegen Majestätsverbrechen erhoben. Der angeklagte König erschien nicht, worauf am 26. April 1313 das Urteil gegen ihn gesprochen, er schuldig erkannt und wegen *perduellio* zur vorgesehenen Strafe des Todes und zum Verlust aller Ämter und seines Vermögens verurteilt wurde[22]. Daraufhin rief der König Klemens V. an[23], der in seiner grundlegenden Entscheidung *Pastoralis Cura* die dingliche Seite der Souveränitätsidee präzise zum Ausdruck brachte und damit einen gewaltigen Schritt zur Erweiterung und Erfassung des Souveränitätsbegriffes selbst tat. Erst durch diese Dekretale[24] hat der Souveränitätsgedanke und -begriff seinen vollen Inhalt bekommen. Der Grund, warum die Dekretale trotz mehrfacher Untersuchungen[25] noch nicht die gebührende Anerkennung in den Darstellungen zur Geschichte der Staatslehren gefunden hat, liegt in der mangelnden Unterscheidung der beiden das Wesen des Souveränitätsbegriffs konstituierenden Elemente. Nur durch präzise Scheidung dieser beiden Sphären (der persönlichen und der dinglichen) kann man zu einer vollen Erkenntnis der Souveränität vordringen[26].

---

[21] "Hanc autem generalem nostram legem extendi iubemus ad praeterita, pendentia et futura ..." loc. cit., S. 965f. Es scheint, daß der Begriff der *regularitas* hier zum ersten Male auftritt, jedenfalls läßt er sich nicht im klassischen oder nachklassischen Latein nachweisen. Über die *tranquillitas* vgl. H. Fichtenau, Arenga (= MIÖG. Erg. Bd. 18 (1957)), S. 69f. Das Gesetz wurde auch als extravagante Novelle unter der Collatio XI dem Corpus Iuris Civ. einverleibt, wo es die Überschrift erhielt: *Quomodo in laesae maiestatis crimine procedatur.* Das Gesetz lehnt sich sehr an die Denkschrift von Anfang 1313 an, insbes. hinsichtlich des Anspruchs auf die universale kaiserliche Jurisdiktion, siehe M. G. H. Const. IV. 2, nr. 1248, S. 1309, Z. 36ff. Nach M. Thilo, Das Recht der Entscheidung über Krieg und Frieden im Streite Heinrichs VII. mit der römischen Kurie (= Hist. Studien, 1938), soll der Verfasser der Schrift Johannes von Calvaroso in Sizilien gewesen sein, s. S. 13, genauere Analyse, S. 68ff.

[22] M. G. H. Const. IV. 2, nr. 946, S. 986—990.

[23] M. G. H. cit., nr. 1253, S. 1369ff.

[24] Enthalten in den Clementinen, II. 11. 2; auch in M. G. H. cit., nr. 1166, S. 1211f. Ich behandle hier nur jene Elemente der Dekretale, die unmittelbaren Bezug auf den Souveränitätsbegriff hatten, und übergehe die lehensrechtliche Komponente, auf die sich der Papst als Lehensherr Roberts beruft. Ebenso enthalte ich mich einer Bewertung des Verhaltens Heinrichs VII. Im Vordergrund steht die Dekretale in ihrer juristischen Bedeutung.

[25] Siehe E. Will (unten Anm. 26); F. Calasso, I glossatori, zit. (oben Anm. 6); W. Ullmann, Engl. Hist. Rev. (oben A. 16), wo des Andreas de Isernia als Wegbereiters der Dekretale gedacht wurde (S. 23ff.); Mario delle Piane, Intorno ad una bolla papale: la Pastoralis cura di Clemente V, Rivista di storia del diritto italiano 31 (1958), S. 23—56, geht trotz seines Bestrebens, Licht in die schwierige Materie zu bringen, auf den rechtsgeschichtlichen Inhalt und Hintergrund nicht ein; P. Costa, Iurisdictio, zit. (oben A. 1), S. 333ff. über Marinus.

[26] Wie sorgfältig der Papst die Sache erwogen hatte, läßt sich aus den einschlägigen Gutachten erkennen, insbes. Oldradus de Ponte (Consilia, ed. Lyons 1550, nr. 43, 69, 88). Über die Übereinstimmung des Gutachtens von Oldradus mit der Dekretale, siehe E. Will, Die Gutachten des Oldradus de Ponte zum Prozeß Heinrichs VII. gegen Robert von Neapel (= Abhandlungen zur mittleren u. neueren Geschichte, Bd. 65 (1917)), S. 45ff. Siehe ferner M. G. H.

Der Schwerpunkt der Dekretale betrifft die juristische Überlegung, daß eine Vorladung vor Gericht außerhalb des Gerichtssprengels des judizierenden Richters rechtsunwirksam ist. In der Übertragung dieses Grundsatzes auf das Gebiet der Staatslehre liegt die Bedeutung dieser Dekretale, denn dadurch wurde erstens dem römischen Kaiser die universale Jurisdiktionsgewalt (wie sie eben erst kürzlich in dem erwähnten Reichsgesetz proklamiert worden war) abgesprochen, was wiederum zur Folge hatte, daß das Kaisertum als universale Einrichtung jetzt auch in ideeller Hinsicht verschwand (faktisch war es schon lange dahin) — eine Folge, die in diesem Zusammenhang nicht weiter zu untersuchen ist[27] — und zweitens, daß die Jurisdiktionsgewalt eines Herrschers sich nur auf ein solches Territorium erstreckt, in dem sie erzwingbar und vollstreckbar ist. Diesem Hauptargument der Dekretale reiht sich noch eine weitere Überlegung an, die, obwohl sie sicherlich auf die Praxis zurückgreifen konnte, nichtsdestoweniger hier, so weit sich feststellen läßt, juristisch und gesetzgeberisch ihre erste klare Formulierung fand. Danach ist Voraussetzung für die Ausübung der Jurisdiktion, daß das Verbrechen auf dem Territorium begangen wurde, in dem sich der Apparat zur wirksamen Verfolgung befindet. Das aber sei der Fall nur innerhalb eines begrenzten Gebietes. Ferner stellt die Dekretale fest, daß der Wohnsitz des Angeklagten von juristischer Bedeutung ist. Eine rechtswirksame Ausübung der Jurisdiktion setzt daher die tatsächliche und nicht bloß juristisch konstruierbare Begehung des Verbrechens auf dem Herrschaftsgebiet voraus, in dem der Täter seinen Wohnsitz hat. Da aber der König sein Land nicht verlassen und sein Domizil nicht verändert hatte, kann die Anklage wegen Majestätsverbrechens gegen den Kaiser nicht erhoben werden. Vom juristischen Standpunkt aus gesehen, legt die Dekretale klar die Zuständigkeit im Rahmen des keimenden Völkerrechts fest.

Die Frage steht obenan, auf welcher juristischen Grundlage der Papst diese Dekretale erlassen konnte. Ist sie auch historisch fundiert? Es fällt nicht schwer, die Frage zu beantworten. Die rechtlich bedeutsamen Grundlagen stammen aus der Rüstkammer des römischen Rechts, des Kirchenrechts und der kirchlichen Praxis und Tradition, die sich bis hinauf ins spätrömische Zeitalter verfolgen läßt. Der Ausgangspunkt der päpstlichen Überlegungen ist unschwer zu erkennen. Der Herrscher wird auf die Stufe eines Diözesanbischofs gestellt. Anders ausgedrückt, auf das Königreich — und andere staatsrechtlich erhebliche Gebiete — werden die für den Bischofssprengel niedergelegten Grundsätze übertragen. Die territorial beschränkte Jurisdiktion des Bischofs

---

Const. IV. 2, nr. 1254 und 1255, S. 1373—1398; besonders das letztgenannte geht mit Scharfsinn auf die rein juristischen Verhältnisse ein. Das juristische Rüstzeug bedarf noch genauerer Analyse.

[27] Schon F. Bock, Reichsidee und Nationalstaaten (München 1943), S. 140, bemerkte, die Kurie „hatte damit theoretisch das Reich als Institution aufgegeben".

gründete sich juristisch offenbar auf das römische Recht[28]. Dieses altrömische Recht wurde durch das Zweite Ökumenische Konzil von Konstantinopel (381) zu einem kirchlichen Rechtssatz erhoben[29] und von hier fand es Eingang in fast alle einschlägigen Kanonessammlungen bis hinunter zu den großen Sammlungen des Hochmittelalters, wo die örtliche Zuständigkeit des Bischofs noch durch eine Anzahl weiterer Dekrete unterbaut wurde[30]. Die rechtliche Zuständigkeit des Bischofs, beschränkt auf seinen Sprengel, war einer der zutiefst verankerten prozessualen Grundsätze des Kirchenrechts. Spätere Päpste haben dann noch diesen Grundsatz ausgebaut, indem sie, wie etwa Innozenz III., dieses Territorialprinzip auf den päpstlichen Legaten anwandten[31] oder, wie Bonifaz VIII., festlegten, daß Statuten, die von einem Diözesanbischof erlassen worden waren, keine bindenden Wirkungen auf dessen Untertanen außerhalb der Diözese ausübten; in dieser Dekretale ging Bonifaz sogar so weit, seine Begründung dem römischen Recht zu entlehnen: „Cum extra territorium dicenti non pareatur impune"[32].

Es läßt sich daher bei näherer Analyse unschwer die einfache und klare Linienführung dieser klementinischen Dekretale erkennen, die, wie nochmals betont sei, keine neuen Grundsätze aufstellte, sondern alte bisher ausschließlich auf das Diözesanrecht (die *lex dioecesana*[33]) Anwendung findenden Rechtssätze auf das öffentliche Recht übertrug. Die in der Dekretale angewandte Terminologie läßt gerade diesen rechtsgeschichtlichen Hintergrund in unzweideutiger Weise erkennen. Die eine oder andere Stelle sei herausgegriffen. Klemens bezeichnet es als geradezu „tamquam notissimum"

quod regem extra districtum imperii, in regno scil. Siciliae notorie ac continue tempore superadicto morantem citare non potuit, nec citatio

---

[28] Dig. 1. 18. 3 und 2. 1. 20. Es sind dies Gesetzesstellen, die sich unter den vielen anderen Stellen finden im Gutachten nr. 1255, quaestio 10, S. 1392, Z. 1ff.

[29] Conciliorum oecumenicorum decreta, hrsg. J. Alberigo et al., 3. Aufl. (Bologna 1973), c. 2, S. 31f.

[30] Hauptquelle in Gratian: IX, qu. 2, c. 7ff.

[31] X: I. 30. 7. Vgl. hier die gl. ord. s. v. Terminos, die sehr interessante Ausführungen über die bischöfliche Zuständigkeit hat. Die Glosse unterstreicht ganz im Sinne Innozenz' den Grundsatz, daß "in aliena dyocesi non potest (episcopus) sedere pro tribunali nec aliquid disponere", daher kann er weder exkommunizieren noch auch lossprechen.

[32] VI: I. 2. 2. Die im Text zit. Worte entstammen Dig. 2. 1. 20. Es wird zu wenig beachtet, daß genau derselbe Grundsatz auch in die Satzungen mittelalterlicher Universitäten eingegangen ist. Das *ius non trahi ad extra* für die Mitglieder der Universität findet sich z. B. in den Statuten der Universität Cambridge aus dem 13. Jh. Vgl. darüber M. B. Hackett, The oldest statutes of the University of Cambridge (Cambridge 1970), S. 26, 53. Einem Indult Gregors IX. gemäß (14. Juni 1233) durften Universitätsangehörige nicht vor ein Gericht geladen werden, das außerhalb des Diözesansprengels des Ordinarius lag. In Paris obwaltete derselbe Grundsatz, obgleich erst später formuliert, vgl. H. Rashdall, Universities of medieval Europe, 2. Aufl. (Oxford 1936), I. 418, Anm. 5.

[33] Vgl. Gratian, XVI. qu. 1, c. 34; auch X, qu. 1, c. 1.

siquam forsan de ipso intra imperii fines fecit, citatum extra imperium constitutum arctavit[34].

Ferner erklärt Klemens, daß der König kein Untertan des Kaisers sei — eine unmißverständliche Absage an die universale Kaiseridee[35] — und folglich der Personalitätsgrundsatz nicht zum Zuge kommen könne. (Rex) in regno praefato domicilium suum fovebat, unde imperator in ipsius personam nulla ratione terrarum huiusmodi (nisi ex natura feudorum) debitam superioritatem habebat.

Schließlich geht der Papst in die materielle Rechtssphäre über, wenn er erklärt, der König könne überhaupt nicht das Verbrechen der Majestätsbeleidigung begehen, eben weil er nicht kaiserlicher Untertan sei, und zwar weder geburtsmäßig noch domizilmäßig[35a].

Die in dieser Dekretale niedergelegten Maxime haben die allgemein staatsrechtlichen Strukturelemente des Souveränitätsbegriffs kräftig umrissen. Die wesentlichste Folge auf dem Gebiete des Staatsrechts scheint mir in der dinglich verstandenen, auf das Territorium bezogenen und von ihm abgeleiteten Komponente zu liegen. Mit anderen Worten, die Verdinglichung der Souveränität hatte zur Folge, daß die herrscherliche Hoheit des Königs an sein Territorium gebunden und insoweit auch begrenzt war. Die sachlichen Grenzen des Territoriums sind zu Grenzen des Rechts geworden[36] — ein wesentlicher Unterschied zwischen diesen herrscherlichen Rechten und den sog. *iura episcopalia*, die ebenso rein judiziell aufgefaßt wurden, bestand nicht[37]. Der Herrscher ist, um die bischöfliche Terminologie anzuwenden, der *(iudex) ordinarius* innerhalb seines Gebietes[38] und, was ganz besonders hervorgehoben werden muß, dieser Grundsatz gilt nunmehr auch für den Kaiser, der eben damit seiner universalen Stellung entkleidet wurde[39]. Anders ausgedrückt,

---

[34] *Pastoralis Cura*, in Clem. II. 11. 2.

[35] Was übrigens die Glosse des Johannes Andreae sofort erkannte: "Per hanc litteram et sequentes patet quod imperator non distringit totum orbem, licet dicatur dominus mundi ...."

[35a] Der König "in eodem regno non, ut praemittitur (in der kaiserlichen Sentenz) in imperio certum continuum et notorium suum habens domicilium ac originem inde trahens, imperatori eo modo non subfuit quod in eum crimen laesae maiestatis commiserit". Diese Frage ist höchst interessant abgehandelt in den mehrfach erwähnten Gutachten, M. G. H. Const. IV. 2, nr. 1254, 1255, S. 1376—1378, 1395—1398.

[36] Wie auch umgekehrt etwas später der Wirkungsbereich der Jurisdiktion die Existenz eines selbständigen staatlichen Gemeinwesens anzeigte, wie es Baldus ausdrückte (Super Feudis, ed. Lyons 1585, in der Rubrik *Quae sint regalia*, fol. 85vb, nr. 2): "Porro territorium non est aliud quam terrae spatium munitum et armatum iurisdictione". Noch viel später, etwa bei Philippus Decius (Consilia, ed. Lyons 1556, cons. nr. 524, fol. 557, nr. 7) finden sich ähnliche Gedanken (vgl. auch sein Consilium nr. 649, fol. 644, nr. 16). Jason de Mayno übernahm die Lehre des Baldus ohne weiteren Zusatz: Consilia (ed. Frankfurt 1609), IV. nr. 166, fol. 577; auch I. nr. 224, fol. 747.

[37] Über die *iura episcopalia*, siehe X: I. 41. 3; II. 24. 27; II. 25. 6; III. 9. 1; III. 39. 21.

[38] Vgl. X: I. 31. 19; auch VI: I. 16. 7.

[39] Wie dies auch allenthalben von der Rechtslehre vertreten wurde, s. Johannes Andreae oben Anm. 35; vgl. Zabarella, Super Clementinas (ed. Venedig 1602), zur *Pastoralis Cura*,

20

die Dekretale stellt, so weit das *imperium* in Frage kommt, einen faktischen Zustand rechtlich fest. Die auf ein räumlich begrenztes Gebiet beschränkte Jurisdiktion — des Kaisers wie des Königs — war aber nichts anderes als die unpersönliche, äußere, zwischenstaatliche oder völkerrechtliche Seite der Souveränität. Zur rein persönlichen Souveränität des Herrschers tritt nunmehr die dingliche, mit dem räumlichen Herrschaftsbereich untrennbar verbundene Souveränität. Man kann hier in der Tat von einer „juristischen Rechtspersönlichkeit des Territoriums" sprechen, wie Otto Brunner einmal geistvoll formuliert hat[40]. Die Landeshoheit hat sich juristisch zu profilieren begonnen als Souveränität im dinglichen Sinne. Letztere hat sich abgespalten von dem rein persönlich verstandenen Souveränitätsbegriff, wird selbständig und beginnt nunmehr erhöhte Aufmerksamkeit auf sich zu lenken, wenn auch noch immer auf ausschließlich juristischer Ebene[41]. Die Vorladung vor ein Gericht wurde richtigerweise als integrierender Bestandteil der Gerichtshoheit verstanden, die in den Landesgrenzen ihre eigenen Schranken fand. Insofern ist die Ausbildung der Souveränitätslehre mit der mittelalterlichen Rechtslehre verknüpft, denn die Souveränität gibt sich unmißverständlich als eine Erscheinungsform der Rechtssprechung zu erkennen[42]. Der aus den beiden Komponenten sich zusammensetzende Souveränitätsbegriff orientiert sich also ganz natürlich und genetisch an der judiziellen Funktion des Herrschers. An der Wiege geordneten Staatslebens stand die richterliche Funktion des Herrschers, und von allem unwesentlichen Beiwerk und Gestrüpp gereinigt, weist der Souveränitätsbegriff des Mittelalters — wie auch der moderne — noch immer die Jurisdiktionsgewalt, die rein richterliche Tätigkeit des Herrschers, als Kernmerkmal auf[43].

---

fol. 89vb, nr. 2: "Papa restringit iurisdictionem imperatoris ad certum districtum ...". Er behauptet auch (ebd.) "quod districtus, territorium et diocesis quasi pro eodem sumuntur et nihil aliud sunt quam universitas agrorum intra fines cuiusvis loci existentes, ubi quis obtinet ius impetrandi ..." (letzteres in Anlehnung an das römische Recht). In ebendemselben Sinn auch Petrus de Ancharano, Super Clementinas (ed. Lyons 1545), zur Pastoralis Cura, fol. 31, nr. 20: "Sententia et decretum imperatoris non extenditur ad personas et loca sibi non subdita ...". Der Kaisertitel wurde demnach als Name ohne besonderen Inhalt verstanden.

[40] O. Brunner, wie oben Anm. 16, S. 148, doch dürfte der Ansatz Brunners die „territorialstaatliche Rechtstheorie kreist seit dem 16. Jh. um den Gedanken der juristischen Rechtspersönlichkeit des Territoriums" viel zu spät sein, weil die Entwicklung schon kräftig seit dem frühen 14. Jh. in Gang gekommen war.

[41] Es sei daran erinnert, daß H. Mitteis den Begriff der Versachlichung in einem ganz anderen Sinne aufgefaßt hatte. Er verstand darunter die Schaffung eines Verwaltungsapparates, einer Behördenverfassung, eines Berufsbeamtentums, op. cit. (Anm. 20), S. 3 u. 8. Aufl., S. 4.

[42] Vgl. etwa Zabarella (wie oben Anm. 39), fol. 90, nr. 6: "Citatio est sententia ... sed sententia extra territorium non ligat ... ergo nec citatio ... citatio est pars iudicii".

[43] In diesem Sinn vgl. Oldradus (oben Anm. 26), consilium nr. 88, nr. 1, mit Berufung auf Nicolaus de Matarellis "qui fuit magnus homo in iure". Ebenso Baldus, Commentaria in Dig. vet. (ed. Venedig 1616), D. 2. 1. 20, fol. 82rb, nr. 13: "Iudex est privatus extra territorium, ita nuntius est privatus extra territorium et non nuntius publicus ...". Ferner Paulus Castren-

Hier reiht sich eine weitere und, wie mir scheinen möchte, wichtige Beobachtung ein. Obgleich man manchmal vom rein historischen Gesichtswinkel aus schon die Beobachtung gemacht hat, hat sie anscheinend noch keine volle rechtshistorische und -dogmatische Würdigung erfahren. Es handelt sich um die offizielle Herrschertitulatur, die zu einem sehr wichtigen Indiz für den Souveränitätsbegriff wird. Wie bekannt, nannten sich im allgemeinen die Herrscher seit der Merowinger- und Frankenzeit Herrscher nicht über ein bestimmtes Gebiet, sondern über Stämme oder ethnische Gruppen — es gab den *Rex Langobardorum, Francorum, Saxonum, Anglorum*, usw. Daneben erscheint seit dem 11. Jh. der *Rex Romanorum* als Vorstufe des *Imperator Romanorum*[44]. Auch die Krönungsordines verwenden durchwegs die personal gefaßten Herrschertitel, insbes. in jenen Gebetstexten, die sich auf die Regierung des dem Herrscher überantworteten Volkes beziehen. Nur gelegentlich kommt das Territorium vor, das *regnum* selbst, aber, soweit sich mit einiger Sicherheit feststellen läßt, nicht in Verbindung mit der herrscherlichen Jurisdiktionsgewalt[45]. Die in den Urkunden usw. verwendete Herrschertitulatur ist sehr bezeichnend, weil sie ausschließlich die persönliche Komponente des Souveränitätsbegriffs ausdrückt — es sind die Franken, Sachsen, Angeln, Römer usw., die dem König untertan sind. Was größere Aufmerksamkeit verdienen sollte, als die Sache bisher auf sich lenkte, ist die langsame Änderung der Königstitulatur, etwa in England vom Ende des 12. Jhs. an, wo unter Richard I. der *Rex Anglorum* mit dem *Rex Angliae*, der *Rex Normannorum* mit dem *Rex Normanniae*, der *Rex Aquitanorum* mit dem *Rex Aquitaniae* wechselweise als die amtliche Königstitulatur auftritt[46], um dann unter seinem unmittelbaren Nachfolger Johann o. L. ausschließlich dem *Rex Angliae* usw. Platz zu machen; und dabei blieb es fürderhin. Es sei vermerkt, daß in der

---

sis, ibid. (ed. Venedig 1593), bes. nr. 10, sowie zur lex 5, fol. 17vb, nr. 3. Alexander Tartagnus, Super Dig. vet. (ed. Venedig 1586), ebda., fol. 50vb, nr. 5: "Iurisdictio cohaeret seu terminetur territorio". Mit dieser Rechtslage — der Herrscher in seiner rein richterlichen Funktion — hat sich H. Hirsch, Die hohe Gerichtsbarkeit im deutschen Mittelalter (Graz-Köln 1940), S. 207 — 209, nur vorübergehend beschäftigt.

[44] Über die Herrschertitel bis zum Ende des 8. Jhs. vgl. das reiche Material bei H. Wolfram, Intitulatio: Lateinische Königs- und Fürstentitel bis zum Ende des 8. Jhs. (= MIÖG. Erg. Bd. 21 (1967)), der S. 27 richtig betont: „Das Objekt (scil. des Funktionstitels) ist naturgemäß zunächst die ‚gens' und erst im späteren Mittelalter das Territorium, das Land". Daher auch die Titulatur *Rex gentis Langobardorum* u. ä. Zur Intitulatio der fränkischen und langobardischen Könige vgl. auch P. Classen, Kaiserreskript und Königsurkunde, in: Archiv f. Diplomatik, 2 (1956), S. 1 ff., bes. S. 38 ff. und 78 ff. Über das Aufkommen des Titels *Rex Romanorum* vgl. R. Buchner, Der Titel Rex Romanorum in deutschen Königsurkunden des 11. Jhs., in: Deutsches Archiv 19 (1963), S. 327 — 38; über die Bedeutung dieses Titels vgl. W. Ullmann, Dies ortus imperii, in: Atti Accursiani, hsg. G. Rossi (Mailand 1968), II. 661 ff., bes. S. 678 ff.

[45] Die Ordines bedürfen noch einer eingehenden Analyse in dieser Richtung, denn viel Staatsrecht und -lehre steckt in ihrer Liturgie, Doxologie und Symbolik.

[46] Vgl. etwa W. Stubbs, Select Charters, 9. Aufl. (Oxford 1948), S. 260 mit S. 261. Vgl. allerdings schon den *Rex Cantiae* bei H. Wolfram (oben Anm. 44), S. 27, Anm. 22.

dürren Urkundensprache des 13. Jhs. der dinglichen Komponente der Herrschersouveränität der Vorzug vor der persönlichen gegeben wurde. Der *Rex Francorum* weicht dem *Rex Franciae*, aber nicht so durchgängig wie in England und in anderen Königreichen, etwa dem *Rex Boemiae*, dem *Rex Poloniae*, usw. Von ganz besonderem Interesse ist die Titulatur Friedrichs II., der sich nannte: *Imperator Romanorum, Ierusalem et Siciliae Rex*. Die Verbindung der persönlichen Komponente im Kaiserbegriff mit der dinglichen im Königsbegriff bei ein- und demselben Herrscher ist von gewisser Bedeutung, denn offenbar ließ sich eine dingliche Komponente der kaiserlichen Souveränität gedanklich nicht fassen. Das ist auch verständlich, weil gerade der in der kaiserlichen Jurisdiktionsgewalt liegende Universalismus sich an kein bestimmtes Territorium binden ließ. Daß sich hier Ungereimtheiten offenbarten, liegt offenbar an den Schwierigkeiten, den Kaiserbegriff in Einklang zu bringen mit dem spätrömischen auf der einen, und dem zeitgenössischen Königsbegriff auf der anderen Seite. Darüber hinaus barg der Begriff der „Römer" noch immer Schwierigkeiten. Wie bekannt sind noch bei Bartolus alle jene „Römer" *(cives Romani)*, die der römischen Kirche folgen.

Andererseits aber hat die amtliche Bischofstitulatur sicherlich seit dem 7. Jh. das unpersönliche Moment hervorgekehrt. Die Beschränkung der Bischofsgewalt auf ein bestimmtes Territorium wird schon in der Amtsbezeichnung klar, denn er ist Bischof einer Kirche, und diese umfaßt juristisch das ihr angeschlossene Gebiet. Der Titel *(archi) episcopus (ecclesiae) Salzburgensis, Remenensis, Cantuariensis, Senonensis, Coloniensis*, usw., beinhaltet keinerlei persönliche Momente, sondern ist dinglich gefaßt. Der Salzburger, der Kölner, usw. kann nicht in seiner amtlichen richterlichen Funktion als Bischof außerhalb seiner Diözese (Provinz) auftreten[47]. Es ist ferner zu bemerken, daß die hierarchisch unter den Königen (und noch mehr unter den Kaisern) stehenden Herzöge schon viel früher als die Könige ihre territoriale Beziehung in ihrem Titel betonten. Diese Verdinglichung der Herzogsgewalt — *Dux Burgundiae, Saxoniae, Sueviae*, usw. — läßt sich noch früher in Deutschland als im Frankenreich wahrnehmen. Dazu kommen noch solche Begriffswendungen wie *Ducatus Bawariae, Turingiae*, usw.[48].

Der Hinweis auf diese Unterschiedlichkeit in der Herrschertitulatur dürfte bedeutsam sein, erstens für das rechtshistorische Verständnis der um die

---

[47] In diesem Zusammenhang sei an die im frühen christlichen Irland anzutreffende Organisation erinnert, dergemäß das Bischofsamt personal verstanden wurde, d. h. ein Bischof für eine zahlenmäßig festgelegte Gemeinde, und nicht für ein bestimmtes Territorium. Soweit mir bekannt, wurde die Bischofstitulatur noch keiner eingehenden Analyse unterzogen.

[48] Siehe das überaus reiche und methodisch vorbildlich gesichtete Material bei W. Kienast, Der Herzogstitel in Frankreich und Deutschland (9. bis 12. Jh.) (München 1968); hier auch S. 149 der sehr interessante Hinweis auf den englischen Heinrich II., der auf seinen frühen Münzen seinen Herrschertitel schon verdinglicht hatte in Bezug auf Aquitannien. In diesem Zusammenhang vgl. noch Wolfram (oben Anm. 44), S. 193f. und C. R. Brühl, Studien zu den langobardischen Königsurkunden (Tübingen 1970).

Wende des 13. und 14. Jhs. einsetzenden rechtstheoretischen Erörterung und schließlichen Fixierung des Souveränitätsbegriffes selbst, und zweitens für die rechtsideologische Blöße, die der *Imperator Romanorum* sich gab im Vergleich mit den „bloßen Königen" — in früheren Generationen seit Gregor VII.[49] verächtlich als *Reguli* gestempelt —, denn für ihn gab es kraft des ideellen Jurisdiktionsanspruchs kein erfaßbares Territorium. Dadurch allein kam er schon ins Hintertreffen. Es würde der Geschichte, der Tradition und vor allem der Kaiseridee selbst einen schweren Eintrag getan haben, hätte man versucht, den Titel „Kaiser der Römer" zu verdinglichen. Damit wäre der ganze ideelle Inhalt des Kaisergedankens in ein Nichts zerflossen. Das Nomen des Kaisers ist eben, wie man auch hier wieder beobachten kann, nicht „nur" eine Titelfrage, sondern bildete am Anfang (Karl d. Gr.) und am Ende ein staatsrechtliches Problem. Eine Verdinglichung der Kaisersouveränität führt, wie eben die klementinische Dekretale dartut, zur Negierung der traditionellen römischen Kaiseridee selbst[50]. Die den Souveränitätsbegriff tragenden Grundpfeiler (der persönliche und der dingliche) klingen noch bis in unsere Tage nach. Erinnern wir uns doch, daß der „Deutsche Kaiser" — wie der preußische König seit 1871 bis November 1918 hieß — nicht „Kaiser von Deutschland" war[51].

Ein weiteres Eindringen in die Strukturelemente der dinglichen Seite muß zwingend dem Wohnsitz rechtserhebliche Bedeutung beimessen. Das Domizil stellt sozusagen das Mittelglied zwischen der Sache (dem Territorium) und der Person des Herrschers dar. Das Domizil schlägt die Brücke zwischen dem Herrscher und Raum in der Person des Untertanen (der sich gerade jetzt um die Wende des 13. und 14. Jhs. anschickt, Staatsbürger zu werden). Durch den Wohnsitz im Territorium wird, soweit der Untertan (Staatsbürger) in Frage kommt, nicht nur ein faktischer, sondern auch ein rechtlicher Nexus zwischen ihm und seinem Herrscher hergestellt. Der erstere bezieht sich auf die dingliche, der letztere auf die persönliche Komponente der Herrschersouveränität. Die päpstliche Dekretale hat dem Wohnsitz jenen Standort im Rahmen der dinglichen Souveränität zugewiesen, der ihm zukommt. Die Faktizität des

---

[49] Gregor VII. in seinem Register, II. 70 (ed. E. Caspar in M. G. H. Epp. sel., S. 230, Z. 14).

[50] Hier sei an den staufischen Versuch erinnert, die Sakralisierung des *Imperium Romanum* durch den Zusatz *Sacrum* (im Gegensatz zur *Sancta Romana Ecclesia*) wieder einzuführen — am Herrschertitel, der nur die persönliche Komponente ausdrückte, änderte sich aber nichts beim Schöpfer dieser Intitulatio, Friedrich I. Über den rechtsgeschichtlichen und ideologischen Hintergrund vgl. meine Short History of the Papacy in the Middle Ages (London 1972), S. 191ff., sowie meinen demnächst im Hist. Jahrb. erscheinenden Aufsatz „Von Canossa nach Pavia".

[51] Vgl. die treffsicheren Beobachtungen bei Bismarck, Gedanken u. Erinnerungen (Ausg. 1921), II. 141f.: „In der Schlußberathung am 17. Jan. 1871 lehnte er (Wilhelm) die Bezeichnung Deutscher Kaiser ab und erklärte, er wolle Kaiser von Deutschland oder gar nicht Kaiser sein ... daß der Titel Kaiser von Deutschland einen landesherrlichen Anspruch auf nichtpreußische Gebiete involviere". Für den Hinweis auf diese Stelle bin ich meinem Kollegen J. Steinberg dankbar.

ordentlichen Wohnsitzes erhebt sich zu einem rechtlich bedeutsamen Element der Souveränität selbst.

Die Territorialhoheit gründet sich nicht, wie dies manchmal in der Literatur vertreten wird, auf den römischen Eigentumsbegriff[52] oder auf patrimoniale Vorstellungen[53], sondern ausschließlich auf die juristische Erkenntnis, daß die richterliche Tätigkeit (d. h. erzwingbare Jurisdiktion) sich nur auf ein umschreibbares Territorium erstrecken kann, und daß die Gerichtsbarkeit der Urgrund der Souveränität ist. In der Rechtslehre hat sich die Diözesanstruktur als Vorbild erwiesen. In der Übertragung der Diözesangrundsätze auf das öffentliche Recht liegt eine der Wurzeln der modernen Rechts- und Staatslehre. Genauso wie die Jurisdiktionsgewalt des Bischofs in den Diözesangrenzen ihre Schranken findet, in ebendemselben Maße erfahren die Hoheitsrechte und insbesondere die richterlichen ihre Schranken im Territorium des Herrschers. Erst vermöge dieser Erkenntnis konnte der Begriff des Staates konkretisiert und ihm der entsprechende Inhalt verliehen werden. Man könnte wohl sagen, daß die wissenschaftliche Erfassung des Staates, angebahnt durch die Entwicklung im 13. Jh.[54], erst jetzt richtig in Fluß kam, weil die Voraussetzungen sowohl ideologischer als auch faktischer Art gegeben waren[55].

Was bisher im Bereich des Königtums höchstens bloße Rechtsübung war[56], wird nunmehr durch *Pastoralis Cura* zu einem für die weitere Staatslehre bedeutungsvollen Grundgesetz erhoben. Durch die Beschränkung des Kaisertums auf ein bestimmtes räumliches Gebiet (und zwar nicht nur faktisch, sondern auch und vor allem rechtlich), wurde das keimende Völkerrecht selbst

---

[52] So etwa A. Verdross, Völkerrecht, 5. Aufl., hsg. S. Verosta u. K. Zemanek (Wien 1964), S. 266.

[53] Vgl. etwa G. Jellinek, Allgemeine Staatslehre, 7. Neudruck der 3. Aufl. (Bad Homburg 1960), S. 470f.

[54] Vgl. Principles of Government (wie oben, Anm. 2), S. 231ff.

[55] Unter die Bedingungen, die die rechtstheoretische Erörterung des Begriffs „Staat" förderten, gehört zweifellos die voraufgehende Landfriedensgesetzgebung; vgl. etwa H. Angermeier, Königtum und Landfriede im deutschen Spätmittelalter (München 1966); weitere Literatur bei P. Fried, Zur „staatsbildenden" Funktion des Landfriedens im frühen bayerischen Territorialstaat, in: Festschrift f. Max Spindler, hsg. D. Albrecht et al (München 1969), S. 283—306. Diesen Erwägungen liegt der Gedanke zugrunde, daß die Sorge um den Frieden zu den hervorragendsten Herrscherpflichten gehörte. Das erklärt auch die tiefere Bedeutung des Herrschers als *Tutor regni* (darüber Carolingian Renaissance, oben, Anm. 3, S. 122f., 177ff.), eine Vorstellung, die keimhaft schon in den Marculf'schen Formeln zu finden ist, wo die Idee der *Tuitio* mit der Munt gekoppelt ist (vgl. etwa M. G. H. Formulae, I. nr. 3, S. 43, Z. 7, sehr häufig dann besonders in Immunitätsverleihungen Ludwigs d. Fr., ebd. in den Formulae imperiales) und so leicht zum spätkarolingischen Begriff des *Tutor regni* führen konnte. Diese Stellung aber — und das scheint mir der Urgrund der mittelalterlichen Staatslehren zu sein — konnte vorzüglich nur durch den Herrscher in seiner Funktion als oberster Gerichtsherr wahrgenommen werden. Das erklärt zum großen Teil, warum es so leicht war, die Grundsätze richterlicher Befugnisse auf die Befugnisse des Herrschers zu übertragen, sei er nun Bischof oder Fürst.

[56] Das Rechtsgutachten über Lyon ist besonders lehrreich, siehe Acta (oben, Anm. 7), nr. 271, S. 199ff.

gefördert. Wenn es ein Merkmal gibt, das das Völkerrecht auszeichnet, dann ist es die in ihm zum Ausdruck gelangende Gleichordnung aller (selbständigen) Staaten. Solange aber das Kaisertum wenigstens im abstrakt-ideellen Sinne als Rechtsinstitution auf universaler Grundlage — wenn auch behaftet mit vielen Einschränkungen, die aber auf der Ebene der realen Tatsachen und nicht auf jener der universalen Rechtsidee lagen — verstanden wurde (und mit dieser Auffassung wollte ja Heinrich VII. Ernst machen in seinem Reichsgesetz), gab es ganz offenbar wenig Möglichkeit und noch weniger Anlaß, die dingliche Seite des Souveränitätsgedankens wahrzunehmen[57]. Es mag wohl sein, daß der Souveränitätsgedanke nicht immer von wohltuendem Einfluß gewesen war, aber es ist ein Gebot der Erkenntnis und des rechten Verständnisses, sich über die Wurzeln des Gedankens Klarheit zu verschaffen.

Diese Überlegungen scheinen umso mehr geboten, als selbst die weltliche kaiserliche Gesetzgebung nach vier Dezennien die dingliche Souveränität der sieben Kurfürsten zum Gegenstand von zwei Kapiteln in der Goldenen Bulle machte. In der am 10. Jänner 1356 von Karl IV. erlassenen Goldenen Bulle wird die Gebietshoheit der Kurfürsten festgelegt in Worten und Begriffen, die sehr an die klementinische Dekretale erinnern. Im 8. und 11. Kapitel wird die Rechtsstellung, d. h. die territoriale Souveränität der Kurfürsten in einprägsamer und detaillierter Weise reichsgesetzlich niedergelegt.

Nullus princeps, baro, nobilis miles ... civis, nulla denique persona eiusdem regni et pertinenciarum eius ubicumque consistencium ... ad cuiuscumque actoris instanciam extra regnum ipsum ad quodcumque tribunal ... citari potuerit sive trahi nec vocari debeat[58].

Diese für den König von Böhmen festgelegte Bestimmung wird mut. mut. auf alle anderen Kurfürsten als anwendbar erklärt. Verständlicherweise tritt bei letzteren an die Stelle des "extra regnum" das "extra territorium et terminos"[59]. Bei den drei geistlichen Kurfürsten bedeutet dies ganz klar, daß deren kirchlicher Amtsbereich vollgültig „verstaatlicht" wurde, während beim Sachsen, Brandenburger und Pfalzgrafen die Entwicklung zur „Verstaatlichung" — und zwar kraft der Betonung der dinglichen Herrscherrechte —

---

[57] Leider ist der Aufsatz von P. Vaccari, Utrum iurisdictio cohaeret territorio: La dottrina di Bartolo, Bartolo die Sassoferrato, (Mailand 1963), II. 737 ff. nicht sehr ergiebig. Die verdienstvolle Studie von M. David, Le contenu de l'hegemonie imperiale dans la doctrine de Bartole, ebd., II. 199 ff. behandelt die durch *Pastoralis Cura* angeregten Fragen nicht eingehend.

[58] Hsg. K. Zeumer in Quellensammlung zur Geschichte der deutschen Reichsverfassung, 2. Aufl. (Tübingen 1913), S. 201. Eine genaue Analyse der in der Goldenen Bulle aufgeworfenen Fragen und deren Verzahnung mit den zeitgenössischen öffentlich-rechtlichen und privatrechtlichen Problemen steht noch aus. Auch die verdienstvolle Studie von A. Wolf, Das kaiserliche Rechtsbuch Karls IV., in: Ius Commune, 2 (1969), S. 1—34, streift die rechtshistorischen Themen bloß (S. 17).

[59] Ebd. Kap. 11, S. 202 f.

eindeutig begann. Am Ende stand die unselige Zersplitterung des deutschen
Reiches, das sich infolge der skizzierten Entwicklung in eine Vielzahl von
(Klein-)Staaten auflöste. Die Festlegung der dinglichen Hoheitsrechte in der
Goldenen Bulle bildete ein zugkräftiges Muster für andere Territorialherren,
was sich bei Rudolf IV. von Österreich ganz kurz nachher zeigen sollte. Es
dürfte wohl keinem Zweifel unterliegen, daß die klementinische Dekretale
jedenfalls rechtstheoretisch der beginnenden Zersplitterung Vorschub geleistet
hat, denn wenige Hindernisse standen dem Bestreben eines Territorialfürsten
entgegen, die in der Dekretale niedergelegten Maxime auf sich selbst anzuwenden.

Ein Blick auf die zivilistische und kanonistische Literatur des 14. und 15. Jhs.
und in Sonderheit auf die reichhaltige und von der Rechtsgeschichte noch nicht
ausgeschöpfte Konsilienliteratur genügt, um darzutun, wie anregend *Pastoralis
Cura* sich erwies. Der rechtshistorischen Forschung stellen sich mannigfache
Fragen, denen in der juristischen Literatur des späten Mittelalters steigende
Bedeutung beigemessen wurde. Diese Fragen betreffen das materielle und das
formelle öffentliche Recht, nicht weniger aber auch das stetig nach vorwärts
drängende Völkerrecht. Vor allem rückt der Begriff des Staatsbürgers und die
Relevanz des Wohnsitzes in den Mittelpunkt der juristischen Diskussion.
Die Bartolinische Lehre von den Statuten ist ganz offenbar mit dem Souveräni-
tätsbegriff auf rein praktischer Ebene verknüpft[60]. Die Frage der richterlichen
Gewalt, einschließlich der Auslieferung eines Beschuldigten, wird im Rahmen
der nunmehr aufgeworfenen Problematik erneut und mit allem juristischen
Raffinement behandelt. Der *locus commissi delicti* erscheint von ganz besonderer Bedeutung innerhalb des Strafprozeßrechts. Daß die dingliche Seite der
Souveränität zum Fragenkomplex der Besteuerung[61] und mit ihr zusammen-
hängender Probleme führte, soll wenigstens angemerkt werden. Ferner er-
regen jene Fragen besondere Aufmerksamkeit, die später einmal im Rahmen
eines internationalen Privatrechts abgehandelt werden sollten, so etwa die
Unterscheidungen, die die streitige und freiwillige Gerichtsbarkeit für Zustän-
digkeitsfragen notwendig machte. Wie weit ist die schriftliche oder durch
Boten übermittelte Ladung eines Beklagten rechtswirksam, wenn er sich
außerhalb des Territoriums, d. h. außerhalb der staatlichen Grenzen, befindet?
Wann und unter welchen Umständen ist Zwang zulässig? Die befruchtende

---

[60] Über die Bartolinische Wendung zur Volkssouveränität (in Verbindung mit seiner Idee
von der *civitas sibi princeps*) vgl. W. Ullmann, De Bartoli sententia: Concilium repraesentat
mentem populi, Bartolo di Sassoferrato (wie oben, Anm. 57), II. 705ff.

[61] Hier sei verwiesen auf ein sehr interessantes, erst kürzlich entdecktes Consilium des
Cynus. Vgl. W. M. Bowsky, A new Consilium of Cino da Pistoia (1324): citizenship, residence and taxation, in: Speculum 42 (1967), S. 431ff., bes. 439ff. Über einen ähnlichen Fragenkomplex im bayrischen Bereich siehe die lehrreichen Ausführungen von K. Bosl, Stände
und Territorialstaat in Bayern im 14. Jahrhundert, in: Vorträge und Forschungen, 14. 343ff.,
insbes. 352ff.

Wirkung, die die nunmehr in das Blickfeld der juristischen Diskussion gerückte Problematik auf die Rechtslehre und mittelbar auf das spätere Recht selbst ausübte, ist noch nicht eingehend genug gewürdigt worden. Ein reiches und weites Gebiet bleibt der Forschung vorbehalten.

SUMMARY

For an adequate understanding of the medieval concept of sovereignty it is advisable to draw a conceptual distinction between the personal and the impersonal component parts of the notion. Throughout the earlier part of the Middle Ages it was overwhelmingly the personal ties between the Ruler and his subjects which made understandable the 'superiority' of the former and the 'inferiority' of the latter. The Ruler formed an estate of his own and was 'major' or 'higher' than the 'subditi', because he alone had been distinguished by God's grace. This was the ground upon which the descending theme of government and law flourished. That this personal side of the Ruler's sovereignty needed supplementation was clearly shown by Pope Clement V's *Pastoralis Cura* which was issued as a rejoinder to Henry VII's imperial law which re-stated in solemn form the universal jurisdiction of the emperor of the Romans.

The hitherto unnoticed advance made by *Pastoralis Cura* lay in that it transferred Roman law principles, Canon law axioms and ecclesiastical practice to public law. The papal decree put into the foreground the principle of enforceability of the law, judicial competence and domicile. It is clearly dependent upon antecedent doctrine and practice that can be traced back to late antiquity. One of its essential points is that the secular Ruler was juristically put on the level of a diocesan bishop who, too, had only a territorially restricted jurisdiction (the *lex diocesana*; the *iura episcopalia*). Thereby the actual physical boundaries of a territory became also boundaries of the enforceable law, and the Ruler himself a *iudex ordinarius* on the episcopal model. The territory acquired a juristic personality. The Ruler appears in this framework exclusively in his judicial function. The Roman law principle of judicial competence limited to a definite territory or space served as a model.

In historical examinations concerning the concept of sovereignty too little attention has been paid to the various intitulations of Rulers, notably the change from the personal title (for instance, the *Rex Anglorum*, the *Rex Francorum*, etc.) to the impersonal (the *Rex Angliae*, the *Rex Franciae*, etc.). On the other hand, episcopal intitulations were generally impersonal and related to the territory within which the individual episcopal church was situated. Similar observations can be made about ducal intitulations. Nevertheless, there were good historical and ideological reasons why the imperial title was not capable of being 'territorialized' and at all times remained 'of the Romans', because by virtue of the function allocated to him he was said to reflect the universality of the papacy. The doctrines set forth in *Pastoralis Cura* facilitated the juristic development of the concept of State in the later Middle Ages.

The effect of this papal decree was threefold. (1) The universality of the empire itself was implicitly and explicitly denied, so that fact and law went once more hand in hand, for as a universal institution the empire had in any case been little more than a German principality for the last decades. (2) The fixation and articulate formulation of the idea of territorial sovereignty which was the reification of the personal sovereignty. (3) The embryonic beginnings of modern international law which operates with independent states, precisely that kind of entity which *Pastoralis Cura* envisaged. A practical application of the territorial concept of sovereignty can be found in the provisions of the Golden Bull.

X

JOHN BACONTHORPE AS A CANONIST

I

THE purpose of this short contribution is to invite attention – albeit in a very sketchy outline dictated by considerations of space – to the early fourteenth-century Carmelite John Baconthorpe, a native of Norfolk, a graduate of Paris and – like the jubiland – a teacher at both Oxford and Cambridge. Baconthorpe's philosophical and theological importance has been fully appraised by modern scholarship,[1] but as far as can be ascertained with any degree of certainty his canonistic contributions have received little or inadequate attention.[2] In fact, his name does not appear in the usual handbooks and *Dictionnaires* of canon law, although his canonistic work and expertise was most certainly on a far larger scale than that of many another scholar who has been given a niche in the ordinary reference works. Leaving aside John of Athona who, incidentally, was an exact contemporary of John Baconthorpe, the fourteenth century did not produce any really memorable English canonistic scholar.[3] Although the edition of his Commentaries on the *Sentences* calls him a *canonista praecipuus* and manuscripts designate him a doctor of both laws,[4] by contemporary standards he could not have

---

[1] See B. M. Xiberta, 'De Magistro Iohanne Baconthorp' in *De scriptoribus scholasticis s. XIV ex Ordine Carmelitarum* (Louvain, 1931), pp. 167–240; supplemented by B. Smalley, 'John Baconthorpe's Postill on Matthew' in *Mediaeval and Renaissance Studies*, IV (1958), 91–145; see also P. Chrysogone, 'Maître Jean Baconthorpe: les sources, la doctrine, les disciples' in *Revue néo-scolastique de philosophie*, XXXIV (1932), 341–65; A. B. Emden, *Biographical Register of the University of Cambridge to 1500* (Cambridge, 1963) pp. 669–70. He lectured at Cambridge by 1330, became Provincial of the English Carmelites and died 1348.

[2] For some remarks cf. Xiberta, 'De Magistro', pp. 180, 182; also Smalley, 'John Baconthorpe', pp. 94, 101, 103, 120.

[3] For a succinct survey of English canonists of this period see L. E. Boyle, 'The *Summa Summarum* and some other English works of canon law' in *Proceedings of the II Internat. Congress of Medieval Canon Law*, ed. S. Kuttner and J. J. Ryan (Vatican City, 1965) at pp. 415–18.

[4] Cf. Xiberta, 'De Magistro', 175f. from Bodley MS. 82: 'Magister frater Iohannes Baconis seu Baconthorpe *doctor iuris utriusque* Parisiensis...' See also J. Bale, *Scriptorum illustrium maioris Brytanniae...catalogus* (edn Basle, 1557), I.382: '...cum summo utriusque iuris ac theologiae magistratu' (in Paris); J. Trisse, 'De magistris Parisiensibus', in B. Zimmermann, *Monumenta historica Carmelitana* (Lérins, 1907), pp. 379–80, says nothing about a degree in law: 'Sextus

been deemed a professional jurist: a Parisian Juris Utriusque Doctor is highly suspect, as there was no study of Roman law after Honorius III prohibited it at the university in 1219. But that he must have received some professional instruction in canon law is beyond question after even a perfunctory perusal of his Commentaries on the *Sentences*. His Commentaries and *Quodlibeta* show a curious lack of knowledge in matters of Roman law and civilian jurisprudence which accords well with the Paris situation.[5]

On the other hand, the relevance, accuracy and manipulation of canonistic jurisprudence and its professional accommodation into theology is sufficient justification for his being accorded a place among the canonists of the fourteenth century. He in fact serves as a particularly good example of the need of integration which a scholar of his standing quite obviously felt.[6] For since the middle of the twelfth century, that is, since juristic theology split up into its component parts[7] as a result of Gratian's *Decretum* on the one hand and Peter Lombard's *Sentences* on the other, specialisation had progressed to such a degree that there was a very real gulf separating the theologians from the jurists, and notably from the canonists, although they treated many matters common to both branches of learning. The earlier *communauté des matières*[8] of theology and jurisprudence was hardly discernible by the thirteenth century. In particular the Fourth Book of the *Sentences* contains numerous topics which were sometimes formulated completely in accord with canonistic style, but contact and mutual fructification, or what is now termed cross-fertilisation, were so rare that for all practical purposes they did not exist, despite the liberal borrowings from Gratian by Peter Lombard.

Here indeed John Baconthorpe is a most notable exception. Only a very lengthy and detailed study could throw the integration of canon law and canonistic jurisprudence in his Commentaries into sharp relief. He pays as much attention to the theologians – some of the relevant

(magister) fuit frater Iohannes de Bachone provinciae Angliae...fuit minimus in persona, sed maximus in sapientia et doctrina.'

[5] I have used the Cremona edn of 1618: *Quaestiones in Quatuor Libros Sententiarum et Quodlibetales*. This has been reprinted by Gregg (Farnborough, 1969). All quotations refer to this edition.

[6] Although rightly emphasising the combination of 'l'élément philosophique et l'élément théologique', P. Chrysogone, art. cit. (above n. 1), p. 341 omits in common with other writers to mention the integration of theology with canon law, which is at least as important.

[7] Cf. W. Ullmann, *The Growth of Papal Government in the Middle Ages*, 4th edn (London, 1970), pp. 359ff.

[8] The expression is J. de Ghellinck's, *Le mouvement théologique du xiie siècle*, 2nd edn (Brussels–Paris, 1948) pp. 422ff.

John Baconthorpe as a Canonist

details are set forth with succinctness and clarity by his modern expositor[9] – as to the law and its interpreters. The hitherto unacknowledged significance of his *Quaestiones canonicae* (i.e. his commentary on the Fourth Book of the *Sentences*) lies precisely in the combination of theology and canonistics.[10] This integration constituted the attempt to restore the unity of the *theologica practica* (or *externa*) as one whole which, as a result of specialisation, had been lost. The *Quaestiones* demonstrate their author's singularly fertile, perceptive and wide-ranging mind with a keen sense for synthesis.[11] With some exaggeration one could say that the Lombard's *Sentences* emphasised the theological aspects of the topics treated juristically by Gratian. What however was originally a difference in emphasis, gave rise to a divisive specialisation, with the result that by the early fourteenth century the unity of ecclesiology itself was seriously threatened. Disintegration and decomposition had begun to corrode what was once one and indivisible, what was once one *totum*.[12]

It is against this background that John Baconthorpe must be seen. His strongly developed aptitude for synthesis and for combinatory and connective thought-processes made him realise the need of integration. The Fourth Book dealt with the sacraments as concrete manifestations of the ecclesiological groundwork. John's commentaries are only loosely linked with the Lombard's subject in the *Distinctiones* and serve as mere *pièces d'occasion*. Let us take a specific example. He introduces the

---

[9] See B. M. Xiberta, art. cit. (above n. 1), pp. 197–212; also pp. 218f.

[10] His *Quaestiones speculativae* (cf. IV.8.1.3, p. 361aD) have been lost: only the *Qu. canonicae* are preserved in MS as well as in the printed editions; see Xiberta, pp. 177–83. In the MS BL. Royal 9 C VII which contains the autograph emendations of the *canonicae*, 22 *Qu. speculativae* are inserted: Xiberta, 'De Magistro', p. 178. The *canonicae* were probably composed in the early 40s, possibly at Oxford.

[11] This is also pointed out – without however referring to his canonistic equipment or use of jurisprudence – in the excellent entry by A. de Saint-Paul, in *Dict. d'Hist. et de Géogr. Ecclés.*, VI (Paris, 1932), 87–9: 'il était doué d'un esprit synthètique...fecondité intellectuelle vraiment exubérante'.

[12] For the same feature in the political field cf. W. Ullmann, 'Die Bulle *Unam sanctam*: Rückblick und Ausblick' in *Röm. Hist. Mitt.*, XV (1974), 45–77. In fourteenth-century England the need of combining theology and canonistics was strongly felt. Cf. the work of William of Pagula, a parish priest writing (c. 1325) for the parochial clergy his *Oculus sacerdotis* which 'is a balance of law and theology', see L. E. Boyle, 'The *Oculus sacerdotis* of William of Pagula' in TRHS, 5th ser. v (1955) at 101; Boyle, *Proceedings* (above n. 3), at p. 424: this work 'is a striking, if unexpected, amalgam of theology and canon law'. See Boyle, 'The *Summa confessorum* of John of Freiburg and the popularization of moral teaching of St Thomas' in *St Thomas Aquinas: Commemoration Studies*, ed. A. A. Maurer, II (Toronto, 1974), 245ff., at 263f. A similar integration is to be found in the *Pupilla oculi* written by the Chancellor of Cambridge, John de Burgh, c. 1385; see Emden, *Biographical Register*, p. 107. This was frequently printed in the early 16th century. There are many other hitherto neglected tracts written in the 14th century.

question of *accidentia* relative to the Eucharist in *Dist.* xii with the very words of the Lombard, but considers that one of the *accidentia* was the juristic protection which the individual churches enjoy and which actually enables them to administer the sacraments, that is to say, ecclesiastical immunity: 'Utrum ecclesia debeat gaudere immunitate?'[13] The answer is given under three headings: the definition of immunity; the kind of immunity churches and their administrators enjoy; and the public duties, imposts, charges and the like which can and cannot be levied on the churches and their incumbents. This procedure allows him to deal theologically and juristically with topics which were commonly outside the purview of canonist[14] and theologian.[15] He did not consider that the Fourth Book covered relevant theological and canonistic topics sufficiently well: he thus hit upon the device of introducing the Fourth Book with a special Prologue consisting of 12 *Quaestiones*, of which the last three concern themselves with the foundations, scope and limitations of the papal government itself.[16] He appends a discussion on the conversion of Jews and infidels to Christianity and on the right of exercising papal jurisdiction in regard to the Holy Land. Here as elsewhere he does not intend and does not pretend to propound any new theories or interpretations, but to pursue a purely didactic purpose by attempting to weave theological and canonistic material together.

Although he could never claim to be a professional jurist, his canonistic equipment was certainly respectable. Here only a bird's eye view can be given of his authorities. Since his knowledge of Roman law and of the civilians was extremely meagre, in technical respects his juristic manipulation of problems left something to be desired. But as regards his knowledge of the canon law itself he cannot easily be faulted. He is thoroughly familiar with the whole Corpus as well as a number of individual decretals issued by Nicholas III, Boniface VIII, Clement V, John XXII and Benedict XII.[17] He has studied Gratian's *Dicta* no less

13 IV.13, qu. un., p. 387bB.
14 In her art. cit. (above n. 1) at p. 142, B. Smalley rightly noted his inclination to use canonists for exegetical purposes: 'By his use of them the fierce little man put a punch into exegesis which it had lacked.'
15 For typical examples contrasting theological and canonistic opinions cf. IV.4.2.1, p. 335aD–E and 336aE; IV.19.1.1, p. 440aE–bA.
16 Q. x–xii, edn cit., pp. 261rb–273rb.
17 Some of these he quoted verbatim, e.g. John XXII's *Vas electionis* directed against Jean de Pouilly in *Extrav. comm.* v.3.2: 'quia non habent omnes constitutionem, ideo hic insero in qua sic dicitur...Datum Avinione 8 kal. Augusti, p.n.a.V' (in IV.15.3.1, pp. 415bD–416bA). He is well acquainted with the condemnation of Marsilius's tract (in *Licet iuxta doctrinam* of 23 Oct.

John Baconthorpe as a Canonist

than the writings of a number of decretists, notably Huguccio, Laurentius, Vincentius, Guido de Baysio, all the *glossae ordinariae*, Raimond de Pennaforte's *Summa confessorum*, Goffredus de Trano's *Summa*, Innocent IV's *Apparatus*, some of the works of Bernardus Compostellanus Junior, Hostiensis' *Summa* as well as *Lectura*, the gloss by Johannes Monachus on the Sext, the commentary of the Archdeacon on the same law book, the glosses by Johannes Andreae on the Sext as well as his *Novella*, Guilielmus Durantis' *Rationale divinorum officiorum*,[18] and so on. There is no doubt that the standard work he consulted on the *Decretum* was the *Rosarium* of Guido de Baysio, to whom he refers not by his usual official designation as Archdeacon, but always as 'Guido'. Any suggestion that John referred to his teacher Guido (Terreni) who wrote an *Expositorium Decreti*, almost contemporaneously with our author's commentary (finished on 17 February 1339), must be dismissed. For Terreni's work was not primarily juristic, but a critical exposition of Gratian's sources and of the use he had made of them.[19] There is no evidence whatsoever that John even knew of his former master's work. The identity of 'Guido' is clear and unambiguous: he used the Archdeacon's work, not only on the *Decretum*, but also his commentary on the Sext (on which Terreni never commented), and the reference in both instances is 'Guido'. Whenever he cites statements of 'Guido' verbatim, they can easily be verified by using the Archdeacon as a control.[20] Considering the respective aims there were hardly any points of contact between Terreni and his pupil.[21] One of the sources frequently referred to by John – even citing the folio – is the *Registrum Romanorum Pontificum*. He obviously consulted this source whenever Gratian had incorporated a canon from one of the early

1327, see O. Raynaldus, *Ann. eccles.*, ed. A. Theiner (Bar-le-Duc, 1872) XXIV, 322–9, nos. 27ff.); or with Benedict XII's *Benedictus Deus* on the Beatific Vision of 29 Jan. 1336 (in H. Denzinger, *Enchiridion symbolorum*, 34th edn Barcelona–Freiburg, 1967) no. 530.

18 But there is only occasionally a reference to the *Speculum Iuris*, e.g. IV.19.2.4, p. 445aD.

19 For a magisterial discussion of Terreni see P. Fournier, 'Gui Terré' in *Hist. littéraire de la France*, XXXVI (Paris, 1927), 432ff., esp. 464ff.; B. M. Xiberta, *Guia Terrena Carmelita de Perpinya* (= Estudios Univ. Catalanis, Barcelona, 1932) II, 60ff.; the object of Guido's writing was 'd'exposar more commentario el text del Decret en sos aspactes no estrictament juridica' (p. 65). The book by I. Melsen, *Guido Terreni iurista* (Rome, 1939), was not accessible to me. Cf. also R. Naz in *Dict. Droit Can.* V, 1011–12.

20 The relevant texts tally entirely: cf., e.g. IV.13.1.1, p. 392bC with the Archdeacon's *Rosarium*, XVII.4.35 (edn Venice, 1523), fo. 236ra, no. 4; IV.18.1.3, p. 429aC with XI.3.31, fo. 184rb; IV.15.3.2, p. 417bE with XVI.1.19, fo. 215vb, no. 3. A comparison with the Archdeacon's commentary on the Sext yields the same result.

21 Terreni was critical, if not hypercritical, of Gratian's use of sources, cf. P. Fournier (above n. 19) 466f., and when theological and canonistic opinions differed, 'taceat Huguccio, quia viri theologi omnes tenent et sequuntur Augustinum' (cit. from Fournier, p. 467).

popes. It is at once evident that this *Registrum* was nothing but Pseudo-Isidore.

About the non-juristic writers and sources very little needs to be said, because all the necessary spade work has been done.[22] What remains to be added is the frequent invocation of Pseudo-Denys whose works apparently never lost their authoritative appeal. There are also isolated instances of quotations from Cicero and Seneca.[23] His great respect for Thomas Aquinas is as significant as is his detached attitude towards Duns and his opposition, if not pathological animosity, to Peter Aureoli. John of Paris is usually viewed with a critical eye. Because hitherto unnoticed it deserves to be pointed out that he records – and apparently accepts – the non-canonical character of the Books of Maccabees: '(Aliqui) dicunt quod libri Machabaeorum non sunt de canone Bibliae, ut dicit Hieronymus in prologis super libris Salomonis'.[24] What needs stressing is the quite remarkable absence of any influence by the new kind of thought-processes as they had become rather fashionable just at the time of his writing. The naturalism, engendered by Thomism and brought into the limelight with particular incisiveness in the writings of John of Paris, Dante, or Marsilius – to mention just a few of his contemporaries – either passed him by[25] or was rejected outright, as in the case of Marsilius to whom he only refers in his citations of the decree of condemnation. There is no proof that he had really understood the implications of this work. Indeed, he may never have read it.[26]

II

The petrinological theme is the backbone in the final *Quaestiones* in the Prologue. Their central subject is the origin, function, scope and extent

---

[22] By Xiberta, *op. cit.* (above n. 1), pp. 197ff. That he also used the *Summa confessorum* is evident, cf. Boyle, *Proceedings* (above n. 3), p. 430 (use of Pagula's *Summa Summarum*).

[23] Cf., e.g., IV.20.2.1, p. 447bE.

[24] IV.45.un., p. 568aB and also E. See St Jerome in his *Praefatio in Libros Solomonis*, in Migne, *PL.* XXVIII, 1243: 'Machabaeorum libros legit quidem ecclesia, sed inter canonicas scripturas non recipit, sic et haec duo volumina legat ad aedificationem plebis, non ad auctoritatem ecclesiasticorum dogmatum confirmandam.' Among the 'aliqui' may have been John of Salisbury, in his *Ep.* 143 (old numbering) in Migne, *PL.* CXCIX.126. Cf. also Peter the Venerable, *Tractatus contra Petrobrusianos haereticos*, in Migne, *PL.* CLXXXIX, 751. But, as far as I can see, the overwhelming view was that these books were canonical. The reference to St Jerome testifies to John's erudition. For an explanation of Jerome's reasons see now J. N. D. Kelly, *Jerome: his life, writings, and controversies* (London, 1975), pp. 159ff.

[25] He knew, how ver, the *Politics*, cf. e.g., Prol. IV.2.1, p. 231bC–D; *Qu* 5.3, p. 245.

[26] In his Postill on Matthew he seems to have adopted a similar course, and 'he shows no sign of having read it' (Smalley (above n. 1), p. 125).

John Baconthorpe as a Canonist

of the papal government itself. His analyses follow well-trodden lines relative to the primatial function of the pope. Nevertheless, his historical perspective is noteworthy. He sees the division between East and West historically conditioned: the unity of the Church was destroyed, he declares, by the 'Greeks' who refused to acknowledge papal primacy. And the arrogation of patriarchal powers by the bishop of Constantinople formalised the schism.[27] And to him the essence of the new Marsilian doctrine was identical with the Greek standpoint: rightly therefore had his heresy, based on biblical-exegetical grounds, been condemned by the papacy.[28] He constantly refers in this context to the 'papal Register': 'Haec habes in libro qui intitulatur Registrum Romanorum Pontificum in decretis Anacleti papae.'[29] Nor is it surprising that the spurious *Epistola Clementis* makes its appearance,[30] and that he approvingly also cites Peter as *cephas* in the sense of *caput* of the apostles. Here our author falls into the same trap into which many before him had fallen, by confusing the term *kephas* with the Greek *kephale*.[3]

An ancillary problem of the papal *plenitudo potestatis* concerned the participation of the cardinals in the creation of the law.[32] 'An papa ex plenitudine potestatis possit sine fratribus suis aliqua statuere de universali statu ecclesiae?' After a lengthy discussion he concludes: 'Omnem legem tam universalem quam particularem licitam, quam cum cardinalibus potest condere, potest per se.'[33] In this function he sees a 'commissario plena potestas generaliter concessa'[34] since the pope has in any case all the laws in his breast.[35] Because for our author

27 Temporarily healed by II Lyon: '...quadraginta tres errores...in concilio Lugdunensi, quos habui de libraria ecclesiae Roffensis...' (Prol., 10.1, p. 262aA–D). In IV.48.12, p. 575bC this becomes 'Libraria de Roccaforte' and in IV.50.1.1, p. 578bA this is: 'Libraria de Rocha forte'.
28 Prol. 10.1, p. 262aC.
29 See P. Hinschius, *Decretales Pseudo-Isidorianae* (repr. Aalen, 1963), p. 79: *Ep.* 2, c.24; *Ep.* 3, c.30, p. 83 = Gratian, *Dist.* XXI. 2, to which he refers.
30 Cf. Ps. Anacletus, *Ep.* 3, c. 29, and Prol. 10.1, p. 262bC–D.
31 Even Innocent III had made the same mistake: *Sermo* II in Migne, *PL.* CCXVII 658A; *Sermo* XVIII (*ibid.* 517B), but cf. *Sermo* XXI (*ibid.* 552C), where he began to have doubts about this meaning. In his decree of condemnation of Marsilius John XXII had the same view: Raynaldus, ed. cit. (n. 17 above), p. 324. It all originated with Ps. Anacletus, *Ep.* 3, c. 33, ed. cit., p. 83: 'Cephas, id est caput.' This is not noted by H. Fuhrmann, *Einfluss und Verbreitung der ps. isidorischen Fälschungen* (Stuttgart, 1972–4).
32 See p. 263aC. On the problem of the divine or human origin of the cardinalate, cf. W. Ullmann, 'Eugenius IV, Cardinal Kemp and Archbishop Chichele' in *Essays in Medieval History presented to Aubrey Gwynn* (Dublin, 1958), pp. 359–86.
33 He quotes the Archdeacon's *Rosarium*, XXV.1.6. (edn Venice, 1523, fo. 274, no. 1) who in his turn quoted Laurentius Hispanus: 'Dicit lau. quod generalem legem universali statui ecclesiae condere non potest papa sine cardinalibus, sed particularem.' John evidently went much further. 34 See p. 263bB.
35 The reference is to the enactment in the Sext by Boniface VIII which made the Roman law passage of C.VI.23.19 the official papal standpoint: VI: I.2.1.

X

the pope was the pivot of the whole ecclesiologically conceived society, 'in omni casu potest per se in quo potest cum cardinalibus'. The sole barrier to papal legislative power he finds in the Old and New Testaments, and in this view he moves along accepted doctrine.

Another contingent question of the papal plenitude of power referred to the pope's right to designate his successor, a topic rarely discussed by the canonists: positive canon law was perfectly plain on the issue[36] which for him was no compelling reason for not examining the problem at length.[37] What exercised his mind was the example of Peter who had appointed his successor in the person of Clement I. Hence could not every pope as successor of St Peter do the same? For Peter 'ordinavit Clementem successorem in auribus totius ecclesiae'. To soothe his conscience John saw this as a genuine election which 'vocatur inspiratio spiritus sancti, quae est canonica'. Once more there was consultation of the book 'qui vocatur registrum Romanorum Pontificum', where in the first chapter he found the 'actual' letter which Clement himself had written to St James in Jerusalem.[38] According to John, Linus and Anacletus were Peter's assistants,[39] whereas Clement was consecrated bishop and after Peter's death became his successor. Indeed, he is quite right in saying that the 'Register of the Pontiffs' (Pseudo-Isidore) had no entry relating to Linus and Cletus (though he might have known that Cletus and Anacletus were identical) from which he concluded that they were no popes.[40] But the problem still remained, despite the Epistola Clementis, for if Clement was the

36 Cf. Alexander III in III Lat., c. 1 (partly in x: 1.6.6) and Gregory X in II Lyon, c. 2 (partly in vi: 1.6.4).

37 From the late 4th cent. the appointment of the Roman archdeacon amounted to his designation as the future pope, as, for instance, evidenced by the decree no. 5 of the Roman synod of 1 March 499: MGH. Auctores antiquissimi, xii.399ff. at 404. The only certain designation of a successor was by Boniface II in 531, see Lib. Pontificalis, ed. L. Duchesne (repr. 1955) I, 281, who appointed the unfortunate Vigilius, but had to retract on protest. The case re-echoed throughout the medieval period, cf. e.g. Peter Damian, Lib. gratissimus, c. 16, MGH. Libelli de Lite, 1.38, lines 30–5; Deusdedit, Libellus contra invasores et symoniacos, c. 13, ibid. ii, 312, lines 4–6; Gerhoch of Reichersberg, Opusc. de edificio Dei, c. 155, ibid. iii, 190f. From one of these sources or their derivatives John learned of the problem. This incident is also the occasion on which the principle that prima sedes a nemine iudicatur was applied, see Lib. Pont., loc. cit.

38 Epistola Clementis, ed. Hinschius, Decretales Pseudo-Isidorianae, pp. 30ff. About details cf. W. Ullmann, 'The significance of the Epistola Clementis' in Journ. of Theological Studies, n.s. xi (1960), 295ff. A check proves that John's quotations are perfectly correct.

39 The gl. ord. on viii.1.1 saw the problem differently and adopted a different solution: '... videns autem Clemens quod hoc esset perniciosum exemplum quod aliquis sibi eligerit successorem, renuntiavit papatui et tunc electus est Linus, eo mortuo electus est Cletus, quo mortuo denuo fuit Clemens electus, et sic Clemens secundum unam computationem fuit secundus, et secundum aliam fuit quartus. Disputat hic mundus, quartus fueritve secundus?'

40 For the various kinds of computation cf. art. cit. (above n. 38), pp. 302ff.

John Baconthorpe as a Canonist

first successor of St Peter, who elected him after Peter's death? 'Per quos fiebat electio Clementis?' His answer is:

Pro illo tempore haec fuit bona electio, nam cum assensu cleri et populi consuevit antiquitus episcopi fieri electio.[41]

In subsequent ages

semper electio pertinuit ad clerum, sed fidelis populi consensus adhibendus erat, quia docendus est populus, non sequendus.[42]

John goes very far in the application of the electoral principle which he bases on Pseudo-Anacletus:[43] the election of a pope was specifically ordained by Christ:

Fuit ex ordinatione Christi, nam Petrus a Christo et per electionem apostolorum fuit institutus in forma electionis in futurum.[44]

In the last resort this unusual view could only be derived from the preamble of the *Epistola Clementis*.[45] According to John the electoral principle was even applied to Christ as can be concluded from Is. 42. 1. He does not, and in all likelihood cannot, adduce any authority for this remarkable thesis.

In the end he shelters behind the example of Moses who was bidden by God not to elect, that is, appoint his own successor, from which he deduces that 'nec summus pontifex debet eligere successorem' partly in order to avoid simony, partly to exclude subterfuges and similar reprehensible devices.[46] Nor could the appointment of Clement by Peter provide a precedent because this was, our author avows, 'prae-difinitum per spiritum sanctum', and what is thus arranged is outside the ordinary laws. He is bound to concede that the papal plenitude of power suffered 'exceptionem in hoc casu'. Indubitably Peter had been

---

[41] Referring to *Dist.* LXIII.20 and 11, and *Dist.* XXIII.1.

[42] He may have had in mind the decree of 769 (*MGH. Concilia*, II, 86, no. 14) embodied in *Dist.* LXXIX.4. The memorable expression *Populus docendus, sed non sequendus* originates with Celestine I, *Ep.* 5, in Migne, *PL.* L, 437, cf. W. Ullmann, *Principles of Government and Politics in the Middle Ages*, 3rd edn (London, 1974) p. 134, though *docendus* was sometimes changed into *ducendus*, e.g., by Alcuin, *Ep.* 132, c. 9 in *MGH. Epp.* IV, 199 (addressed to Charles); here also the rejection of the adage: *Vox populi, vox Dei*, 'cum tumultuositas vulgi semper insaniae proxima sit.' For the Roman synod in 898 under John IX it was also self-evident that 'populum non sequendum esse, sed docendum', see J. D. Mansi, *Conciliorum Collectio* (Venice, 1773) XVIII, 223E.

[43] *Dist.* XXII. 2 = Ps. Anacletus, *Ep.* 3, c. 32, ed. Hinschius, *Decretales*, p. 83.

[44] Prol. x.3, p. 264bD: 'Ipsi (apostoli) inter se idipsum voluerunt, ut reliquis omnibus praeesset apostolis et caput...'

[45] See *Epistola Clementis*: 'vocatus et electus,' ed. Hinschius, *Decretales*, p. 30.

[46] Invoking Gratian, VIII.1.6.

chosen by the apostles as their head, and it was they who had bequeathed this arrangement to posterity as an immutable law:

Dices igitur canones apostolorum, qui reperiuntur in registro Romanorum pontificum, sunt immutabiles.

Pseudo-Isidore had not yet spent his force in the fourteenth century. There were very few canonists, or for that matter theologians, who had taken the trouble to consult the 'original source'. From the canonistic standpoint it is the consultation of the source rather than the substance of the novel argumentation which is significant, especially when one considers how stereotyped, if not monotonous, fourteenth-century canonistic literature had become. The novelty of approach (as well as of interpretation) is all the more refreshing as it was advanced by a scholar whose mind was not, by training, cast into the somewhat rigid mould of the jurist who was hypnotised by the lex lata.[47]

The electoral principle entails consideration of the cardinalate. Not apparently much exercised by the contemporary discussions concerning the divine or human origin of the cardinalate as an institution, his point d'appui is once again the Epistola Clementis – 'ut in registro Romanorum pontificum, cap. I'. According to John's interpretation, the cardinals had existed before Nicaea because, like patriarchs and archbishops, they had been appointed by the apostles.[48] Peter himself had assistants: what is therefore of particular importance in this context is that the cardinals had an intimate connection with the Roman Church which (Ps.) Anacletus (Dist. xxII.2) called 'cardo (et caput) omnium ecclesiarum'. From here it was only a short step to the explanation of the cardinals as cardines which indeed was the common standpoint.[49] Of the Innocentian view concerning the Levitic origin of the cardinals there is no allusion anywhere.[50] Instead at great length and with exact folio reference he quotes from the 'papal register' that the earliest popes had considered the prelates appointed by the apostles as collaterales assistentes or counsellors.[51]

The relationship between the cardinals and other ecclesiastical

---

[47] About the different approaches of theologians, philosophers and jurists to the idea of justice and law, cf. Ullmann, Principles (above n. 42), pp. 290ff.

[48] 'Ante illud concilium sub Sylvestro (!) celebratum instituti fuerunt...'

[49] This view of cardo-cardinalis has a long history and was also quoted in the Leo–Humbert letter to Kerullarios (cited in Growth, above n. 7), p. 321. For the early historical (as distinct from 'doctrinal') development see S. Kuttner, 'Cardinalis' in Traditio, III (1945), 129ff. which is basic.

[50] For details cf. W. Ullmann, art. cit. (above n. 32), esp. pp. 369ff.

[51] 'Haec in Registro Romanorum Pontificum, fo. 5 et fo. 19...'

John Baconthorpe as a Canonist

dignitaries constituted one of the most hotly debated questions in medieval juristic scholarship.[52] In a concise and succinct manner John makes the very distinction that was to become the official standpoint exactly a hundred years later. He maintained that basically the *ratio ordinis episcopalis* and the *ratio iurisdictionis papalis* determine the relationship between cardinals and other prelates. The distinction between what is technically called the *potestas ordinis* and the *potestas iurisdictionis* supplies a firm juristic basis for establishing the right order. A century later Eugenius IV was to make exactly the same distinction in unravelling the cluster of problems surrounding the archbishop's relations to a cardinal. Let our author speak himself:

Licet archiepiscopi et patriarchae sunt maiores ratione ordinis episcopalis, tamen cardinales sunt maiores ratione iurisdictionis papalis.[53]

It is evident that he considered the cardinalate an ecclesiastical office that could be attached to any rank: hence the cardinal-deacon was hierarchically superior to an archbishop. For him the cardinals are judicial assistants of the pope, again the view authoritatively expressed later by Eugenius IV. According to John they assist the pope in trials concerning bishops, archbishops, patriarchs, in controversial matters relative to faith and morals, and evidently in the formulation and enactment of legislative measures.[54] Furthermore, by reason of their intimate judicial link with the pope they are called *legati a latere*, because they form part of the pope's body, an adaptation of the respective Roman law statement that the senators formed part of the emperor's body.[55] This topic leads our author to discuss the legatine system and the prerogatives which the cardinals enjoy in the exercise of their functions as *legati a latere*. He presents a neat and competent summary of the respective enactments[56] and devotes considerable space to the powerful protection of the cardinals, notably in respect of offences committed against them. These offences are to be treated as high treason, because the eventual target of the crime was the papal majesty itself. Hence punishment was

---

52 For this cf. W. Ullmann, 'The legality of the papal electoral pacts' in *Ephemerides Iuris Canonici*, XII (1956), 312ff.

53 Art. 4, p. 265bE–266aA.

54 The wording of Eugenius IV's decree *Non mediocri dolore* (details in art. cit., above n. 32), should be compared with that of our author.

55 See C. IX.8.5, incorporated in Gratian, VI.1.22. He also adduces the *gl. ord.* on X: 1.30.9 which concedes that this judicial function also applies to the *capellani papae* when acting as papal legates.

56 Cf. X: 1.30.8, 9, 10; he also refers to X: V.33.23 (= IV Lat. c. 5) and VI: 1.15.1.

extended beyond the actual wrong-doer to his descendants in direct line as well as to collateral relatives.[57] The crime entailed the social, economic and moral ruin of the defendant, his family and relations, as they were deprived of the right to acquire property or to dispose of it by testamentary means. Hardly any other crime incurred such stringent penalties as the crime of *lèse majesté*, in itself a first-rate pointer to the underlying governmental ideology.

The substance and meaning of the papal vicariate of Christ presupposed clarification of Christ's own powers: here he follows Thomas Aquinas' *Summa theologiae* (III.59) closely and contributes little in substance. Since in common with Thomas he considers that Christ had judicial powers (*iudiciaria potestas*) in regard to all human things (*quantum ad omnes res humanas*), John can readily employ the teleological argument:

Res humanae ordinantur, *ut* per earum usum debitum assequetur homo vitam aeternam, et vitae aeternae iudex est Christus.[58]

This is the message of the wholeness point of view: the totality of the life of a Christian *qua* Christian matters. No conceptual distinction can be drawn between religious, moral, political and other norms. This indivisibility was a basic Christian presupposition and furnishes an easy explanation for the view expressed by an exact contemporary of Baconthorpe that life was merely a *vita transitoria* in which the worldly things are no more than 'organa et instrumenta ad finem ultimum ordinata'.[59] Indeed, it was the standpoint that had been argued in countless tracts from the fourth to the fourteenth centuries. Further, according to John, Christ had 'potestatem dispositivam, distributivam et translativam quantum ad omnes res huius mundi'.[60] Consequently, Christ was 'rex regum super omnes reges terrae'. In this very same context John viewed property as an effluence of grace, a claim unbeknown to him already made by Gregory VII,[61] and by Innocent IV and Hostiensis (whom he invokes).[62] Therefore, 'potest dominium dare aliis et con-

---

[57] See VI: v.9.5. On this cluster of problems cf. W. Ullmann, 'The significance of Innocent III's decretal "Vergentis"' in *Études...dédiées à Gabriel Le Bras* (Paris, 1965), 729ff.

[58] At p. 267aA.

[59] Hermannus de Schilditz, *Contra haereticos*, ed. R. Scholz, *Unbekannte kirchenpolitische Streitschriften des 14. Jahrhunderts*, II (Rome, 1914), 135, cf. also 142. This totality standpoint was expressed lucidly by another contemporary of John, Conrad of Megenberg, *De Translatione Romani imperii*, c. 12, ed. *ibid.* II, 292: 'Liquidum est religionem christianam quodam *totum* esse.' [60] At p. 267aB, referring to Ps. 23:1.

[61] *Reg.* VII.14a, ed. E. Caspar, *MGH, Epistolae Selectae*, t. II (repr. Berlin, 1955), 487: the two apostles can 'omnium hominum possessiones pro meritis tollere unicuique et concedere'.

[62] Innocent IV in his *Apparatus* (edn Frankfurt, 1535), ad X:III.34.8, fo. 430vb, no. 10; Hostiensis, *Lectura in Decretales* (edn Paris, 1512), *ibid.*, fo. 124va.

cedere sicut placet'.[63] Property was not based on any natural law or natural rights, but was a favour, a grace, a *beneficium* conceded.[64]

To these views John adjoins his very detailed analyses concerning the substance and ramifications of papal power. In a different context he had stated that the pope's function was principally juristic: 'Papa est arca iuris, cuius est omnes libertates ecclesiasticas statuere.'[65] Although he did not operate with the concept of the pope as *indignus haeres b. Petri*, he nevertheless assumed the juristic transfer of powers to have taken place topographically: 'Locus autem quem elegit Dominus est sedes Petri et apostolica.'[66] And this transfer concerned the same rights he had attributed to Christ – the *ius dispositivum, distributivum* and *translativum*, a categorisation and a thesis all his own: I have not found it before, nor does he himself cite an authority. For the function of the pope as universal monarch he invokes partly the law and partly doctrine.[67] Innocent III's thesis that 'Romanus pontifex non tantum puri hominis, sed veri Dei vicem gerit in terra et divina auctoritate fulcitur'[68] is correctly seen by John as the expression of papal *maioritas*, that is, legal and judicial sovereignty concerning all Christians 'totius orbis indistincte'.[69] His exegesis presents the traditional unipolarity point of view. What is here remarkable is the absence of any reference to *Unam sanctam* or the numerous other unambiguous and relevant papal statements nor is there any recourse to a two-sword theory or the juristic implications of the Donation of Constantine. Evidently, papal sovereignty includes the non-justiciability of the pope: the papal tribunal was the final court of appeal 'in omni causa tam civili quam ecclesiastica'.[70] This unappealable jurisdiction extends also to the deposition of kings – the relevant passage is a literal copy of the Arch-deacon's[71] – as well as of emperors.[72]

Let us now briefly survey the last *Quaestio* in the Prologue in which

---

[63] At p. 267aC.
[64] About this concession principle, cf. *Principles* (above n. 42) pp. 54f., 76f.
[65] IV.3.2.2, p. 318bD, referring to *Dist.* XXI.1 and 2.   [66] Art. 4, p. 269aA.
[67] Such as X:I.7.3; IV.17.13, and the relevant glosses and commentaries, as well as to *Dist.* XXII.1, which is attributed to Nicholas I, but is Peter Damian's. For the genesis and later development, cf. *Growth*, (above n. 7), p. 437 n.4, to which should be added another statement of Damian's in his letter to Hildebrand: *Opusc.* 5, in Migne, *PL.* CXLV, 91.
[68] X:I.7.30; cited at p. 268bB.
[69] Referring to the *Lectura* of Hostiensis, ad X:IV.17.13 (edn Paris, 1512), fo. 38va.
[70] Art. 4, p. 269aA. For some observations on this topic cf. W. Ullmann, 'The medieval papal court as an international tribunal' in *Virginia Journal of International Law* (= Essays in honour of H. C. Dillard), XI (1971), 356ff.
[71] *Rosarium* ad XV.6.3 (edn Venice, 1523), fo. 213rb.
[72] Relying on X:I.6.34 and the *gl. ord. ibid.*

he deals with two seemingly unrelated problems, the conversion of Jews and infidels, and the papal rights in regard to the Holy Land. This at first sight unusual grouping can be explained by a common denominator: the treatment and position of non-Christians by Christians. Law and doctrine had never left any doubt about the essential element of consent in baptism.[73] Yet, he holds, papal legislation shows that there were ways and means by which indirect and gentle pressure could be exercised to make the Jews convert:[74] the Church 'indirecte quodam modo eos cogit'.[75] Moreover, as Huguccio had already pointed out, Jews could be subjected to higher public payments, 'ut sic facilius trahantur ad fidem'.[76] The pope may prohibit usury among Jews because 'hoc est contra utrumque testamentum'.[77] Christians have an undoubted right to send missions to infidel countries: if they object, secular princes may be called upon to assist missionary efforts: 'potest ergo papa cogere infideles ad fidem coactione (saltem indirecta)'. In regard to the Holy Land John considers that numerous statements in both the Old and the New Testaments amply justify papal intervention which is also warranted by history, he declares: the conquest of the Persians by the Emperor Heraklios in 628–9 who rescued Palestine from the infidels[78] – a most unusual argument which no other author had adduced – and the eventual reconquest by Godfrey of Bouillon through which a *ius conquisitionis* accrued to the papacy. And since the pope *qua* pope succeeds Christ – 'quia Romanus pontifex succedit Christo' (a debatable formulation) – he was juristically the *haeres terrae promissionis*. However, all this was by then a purely academic discussion.

Additional canonistic points came also to be treated in John's *Quodlibeta*.[79] One of these concerned the petrinological thesis in regard to the revocation of a previous papal decree or statement. The *Quodlibet*

---

73 Prol., *Qu*. x, p. 270aE.

74 x:v.6.4, 15; also 8, 10, 13; Gratian, xxviii.1.13.   75 At p. 271aB.

76 In the *Rosarium* ad xxiii.6.4 there is no mentioning of Huguccio which proves that John had consulted him directly (and most Huguccio MSS are of fourteenth-century provenance). The Archdeacon said this: 'Nota argumentum pro consuetudine hispanie ubi exiguntur tributa a sarracenis et iudaeis, etsi terras non habebant secundum la.' Apart from Laurentius no other canonist (or civilian) is quoted.

77 Innocent IV in his *Apparatus* ad x:iii.34.8, fo. 430v. Hostiensis in his *Lectura, ibid.* (edn Paris, 1512) fo. 124va, is of the same opinion, though he does not mention Innocent: 'Oves autem non sunt solum fideles, set etiam infideles per creationem, licet non sint de ovili, unde sequitur quod papa super omnes habet potestatem et iurisdictionem de iure, licet non de facto.'

78 For this see G. Ostrogorsky, *Geschichte des byzantinischen Staates*, 3rd edn (Munich, 1963), 86f. Heraklios returned the Cross to Jerusalem in 630.

79 Appended to the Cremona edn of 1618. Their exact chronological relationship to the Commentaries needs to be established. There may be several recensions.

John Baconthorpe as a Canonist

in question[80] was a sequel to the Marsilian attack on the petrinological theme and to some pronouncements by John XXII: had the pope by virtue of his primatial position the right to revoke a decision of his precedessor? Indeed, this problem was later to assume major dimensions in the shape of papal infallibility. He had already touched on the power of the keys in the appropriate places of the *Sentences*.[81] The *Quodlibet* is headed by the carefully worded question:

Utrum illud quod est ordinatum per *clavem scientiae* in fide et in moribus semel per Romanum pontificem ita perseveret immobile, quod successori revocare in dubium vel contrarium asserere non licuit, sed de his, quae per *clavem potestatis* ordinaverit, secus sit.

Restrictions of space do not allow a detailed examination of this problem here, but so much may be said with confidence that John made a distinct contribution to this important issue, because he viewed it from both the theological and canonistic angles. Indeed, by a very dexterous handling of the law, including decrees which were of no universal interest, such as Clement V's *Meruit*, he trod a path which is far from being appreciated by modern scholarship. Not the least significant feature (which appears to have gone unnoticed) of this *Quodlibet* is that in it he touches on, and examines, the meaning of such technical matters as the clause employed in papal documents (the *Privilegia*): 'salva auctoritate Romanae ecclesiae'.[82] That he did concede to the pope revocatory powers, has recently been pointed out.[83] But his argumentation demands that degree of close attention and respect which it has not yet received. As soon as the problem was aired, he realised its explosive potentiality. To him the problem of revocability or infallibility had nothing to do with sovereignty: this was an exclu-

[80] *Quodlib.* III.17, pp. 774–9.
[81] IV.17. His Postill on Matthew is an appendix to his IV.19 about which see Smalley, art. cit. (above n. 1), especially p. 103.
[82] See p. 778aE and 779aA. For this clause cf. F. Thaner, 'Entstehung und Bedeutung der Formel *Salva...*' in *Sitz. Ber. Vienna, phil. hist. Kl.*, LXXI (1872), 807–51; J. B. Sägmüller, *Zur Geschichte der Entwicklung des päpstlichen Gesetzgebungsrechts* (Rottenburg, 1937). The formula is Ps. Isidorian: Ps. Stephen, *Ep.* 2, c. 9, ed. Hinschius, p. 185; Ps. Julius, c. 12, *ibid.* p. 469. It appeared in Gratian, *Dist.* LXXX.1; III.6.12 and 9.7, also in the famous D.p.c.15, XXV.16. In view of W. Holtzmann's thesis in *Studia Gratiana*, I (1953), 325–49 that Gratian had no influence on the papal chancery before Clement III and the consistent use of this formula from the 40s onwards, the problem is in need of examination. The significance of this diplomatic matter has not fully been realised by H. Fuhrmann, *Einfluss und Verbreitung*, p. 352, n. 291; cf. also W. Ullmann in *Zeitschrift der Savigny-Stiftung, Kan. Abt.*, XLVI (1960) at 432.
[83] B. Tierney, *Origins of Papal Infallibility* (Leiden, 1972), p. 188, who is perhaps a shade too brief in the citation of passages (e.g. of that on p. 779a–b). Cf. also IV.17 and 15.11, pp. 515–518bC.

sively legal concept which could not be accommodated within the terms of the *magisterium*. Sovereignty was the effluence of the exercise of the *clavis potestatis* and concerned government: it is a meaningless concept within the precincts of the *magisterium* or teaching where the *clavis scientiae* operates. He used perfectly understandable terminology. Hence whether a statement or decree was revocable depended on whether it was issued by a pope in his capacity as a *gubernator* or in that as a *magister*. In the former capacity he acted as a sovereign monarch whose rulings could be modified or revoked by a (sovereign) successor, in the latter capacity he acted as a teacher, and the idea of sovereignty simply did not enter here.

Although it might at first sight seem strange, John also treats the Immaculate Conception within the petrinological framework. This instance testifies once more to his principal aim to achieve an integration of theological and liturgical matters which had elements in common with canon law. As his contribution has only been cursorily touched on by modern scholarship, a few remarks seem apposite. In a number of places[84] he attempted to prove the thesis that Mary was free from original sin and was conceived immaculately.[85] He draws his arguments partly from Augustine's *De natura et gratia*,[86] *De Genesi ad litteram*[87] and other exegetical works and some New Testament passages, here and there supported by snippets from Aristotle, by Anselm's *Cur Deus homo*[88] and Pseudo-Anselm's *De conceptu virginali* – the author of this *De conceptione B.V.M.* was Eadmer[89] – a tract, he says, that is to be seen in many places:[90]

Inveni istum librum in domo Fratrum Minorum Cantabrigiensium et postea inveni Parisiis eundem tractatum in manu unius communis stationarii.[91]

[84] III.3.2.4–5, pp. 34ff.; IV.2.3.3–5, pp. 307ff.; IV.3.1.2–3, pp. 314ff.; *Quodlib.* III.13–14, pp. 763ff.
[85] In II.2.30.2–3, pp. 642b–645b, he had propounded a different view which is singled out by I. Brady, 'The development of the doctrine of the Immaculate Conception in the 14th cent. after Aureoli' in *Franciscan Studies*, XV (1955), 175ff., at 195. John's contemporary, Hermann de Schilditz, wrote the first tract in Germany on the topic, *c.* 1350: *Tractatus de conceptione gloriosae virginis Mariae*, ed. A. Zumkeller (Würzburg, 1970), pp. 109ff. For the three MSS of this tract cf. editorial comment, pp. XIVff.
[86] Ed. in *Corpus scriptorum ecclesiasticorum latinorum* (Vienna), XL, 233–99.
[87] Ed. *ibid.* XXVIII, 1–435.   [88] Esp. cc. 16, 18, see p. 309bD.
[89] Ed. in Migne, *PL*, CLIX, 301–18 and by H. Thurston and Th. Slater, *Tractatus de conceptione s. Mariae* (Freiburg, 1904). Details in R. W. Southern, *St. Anselm and his Biographer* (Cambridge, repr. 1966), pp. 290ff. Apparently M. Manitius, *Geschichte der lateinischen Literatur im Mittelalter*, III (Munich, 1931), 92 still considered this a genuine Anselmian product.
[90] 'Hunc librum vidi in multis locis...incipit autem liber Anselmi de conceptione sic: Principium...' (p. 309bE).
[91] *Quodlib.* III.13, p. 763bB, also quoted by Xiberta, 'De Magistro Iohanne', p. 207 and Southern *St. Anselm*, p. 295 from Brady, 'Immaculate Conception', p. 196, n. 77.

John Baconthorpe as a Canonist

But in order to strengthen his case, a juristic buttressing appeared to him advisable, hence his invocation of a number of canon law passages.[92] The institution of a formal feast day celebrating the Immaculate Conception was to his mind long overdue. To this end he makes a passionate plea to the papacy that by virtue of its primatial function it should decree the establishment of this feast. In support of this plea he refers to the many relevant discussions among theologians in Paris, Oxford and Cambridge who were all of one mind:

Nam a multis annis disputatum est inter theologos in universitatibus Parisiensi, Oxoniensi ac Cantabrigiensi, et ubique determinatur, quod sanctum est conceptionem b. Mariae celebrare, habito respectu ad eius sanctificationem, et in dictis universitatibus celebratur per statutum.[93]

Only the papacy could put its seal on this custom, for its magisterial primacy extends also to liturgical matters. Both Innocent III[94] and Gregory X had shown the proper dimensions of this function,[95] and so did contemporary popes, such as John XXII and Benedict XII.[96] But there was even more justification for the papacy to act in the matter of the Immaculate Conception, because the Roman Church itself celebrated this feast;[97] and, since the true religion was preserved in the apostolic see,[98] it was only right and proper for the 'vicarius Dei in terris' to confirm this custom. Papal silence would inflict damage on religion.[99] John quotes lavishly from Pseudo-Anselm (i.e. Eadmer) and goes into the details of the miracle that was revealed to the abbot of Ramsey, Elsinus, apparently the first to have introduced this feast, at least in his abbey.[100] The *Quodlibeta* also refer to the opponents of the feast: there was the *glossa ordinaria* on the *Decretum* which poured ice-

---

[92] On the nature of Privilegia (which John invokes) see Innocent III in x:v.40.5, refined and elaborated by Innocent IV (vi:v.7.1) and commented on by himself in his *Apparatus* ad x:v.33 in fine (edn Frankfurt, 1535, fo. 538rb).

[93] iv.3.1.3, p. 316bB; *Quodlib*. iii.14, p. 767bB. See also iv.2.4.2, p. 316aC concerning the sermon preached by Alexander Neckam at Oxford. Duns and his teacher William of Ware were also advocates of the feast, cf. K. Binder, 'Heinrich von Gent über die Empfängnis der Gottesmutter' in *Festschrift für Franz Loidl* (Vienna, 1970) pp. 13–29, at 23f. Henry was an opponent.

[94] See x:1.1.2.   [95] vi:1.1.c.un. = II Lyon c.2.

[96] On the Beatific Vision. The date (29 Jan. 1336) gives some clue to the time of his writing. The same problem also forms the topic of iv.50.1 and 2, pp. 579ff.

[97] See iv.2.4.2, p. 316bE.

[98] He refers to Gratian, xxiv.1.11.   [99] Referring to xxiv.1.13.

[100] *Quodlib*. iii.14, p. 765bE: '...ibi recitat (scil. Anselmus) quomodo istud festum fuit miraculis revelatum abbati Helsmo Ramensi in Anglia...' See also *ibid.*, p. 767aE. This is from the *Miraculum s. Mariae*, in Migne, PL. cxix, 323–6. For details and background see R. W. Southern, 'The English origins of the "Miracles of the Virgin"' in *Mediaeval and Renaissance Studies*, iv (1958), 176ff., at 195–8.

cold water on this concept.[101] The professional canonists moved in good company, as he tells us, since no lesser man than Bernard of Clairvaux had strongly opposed the formal celebration of the Immaculate Conception.[102] It is understandable that John was gratified by the recent statute issued by the provincial council of Canterbury in January 1328 which decreed the observation of this feast.[103]

III

Space can here be found for only a few remarks on the numerous other topics treated by this much-neglected juristic theologian. A selection is not easy because his commentary on Book IV ranges over a very wide field of canonistic jurisprudence. His exposition is only loosely linked with the topic set by the Master of the *Sentences*. As a characteristic instance of John's method may be taken his commentary on *Dist*.vii. Its subject, the sacrament of confirmation, was dealt with by the Lombard in two short Articles, one on its essence, the other on its relation to baptism. Now John briskly deals with the theological side of confirmation,[104] only to hasten to the juristic question concerning the legitimate administration of the sacrament. Apart from Thomas Aquinas, Richard Middleton, and others, his main authorities are the relevant chapters in Gratian's *De consecratione*. John appends a number of associated problems, such as consecration of chrism, the power of the local bishop to delegate confirmation to priests in his diocese, and so on. But all this is merely an introduction to the quite unexpected question of the exact relationship between confirmation and election. Clearly, of this the Lombard had said nothing, but John joins the two topics and devotes three lengthy *Quaestiones* (fourteen columns) to them. Here he

---

[101] See *gl. ord. (De cons.* III.1; I used the edn Antwerp 1537): 'De facto conceptionis nihil dicitur, quia celebrandum non est sicut in multis regionibus fit, maxime in Anglia, et haec est ratio, quia in peccato concepta fuit.' To judge by the siglum, this was Huguccio's view. In his *Rosarium (ibid.,* IV.3, edn Venice, 1523, fo. 338vb) the Archdeacon treats this in connection with 'the two births' (of St John 3:3–5): '...unde conceptio b. Mariae non debet celebrari, sed nativitas ex utero bene celebretur et s. Johannis, quia fuerunt in utero sanctificati et eis fuit dimissum originale peccatum, secundum hu'. For Henry of Ghent, see above n. 93.

[102] See p. 764bC and p. 768aD. Bernard's letter to the canons of Lyon in Migne, *PL.* CLXXXII, 332–6.

[103] See p. 765aA: '...concilium provinciale Cantuariense noviter anno Domini MCCCXXVIII, mense Januario declarat...'. See D. Wilkins, *Concilia* (edn London, 1737), II, 552. W. Lyndwood, *Provinciale* (edn Oxford, 1679) comments on this decree under the title 'De Feriis' (p. 101a–b), where in addition to many canonists he also quotes Bernard's letter. With the exception of the last word ('libenter') the quotation is faultless.

[104] IV.7.1–3, p. 348b–349b.

John Baconthorpe as a Canonist

poses virtually all important matters relative to election: the qualification of electors, of the elected, personal and impersonal conditions of
valid elections, impediments to ratification, the principles of quantita-
tive and qualitative majority, the various forms of election procedures, the
rôle of scrutineers, voting by proxy, factors nullifying an election, such
as participation of excommunicated persons or of suspended officers,
and so on. Based on a thorough knowledge of canonistic literature, this
is a very respectable canonistic *opusculum* on elections, the importance
of which is only heightened by the appended question on the effects
of customary law and usages on elections.[105] It is in this partly
theoretical, partly practical context that he treats of the concept of
customary law, its juristic ingredients, its derogatory power, the
relative importance customary law may display in the elections of
various officers, such as in abbatial or episcopal elections, and similar
questions. No doubt this was an ingenious way of introducing his
audience or his readers to a jurisprudential topic of considerable magnitude. Dexterity of manipulating complex matter can certainly not be
denied to our author – witness his handling of customary law in relation to (what he himself calls) *ius positivum*,[106] or his anatomy of the
Roman-law-based view that *pontifex omnia iura suo pectore habet.*[107]

Another subject only remotely linked with the *Sentences* is that of
excommunication, its validity and effects.[108] Since excommunication
was a juristic act and therefore the effluence of jurisdictional power, he
reverts to the exercise of the *potestas clavium* to throw light on it from
yet another angle. Of the theologians – and he ranks himself among
them: 'cum igitur nos theologi concedimus...'[109] – he singles out
Thomas, Duns, the *Scoti*, Peter Aureoli, not without crossing swords
with him once again, while within the field of canon law he invokes the
whole galaxy of eminent canonistic names as well as the enactments
from Gratian down to the Clementines. This is a veritable tract on
excommunication.[110] Among the topics examined are the constitutional and ecclesiastical qualifications of the officiating organs; the rôle
of the unjust and unlawful sentence, including the famous statement by
Gregory I ('Utrum iuste vel iniuste obliget, pastoris tamen sententia
gregi timenda est');[111] *error iuris* and *error facti* as well as *ignorantia iuris* in
relation to the validity of the sentence; the distinction between ex-

---

[105] *Qu.* 4, p. 355aC.   [106] *Ibid.* p. 355bA.   [107] *Ibid.* p. 356aA (VI:1.2.1).
[108] *Sentences*, IV.17–19.   [109] Art. 3, p. 425aC.   [110] See pp 426aE–439bD.
[111] On this and its transmission cf. *Principles* (above n. 42), p. 107, to which should be added:
Anselm's *Collectio canonum*, ed. F. Thaner (repr. 1965), VI.139, p. 334.

communications which are null and void *ab initio* and those which are unjust; the grounds of appeal; the social consequences of excommunication; and so on. A highly significant feature of this 'tract' is the attention it gives to the excommunication of juristic persons, one of the really thorny problems after Innocent IV. Considering that he was a theologian, John shows himself extraordinarily well-informed on this topic. To him the *universitas* as a juristic person was a *persona imaginaria et non vera*: it possesses no *animam rationalem veram*,[112] and therefore, notwithstanding contrary opinions, excommunication can be decreed only against *universos animatos*, but not against the *universitas* itself.[113]

The obligatory character of commitments solemnly undertaken in an oath was frequently discussed since the problem first emerged during the Investiture Conflict:[114] John clearly saw the necessity of dealing with this question. The baptismal vow serves him as a springboard for an analysis of other vows (simple and solemn) and of oaths.[115] The canonistically important conclusion relates to papal dispensatory powers from vows and oaths.

Licet de plenitudine potestatis dispensare possit (scil. pontifex Romanus) super omne ius ecclesiae, ubi tamen erraret contra voluntatem Dei, non posset valere, quia ubi errat commissarius ab intentione committentis, nihil valet.[116]

Another practical problem he discusses was the modification of the promises contained in a vow or oath by extension or restriction, and the possible need of dispensation,[117] necessitated by changing circumstances or by misunderstanding or error.

In an ecclesiological context the descending theme of government and law assumed its concrete shape in the hierarchical ordering of society, hence the prominence of ecclesiastical ranks, their gradation and validity, notably of orders conferred by heretics. The divergence between theologians and canonists on this latter problem was an additional incentive for our author to find a synthesis, precisely because the topic embodied all the classical features of the *communauté des matières*.[118] Even the briefest of outlines of all the problems covered in

---

[112] Art. 3, p. 437aC–E.
[113] See VI:V.11.5. On the subject of excommunication of juristic persons see P. Michaud-Quantin, *Universitas* (Paris, 1970) pp. 327ff.
[114] Cf., e.g., Bernard of Constance, *Liber canonum*, in *MGH.*, *Libelli de Lite*, I.507, c. 37.
[115] IV.3.3.2, p. 321ff.
[116] Art. 3, p. 328bE, referring to X:III.8.4 and 5.38, which is really ingenious. For the *commissarius* cf. above at n. 34.
[117] *Ibid.* Art. 4, p. 330a–b, and Art. 5, pp. 330–332bE.   [118] IV.25, pp. 495ff.

John Baconthorpe as a Canonist

over sixty columns would assume monographic dimensions. Evidently, the 'hardy annuals' receive their due attention, such as the constituents of the sacramentality of orders;[119] whether the episcopal rank was an order or merely a higher grade of the priesthood; ordination impediments; dispensation from irregularities; and so on. In parenthesis it should be observed that this discussion too has a strong practical tinge, notably in regard to servitude and villeinage, property, manual labour and *mendicitas*.[120] Nor does he omit to deal with the nuns.[121] There is an inner coherence in this quite remarkable 'tract' on the orders, within which obedience and its consequences occupy an important place.[122]

Compensation for wrongs inflicted and restitutions of illegitimately acquired rights are characteristic of all legal systems. The medieval canon law, too, dealt with these subjects.[123] Despite the technicalities involved, John does not shirk this issue which was quite obviously of practical concern. Here again the *Sentences* provided only the most tenuous link with the topic of legal restitution. Under this heading[124] John treats of the need of turning a moral obligation into law and of the responsibility of the church (as distinct from its incumbent) for restitution. How far have the judicial personnel and the officers employed in and by the courts a duty of restitution and compensation?[125] Are arbitrators, auditors, executors, assessors, judges delegate, notaries, bedells, messengers and similar officers included in this personnel? In this lengthy examination of another sixty columns he also deals with such subjects as the withholding of just wages, excess of fair profit, compensation for damage caused by simony or usury,[126] indemnification for breach of contractual obligation, compensation for crimes committed in the prosecution of war, such as personal injuries, outrage against the person (rape),[127] restitution for shipwreck suffered, and so on. The mass of material here digested and dexterously manipulated is indeed most impressive.[128]

---

[119] *Ibid.* pp. 512–513bA. This topic prompted even the Archdeacon to consult Thomas Aquinas: *Rosarium*, xxv.1.6, no. 5, (edn Venice, 1523) fo. 275ra: 'Dicit Thomas in summa sua, quod...'.

[120] *Ibid.* pp. 500–501b; 520bE–523aD.   [121] iv.25.6, p. 512.

[122] *Qu.* 14, pp. 523ff.   [123] x:ii.13; vi:ii.5; *Clem.* 1.39; Gratian ii.2; iii.1.

[124] iv.21–22, pp. 452ff.   [125] Art. 4, referring to vi:ii.14.1.

[126] *Ibid.* pp. 466bA–475bB; *Qu.* 5–6, pp. 475ff.   [127] *Ibid.* pp. 459ff.

[128] Mention should at least be made of other practical canonical problems, such as the reasons and effects of the interdict and the qualification of those who can pronounce and dispense from it; clerical immunity (iv.11.4, pp. 384ff.); the right of asylum, its *raison d'être* and foundation in ecclesiastical doctrine (iv.13.1, pp. 392ff.); matrimony (iv.26ff., pp. 533ff.); consecration, desecration and reconsecration of churches and cemeteries, the appropriateness of the locality for divine services, etc. This exposition is a full-length commentary on x:iii.40.10; vi:iii.21.

Lest it be thought that John was only interested in substantive law, two topics in procedural law should at least receive a passing remark. The multitude of civil litigations and criminal trials prompted the introduction of simplified proceedings known as 'de plano et sine strepitu ac figura iudicii'.[129] John stipulates a number of safeguards so that the cause of justice does not suffer, although the procedure is 'contra ius commune'.[130] The other procedural point concerns the probative value of evidence. He treats this as an issue of the difference between the private and public knowledge of the judge.[131] It was an old problem and had excited many jurists: should the judge adjudicate or sentence on the basis of the evidence given in court, or can he also use his own privately acquired knowledge?[132] Here he adopts an independent attitude and rejects the canonists' general opinion that the judge should reach his verdict 'secundum allegata et probata'.[133] This rejection betrays his theological outlook and lack of practical experience in the administration of the law: his reasoning commands respect, nevertheless. Suppose, he says, that the defendant John is charged with committing theft in London on 10 December, and on the evidence before the judge the charge is proved, yet the judge knows perfectly well that John was in Rome on that day. If he now sentences John, he acts against his better knowledge and therefore sins; if he acquits him, he acts 'contra iustitiam publicam'. In disagreeing with the *communis opinio* he applies the descending theme of government and law in a rather unusual way. To him the *iudiciaria potestas* has to decide a case finally and, within an ecclesiological society, this power was first given to St Peter and thence to his successors who hand it on to lower placed officials. The pope (or, for that matter, a lower judge) cannot himself decide against the truth. This analysis is, perhaps, one of the best instances of our author's utter integrity. What makes this section still more significant is the light it sheds on the concept of law when seen in the pure and unadulterated air of theological premisses.[134] This topic,

c.un. and 23.2. He examines such questions as nose bleeding of the celebrating priest at mass (because blood is being shed); someone entering the church having been wounded outside in an affray; death occurring as a result of violence inside or outside the church; 'coitus maritalis sive extramaritalis' inside the church, all with further distinctions and subdivisions: IV.10.1–2, pp. 376ff.

[129] X:II.19.11 and *Clem.*: V.11.2 and II.1.2.   [130] IV.25.16, pp. 531–3.

[131] IV.1.3, pp. 282ff.; also II.40, pp. 688ff.

[132] Cf. W. Ullmann, *The Medieval Idea of Law* (London, repr. 1968), p. 129 and the civilian passages cited there.   [133] IV.1.3, p. 283bD–E.

[134] See Art. 3, p. 284aE: Judicial decisions should conform to truth. 'Ergo ius humanum desinit esse eius ligans aut solvens apud eum, qui certus est de veritate contraria.'

John Baconthorpe as a Canonist

as so much else in John Baconthorpe's work, would repay thorough study by medievalists whose concern is historical jurisprudence.

In studying John Baconthorpe, the reader is confronted by a man of exceptional erudition. He is conversant with a far greater number of academic disciplines than most of his contemporary academics. His *Quaestiones canonicae* are primarily didactic and may well be classed the forerunner of the comprehensive academic handbook which synthesised theology and canonistics and aspired at an integrated practical theology. This integration was to overcome the fragmentation that threatened the traditional unity of outlook. What others of such divergent persuasion as Dante, Engelbert of Admont, Alvarus Pelagius and Augustinus Triumphus tried to do in the field of government and society – that is, to restore the latter's unity by the universality of the monarch's rule, in order to neutralise the new disintegrating forces – the Carmelite attempted to do by returning to the one and indivisible juristic theology. His *Quaestiones* are simultaneously more and less than the conventional canonistic works. They are more, because they attempt to bridge the yawning gap between theology and jurisprudence; they are not tied to specific juristic categories; they are not intended as professional expositions of canonistic jurisprudence, but are conceived on a comprehensive scale. But against these indubitable merits must be set some demerits: there is hardly any Roman law or the viewpoint of a civilian taken into account. And were not many of the problems common to both canonist and civilian? Did not the very first titles of the first Book of the Codex deal with precisely the topics which formed a large part of our Carmelite's commentaries? Is not in fact canonical jurisprudence built on the firm foundations of Roman jurisprudence? Then as now, nobody could profitably pursue any canonistic topic unless he had at least an elementary grounding in Roman law. This grounding he lacked, as a perusal of his commentaries soon reveals. And within canonistic jurisprudence there are some notable lacunae, such as the lack of consultation of the numerous *ordines iudiciarii*. The topics are unevenly and selectively treated.

Yet whatever shortcomings there are, they are heavily outweighed by the positive achievements of the work. Our knowledge of the intellectual landscape of the fourteenth century would be materially enriched, if this undeservedly neglected canonistic theologian were to find a sympathetic interpreter and expositor who can be assured of a rich harvest. The achievements of lesser men have had a greater share of attention than this man's efforts, aiming as he did at a practical integration of several disciplines. Here indeed lies a vast and fallow field of research.

XI

THE MEDIEVAL INTERPRETATION OF
FREDERICK I's AUTHENTIC «HABITA»*

* The following editions of medieval works have been used:

A - *Civilians*

Accursius, *Glossa Ordinaria*.

Azo, *Summa Codicis*, Bâle, 1663.

Baldus de Ubaldis, *Commentaria in Codicem*, Venice, 1615.
—   —   *Digestum Vetus*, Venice, 1615.
—   —   *Infortiatum*, ibid. 1615.

Bartholomaeus Salicetus, *Super Codicem*, Venice, 1574.

Bartolus de Sassoferrato, *Commentaria in Codicem*, Aug. Taur., 1577.
—   —   *Digestum Vetus*, ibid., 1577.
—   —   *Infortiatum*, ibid., 1577.
—   —   *Digestum Novum*, ibid., 1577.

Cynus de Pistoja, *Commentaria in Codicem*, Francofurti, 1578.

Jacobus de Arena, *Super Jure Civili*, Lugduni, 1541.

Jacobus Butrigarius, *Lectura super Codicem*, Parisiis, 1512.

Jacobus de Ravanis, *Lectura super Prima Parte Codicis*, Parisiis, 1519.

Johannes de Platea, *Commentaria in Tres Libros*, Venice, 1563.

Lucas de Penna, *Commentaria in Tres Posteriores Libros*, Venice, 1597.

Odofredus, *Lectura in Codicem*, Lugduni, 1552.
—   —   *Digestum Vetus*, Lugduni, 1552.
—   —   *Infortiatum*, Lugduni, 1552.

Paulus Castrensis, *Commentaria in Codicem*, Venice, 1594.
—   —   *Digestum Vetus*, Venice, 1594.

Raphael Fulgosius, *Commentaria in Codicem*, Lugduni, 1547.

B - *Canonists*

Archdeacon (Guido de Baysio), *Rosarium*, Venice, 1577.

Goffredus de Trano, *Summa Titulorum Decretalium*, Venice, 1586.

Guilielmus Durantis, *Speculum Juris*, Bâle, 1584.

Henricus de Segusia (Hostiensis), *Summa Aurea*, Coloniae, 1612.
—   *Lectura in V Libros Decretalium*, Parisiis, 1512.

Johannes Andreae, *Novella super Decretalibus*, Venice, 1505.
—   *Novella in Sextum*, Venice, 1581.

Panormitanus, *Lectura in Decretales*, Venice, 1513.
—   —   *Sextum*, Venice, 1592.

Zabarella Franciscus, *Commentaria super Decretales*, Venice, 1602.

Mirari profecto jamdudum non desino, cum nemo unus Doctor hactenus de privilegiis scholasticorum abunde scripserit[1]. Written well over 400 years ago, these words of Petrus Rebuffus introducing his lengthy tract *De Privilegiis Scholarium* are still applicable to-day. The constitution of Frederick I, *Habita*, is justifiably referred to in the standard books on medieval universities as one of the great land marks in the development of the medieval *studia generalia*[2]. It « marks one of the great moments in the history of medieval learning [3]». That the great eighteenth-century English lawyer, William Blackstone, still recognized the validity of the authentic[4], cannot cause much surprise, although by no stretch of imagination could it be said that England formed part of the medieval empire[5]. But

---

C - *Manuscripts*

Glossa Ordinaria ad Comp. III (Tancred): Gonville and Caius College, Cambridge, MS n. 17.

Apparatus ad Comp. I, Cistercian Monastery, Zwettl, Lower Austria, MS no. 162.

Huguccio, *Summa Decretorum*, Lincoln Cathedral Chapter Library, MS no. 2, and Pembroke College, Cambridge, MS no. 72.

Johannes de Petesella, *Summa Decretalium*, Vatican Libr., MS Lat. 2343.

Thomas of Chabham, *Summa Confessorum*, University Library, Cambridge, Add. MS 3061.

[1] Contained in *Tractatus Illustrium Jurisconcultorum*, tom. XVIII, fols. 32va-67rb; also in *Tractatus Varii Petri Rebuffi*, Lugd., 1581, pp. 471-607.

[2] H. DENIFLE, *Die Universitäten des Mittelalters*, pp. 48 ff., G. KAUFMANN, *Geschichte der Deutschen Universitäten*, vol. I, pp. 163-6; H. RASHDALL, *The Universities of Europe in the Middle Ages*, ed. F.M. Powicke and A.B. Emden, vol. I, pp. 143-5, 180-1; S. D'IRSAY, *Histoire des Universités Françaises et Etrangères des Origines a nos Jours*, vol. I, pp. 90-1. The authentic was iussed in November 1158 at Roncaglia. On the background and genesis of this constitution see the stimulating and penetrating article by F. KOEPPLER, *Frederick Barbarossa and the schools of Bologna: Some remarks on the authentic Habita*, in « English Historical Review », vol. liv, 1939, pp. 577-607; here also a much improved text of the authentic will be found, pp. 606-7.

[3] Sir MAURICE POWICKE, *Three Studia Generalia*, in «Prague Essays», ed. R.W. Seton-Watson, 1949, p. 32, where the contents of the authentic are admirably summarized.

[4] Cited by POWICKE, *loc. cit.*; see W. BLACKSTONE, *Commentaries on the laws of England*, 6th ed., Dublin, 1775, Bk. III, vol. II, pp. 83-5. Although Roman law as such was never received in England, some of its general principles were adopted, cf. E. WOHLHAUPTER, *Der Einfluss naturrechtl. und kanonistischer Gedanken auf die Entwicklung der englischen Equity*, in « Acta Congressus Juridici Internationalis », 1935, vol. II, pp. 444 ff.

[5] Whatever the facts, late twelfth-century doctrine certainly maintained the opposite. The great canonist Huguccio (Innocent III's master) gave several opinions

neither did Spain and France, and yet Frederick's authentic was
as much recognized there as in the empire proper. It has been remarked with great truth that more than a vestige of the medieval
privileges can be observed in modern Oxford and Cambridge[1].
And, until fairly recent times, the immunity of the continental university
buildings from the power of the police (the so-called « Freiheit des
akademischen Bodens ») was one more reminder of the privileges
enjoyed by medieval students and masters.

Although the authentic enacted nothing startlingly new, its interpretation by the medieval jurists led to the fixation of a number of
privileges which came to be recognized as the *privilegia scholarium*,
allegedly based on Frederick's constitution. The jurists were the
only competent authorities to interpret the authentic, since, quite
apart from its insertion in the Codex of Justinian, the authentic was
living law, unlike so much else in the Justinianean codification; moreover, the jurists themselves were personally affected by this law, in
their former capacity as students as well as in their present function
as academic teachers. The — at times — rather liberal and extensive
interpretation of the authentic resulted, then, in the emergence of a
peculiar *privilegium scholarium* which held its own by the side of the
much older *privilegium clericorum*, comprising as it did the *privilegium immunitatis, canonis* and *fori*. The statutes of Bologna and of
Padua, to mention only two outstanding examples, bear witness to

---

of why the English and the French were subjects of the empire. Because his theory
is not as widely known as it deserves to be, we quote the passage in full. *Summa Decreti*, ad Dist.i, cap. 12, MS Pembroke College, Cambridge, no. 72: *Sed quid de Fran-
cis et Anglicis et aliis ultramontanis, numquid ligantur legibus romanis et tenentur vivere secundum eas? Respondeo, utique, quia subsunt vel subesse debent romano imperio,
nam unus imperator in orbe, ut VII, q. I In apibus; sunt in diversis provinciis diversi
reges sub eo, VI, q. III Scitote. Preterea quicumque utuntur lingua latina, dicuntur romani. Unde et lingua latina romana dicitur, ut de Consecr. Dist. IIII Retul., et ideo
romani hic intelliguntur omnes latini et hoc jure omnes latini astringuntur. Item saltem
ratione romani pontificis subsunt romano imperio; omnes enim christiani subsunt apo-
stolico et ideo omnes tenentur vivere secundum leges romanas, saltem quas approbat ecclesia.* This passage is now also transcribed by MOCHY ONORY, *Fonti Canonistiche
dell'Idea Moderna dello Stato*, 1951, p. 174-5; cfr. also the passage quoted from Magister P (Beneventanus ?) by A. M. STICKLER in *Salesianum*, 1952, p. 491. The
monumental work of Huguccio is still not edited; for a proposal to edit the *Summa*, see N. DEL RE, *I Codici Vaticani della Summa Decretorum di Uguccione*, 1938,
and particularly the forthcoming study of L. PROSDOCIMI, *La Summa Decreti di
Uguccione da Pisa*, in the « Studia Gratiana ».

[1] Sir MAURICE POWICKE, *loc. cit.*, p. 34.

this equality of the two *privilegia*[1]. This is all the more important to keep in mind, as the lay scholars, for whom (as we shall presently see) this authentic was primarily issued, were, compared with their clerical brethren, at a decided disadvantage in the matter of protection: as a group they had none of the great privileges which, as a matter of course, even the lowest tonsured clerk could claim. Although originally intended for the law scholars, the authentic also came to apply to all the lay scholars in other faculties.

This brings us to the motive which prompted the emperor to issue *Habita*. With great ingenuity and acumen it has recently been suggested that this law was granted upon the request of the professors at Bologna[2]. But it seems, if we can rely on the testimony of later jurists, that it was the *scholares* who submitted their request to the emperor[3]. Whatever the facts at Roncaglia might have been, we would be well advised to bear in mind the time and the temper of the time that witnessed the promulgation of this law. For nobody else appreciated the enormous political and ideological advantages that could be derived from the resuscitated Roman law more than Frederick and his able imperial chancellor, Rainald of Dassel. « Dassel knew the part that Roman lawyers could play in his new forward policy »[4], and « Dassel adopted all principles of law that served Barbarossa's interests »[5]. But serious difficulties and impediments had to be overcome by those who undertook the long and arduous

---

[1] See the Statutes of Bologna, cap. LXXXX, in H. DENIFLE, *Archiv für Literatur und Kirchengeschichte*, vol. III, p. 369; Statutes of Padua, cap. V (6); DENIFLE, *ibid.*, vol. VI, p. 491. Cf. also *Cartulaire de l'Université de Montpellier*, vol. I, no. 6, p. 192. Considering the French legislation at the University of Paris, M.-M. DAVY, *La situation juridique des étudiants de l'Université de Paris au XIIIe siècle*, in « Revue d'Histoire de l'Eglise de France », 1931, pp. 297-311, very pertinently says, pp. 300, 310: « Les écoliers... sont assimilés aux clercs ». But he does not associate *Habita* with this development.

[2] KOEPPLER, *loc. cit.*, p. 596.

[3] Cynus in his *Casus* introducing his commentary on *Habita*, fol. 206rb.

[4] KOEPPLER, *loc. cit.*, p. 606. The « forward policy » is well summed up by F. HEER, *Die Tragödie des Heiligen Reiches*, 1952, p. 151: « Unter der Parole von der Wiederherstellung der Einheit der Christenheit wollen Rainald und Friedrich die tatsächliche Unterordnung des Papsttums unter die Generallinie der Reichspolitik erkämpfen ».

[5] KOEPPLER, *loc. cit.*, p. 583. And yet, it does not seem that Rainald had studied Roman law at Paris, see KOEPPLER, *ibid.* and J. SPÖRL, *Rainald von Dassel und sein Verhältnis zu Johannes von Salisbury*, in « Eichmann Festschrift (Hist. Jb.) », 1940; p. 251.

journey to medieval Bologna. The professors themselves complained to the emperor about the practice of reprisals to which the students (and here the law students only could come into question) were effectively subjected[1]. But quite apart from the reprisals, there were innumerable other dangers that beset the scholar travelling from distant parts of Europe to Bologna. Hence, if Frederick wished to promote the scientific study of Roman law, from whose elaboration and application he expected so much in the political and ideological sphere, he had to find ways and means to facilitate attendance at the schools and to give the scholars that feeling of security which to all intents and purposes they lacked.

Yet, were these the only considerations that moved Frederick and his chancellor to issue the authentic? *Habita*, next to its apparent humanitarian character, certainly also had to its credit a purely political aspect which, we venture to add, was the more important one of the two. The fifties of the twelfth century witnessed an unparalleled upsurge of canonistic studies after the publication of Gratian's *Concordia discordantium canonum*[2]. As is well known, the work of Gratian was at once accepted in the school; and the tenor of this work leaves no room for doubt that at the time it presented the most appropriate weapon for the papacy, exactly fulfilling the dreams of a Gregory VII. If such a broad generalization is allowed, it is this: on the one hand, Gratian's *Decretum* was closely modelled on Roman law[3], and on the other hand, the prerogatives of the papacy

---

[1] See GIESEBRECHT, in *Sitzungsberichte der Bayrischen Akademie der Wissenschaften*, phil. hist. Cl., 1879, vol. II, p. 285; MONACI, in *Fonti per la Storia d'Italia*, vol. I, and DENIFLE, *op. cit.*, p. 49, and KOEPPLER, *art. cit.*, p. 596. For an example of how many « foreign » students flocked to medieval seats of learning, see A. L. GABRIEL, *English Masters and Students in Paris during the 12th century*, in « Analecta Praemonstratensia », 1949, pp. 51-95.

[2] For the date of its publication see the late MGR. DE GHELLINCK, *Le Mouvement Théologique du XIIe Siècle*, 1948, p. 212, and ST. KUTTNER, *De Gratiani Opere Noviter Edendo*, in « Apollinaris », 1948, pp. 118 f. A tentative suggestion is made in the forthcoming *Studia Gratiana* that the *Decretum* in the form in which we know it, had gone through three main phases, of which only the first belonged to the Gratian period proper.

[3] See esp. A. VETULANI, *Une suite d'études* etc., in « Revue Historique de Droit français et étranger », 1936, pp. 343-58; 1937, pp. 461-79, 674-92; 1947, pp. 11-48; *Idem*, in « Apollinaris », 1948, pp. 23 ff. Cf. further the late VAN HOVE, *Droit Justinien et Droit Canonique depuis le Décret de Gratien jusqu' aux Decretales*, in « Miscellanea Historica in Hono ,m Leonis van der Essen », 1947, vol. I, pp. 257-71. On the later

figure most prominently in it[1]. The proper science of canon law dates from the appearance of Gratian's *Decretum*. A glance at Bologna in the fifties of the century will show us what eminent and capable canonists, quite apart from Gratian himself, had been teaching there and making their influence felt[2]. But, politically speaking, what they learnt and studied and taught at Bologna was in no wise in harmony with what Frederick desired. And their ideological basis was the law, just as it was to be Frederick's new support. It would be idle to deny that the emperor or Dassel had not recognized this danger that constituted a threat to the future of Roman law studies. It is equally undeniable that all those students of canon law at that

---

influence of Roman law see especially the illuminating study by G. LE BRAS, *Le Droit Romain au service de la domination pontificale*, in « Revue Historique d. Droit franç. et étrang. », 1949, pp. 377-98.

[1] Cf. G. LE BRAS, *Les écritures dans le Décret Gratien*, in « Zeitschrift der Savigny Stiftung f. Rechtsgeschichte », Kanon. Abt., 1938, pp. 77 ff. The opinion of A. M. STICKLER, *Magistri Gratiani Sententia de Potestate Ecclesiae in Statum*, in « Apollinaris », 1948, pp. 36 ff., that the *Decretum* presents a dualism, is wholly erroneous. This « dualist » view is unhistoric and contradicts the ideological development from the times of Leo I and Gelasius I onwards; it is distorting since the anti-thesis of « State and Church » was quite alien to the medieval mind (the term *Status*, it will be noted, had to be invented to express what Gratian — or anyother contemporary — could not express, because it was not there); it solely operates with the twentieth-century concept of *ecclesia* and entirely neglects the central (Augustinian) idea of *ecclesia* which was the *fons et origo* of all medieval ecclesiastico-political thinking; it pays no regard to the ferment of the medieval universalist ideology, itself the resultant of Roman (imperial) and Christian universalism; it does violence to the tenet of the primatial position of the Roman Church and implicitly restricts the pope's function as *vicarius Christi*; it overlooks the fundamental difference between the *ordo sacerdotalis* and the *ordo laicalis*; it therefore rests, above all, on a profound misconception of the medieval *Respublica Christiana*, consequently disregards its most essential feature, its functionalism, and results in an interpretation which amounts to a perversion of what a Nicholas I had once called the *catholicus ordo*. Indeed, such dualistic « interpretations » breath the spirit of the papally condemned anti-papalist literature and arguments of the 13th and 14th centuries. The failure of the modern interpreters is on a par with the eventual failure of the medieval anti-papalists.

[2] Of the most eminent only the following should be mentioned: Paucapalea, Rolandus (how ominous for Frederick after the « beneficium » controversy), Omnibonus, Rufinus, Albertus (the later Gregory VIII, about whose importance for the hierocratic system and legislative power see W. HOLTZMANN, *Die Decretalen Gregors VIII*, in « Mitteilungen des Instituts f. oest. Geschichtsforschung », 1950, pp. 113-123), Cardinal Laborans, etc. For the whole intellectual climate at Bologna see especially DE GHELLINCK, pp. 416 ff.

time were clerks and were automatically protected by the very law they studied; the previously mentioned *privilegia* were all incorporated in the *Decretum*. Here was a lively scholarship, attracting scholars from far and wide who by virtue of their tonsure were effectively protected — there was the Roman law, perhaps equally lively, but whose students were always exposed to numerous vicissitudes and humiliations. Despite its youth, canon law and canonistics were already a serious competitor to Roman law. In order to put lay scholars wishing to study Roman law on something like an equal footing with the clerical scholars studying canon law, Frederick I issued *Habita*. The authentic was as much directed against high-way robbers and other undesirable elements as against the canonists: it is a very able, far-sighted and diplomatic move against the clerical exponents of hierocratism, reared and schooled as they were in canon law. However hypothetical, it is nevertheless tempting to ponder on what would have happened to medieval (and perhaps modern) Roman law studies, had there been no *Habita*[1].

Set thus against the time and its temper as well as against the place, Bologna, the promulgation of this law had of course nothing to do with any gratitude on the part of Frederick I towards the Four Doctors[2]. Indeed, the only place in which the decree could have had any value at all, was Bologna[3], whither the canon law students could travel in comparative safety, whilst the Roman law students were subjected to all sorts of maltreatment. Whether the narration of the poet who depicted the scenes before Bologna in 1155 in a rather dramatic form had any factual basis is still more doubtful after the real motives of the emperor are set into proper perspective[4]. That Frederick did not publicy give his reasons, namely, to create

---

[1] The clerks had already been protected in a manner in which the lay students were now to be protected. The *Privilegium fori*: C. XI, q. i, per totam, cf. also C. XXI, q. V, and C. II q. VII; the *Privilegium immunitatis*: C. XII, q. II, c. 69, cf. also *Cod. Theod.* XVI, 2, and *Cod. Justin.* I, 3; the *Privilegium canonis*: C. XVII, q. IV, esp. c. 29.

[2] « The emperor's reward to the Bolognese teachers of law was his authentic Habita », KOEPPLER, p. 588.

[3] See A. SORBELLI, *Storia della Università di Bologna*, 1944, vol. I, p. 153, though he does not see the connexion.

[4] DENIFLE, *Universitäten*, p. 54, after discussing the value of this narration, declares that it is wiser « die Erzählung vorderhand mit Misstrauen aufzunehmen. Ein historisches Faktum kann ich bis jetzt noch nicht darin erblicken ».

an effective counterweight to the canonists needs no explanation, if one takes into account the year of the eventual promulgation (1158) and the rising tide of political papalism[1]. The real motives of Barbarossa were however exceedingly well covered up by the altruistic, humanitarian and beneficent façade that cloaked the authentic. The rôle which the emperor was fond of playing, namely that of the *dominus mundi*, so much trumpeted about in the Roman law books, afforded at once a further stimulus to protect wretched creatures desirous of studying the « sacrae et divinae leges » and devoid of any protection, as well as a welcome shelter behind which he could lodge a well-thought out and effective attack on the ominously rising canon law school at Bologna. In pursuance of his ideology the emperor bestows his special care on those scholars by whose scholarship the world is illuminated — « quorum scientia *totus* illuminatur *mundus* ». Measured against the ideological background of the « imperium mundi » and the «dominus mundi», the illumination by the scholars of the whole world acquires a decided political flavour[2].

Moreover, this scholarship, according to Frederick in his *Habita*, « makes men obey God and Us »[3]. When we now bear in mind that the *beneficium* is granted «maxime» to those who « profess » the sacred and divine (civil) laws, the underlying political idea emerges also quite plainly. The study of Roman law will teach men to be obedient to God and the emperor — or differently expressed: it will safeguard the continued working of the imperial ideas. The emperor, in this decree, gives away his eventual political design, that is, a world government in which the civil (Roman) laws reign supreme, and not the canon law. It was but one means, however innocuous in appearance, whereby the ancient imperial design was to be brought nearer to its realization, that is, a universal dominion of the emperor with unlimited claims to obedience. Since the controversy of empire *versus* papacy

---

[1] In a very ingenious manner KOEPPLER draws attention to the drafting of the constitution: « We may imagine how, only five months after this patent excuse (*i.e.*, of the *beneficium*) the chancery clerks enjoyed rubbing it in, when they wrote in the authentic that the emperor gave this *beneficium* to the academic population », *art. cit.*, 606.

[2] For an ideological interpretation of this Staufen tenet see now F. HEER, *op. cit.*, pp. 159 ff.

[3] *Ut. . omnes eos, quorum scientia mundus illuminatur, ad obediendum Deo et nobis.*

was in reality a struggle for the supremacy of Roman and Canon law, Frederick's authentic bears witness to the political wisdom of its author and heralds the battle which was to be faught with the weapons of the law. Even later medieval jurists had grasped the inner significance of this authentic; so when Baldus, in commenting upon the words *ad obediendum Deo et nobis*, emphasizes that the emperor was a minister and servant of God, and not of the Church, that the source of imperial power was celestial, and not terrestrial, and, lastly, that imperial power *rationabiliter* possesses *universam terram, quae ascendentem videt et occidentem solem*[1]. To anyone acquainted with the politico-legal phraseology of medieval jurists, these words of Baldus bear a very great significance, precisely because they are used in this context; or what Baldus wishes to say is that Frederick with this authentic attacked the hierocratic scheme which made him a « minister and servant of the Church ». *Habita*, we hold, presents Staufen ideology in a classic form[2]. Or should one really and naively assume that the motive of Frederick I was so very self-less and that he was purely impelled by pity for the economic and financial plight of the lay scholars going to Bologna to study there the hallowed civil laws? Indeed, Accursius, when explaning the term *injuria* of the authentic, rejects the idea that the emperor by punishing an *injuria* inflicted upon a scholar, thereby had created some new legal maxim: an *injuria* had always been illegal, but the emperor had threatened heavy sanctions, « so that the scholars may not feel neglected »[3]. Moreover, as we shall presently see, it was the *communis opinio* amongst civilians and canonists, that the authentic did not concern clerical scholars. To the initiated the authentic is a conciser political document

---

[1] BALDUS ad auth. *Habita*, n. 26.

[2] Although its juristic formulation leaves a good deal to be desired: and this may reflect on Dassel's lack of training, provided that he was the draughtsman, see *supra*, p. 6. That Dassel however was considered the « evil spirit » behind the throne, John of Salisbury testifies. Speaking of the schism afterwards, he says, for instance, *Ep.* CCLXXXVIII (MIGNE, *Patr. Lat.*, vol. CXCIX, col. 268 D): *qui* (scil. *Coloniensis*) *totius schismatis faber erat, incentor, et signifer, et a sede apostolica condemnatus ex nomine; Ep.* CLXXXIX, col. 200 A, characterizing Dassel as *contemptor ecclesiae semper, quantus incentor et auctor schismatis, ex quo potuit, ille Coloniensis praesumptor ecclesiae, maximus inter locustas bestiae...* See also J. SPÖRL, *art. cit.*, pp. 252-3, esp. note 31 (referring to Alexander III's characterization of Rainald as *ille auctor et caput turbationis*: JL. 11033). Cf. now also W. HOLTZMANN, *Das mittelalterliche Imperium*, 1952, p. 22.

[3] *Gl. ord.* ad auth. Habita, s.v. « *scholaribus* »: *Nec enim licet alicui inferre injuriam, sed ideo de his dicit specialiter, ne videantur negligi*; s.v. « *speciali* »: *Nam licet omnes debeant ab injuriis defendi, hi maxime, ne videantur negligi.*

than the verbose utterances of contemporary political writers. It is a testimonial to the man who « die höchsten weltlichen Zeitideale verkörperte »[1]. That it did not fulfil the political mission which it was designed to play, was not indeed the fault of its author.

Further corroboration of our point of view may be found in the other enactment of the authentic, namely, that the scholars should live and travel securely and that the emperor would defend them by virtue of his special love (speciali dilectione) he had for them. That again was nothing new and the reason why Frederick singled aout his special care for them was, in the words of the gloss: ne videantur negligi. Quite apart from the fact that the emperor was not entitled to legislate on such a vital matter affecting the forum of the clerks[2] who in any case were sufficiently protected, who else was there who needed a special re-assurance of imperial watchfulness if not the Roman law scholars? They should not feel neglected when comparing themselves with their clerical brethren. Moreover, it was surely so-

---

[1] So the late HAMPE, Deutsche Kaisergeschichte in der Zeit der Salier und Staufer ed. F. Baethgen, 1949, p. 142; see now also F. HEER, op. cit. (supra, p. 6, n. 4), pp. 148 ff., 182 ff., 205 ff. This is not the place to go into details concerning the political aims of Frederick — who it must be remembered coined the technical term sacrum imperium, a term that sums up the whole Staufen ideology — and of his advisers, but in this context mention must be made of the enduring influence on the emperor by Bishop Eberhard II of Bamberg who negotiated with Frederick (before the latter's election) in 1152 de reformando et componendo regni statu (Guttenberg, Germania sacra, vol. II/1, p. 143, quoted FICHTENAU, Bamberg, Würzburg und die Stauferkanzlei, in « Mitt. d. Inst. f. oest. Geschichtsforschung, 1939, p. 245); John of Salisbury reports, Ep. lix (PL, vol. CXCIX, col. 39): Scio quid Teutonicus moliatur... promittebat enim se totius orbis reformaturum imperium et urbi subjiciendum orbem... The age of Frederick was, as FICHTENAU remarks, p. 255, « kein religiöses, sondern ein eminent politisches ». See also W. FOEHL, Mitt. d.'Inst. f. oest. Geschf., 1936, pp. 119 ff., on Eberhard's rôle after Besançon. The authentic Habita, we hold, was one more means by which the status regni and the reformation totius orbis were to be ordered. The rising hierocracy made this in 1158 more than ever imperative. Habita was the expression of laical ideology concerning the government of the Respublica Christiana.

[2] One has only to look a few years ahead and to recall the conflict between Henry II of England and Thomas Becket, where the question of the forum played such a conspicuous rôle. But cf. Cynus, infra p. 32, n. 1. It would be rash to read into Alexander III's communication (written 1170 – 1172 and printed in Chartularium Universitatis Parisiensis, ed. DENIFLE and CHATELAIN, vol. I, Intr., p. 5) a papal corroboration of Frederick's Habita. The case touched upon many and rather unusual points and was complicated by the scholars being clerks. See esp. the remarks in RASHDALL-POWICKE, vol. I, p. 290 note 1, and also the observations of LYNN THORNDIKE, University Records and Life in the Middle Ages, ed. 1949, at no. 8, p. 19.

mewhat superfluous for a medieval emperor to state that people should live and travel securely, when the numerous enactments in the Justinianean codification dealing with this point are taken into account. The medieval jurists, perhaps possessing a better knowledge of Roman law than the draftsman of *Habita*, clearly realized this superfluity: is not everyone according to the *jus commune* protected and supposed to travel securely, asks Bartolus, and answers: « nam scitis quod grassatores puniuntur »[1]. The only meaning which the jurists could attach to this peculiar enactment was that the scholars were to be exempted from paying tolls on their journey to the *studium* — and this was what *Habita* did not say. But we can perhaps appraise the embarrassment of the jurists when we quote Bartolus again. The word *securi* means *quod non teneantur solvere pedagia, alias haec constitutio nichil relevaret, et ita tenent omnes doctores*. Apart from the drastic sanction and the fixation of the judicial tribunal[2] there was nothing new in *Habita*, and the gloss puts the finger on the right spot when it says: the scholars should not feel neglected. But no clerical scholar had any reason for feeling neglected, tenderly watched as he was by the various canons in the *Decretum*, and particularly in the later *Decretales*.

Protection by the emperor meant protection by the public authority. In as much therefore as public authority was forced to act on the basis of the law, it did this in the public interest. Protection of the scholars, and we may qualify: of the lay scholars, was a matter of public concern. Jacobus de Arena succinctly pointed to the association between *Habita* and the public interest: *Publica versatur utilitas in scholaribus, cum per sapientiam, quam addiscunt et quae docetur in scholis, mundus illuminatur*[3]. Infliction of an injury on a scholar was at the same time an injury inflicted on the whole public weal[4]. And Nicholas Matarellus thinks that the authentic « denotat causam communis boni »[5]. Protection, within the terms of *Habita*, is an effluence of *publica utilitas*, and hence Baldus counsels that the secular power has the duty to protect the *studium*, if need be, by force,

---

[1] Bartolus in the « Antiqua Lectura » on auth. *Habita*, fol. 129vb.

[2] But this again was not entirely new, cf. Justinians' constitution *Omnem*.

[3] Jacobus de Arena, *Infortiatum*, De Solut. Matr., Dotis Causa, no. 9, fol. 88vb.

[4] *Ille, qui nocet scholaribus, nocet publico, ut praeallegata authentica, ergo debet prohiberi, sicut qui ab edificando nocet in publico*, Jacobus de Arena, *ibid*.

[5] As reported by Baldus, ad auth. *Habita*, no. 20.

since an offence against it is not unlike committing a sacrilege[1]. That the original political character of the authentic had not been lost sight of, can perhaps best be seen by the claims advanced by the jurists on behalf of the secular authority that it had the right to legitimize bastard scholars in papal territory[2]. As we know, the legitimation of illegitimate children was of great political importance and constituted one of the most controversial points in political literature[3]. The phrase adopted in this context that the scholars were, so to speak, the « spiritual sons of the emperor », should not pass without notice on account of its revealing nature: no doubt, an approximation of the secular power to the spritual authority was thereby implied.

With due respect to the giant of medieval juristic thought, Bartolus, it should be noted that a careful reading of C. IV, 61, 5 would have elicited the ruling[4] that the students travelling to a *studium* should be freed from paying a toll, at least as far as their personal belongings were concerned: *Quae ad usum proprium deferantur vectigalium immunitate gaudent.* Baldus moreover lectured that books and personal things *quae circumducuntur causa studii* were to be free from tolls[5]. Jacobus Butrigarius maintained that it would be impossible for a student to attend the schools, were he not allowed to transport his books[6]. The freedom of clerical scholars from tolls was based on the idea that their exaction would be an infringement of the liberty of the Church, and hence was prohibited[7].

---

[1] *Ideo priores, quando expedit, debent mittere armatos ad domum sapientiae, nam est quoddam sacrilegium ibi offendere,* Baldus, ad auth. *Habita,* no. 27.

[2] *Scholares non legitimi nati etiam de terris ecclesiae possunt legitimari a principe tamquam filii spirituales, quod est notabile,* Baldus, *ibid.,* no. 22.

[3] See *Gregoriana,* IV, XVII, 13, and commentaries and lectures on it by the canonists.

[4] To which Bartolus himself draws our attention in his lecture on Dig. 39. 4, lex fin.

[5] BALDUS, *loc. cit.,* no. 7.

[6] Jacobus Butrigarius, ad auth. *Habita,* fol. 121ra: *Sed an de rebus suis debent solvere pedagium, et dic quod non, quia cum sine ipsis non possit esse, videtur concessum, ut et eas portet libere... nam de rebus, quas quis portat ad suum usum nichil debet solvere.* The provisions for the students at the University of Lérida in Spain, were still more liberal, see J. VILLANUEVA, *Viago literario a las iglesias de Espana,* Madrid, 1851, p. 205. See also the very generous terms granted by Philip VI to the scholars at the University of Montpellier, *Cartulaire de l'Université de Montpellier,* vol. I, no. 57, pp. 286-7.

[7] See Innocent IV in *Chartularium Universitatis Parisiensis,* ed. DENIFLE and CHATELAIN, vol. I, no. 164, p. 194, and no. 211, p. 237.

Two important consequences were drawn from this. In the first place, the freedom from tolls naturally concerned only the travelling scholars, hence the citizens of the university town were not affected by it. This followed clearly from the wording of the law itself and was repeated by nearly every glossator and commentator. But the fact that a university town put foreign scholars on the same footing as its own citizens made no difference to their status[1]. Moreover, in the fourteenth century, juristic doctrine advanced the point of view that although scholars had no domicile in the town, they nevertheless were entitled to the same privileges as the citizens proper. This was, for instance, the opinion of Johannes de Platea[2]. On the other hand, the students could not be subjected to the duties incumbent on the citizens themselves, as a decree of Charles VI of France conceded to the students at Paris, and also at Montpellier[3]. Hence they could not be forced, even in times of war or other emergency, to do guard duties or any other duty to which the citizens were liable. The scholars enjoyed the privileges of the citizens, but did not share their burdens[4].

Secondly, this freedom from tolls and customs could be claimed only if the scholars travelled to a recognized *studium generale*. Although the constitution did not stipulate any qualification of the towns to which the scholars travelled, at least the earlier interpreters held that only *regiae urbes* or *legitima studia* came into question. Jacobus de Arena, for instance, said that the place to which the scholar travelled must have the privilege conferred upon it (by emperor or pope) or at least must be able to claim a habitual teaching of law « tanto tempore cuius initii non extat memoria »[5]. In speaking of Bologna

---

[1] *Sed pone, statuto bononiensi cavetur, ut scholares forenses pro civibus habentur in omnibus, an tunc habebunt privilegium huius authenticae. Ego tenui, licet transitorie, quod sic... et idem nunc teneo,* Barth. Salicetus, ad auth. *Habita,* fol. 116rb.

[2] Johannes de Platea, ad X. De incolis, l. cives: *Licet scholares non habeant domicilium in loco studii, tamen adhuc gaudent privilegiis illius civitatis, in qua student.*

[3] See *Chart. Univ. Paris.,* ed. cit., vol. IV, no. 2123, p. 359, no. 2135, p. 367; cf. also *Les Ordinances des Rois de France,* vol. XI, p. 6.

[4] Padua enacted this: *Statuimus, quod scholares computentur cives quantum ad commoda, et non quantum ad incommoda,* in « Statutes », VI (15), ap. DENIFLE, in *Arch f. Lit. & Kirchgesch.,* vol. VI, p. 517, cf. also *ibid.,* p. 531. Rather scornfully Johannes Hispanus de Petesella remarks in his *Summa* that *multi scholares facti sunt cives bononienses, qui in decrepita aetate dies suos volunt consumare,* vol. 161vb.

[5] The whole passage runs: *Quid ergo si civitas hoc privilegio careat? Sed in ea studium juris est habitu tanto tempore, cuius initii non extat memoria, ut est bononiae*

the jurists understandably lost their sense of historicity[1], and statements like that of Baldus that for some 1000 years the study of law had flourished at Bologna, were not uncommon[2]. That the position of Bologna as a *legitimum studium* was never questioned, goes without saying. Bologna was considered the « regia civitas » par excellence, because Emperor Theodosius had founded the city, which « historical fact » was deduced from the legend of St Ambrose; this peculiar interpretation was in vogue since Johannes Bassianus and Azo, as Odofredus tells us[3]. Bologna was the « nutrix et mater legentium », since it was the intellectual birth place of so many cardinals and other luminaries on the horizon of the law[4]. Padua, too,

---

et paduae. Respondeo licite potuerunt jura docere ibidem, cum ex tanti temporis patientia principis remississe prohibitionem suam et permisisse fingatur, Jacobus de Arena, *Dig. Vet.,* Proem., fol. 61vb, no. 13.

[1] About the lack of historical sense at that time, cf. the fine observations of P. KOSCHAKER, *Europa und das römische Recht,* pp. 48 ff.

[2] *Nota, quod hoc habet locum in pergentibus et stantibus, ubi exercentur studia, hoc est, ubi legitime docentur jura et aliae scientiae, quia civitas habet hoc ex privilegio vel ex antiqua seu longissima consuetudine, sicut est illustris civitas bononiensis; inviguit studium forte annis mille... et idem dicendum est de civitate paduae, et de hac inclyta civitate,* Baldus ad auth. no. 10; the last named city was Perugia, where Baldus lectured when writing his commentary on the authentic.

[3] Odofredus also shows us that even at Bologna a distinction was made between the old part of the city (which was considered a *civitas regia*) and the new part beyond the river (*ultra Aposam*): hence Azo lecturing in this latter district was petitioned to transfer his lectures to the old part of Bologna. In his own lecture Odofredus said this: *Custodiatis vos hic propter unam glossam hic scriptam, et est domini Johannis et Azonis, et hi glossant hic: remissionem non habent, igitur doctores, qui docent ultra Aposam, non debent habere immunitatem, de quo docebat dominus bagerotus, unde procedebat hoc. Scholares voluerunt, quod dominus Azo legeret in platea sancti stephani; dicebant ipsi, bononia est regia civitas, ut invenitur in legenda ambrosii et sancti petronii, et bononia est ab aposia citra, unde dicebant ipsi: si nos docemus in regia civitate debemus habere immunitatem, si citra aposam, si ultra non... unde qui regunt in regiis civitatibus recte doctores, alias non dicuntur jura docere,* Odofredus, *Infort.,* De excusat. tut., Si duas, fol. 52rb. On Bagerottus see SAVIGNY, *Geschichte des römischen Rechts,* vol. V, pp. 125 ff. See also Bartolus, *Dig. Vet.,* Prima Const., § Haec autem, fol. 5ra: *Unde dic, quod in civitate bononiae possunt jura doceri, quia est civitas regia, nam fecit imperator theodosius jussu beati ambrosii, ut in legenda beati ambrosii reperitur, quae est apud s. victorem, locum religiosum, ubi ego steti per magnum tempus ad studendum et revidendum libros per meipsum.*

[4] *Bononia nonnullos pene infinitos genuit cardinales et lumina mundi, et ideo non est disputandum de bononia,* Baldus, *Dig. Vet.,* Prima Const., § Haec autem tria, fol. 5vb, no. 1.

and Perugia were held to be places appropriate for law studies because they could claimits customary teaching[1]. The reason for looking somewhat askance at the other cities, was stated by Bartolus. He thought that any other science but the law could be taught *in qualibet civitate* but the law only *in civitatibus privilegiatis*, and therefore those who went to the former in order to study law, attended a *studium adulterinum*[2]. Bartolus also came to speak of this in his lecture on the *Digestum Vetus* where he said that the reason why the law should not be taught in just any locality was that there *jura perverterentur et falsoficarentur* since in these places there were neither great numbers of experienced jurists nor could the proper books be consulted[3]. Nevertheless, there were some « moderni », such as Ricardus Malumbra, who held that law could legitimately be studied *in qualibet civitate vel castro*, but their opinion met with a curt phrase of disapproval on the part of Bartolus: *quod mihi non placet*. But the *moderni*[4], were by no means as modern as Bartolus would have liked them, since long before Ricardus Malumbra the great glossator Pillius had declared (although only after his migration from Bologna to Modena) that considering the actual political state of affairs, the Eastern and Western empires were separate entities, and therefore the monopoly of the two cities (Constantinople and Beyruth) had ceased to have any meaning for the West: *Coeperunt quoque jura quovis loco tradi et maxime Bononiae*[5].

The requirement of a recognized *studium* was also of some importance as regards the clerical scholars: they were in no position to enjoy the prebends of their benefices, if they did not reside at one of the genuine *studia*. Innocent III in a decretal letter replied to the query of a bishop that, generally speaking, the canons who, though having episcopal permission, nevertheless migrated from a *studium* to some other small locality, should be deprived of their

---

[1] Baldus, *ibid.*; for Padua see also Jacobus de Arena, *ibid.*, no. 13, and Bartolus, no. 2. A royal foundation in the strict meaning of the term was Lérida, see RASHDALL, *ed. cit.*, vol. II, p. 92.

[2] Bartolus in the « Antiqua Lectura », ad auth., fol. 129vb, no. 3.

[3] Bartolus, *ibid.*

[4] Richardus Malumbra ridiculed those who treated *scientiam nostram modo sillogistico, sophistico et dialectico, et dicebat considerari debere, quod scientia nostra tradi non debet hoc modo*, see the passage transcribed by E. M. MEIJERS, *De Universiteit van Orléans en 13 euuwe*, in « Revue d'Histoire du Droit », vol. II, p. 491, note 2.

[5] See the passage transcribed by KAUFMANN, *op. cit.*, vol. I, p. 175, n. 1.

prebends[1]. It is interesting to observe that Johannes Teutonicus in his gloss on the *Compilatio Tertia* (which contained this Innocentian decretal) interpreted « villas » in no may different from that of his civilian colleagues: to him Innocent III merely had in mind the study of law[2]. As it befitted a canonist of Hostiensis's standing, he interpreted that Innocentian decretal correctly and at the same time realistically. Clerics, who because of the reason of war or other contingency were unable to reach Bologna, could nevertheless study in some appropriate place or even castle, provided that they had a competent master[3]. The opinion of Guido de Baysio (the archdeacon) that episcopal permission alone was a sufficient guarantee of the clerical scholar's receiving his prebend[4], no matter whether or not the *studium* was recognized as a *generale*, did not meet with the approval of later canonists, such as Johannes Andreae, who curtly stated refuting the theory of his master: *Tu dic contra, quod sola licentia, quam dat episcopus existendi in studio, non sufficit, nisi esset studium privilegiatum in hoc*[5]. A general papal permission, however, was a sufficient presupposition for the further enjoyment of the clerk's prebend whilst « in scholis »[6].

That students travelling to an interdicted locality could never

---

[1] Innocent III in *Gregoriana*: III. iv. 12. But cf. the invective of the Dominican prior, Philip, against the clerics flocking to Paris, in M. M. DAVY, *Les Sermons Universitaires Parisiens de* 1230-1231, p. 397.

[2] Johannes Teutonicus in the *gl. ord.* on *Comp. III*, fol. 238va, s.v. « villas » *In regiis civitatibus, non tamen in parvis, jura docenda sunt, ut in prohemio fforum. Jo. ».* It should be noted that at the time when Johannes wrote his gloss (1210-1215), the idea of papal authority for the foundation of the *studia generalia* was not yet known. Hostiensis also operated with the term *regia civitas*, see his *Lectura*, De cler. non res., c. Tuae, fol. 10vb.

[3] Hostiensis, *loc. cit.*, s.v. « committunt »: *Numquid enim si propter guerram non audent ad praesens scholas bononiae accedere? Licebit eis citra montes etiam in castris, si competentem magistrum habeant studere? Sic , quia non fit in fraudem,* vol. 10vb.

[4] Archdeacon, *Rosarium*, ad *Dist.* XXXVII, c. De quibusdam, fol. 50va, no. 14: *Potest dici, ubi scholaris est in studio de licentia episcopi quod tunc habebit suos redditus, nam cum episcopus possit licentiare clericum, ut vadat at scholas, immo clericus alias ire non debeat, extra, de cl. non res., relatum.*

[5] Johannes Andreae, *Novella in Decretales*, De cler. non resid., Tuae, fol. 12ra. He summarizes the decretal in these words: *Privilegiatus quod absens in studio fructus praebendae percipiat; studens in studio particulari privilegio non utetur, h.a.*

[6] Cf. Innocent IV in *Chart. Univ. Paris.*, ed. cit., vol. I, no. 158, p. 191; no. 185, p. 215, and John XXII, in *Cartulaire de l'Université de Montpellier*, vol. I, no. 59, p. 289-91.

claim any privileges, went without saying. There was, on the whole, general agreement amongst the jurists, whether civilians or canonists[1]. The interdict was on the same level as a *capitis diminutio* in Roman law[2].

The growng importance of the pursuit of knowledge in a *studium generale* and of the study of law in particular accounted for the elaboration of a number of privileges which were held to be have been based on the idea of public interest. The scholar on arrival might have had difficulties in finding lodgings, and the French civilian, Guilielmus de Cuneo, in his commentary on the Codex, stated as a matter of fact, and not as a matter of opinion, that compulsory billeting could be invoked. *Si scholares non inveniunt domos, possunt cogi domini ad locandum eos*[3]. The lodgings themselves were protected in a manner which a modern scholar would envy. The prevention of noise in the neighbourhood of the schools or the scholar's rooms was one such privilege. Treating of this, Bartolus neatly puts the proper reason in the foreground. With scholars, he says, *versatur publica utilitas in communi et in quolibet particulari* and if there was an artisan or a workman next to the student's house or the school, who created noise or bad odour (such as the brimstone workers) that distracted the students, he could be compelled to remove his work-

---

[1] Baldus, ad auth. *Habita*, no. 11: *Sed quaeritur, numquid studentes in civitate damnata propter rebellionem habent ista privilegia, et dic, quod non, quia talis civitas habetur pro mortua, ut notat Inno. c. grave, De sent. exc.* Johannes Andreae, Gloss ad Sextum, De reg. juris, c. privilegia: a *civitas interdicta* cannot have the *privilegia studii, quia organa sunt suspensa.*

[2] Baldus, *loc. cit.*: *Quia interim est capite minuta, cum excommunicatio et interdictum sunt quaedam mors, ut notatur Inst., De cap. dim.,* § 1.

[3] Guilielmus de Cuneo (about whose influence see E. M. MEIJJERS, *art. cit.*, vol. II, pp. 506 ff., especially p. 508) in his commentary on C. De epp. et cler., Decernimus, repeated by Baldus, *Infort.*, De soluto matr., lex 1, fol. 43va, no. 19. The statutes of Bologna made it difficult for lodging house keepers to eject students from their houses, see *Statutes*, cap. LXXII, p. 355, *Arch. Lit. & Kirchgesch.*, vol. III; the destruction of these houses was also made difficult, cap. LXXIII. For Padua see *Statutes*, cap. V, 22, 23, *Archiv etc.*, vol. VI, pp. 504, 505. At Toulouse Innocent IV gave a mandate to the bishop to accomodate poor scholars in « hospitalibus de Tolosa », see MARCEL FOURNIER, *Les Statuts et Privileges des Universités Françaises*, vol. I, no. 520, p. 450. It should be borne in mind that according to canon law, Doctors and scholars were not allowed to have students in their houses, see *gl. ord.*, ad *X*. III. XVIII. 1; on this see also Bologna Statutes, cap. LXVI, and Paduan Statutes, cap. V (16).

shop[1]. In his usual spectacular manner Odofredus told his audience: Or signori, *haec lex potest allegari contra malos vicinos scholarium, qui impediunt eos legere, si moniti nolunt abstinere*[2]. According to Jacobus de Arena, however, a distinction should de drawn, according to who preceded whom upon the spot. If the workman was there first, there was no means of removing him[3], but Bartolus strongly objected to this somewhat democratic reasoning, because privileges could not be considered from the point of view of priority in time[4]. The life of a jurist was in no way inferior to the contemplative life of a monk or of a friar, and hence both should be treated on the same level, declared the canonist Hostiensis[5]. The schools themselves enjoyed immunity in so far as the scholars whilst actually inside the building, could not be arrested: *studium ex consuetudine gaudet immunitate*, and just as nobody could be captured in the cloister, in the same way nobody could be arrested in «the schools»[6].

It was also in the public interest that the scholars should be permitted to work on *diebus feriatis*, that is, on holidays of obligation, *totis nervis* because this activity was no different or less important than eating and drinking on holidays[7]. In another respect, too, the

---

[1] *Scholares vel doctores possent repellere fabrum, qui stat juxta scholas vel compellere ne malleat propter publicam utilitatem, ut res publica peritis hominibus repleatur,* Bartolus, *Infort.*, De sol. matr., lex 1, fol. 4ra, no. 30.

[2] Odofredus, *ibid.*, fol. 2va. For another source of disturbance to scholars, especially at Cambridge, see THOMAS FULLER, *History of the University of Cambridge*, ed. 1840, pp. 25 f.

[3] See Jacobus de Arena, *Infort., loc. cit.*, fol. 88vb.

[4] *Praeferuntur etiam ei (i.e., fabro), qui prior est tempore, quia privilegia non considerantur ex tempore... idem dico, si faber est juxta domum unius scholaris. Et ad hoc proprie facit lex nostra, quia hic versatur utilitas publica respectu universi... quia propter scientiam efficitur doctor ut leget vel erit magistratus vel papa vel cardinalis, ut tota die vidimus,* Bartolus, *Infort.*, loc. cit., no. 30, fol. 4ra. Cf. also Hostiensis, *Lectura,* De jud., c. fin., and Panormitanus, *ibid.* This provision was actually laid down in the Statutes of Lérida: *...ne possint in suis lectionibus per alios cives vel extraneos promiscuis actibus perturbari*, see the document printed by DENIFLE, *Urkunden zur Geschichte der mittelalterlichen Universitäten*, in «Arch. f. Lit. & Kirchgesch.», vol. IV, pp. 256-7.

[5] Hostiensis in his *Summa*, Proem., § Unde.

[6] See Panormitanus, De consuet., c. 2, fol. 23va. The houses of scholars (and of Doctors) in the university of Lérida could not be searched by royal officers, see the *Carta ordinationis et immunitatis studii generalis Ilerdensis*, in J. VILLANUEVA, *Viago literario* etc., vol. XVI, pp. 200-207, at p. 203.

[7] Lucas de Penna, C. XI, De agric., lex 1. The holidays at Montpellier seem to

idea of public utility received a rather unorthodox interpretation. According to the *jus commune* of the time, the association between Christians and Jews was frowned upon, and in fact their living together was prohibited[1]. The association in the schools, however, does not seem to have been expressly forbidden, the reason being that the Jews could thereby be brought nearer to the Christian faith[2]. Moreover, in view of the strong ideological support which the French monarchy received from the lay scholars at the turn of the thirteenth and fourteenth centuries, it took an increasingly lively interest in their welfare and protection. It was considered contrary to the public interest — *cadit in detrimentum rei publicae* — if scholars under whatever pretext were to be prevented or kept away from attending schools, for in this way the public would suffer, and it was of no lesser moment than a disturbance caused to sacred things. This was made the subject of a decree issued by Philip IV in 1306, and repeated and confirmed by Philip VI in 1341 and 1345[3]. In some respects this special protection offered by the French kings to the scholars appears to be an elaboration of the protection given by Pope Gregory IX in 1231 and repeated by Innocent IV to the masters and scholars of Paris[4].

The heavy penalties inflicted upon those mentioned in the constitution of Frederick, disregarding its provisions, gave an added sense of security and protection to the scholars. The prohibition of reprisals against scholars was only one specific point, and it is noteworthy that in his famous *Parens scientiarum* of April 1231 Gregory IX[5] extended this prohibition to the capture of any master or scholar *pro*

---

have been rather frequent, see *Cartulaire* etc., vol. I, no. 65, pp. 311 f., but according to the Statutes of Toulouse lectures on canon law were allowed on public holidays, see M. FOURNIER, *Les Statuts* etc., vol. I, no. 545, p. 484, sectio IX.

[1] *Decretum*, C. XXVIII, q. I, c. 13; cf. also C. XXIV, q. I, c. 24, and *Extra*, V. VI.

[2] Cf. Panormitanus, De jud., c. 1.

[3] *Chart. Univ. Paris.*, vol. II, no. 657, p. 120; no. 1044, p. 507; no. 1119, p. 574. The decree of Philip VI was probably also applicable to Montpellier, see *Cartulaire*, vol. I, no. 73, p. 380. The Statutes of Lérida had a similar provision, see VILLANUEVA, *op. cit.*, p. 202. Cf. also the letter of Philip V to the bailiff at Orleans, in M. FOURNIER, *Les Statuts* etc., vol. I, no. 48, p. 44, and of Philip VI, no. 88, p. 80.

[4] *Chart. Univ. Paris.*, vol. I, nos. 95 and 113, pp. 147, 160, and no. 162, 209, pp. 192, 236. See also Innocent IV's letter to the archdeacon of Bologna, in SARTI-FATTORINI, *De Claris Archigymnasii Bononiensis Professoribus*, vol. II, p. 174.

[5] *Chart. Univ. Paris.*, vol. I, no. 79, pp. 136-9.

*debito contractu, cum hoc sit canonicis et legitimis sanctionibus inter-
dictumo*.[1] Padua also extended the prohibition of reprisals to those
who brought food to the city. But of perhaps greater practical significance was the protection which our constitution afforded with regard to injuries inflicted upon scholars[2]. The jurists were unanimous
in their verdict that the term comprised corporeal as well as incorporeal injuries[3]. Of course, self-defence in case of an attack by the
scholar himself was always permitted[4]. The question whether the
tearing of clothes and of bridles constituted a corporeal injury, was
usually answered in the affirmative[5], but the question whether
malicious slander of a scholar was also an injury in the strict meaning
of the term, was not decided; for example, was it an injury to the
scholar if, for however a praiseworthy motive he might have gone
to the house in which a girl lived, it was said of him that he did not
go there to teach her the » Our Father »[6]? There was general agreement amongst the jurists that the scholars had the right to appeal to
the emperor directly in case of any *gravamen*, however indefinite this
might have been in the particular instance. Since they formed « unum
corpus » with the scholar himself, his parents and his sisters, in short

---

[1] See also a similar regulation for Lérida, VILLANUEVA, *op. cit.*, p. 202, and the
bull of Clement V for Orleans, FOURNIER, *Statuts*, vol. I, no. 21, p. 14.

[2] See Statutes, cap. VI (9). For Oxford, see also the *Indenture between the University and the town*, in « Munimenta Academiae Oxoniensis », Rolls Series, ed. H.
ANSTEY, p. 346.

[3] See *gl. ord.*, ad auth. *Habita*.

[4] *Gl. ord.*, *ibid.*

[5] See Baldus, ad auth. *Habita*, no. 32.

[6] Baldus, C. IV, De Probat., no. 3, fol. 38vb This case is to be found also in a
somewhat embellished form in STENO BIELKE's *Commentatio de academiis*, transl. by
THORNDIKE, *op. cit.*, p. 390, no. 174. The *gl. ord.* on the *Decretum* (C. XI, q. III, c.
absit) would have none of an injurious presumption against a clerk who embraced a
woman: the theologian, on the other hand, had a somewhat stricter point of view in
these matters, if Thomas of Chabham (sub-dean of Salisbury, 1214-1230) is any indication: *Si aliquis inveniret clericum cum uxore sua et amputaret virilia, non incideret
in canonem latae sententiae nec esset excommunicatus*, fol. 30va of his *Summa Confessorum*, MS Univ. Libr., Cambridge. On this much neglected work see A. TEETAERT,
La confession laique dans l'Eglise latine, pp. 347 ff. The university of Lérida did not
include incorporeal injuries, see the document printed by DENIFLE, *Archiv*, vol. IV,
p. 258, but corporeal injuries met with drastic sanctions. Papal legislation permitted
suspension of lectures in case of injuries, see *Parens Scientiarum*, Innocent IV to
the University of Toulouse, FOURNIER, *Statuts*, vol. I, no. 523, p. 451, and Clement
V to Orleans, *ibid.*, no. 19, p. 12.

his nearest relatives partook in the privileges of the scholar, when they visited him at the *studium*. *Et idem dico, si pater et mater vel soror vadant at visitandum scholares, qui quoddam modo unum corpus sunt*[1].

As far as applicable the privileges which we enumerated, also applied to the scholar on his journey home, whether it was after concluding his studies or whether he temporarily left the *studium* for some special reason. In the latter case the presupposition was that he had the *animus revertendi*[2]. Another presumption was that he was not allowed to be absent for more than five years, as Baldus and Salicetus emphasized[3]. If the scholar was prevented from reaching the *studium* within the prescribed five years by wars, epidemics, illness, and so forth, he could claim a *justa causa* and the time thus lost was not computed within the *quinquennium*. A just case for absence from the *studium* might be, according to Lucas de Penna, that the scholar wished to prepare himself for the following year, *nam et tempus quod datur ad preparationem, datur in absentia causa reipublicae*[4]. The need to supply himself with more money or other necessities of life was also held to be a just cause of absence, but in this case it seems that he needed the permission of his Doctor[5]. Even if the student spent more than ten years in the *studium* without completing his courses, he could not acquire legal domicile there, and hence the peculiar privilege of having the choice of three judges, still applied, always provided that he devoted himself to his study[6]. Nevertheless, there is the isolated opinion of Guilielmus de Cuneo that after ten years of residence the scholar would acquire legal domicile in the place of the *studium*. But, according to Paulus Castrensis, Raynerius de Forlivio and Jacobus de Ravanis had impugned

---

[1] Baldus, *loc. cit.*, no. 34.

[2] See Lucas de Penna, C. XI, De privil. schol., lex 2, no. 4, p. 798.

[3] Salicetus, ad auth. *Habita*, no. 30, fol. 116ra, and Baldus, ibid., no. 42. Cf. also Statute at Padua, cap. VI (4).

[4] Lucas de Penna, on C. X, 39, 2, no. 7.

[5] *Idem*, on C. XII, 19, 9 no. 1: *Si autem de licentia sui doctoris aut rectoris discedat a studio, ut profiscatur pro necessariis suis, gaudeat privilegio scholaribus indulto, supra Ne fil. pro patre, Habita, secus, si absque licentia.*

[6] Cf. again Lucas de Penna, on C. X, 39, 2 no. 7: *Nam si per mille annos staret scholaris in studio animo studendi et non incolatum vel sedem suam constituendi, non constitueret ibi domicilium.* See also Paulus Castrensis, *Dig. Vet.*, De judic., Haeres. abs., § Si quis, no. 12, fol. 125ra, and *Speculum Juris*, Lib. I, part. II, De Reo, § Dicto, no. 5, fol. 185.

this standpoint, and neither did Paulus see any reason to adopt Guilielmus's strange opinion, since the scholar always had the *animus recedendi finito studio*[1]. The canonists, too, were of the same mind as the overwhelming part of the civilians[2]. In practical terms this meant that the scholar was not incorporated in the diocese in which the *studium* was situated[3].

The question of domicile was not of mere academic interest, since according to the law as laid down in C. X. 39. 2, the *forum competens* was at the locality in which the contract was concluded or in the domicile of the defendant[4], and not in the place of the *studium*. Consequently, if the scholar had acquired domicile in the *studium* through ten years residence, he could have been sued there, and not in the district in which the contract was made. But the jurists were quite unanimous in their doctrine that the authentic had not changed the ordinary *forum competens* for contracts entered into elsewhere. The choice of the judge which Frederick had given to the scholars, did not therefore apply to those litigations which resulted from contracts concluded outside the *studium*. Cynus asks: *Quaeritur, numquid scholaris de contractibus initis partibus suis, possit Bononiae conveniri?*, and he replies that he cannot[5]. Before him, Jacobus de Ravanis was of the same opinion, namely, that the privilege of being able to choose one of the three judges was concerned only *de contractibus ibi habitis*[6]. Even if the scholar had promised payment or fulfilment of his obligation contracted somewhere else, at the place of the *studium*, the privilege of choosing his judge would still not apply. This was of

---

[1] Paulus Castrensis, C. De jurisd. omn. jud., Juris ordo, no. 3, fol. 131ra. But see also Jacobus *infra* note 6.

[2] Archdeacon, on VI: De temp. ord., c. Eos, no. 2, fol. 42vb.

[3] See Johannes Andreae, *Novella in Decretales*, Proem.

[4] This was also the teaching of the canonists, see, for example, Johannes de Petesella in his *Summa*, De foro comp., fol. 161rb: in the case of several domiciles he could be sued at one of them: *Si in pluribus locis habeat domicilium, in quolibet potest conveniri*. On the whole question of the appropriate *forum* see especially G. ONCLIN, *De territoriali vel personali legis indole*, 1938, pp. 42 ff. and 100 ff.

[5] Cynus, ad auth., no. 9.

[6] Jacobus de Ravanis, ad auth., fol. 176rb.: *Dico, quod coram episcopo potest conveniri de contractibus eo loco habitis. Unde si ego non contraxissem hic et de contractu alibi habito me conveniret, hic non responderem, nisi contraxissem domicilium, quia per decem annos hic mansissem in studio, quia tunc haberem domicilium... unde hic intelligitur, quod convenitur scholaris coram episcopis locorum de contractibus ibi habitis, et poterunt eos declinare et eligere doctorem.*

practical importance in those cases in which the student absented himself and entered into an obligation somewhere else, but promised fulfilment whilst *in scholis*. Andreas de Barulo was quite precise about it: *Hoc privilegium datur personae in factis in loco, non extra locum factis* [1], and Baldus adopting the opinion of Andreas pointed out that in these legal transactions the student did not assume the rôle of a scholar on whom the privilege was conferred: *Licet conferatur solutio in loco, non confert ut scholaris nec contrahitur cum eo tamquam cum scholari* [2]. The real need for this restriction is not difficult to see considering the numerous loopholes.

All this brings us to the perhaps most celebrated clause in the constitution *Habita*, that is, the privilege of choice of judicial tribunal. The authentic stated that a scholar when sued might choose between his *Dominus*, that is, his own teacher in civil law (the *Magister* in other faculties) [3], and the local bishop. The magisterial jurisdiction was based on the idea that the Doctores were the *studii gubernatores* to whom the care of the scholars was committed [4]; the *paternitas doctoralis* was a sufficient guarantee for the Doctor's impartiality [5]. A third judge was optional, namely the local Podestà, since the authentic did not abolish the latter's ordinary jurisdiction, but merely added two new optional judicial authorities: in view of the fact that *Habita* had a well-known predecessor (*i.e.*, the constitution *Omnem*) [6], the competency of the Podestà was not doubted, whose power remained therefore untouched. It was based on the *jus commune*, as Jacobus Butrigarius stated [7]. In France his place was taken

---

[1] See the report of Baldus, *loc. cit.*, no. 43.

[2] Baldus, *ibid.*

[3] On these terms see *gl. ord.*, s. vv.

[4] Jacobus de Arena, *Dig. Vet.*, Proem. no. 13, fol. 61vb. See furthermore E. M. MEIJERS, *art. cit.*, vol. II, p. 476, note 2 (Petrus de Bellapertica). On the temptation to misuse the privilege see the delightful passage in FULLER's, *History* p. 22.

[5] See Baldus, no. 59, and Statutes at Bologna, cap. LVII. It was perhaps the *paternitas doctoralis* which prompted the examiners to report on the performance of a canon law student at his examination, in the following paternal manner: *Reperimus, quod ipse satis debiliter se habuit in dicto examine, et credimus, quod propter timorem, ut apparet prima facie. Et ego Savaricus Christiani, Decretorum Doctor, sum in eo expertus, quod est timorosus et modicum scit attento tempore, quo audivit*, transcribed from an Avignonese MS by DENIFLE, *Archiv*, vol. III, p. 334 note.

[6] See DENIFLE, *Universitäten*, p. 57; KOEPPLER, *art. cit.*, p. 605, and all the medieval jurists on this point.

[7] Ad auth., fol. 121ra. The scholars at Lérida could choose between the rector, their master and the bishop, see VILLANUEVA, p. 201-2. The university of Salamanca

by the bailiff, as Jacobus de Ravanis tells us[1]. It is however a sign of the growth of rectorial powers by the turn of the thirteenth and fourteenth centuries that a scholar could also be summoned before him. The extra-legality of this procedure was undersood by contemporaries, but it had become the *consuetudo*, and hence the tribunal of a fourth optional judge came into being: a summons before the rector did not entail the heavy penalties of the authentic[2].

This privilege of being able to choose his judge was not, however, conceded, if the scholar was sued by a widow or others who enjoyed certain procedural benefits[3]. Although the provisions of the authentic came into full play, if a scholar sued another scholar, they did not touch the privileges of the widows and orphans (the so-called *personae miserabiles*), and the reason was that they *debiliores sunt et etiam omnem parvam potentiam perhorrescunt*[4]. In practice this had

---

adopted the provisions of *Habita*, see RASHDALL, *ed. cit.*, vol. II, pp. 79 f. For the *justiciarius scholarium* at Naples, a royal official, who dealt with criminal cases, whilst the choice of bishop and master was retained, see J. C. GIUDICE, *Codice Diplomatico del Regno*, vol. I/1, p. 253; DENIFLE, *op. cit.*, p. 454; RASHDALL, vol. II, p. 25; cf. also the foundation charter of Frederick II in HUILLARD-BRÉHOLLES, *Historia Diplomatica Friderici II*, vol. II, p. 450. For the origins of the *conservatores* at Paris, see the charter of Philip Augustus, *Chart. Univ. Paris.*, vol. I, no. 1, pp. 59-61, RASHDALL, vol. I, pp. 295, 416-7. The 16th cent. editor of Jacobus Butrigarius's *Lectura* appended a note to the lecture of Jacobus and makes fun of the view of Cynus that even at Paris the scholars were summoned by the secular justice; the editor exclaims: *Parcet mihi Cynus, parisius est judex specialis scholarium, qui est ecclesiasticus, qui vocatur judex conservator privilegiorum*, fol. 121va. Cf. also the appointment by Innocent IV of the bishops of London and Salisbury as conservators at Oxford, *Cal. Papal Reg., Letters*, ed. Bliss, vol. I, p. 306, and the observations in RASHDALL, vol. III, pp. 115 f.

[1] Jacobus de Ravanis, ad auth., fol. 176rb. At Oxford the Chancellor's court alone was competent, see for details, *Munimenta Acad. Oxon.*, ed. cit., pp. CI, 303 f, 510, 719, 769, and Edward I's Letter patent of 30 October 1275, *Cal. Pat. Rolls*, Edw. I, 1272-1281, p. 108. For Cambridge where the Chancellor's court had extremely wide powers, see *Statuta Antiqua*, chapters 33, 36 (in *Documents relating to the University and Colleges of Cambridge*, 1852, vol. I, pp. 327, 328); cf. also Hugh of Balsham's communication in FULLER, pp. 47-51, and the Letters patent of Henry III, Edward II and Edward III, and the charter of Richard II in G. DYER, *The Privileges of the University of Cambridge*, vol. I, pp. 63, 68, 74, 79, 86.

[2] See Jacobus Butrigarius, ad auth., fol. 121ra, discussing the possibility ef rejecting the Podestà in favour of the rector. The choice of a fourth judge was based on the medieval theory of corporations which were granted to elect their own rector. For Orleans in particular see the passage transcribed by MEIJERS, *art. cit.*, vol. II, p. 477, note 1.

[3] See C. III, 14. 1.

[4] Baldus, ad auth., no. 61.

the consequence that the widows and orphans still retained as their own judge the ecclesiastical tribunal, and our authentic changed nothing in this[1].

A rather great variety of opinion was expressed on the applicability of the authentic to criminal cases. Perhaps the diction of the law itself was not most happily chosen, since *lis* and *negotium* could be interpreted in various mays. But, on the testimony of Odofredus, it seems that for a considerable time after its promulgation the authentic was also applied to criminal case softhe scholars at Bologna, in fact down to the time of Azo[2], when the scholars decided to renounce the privilege as far as it concerned criminal cases. Whether the reasons which according to Odofredus had prompted the Bolognese scholars to renounce the privilege, were the real ones, may be doubted, but the fact of this renunciation seems indisputable[3]. Jacobus de Arena taught that the authentic was applicable to civil cases only, whilst criminal cases were outside its scope altogether[4]. Jacobus was joined by Nicholas Matarellus who interpreted the terms *lis* and *negotium* in the strict meaning, because *significant hominum commercia, non delicta*[5]. But the opinion of Jacobus and Nicholas was of little interest to their colleagues. What was of interest to them was whether this renunciation of the Bolognese scholars was binding upon their successors. Cynus expressly denied that it had any binding character, referring to the old legal maxim *res inter alios acta, aliis non praejudicat*[6]. That French civilians, such as Jacobus de Ravanis, rejected the Bolognese step as far as French *studia* were concerned, is in no need of emphasis[7]. It is somewhat strange that the real

---

[1] For the *personae miserabiles* see *Gregoriana*, II. II. 10, 11, 15, and I. XXIX. 38. Cf. also the practical case envisaged by Cynus, ad auth. *Quas actiones*, (D. Ce ss. eccl.), fol. 12va, no. 6. In this context the passage of Petrus de Bellapertica (transcribed by E. M. MEIJERS, *art. cit.*, vol. I, p. 128, note 1) should be referred to.

[2] The explanation given was that the constitution *Omnem* also included both civil and criminal cases, and that Frederick merely wished to expand *Omnem*.

[3] See Odofredus ad auth. *Habita*, fol. 204 ra. See also *gl. ord.* ad auth.

[4] Jacobus de Arena, ad auth. *Habita*, fol. 20va.

[5] See the report of Baldus, no. 51.

[6] Cynus, ad auth. no. 6: *Dicit glossa, quod bononiae pro parte renuntiaverunt scholares istud privilegium in criminalibus. Sed certe istud nichil ad nos, quia per renuntiationem ipsorum non potest nobis aliquod praejudicium generari, cum res etc. Item, licet scholares jamdiu renuntiassent, qui modo mortui sunt, propter hoc non fit praejudicium nunc existentibus in studio...*

[7] Jacobus de Ravanis, ad auth. *Habita*, fol. 176rb: *Bononiae renuntiatum est*

difficulty in the case of criminal cases was not pointed out before Baldus: if the bishop was chosen by the accused and capital punishment was to be the sentence, the bishop was obviously in no position to deal with the case: *unde ex qualitate judicum apparet, quod in criminalibus non potest ista authentica intelligi*[1].

At the latest before the *litis contestatio* the scholar had to declare whether or not he wished to avail himself of his right to choose between the three judges[2]. And once the choice was made before the summoning judge, the scholar could no more withdraw and change his mind. But the possibility had to be faced that despite the rejection of the summoning judge (implicit in the choice of one of the other two judges) the latter nevertheless overruled the objection. Technically speaking, the decision of this judge was an *interlocutoria sententia*, and the question arose whether the scholar should appeal at once, or defer the appeal until the eventual decision of this judge. Whilst Nicholas Matarellus would have chosen the latter alternative, obviously basing himself on the regulation which forbade appeals of this kind[3], it seems that the opinion of Cynus prevailed that, namely, appeal from the *interlocutoria sententia* should be lodged at once, because this lack of judicial competency could not be made a gravamen in the appeal from the *sententia diffinitiva*[4]. Although the constitution did not distinguish between the three judges and considered them of equal rank, the jurists nevertheless established some sort of judicial hierarchy. If the *sententia interlocutoria* was given by the Doctor, the appeal went to the Podestà or to the Bishop (if the Doctor was a clerk), unless one of these had previously been refused by the scholar; if the Podestà took the decision, the appeal went to the Bishop in any case, who was considered *tamen in se simpliciter major* than the Doctor[5]. The execution of the *sententia diffinitiva* lay in the hands of the Podestà, upon request of the Doctor

---

isti electioni, quantum ad criminales conveniuntur coram potestate nec possent doctorem suum eligere... sed illud, quod factum fuit ibi, non praejudicat.

[1] Baldus, no. 51. For criminal cases at Cambridge cf. *Statuta Antiqua* (*supra*, p. 26 n. 1), chapter 33.

[2] The opinion of the *gl. ord.* that the choice could also be made after the *litis contestatio* was unanimously rejected.

[3] C. Quo appell. non rec., Ante sententiae.

[4] Cynus, ad auth. *Habita*, no. 14.

[5] Bartolus, ad au:h., no. 6, fol. 130ra : *Appellabitur ad proximum superiorem. Unde si doctor vel rector est laicalis, appellabitur ad potestatem, si clericus ad episcopum.*

or the Bishop[1]. According to Johannes Andreae in his *Additiones ad Speculum* there were some civilians who held that the Podestà could only then execute the sentence at the place of the *studium*, if the scholar had sufficient goods there to make the execution worth while; if he had not, the Doctor (or Bishop) would have to request the appropriate authority of the place in which the scholar's goods were situated[2].

It was in connexion with the option of choosing one of the three judges that the canonically sanctioned privileged position of the clerical scholars received particular attention. There was general agreement (for reasons which are not relevant to this enquiry) that the emperor at that time at least was no more entitled to legislate on matters directly affecting the clerics, and most decidedly not on a matter that had been considered as of vital importance, such as the trial of clerics before a secular tribunal. Hierocratic doctrine and practice tenaciously clung to the *privilegium fori* of the clerics[3]. But although nobody admitted that the authentic was applicable to clerical scholars, would it not be possibile to say that they could at least renounce their *privilegium fori*, and in this way apply the authentic to themselves? This question had some basis in the law, though not in canon law, but in the *Codex*[4], according to which it was possibile for clerics to be tried by a secular justice, if they agreed voluntarily; within the framework of this law, then, clerics could effectively choose between their bishop and their local magistrate. In his usual dry manner the Archdeacon of Bologna, Tancred, curtly stated that *haec lex secundum canones hodie non valet*[5], hence a renuntiation on the part of the cleric was excluded, at least one that would have derived its force from the law. Yet, could it not reasonably be maintained that, apart from positive law, the cleric could renounce his *privilegium fori* on general grounds?

This question engaged Johannes Teutonicus to a considerable extent. In his gloss on the *Compilatio Tertia* (as incorporated by

---

[1] Jacobus de Arena, ad auth., no. 2: *Dic, quod doctor potest suam sententiam executioni mandare per judicem saecularem.* See also *Speculum Juris*, De executione sententiae, lib. II, partic. III, § Nunc, no. 12, fol. 817.

[2] Johannes Andreae, ad *Speculum Juris, loc. cit.* (preceding note).

[3] See R. GENESTAL, *Le Privilegium Fori en France*, vol. II, pp. 3 ff. Cf. also *idem, Les Origines de l'appel comme d'abus*, 1951, pp. 1-2.

[4] C. II. 3. 29.

[5] s.v. « renuntiare », fol. 191rb.

Tancred in the *glossa ordinaria*) Johannes, quite in agreement with contemporary doctrine held that the validity of a renuntiation of a privilege depended upon the kind of privilege. If a particular privilege was given only for the personal benefit of certain persons, this privilege could be renounced; this was the case with the *Velleianum* which could be renounced by the woman. It was an entirely different matter, however, if the reason of granting a privilege was the protection of the privileged individual from otherwise lawful interferences by others, as was the case with the *Macedonianum*, the benefits of which could not validly be renounced.

Now, if these principles are transferred to the *privilegium fori* of the clerics, Johannes Teutonicus says, we shall see at once that, generally speaking, the clerk cannot validly renounce it. For this privilege belongs to the second category, *quod non tam in favorem clericorum quam in odium laicorum est introductum; ipsi enim oppido infesti sunt clericis, ut II, q. VII Laicos*. Hence, if an apostate cleric, though personally losing the *privilegium fori*, is beaten by a layman, the *privilegium canonis* will nevertheless play its full force. *Si tamen talis percutitur a laico, potest uti privilegio, licet illud quantum ad se perdidit*. Moreover, if a cleric is beaten by a layman, he can renounce all personal claims arising out of the damage inflicted upon him, but he cannot dispose of the claims which the Church as a whole has against the layman[1].

All this is true, Johannes declares, when we consider formal and explicit renuntiations of a cleric. For, according to him, the cleric *can* renounce his privilege by tacitly consenting to being tried by a secular judge; he can do this effectively by simply obeying the summons of this judge[2]. After all, the pope himself can voluntarily submit himself to the judgment of the emperor[3], or to that of a synod[4]. There are many things to which we can agree by implication, though not formally and explicitly Therefore, by implicitly recognizing the authority of the secular tribunal, the cleric can avail himself of the privilege set out in *Habita*, « for otherwise the privilege

---

[1] *Si clericus est verberatus a laico, potest remittere injuriam quantum ad se, licet non quoad ecclesiam, ut XXIII, q. IV, Si quis.* In modern terminology this would amount to a distinction between private and public law.

[2] *Licet clericus per pactum non possit renuntiare foro suo, posset tamen tacite renuntiare foro respondendo coram laico.*

[3] C. II, q. VII, c. 41.

[4] C. II, q. V, c. 10.

of Frederick that every scholar can choose his judge, would vanish into the air » [1].

If ever a theory was unanimously rejected, it was this theory of Johannes Teutonicus [2]. With the ascendancy of the extreme forms of papalism as the century wore on, on the one hand, and with the promulgation of Frederick II's authentic *St..tuimus*, on the other hand, there was non room for such an accomodating standpoint as that of Johannes. Bartholomaeus Brixiensis, for instance, who brought the *glossa ordinaria* on the *Decretum* up to date, faithfully incorporated Johannes's gloss into his own *Apparatus*, but added these words: *Quicquid dicat Johannes, hoc tene, quod in laicum nullo modo consentit clericus*. Whatever doubt may have remained on the possibility of a cleric standing his trial before a secular justice, it was dispelled by *Statuimus* which was also inserted in the Codex [3]. Perhaps Cynus was clearest in his exposition. It should be remembered that he was one of the fiercest antagonists of the canonists and of political papalism, and he very grudgingly conceded any privilege which the clerics might enjoy. But now that Frederick II had exempted the clerics from the jurisdiction of secular tribunals, not even Cynus could quarrel with the canonists about the privileged position of the clerics:

---

[1] *Alioquin nisi hoc dicatur, exsufflatum erit privilegium frederici, quod quilibet scholaris potest eligere coram eo, quo iudice respondere velit, ut Ne fil. pro patre, Habita.*

[2] It might be that his own political bias made him propound this view.

[3] Under the title De epp. et cl., ante l. 34. Parts of this long decree of Frederick II were also adopted by papal legislators, beginning with Innocent IV, see *Bullarium Romanum*, vol. III, pp. 503 ff; cf. also Alexander IV, *ibid.*, pp. 612 ff., 652, 669 f., and it was eventually incorporated in Boniface's *Sextus*, V. II. 18. About this see now A. C. SHANNON, *The Popes and Heresy* etc., 1950, pp. 113-4. It should be noted in parenthesis that Urban IV's adoption of Frederick II's heretical decrees which is neither in his Registers nor in the *Bullarium Franciscanum*, can be found in a specifically Franciscan collection of « heretical » laws preserved in the hitherto un, detected MS no. 9 in the Collectio Rosminiana at Stresa: no. 17 of the collection-fol. 57; here is also Clement IV's endorsement of Frederick II's decree, no. 19, fol. 58, which is not registered, but is in the *Bullarium Franciscanum*, vol. III, no. LII, p. 47a. Most of the decretals collected here are not in the Archives at Assisi, cf. F. PENNACCHI, in *Arch. Franc. Hist.*, vols. VIII, X-XIII. This interesting miscellaneous Codex also contains a *Consilium domini Guidonis Fulgonis qui postea fuit papa Clemens IIII* on a number of practical points arising in heretical proceedings; it shows this pope extraordinarily conversant with the roots of inquisitorial procedure in Roman law The fols. 1-52 contain the hitherto unknown *Casus summarii decretalium* of Guido de Leonico. About all this we hope to report in due course. The *Consilium* of Clement IV, hitherto unknown, is also in MS 69, set VIII, fol. 11-51, of the Studienbibliothek, Linz.

Licet vellent (*scil.* clerici scholares) *hodie habere dictam electionem, non possunt, quod est verum de scholaribus tonsuram habentibus*[1]   In this as in so many other points, Cynus loyally followed Jacobus de Ravanis[2]. The general doctrine was that the authentic did not apply to clerical scholars at all.[3]. We may call as a last witness the Bolognese professor of canon law, Johannes de Petesella, a Spaniard, who wrote the first *Summa* on the *Gregoriana* the year after it was published.   Reviewing the position of clerical scholars he says this: *Nec huic privilegio potest clericus abrenuntiare... ut est videndum in scholaribus, qui habent tres judices, ut habetur in privilegio Frederici, quod est positum C. Ne Filius pro patre, Habita. Sed ego non admitto illud in scholaribus clericis, quos de necessitate dico coram espiscopo conveniendos, quia privilegium imperiale non potest constitutionem apostolicam immutare.* The *privilegium fori* was not *tale beneficium, quod possit renuntiari*[4].

Nevertheless, what was the position of a cleric « in scholis », if he was sued? Who was his judge? According to canon law, it was *his* bishop, that is, the local ordinary, but who was his ordinary, say, at Bologna, if he came from *citra montes*? Here Goffredus de Trano advanced the very strict point of view, namely, that the clerics had to be judged by their own bishop: the Bolognese clerics, that is, those who were citizens of Bologna, by the local bishop, the foreigners by their own ordinary[5]. But this strict, and we may add unrealistic, opinion of Goffredus de Trano did not meet with the approval of the

---

[1] Cynus, ad auth. no. 6: *Haec sententia facta fuit ante auth. Statuimus, quam habemus supra, quoniam facta fuit eo tempore quo imperator habuit potestatem concedendi clericis privilegium* (!). *Haec authentica fuit antequam fuissent exempti a sua jurisdictione et facti de jurisdictione ecclesiae, de qua facti fuerunt per auth. Statuimus... ideo licet vellent...* Hostility to canonists was not confined to civilians, see the interesting paper of M. MACCARRONE, *Teologia e Diritto Canonico nella Monarchia III, 3* in « Rivista di Storia della Chiesa in Italia » 1951, pp. 7-42.

[2] See Jacobus de Ravanis, ad auth., fol. 176 rb: *Scholaris non clericus, sed laicus habet electionem trium judicum, per auth. Statuimus.*

[3] The injunctions issued by Innocent IV to the University of Bologna contain nothing new; they are printed by DENIFLE, in *Archiv*, vol. IV, p. 245.

[4] *Summa*, De foro comp., fol. 161va. On Johannes himself see SCHULTE, *Beiträg ezur Literatur über die Decretalen Gregor's IX*, in « Sitzungsberichte d. kaiserl. Akademie d. Wiss. », phil. hist. Cl, vol. LXVIII, pp. 61-83.

[5] Goffredus de Trano, *Summa Titulorum*, De foro comp., fol. 72va. It appears that this was the older doctrine, see, for instance, the anonymous author of the *Apparatus* on *Comp. I* (based on Ricardus Anglicus?) who says that to be tried by his local bishop was a privilege of the cleric who therefore had to be asked for his consent if he was to be tried by some other bishop: De foro comp., fol. 11va.

other great canonists of the thirteenth century. Hostiensis, for instance, after stating that the authentic did not concern clerical scholars at all[1], confessed that there was no question of depriving a cleric of his dishop whilst *in scholis*, but that the permission of his local ordinary to attend the *studium* also signified the approval of his Bishop for the jurisdiction of the bishop in the *studium*[2]. As far as one can see, this was the generally accepted opinion amongst the canonists.

One last problem remained to be solved. Should the clerical scholar not have the option between the Bishop and his Doctor, if the latter was also a cleric? Ubertus de Bobio and the continuator of his work, Johannes de Deo, avowed that then the clerical students should be given the choice[3]. It was not difficult to see that this doctrine was originally set forth by a civilian, such as Ubertus was. According to the Archdeacon this opinion had been rejected by Guilielmus Naso, one of the pupils of Alan[4], the great English canonist at the beginning of the thirteenth century: Guilielmus had argued that the emperor could not possibly confer jurisdictional powers on Doctors as regards clerics which the former had not already possessed. *Nam jurisdictionem imperator non potest dare magistris sive doctoribus, quam in clericos non habebat.* Only Johannes Calderinus of the fourteenth-century canonists adhered to the opinion of Ubertus de Bobio and Johannes de Deo[5], whilst the thirteenth-century Speculator reported it, without deciding on its acceptability[6].

If the secular justice were to try clerical scholars, he and his *consiliarii et fautores* were to excommunicated[7]. It is also of interest

---

[1] *Puto verius, quod prius dixi, scil. quod in scholaribus saecularibus tantum habeat locum constitutio et quod clericos non includat.*

[2] Hostiensis, *Summa Aurea*, De Magistris, col. 1347, no. 10.

[3] See the report of the Archdeacon, *Rosarium*, ad C. XI, q. I, c. 42, fol. 211rb., no. 3; Panormitanus, De foro comp., Si diligenter, no. 52, fol. 56ra. Johannes de Deo wrote this in his tract *De Cavillationibus*, about which see SCHULTE, *Quellen und Literatur*, vol. II, pp. 104-6; VAN HOVE, *Prolegomena*, p. 491; also SAVIGNY, *op. cit.*, vol. V, pp. 132-6. Martin IV attended the lectures of Ubertus de Bobio on civil law at Parma, see SALIMBENE, *MGH.*, *SS.*, vol. XXXII, p. 508.

[4] See SARTI-FATTORINI, *De Claris Archigymn. Bonon. Prof.*, vol. I, p. 417, and R. TRIFONE, *Gli scritti di Guglielmo Nasone* etc., in « Rivista di storia del diritto Italiano », vol. II, pp. 242-60.

[5] See Panormitanus, De foro comp., Si dilig., no. 25, fol. 56ra.

[6] *Speculum Juris*, Lib. I, partic. II, De Reo, § Dicto, no. 9, fol. 185.

[7] Goffredus de Trano, *Summa*, De immun. eccl., c. adversus; and Hostiensis, *Summa*, ibid.

to note that the Master in the schools teaching a cleric who had grown a beard or had put down his clerical habit, was excommunicated *ipso facto*[1]. A nice problem constituted the question what should be the position of the defendant before a secular judge, if during the proceedings he becomes a cleric? *Dicunt omnes, quod coram eodem judice finiet*[2], but if the case was a criminal one, the ecclesiastical judge would have to step in, because not even the most newly fledged clerk could be punished by the secular authority[3].

It now remains to circumscribe as closely as it is possible the circle of individuals who benefitted from *Habita*. And here in the first place, the term scholar demands our attention. There was, on the whole, general agreement amongst thirteenth-century writers that the authentic not only wished to confer privileges on the legal scholars in the narrowest meaning of the term (that is, the Roman law students), but also on the scholars of every faculty. Yet, it is worthwhile pointing out that some jurists only grudgingly included the scholars *cuiuscumque scientiae*, as is evidenced by Jacobus Butrigarius. But it was difficult to overlook the work *maxime* in the authentic, and therefore students in non-legal faculties had of necessity to be included[4]. Consequently, also the arts (grammar) students were understood to have benefitted from the authentic, « because without grammar the knowledge of the civil law was not possibile »[5]. The formal presupposition was that the student was properly matriculated; a suspended student did not enjoy the privileges. Proof that he was a student could be furnished, apart from registration in the university *matricula*, by circumstantial evidence[6]. Whilst the material presupposition was that the scholar devoted himself to his studies entirely: that those who only went to a *studium* for the sake of non-scholastic activities and cut lectures were not considered worthy of the pri-

---

[1] And of course the scholar too: Archdeacon, *Rosarium*, ad Dist. XXIII, Si quis, fol. 32vb, no. 2.

[2] *Speculum Juris*, loc. cit., no. 5.

[3] *Idem, ibid.*

[4] Jacobus Butrigarius, ad auth. *Habita*, fol. 121ra: *Numquid habeat locum in omnibus scholaribus aliis quam legum? Respondeo, quod licet quaedam rationes adaptentur solum scholaribus legum, tamen et quaedam sunt generales ad omnes scholares aliarum scientiarum et decretalium et medicinae et grammaticae et logicae, et hoc probatur dictione « maxime », quae est in textu.*

[5] Jacobus Butrigarius, *loc. cit.*

[6] Bartolus, ad auth., no. 3, fol. 129vb.

vileges[1]. Those little deserving students, though formally matriculated, who looked like warriors and lounged about most of their time, were called *ostentatores*[2]. Studying was a *personalis actus*, and hence required personal attendance at lectures[3]. The pursuit of knowledge was not unlike leading a contemplative life: just as it was forbidden by Innocent III that married clerks should have ecclesiastical benefices, since *cythara cum psalterio male concordat*[4], in the same way the married scholars were frowned upon[5]. *Ratio est, quia non possumus libris et uxori pariter inservire.* Even if the scholar attended a recognized *studium generale*, he would not benefit from the privileges, when devoting himself to so-called forbidden branches of learning, such as necromancy: he was not then considered enrolled *in literatoria licita facultate*[6].

The circle of persons to whom the scholar's privileges were applied, was drawn rather liberally. The household of the scholar was also included in the privileged class — and this, incidentally, gives us some insight into the social standing of the medieval university population — since no scholar (and master) was supposed to be able to live without his entourage: the servants were therefore in exactly the same position as their masters, for so lang as they were in their actual service. For, as Panormitanus put it, one could not expect a scholar to cook his meat and do other « vile things » which necessarily

---

[1] See Baldus, ad auth., no. 38: *Quaero igitur, qui dicantur scholares? Respondeo illi, qui de facto et animo sunt scholares, non illi, qui fingunt et non student et intrant scholas et vadunt vagando.* Lucas de Penna, C. X, 49, 1 no. 9: *Item debent studiose et diligenter agere circa scientiam, non delitiis aut voluptatibus occupari.* See also Johannes de Lignano, as reported by Panormitanus, De jud., c. 1, fol. 6va; and for Cambridge, see *Statt. Antt.*, chapter XLII. About the difficulty of protecting the university from false students, see Canon A. L. GABRIEL, *La protection des étudiants a l'Université de Paris au XIIIe siècle*, in « Revue de l'Université d'Ottawa », 1950, p. 50 (lamentation of the chancellor) and p. 55; cf. also M. M. DAVY, *art. cit. (supra* p. 6, n. 1), p. 309 *(vagi scholares).*

[2] Rapheal Fulgosius, C. De transact., Sub praetextu.

[3] See Baldus, C. De caduc. toll., lex 1, § Ne autem.

[4] *Gregoriana*: III. III. 5.

[5] *Cythara* was the symbol of *vita activa*, whilst *psalterium* that of the *vita contemplativa*, see *gl. ord.* ad *decret. cit.* At Cambridge Edward III ordered *quod nulla publica mulier infra dictam villam Cantabrigiae vel suburbium* (beyond St Giles?) *eiusdem conversetur seu moretur.* Cf. also the arenga of this: G. DYER, *The Privileges of the University of Cambridge*, pp. 76-77. For Oxford see RASHDALL-POWICKE, vol. III, p. 91 note 5.

[6] Baldus, ad auth., no. 49.

detracted from the pursuit of knowledge[1]. The scribes, too, were included[2], provided that they were not married[3]. The Statutes of Bologna and Padua considered the booksellers, purveyors of writing material, and any workmen attending to the schools, worthy of the same privileges as the scholars themselves[4]. This very wide extension of the constitution was usually based on the rather harmless looking clause employed in it, namely, that the *nuntii* of the scholars should also benefit from the privileges.

Even a Doctor himself could advantageously apply the provisions of *Habita* to himself, if in some capacity he was still a student; so, for instance, if a Doctor of civil law began to study canon law under a canonist, he would then partake in the privileges conferred upon both groups of academic members. *Iste est doctor quoad quid, et scholaris quoad quid* was the opinion of Nicholas Matarellus[5]. The student who had received the lowest degree, the *Licentiatus in legibus*, or *in decretis*, or *in artibus*, could claim the privileges of scholars[6].

Could it be maintained that the whole corporation, the whole *universitas scholarium*, should be favoured, at least as far as this was reasonable and applicable, mainly as regards the privileged *forum competentiae*? Salicetus directs our attention to this problem, with which he deals at some length. There are some, he reports, who would deny any privileged position to the whole *universitas*; consequently, any action against it should be brought before the ordinary judge, the Podestà, *quia ipsa est quoddam corpus repraesentatum*[7]. But Sali-

---

[1] Panormitanus, VI: De priv., c. 1.

[2] Baldus, *loc. cit.* no. 10: *Nota, quod scriptores sunt sub eodem foro sicut scholares, et sunt sub praeside, episcopo et doctore.*

[3] *Gl. ord.*, Extra: III. XVIII. 1, s.v. « scholarium ».

[4] See cap. X, and cap. VI (16) respectively. The household of the scholar was expressly protected at Lérida, see the document printed by DENIFLE, *Archiv*, vol. IV, p. 258. A similar provision extending to barbers, parchment makers, book binders, bell ringers, cooks, etc., will be found at Oxford, see *Munim. Acad. Oxon.*, ed. cit., p. 52, cf. also pp. 344-5. It is well known that the Oxford tradesmen and servants claimed the privileges of the scholars in Elizabethan times. For the protection of the scholar's household at Cambridge, see *Statt. Antt.*, ch. 33. At Naples the *apothecarii ac ceteri, qui ibidem ratione scholarium morantur* were privileged, see GIUDICE, *Codice Dipl. del Regno*, vol. I, p. 253. An interesting case involving the protection of the household in *Cartulaire de l'Université de Montpellier*, vol. I, pp. 706-12.

[5] See the report of Baldus, no. 9.

[6] *Idem, ibid.*, no. 39, and Salicetus, ad auth. no. 12.

[7] Salicetus, *loc. cit.*

cetus does not agree with this point of view, for if the scholars have
their own *forum*, which they may elect — and they have it simply
because they are members of the *universitas* — why should not the
whole body have it, since *universitas nichil aliud est quam scholares
ipsius*. Therefore, the corporation of scholars, like the individuals,
must be conceded the privilege of choosing either Podestà, Bishop or
Doctor. But another difficulty arose here — who was the Doctor, as
there were many Doctors in the same corporation? According to
Salicetus the answer was *omnes doctores legentes habentur loco eius
vel saltem collegium* whilst according to Baldus, it was the rector, just
as a chapter could also be convened before the abbot, as Cynus had
taught [1]. But as there were necessarily lay and clerical Doctores
amongst the regents, a further difficulty presented itself: if all of
them were to sit as judges the case might arise in which they would
have to render a judgment in a cause that could not legitimately be
decided by lay persons, even if there were some clerics on the bench.
Quid juris? Bartolus [2], and, follwing him, Baldus, drew a neat di-
stincion. If the corporation was composed solely of lay persons, or
solely of clerics, there was no difficulty at all, but if the corporation
was a mixed one, it depended on the larger proportion of laical or
clerical members. If the latter were represented in greater numbers,
trahunt ad se laicos, although Baldus expresses himself cautiously
concerning the greater number of laical students: *aut major est pars
laicorum, et tunc inspicitur major pars, quia alia accessionis locum
tenet, licet precisior sit* — and he left it at that. Bartolus was more
consequent and admitted that in such a case the laical rector would
have no jurisdiction over the clerics [3]. Quite in typical medieval
fashion Baldus also faces the possibility of laical and clerical scholars
having equal numbers; his (quite unusual) laconic answer was:
Tunc laici accedunt clericis tamquam dignioribus. Salicetus threw away
all subtle distincions concerning the numerical strength of laical and
clerical students and avowed that despite a numerical preponderance
of laical scholars, the *universitas* as such should be taken as a *corpus*

---

[1] C. Ne quis in sua causa, lex 1.
[2] Bartolus, *Dig. Nov.*, 47, De coll. illic., l. sodales, fol. 148va, no. 12.
[3] Bartolus, *ibid.*

ecclesiasticum [1], and accordingly the Bishop or the clerical rector should be the competent judges for a mixed *universitas scholarium* [2].

Many more topics could be treated to show how minutely and at the same time how liberally the medieval jurists interpreted Frederick I's constitution. It furnished a welcome occasion to elaborate a detailed system of scholars' privileges of which it was the basic law. That *Habita* was of vital concern to the civilians and of little or no interest to the canonists, will have become sufficiently clear. The authentic was an imperial insurance for the Roman law students; it was to give them that sense of security which they lacked in comparison with the canon law students; it was the solemn pledge of the supreme secular authority to protect those who engaged themselves in the study of the secular law; it was the ecumenical legislative act which was to rescue the study of Roman law from the threat of absorption and extinction by its rival, the canon law. That it fulfilled this role, even if the wider political hopes of its author were unrealizable, is amply proved by the exuberant flourishing of Roman law studies in Europe throughout the Middle Ages. For the service to the intellectual unification of Europe and the world at large, rendered by Frederick's *Habita*, civilized man owes him a great debt of gratitude: in his own way he contributed effectively to the intimate association of

EUROPA UND DAS RÖMISCHE RECHT.

---

[1] That the *studia generalia* were « kirchliche Anstalten » was the theme of F. Stein, *Die akademische Gerichtsbarkeit in Deutschland*, 1891, and the attacks directed against him by some of his contemporaries therefore appear to have been misdirected.

[2] It is not without significance that at Bologna the rector had to be a clerk. On the difficulties of mixed universities see also the remarks of Kaufmann, *op. cit.*, vol. II, pp. 104-5.

XII

THE DELICTAL RESPONSIBILITY OF MEDIEVAL CORPORATIONS

FEW subjects have engaged the interest of jurists and commanded the attention of practical lawyers to a higher degree than the criminal liability of corporations. Broadly speaking, interest and attention were less focussed on the essence, structure and theory of a corporation than on the practical question of whether sanctions against a corporation were permissible. In his monumental work Gierke somewhat oversimplified the issues, and this was particularly true as regards his presentation of the medieval doctrine on the liability of corporations. His own ' realistic ' views on the nature of a corporation were apt to colour his interpretation, and selection, of quotations. Moreover, this problem of a corporate criminal liability is one that has continually engaged the attention of the higher courts.[1] A brief restatement of the medieval doctrine on this point seems worth while. We should keep in mind, however, that a theory in the strict meaning of the term had not been conceived until the late thirteenth century, and not developed before the middle of the fourteenth century. If we can take Azo and Bracton as typical representatives of thirteenth-century legal thought, we may well agree that the problematical nature of a corporate criminal liability was at that time not even perceived, quite apart from the larger question of the nature of a corporation.[2] This lack of any constructive thought on the part of these two great jurists is not indeed surprising, as Roman Law itself cannot be considered to have been as clear a guide on this topic as in some other respects. The Roman lawyers, it appears, were vague and elusive. Speaking of Ulpian's dictum in D. 4. 2. 9. 1, a modern authority claims that he ' is certainly not making a considered statement on corporate delictal responsibility '.[3] Although one might, by way of a skilful interpretation, deduce from section 3 of

---

[1] See especially *R.* v. *I.C.R. Haulage, Ltd.,* [1944] K.B. 551; but see also *Pearks, Gunston & Tee, Ltd.* v. *Ward,* [1902] 2 K.B. 1, where the remarks of Mr. Justice Channell (p. 11) deserve full quotation : ' By the general principles of the criminal law, if a matter is made a criminal offence, it is essential that there should be something in the nature of a *mens rea,* and therefore in ordinary cases a corporation cannot be guilty of a criminal offence . . . but there are exceptions to this rule '.

[2] See Pollock and Maitland, *History of English Law,* 2nd ed., vol. i, pp. 494, 495–6.

[3] Professor P. W. Duff, *Personality in Roman Private Law,* pp. 91–2; cf. also F. Brendan Brown, *The Roman Conception of the Juristic Person,* Washington, 1926, Ch. II *passim.*

this same *lex* that a corporate body can commit a crime and can be punished, there is hardly any evidence in classical Roman law for making corporations, such as colleges, criminally responsible.[4] Moreover, Ulpian appeared to be disinclined to allow an *actio* against a corporation when he replied to the question of whether a town was suable: ' Puto ex suo quidem dolo non posse dari (scil. actio) ', posing the somewhat rhetorical question, and anticipating the answer to it: ' Quid enim municipes dolo facere possunt ? '[5] It was only at a later date that some specifically mentioned bodies were held liable for criminal offences committed by their members.[6]

Nevertheless, Ulpian's doubts left the glossators unmoved. They were bold enough to proclaim the corporate criminal liability, without however attempting to justify it on the strength of the sources available. The glossators, as Gierke has shown us,[7] did not develop any theory about the structure of a corporation, and, yet they took its criminal liability for granted. The disquisitions on this point are extremely scanty, brief and, very frequently, not to the point at all. So, for instance, the glosses contained in the so-called *Brachylogus*[8] simply reiterated Ulpian's dicta,[9] but it is already noticeable in this collection that D. 4. 3. 15 received an interpretation which certainly did no great honour to the glossatorial interpretative methods. This was an interpretation, however, that came to be generally accepted by contemporary doctrine. When Ulpian sceptically asked whether a corporation could act with *dolus* and by this very question implied the impossibility, the glossators, apparently encouraged by the doubts of Ulpian, interpreted the ' Quid enim dolo facere possunt ? ' as meaning that a corporation could ' not easily ' act fraudulently. Azo supplied the answer to Ulpian's question in this way: ' Nihil facile propter naturalem hominis ad dissentiendum facilitatem '.[1] Nor was Azo unique in this courageous interpretation of the Roman law. The *Glossa ordinaria* also maintained that a ' facile ' should be inserted to make the text intelligible: ' Quod contraria lex dicit " quid enim etc." supple facile '.[2] The reason why the glossators upheld this view

---

[4] See Duff, *op. cit.*, pp. 92, 157.
[5] D.4.3.15.
[6] *Cod. Theod.* 16.4.5, and Duff, p. 157, note 6, p. 158.
[7] *Das Deutsche Genossenschaftsrecht*, vol. iii, pp. 178–238, at pp. 189, 195, 203.
[8] *Corpus Legum sive Brachylogus Juris Civilis*, ed. C. Böcking; about the date of its composition see Fitting, *Ueber die Heimat und das Alter des Brachylogus*, Berlin, 1880.
[9] II.1.10 and 12; II.1.14, and IV.5.5.
[1] Azo, *Summa Codicis*, II.19, no. 17, and II.20, no. 12: ' Licet contingat cum difficultate, ut universitas consentiat in dolo vel metu vel similibus committendis, et ideo etiam dicitur municipes non posse fieri dolum, subaudi facile '.
[2] See *Glossa ordinaria*, D.4.2.9.1, s.v. ' collegium ': ' vel dic, quod verius puto, quod universitas dolum et metum committit, ut hic dicit, et quod contraria lex . . . '.

may be seen from the gloss on Ulpian's text itself.[3]   Here the glossator explained that corporations could not reach a decision easily, because of the difficulties inherent in the nature of an organised body: ' Quia nec consentire facile possunt, sed tamen possunt cum difficultate, ut pulsata campana, quia videbantur omnes facere, quod concilium facit vel major pars, et metum inferunt . . . '.[4]   The great glossator and pupil of Placentinus, Pyleus, put forward a very similar, but seemingly independent, opinion in his *Summa in Tres Postremos Codicis Libros*.[5] He too was bent on establishing a criminal responsibility of a corporation and, therefore, anxious to rid himself of Ulpian's weighty dictum; he even seemed to read in it that the Roman spoke of a corporation's inability to be of the same mind in any point of discussion; and Ulpian had merely attempted to state the difficulty, and not the impossibility, of a corporation's reaching agreement. ' Quamvis dicatur alibi, quod universitas consentire non poterit vel dolo facere, illud enim non impossibilitatem, sed facti notat difficultatem '.[6]

After having dispensed with the obvious stumbling block presented by D. 4. 3. 15. 1, it was not difficult for the glossators to propound in general terms a corporate criminal liability. This was so much a self-evident idea to them that their statements, if any, were extremely laconic.[7] And when we find some longer statements, they show quite plainly that the glossators had failed to grasp the idea of a corporate delict. The *Glossa Ordinaria* on D. 3. 4. 7. 1 put this question: ' Quid, si quilibet de universitate tibi intulit injuriam?' To make the juristic meaning of the question clear, the gloss continued: ' Numquid universitas dicetur hoc fecisse et poterit a te conveniri?'[8] It seems, said the glossator, that the corporation was not suable, because one could not maintain that it had acted ' ut universitas ', but rather that the perpetrator had become active on his own initiative. Nevertheless, the final decision of the gloss was that the corporation should be held liable: ' Quia universitas nihil aliud est nisi singuli homines, qui ibi sunt '.[9] The only condition, according to the glossators, for the criminal liability of a

---

[3] *Glossa ord.*, D.4.3.15.1, s.v. ' facere possunt '.
[4] See also the gloss to D.41.2.1.22, s.v. ' non possunt ': ' subaudi hic facile vel commode; and gloss, D.38.3, s.v. ' non possunt ': ' scilicet facile '.
[5] This *Summa* was begun by Placentinus and completed by Pyleus; see Guido Panzirolus, *De Claris Legum Interpretibus*, lib. ii, cap. xxi, p. 109.
[6] *Summa*, XI.29, no. 12.
[7] A number of glossators did not touch on the point at all; so, for instance, Bulgarus in his *Ordo Judiciarius* (ed. Kunstmann, *Krit. Ueberschau*, II), or the *Ordo Judiciarius Magistri Richardi Anglici* (ed. C. Witte), or *Othonis Practica* (Otto Papiensis), ed. Venetiis, 1567.
[8] *Gl. ord.*, s.v. ' non debetur '.
[9] The reason why an *actio* should be denied was: ' Quia non ut universitas, scil. concilio habito et campana sonata vel alias eis convocatis, fecisset, sed quilibet suo motu '.

80

corporation was some vaguely conceived corporate will to commit
a crime: the liability was denied only when it was clear that the
corporation had not acted ' ut universitas ',[1] but for a detailed
discussion of this most important criterion we search in vain
amongst the glossators.[2]

A notable exception, however, was the great twelfth-century
glossator and teacher of Azo, Johannes Bassianus, to whom Gierke
failed to give due consideration. It appears that Johannes was one
of the first to whom a concrete instance was submitted for decision.
And with him the distinction between corporate acts of the organisation and the individual acts of its members became a decisive
feature in attributing corporate delictal liability. The facts of the
case were these.[3] The Archbishop of Ravenna was the owner of a
forest in which citizens of a certain village were wont to fell trees.
Upon the request by the archbishop they promised to abstain from
interfering with his property, and in particular from felling trees.
But soon afterwards a peasant ('rusticus') again began to fell
trees: the household of the archbishop seized the man and beat
him—'egregie verberaverunt'. The victim of the outraged episcopal household ran back to his village and reported his experiences
in the forest by crying and shouting throughout the village. Where-
upon all the inhabitants of the village provided themselves with
arms and revenged themselves by depredations on the forest.[4] The
problem put to Bassianus was, therefore, whether the whole village
community as a corporate body should be liable for the damage, or
whether the archbishop would have to sue the perpetrators
individually. D. 3. 4. 7. 1 and *Inst.* 2. 1. 6 would indorse an *actio*
against the individuals, ' quia singuli constituunt universitatem '.
But Bassianus was not satisfied with this legalistic opinion of his
predecessors and contemporaries. For him the decisive criterion
lay in the action as a corporate action of the whole community. Did
they proceed to the action as a corporate body, or merely as
' singuli '? If it could be proved that there was some external
means which called the villagers together, such as ringing of the

---

[1] See especially the gloss to D.3.4.7.1, s.v. 'non debetur'.
[2] If we can believe Odofredus, there were some 'antiqui doctores' who denied the
criminal liability of an organisation altogether 'propter naturam difficilem ad
consentiendum, facilem ad dissentiendum '; see his lecture on D.4.2.9 (§ *Animadvertendum*), no. 1, fol. 150 *verso*. It may be that he had in mind the canonist
Johannes Teutonicus.
[3] The case is reported in Jacobus de Arena, *Commentarii in Universum Jus Civile*,
D.3.4.7, fol. 29, of the edition Lugdunum, 1541; Albericus de Rosciate, *Commentaria in Digestum Vetus*, D.4.2.9 (§ *Animadvertendum*), fol. 254; Odofredus,
loc. cit., no. 2; Cynus, *Commentaria in D.V.*, D.2.2.1, no. 14, fol. 31; Petrus
de Bellapertica, *Commentaria in Codicem*, C.I,8,14, and Oldradus de Ponte,
Consilia, cons. 315.
[4] 'Rustici armaverunt se omnes et iverunt ad silvam et dederunt eis magnum
damnum '.

bells, blowing of trumpets, or beating of drums, and the like, and
if thereupon the villagers marched to the forest, the whole community must then be held liable. ' Aut illud maleficium factum fuit
ad sonum campanae vel tubae vel cornu vel ad tubulam pulsatam,
quo casu universitas dicitur fecisse maleficium.' According to
Bassianus, another symptom of a communal action would have been
that the village standards were carried ahead of the procession and
that the village authorities were amongst the crowd—in this case
too the community as a body was answerable for the charge.[5] If,
however, neither of the two conditions could be proved, the archbishop would have to charge the perpetrators individually on the
basis of the *Lex Aquilia*.

This theory of Bassianus was certainly a step forward as
compared with the coarse, uncouth and immature opinion of his
contemporaries, and even of his own pupils, such as Azo. But it
would be rash to say that his view came to be generally accepted
in the thirteenth century. No lesser jurist and canonist than
Innocent IV offered a somewhat novel theory which has often been
misunderstood, misconceived and misinterpreted, mainly because
it laid itself open to misinterpretation. His ideas, though clad in
typical medieval parlance, deserve our attention, not only on
account of the subject itself, but also for the sake of its wider
implications. The misunderstanding of Innocent's theory results
chiefly from the somewhat ambiguous nature of the terms
' criminal ' and ' civil '. Innocent's application of these terms is
not identical with that in common usage. What must never be
forgotten when reconstructing Innocent's theories is that he was a
canonist, and it was as a canonist that he examined the liability of
a corporation. And when he spoke of ' delinquere ', ' punire ', and
the like, he generally had in mind canonical crime and punishment—
which latter was, of course, excommunication. Innocent IV treated
of this problem in two places, that is, in his commentaries on
Decretales V. 3. 30 and V. 39. 52.[6] After briefly reviewing the
common point of view, this Pope maintained that a corporation
could be neither accused nor punished—only the wrongdoers themselves were liable to prosecution and punishment—although a ' civil '
action might well lie against a corporate body involving it in a
pecuniary punishment. ' Nos dicimus ', said Innocent, ' quod
universitas non potest accusari nec puniri, sed delinquentes tantum,

---

5 ' Sed et si non venerunt campana sonata vel tuba vel cornu, vel tubula pulsata,
   sed portaverunt signa sua cum potestate eorum vel consule eorum, tunc universitas dicitur deliquisse, et cum ea erit agendum '.
6 *Commentaria in Libros Quinque Decretalium*, De Simonia, Dil. fil., fol. 500
   verso; De Sent. Excomm., Canon. Inst., fol. 557, of the edition, Francofurti,
   1570.

civiliter autem conveniri et pecuniariter puniri possunt ex delicto rectorum '.[7] The reasons that prompted Innocent IV to put forward this view which, seen in its proper perspective, was by no means as revolutionary as some moderns would have it, were the following. A ' criminal ' punishment of a corporation—' civil ' condemnation was admitted by Innocent as legitimate—would entail that ' punishment ' be inflicted not only on the criminals themselves, but also on innocent persons, such as infants, unborn children, etc., who had never consented to the wrong action. The consequences of a ' criminal ' condemnation would visit also those who would be born long after the commission of the crime. Consequently, as a canonist he declined to admit excommunication as a legitimate sanction against a corporate body. ' Eadem est universitas, quae est tempore delicti, et quae futuro tempore, quae nullo modo delinquunt: esset autem multum iniquum, quod huiusmodi, qui nullo modo delinquunt, excommunicarentur '.[8] But apart from these extra-legal considerations, Innocent also advanced purely legal views to support his plea against the excommunication of organised bodies. First, a corporation can do no wrong—' universitas nihil potest dolo facere '—by which dictum he obviously meant ' no canonical wrong ' [9]; second, a corporation is a legal abstraction, and not a living reality—' impossibile est, quod universitas delinquat, quia universitas, sicut est capitulum, populus, gens, et huiusmodi, nomina juris sunt et non personarum, et *ideo non cadit in eam excommunicatio* '.[10] From these transcribed passages it follows quite plainly that all Innocent IV was interested in proving was the legal inadmissibility of excommunicating a corporate body. For the legal possibility of a ' civil ' liability was fully admitted by Innocent, provided certain conditions were fulfilled; so, for instance, actions undertaken by the officials of the body upon the explicit ' mandatum ' of the community, or actions of the officials undertaken without a ' mandatum ' but with later corporate approval. Innocent envisaged as ' civil ' sanctions the interdict and suspension which could be inflicted only on ecclesiastical bodies. More than that: he even acknowledged that criminal proceedings may be instituted against a corporation and he advised that the capital punishment should be transformed into a fine: ' Item poena capitali

---

[7] *Decretales*, V.3.30, fol. 500 *verso*.

[8] With a reference to the *Decretum*, xxiv.3.1, where St. Augustine spoke of the problem of excommunicating a family on the grounds of the sins committed by one member of the family; he would have refused excommunication. Gratian himself commented on the same problem in the *Rubrica*: ' Non ergo pro alicuius peccato tota familia excommunicanda est '.

[9] With a reference to D.4.3.15.1.

[10] In *Decretales*, III.36.7, fol. 437, he says that a ' universitas est corporalis ': here he expressly deals with civil actions against a corporation.

Delictal Responsibility of Corporations   83

vel mortis vel relegationis punietur universitas, *si contra eam agatur criminaliter*, sed poena capitis mutabitur in pecuniariam '.[1] Lastly, this Pope, to leave no doubt in the minds of his readers, reaffirmed the principle that ' pro peccato unius punitur alias infamia '.[2] The apparent contradiction between the passage in which Innocent denied that a corporation could commit a crime, and the other passages just quoted, can be solved, I believe, by the adequate evaluation of the term ' delinquere ' which he reserved for those offences which entailed canonical punishment, that is, excommunication. Or should one really assume that a jurist of Innocent's calibre did not require *mens rea* in cases of civil tort? But apart from the differences of terminology there is very little difference between him and his contemporaries in principle.[3]

Moreover, Albericus de Rosciate, who wrote well over a century after Innocent had completed his commentaries, entertained no doubt that this Pope took the ' secular ' punishment of a corporation for granted. Dealing with this particular problem Albericus stated that a corporation must be considered in the same manner as any ordinary individual—' Curia et societas vicem personae sustinent '—that corporations can therefore commit crimes and that appropriate punishment could be inflicted: ' Eadem fictione delinquere possunt, et puniri ea tamen poena, quae possit cadere in eos '.[4] *And for this reason Innocent said*, Albericus reported, that a corporation was to be deprived of its privileges: ' Et ideo dicit Innocentius, quod privetur privilegiis et sic capite minuitur '. We find further confirmation for our interpretation in the commentaries of the same jurist on the *Digestum vetus*. Here Albericus asked whether a corporation could be excommunicated, and the reply was in the negative.[5] As regards ordinary punishment, however,

---

[1] *Decretales*, V.39.52, no. 2, fol. 5557. He refers to D.48.8.1, which reference seems to show that Innocent considered the possibility of a common crime being committed by a corporate body.

[2] *Loc. cit.*, no. 3, with a reference to the *Decretum*, vi.3.17.

[3] We purposely abstained from going into the question of whether Innocent can be called the originator of the ' Fiction Theory ', so Gierke, vol. iii, p. 280, or whether he belongs to no particular school of thought in the modern sense. We think that, in assessing Innocent, his position as a canonist is usually left out of account. Bernardus Parmensis in his gloss on *Decretales*, III.50.7, s.v. ' eis ', also maintains that a ' universitas delinquere potest '.

[4] C.IX.2.7, no. 15, fol. 184.

[5] D.4.2.9 (§ *Animadvertendum*), no. 7, fol. 254: ' An universitas possit excommunicari? Dic quod non '. Before Innocent IV's resolution at the council of Lyons (1245) was embodied in the *Liber Sextus* (V.11.5), canonists opined, like him, that a corporation could not be excommunicated; cf. the Archidiaconus (Guido de Baysio) in his *Rosarium* (written before the promulgation of Boniface VIII's *Sextus*), *causa* xii, *quaest*.2, *can*.56: ' Universitas non habet animam, quae per excommunicationem traditur Sathanae '. See also *Speculum Judiciale*, IV.4, fol. 520, and Zenzelinus in *Extravagantes*, I.2, and V.1: ' censurae ecclesiasticae non capax '.

84

Albericus counselled that either a fine could be imposed or, in a case of capital punishment, the corporation should be destroyed.[6] To sum up: Whilst Innocent admitted civil punishment, he excluded the excommunication of a whole corporation; capital punishment ought to be commuted into a fine.

That Innocent's theory was not unique amongst his contemporaries can be clearly seen from the independent theory of Jacobus de Arena. He, too, fully admitted the possibility of punishing a corporation for a crime that was committed on its behalf, but said that any capital punishment should be commuted into a fine. ' Sed pone, quod civitas facit homicidium, cui abscinditur caput? Universitas enim non habet caput neque animum.' The answer he gave was that the corporation ' punietur pecuniariter ', whilst the actual perpetrators should suffer punishment according to the ordinary rules. This, incidentally, was also the reason why in the opinion of Jacobus de Arena a corporation was entitled to a syndic: ' Hinc est, quod potest intervenire pro ea syndicus '.[7]

According to all medieval jurists, the criminal action must be a corporate action. The usual way of assembling the members for the purpose of acting corporately was by some visible or audible means, such as ringing of the bells, beating of the drums, and the like. If the use of such summonses could be proved, the corporation as such was held liable. An interesting case was reported by Odofredus when he treated of the liability of chapters and prelates for a crime committed on their behalf by capitular members. This crime was considered to be a crime for which the church itself was liable. At the occasion of the arrival of a papal legate at a monastery the abbot rang the bells to assemble all the monks; he told them that the legate came to make some demands which the abbot was not prepared to grant. The monks themselves did not appear to be willing either, and cried: ' Where is the legate? We will see that he will never return to Rome '. Thereupon the legate was seized and killed by some monks. Odofredus maintained that this was a crime for which the whole chapter was responsible—' sic fuit delictum totius capituli '—because the murder was a corporate action: if the abbot had omitted to ring the bells, he alone would have been answerable for the crime, and not the chapter and the church. ' Unde ', Odofredus concluded, ' bene redundat in damnum ecclesiae, sicut delictum alicuius populi redundat in damnum suae

---

[6] ' Et ubi esset tale delictum, quod exigeret poenam capitalem, poena capitalis civitatis est, quod patiatur aratrum et destruatur '.
[7] Exemplifying this by a reference to C.XII.36.18. Jacobus's theory was still quoted by Albericus, C.VIII.4.7, no. 6, fol. 142 *verso*.

civitatis '. [8] In a similar direction ran the thoughts of the Frenchman Petrus de Bellapertica.[9]

It was left to the 'juristic giant of the fourteenth century, Bartolus, to make a great step forward in the juristic apprehension of corporate liability. Bartolus, whose doctrines did not receive that attention by Gierke which their merits warranted, quite clearly grasped the implications and difficulties inherent in this problem, and that to a degree which makes him tower above his contemporaries. It will be worth while reconstructing his thoughts on this topic and devoting some little space to his doctrines. This will be all the more instructive as Bartolus shows himself a thorough-going positivist whose approach to the subject was far more ' fictionist ' than, say, of Innocent IV. After expressing his dissatisfaction with the gloss on D. 48. 19. 16, on the grounds of its vagueness and unsatisfactory arguments for the milder punishment of a corporation, Bartolus succinctly stated that a sharp distinction must be made between the corporate capability to commit a crime, and the corporate capability to suffer punishment. ' Ista quaestio est multum subtilis judicio meo ', declared Bartolus gently approaching the subject,[1] ' nam prius est videndum, an universitas possit delinquere, secundo, an possit puniri '. Some jurists maintained, Bartolus said, that a corporation could commit no crime, because ' universitas est nomen juris et non habet animum nec habet intellectum, ergo non potest delinquere '.[2] This opinion was held by Innocent, Bartolus declared and thereby seemed to have laboured under the same misapprehension as his brethren some centuries later: Bartolus, therefore, appeared to take the term ' delinquere ' in the sense in which the civilians alone took it, that is, as referring to the commission of a common crime. Others again taught, Bartolus continued his report, that corporations were capable of crimes of omission only, and not of those of commission.[3] These jurists might find some superficial support in C. I. 2. 10, although recent imperial legislation disproved the correctness of this line of argument: this opinion was dismissed by Bartolus with a categorical ' hoc non placet ', explicitly referring to a constitution of Frederick II.[4] ' Quid dicemus ? '

Before dealing with the delictal capability of a corporation, Bartolus wanted to clear the ground by asking the preliminary question, In which relation do the members of a corporation stand

---

[8] Odofredus, C.I.2.10.
[9] See his lecture on C.VIII.4.7, fol. 269. Cf. Andreas de Isernia, *In Usus Feudorum*, II.40 (§ *Item si clericus*).
[1] Fol. 200, no. 1.
[2] *Loc. cit.*, no. 2.
[3] He apparently alluded to Jacobus de Arena who had disinguished between ' delicta negligentiae ' and ' delicta operationis '.
[4] See *Constitutiones I.3*, inserted as *Authentica* in C.I.3.2.

to the corporation itself? 'Ad intellectum huius quaestionis debemus videre primo, an universitas sit aliud quam homines universitatis?' Some had declared that the members and the corporation were notionally identical. It was especially the canonists and, above all, 'omnes philosophi' who held that the whole did not differ from its parts 'realiter'.[5] All this is true, Bartolus avowed, as long as we speak of a corporation 'realiter, vere et proprie', for the community of students is indeed nothing else but the students themselves.[6] But, and this is where his argumentation is simply based on an *a priori* premise, 'we jurists' ('nos juristae') must start from the 'fictio juris', and in that case these canonists and philosophers must be considered wrong, 'for the corporation represents one person who is notionally something different from the members constituting it '.[7] This fictitious character of a corporation becomes clear, according to Bartolus, if due consideration is given to the idea of continuity inherent in every organised body: all the present students may die, all the contemporary members of a nation may perish—and yet the group remains the same. In other words, the corporation is notionally different from its constituent members. There are therefore two clearly distinguishable persons. 'Et sic aliud est universitas quam personae, quae faciunt universitatem secundum juris fictionem, quia est quaedam persona repraesentata.'[8] Now it is certainly interesting to note that Bartolus claimed the support of only one legal text, and that was the same single passage which Savigny adduced to prove his 'Fiction Theory' precisely five centuries later,[9] that is, D. 46. 1. 22.[1]

---

[5] 'Et hoc tenent omnes philosophi et canonistae, qui tenent, quod totum non differt realiter a suis partibus ', *loc. cit.*, no. 3. This may be, *inter alia*, an allusion to Aquinas's *Commentary on the Nichomachean Ethics*, lib. I, lectio 2, and his *De Regimine Principum*, lib. I, cap. 14.

[6] 'Veritas est, quod si quidem loquamur realiter, vere, et proprie, ipsi dicunt verum. Nam nil aliud est universitas scholarium quam scholares '.

[7] 'Secundum fictionem juris ipsi non dicunt verum, nam universitas repraesentat unam personam, quae est aliud a scholaribus seu ab hominibus universitatis '.

[8] Cf. also his lecture on D.41.1.22, no. 3: a corporation 'non est propria persona, sed repraesentata ', and lectures on D.47.22.1.1.

[9] Savigny, *System des heutigen Roemischen Rechts*, vol. ii, p. 241.

[1] We are not here concerned with the question of whether Florentinus's passage is typical and merely an epitome of a generally held opinion, so, of course, Savigny, and presumably also Bartolus, or whether this text is 'unique ', so Duff, p. 225, but see also Brown, *op. cit.* In any case, it was less Innocent IV who can be called the predecessor of Savigny's Fiction Theory, as Gierke thought, than Bartolus. The argumentative acumen sometimes displayed to destroy Gierke's assertion therefore appears misplaced. Gierke's whole doctrinal edifice was vigorously assailed by De Wulf, 'L'individu et le group dans la Scolastique du XIIIe Siècle ' in *Revue Néo-Scolastique de Philosophie*, vol. xxii (1920), pp. 341 ff., *idem*, *Philosophy and Civilisation in the Middle Ages*, Ch. X *passim*, and E. Lewis, 'Organic Tendencies in Medieval Political Thought ' in *American Political Science Review*, vol. xxxii (1938), pp. 849–76; see also F. Brendan Brown, 'Canonical Juristic Personality ' in *The Jurist*, vol. i (1941), pp. 66–73. On the other hand, see John Neville Figgis, *Churches in the Modern State*, cap. II, esp. at pp. 58–86. Of course it would be absurd to say that Bartolus

Proceeding from this premise Bartolus sees no great difficulties in attributing to a corporation the capability of committing crimes. Nevertheless, it was incompatible with his theory for him to speak of a ' persona repraesentata ' as a person really perpetrating a crime in the ordinary sense of the term. ' Proprie ', declared Bartolus after repeating his question,[2] ' non potest delinquere ', since a corporation is not ' proprie ' a ' persona ', but ' something fictitious put in the place of the true '—' tamen hoc est fictum positum pro vero, sicut ponimus nos Juristae '. As regards crimes of omission Bartolus unhesitatingly declares that with this category of crime a corporate body may well be charged: ' Peccatum omissionis potest committere universitas '. If a corporation omits to carry out its legal duties and obligations, the corporation as a whole should be made responsible, although negligence may be attributable only to its officials.[3] As to crimes of commission Bartolus introduces a rather attractive distinction. A corporation was held liable by him only for those crimes which the corporation *qua* corporation could commit, or, in other words, which ordinary citizens were incapable of committing. In this category of crime Bartolus placed offences which the corporation committed through legislation, taxation, conferring of jurisdictional powers, and the like. This Bartolus found proved in the above-mentioned constitution of Frederick II.[4] The necessary presupposition was, however, that the corporation was constitutionally entrusted with the legal right to impose taxes or to legislate, etc., though not, of course, for criminal purposes. This specific right Bartolus called a ' jus residens ': ' Hoc facit ipsa universitas, in qua est illud jus residens '.[5] What would have happened in default of this presupposition, Bartolus is cautious enough not to ask. A very natural corollary of Bartolus's standpoint was his denial of a direct corporate liability for crimes which ordinary citizens were also capable of committing. For these common crimes require a ' persona vera ' and therefore cannot be committed by a corporation ' proprie '. The corporation, however,

---

was the originator of a Fiction Theory: it was, most likely, through a misunderstood conception of Innocent's view that Bartolus adhered to this opinion, although, no doubt, Bartolus quoted precisely those Roman passages which Innocent naturally had no reason to quote, but which were quoted exclusively by those who desired to prove the Roman genesis of the Fiction Theory.

2 *Loc. cit.*, no. 4.

3 ' Licet hoc contingeret negligentia regentium universitatem, tamen ipsa dicitur negligere ', referring to C.I.2.10 which, in his opinion, should be read in conjunction with D.17.1.8.4.

4 ' In delicto vero commissio, seu quid committitur faciendo, deberes advertere. Nam quaedam sunt, quae tantum fieri possunt per ipsam universitatem, ut facere statuta, dare jurisdictionem, imponère collectas et similia, isto casu potest universitas delinquere, d.auth.nulla communitas, C.De ss.eccl. in auth.cassa . . . nec enim potest dici, quod aliquis privatus hoc faciat.'

5 Referring to D.1.1.9.

is said to commit these crimes, such as murder, rape, etc., 'improprie', through its officials and agents.[6]

Turning to his second question, *i.e.*, whether a corporation can be punished, Bartolus again reviews the state of opinion, singling out Innocent IV as the only one denying the corporate body's capability of suffering criminal punishment. There can be no doubt, Bartolus declares, that civil sanctions are admissible. Whatever a corporation acquired in a criminal way, could be recovered by a civil action.[7] Moreover, he states that wherever a criminal offence did not entail any acquisition retrievable from the corporation, no distinction should be made between civil and criminal proceedings. ' De eo vero, quod non pervenit, an civiliter vel criminaliter conveniri, puto idem juris esse.' He then proceeds to elaborate this rather vaguely formulated, though important point. In a number of crimes, he maintains, proceedings (be they criminal or civil) instituted against a father may involve punishment, not only of the father himself, but also of the son: the latter is then punished because of his father's conduct. ' Quaedam sunt delicta, propter quae filius punitur propter patrem.' And Bartolus sees no reason why this principle should not be applied to corporations also; in fact, the destructions of Troy and of Carthage may be taken as practical applications of this principle. The crimes and passages to which Bartolus makes explicit reference in order to support his opinion were these: D. 48. 4. 11 in conjunction with C. IX. 8. 5. 1 (*crimen laesae majestatis*) and *Liber Sextus* V. 2. 15,[8] and V. 9. 5.[9] Bartolus considers that the condemnation of the Templars and their Order by Clement V (and not, as he erroneously states, Boniface VIII) for the crime of heresy committed by some knights only was a proof of the correctness of his ideas.[1] Futhermore, Bartolus's positivist leanings and his unquestioned, almost uncritical acceptance of ' what is, is right ', leads him to adduce another example to show that his opinion is not only deduced from the letter, but also from the concrete application, of the law. Emperor Henry VII's brutal condemnation of the rebellious city of Brescia

---

[6] ' Quaedam sunt, quae non respiciunt ista jura residentia apud universitatem, ut committere homicidium, vel facere violentiam, et tunc universitas non potest hac facere proprie, quoniam ista requirunt personam veram . . . sed dicitur committi improprie per alios regentes civitatem, seu alios, quibus civitas commisit vigore statuti.'

[7] *Loc. cit.*, no. 5.

[8] Concerning the *crimen haeresis*, condemnation for which involves, according to the intention of the legislator, Boniface VIII, punitive sanctions against the descendants.

[9] Assault against a cardinal, which crime, according to Boniface's expression, was on the same level as high treason, and therefore also entailed heavy sanctions against the (possibly quite innocent) descendants of the accused.

[1] The report of Gierke, vol. iii, pp. 408–9, is not quite accurate and omits important details.

in 1311 appeared to Bartolus as the external manifestation of the principle laid down in C. IX. 9. 5; more than that, whatever the Ruler does, has the force of law. Consequently, Innocent's arguments against the criminal punishment of corporations are to be dismissed as incompatible with the law.[2] And yet, Bartolus is content with the mere statement ' quaedam sunt delicta . . . ' in which punishment inflicted on the father also involves his descendants. Whether Bartolus considers these two cases, *i.e.*, high treason and heresy, as the only cases or as examples of a general principle, cannot be decided on the basis of the material available.[3]

On the other hand, ' there are some crimes ' in which this principle of ' extensive punishment ' cannot be applied. If we understand Bartolus aright, he has in mind cases in which the members of a corporation are presumed to be guilty in the eye of the law, and in which there is no question of obviously innocent people being punished. It will be worth while quoting Bartolus himself : ' Quaedam sunt delicta, in quibus filius non punitur propter patrem, et hoc in casibus, in quibus dixi universitatem delinquere, universitas ipsa punitur '. This dictum of Bartolus is somewhat clarified by his distinction between punishments which are directly inflicted on the corporation as such, and not on its members—and punishments through which corporation and members alike suffer. To the first category belong confiscation of corporate goods, whilst a fine imposed on the corporation is a punishment ' quae aeque cadit in universitatem et in singulos '.[4]

This latter case merits a further differential treatment, according to Bartolus, whose theory on this point unmistakably tries to satisfy, on the one hand, the demands of justice, and, on the other hand, to execute a scheme that was fundamentally opposed to an idealistic conception of justice and equity. To be sure, Bartolus is well aware of the ' collective ' nature of crime and punishment, particularly in the last-named category. And his theory attempting as it does to harmonise two conflicting notions, shows, firstly, the inherent weakness of his doctrinal edifice, and, secondly, Bartolus's tacit admission of this weakness. Punishment that falls on corporations and members alike must take into the question the size of the corporation. If the body was small, especially in the case of limited membership, for instance, in cathedral chapters, the fine is to be imposed only on the guilty members, that is to say, on those who have explicitly consented to the commission of the crime. In the opinion of Bartolus this is laid down in D. 17. 1. 1. But after all

---

[2] *Loc. cit.*, nos. 5 and 6.
[3] He also treated of this problem in his tract on the Constitution *Qui sint rebelles* of Henry VII, but here too he did not give any clue.
[4] *Loc. cit.*, no. 7.

his subtle distinctions Bartolus advances the somewhat startling idea that in the case of a large body, such as a municipality or a nation, the innocent must suffer with the guilty, because 'it would be difficult to distinguish between the consenting and dissenting members'. Consequently, the whole group must suffer punishment.[5]

All these somewhat cumbrous considerations are to apply only to those crimes which a corporation can commit 'proprie'. If the crime were one of whose commission a corporation were only 'improprie' capable, such as murder, a corporation should then share the fate of any individual wrongdoer provided the punishment in question can be meted out against a corporate body. If this should prove impossible, the punishment should be commuted into a fine—and thus by a very circuitous way Bartolus arrives at a conclusion not unlike that of Innocent. The reason for the modification of punishment Bartolus finds in the impossibility to inflict capital punishment on a corporation which 'non habet caput verum, sed fictum'. Nevertheless, Bartolus himself seems to have felt the inconsistency of his doctrine when he defends himself against Innocent's point of view who, it will be recalled, refused to admit excommunication against a whole community on the ground that the innocent would thereby suffer. Now, Bartolus says, this is certainly true as regards a fine, 'quae imponitur illis, qui non deliquerunt' and he concedes the plausibility of Innocent's objection—'et in veritate ego concederem istud'. The only way out of this injustice is, according to Bartolus's advice, that the innocent members should make no contribution to the fine, whilst again he points out that this advice is based upon the law, D. 17. 1. 1, as well as upon a decision given by Emperor Henry VII himself: ' Et hoc vidi in quadam sententia definitiva imperatoris Henrici '.[6]

The really valid criterion for a corporate crime Bartolus, in common with the general opinion, sees in a communal resolution arrived at after adequate deliberations; otherwise one would be entitled to speak only of a crime committed by individual members. Bartolus refers us here to D. 43. 24. 15. 2 for confirmation, apparently basing himself on Ulpian's words which were obviously not used in a directly applicable context. Until the contrary is proved Bartolus suggests that proceedings should be instituted only against the actual perpetrators. The deliberations preceding the resolution are an indispensable requirement for corporate delictal liability, although subsequent approval ('ratihabitio') by the community would compensate for the lack of deliberations. Hence the violent

---

[5] *Loc. cit.*, no. 7: ' Sed si esset collegium magnum et diffusum, ut est populus seu aliqua communitas, tunc quia discernere consentientes a non consentientibus esset defficile, tota civitas et tota universitas punietur '.

[6] *Loc. cit.*, no. 8.

ejection from a castle by its inhabitants would entail the punishment of the whole group if they remained in possession of it.[7]

In this context Bartolus's theory about the representative character of the officials of a corporation becomes interesting. ' Quaero, an ex delicto officialis teneatur universitas ? ' He denies the liability of the corporation on the ground that the officials had no power to commit a crime: if it were proved, however, that there was a preceding instruction by the corporation to the officials, or that the corporation approved of the crime subsequently, Bartolus counselled that the ordinary rules of corporate criminal liability should be applied.

One more important point was touched upon by Bartolus. The significance of this point apparently escaped his contemporaries and successors. This point incidentally shows that he followed up his scheme logically and consistently. He asked whether after the punishment of a corporation its individual members also incurred liability.[8] It might seem that the principle ' ne bis in eadem re ' resisted their individual punishment, but Bartolus declined to accept this view and again drew attention to his own differentiation of corporate crimes.[9] If the crime was of a nature that could be committed by a corporation ' proprie ' the latter should be punished as the actual perpetrator, whilst individual members could be charged as instigators to the crime.[1] But in the opposite case, Bartolus suggested that the individual members should be held liable as the perpetrators, like any other private person, and the corporation should incur liability as the instigator of the crime.[2]

It will cause no surprise if we find this Bartolist doctrine accepted by almost the whole of the succeeding lawyer generation. The conciseness, crispness and apparent clarity of his theory could not fail to win adherents. His typically scholastic distinctions and subtle differentiations, however much they might have been removed from the work-a-day world, were eagerly snatched at by his great

---

[7] *Loc. cit.*, no. 10: ' Puto tamen, quod posset sequi ratihabitio, quod sufficieret ad puniendum universitatem, ut si per vim expulerint me de castro et universitas illud sibi retinet '.

[8] *Loc. cit.*, no. 12: ' Quaero, si est punita universitas, an possint puniri aliqui homines singulares? '

[9] Lucas de Penna, independent of Bartolus, had a very similar view in his commentary on C.XII.60.3 *Rubrica*, and before him Cynus in his lecture on C.VIII.4.7, no. 16.

[1] *Loc. cit.*, no. 12: ' Quaedam sunt delicta, quae dicuntur fieri per universitatem, ut dixi, et in illis sola universitas potest puniri tamquam faciens, alii singulares poterunt puniri tamquam instigatores et fieri facientes '.

[2] ' Sed in delictis, quae non fiunt per universitatem, erit totum contra, quia facientes punientur de delicto; universitas vero punietur tamquam fieri faciens vel tamquam ratm habens suo nomine.'

pupil, Baldus.[3] But it was not only the civilians [4] who adopted and propagated Bartolus's views, but also the canonists: whilst the latter recognised some fundamental theoretical incompatibilities between Innocent and Bartolus, they saw extremely little practical difference between the two great jurists.[5] Nor, of course, was there any lack of enthusiasm on the part of the post-Bartolist generation to ' improve ', reinforce, expand, and deepen the scheme of their great master, by drawing more and more subtle distinctions, until the original scheme resembled an almost impenetrable cobweb of finely woven ' distinctiones ' and ' divisiones '. The reconstruction, however, of these later mosaic-like schemes, overburdened with theoretically valuable, though practically unrealistic sub-divisions, would be of little modern interest. In passing we may mention the opinion of Baldus which he expressed in his lecture on D. 4. 2. 9. 1. Examining the criminal liability of a corporation he taught his pupils that they should clearly distinguish between corporations in which all the members were considered ' capaces doli ', and those bodies whose members lacked that capability; this latter was the case with a whole nation. Now the former category incurred criminal liability, if their legitimate council or their representatives had decided on the perpetration of a crime: in this case ' omnes delinquunt '; consequently, ' collegium delinquit et vere '.[6] The second category was held liable by Baldus only ' interpretative ', provided the perpetration of the crime was preceded by a formal resolution on the part of the councillors. One might speak here of an indirect liability incurred by the nation through the criminal activity of its ' government '.[7] But Baldus seems to have denied a direct liability of a nation; this was indeed the interpretation which later jurists placed on his theory: ' Et sic sentit (scil. Baldus), quod populus per se non delinquat '.[8]

Of the jurists who explicitly refused to follow Bartolus's lead, we may mention Bartholomaeus Salicetus who put forward a practically unworkable view: according to him, the perpetrators of a

---

[3] See his lecture on D.12.1.27, no. 7, and D.3.4.7, no. 18, and 3.4.1, no. 5, where he speaks of the majority principle as the principle which justifies the criminal liability of a whole corporation.

[4] Cf. Angelus Aretinus, *Institutiones*, I.2.5; Paulus Castrensis, D.3.4.7, no. 5; Angelus de Ubaldis, *Consilia*, cons. 165, no. 24, etc.

[5] See, *e.g.*, Antonius de Butrio, *Decretales*, V.3.30, no. 10; Cardinal Zabarella, *ibid.*, nos. 6–8, and Petrus de Ancharano (a pupil of Baldus) in *Sextus*, V.11.5, nos. 7–9, and I.3.5, no. 4, where Bartolus was called a ' lumen juris ' greater than Innocent.

[6] *Loc cit.*, no. 8.

[7] ' Aut est talis universitas, in qua non sunt omnes dol: capaces, ut populus, et tunc quando regimina deputata delinquunt concilio solemniter congregato, tunc interpretative delinquit totus populus. '

[8] So the wording in no. 13 of the *consilium* of Philippus Corneus to which we will turn presently.

crime had acted on behalf of the corporation and therefore in
the name of those members only who had given their consent;
punishment, consequently, should be suffered, not by the whole
corporation, but only by the ' consentientes '.[9] There is, however,
one post-Bartolist opinion that merits a little closer examination;
it is one that is expressed in a very lengthy *Consilium* of Philippus
Corneus.[1]

The facts as we can gather from the *Consilium* were these. One
day in a certain municipality the senators, councillors, and ' quasi
totus populus ' left the palace (probably the town hall) all having
equipped themselves with arms and shouting loudly and wildly
' arma, arma, carne, carne '. The drums were beaten and the whole
procession moved in greatest commotion to the house of a Johannes
de Camosa where a certain Petrus Saccus and a Persantes lived.
The crowd broke into the house—whose owner was not present—
and angrily and threateningly demanded these two men. These,
however, fled, escaped from the crowd and, apparently to save
themselves, jumped over the city walls. A short while later Petrus
Saccus was found bleeding to death as a consequence of a serious
abdominal wound, whilst Persantes was hanging in front of the
town hall. The juristic problem was: could the whole municipality
be held liable for the murder of these two men?

Philippus Corneus denied a corporate liability in this case. He
made the preliminary observation that, in order to make a corporation liable, the criminal action must be the expression of a communal
will. But the presupposition for a will accountable to a corporation
was a formal resolution on the part of those who governed the
municipality.[2] Not only were there no witnesses who had actually
seen who hanged Persantes or who stabbed Saccus, but there was
also no evidence as to a formal resolution on the part of the city
council. It would ill behove a jurist were he to follow glibly the
witnesses in declaring that the corporation was liable, because ' quasi
totus populus ' was seen marching from the town hall to the house
of Johannes. For the people was nothing but a ' corpus imagin-
arium ',[3] an abstract notion which could not serve as an adequate
basis for juristic thought. If a whole people was to be held liable,
then all its members must have become active: but which witness
was in a position to see which of the people was missing in the

---

[9] See his lecture on C.IX.30.1, nos. 6–7; a view not unlike that of Salicetus was
propounded by Paulus Castrensis in his lecture on D.36.1.1.15, no. 5, and,
according to later reports, also by Guilelmus de Cuneo in his lectures on the
Digestum Vetus.

[1] *Consilia*, lib. iv, cons. 224, fols. 209 *seq.*; this *consilium* has ten folio columns.

[2] ' Ad hoc autem, aut universitas ex gestis per homines teneatur, requiritur, quod
fuerint gesta communicato concilio ', no. 13.

[3] This was apparently the counterpart of the ecclesiastical *corpus mysticum.*

crowd ? [4]   The liability of the municipality was deduced from the
fact that the drums were beaten, which fact had fulfilled the formal
requirement of validly convoking the council.   But Corneus very
appropriately pointed out that this had happened after the crowd
had left the town hall, and therefore had no bearing upon the formal
communal resolution.   This external call was necessary, he stated,
to convoke an assembly which was to deliberate on some points;
but it was not devised to gather people to carry out a resolution.
It was only natural that the crowd grew rapidly as a consequence of
the beating of the drums, because curious onlookers could always
be assembled.

This latter point brings Corneus to a statement of some importance.   He declared that the convocation of a city council must have
proceeded in a certain formal manner.   The usual way was the
beating of the drums, or the like, but this was not sufficient in his
opinion.   The call to assemble must have originated with the
constitutional authority, that is, in most cases with the podestà.
Should, therefore, a council meet without this condition having been
fulfilled, the resolutions passed would be of no legal validity.   As
Corneus said, most municipal statutes contained special regulations
on this point.   ' Nam debet concilium convocari auctoritate magistratus, prout solent esse praesides seu potestates locorum.'   The
resolution of the council in the concrete case, convoked as it was
without the podestà's authority, was therefore ' contra formam
statutorum et consuetudinis dictae terrae '.   Moreover, that council
because of this constitutional defect, ' non censetur repraesentare
communitatem '.

Closely allied to the foregoing consideration is the further point
of Corneus also touching upon a constitutional aspect.   He suggested
in his *Consilium* that the council of a municipality should not be
held to possess unlimited, discretionary powers to pass any kind of
resolution: the powers of the council must be based upon the
municipal statute, and here again most statutes provided specific
regulations.   There can be no doubt that Corneus considered the
council as a body to which certain powers had been delegated.[5]
A distinction should be drawn between the validity of resolutions
passed by a council legitimately entitled to unlimited powers, and
the validity of resolutions passed by councils whose powers were

---

[4] *Loc. cit.*, no. 17.
[5] This medieval idea of delegation should not be confounded with the modern idea
of delegation.   Although Corneus did not say it, we may safely assume that the
powers of the council were not delegated by the municipality.   It would be
quite wrong to see in this ' delegated ' power any democratic conception.   The
council certainly was thought of as a representative of the people and the
councillors as the deputies, not, however, in the modern sense, but in the sense
of the people's welfare and interests.   Cf. also following note.

restricted by statute or custom. Let us quote the relevant passage:
' Concilium civitatis vel terrae eatenus repraesentat communitatem,
et obligat illam, quatenus se extendit potestas ei concessa '.[6] Now
if a council of the latter category passed a resolution that was beyond
the powers conferred, the resolution would clearly have been *ultra
vires.* And this was the case in the concrete instance. The action
of a council could legally bind a city, nation, etc., only in so far as
the action emanating from the resolution was *intra vires* of the
council: the councillors were delegates of the municipality, etc.:
' Concilium eatenus obligat vel afficit communitatem vel eius gesta
censentur gesta communitatis, quatenus sunt deputati, ut universi-
tati praesunt ex forma, scil. statutorum vel consuetudinis, et sic
quatenus universitatis dicto modo vices gerit '.[7] If, however,
statute or custom conferred powers on the council ' generaliter,
simpliciter et absolute ', its members then were considered to be
' generaliter praepositi ad regimen civitatis '.

In our survey of the medieval corporate liability, as short as is
compatible with historical accuracy, we have merely tried to indicate
the salient features in the medieval development of this thorny
problem. One concluding observation may be allowed. Is it
true, as Gierke so insistently proclaimed, that the medieval theory
constituted a contradiction? Without noticing this irreconcilable
Zwiespalt, Gegensatz, circulus vitiosus,[8] the medieval scholars were,
on the one hand, alleged to have considered a corporation a *persona
ficta*—that is a body fundamentally a-personal, soulless and lifeless
into which only the State infuses life—and, on the other hand, a
persona vera—that is, a ' real ' organism with an inherent life and
purpose, a ' real ' thing. The former, the absolutist doctrine, was
the romanistic-canonistic conception, the latter the germanistic and
' properly medieval ' idea of a corporation.[9] Within the conceptual
framework of the ' Fiction Theory ', there can be no question of a
mens rea, as a fictitious body is without a mind—and, yet, the
medieval jurists attributed to the corporation the capability of
committing crime and of suffering punishment. In the theory of
criminal liability of corporations Gierke perceived the contradiction
between the two notions to be particularly glaring.[1] But does not
Gierke make the pardonable mistake of attempting to fit medieval

---

[6] *Loc. cit.,* no. 10. We may well agree with Professor Lewis that ' medieval
political theory was given an incorrigibly paternalistic character, and in its
premises was completely alien from democratic and liberal tendencies ', *loc. cit.,*
p.863.

[7] *Loc. cit.,* no. 10.

[8] Gierke, *op. cit.,* vol. iii, pp. 366, 390, 425, 430, etc.

[9] See Maitland's translation, p. 3, and Gierke, p. 512.

[1] Gierke, p. 390: ' Denn nicht Ein Legist dieser Zeit bekennt sich zu dem der
Fiktionstheorie im Grunde unabweislich entspringenden kanonistischen Axiom,
dass die Korporation als solche willens- und handlungsunfähig ist '.

modes of thinking into a modern pattern? This latter however, resting upon the ' Fiction Theory ' and the ' Realist Theory ', is indeed the creation of the modern analytical mind. To say that medieval jurists did not see the inconsistency in their thinking about corporations, is, of course, only one way of propounding one's own point of view. What seems to be far more likely and far more in consonance with medieval modes of thought was that their theory of corporation, if one could speak of one theory only, could not be constrained within the rigidly logical scheme of the modern pattern, presenting as it does a strait-jacket of an *aut-aut*: either Fiction Theory or Realist Theory. In the medieval doctrines we may well have a *tertium* that still awaits the scientific and accurate elaboration without a spirit of partisanship.

A DISPUTABLE CONSUETUDO CONTRA LEGEM IN THE LATER MIDDLE AGES*

AT ALL TIMES legal doctrine no less than legal practice understandably showed great reluctance to ascribe the character of law to those customs which developed in direct opposition to an explicit legal enactment. Whilst medieval doctrine—both civilian and canonist—considered a *consuetudo secundum* and *praeter legem* as auxiliary and supplementary to written law—"*consuetudo est optima legum interpres*"[1]—and accorded these two kinds of custom full enforceability, the third kind, that of a *consuetudo contra legem* was, for obvious reasons, viewed with far less favour.[2] To the medieval jurists it was clear that too great a latitude allowed to customary practices in direct contravention of the *lex scripta* would result in an altogether undesirable diminution of the latter's authority.[3] Moreover, a custom that had developed in opposition to statute law impugned in no unmistakable terms the authority of the legislator himself—and as far as medieval Roman law and Canon law were concerned that legislator was a monarch, either in the shape of the emperor or in that of the Pope—and if such custom were accorded force of law, the legal sovereignty of the monarchic legislator would be severely undermined in favour of an authority vested in the *populus* itself.[4] The very idea of monarchic government militated against the recognition of a mere custom, of whatever long *vetustas*, as a sufficient basis of law.[5]

---

[1] *D*. 1.3.37 (Callistratus).

[2] For some discussion of the principles of customary law cf. the present writer's "Bartolus on Customary Law" in *Juridical Review*, Vol. 52 (1940), pp. 263 ff.; idem, *The Medieval Idea of Law* (London, 1946), Ch. IV *passim*.

[3] It is different with *desuetudo* which consisted merely in the non-usage of certain legal enactments, cf. Bartolus, *ubi supra*, p. 280, note 4.

[4] In the history of customary law this aspect has not received that attention which is surely its due. It is certainly no coincidence that the whole doctrine of customary law came to be elaborated by the Postglossators from the thirteenth century onwards, when the issue of political and legal sovereignty of the people was not only becoming a central item of doctrine but also, and perhaps more so, of practice. The elaboration of this doctrine necessarily led to the conception of the *populus liber* who not being subjected to a superior, could legislate for itself, and consequently the doctrine of customary law is a highly important aspect of the growing thesis of popular sovereignty which, within the framework of jurisprudence, appears as the legal sovereignty of the people. The development of political sovereignty of the people entailed a considerable modification of what may have been held the theory of customary law as contained in Roman law. As so often, historical jurisprudence and the history of political ideas are so intimately connected that they can be regarded as one and the same thing seen from different angles. In modern times the problem was of course fully appreciated by Austin.

[5] Cf. *C*. 8.53.3, where a *consuetudo contra legem* is expressly excluded as a source of law. As for Canon law, Innocent III expressed his view on a custom opposed to statute law thus: "*Consuetudo quae canonicis obviat institutis, nullius debet esse momenti*" (*Extra:* I.iv.3), though he recognized, in common with Roman law, the supplementary character of customs: *ibid.*, *cap*. 8, where he quotes approvingly *D*. 1.3.37. The criterion was the nature of the custom as "*rationabilis*." On the presupposition of a true monarchic government this criterion amounted, however, to very little.

* A footnote to the lecture given by Herbert Jolowicz at the Riccobono Seminar, "The Stone that the Builders rejected," posthumously published in *Seminar*, Vol. 12, (1954), especially pp. 44 ff.

86

Whatever view may have been taken of the legal validity of a custom opposed to statutory pronouncements, there can be no doubt that its basis must have been longevity, that is, longevity of actual practice and usage. A question that is perhaps of theoretical rather than practical interest is whether juristic doctrine alone can supply a sufficiently strong basis for creating a *consuetudo contra legem*. Generally speaking, by the fourteenth century it was unanimously held that a *consuetudo contra legem*, provided that all other requirements were fulfilled, displayed full legal effects, so that the *lex* in this particular instance was effectively abrogated.[6] But the presupposition was still that the foundation of this *consuetudo* was usage and practice of the same act through a more or less definite period. But legal scholarship as such was not of course concerned with acts and usage—and yet there seems at least one instance in which legal doctrine was recognized as sufficient basis for a *consuetudo contra legem*.

The law embodied in Justinian's *Codex* and originally issued in 398 A.D. by Arcadius and Honorius, dealt with criminals who were condemned to death; it forbade, *inter alia*, all intervention by clerics on behalf of the condemned prisoners.[7] If ever a prohibition was clear, it was this. And yet, in the later Middle Ages a specific custom in contravention of this explicit law had been asserted according to which the condemned man was free if on his way to the place of execution he was fortunate enough to meet a cardinal.

In no gloss, commentary or lecture before the middle of the fourteenth century can there be found any hint of the existence or of the growth of this custom: neither civilian nor canonist apparently knew of it. The first notice of this "custom" appears in the great work of Albericus de Rosciate on the *Codex*. In his commentary on *C*.1.4.6, he said this:[8]

> *Existendo in Romana curia Avinionensi audivi a fide dignis quod si aliquis ducebatur ad justitiam etiam ultimi supplicii et obviabat alicui cardinali, quod justitiarius eum dimittebat ob reverentiam cardinalis.*

Now Albericus de Rosciate's information is all the more interesting as he never taught at any University, remaining most of his life a mere practitioner.[9] In 1340 he was the ambassador of the Visconti to the papal court at Avignon[10] and it was very likely on the occasion of this visit that he heard of this peculiarly privileged position of a man condemned to death. Albericus himself does not enlarge upon the legal ingredients or the juristic nature of this alleged custom: according to him, the prisoner was automatically free and saved from the gallows by the mere fact of meeting a cardinal in public whilst on his way to the scaffold. The *raison d'être* of this liberation lies, in his opinion, in the reverence due to a cardinal. Moreover, the privileged position of the prisoner himself was for Albericus in some way the indirect effluence of the clerical status in

---

[6] Cf. Bartolus, *ubi supra*, pp. 280 ff.

[7] *C*. 1.4.6; cf. also *C*. 7.62.29 (*Addictos*).

[8] Albericus de Rosciate, *Commentaria ad Codicem* (Lyons, 1545), fol. 36ra.

[9] Cf. F. Savigny, *Geschichte des römischen Rechts im Mittelalter* (2nd ed., Heidelberg, 1850), Vol. 6, 127. Cf., furthermore, *Dictionnaire d'histoire et de geographie ecclésiastique*, s.v. Albéric de Rosate.

[10] Cf. his own narration in his commentary on *C*. 1.2.14.

general: clerics were supposed to help those who were in need of help. For immediately preceding the passage quoted he says: *"Multi clerici dicentes suum esse officium juvare positos in necessitate et illos qui ducuntur ad mortem,*[11] *sed illud supplicando non eripiendo nisi manifeste appareret eum condemnatum inique"* in which case he implies that clerics may even use force to save the condemned man from the gallows.

Although, strictly speaking, Albericus did not maintain that this custom had in fact grown up, his younger contemporary, Baldus de Ubaldis, spoke of a custom derived from a privilege. On the other hand, the passage in Baldus would not go to show that the liberation was automatic, as it appeared to be the case with Albericus: release was apparently left to the discretion of the cardinal himself; it depended on him whether or not he wished the prisoner to be freed, for Baldus stated that the cardinal *could* liberate the condemned man. His statement was rather laconic and there is no possibility of ascertaining by what means the cardinal could produce the alleged effect.[12]

> *Nota, quod contra hanc legem faciunt cardinales quodam privilegio, nam si obviant ei qui ducitur ad mortem, habent ex consuetudine hoc privilegium, quod possunt eum a morte liberare.*

It is difficult to say whether Baldus was influenced or merely inspired by the information which Albericus gave: the shortness of the passage together with all lack of references to facts would indeed justify some suspicion that Baldus without giving his source made Albericus's statement his own, but modified it by asserting the discretionary power of the cardinal. Nevertheless, he explicitly declared that this was a custom.

It was a contemporary of Baldus, Bartholomaeus Salicetus, who, as far as I could ascertain, supplied what Baldus had omitted to state, namely, how the discretionary powers of the cardinal were to be exercised: the cardinal could liberate the prisoner if he put his red hat on the former's head.

> *Ultimo scias, quod cardinales non servant hanc legem in principio habentes ex consuetudine privilegium, ut si obvient ei qui ducitur ad supplicium* possint *mittendo suum pileum illum liberare a morte.*[13]

That a cardinal had this right of saving a prisoner from the gallows was also asserted by Paulus Castrensis who seemed to have conflated Albericus and Baldus and to have been oblivious of Salicetus. He too explicitly declares that this right of the cardinals was customary—*"ubique audivi divulgatum"*—and that it was in fact acted upon: the court officials at Florence, where the papal *curia* stayed—between 1433 and 1442—were anxious not to take a prisoner through those streets in which a cardinal was likely to be met. *"Tempore quo curia erat Florentiae, sicut hodie,*

---

[11] With a reference to Gratian's *Decretum*, C. XXIII, qu. 3, c. 37.

[12] Baldus de Ubaldis, *Commentaria in Codicem* (Venice, 1615), *ad C.* 7.62.29 (*Addictos*), no. 1, fol. 10rb. For Baldus see Savigny, *op. cit.*, Vol. 6, pp. 208 ff; *Dictionnaire du Droit canonique*, s.v. Baldi; W. Ullmann in *Law Quarterly Review*, Vol. 58 (1942), pp. 356 ff.

[13] Bartholomaeus Salicetus, *Lectura ad Codicem* (Lyons, 1549), *ad C.* 7.62.29, no. 4, fol. 56va. For Salicetus see Savigny, *op. cit.*, Vol. 6, pp. 262 ff. The red hat as a distinctive sign of the dignity of cardinals was introduced by Innocent IV in 1245, cf. P. Hinschius, *Kirchenrecht* (Berlin, 1869), i.357; also W. Plöchl, *Geschichte des Kirchenrechts* (Vienna, 1955), ii.87 (with further literature).

cavebant rectores ne cardinales irent per loca, per quae criminosi duce-bantur."[14] In the second place in which Paulus treats of this matter, he confirms that this custom was actually observed: "*Et ita servatur de facto.*"[15] Like Albericus before him, Paulus Castrensis also holds that the *raison d'être* of this liberation was respect and reverence for the dignity of the cardinal, although, naturally enough, no legal passage could be quoted in support of this allegation.

It should not, however, be assumed that only North Italian and specifically Bolognese jurists knew of this alleged right of the cardinals. In the fifteenth century the famous Neapolitan jurist, Paris de Puteo, also declared that a cardinal could save a prisoner from the gallows. His explanation, however, was different from that offered by Baldus (a privilege based upon custom) or Albericus and Paulus Castrensis (respect for the cardinal's dignity): according to him, the cardinals have this right because they are the equals of kings—"*cardinales sunt instar regum.*" The *mystique* of medieval kingship was apparently transferred to the cardinals who, because no express law could be quoted, were endowed with rights which derived from extra-legal premises.[16] This reasoning by one of the foremost jurists of the fifteenth century would indeed indicate that he himself was still searching for some plausible explanation of this supposed right. And it is some reflection on the Neapolitan's frame of mind that he so easily takes recourse to an application of the conception of kingship.

Of other fifteenth-century authors two deserve special mentioning, partly because both were academic jurists as well as practical lawyers, and partly because both enjoyed a very high reputation in their own and subsequent times. Each is quoted by later writers as the authority on matters of actual practice. The one is Bartholomaeus Caepolla, of Verona, and professor at Bologna, who in his influential *Tractatus Cautelarum* reports the doctrine of Albericus and Baldus without adding any new doctrinal point. Since Caepolla's book was written on the basis of his

---

[14] Paulus Castrensis, *Commentaria ad Codicem* (Venice, 1594), *ad C.* 1.4.6, no. 10 ' fol. 23rb: "*Ultimo dicit Albericus se audivisse in Romana curia, licet hoc jure non reperiatur cautum, sed ubique audivi divulgatum, quod quando criminosus ducitur ad justitiam et obviat alicui cardinali, quod ille talem criminosum potest auferre de manibus familiae, et familia non debet sibi resistentiam facere, sed ob reverentiam dignitatis sibi tradere, et tempore quo curia erat Florentiae ,sicut hodie, cavebant rectores ne cardinales irent loca, per quae criminosi ducebantur.*"

[15] Idem, *ad C.* 7.62.29, no. 2, fol. 140vb: "*Dictum (scil. huius legis) fallit in cardinalibus, qui habent hanc prerogativam ex consuetudine, ut inquit Baldus, quod si obviant alicui, qui dicatur ad justitiam, possunt ipsum eximere de manu familiae ponendo capellum super caput eius, et ita servatur de facto.*"

[16] Paris de Puteo, *De sindicatu*, edited in *Tractatus Illustrium Jurisconsultorum*, Vol. 7, fol. 294vb: "*Numquam enim capitalis condemnatio est differenda, nisi ex causa et supra vel ratione alicuius casus emergentis, ut quia condemnatus obviaret cardinali, quia ipsi habent ex consuetudine ,quod si obviant damnato ad mortem, quod possunt eum liberare, ut dicit Baldus . . . cardinales sunt instar regum.*" Paris de Puteo reports a rather interesting and amusing case of a liberation from the death penalty in which the Pope himself was involved, though I am unable to verify the details of the case reported, *ibid.,* no. 1: "*Cum quidam nobilis Romanus fuisset condemnatus ad mortem, dixit velle ex causa necessaria alloqui papam Joannem Cossam Neapolitanum, quod cum senator ei hoc permisisset ille damnatus, cum fuit coram papa, dixit sibi 'Tu vis me decapitari facere, ego non sum dignus ista poena, sed es tu dignus, quia es papa et majora crimina commisisti.' Propter quod papa indignatus mandavit senatori, quod eum decapitaret, quo audito ille damnatus exclamavit, quod papa erat irregularis, quia mandavit hominem occidi et in tantum clamavit super irregularitatem papae, quod fuit liberatus ne diceretur pontificem propterea irregularitatem incurrisse.*" Cf. also *infra*, note 30.

XIII

practical experience, one may safely gather from his exposition that this
cardinalician right was in fact observed, as it also becomes clear from the
advice which he gives: *"Sed Dominus justitiae . . . debet esse cautus ne duci
faciat condemnatum per loca, in quibus obviari possit aliquis cardinalis."*[17]
The other (late) fifteenth-century writer was Hippolytus de Marsiliis who,
like Caepolla, makes the release of the prisoner conditional upon the
exercise of the right by the cardinal, but asserts that the prisoner be given
i nto the custody of his liberator.

> *Ipse cardinalis potest illum reum auferre de manibus familiae, et familia
> non debet sibi facere aliquam resistentiam, sed ob reverentiam ipsius
> cardinalis eum sibi tradere.*[18]

Lastly, a brief reference may be made to the great Jason de Mayno who
in his lecture on the *Codex* merely in passing drew the attention of his
audience to this right of the cardinals,[19] and to the influential and outstanding French jurist Alexander Tiraquellus.[20]

It will be seen that neither the original reporter and author (Albericus
and Baldus) of this practice nor their *sequaces* in the fifteenth and sixteenth centuries were in a position to quote a single passage in law—and
we may recall the caustic remark of Paulus Castrensis: *"licet jure non
reperiatur cautum"*—or a *privilegium* which would have supported this
alleged right, and yet from the statements quoted it becomes abundantly
clear that this custom had in fact grown up in certain parts of Europe.
In default of any secure basis the jurists operated either with considerations
of a general nature, such as the dignity of the cardinals, or with a trans-
plantation of the *mystique* of medieval kingship to the senators of the
Pope, the cardinals.[21] The only firm conclusion which can safely be
drawn from the all too brief expositions is firstly that this right of the
cardinals was not asserted as customary before the middle of the fourteenth century and secondly, that because of this assertion in the works

---

[17] Bartholomaeus Caepolla, *Tractatus Cautelarum* (Frankfort, 1582), *cautela* ii, p.
2a: *". . . et ita de facto observatur, et ideo tu posses esse cautus quando aliquis esset
condemnatus ad mortem, ut procures, ut quidam cardinalis sibi obviam fiat, et super
caput eius capellum imponat, quia hic a morte liberatur. Sed dominus justitiae, si hoc
vellet evitare, debet esse cautus, ne duci faciat condemnatum per loca, in quibus obviari
possit aliquis cardinalis."*
[18] Hippolytus de Marsiliis, *Singularia* (Frankfort, 1596), no. 273, p. 665a, no. 15.
[19] Jason de Mayno, *Commentaria ad Codicem* (Lyons, 1569), *ad Cod.* II, xiv,
Rubrica, no. 2, fol. 111vb: *"Quarto limita in causis criminalibus, in quibus ingeritur
poena sanguinis. Nam licitum est sanguinem suum qualitercumque redimere . . . et qui
obviant cardinali, dum dicitur ad patibulum, debet liberari a poena mortis."*
[20] For Alexander Tiraquellus cf. J. Brejon, *Un jurisconsulte de la Renaissance: A.
Tiraqueau* (Paris, 1937). By his time it was possible to refer to quite a formidable
array of authorities, but he himself does not add greatly to our knowledge. See his
tract *De poenis* in his *Opera omnia* (Frankfort, 1574), *causa* 55, p. 119. His Italian
contemporary, the great criminologist Julius Clarus, amasses still more literary material
than Tiraqueau, but cautiously remarks that although he had never had an opportunity
of observing this custom in practice—*"Ego numquam vidi hoc in practica contingere"*
—out of respect for the dignity of the cardinals *"qui aequiparantur regibus"* the death
penalty should be commuted into some other form of punishment: *"Si tamen casus
contingeret, essem in sententia, ut posset poena mortis mitigari et reus ad triremes trans-
mitti, et hoc ob reverentiam amplissimi ordinis cardinalium, qui aequiparantur regibus et
in quibus residet tota fere majestas Christianae reipublicae,"* Julius Clarus, *Receptarum
sententiarum opera omnia* (Frankfort, 1590), *lib.* V, § fin., *quaestio* 98, p. 410, no. 5.
[21] For this function of the cardinals cf. J. B. Sägmüller, *Die Tätigkeit und Stellung
der Kardinäle bis auf Bonifaz VIII* (Freiburg, 1898), pp. 156 ff.; and now W. Ullmann,
The Growth of papal government in the Middle Ages (London, 1955), pp. 319 ff.

of two such influential writers (Albericus and Baldus) later practice in fact observed and respected this supposed right of the cardinals. It is therefore interesting to note that the mere assertion by two eminent jurists of a custom allegedly based upon a privilege conferred on cardinals, was sufficient in itself to create the very custom that they had maintained had already been in existence. This surely must be a unique instance of the creation of a customary law, not by the ordinary means of actual usage and practice, but by legal scholarship alone; and, what is more, it was a customary law that was directly in opposition to the written law.

Two reasons may tentatively be suggested for the comparative ease with which the passage from a mere assertion of a custom to at least partial observation of a custom was effected. It will be recalled that the first information about this practice came from Avignon where the papal *curia* then stayed. Now in the history of the papal constitution, the Avignonese sojourn of the *curia* signifies the period in which the cardinals at least factually assumed for themselves rights in the government of the Church which when logically pursued, were certainly apt to change the whole traditional monarchic constitution of the Papacy.[22] We recall the thesis of several authors that the cardinals were the equals of kings and that the privilege accorded to them was in reality an acknowledgment of their representing the "whole majesty of the *respublica Christiana*" (Julius Clarus). Differently expressed: the cardinals claimed to embody in their persons true governmental powers and, by extension of the medieval-Roman principle that the prince was not bound by the law[23]—"*princeps legibus solutus*"—the transference of the *mystique* of kingship to the cardinals could be effected without undue difficulties; and hence also the blatant violation of the statutory enactment in *C*.1.4.6 may become accessible to understanding and explanation.[24] Although of little direct significance, this problem belongs to historical jurisprudence no less than to the sphere of ecclesiastical constitutional history: it is an aspect which from a quite unexpected angle—i.e. from that of the sources of the law —throws into clear relief the ambitions of the cardinals, for there can be

---

[22] Cf. G. Mollat, *Les papes d'Avignon* (3rd ed., Paris, 1951); W. Ullmann, *The Origins of the Great Schism* (London, 1948), pp. 183 ff.; and on the genesis of this problem see idem in *Studi Gregoriani*, Vol. 4, (1952), pp. 112 ff.; and B. Tierney, *Foundations of Conciliar Theory* (Cambridge, 1955), pp. 193 ff.

[23] For the medieval development of this see the illuminating remarks of H. F. Jolowicz, *art. cit.*, pp. 40-1. Cf. also Fritz Schulz in *English Historical Review*, Vol. 60 (1945), pp. 157 ff.

[24] It might conceivably have been the case that this right of the cardinals was considered analogous to the right of asylum and the subsequent immunity of the criminal. Cf. *C*. 1.12 (*De his qui ad ecclesiam confugiunt*) and *Extra:* III.xlix (*De immunitate ecclesiarum*). It was already an extension of the right of asylum and of the *ratio* underlying this right when a criminal embraced in the street a priest who carried the Host: the prisoner was granted immunity from arrest. Cf., e.g. Ludovicus Romanus Pontanus, *Singularia* (Frankfort, 1594), no. 339, p. 51a: "*Quid si videns corpus Christi per civitatem ire, amplexus est sacerdotem illud portantem, an licite potest capi? Hanc quaestionem habui de facto in Urbino.*" He advised against the legality of the arrest. An editorial note *ibid.* refers to the tract of Ludovicus Gomez, *Institutiones de actionibus* (which was not accessible to me) in which he said: "*Si hoc ecclesiae concessum est propter Christum, a fortiori concedi debet sacerdoti portanti Christum.*". Very much the same argumentation was already advanced by Hostiensis in his *Summa aurea* (Venice, 1570), 3.49, no. 12, fol. 317vb: "*Ex mente juris est, ut ubi est major ratio fortius extendatur*" and hence the criminal attaching himself to a priest carrying the Host enjoys the same immunity as if he had fled into a church "*quamvis non sit expressum in jure.*"

little doubt that the original report by Albericus was inspired by them. Furthermore, papal legislation in the thirteenth century bears out what is here suggested, for resting on the conception that the cardinals in a specific way partake in papal power, Boniface VIII decreed that an injury inflicted upon a cardinal constituted the *crimen laesae majestatis*.[25] Consequently, the view that the cardinals were the equals of kings and that therefore kingly prerogatives could be transferred to them, received some support in papal legislation itself or was even possibly engendered by the latter. In any event, the usual means at the disposal of positive historical jurisprudence are quite insufficient to explain this remarkable development.

The second reason for this emergence of a "customary right" may have been the desire of the scholar jurists to reduce the all too frequent incidence of actual executions.[26] One may even go further and say that this development proceeded concomitantly with the rising tide of humanism. Although considering its inflexibility and the legislative processes involved, a change of positive law in this respect was virtually out of the question, the scholar jurists on the other hand welcomed the opportunity, on however flimsy grounds, to keep down the number of executions. In other words, this development appears to have been an issue of late medieval *Kriminalpolitik*.[27]

One of the most curious features presented by this problem was the lack of interest the professional canonists displayed in this question. So far all our witnesses have come from the civilian camp. None of the fourteenth-century canonists knows anything of this privileged position of the cardinals. Amongst the fifteenth-century canonists I could find only two who treated of the matter: both appear to support the doctrine,

---

[25] *Liber Sextus*, V.ix.5.

[26] Cf. on this topic G. Dahm, *Das Strafrecht Italiens im ausgehenden Mittelalter* (Berlin & Leipzig, 1931), pp. 301 ff.

[27] Considerations of this nature came more and more to the fore, so that in the sixteenth century writers like Thomas Ferratius and Marcus Antonius Blancus in their intensely practical works on *Cautelae* devoted long sections to those cases in which the execution of the death penalty could not be carried out. An interesting case was that of a Jew who after having committed a crime sanctioned by capital punishment, became a Christian. It was held that this converted Christian was not liable to any punishment, let alone punishment by death, because the effect of baptism was to remit all punishment, spiritual and temporal. Cf. Thomas Ferratius, *Tractatus Cautelarum* (Frankfort, 1582), *cautela* XXIV, p. 133b, no. 4, who refers to an actual case having occurred at Padua: "*Et ita fuit hic Paduae obtentum in causa cuiusdam Judaei, qui commiserat unum enorme furtum, quo commisso fecit se Christianum in qua causa pro et contra intervenerunt sollenniores doctores totius gymnasii et ultimo loco fuit liberatus ab omni poena corporali.*" Cf. also Marcus Ant. Blancus, *Cautelae criminales* (Frankfort, 1582), p. 309a, no. 3: "*Item etiam liberatur si esset Judaeus, qui dum ob delictum ad supplicium duceretur, petiit se fieri Christianum et revera se Christianum fecit . . . quia baptismus habet tantam efficaciam et tantam virtutem quod non solum liberat hominem ab omni poena spirituali, quoad Deum, verum etiam ab omni corporali, quoad mundum.*" The *glossa ordinaria* on the *Decretum, De consecratione, Dist.* iv, *cap.* 99 (*Sine poenitentia*), s.v. *baptismate*, had said this: "*In poenitentia etsi dimittatur peccatum per contritionem, remanet tamen temporalis satisfactio: in baptismo non. Nam tanta est vis sacramenti, quod nec etiam temporalis satisfactio remanet in baptismo pro peccatis . . .*" The same opinion was expressed by St. Bonaventure, *In libros IV sententiarum* (Rome, 1570), IV, iv. art. 1, qu. 2, p. 52. Innocent IV, on the other hand, limited the effects of baptism to spiritual punishment only: "*quoad accusationem et poenas, alias non spirituales, bene ligabitur post baptismum,*" *In V Libros Decretalium* (Frankfort, 1570), *ad Extra:* IV.xix.8, no. 3, fol. 483va. Thomas Aquinas advocated a remission of punishment by the prince on grounds of charity: *Summa Theologiae* (Venice, 1593), III, qu. 69, art. 2, fol. 221.

92

though neither added anything worth while. The one is Felinus Sandaeus[28] and the other is Martinus Laudensis who, although having written two lengthy tracts on the cardinals, devoted only two sentences in his second tract to this problem which, for him, was no more than a *"pulchra quaestio."*[29] A possible, though not entirely convincing explanation for this lack of interest amongst canonists may be found in the fact that this was a matter that concerned the execution of a man, i.e. a *judicium sanguinis*, and by law clerics were forbidden to partake in these proceedings;[30] hence this problem may not have been of topical interest to the canonists.

But there was one fifteenth-century canonist of repute who whilst outspokenly hostile to this privilege claimed for (or by) the cardinals nevertheless indirectly proves that this custom was in fact observed. Andreas de Barbatia[31] writing his tract *De praestantia cardinalium* shortly after 1450, divided the treatment of this problem into two parts. In the first he flatly denied, on juristic and meta-juristic grounds, that the cardinals could have, or could have been given, this privilege; in the second part he apparently makes a concession to legal reality—*"sed posito quod domini cardinales habeant istud privilegium"*—by attempting to exclude a number of cases in which this privilege should be inoperative.

To Andreas de Barbatia, it seems, only strictly juristic arguments appealed. According to him, neither the fact of being a cardinal nor that of being a papal cardinal legate can be a sufficient ground for claiming to do something *"contra ordinem juris."*[32] The law lays it down explicitly that a condemned man cannot by any means be saved from the gallows.[33] If this were claimed by reason of a privilege *"scirem libenter a quo tale privilegium emanaverit."* It cannot be said, he holds, that the Pope would grant a privilege by which the ordinary course of justice would be interfered with: both Roman and Canon law enjoin the execution of a sentence

---

[28] Felinus Sandaeus, *Commentaria in Decretales* (Lyons, 1587), *ad* I.xxix.26, no. 6, fol. 206ra: *". . . si ductus ad mortem obviat uni cardinali, qui cooperiat eum pilleo suo, quia debet liberari a morte, ita Baldus et Paulus de Castro in l. Addictos, C. De appellationibus."* For Felinus see J. F. Schulte, *Geschichte der Quellen und Literatur des canonischen Rechts* (Stuttgart, 1877), ii. 350 ff; A. van Hove, *Prolegomena* (2nd ed., Mechlin, 1945), pp. 498 ff., here also further literature.

[29] Martinus Laudensis, *Tractatus alter de cardinalibus* (edited in *Tractatus tractatum*, Lyons, 1548), *quaestio* 47, fol. 381ra: *"Quaestio pulchra est, an dominus cardinalis si obviat ei qui ducitur ad mortem, possit eum liberare a morte. Respondet Baldus quod sic . . ."* On Martinus cf. Schulte, *op. cit.*, ii. 395 ff.

[30] Cf. Gratian's *Decretum*, XXIII, v. 7, and *Extra:* III.l.5 and 8. Having taken part in these proceedings as a layman constituted a case of *irregularitas*, i.e. inability to obtain clerical orders except by dispensation. This case of "irregularity" was usually considered under the heading of *"defectus perfectae lenitatis"* and applied to soldiers, judges, prosecutors, notaries, military escorts, executioners and their assistants, and so forth. Cf. *supra*, note 16, where the prisoner somewhat untechnically had this "irregularity" in mind; he should have declared the Pope's order unlawful.

[31] On Andreas de Barbatia, cf. Schulte, *op. cit.*, ii. 306 ff.; Van Hove, *op. cit.*, 500 with bibliography; and H. Jedin, *Geschichte des Konzils von Trient* (Freiburg, 1949), i. 64, 68, 490, note 19.

[32] His tract is edited in *Tractatus universi juris* (Lyons, 1549), Vol. 13. Cf. fol. 375vb: *"Nona quaestio:"* *"Sed tu pondera primo cardinalis non potest facere ex eo quia est cardinalis, nec etiam ex eo quod est legatus a latere. Nam non potest disponere contra ordinem juris."*

[33] *Ibid.:* *"Sed lege est expressum quod damnati ad supplicium eximi non possint, ut in l. Addictos, C. De espiscopali audientia (C. 1.4.6), ergo sequitur quod nec ut cardinalis nec ut legatus de latere hoc potest."*

legally and validly pronounced. Moreover, it is in the interest of the *respublica* itself that criminals be brought to justice.[34] A privilege of this kind would be *"contra omnem legis dispositionem"* and consequently null and void. Nor can it be maintained, according to Andreas, that this privilege could be validly derived from custom—as in fact Baldus and the other jurists had held—because this privilege would be *"contra jus divinum"* and directed against the security of the State itself: it would simply open the doors to delinquency.[35]

> *Et ideo huiusmodi privilegium non est sine dubitatione; nec esset bonum exemplum honeste et recte vivere volentibus, si cardinales uterentur illo privilegio.*

But even if the cardinals had this privilege, Andreas goes on to say, it should not be used in every case. A prisoner found guilty of the *crimen falsi*[36] should not be freed, because as Angelus de Ubaldis had once said in a public disputation, this kind of criminal was even excluded from benefiting from the proclamation of a general amnesty.[37] And the same argument applies to the prisoner who was found sentenced for a *"crimen commissum contra patriam '*—a significant extension of the conception of the *crimen laesae majestatis*—and he too should have no hope of liberation: *"in generali concellatione bannitorum non venit bannitus propter crimen commissum in rempublicam"* and therefore there is all the more reason for carrying out the death penalty on him. This privilege should not be operative furthermore in the case of a crime committed against the imperial majesty, that is, against the person of the emperor, and in cases of heresy.[38] Lastly, if the crime was *"atrox et horrendum"* no justification

---

[34] *"Durum est credere quod a Romano pontifice emanasset tale privilegium, nam scriptum est non permittas maleficos vivere super terram, nec est crudelis qui maleficos occidit*, 23 qu. 5, Non est crudelis et c. Qui homicidas (*Decretum:* XXIII, v. 28 and 31). *Nam reipublicae interest delinquentes punire, l. Ita vulneratus, ff. Ad legem Aquiliam* (D. 9.2.51), *et c. Ut famae, De sententia excommunicationis* (*Extra:* V.xxxix.35).

[35] *"Si vero dicimus tale privilegium emanasse a consuetudine, et ita ponit Baldus et Salicetus ibi dicentes privilegium illud competere et procedere ex consuetudine, videtur talem consuetudinem non tenere, primo quia est contra jus divinum quod disponit Non permittas maleficos vivere super terram* (cf. *Exod.* xxii.18), *est etiam contra rempublicam, quia reipublicae interest ne maleficia remaneant impunita. Item quia per talem consuetudinem paratur via ad delinquendum."*

[36] About this crime which included many offences, see Dahm, *op. cit.,* pp. 501 ff. The main offences were: counterfeiting, perjury, change of name, change of weights and measures, falsification and forging of documents, etc. Death was decreed only for the first-mentioned offence.

[37] *"Unde credo non habere locum cum quis damnatus esset de crimine falsi; dicit Angelus in disputatione incipiente 'Exorta guerra' quod si ex mandato dominorum fiat generalis cancellatio bannitorum, non venit bannitus de crimine falsi."*

[38] Andreas here refers to the well-known case of Richardus Malumbra who was condemned for heresy, but for whom his Bolognese colleagues intervened: *"Quarto non habet locum in haeretico, quia tunc nemo debet illum fovere . . . et propter hoc male fecit collegium Bononiense supplicare pro illo haeretico* (scil. Ricardo Malumbra). *Nam si hic est verum in crimine laesae majestatis imperatoris, ergo multo magis in crimine laesae majestatis ipsius Dei vivi. Nam crimen haeresis et crimen laesae majestatis aequiparantur, l. Si quemquam, C. De epp. et cl.* (C. 1.3.31), *c. Infidei favorem, De haereticis in VIo* (*Sextus:* V.ii.5), *c. Licet Heli, De simonia* (*Extra:* V.iii.31)." The prominent colleagues of Richardus Malumbra were Jacobus Butrigarius and Jacobus de Belvisio; the case occurred in 1325 when a papal commission was appointed to investigate the case. Cf. Raynaldus, *Annales ecclesiastici* (Lucca, 1724), xiii, *ad annum* 1326. Jacobus Butrigarius himself in his lecture on C. 1.3.14 refers to it: *"Et ideo collegium doctorum fuit fortiter reprehensum a domino legato dum doctores supplicabant pro domino Ricardo Malumbra qui erat de haeresi damnandus."* The charge of heresy

94

could be found, according to Andreas, for even a commutation of the death penalty. In this case he advocates that the prisoner "*debet dari bestiis ad comedendum et ad dilaniendum.*"

There is no doubt that Andreas de Barbatia clearly perceived the intrinsic juristic problem, that is, whether a privilege that is detrimental to the well-being of the State, because diametrically opposed to the law, could produce a customary right, even if it were proved that such a privilege was ever conferred or that it grew as a result of custom: in this latter case the further problem arises whether a privilege in the strict meaning of the term could ever be derived from mere custom. At the same time there can be no doubt that already in the time of Andreas, that is, the middle of the fifteenth century, this peculiar custom was in fact observed: one may be tempted to say that considerations of *Kriminalpolitik* which had moved his opponents to propagate this "custom," prompted him to restrict its application. Nevertheless, even in this negative manner he is a witness of the existing right, the scope of which may well have been a matter of dispute. It is certainly worth mentioning that the negative attitude of Andreas de Barbatia found so little favour amongst later writers that I have not detected a single author who would have made a reference to him. On the contrary, despite the obvious predilection of the jurists in the fifteenth and sixteenth centuries—the great *malaise* of medieval legal scholarship in its declining years—to quote and amass an imposing literary apparatus, not one considered it necessary or even advisable to draw attention to the indubitably well-argued juristic opinion of Andreas de Barbatia.[39] From the point of view of historical jurisprudence it remains true, however, that the growth of this custom had its roots, not in actual practice, but in the repeatedly asserted doctrine of the academic jurists: practice followed doctrine. This case may well be an instance of a genuine *Juristenrecht*.

---

was based partly on the teaching of Richardus that trade with the Saracens was lawful and partly also on his adherence to Louis the Bavarian during his conflict with John XXII.

[39] Cf., e.g., Petrus Duenas, *Fallentiae regularum juris* (Venice, 1571), *regula* 81, p. 85. As late as the beginning of the eighteenth century canonists referred to this right of the cardinals, cf. Ludwig Engel, *Collegium universi juris canonici* (Salzburg, 1706), I.33, no. 20, p. 219: "*Privilegium ex consuetudine introductum habere dicuntur (scil. cardinales), quod ad supplicium ductum possint veste aut pileo tegendo liberare.*"

XIV

A Greek Démarche on the Eve of the Council of Florence

Despite the superabundance of material available for the historical preliminaries and the progress of the Council of Ferrara-Florence, there is a source which to all intents and purposes has been neglected and has, therefore, remained outside the purview of the historiography concerning this critical Council. In more than one respect this source sheds significant light on the attitudes, mechanics and state of mind of at least some Greek sections and their aspirations in the matter of the union of the Greek and Latin Churches. The source is not an official document but, as we shall presently see, a memorandum or, to use Foreign Office jargon, a minute by a highly placed official who was not either in his private or public capacity in any way involved in the matter reported. The memorandum demands attention on several counts. It records an unexpected approach on the part of some Greeks to the duke of Milan shortly before Eugenius IV decided to transfer the Council from Ferrara to Florence. The record reveals, like a flashlight, how much diplomatic activity was going on in the corridors of power, in the couloirs, in the backrooms safely removed from the gaze of the public, of the annalists, official shorthand writers, and the forerunners of the modern journalists and of the media, that is to say, the diarists, eavesdroppers and reporters appointed by the various European courts at the seat of the Council. This memorandum or minute is the only source that informs posterity of an abortive, but nonetheless very symptomatic approach intended to settle the question of the union by radical means. Above all, the memorandum faithfully reflects the age-old Byzantine ideology which reached back into the somewhat hazy ancient Roman period and which had matured over more than a millennium that manifestly linked *Nea Roma* with Roman antiquity. The core and tenor of this approach associates historical continuity with historical Roman law, a combination that had served as the very ingredient, nay, as the *anima* that gave birth to, and shaped the future of, the Church in Byzantine realms.

In order to appreciate the nature of this Greek démarche a few introductory remarks on the wider background and the setting seem advisable. It will be recalled that the continuing menace of the Turks at most of the vulnerable frontiers of the economically, financially, territorially and, above all, ideologically and constitutionally weakened empire had prompted several approaches by the Greeks to the West since the return of Michael Palaeologus: I leave out the proposal made in 1274 to the papacy for a union of the two Churches in order to ward off the threatening designs of Charles of Anjou, the papal vassal. But it may well be that this step, however unsuccessful it proved in the end, served as a model for John v in 1369 when, in the face of Turkish threats, he submitted several proposals to the papacy culminating in the promise of a union and in his undertaking to lead the Greek people and clergy to Roman Christianity: apparently the domestic response to this plan in the empire and in Constantinople was far from favourable, nor did Innocent vi show much appreciation of the proposed measures.[1] Although there was apparently some greater willingness on the part of the Greeks in 1399 to appeal to the West for help, the West was evidently in no position to render any: the Schism within the Latin Church had split it from top to bottom, and any assistance to Constantinople was quite out of the question. Moreover, the Hundred Years War was raging between the chief powers in Western Europe. In these circumstances the appearance of Manuel ii in Paris and London in 1400 to solicit help personally, could not but evoke deep sympathy with the Byzantine plight, but little more.[2] This brings me to the last rapprochement between the Eastern and Western Churches. John viii was hard pressed by the Turks on all his nerve centres, and this included Constantinople itself, and the only sensible step appeared to him—though by no means to all sections of the city's or the empire's populace—to pursue a vigorous campaign to enlist Western help in return for the promise of uniting the two Churches.

Now the papacy under Eugenius iv was—as were the somewhat

---

[1] For details cf. G. Ostrogorsky, *Geschichte des byzantinischen Staates*, 3rd ed. Munich 1963, 444 ff.; and for the background see especially D. M. Nicol, 'Byzantine requests for an oecumenical council in the fourteenth century' in *Annuarium Historiae Conciliorum*, i (1969), 69–95.

[2] He saw the king, Henry iv, on 21 December 1400 and spent Christmas with him at Eltham: *Chronicon Adae de Usk A.D. 1377–1421*, ed. E. M. Thompson, with English translation, London 1904, 56 f. and 219 f. Adam of Usk has locc. citt. quite a perceptive description of the appearance of the emperor in the streets of London: 'The emperor always walked with his men dressed alike and in one colour, namely white, in long robes cut like tabards; he finding fault with the many fashions and distinctions in dress of the English, wherein he said that fickleness and changeable temper was betokened. No razor touched head or beard of his chaplains. These Greeks were most devout in their church services which were joined in as well by soldiers as by priests, for they chanted them without distinction in their native tongue . . .'. The emperor was 'also comforted at his departure with very great gifts'. See further *Eulogium Historiarum Continuatio iii*, ed. F. S. Haydon, in Rolls Series, London 1863, at 388: 'Hoc anno (i.e. 1400) imperator constantinopolitanus venit in Angliam ostendens indulgentiam papae omnibus . . . et petiit auxilium a rege contra Turcos et infideles. Qui habebat quotidie missam per notam in camera sua ab episcopis suis ritu Graecorum, et quotidie imperator et omnes sui communicabant. Quem rex honorifice recepit et omnes expensas suas in Anglia persolvit . . .'. The emperor left in February 1401 and received a grant of some £2,000: see E. F. Jacob, *The Fifteenth Century 1399–1485*, repr. Oxford 1969, 76–77; D. M. Nicol, 'A Byzantine Emperor in England' in *University of Birmingham Hist. J.*, xii (1971), 204 ff.

excitable and vociferous Basleans—very keen on this union, so that one could speak of a three-cornered interest in the union: the emperor John VIII, the pope Eugenius IV, and the Baslean conciliarists.[1] Evidently, the respective motives differed widely and on fundamental grounds. The pope was anxious to boost the papal primatial function with all its attendant consequences (the application of the descending theme of government, immunity from judgments, and so on), precisely the function that was anathema to the radical conciliarists at Basel who were eager to implement the ascending theme of government as well as the other respective decrees of Constance, and they therefore hoped to find in the imperial government of Constantinople an effective ideological ally for their own designs against the monarchic papacy.[2] In assessing the situation in the thirties of the fifteenth century one should never lose sight of the conspicuous hardening of the papal and conciliarist fronts. This was the very legacy of the Great Schism that had shattered so many illusions and—what might appear in retrospect—preconceptions which made it imperative for the papacy to achieve a demonstrable success, if only to preserve the claim to monarchic government. Since the relations between the papacy and the Basleans had rapidly and very swiftly worsened from 1435 onwards, there was all the more reason for the papacy to act in a decisive manner so as to produce a striking and tangible success. Hence Byzantine intentions and Western aspirations complemented each other rather well, however much their motives differed. That in the end it was the papacy which, so to speak, raced the conciliarists, was entirely due to its greater expertise in this kind of activity, to its resoluteness and planning as well as to its quick and correct assessment and evaluation of the developing situation. Both, therefore, the monarchic papacy and the Baslean conciliarists, despatched a fleet to Constantinople to fetch the Greeks and transport them at their respective costs. To make the picture complete, mention should at least be made of the absence of an emperor in the West during the winter months 1437–1438. The emperor Sigismund had died on 9 December 1437 at Znaim in Moravia, and no successor had yet been chosen. Albrecht II having been elected king of the Romans in March 1438[3] showed little interest in the squabbles between Eugenius IV and the conciliarists, and also had his hands full in Bohemia, Austria, Hungary and Poland. Nobody would have dared to predict in 1438 that this king

---

[1] The 'three-sided situation' is rightly pointed out by D. I. Geanakoplos, 'The Council of Florence (1438–1439) and the problem of union between the Greek and Latin Churches' in *Church History*, xxiv (1955), 324 ff., at 328.

[2] For some remarks on this topic cf. H.-G. Beck, 'Byzanz und der Westen im Zeitalter des Konziliarismus' in *Vorträge und Forschungen*, xii (1960), 135 ff., at 146, though this focal point might have been emphasised a little more.

[3] For his election as king of Hungary on 18 December 1437, see *Deutsche Reichstagsakten* (abbreviated: *RTA*.), ed. G. Beckmann, Stuttgart-Gotha 1925, xiii. 168 n. 1; and for his election as king of the Romans see the proceedings and official *acta*, ibid., nos. 28 ff., at 73 ff.; the final voting was on 20 March 1438, nos. 36–37, at 92 f. For some details (based on inadequate source material) cf. W. Wostry, *König Albrecht II.: Prager Studien aus dem Gebiete der Geschichtswissenschaft*, ed. A. Bachmann, fasc. 12 and 13, 1906–1907.

was to begin the long and uninterrupted line of Habsburg rule in Central Europe that lasted until 1918.

In any case it was not merely the physical existence of the empire in Constantinople that was at stake. What weighed perhaps even more with many intellectuals as well as with the mass of the population was the threat and possible disappearance of the mystique that had sustained the empire throughout the millenium of its lifetime, and which culminated in the one, basic and unquestioned ideological tenet which without fear of contradiction can be called the life blood of the empire: that is, its notional universality, its universal mission, the veritably cosmic role it believed it had to play as an instrument of divinity: the Autokrator was the vicegerent of the Pantokrator.[1] Being the legitimate successor of the ancient Roman empire, albeit in a Christian complexion, this Greek empire inherited also the function and position of the emperor in regard to the creation, administration and application of public law, and this really is the fundamental theme which—however little this is realised by modern historians—necessarily determined the role of the emperor himself in regard to ecclesiastical matters. This application of the ancient Roman public law is the key to the understanding of the development of the Church under the βασιλεὺς τῶν ῥωμαίων, for the *ius publicum in sacris, sacerdotibus et magistratibus consistit.*[2] Hence the constitutionally fixed and legally anchored intervention of the emperor in all ecclesiastical and religious matters, including the convocation of councils, appointments of ecclesiastical officers, their dismissal, transfer, and so on. Far too little importance is attached to this unquestioned constitutional basis of the Byzantine imperial government, which, in this vital respect, most conspicuously manifested its claim to be a legitimate continuation of the ancient Roman empire.[3] While its complexion had become Christian, in its structure the Byzantine empire inherited the universality of the ancient Roman empire. Consequently, the imperial universality in its

---

[1] For this topic only a few specimens can be given, since the literature is too rich to be quoted here. Cf. L. Bréhier, *Les institutions de l'empire byzantin*, 2nd ed., Paris 1949, esp. chapters 1 and 2, at 1 ff. and 52 ff.; K. Jäntere, *Die römische Weltreichsidee* (=*Annales Universitatis Turkuensis*, series B, xxi (1936) 128–42); L. Cerfaux and J. Tondriau, *Le culte des souverains*, Paris 1956, 439 ff.; O. Treitinger, *Die oströmische Kaiser- und Reichsidee nach ihrer Gestaltung im höfischen Zeremoniell*, 2nd ed. Darmstadt 1956; A. Michel, *Die Kaisermacht in der Ostkirche*, Darmstadt 1959; H. Rahner, *Kirche and Staat im frühen Christentum*, Munich 1961, esp. chs. 3 ff.; F. Dölger, *Byzanz und die europäische Staatenwelt*, Darmstadt 1964, esp. 9 ff., 34 ff., 282 ff.; H.-G. Beck, 'Reichsidee und nationale Politik im spätbyzantinischen Staat' in *Byzantinische Zeitschrift*, liii (1960), 86 ff.; id., 'Res publica Romana: Vom Staatsdenken der Byzantiner' in *Sitzungsberichte der Bayrischen Akademie der Wissenschaften*, phil. hist. Kl., 1970, fasc. 2.
[2] Ulpian's classic definition in *Dig.* 1.1.1 (2).
[3] For this cf. W. Ullmann, *A Short History of the Papacy in the Middle Ages*, 2nd ed. London 1974, 7, 23, 29, 41, 43 45. It is, nevertheless, interesting to see that in course of time the ecclesiastics began to assert their own independent position: the imperial rights concerning the ecclesiastical organism became questioned in the fourteenth century when the right of the imperial government to translate bishops from one see to another was no longer accepted and, in fact, disputed. It is the great merit of H.-G. Beck to have stressed this important feature, in *Sitzungsberichte*, cit., at 36–38.

Christian garb necessarily entailed the claim to ecclesiastical universality.[1] It was precisely at this point that after some skirmishes in the fourth century the imperial government in Constantinople openly clashed with the papacy in the fifth century—and the consequences are all too well known: first alienation, with the aftermath of the Acacian schism, through the stages of the iconoclastic controversies, the Photian schism, the final solemn break in 1054, down to the crusading idea that had as one of its motivating incentives the establishment or re-establishment of papal primacy in the East eventually achieved in 1204.[2]

Two cosmologies confronted each other. They were both universalist, though each setting out from different premisses which paradoxically enough claimed Roman parentage. These premisses make understandable that a genuine and enduring reconciliation of the Greek Church with the Latin Church was beyond human ingenuity. The crux of the matter was the papal writ—how far did it run? Acknowledgment of papal primacy was a precondition for any real lasting union. But by the thirties of the fifteenth century there was little likelihood that any modification of the petrinological theme as developed and applied by the papacy could be envisaged: it had by then a respectable historical-exegetical background reaching back to exactly the same age in which the Byzantine imperial government had begun to evolve its own standpoint and, what is immediately important, any modification of papal petrinology could have had far-reaching consequences in regard to the conciliarists assembled at Basel, who would have considered any concessions to the Greeks within the scope and extent of the primatial function a victory for their own cause. The subsequent discussions with the Greeks reflected the serious difficulties of the papacy that unless it was willing to endanger its own position by simply setting aside the development of a millenium, it could not be expected to make adjustments in regard to its primatial-monarchic functions merely to pacify the Greeks and at the very juncture when the Basleans were, so to speak, breathing down its neck. On this count alone no *aggiornamento* was possible. It is superflous to reiterate that the papacy had never officially confirmed the decrees passed at the Council of Constance.[3] And the eventual acceptance of the pope's primacy by the Greeks in the final decree *Laetentur coeli*[4] was, from the historical angle,

---

[1] This is incontrovertibly demonstrated by the designation of the patriarch of Constantinople as *universalis patriarcha* which indeed was officially used by the imperial government in the sixth century, cf., e.g., Justinian's *Novella* 83, proemium, designating the patriarch Mennas as 'universalis patriarcha'. Cf. in this context the highly significant letter by Felix III in 483 to Acacius, the patriarch, in which the pope expressed his astonishment at the temerity of the patriarch's calling himself 'totius ecclesiae princeps': cited in W. Ullmann, *Growth of Papal Government in the Middle Ages*, 3rd–4th ed., London 1970, 15 n. 9.

[2] On this cf. *Short History of the Papacy*, cit., 150, 211, 215 f.

[3] Ibid., 303 f.

[4] Text in *Conciliorum oecumenicorum decreta*, ed. J. Alberigo et al., 3rd ed., Bologna 1973, 523 ff. For an authoritative commentary by an eminent participant of the Council see Johannes de Turrecremata on the relevant passage in the decree: E. Candal (ed.),

barely a victory for the papacy, since the Greeks were hardly in a position to resist it after all the protracted and embittered discussions and in the face of the alarmingly increasing Turkish menace. The hostile reception of this decree in Constantinople was, perhaps, the best proof of the irreconcilability of the opposing standpoints.

The appearance of a large papally financed fleet at Constantinople on 3 September 1437 was cordially welcomed by the Greeks.[1] The Baslean fleet arrived exactly a month later, on 3 October, and could not compare in equipment or men or financial resources and backing with those at the disposal of the papacy in the autumn of 1437.[2] The impression they made on the imperial court left it in no doubt whose fleet it should use. The decision to sail in the papally financed fleet was not difficult to reach.[3] The papacy had taken great care to despatch notable scholars to the Greeks—among others there was Nicholas of Cusa[4]—for conducting any preliminary negotiations, although the Greeks took the matter no less seriously and included among their numbers equally prominent men of letters, quite apart from the professional theologians. What must have appeared as one of the largest convoys in peacetime—considering the quantity and quality of the men on board ship—set sail on 27 November 1437 for Italy and landed at Venice on 4 February 1438. From Venice the Greeks betook themselves to Ferrara, where they arrived early in March 1438.[5] Altogether there were some 700 Greeks, including the emperor himself, surrounded by all the pomp and ceremony appropriate on such occasions, accompanied by the patriarch of Constantinople, no less attended by splendour and display corresponding to his position and

---

Apparatus super decretum Florentinum unionis Graecorum (= *Concilium Florentinum,* ii (1942)) at 96–114. For the Byzantine reaction in Constantinople after the return of the Greeks see the illuminating account by Syropoulus, in his report: *Les 'Mémoires' du Grand Ecclésiarque de l'Église de Constantinople Sylvestre Syropoulos sur le Concile de Florence* (= *Concilium Florentinum,* ix (1971)), ed. V. Laurent, at 546 ff. This magnificent edition of the Greek text (with French translation) is the first full-scale edition of Syropoulos's large work and is the fruit of some four decades of editorial labour.

[1] For details cf. J. Gill, *The Council of Florence,* Cambridge 1959, 77 ff.; id., *Constance et Bâle-Florence* (in *Histoire des conciles,* ix (1965)), 214 ff.

[2] Cf. J. Gill, *Florence,* 80 ff. H.-G. Beck (*Vorträge und Forschungen,* cit., at 146) rightly points out that because the Greeks knew very well that Basel as well as the papacy needed them for their respective programmes, they would be in a position to put all their expenses on Western shoulders. On 25 October 1437 the imperial government replied to the Basleans that the Greeks would sail in the papal fleet: see F. Dölger, *Regesten der Kaiserurkunden des oströmischen Reiches von 565 bis 1453,* Munich 1965, no. 3476. For a detailed and lively account, see Syropoulos, *Mémoires,* ed. cit., at 160 ff.; here also the severe economic difficulties which faced the Greeks, ibid., 188 ff., 296 f.

[3] Gill, op. cit., 88 ff.

[4] It would seem that he conceived some of the basic ideas set forth in his *De docta ignorantia* on his voyage; cf. the dedication of the work to Cesarini, ed. Heidelberg Academy (1932). For some details cf. *Nikolaus von Kues als Promotor der Oekumene,* ed. R. Haubst, Mainz 1971 (= *Mitteilungen und Forschungsbeiträge der Cusanus Gesellschaft,* ix).

[5] On 25 February 1438 the emperor wrote to the Basleans and suggested that they should join him at Ferrara in the Council: *Reg.* no. 3478.

GREEK DÉMARCHE ON THE EVE OF THE COUNCIL OF FLORENCE

mission, followed by the astonishingly great number of scholars and highly respected men of letters.[1]

At Ferrara the dialogue between Latins and Greeks was predictably beset by all sorts of difficulties of a doctrinal nature, though the economic and financial plight began to afflict both parties. The pope who bore the brunt of the expenses of the Greeks and also a good deal of the Western participants of the Council, found his treasury rapidly facing 'liquidity problems', especially when the Ferrara business community realised the unique distinction and opportunity of having such a galaxy of the world's prominence within its walls: the temptation to raise prices proved too strong to be resisted. Escalation of food prices resulted in a 100 per cent. inflation, and with an empty treasury the pope was forced to borrow money from the Medicis at Florence, otherwise he would have faced bankruptcy. However, on the main front, that is, the desired union, there was no progress either: the speeches and endless discussions produced no tangible result. So in the end, the unhealthy climate at Ferrara—economically, physically, politically, theologically, and hygienically[2]—made the papacy decide to leave for Florence, which had, indeed, made tempting financial offers in the later autumn of 1438.[3] The respective decision was taken by the full Council at Ferrara on 10 January 1439. It was published on the same day.[4] The Greeks had no alternative but to acquiesce in the move. The first solemn session at Florence opened on 2 March 1439.

Meanwhile, at Basel, there had arrived on 5 December 1438 the German legation despatched by Albrecht II.[5] It consisted of five well-known and respected men: the bishops of Passau, Lübeck and Augsburg together with the imperial chamberlain Conrad XIII of Weinsberg accompanied by John of Eycke. The legation was empowered to take all

---

[1] For some personalities see J. Gill, op. cit., 89 n. 2, and now especially Syropoulos, *Mémoires*, ed. cit., at 184 ff. Further, J. Décarreaux, 'L'arrivée des Grecs en Italie pour le concile de l'union des églises d'après les mémoires de Syropoulos' in *Revue des études italiennes*, vii (1960), 29–59; ix (1962), 33–99; id., 'L'union des églises au concile de Ferrare-Florence' in *Irénikon*, xxxix (1966), 46 ff. and 177 ff. Cf. also J. P. Arrignon, 'Les Russes au Concile de Ferrare-Florence' ibid., xlvii (1974), 188–208.

[2] The point is made by Syropoulos in his *Mémoires*, ed. cit., at 298 f.

[3] For the bankruptcy of the papacy see J. Gill, *Florence*, 173 ff. and for the relations between Eugenius IV and Florence, see J. Kirshner, 'Papa Eugenio IV e il monte comune' in *Archivo storico italiano*, cxxvii (1969), 339–82. Cf. also *Acta camerae apostolicae et civitatum Venetiarum, Ferrariae, Florentinae, Ianuae de concilio Florentino*, ed. G. Hofmann (=*Concilium Florentinum*, iii. 1 (1950)) nos. 54 ff., at 45 ff.

[4] See *Decreta* (cit. above, 341 n. 4) at 523.

[5] See Johannes de Segovia, *Historia Gestorum Generalis Synodi Basiliensis*, xiv. 13, ed. in *Monumenta conciliorum generalium saeculi XV* (Vienna Academy, Vienna 1857–86) iii. 183 ff. For Johannes de Segovia, see U. Fromherz, *Johannes von Segovia als Geschichtsschreiber des Konzils von Basel* (in *Basler Beiträge zur Geschichtswissenschaft*, ed. E. Bonjour and W. Kaegi, lxxxi (1960)) esp. 67 ff. Of particular merit is H. Diener, 'Zur Persönlichkeit des Johannes von Segovia: ein Beitrag zur Methode und Auswertung der päpstlichen Register des späten Mittelalters' in *Quellen und Forschungen aus italienischen Archiven und Bibliotheken*, xliv (1964), 289–365.

necessary steps to achieve peace between the papacy and the Council.[1] In the question of the union of the Latin and Greek Churches the German government showed no particular interest and was to all appearance indifferent to the issue.[2] It would seem that the three bishops played only an insignificant role in the Council,[3] and that the main diplomatic activity was in the hands of Conrad of Weinsberg who, in fact, was appointed Protector of the Council of Basel.[4] He clearly was a highly versatile man with plenty of experience in handling delicate matters: he was above all an astute and adroit diplomat and had been the confidant of the emperor Sigismund who had appointed him imperial chamberlain in 1411. Conrad was in charge of numerous legations, was present at most of the imperial diets and other official gatherings, and appeared as the spokesman of the imperial electors (he himself of course was not an elector) whom they sent to the court of Albrecht of Austria to inform him of their election in March 1438.[5] Under the new Ruler Conrad kept his function as chamberlain. Among his notable attainments was also expertise in taxation, evidenced by his introduction of a special tax on the Jews as an additional source of income for the government.[6] His standing and reputation in high ecclesiastical councils can be seen from his presence at the election of the last anti-pope ever to be elected, Felix v.[7] After Albrecht II's early death in October 1439 Conrad's official position was confirmed by the regent of Germany.[8]

Evidently, a man of this stature had his observers, reporters and recorders in the important places and courts of Europe. It is also plain that he received reports from Greek quarters as well as from the duke of Milan, Filippo Maria Visconti, one of the most ambitious and determined

[1] The royal document appointing the ambassadors and giving them full powers of attorney is in Johannes de Segovia's *Historia*, cit., iii. 185–6; and in *RTA.*, xiv. 6, no. 1, dated 13 November 1438 at Görlitz. The relevant passage runs: '... nobilem Conradum de Winsperg eiusdem imperii camerarium et venerabilem utriusque iuris doctorem magistrum Johannem de Eyke (he was professor ordinarius of both laws at the university of Vienna) oratores et consiliarios nostros devotos et fideles dilectos, dantes et concedentes ipsis plenariam facultatem et omnimodam potestatem coram prefato reverendissimorum patrum cetu nostri parte comparendi, desiderium quod gerimus ad conservandam tutandamque ecclesiasticam unitatem proponendi, omniaque media pro tollenda huiusmodi differencia apperiendi ...'.

[2] G. Koller, *Princeps in ecclesia: Untersuchungen zur Kirchenpolitik Herzog Albrechts II. von Österreich*, Vienna 1964, stops before Albrecht's election as king of the Romans.

[3] Cf. G. Hödl, 'Zur Reichspolitik des Basler Konzils: Bischof Johannes Schele von Lübeck' in *Mitteilungen des österreichischen Instituts für Geschichtsforschung*, lxxv (1967), 46 ff.

[4] Cf. above n. 1 and *RTA.* xiv. 57 f., no. 21, and Johannes de Segovia, *Historia*, ed. cit., iii. 186. Details in H. Welck, *Konrad von Weinsberg als Protektor des Basler Konzils*, Schwäbisch Hall 1973.

[5] *RTA.* xiii. nos. 41, 47 at 97 f., 110, esp. 112 n. 1.

[6] See K. Schumm, 'Konrad von Weinsberg und die Judensteuer unter Kaiser Sigismund' in *Württembergisch Franken*, new series, liv (1970), 20–58 (reference kindly supplied by Mr. E. Gindele, University of Tübingen). Cf., e.g., *RTA.* xiii. nos. 347 ff. For his other plans, cf. now H. Koller in Festschrift H. Heimpel, ii, Göttingen 1973, at 70 f.

[7] Details in Johannes de Segovia, *Historia*, ed. cit., xvi cap. 15, in ed. iii. 455, lines 7 ff.; and cap. 17, at 464, line 18 f.; also cap. 28, at 495, lines 6 ff.

[8] See *Allgemeine Deutsche Biographie*, xli (1896), 519.

GREEK DÉMARCHE ON THE EVE OF THE COUNCIL OF FLORENCE

contemporary Rulers—the type of man whom only Renaissance Italy could produce: astute, crafty, aggressive and ruthless, qualities no doubt known to the papacy and to the Greeks. Now Conrad of Weinsberg was not only a versatile diplomat, but was also a characteristic higher civil servant. He kept meticulous accounts of expenses as well as having copious notes made, including records of reports received, and copies of decrees and orders, and the like. He even had his own *reigister*.[1] The expenses accounts he kept for the year 1437–1438 have long been edited.[2] His personal file (now in the Hohenlohe Archive in Neuenstein, Germany)[3] concerning the planned union of the Churches and the papal-conciliarist tussle, and relating to his sojourn in Basel, has, however, hardly attracted any attention,[4] although it contains a number of most interesting entries[5] of which the memorandum concerning the démarche of the Greek embassy is perhaps the most noteworthy.[6] This memorandum is under the general heading of: 'Novitates de domino nostro papa, duce mediolanensi, venetis et florentinis'. The report in question is on the reverse of a single folio. On the recto there are undated details of an embassy by the duke of Milan to Eugenius IV (of which no other record seems to exist) which tried to mediate between Basleans and the pope and to affect a cancellation of the pope's deposition by the Council at Basel; and there is also a mention of the pope's intention of going to Florence with the eventual aim of resuming residence in Rome.[7] The last entry of this first section of *Novitates* on the recto is somewhat cryptic and runs: 'Item dominus noster papa omnes suos actus et negocia dirigit et diriget contra Romanum imperium.' This memorandum of four parts is followed by a copy of the decree that transferred the Council from Ferrara to Florence. Interestingly enough the Council is here called a mere *conciliabulum*. This is the only piece that bears a date (10 January 1439).

About the reliability of Conrad of Weinsberg as a civil servant no doubt is permissible. He was exact, hard-working, painstaking, qualities which are matched by the absence of imagination, inventiveness and originality which at all times have been the hallmark of the civil servant in the higher echelons. Conrad does not tell us in the entry to which I will presently turn, where or how he had obtained his information, who gave

---

[1] See H. Weigel (ed.) in *RTA*. xiv. 57 n. 4. There are numerous and illuminating entries, ibid., nos. 160–167, at 278–95.

[2] J. Albrecht (ed.), *Einnahmen und Ausgaben Conrads von Weinsberg aus den Jahren 1437 und 1438* (= *Bibliothek des literarischen Vereins in Stuttgart*, xviii (1850)).

[3] It is in the Gemeinschaftliche Hausarchiv (GA), part IV, G59, no. 25. I would like to thank the Chief Archivist, Dr. Taddey, for his help and the supply of photocopies.

[4] There is a brief mention in G. Beckmann, *Der Kampf Kaiser Sigismunds gegen die werdende Weltmacht der Osmanen*, Gotha 1902, 62 n. 2.

[5] Ed. H. Weigel in *RTA*. xiv. 56–57.

[6] Referred to by G. Beckmann, loc. cit. and ed., loc. cit., at 57.

[7] Ed. cit: 'Animo ulterius Romam iturus se ad Florentiam transferret'. The pope explained to the Milanese ambassadors that he had no intention of going to Florence with a view to entering into an alliance with the Venetians, Genoese and Florentines against the duke of Milan.

it to him, or similar details.[1] But as this was clearly a most delicate and sensitive issue, one would hardly expect that a civil servant would give his source of information. At any rate, this minute might well reveal to us far more than do all the reported long-winded and inconclusive theological and abstruse discussions between the orthodox and Latin Churches at Ferrara-Florence. The memorandum is a dry, matter-of-fact report which I am inclined to think was put down in the way in which it was received. As indicated, there is no date attached to it, but it must have come to Conrad's notice before the decree transferring the Council from Ferrara to Florence reached him, otherwise there would have been little point in keeping a record of it. On the other hand, Conrad himself had not arrived at Basel before 5 December 1438. Hence the receipt of this report can be narrowed down to the weeks between early December and the time the decree concerning the transfer to Florence became known in Basel (probably in late January 1439).[2] And the report itself makes clear that when the Greek approach to the duke of Milan was made, no decision in regard to the future place of the Council had yet been taken. It does, however, confirm that the search for a 'third place' was still continuing.[3]

Were it not that the substance of this report had all the appurtenances of Greek-Byzantine ideology, embedded as this was in a by-now ossified historicity, one would be inclined to dismiss it as the plan of fantastic dreamers. What I think this revealed was—and there can be no doubt that the plan was hatched in the latter part of 1438 or the very early days of 1439—that some of the Greeks still assembled at Ferrara had become disillusioned by the wholly unpromising progress of the discussions and had decided on a radical surgery, possibly with a view to forcing the hands of the emperor himself. The Gordian knot was to be cut. It is well known that among the Greeks in Ferrara (and later also at Florence) there was quite a strong contingent which was desirous of a union on Greek terms only. There was, to mention just one prominent and vociferous section, led by the metropolitan Markos Eugenikos of Ephesus, which was bitterly opposed to making any concessions in substance.[4] It is, therefore, likely that the plan outlined in the memorandum of Conrad of Weinsberg had not the official support or sanction of the imperial government itself but reflected the views of those who were adamant about preserving the mystique of true Roman universality. They looked askance at the idea of a union involving as it did acknowledgement of

<hr />

[1] To judge by the entries ed. in *RTA*. xiv. 278 ff., he really had his antennae everywhere and was in touch with virtually everyone of consequence.

[2] See Johannes de Segovia, *Historia*, ed. cit., iii. 216; R. Bäumer, 'Eugenius IV. und der Plan eines "Dritten Konzils"' in *Reformata Reformanda: Festgabe für Hubert Jedin*, ed. E. Iserloh and K. Repgen, i, Münster 1965, 87 ff., at 95 (1 February 1439). For the original Greek reaction to a third place see Syropoulos, *Mémoires*, ed. cit., 130, 146.

[3] See Johannes de Segovia, *Historia*, ed. cit., iii. 197.

[4] Cf. J. Gill, *Florence*, 226, 234 f., 248 f., 250.

papal primacy and the acceptance of a number of hitherto hotly contested dogmatic points.[1] Nevertheless, the possibility that the plan here outlined, was merely a kite to see how far the duke of Milan was willing to go with the Greek proposals, so that the next phase would have been an official imperial approach, should not be dismissed altogether. As it is, the plan seems to have run itself to the ground: there is no record in any of the official Registers[2] or in the accounts of annalists or diarists. All of this only goes to prove the highly secret or private character of the mission. One has but to imagine what would have happened if the plan had come to the knowledge of the papacy or other negotiators at Ferrara—the whole carefully erected edifice would have collapsed in ruins before an astonished, if not stunned, world.

The tenor of the démarche is characteristically Byzantine: historical, universalist, and stressing the hallowed Byzantine standpoint that the ecclesiastical division between East and West was the consequence of the establishment of an empire in the West. If we translate this into a more comprehensible language, the démarche was based on the one fundamental and primary consideration to which the East had always adhered, that is, that it represented the one and only historic legitimate successor to the ancient Roman empire. The breakaway of the West was entirely the responsibility of the Germans, and it was this rupture which lay at the roots of the ecclesiastical division. In a word, the ecclesiastical division was contingent on the division of the once undivided Roman empire. It may very well be that by shifting all the responsibility onto the Germans the part played by the papacy in the division was to be minimised—a tactical manoeuvre to prevent possible damage to the prestige of the papacy. It may, however, also be that Conrad was not supplied with all the details or recorded them in a mangled way. The historical precedents recorded show, nevertheless, that either reporter or recorder were perhaps not as much adrift in their history as might at first sight appear: the historical precedents were telescoped so as to make them adjustable to the purport of the message to be conveyed to the duke of Milan. The style is, as one would expect in a minute of this kind, unadorned, direct and without flourish, in fact, a mere recording without much attention to style or linguistic or grammatical detail. It is perhaps best to describe this as extended notes or jottings written down in some

---

[1] F. Dölger, 'Politische und geistige Strömungen im sterbenden Byzanz' in *Jahrb. der österreichischen byzantinischen Gesellschaft*, iii (1954), 3 ff., at 12 ff. gives a survey of the various sections and parties in Byzantium and their aims. The overwhelming part of the civil service and of the higher clergy formed one such segment which would have no union with the West under any circumstances, even if Constantinople were to become an easy prey to the Turks.

[2] The *Reg.* have no entry that even faintly could bear upon this démarche: *Reg.* nos. 3484 and 3485, both of December 1438, deal with entirely different matters. Nor is there any mention of the embassy in the *Vita Philippi Mariae Vicecomitis Ducis III*, ed. in L. A. Muratori, *Rerum italicarum scriptores*, xx (= *Rerum Mediolanensium Historia*, ii), Milan 1731, 985–1020. There is no reference or allusion to it in Syropoulos's *Mémoires*. Nor have I found any reference to it in a modern work, except as noted above, 345 n. 4.

haste, since this was obviously a routine cancellarial matter designed only for internal use.

The memorandum begins thus: 'Recently some high-placed Greeks were sent from Ferrara to the duke of Milan and explained to him that in the earliest days of the Church the universal government of the world was one and whole'. This opening is not without significance. From the outset the Greek legation linked the fate of the Church with the universal monarchy of the Roman principate and empire. Indeed, the government of the emperor could then be called a *universalis monarchia orbis*,[1] and this was still the case in the Constantinean period and afterwards. The memorandum continues by saying that the *gubernacula* remained undivided 'until Nikephoros and Michael (Rangabe) (811–13) for the better management of the world government (*pro utiliori gubernacione orbis*) called upon the assistance of Charles the Great and entered into an agreement with him to the effect that Charles and his heirs should rule Rome together with the Occident, and they themselves Greece and the whole of the Orient, and they agreed that they were each other's brothers, should call each other this way and render mutual assistance'. However exaggerated in this somewhat simplified manner, there is a grain of truth in the assertion. Although the Eastern emperor—the βασιλεὺς τῶν ῥωμαίων— stood at the head of the family of all nations as their father, he nevertheless distinguished some by addressing them as ἀδελφοί, whereas others were mere φίλοι. In fact, there was a full hierarchy of nations according to the degrees of family relationship.[2] In actual fact, however, it was Charlemagne who according to the testimony of Einhard, entirely supported by the official correspondence, first addressed Nikephoros and Michael I as 'Brother'.[3] In other words, Charlemagne soothed the susceptibilities of the Byzantines by not claiming any universality for his government[4] by adopting a Byzantine device which had an entirely different origin and connotation from that given to it by the Frank. Yet now on the eve of the collapse of Byzantium, it was its government which made so to speak a virtue out of necessity and claimed to be entirely in accord with Charlemagne's intentions. They conveniently overlooked the rich development of the Latin Church by the time of the Carolingians on lines quite

[1] See the *Lex Rhodia*, in *Dig.* 14.2.9. Literature and significance in W. Ullmann, *Law and Politics in the Middle Ages*, London 1975, 57 f.
[2] This was first recognised by O. Meyer, 'Εἰς τὸν ῥῆγα Σαξωνίας' in *Festschrift für Albert Brackmann*, Weimar 1931 123 ff., at 130 ff.; see further G. Ostrogorsky, 'Die byzantinische Staatenhierarchie' in *Seminarium Kondakovianum*, viii (1936), 41 ff. and F. Dölger, 'Die Familie der Könige' op. cit. (above, 340 n. 1), 34 ff.
[3] Einhard, *Vita Karoli*, 5th ed. by G. O. Holder-Egger, in *M. G. H. Scriptores Rerum Germanicarum*, Hannover-Leipzig 1905, cap. 28, at 28: 'Quo tempore . . . vicitque eorum contumaciam magnanimitate . . . mittendo ad eos crebras legationes et in epistolis fratres eos appellando.' See further *M. G. H. Epistolae*, iv, no. 37, at 556 (anno 813); in 811 he apostrophised Nikephoros 'tua fraternitas', ibid., no. 32, at 546. See also O. Meyer, art. cit., at 135; F. Dölger, op. cit., 45 f. and W. Ullmann, *Growth* (as above, 345 n. 1) 113 n. 3.
[4] Cf. *Growth*, 104 ff.; *Short History*, 85 ff. The passages cited clearly prove that the idea of a division into an occidental and oriental empire was Charlemagne's.

independent from those in the East which had been firmly controlled by the imperial government.

The demise of the Carolingian line was, the Greek embassy declared, the beginning of the division of the empire and therefore also of the Church itself, because *extranei* emerged as usurpers: at one time they were Italians, at another Germans and—it is interesting to see how their message slid over the numerous troubles, such as the iconoclastic matters, the Photian schism, the final break as well as over the later period in which there were plenty of instances in which the Byzantines called the Western Rulers ἀδελφοί[1]—'at long last (*tandemque*) it was established in the West beyond and contrary to the will of the Greeks that there should be electors who should have the power to choose from the midst of the Germans emperors of the Romans or of the Occident whom the Roman pontiff had to crown and to approve (in this order!), with the result that the empire was no longer in the hands of the Greeks—to whom the *principatus monarchicus* belonged by right—but was divided.' This *divisio monarchiae*, this division of the one undivided government into an occidental and oriental half,[2] resulted in the collapse of the empire in the East as well as in the West, and consequently in the division of the *monarchia ecclesiastica*. This was the reason why the Church was afterwards divided and why it has remained so ('monarchia ecclesiastica *post hec* et *propterea fuit* et *est* divisa'). Here is presented to us in an almost classical manner the clearest possible evidence of how the real universal monarchy as claimed by the Byzantines was a precondition for the existence of a universal and undivided Church. This message of the embassy most faithfully reflects the Byzantine way of thinking in a concise and economical way, and for this reason alone should long have attracted attention.

However, this was only so to speak the historical introduction to the constructive proposal they put before the duke of Milan. He was to use his good offices to ensure that an ecumenical council should be assembled in a place to which the pope could conveniently come so that discussions could take place, and these discussions were to concern the re-establishment of the universal monarchy.[3] For only when this was achieved, could the ecclesiastical monarchy *facillime* also be restored. And this general proposal was followed by the bait the Greeks held out to the duke: once this

---

[1] Cf. the numerous examples quoted by F. Dölger, op. cit., at 46 ff.

[2] The unitarian theme—imperial unity (*Reichseinheit*) as a precondition of ecclesiastical unity (*Kircheneinheit*)—was first concretely applied after Constantine when imperial governments adopted the policy of compulsory ecclesiastical union (see E. Caspar, *Geschichte des Papsttums*, i Tübingen 1930, 167 ff) and found in Justinian its most consistent representative. Cf. on this the literature cited above, 340 n. 1; *Growth*, 31 ff., 75 ff.; *Short History*, 41 ff. For the doctrinal side of the problem see H.-G. Beck, *Kirche und theologische Literatur im byzantinischen Reich*, Munich 1959, 32 ff., 626, 682. This Byzantine view would have been directly relevant to the important thesis advanced by W. Ohnsorge, *Das Zweikaiserproblem*, Hildesheim 1947.

[3] This makes it clear that the search for a 'Third Council' was still going on. Whether the Greeks would have accepted the Basleans' suggestions (above, 342 n. 5) is far from certain in view of their earlier rather vehement rejections.

universal monarchy was restituted—*reparata monarchia orbis*—it would be necessary to constitute an imperial tribunal in Italy and to appoint a perpetual vicar of the empire in Italy who would have to act on behalf of the emperor and to deal with all emerging imperial cases, as far as they concerned the Occident, and who would have to hand out imperial fiefs to princes, counts and barons. And this perpetual vicar was to be none other than the duke of Milan himself and his heirs: 'Ipse suique heredes perpetui vicarii imperii constitui deberent'. It is perhaps not without interest to note that the memorandum has *consolando ducem*, which clearly indicates that the minute itself recorded merely the gist of the information obtained in indirect speech and was by no means intended to be a verbatim report.

In the characterisation of the offer made to the duke as a consolation one can detect a slight irony on the part of the reporter or the recorder himself, a subtle gibe as it were at the ignorance of the Greek embassy concerning Italian or Western conditions. As a matter of fact, the duke of Milan had been perpetual vicar (of the Western emperor) for nearly 150 years. In 1294 Adolf of Nassau had appointed Matteo Visconti imperial vicar of Milan, and the office became hereditary in 1349. In 1395 king Wenceslaus raised Giangaleazzo to the rank of a prince of the Roman empire (in the West) with the title of duke of Milan.[1] It is certainly worth a remark that the constitutional position and function of the duke of Milan had become a focal point of a number of juristic and political problems in the course of the fifteenth century. I happen to know of at least two lengthy *Consilia* by most eminent jurists, one given by Paulus Castrensis and the other by Alexander Tartagnus, both dealing with the scope and extent of the duke's power. Paulus Castrensis, an outstanding civilian, who taught at Siena and Avignon universities, and also at Bologna and Perugia (died 1441),[2] went into great detail in his long *Consilium* relative to the duke's legislative powers.[3] He concluded that the duke was in possession of *omnis potestas imperialis* and that in his own domain (which included virtually the whole of Lombardy) not even the emperor himself could exercise jurisdictional powers.[4] Alexander Tartagnus was a no less eminent jurist and in fact a pupil of Paulus Castrensis,[5] who likewise arrived at the conclusion that the duke occupied

---

[1] For these details see D. M. Bueno de Mesquito, *Gian Galeazzo Visconti, Duke of Milan: a study in the political career of an Italian despot*, Cambridge 1941.

[2] Details in F. C. von Savigny, *Geschichte des römischen Rechts im Mittelalter*, 2nd ed. vi Heidelberg 1850, 281 ff.; N. del Re, *Paolo di Castro, dottore della verità* (=*Studi Senesi*, lxxxii (1970)); N. Horn, 'Die legistische Literatur der Kommentatorenzeit' in *Handbuch der Quellen und Literatur der neueren europäischen Privatrechtsgeschichte* ed. H. Coing, Munich 1973, 276, 340.

[3] Ed. *Consilia*, Frankfurt 1582, pars II, *Cons.* 34, fol. 18rb–19vb. On him as a *Consiliator* cf. H. Lange, Die Rechtsquellenlehre in den Consilien von Paul de Castro' in *Gedächtnisschrift für Rudolf Schmidt*, Berlin 1967, 421 ff., cited by N. Horn, loc. cit., 340.

[4] *Cons.* cit., fol. 19vb; here also the statement concerning the right to wage wars like kings 'de plenitudine potestatis'.

[5] Details in Savigny, op. cit., vi. 312 ff.; N. Horn, loc. cit., 273.

in fact and in law the same position as the emperor himself had.[1] In other words, Western contemporaries were thoroughly familiar with the duke's imperial vicariate. No doubt, he made the most of it, as the disputes concerning his constitutional standing amply prove. The proposal, therefore, to appoint him now an imperial vicar of the Greek emperor can hardly have made a profound impression on him. It causes no surprise that nothing further was heard of this embassy or its suggested radical solution or of the duke's reaction.

Yet despite its fantastic character this step—assuredly unofficially taken with a view to ascertaining the duke's attitude—demands attention because it symptomatically reveals the complete lack of realistic assessment on the part of what the memorandum calls 'high-placed Greeks'. It shows that even at this late hour some Greek sections or factions were unable to free themselves from the by then wholly unrealistic, petrified ideology and preferred to withdraw into what had become a mystique of the empire's origin and raison d'être. The démarche manifests some quite alarming dimensions of unfamiliarity with the actual conditions in the West and pursues illusory, if not grotesque, aims. But assuredly this was not the only illusion and the only manifestation of contemporary unrealism. Was the Florentine declaration of the union any more realistic? Was the attitude of the Basleans during the crucial year of 1439 that witnessed the 'healing' of the East-West schism as well as the election of an anti-pope and thus the emergence of a (new) schism within the Western Church, any more realistic? What permits of no doubt is the crucial role which Constantinople played at the very beginning of the medieval era and towards its end.[2] In the early period it was the vigorous and sustained challenge to the West which the papacy accepted with alacrity—in the late medieval period Constantinople was a mere phantom that believed in its own mystique which was dissociated from all contact with reality. Nevertheless, a not dissimilar observation could be made about the Latins: they employed blunted, stale and worn theses. It was as if the via moderna had not yet made its entry upon the milieu of the governing strata of society: both Greek and Latin had not only grown old and fatigued, but were also impervious to the change of wind. They fought the same old battles all over again, oblivious of the indisputable and fundamental changes in the intellectual, religious, social and political fields, changes that is which left their indelible imprints on many sections of contemporary society. They, however, were as yet—due to a long historical process—unable to enter the precincts of decision making bodies in an effective and constitutional way. Yet both Greek and Latin were soon to share a common fate and to live through traumatic experiences—the one at the hands of the Turks who came as the invading destroyer and foreign enemy; the other, a generation later, approached

---

[1] Ed. Consilia, Lugdunum 1585, vol. i, Cons. 2, fol. 4ᵛ, no. 9.
[2] For some reflexions on this topic cf. Short History, 306 ff.

the precipice of self-destruction and self-mutilation as a consequence of self-inflicted wounds and fratricidal internal strife that was to break asunder what within the Latin orbit had been one undivided Christendom. It was a split that was to shape the destiny of Europe to this day. But all these are reflexions which are outside my topic, however much prompted by a neglected source, the historic significance of which lies in its illustration of the frame of mind of influential Greeks on the threshold of Byzantium's last agony.[1]

[1] The importance of the memorandum makes it advisable to append the entry in full. I have collated the original with the text in *RTA*. xiv. 57 without adopting the latter's questionable punctuation. I would like to thank Mr. R. V. Kerr, of the University Library Cambridge for his help with some textual problems.

Appendix
Report of a Greek approach to the duke of Milan: late 1438–early 1439

O: Original in Hohenlohe Archives: Neuenstein, Germany: GA, part IV, G59, no. 25, saec. xv.

W: Ed. H. Weigel in *RTA* xiv. 57, no. 20.

Nuper quidam honorati greci de ferraria missi ad ducem mediolani exposuerunt quod in primordio ecclesie universalis monarchia orbis fuit integra.[a] Indivisa gubernacula eius rememorando tempora constantini semper apud grecos remanserant usque nichephorus et michahel imperatores pro utiliori gubernacione orbis assumpserunt sibi in adiutorium karolum magnum, cum quo pacta inierunt, ut karolus romam cum omni occidenti suique heredes gubernare deberent,[b] ipsi vero greciam et totum[c] orientem, alter alterius frater esse et appellari deberet et semper alter alterum iuvare. Defunctoque karolo suisque heredibus extranei sibi usurpaverunt imperium occidentis modo ytalici, modo germani. Tandemque in occidenti ordinatum fuerat preter et contra voluntatem grecorum quod in germania essent electores qui haberent imperatorem romanorum[d] sive occidentis[e] eligere de germanie gremio. Romanus eciam pontifex illum coronare et approbare haberet sicque, quia in preiudicium grecorum, apud quos principatus monarchicus esse debuit, hec divisio monarchie facta extitit,[f] imperium tam in oriente quam in occidente collapsum videtur. Monarchia ecclesiastica post hec et propterea fuit et est divisa: exhortando ducem quatinus operam daret ut ycumenicum[g] concilium in loco ad quem romanus pontifex commode venire posset, in ytalia presertim, celebraretur ibique de reparacione et reintegracione divisi orbis monarchie laboraretur eaque reintegrata facillime[h] ecclesiastica monarchia posset reuniri. Reparata monarchia orbis necessarium[i] foret in ytalia ordinare primo imperiale tribunal occidentis unumque perpetuum vicarium imperii coram quo universe[j] imperiales cause tractentur quique haberet feuda imperialia porrigere principibus comitibus et baronibus, consolando ducem quod ipse suique heredes perpetui vicarii imperii constitui deberent.

[a]W: reads *integra indivisa: gubernacula* . . .
[c]O and W: *totam*
[e]W: *occidentalem*
[g]O and W: *ycomenicum*
[i]W: *necesse*
[j]O: has *fere* or *fori* between *universe* and *imperiales*; W has *fere*, but queries original's *fori*.

[b]O: *deberet*; W: *deberent*
[d]W: *Romanum*
[f]W: reads *extitit; imperium* . . .
[h]O and W: *facilime*

352

XV

THE FUTURE OF MEDIEVAL HISTORY

Some seven years ago I had the privilege and honour
to deliver an inaugural lecture in which I attempted
to show why and in what way medieval ecclesiastical
history was relevant to the understanding of the
medieval period. Today I would like to address
myself to a different topic, one that has engaged my
attention for some time as no doubt it has occupied
the attention of many others. It would be somewhat
unrealistic to deny that the present state of medieval
studies causes some concern and calls for some re-
thinking and re-examination.

Leaving aside the malaise that afflicts all humanistic disciplines in a technological age, in which the
computer plays an increasingly decisive role, there
are some specific grounds that would seem to apply
with particular force to the medieval branch of
historical studies. One explanation for the retarded
progress and the lessening appeal of medieval studies
is what one might call over-specialisation of academic historical pursuits, conspicuous as this over-
specialisation is in chronological as well as topical
respects. There is an increasing and stifling concentration on smaller and smaller spans of time, and
allied to it there is a self-imposed confinement to
highly specialised topics within a small period.
Taken together these two features quite naturally
tend to make the study of medieval history less

appealing than it once was. Further, this self-imposed straitjacket leads to undesirable consequences: it leads to a special kind of Parkinson's law. The narrowing of historical interest generates its own momentum and is self-perpetuating, because the detailed, minute, not to say myopic examination brings forth its own offspring, only still smaller, more minute and more esoteric, produced by what Louis Halphen once called *le spécialiste de l'insignifiant*. Although my own work would appear to make this protestation unnecessary, let me nevertheless say as emphatically as I can that I am not against the examination of detailed questions, or against monographs, but what I would maintain is that they must not be an end in themselves, but merely a means to an end. It is excellent professional practice if the research student is made to edit a tract, some charters, a register, a *summa*, a badly neglected chronicle, and the like. This kind of work prevents him from making large, unsupported and unsupportable generalising statements, since he has to chart his way through a sometimes heart-breaking and nerve-racking thicket of obstacles and hurdles. No less beneficial is the diplomatic and paleographical examination or the detailed analysis of the influence of a particular literary movement or public institution. But, and this is a point which I would like to stress, this same scholar has a social duty to allow wider sections of the populace to partake in his own knowledge and expertise. In a word, the historical scholar and quite specifically the medievalist, has a twofold duty: one to his own speciality, to his own chosen field of scholarship, where he can justifiably claim expertise, and the other to society which after all maintains him and which makes it possible for him to apply himself with singular zeal to his own research. But this duty to society makes it imperative for him to return to it the fruits of his own research work and learning by putting his specialist work into a broader perspective. In many instances he will do this all the better and with all the greater success if he tries to apply his methods, techniques and topics to periods antecedent to and succeeding those which originally fired his research enthusiasm.

Among medievalists scores of most eminent scholars can be mentioned who have abundantly fulfilled these requirements. They were editors of the severest standards or profound analytical researchers of difficult historical, textual or seemingly minute specialist problems, yet they were also expositors of brilliant large-scale syntheses of wide stretches of medieval history. Because their expositions were based on their own research and expertise, they made wide sections of the populace share in their own knowledge. None had the benefit of secretaries, typewriters, xerox machines, microfilms, dictaphones, computers, and yet, we cannot do without the labours and the illuminating syntheses of, say, Louis Duchesne, Achille Luchaire, Fustel de Coulanges, or of Georg Waitz, Albert Hauck, Erich Caspar, or on this side of the Channel, William Stubbs and our own Maitland, not to mention those still happily among us. What they – and so many others of a bygone generation – did was to progress from scholarly analysis to scholarly synthesis, and what we are inclined to do is to stop at analysis and to be

3

impervious to the demands of the whole. The nowadays so generally favoured process of atomisation without any attempt to show how the individual parts fit into the whole and how they are bonded together to make the whole intelligible cannot be conducive to the promotion of medieval history and tends to make it esoteric. There is no such thing in medieval history as *pars pro toto*. No doubt, here is a very serious problem: on the one hand there is the text-book writer who keeps a most respectful distance from the sources, but in compensation adopts a condescending tone and lavishly supplies glossy pictures which are the centre piece of attraction on the coffee-table; on the other hand there is the pure researcher who is so immersed in his microscopic problems that he does not see the wood for the trees. I believe there is a way of steering safely between Scylla and Charybdis not necessarily by large-scale syntheses, but by turning a number of topics which now lead a semi-autonomous existence into integral parts of the study of the Middle Ages. What I would plead for is integrative history. Permit me therefore on this occasion to indicate the way in which an integrative history can become fruitful and useful.

Since a great deal of history is concerned with public occasions, events, movements, developments, the material of history must be verifiable which explains the fundamental importance of records, mainly in written form relating as they do to externally detectable, tangible and concrete acts. Viceversa, the internal element, attitudes, moods, intentions, mental reservations, are of interest only in so far as they are relevant to the explanation of public-external acts, and verifiable by, or at least deducible from, concrete evidence. By general consent the individual, personal character measured by purely ethical and subjective standards, is not a prime object of serious historical study.

A distinctive mark of medieval historiography is its impersonal trait. The paucity of the other sources which would enable the historian to compose a picture of the actuality of social and public life, is similarly noteworthy: personal mémoirs, diaries, autobiographies, personal correspondence, confidential reports, private letters, pictorial fixations of moments and situations, and the dozens of other sources of information available to the modern historian in superabundance, are absent. Yet it is undeniable that these readily accessible materials harbour some dangers in so far as they are liable to convey a subjectively coloured appraisal or assessment and tend to impress upon the mind an album of unrelated photographic reproductions.

Because he has no such easy access to this kind of information, the medieval historian admittedly suffers from a disadvantage which on closer inspection however turns out not to be without benefit, because he is forced to focus on the one unimpeachable, unassailable and reliable source – the law. In order to compose an adequate picture of social and public life, there can be no better qualified guide than the law. The law was the one vehicle, the one instrument that barred subjective assessment and imprinted itself indelibly upon the whole age. By its very nature law has objective standards and addresses itself only to external actions, to those which can be verified by hard-cash proof. Law as a norm and as a vehicle embodying as it does a theory, or an ideology, refers to the generality and again by definition excludes the specific individual elements. Law presupposes a collective entity, it presupposes a corporation (to use the all-pervading medieval concept). If he is to live up to his vocation, the medievalist has to bear in mind this basic view of society as a corporation. The concepts of law and of the corporation are complementary to each other. They have, moreover, a very distinguished ancestry: they are as much of Hellenistic provenance, as of biblical parentage and of Roman origin.

This brings me to my first postulate. In order to understand the substance, the very core of historical development in the Middle Ages it is indispensable to have at least a smattering of knowledge relative to basic jurisprudential principles. For that law which the medievalist meets at every turn and especially in the context of public and governmental actions, was alleged to be the external manifestation of the Christian faith. For very large stretches, if not for most of the essential issues, the law was held to be the vehicle which turned a number of Christian principles into a social standard of conduct and became thus a most conspicuous instrument of power. Law was the means which distilled a religious theme into the language of an objective norm.

This close link between a religiously orientated cosmology and the law is, I believe, unique to Western Europe. The link furnishes an explanation in a twofold respect. First, the standard of judgment and assessment is entirely objective: because no law addresses itself to a particular individual, it precludes subjective, personal or moralising evaluations, the refuge of the incompetent historical ignoramus. In so far, then, the law is more reliable than its subjective counterpart in the form of narratives which are necessarily of an episodical, if not ephemeral character. And because of the overwhelming importance attached to the law, its transmission is in a better shape than chronicles or other written records. Further, the overbearing weight of the law and the inseparably linked collectivist view explains why the individual personality was credited with so little importance in the historical process and why medieval historiography was on the whole impersonal. In itself the sharply accentuated objective standpoint is related to the uncontested medieval thesis of the establishment on earth of a divine order of things inaccessible to man's interference. The divine world order was held to be purely objective because impersonal and external to man himself. This dominant collectivist or corporational theme for understandable reasons relegated the individual traits to the background.

In close proximity to this theme stands the very character of the governmental programme which in some instances amounted to a blueprint. The king,. the bishop, the emperor, the pope, in short every governor was held to be the executive organ of a programme that was fixed for him, in admittedly general terms, on the occasion of his enthronement or his consecration, but which nevertheless provided a fairly circumscribed framework of governmental actions and functions to be fixed and formulated by the law. In formulating the law the governor was as often as not the expositor of vital governmental ideas and principles, and in so doing personified an indissoluble link between theory and practice, assuredly unparalleled in any other historical context.

The second and equally important explanation supplied by the close link between Christian cosmology and its outward social manifestation, the law, has reference to what should be one of the first lessons any undergraduate has to learn before he embarks upon medieval history, that is, the wholeness point of view, the totalitarian standpoint upon which the law and its underlying ideology rested. We are so easily inclined to differentiate between the various mental categories of the religious, moral, political and so on, that we forget how recent this atomisation really is. What counted was the whole man as a Christian, and not his political or religious facets. His actions, private or public, were directed towards (or were said to be directed towards) the attainment of an end that was not mundane, not of this world: the observer is here confronted by a concatenation of a religious axiom with the social phenomenon of the law, based as it was on the inseparability of life in this and the other world. Unilinearity or unipolarity were the axiomatic foundations, and not a bipolarity or multipolarity of social life, as there was no pluralistic society.

If law and jurisprudential principles were given their proper standing, a number of fascinating topics would be opened up. There is general agreement that in the earlier medieval period an amalgamation of Roman, Christian and Germanic elements took place. But how did this amalgamation manifest itself if not in jurisprudence? We have no contemporary tracts or books on this process of coalescence and yet it progressed steadily. Law provided the common platform on which this fusion could effortlessly take place. And law as a social phenomenon must by its nature be flexible and adjust itself to social realities. Translated into concrete terms this means that there was an approximation of Roman law to Germanic customs and practices, notably between the sixth and ninth centuries as amply evidenced by the codes of which the Visigothic example was but one conspicuous instance. Further, the kind of Christianity that fertilised the fallow soil of Western Europe, had already been imbued with legal elements that betrayed a powerful parentage, that is the legalism of the Old Testament in conjunction with Roman jurisprudence. It was a singularly potent combination, all the more so when Roman jurisprudence was infused into the very body of early Christianity. Tertullian's influence was to reverberate throughout the medieval period and beyond, and together with the Vulgate which employed Roman law language to convey the meaning of the ancient Hebrew and Greek text, proved to be an irresistible force in Western Europe. And yet because of the variegated character of this biblical, Hellenistic and Roman fusion it was highly elastic and adjustable and could without much effort absorb alien Germanic elements into its own system. Medieval studies have hardly begun to penetrate into this integrated matrix of the period. Only recently have we been enabled to have glimpses of the ideological kinship between the Germanic *Munt* and the Roman *tutela* and the Pauline background. It was a singularly effective harmony which yielded one of the most influential governmental principles relative to rulership in a Christian setting. The same accord can be witnessed in the fusion of Roman with Christian cosmology before the very first century of the Christian era was out: I refer to the genuine *Prima Clementis* which was the basis of the hierarchical ordering of society throughout the subsequent ages. How many medievalists are aware of the roots of functionalism, of order, of the social grading, and of the hierarchy of ranks? How many think of, let alone investigate, the possibility that the prohibition on the alienation of public rights and goods had some of its roots in the Pauline arsenal? And if there is the one or the other who points to a particular strain in the integrated whole, he meets with nothing but blank looks or with horrified amazement at his intellectual adventurousness. A good deal of intellectual parochialism has to be overcome if medieval studies are to make tangible progress.

A further observation is called for. For understandable reasons there is especially in the earlier period an intimate connection between jurisprudential and religious thought. The result of this link was what for want of a better term I call juristic theology. It was this juristic theology which affected virtually all segments of public life. The most obvious instance of juristic theology was baptism which is always thought of as a mere sacramental–liturgical act: certainly it was this, but the medievalist who wishes to penetrate into the texture of medieval society, realises that baptism was also an eminently (and perhaps even pronouncedly) juristic act. It was a rebirth of hitherto unsuspected dimensions which can adequately be assessed only if the ideological, social and constitutional consequences of this juristic act are correctly assessed. If the incorporation of the individual into the body public is disregarded, one will find it difficult to explain on the one hand why excommunication was so formidable a legal and social measure, and on the other hand it is hardly possible to comprehend the renaissance of man, which resulted from the transformation of the mere subject into the citizen in the political field – one of the major historical revolutions, when the wholeness point of view began to give way to departmentalisation and atomisation. What I would plead for is that the rudiments of jurisprudence and basic religious–biblical knowledge be integrated into medieval historical studies. By this integrating process justice would be done at long last to the wholeness point of view on which all shades of opinion in the Middle Ages were agreed.

There is one more genre of sources to which I would like to draw special attention, because they are in urgent need of integration. These sources embody so to speak applied juristic theology in the shape of concrete symbolism. The various Orders for the ritual of royal coronations, imperial coronations, papal consecrations and coronations as well as the actual symbols used, including the clothing and other apparel which served as objects that were readily comprehensible as typifying specific power associations, should constitute an integral part of medieval studies. Symbolism partakes of theology, liturgy and jurisprudence and the Orders epitomise the essential functions of the gubernator and demonstrate by their own language the structure of governmental power. The great value of symbolism lies in that the meaning of the ritual is not accessible to several interpretations, but to one only, because the meaning of the idea to be symbolically expressed by special gestures, actions, prayers, etc. had to be grasped by the most dull-witted contemporary. Hence in order to exclude ambiguity, a very great deal of mental labour went into the ritual instructions. Medieval symbolism was the instrument that clothed the invisible abstract idea in the visible and readily comprehensible concrete gesture or emblem. The significance of whole ideological programmes was conveyed in this practical manner. Above all, the symbols were the easily discernible signposts of the structure of power in the Middle Ages. Fortunately, much excellent pioneering work has been done in recent decades – I only need to mention Eichmann, Schramm, Heinrich Mitteis, Elze, Folz – so that present-day research can build on very secure foundations.

The opulence of symbolism enshrined in the *Ordines* is at times quite overwhelming – and yet how little use is made of it. There is a pressing need for detailed comparative studies of at least the royal coronation *Ordines* – the English, French, German and Spanish are almost all now accessible to research – which show the genesis and mutual influences and individual strains not merely in the *Ordines* but above all in the respective constitutional developments. Of no less interest are the ideological contents of the imperial and papal coronation *Ordines,* because they distilled the relative functions of pope and emperor into the unmistakable language of symbolism. Take unction and compare its imperial development with that of its royal counterpart, and no dispute can arise about the role allocated to the emperor by the papacy; or take the total absence of unction in the papal coronation; or take the highly revealing omission of an enthronement in an imperial coronation service and you will get the proper measure of the function of the emperor far more reliably than from any medieval or modern discussion. One can go as far as to say that because modern medievalists – and not all of them are obtuse – have disregarded medieval symbolism, a number of wholly unnecessary confusions has arisen, and one of them concerns the very standing and function of a so-called Roman emperor created by the pope. A great deal of work has still to be done relative to the fructifying effects of royal anointings upon episcopal functions and the concomitant constitutional and social consequences. What were the actual intellectual feeders of this development? The interactions and differences between Byzantine coronations and their Western imitations are topics which have been shelved for far too long. By what stages and by what media did this imitation come about? The *Ordines* are more faithful mirrors of constitutional developments than the commonly available written documents, which as often as not are fragmentary and incompletely transmitted. A rather notable instance is the 4th clause in Edward II's coronation promise which

13

mirrored the constitutional development unsurpassably well: no writing, no tract, no gloss, could have conveyed the meaning as succinctly as this source. Do not the English coronation Orders of the fifteenth century rather faithfully mirror a strong theocratic resurgence? Would this not possibly help to explain the fortunes of the monarchy a generation or two afterwards? What vast virtually untapped sources of information have been neglected by failing to integrate medieval liturgical symbolism into the study of medieval history. Instead of taking a panoramic view of all the essentials, modern medievalists all too often focus their vision on the parish pump and take offence if they are reminded of the numerous and substantial segments of which they are blissfully ignorant, but which only in their totality can yield a historically correct portrait.

What is true of inauguration symbolism, can *mutatis mutandis* be applied to coins and written documents. The former are not only very reliable and succinct guides to the reconstruction of basic governmental conceptions as demonstrated by their inscriptions, but they also are – and perhaps foremost – means that provide us with hard-cash evidence with which to fathom the economy at a given time. Apart from this, coins have in the course of their long development, served a great many other purposes: they constituted ready-made devices for the propagandistic dissemination of particular political ideologies. But it is superfluous for me to elaborate this topic, since the relevance of numismatics to history has been shown in a most authoritative manner. Indeed, it is gratifying to record that this University has for many years shown itself alive to the importance of the subject.

As to official documents, it is, I think, high time that the view was discarded according to which formulae in documents are no more than 'mere' formulae. Diplomatic, administrative and institutional history peremptorily demand that the formulae be credited with the importance which they intrinsically po⸱sessed. Of course, chancery products employed stereotyped formulae, but they were pregnant short-hand devices embodying whole programmes. Take the case of the change of intitulation from a *Rex Anglorum* or *Rex Francorum* to that of *Rex Angliae* or *Rex Franciae* and you will at once see the deep significance of this for the development of territorial sovereignty that in course of time was to replace personal sovereignty. A chain reaction follows if one tries to ask necessarily related questions: why, for instance, was the episcopal intitulation always territorially orientated? – you do not hear of an *episcopus Eliensium* or *Lincolniensium* and you always have an intitulation which is related not to persons, but to things. This contrast between the personal sovereignty of the king and the reified position of the bishop – or for that matter of the duke or markgrave – is surely a matter urgently needing investigation to which the 'mere' diplomatic formulae give rise. The *Rex Dei gratia* a mere formula or an expression of devotion? How naive. The vast theme of grace–disgrace, *Gnade–Ungnade*, *gratia–indignatio*, was telescoped into the briefest formula. To call all these mere formulae is an ineffectual disguise for intellectual sloth and torpor.

Recent diplomatic researches have shown what rewarding insights even such brittle charter materials as the Carolingian documents have yielded, notably in respect of the history of personages and the very revealing manner in which governmental ideology could be expressed in otherwise innocuous looking formulae.

No more than a rudimentary but integrated knowledge of jurisprudence combined with a smattering of liturgy and theology is necessary to enable us to have a better understanding of the presuppositions which gave rise to the idea of the rule of law, to the very medieval concept of the *Rechtsstaat* which the medievalist meets at every turn. It was a concept that was fundamental to society, even if in practice numerous exemptions from the rule were observable, such as dispensations, immunities, and so on, but even so, the exemption itself was a juristic measure within a due process of law. The rule of law was one of the numerous beneficial bequests of the medieval world: it meant primacy of reason over violence and brute force.

The overwhelming significance attached to the idea of law explains the exuberance of juristic symbolism. This juristic symbolism manifested itself in a number of ways which are particularly important from the point of view of integration. Heraldry is a notable part of social and constitutional history and is above all a means which allows us to understand the social stratification in the Middle Ages and to comprehend the internal development of the estates – of the higher and lower aristocracy, the knights, etc. – as well as of the later extension of armorial rights to institutions and corporate personalities, such as towns, guilds, colleges. Armorial language is precise, concise and mirrors political and constitutional designs faithfully. And because law played so vital a role, the importance of the other kind of juristic symbolism is easily understandable, that is, the significance of the seal as the necessary means of authentication of documents. The documentary seal had additionally served as a vehicle of governmental propaganda, and the types and kinds of portraits, the choice of the inscription and the architectural impregnations on the seal were first-rate symbolic indications relative to status and political–governmental intentions. Heraldry is also as much part of the history of art as numismatics forms an essential part of economic history. Sphragistics as much as heraldry, numismatics and diplomatic are all long overdue for a full integration into the medieval historical syllabus.

The growth of medieval universities offers persuasive proof of the importance which jurisprudential themes had assumed. The very first European seats of learning were the law schools at Pavia, Ravenna and above all the queen of all legal studies, Bologna. Not only was jurisprudence the first subject that was academically studied, and therefore the begetter of the universities (chronologically preceding Paris) but it was also the subject that became instrumental in the eventual emancipation of the layman. One must never forget that it was exclusively lay people who originally populated Bologna; it was lay people who created what had not existed in the ancient world, that is a university which was appropriately

17

enough called a corporation of masters and students. Precisely because it was the law that constituted the central issue in the Investiture Contest, the layman came to realise what the claims of the hierocratic party signified, and he fought back with the at the time superior weapon, the mature and richly developed Roman law, thereby setting in train an evolution that only now begins to be slowly appreciated: it was the process of secularisation that affected constitutions, institutions, organisations, thought as well as governments. In meeting the challenge the laymen potently prepared the revolution of the thirteenth and fourteenth centuries wrought by the rediscovery of Aristotle. The emergence of the secular or ancient Romanism was but one though perhaps the most important result of this process of emancipation: ecclesiastical Romanism was relegated to its proper role. A great deal of correction is required to rid modern generations of the one-sided view of clerical monopoly in the Middle Ages.

This last reflection leads me to a related topic. There are several points of contact between the medievalist and the modern social scientist, and the great popularity which the social sciences enjoy is explicable by the urge to find out the internal mechanics and the working principles of our present society. The medievalist has here a slight advantage in that he is in the enviable position of standing on very firm evidential ground: at his disposal is the surest social guide, the law. In his inimitable and concise manner the Olympian of this University once said that 'Law was the point where life and logic

met.' There are some very rewarding fields of enquiry for the historical sociologist (if the species does
not exist, it is high time it came into being) or his
more modest colleague, the social historian. To
begin with there was the legislation of the numerous
medieval councils in all parts of Western Europe.
In this context the very function of law as the social
norm comes to its fruition, since it sanctions or
ostracises certain modes of conduct. The councils
– general, provincial, diocesan – were chief instruments which put Christian precepts into the concise
language of the law. They were composed of men
who not only overwhelmingly came from the very
strata of society for which they legislated, but also
knew from first-hand experience what needed to be
done at the grass-roots of society. Conciliar decrees
were a mirror of social practices to be enforced and
strengthened, of social malpractices and abuses to be
eliminated, of usages which one age was to consider
essential for the functioning of society and another
age to declare superstitious. The social historian has
here a literally speaking untapped reservoir; the
councils were barometers of public opinion, for the
synodists could hardly declare law what was unacceptable to those who were to live by it. The neg-
lect of this source essential for social (and also constitutional) history is all the more regrettable, as at
least for the central medieval English period an
exemplary and authoritative edition of the synods
and councils with a wealth of ancillary material is
now readily at hand, the result of decades of in-
defatigable work by my distinguished predecessor
in office. Further, of all the numerous medieval

assemblies the councils are the only ones of which we frequently know the names and the standing of the participants. New and profitable perspectives can be gained from a study of these personalities: who were they? what was their social, cultural, educational, economic background? are some of the questions which impinge themselves upon us. These indeed are gates to untapped sources of *Persönlichkeits-forschung*. What rich material the conciliar decrees have for comparative studies, let alone for comparing the state of religious–social affairs East and West! Several books on the sociology of religion have in recent years appeared full of speculative reflection and little evidential support – but here within a firm historical framework and hard-cash evidence in abundance a very rich field still awaits the expositor.

In proximity to this topic stands another source of social history that is badly in need of integration. I refer to the *Consilia* of the jurists from the thirteenth to the sixteenth centuries. They were approached from all parts of Europe and functioned like un-official courts of justice: their well-considered opinions had the stamp of finality. Now these *Consilia* are not only interesting in themselves as first-class juristic exercises in which the juristic scalpel was wielded with great skill, but above all they are important documents which illuminate social conditions: the status of an individual or a corporation such as a guild or a municipality, relations between a monastery and a town, the growth and decay of privileges appertaining to groups or classes, the growing nationality principle and the application of the idea of territorial sovereignty to problems of taxation, liability to military dues, advisability of undertaking a military campaign or even a crusade, problems of citizenship, its acquisition and loss, mining rights, fishing rights, maritime law – these are just a few most frequently occurring topics one meets in the *Consilia*. They reflect reality to a degree to which hardly any other source can aspire. The great issues of the day were also submitted to the jurists, such as difficult border conflicts, questions of validity of elections, termination of schisms within the Church, the validity of royal or papal electoral pacts (the Capitulations), and so on. Literally speaking thousands of *Consilia* of the late medieval period are still hibernating in dusty and worm-eaten tomes. Baldus alone wrote not less than 2061 *Consilia*, many of them lengthy tracts. Paulus Castrensis had 1206 *Consilia* to his credit, while Philipus Corneus reached the respectable number of 1358. There was hardly a jurist who had not written several hundred *Consilia*.

The public and its opinion have been major forces in modern society for some time. From a purely genetic point of view there should long have been an attempt to discover how and why the public at large came to play a determinative role in social and political life, or to put the question technically, what contributed to the replacement of the descending theme of government and law by its ascending counterpart? Posed from this angle, the topic needing immediate attention is the polemical and publicistic literature of the late eleventh and early twelfth centuries, its social impact and the slow

channelling of these private efforts into official
avenues, so that what was once pure scholarship
becomes by the mid-thirteenth century centralised,
governmental propaganda in the shape of manifestoes, encyclicals, appeals, and so on, composed by
able ghost-writers, only to give way a generation or
two afterwards to the universities which became the
platform for influencing public opinion – witness
France in the early fourteenth century – and later
throughout Europe the bearer of the anti-Establish-
ment forces, culminating in the Conciliar Movement.
It would be a fascinating and urgent study to pursue
the means by which the public and its opinion came
to assume the dimensions which they did, so much
so that by the mid-fifteenth century they acted
like powerful subterranean agents pressing upwards
from below the surface. The emancipation of the
third estate was firmly embedded in this process.
The forces of the Establishment reacted not unexpectedly: like frightened sheep they huddled together to resist the onward march of the third
estate – fear of the amorphous multitudes was what
drove the Establishment forces together (witness the
Concordats in the fifteenth century, the wholesale
flight of the conciliarists, the prophesies of doom and
disaster in the diets of the mid-fifteenth century at
the prospect of the new masses being admitted into
the political arena). Most of the relevant material is
easily available – what is needed is a study in the
growth of education and the role governments
played in fostering higher education, with consequences not always foreseeable by, or welcome to,
the patrons. That herewith detailed comparative

studies would necessarily follow, seems evident enough. A rewarding by-product would be a considerable advance of our knowledge and understanding of the infrastructure of society and linked with it the emergence of its conceptual abstraction, the State.

It is certainly worth mentioning that whereas throughout the fifteenth century the idea of Europe widens externally in the age of explorations, it divides itself internally and loses much of its inner coherence and consistency as a result of the collapse of a religiously united Europe. It would seem that the Reformation and the internal shrinkage of Europe have insufficiently attracted the attention of the medievalists. Correctly seen, the Reformation is not so much the beginning of a new age, as the final phase of the medieval period. The forces which were to display their full effects, had assuredly been observable for several generations before the Reformation. The aversion from the objective, collectivist, corporative conceptions and the predilection for the subjective, individualistic view point with the ancillary postulate of freedom of choice and consent and similar manifestations of the *pre-Reformation* era, can adequately be appraised, assessed and evaluated only by the medievalist, because he has seen the infancy, puberty and growth of the ideology that was now rapidly being replaced, and he therefore is all the better equipped to judge the to my mind crucial development historically. But how many medievalists do this? How many have seen that there was a problem or the extent of the change between, say, the early fourteenth and the mid-fifteenth centuries?

The division of Europe from the early sixteenth century onwards warrants a few observations which are particularly apposite from the point of view of integrative history. For this division proceeded on lines not at all dissimilar to those which in an earlier age conditioned the division of Europe into its Latin and Greek half. In both it was juristic theology which furnished the backcloth and largely explained the subsequent evolution. The lack of integrative history makes itself quite specially felt in this context, for one of the weightiest and most serious deficiencies in medieval history is the omission of Constantinople as one of the potent forces which directly or indirectly contributed to the making of Europe and of its history. The excision of Byzantine history from medieval European studies does indeed seem to me an unforgivable offence against the very spirit of history.

It was juristic theology which had so conspicuously formed the physiognomy of medieval Europe, precisely that kind of Christianity against which Luther rebelled. But historically speaking this juristic theology was itself the result of the challenge which New Rome had issued to Old Rome. Old Rome epitomised by the Church of Rome, considered the relevant governmental actions of New Rome, of Constantinople, a challenge to its own existence, a challenge to its survival as a governing institution, a challenge to its vocation and profession. Challenge frequently mobilises latent forces and resources. In meeting this challenge of New Rome, the Church of Old Rome constructed a conception of Christianity with the most Roman of all Roman tools – the

Roman law. This kind of Christianity was however unacceptable to New Rome for reasons which I have tried to explain elsewhere. The emergence of the ideological notion of Europe in the eighth/ninth centuries held together by the faith fixed and formulated by means of the law, was historically speaking indissolubly linked with the rift between Old and New Rome. It was on the débris of Old Rome that Europe as a Latin-orientated unit came into being in the process of which ancient Germanic customs were either absorbed or swept away. The geographical extent of Europe no longer corresponded to the ideological concept. For a better understanding of the structure and infrastructure of the course of medieval history it is imperative that attention be paid to the genesis of a divided medieval Europe. Papal Rome and imperial Constantinople were indeed the two cornerstones upon which the development of medieval history rested. The omission of Constantinople from our medieval history syllabus is as grave a deficiency as the omission of the USA or of the USSR would be from a course that dealt with modern twentieth-century Europe. Was Byzantium not part of Europe? Was its theology, philosophy, historiography, poetry, its civilisation Asiatic? Was it not in fact the consummation of Rome and Hellas? Is it not a sign of arrogance on the part of us Westerners to regurgitate in an unthinking manner the medieval–ecclesiastical view that Byzantium was not European? The theme of Old and New Rome was the one theme that accompanied the course of medieval history from the first to the eleventh Constantine. The theme is observable in religious, ecclesiological, cultural, social, theological and above all in governmental respects, and this from Sicily to Scotland, from Iberia to Poland and Hungary. The rivalry sometimes erupted into open schisms and conflicts, sometimes giving rise to military undertakings, sometimes to formal and stately meetings between the contending parties, but it was always there in one form or another. Without the integration of Byzantium any study of the genesis and evolution of medieval Europe is bound to remain fragmentary, if not misleading, intellectually parochial, if not disingenuous, and historically suspect.

This postulated integration would of itself promote comparative studies, and one of the topics that requires close analytical treatment is the social and governmental effect exercised by language. We forget so easily that in the West Latin was a foreign language to most people in the Middle Ages. As a spoken language Latin had died out in the sixth century. The language in the official documents as well as the language of the learned writer and the polished historiographer and poet remained Latin, which was also the language of the Church services. Ordinary folk spoke as little Latin as they do today. When the vernacular became recognised as a legitimate medium of communication in the West, it heralded, if it did not accompany, one of the really great intellectual revolutions effected as this was by Aristotelian cosmology. From the thirteenth century onwards the picture began to change radically. When we now look at Byzantium the official, learned and literary language was Greek, but it was also the language of ordinary folk, however demotic, however vulgarised their Greek was. They could understand, at least as far as language went, the official documents, and they could follow the Church services; they could read poetry and sing hymns in a tongue which was neither dead nor foreign to them, even if it may not have been their own private medium of communication. But this is an observation which can be made about any present-day language. Go into any Alpine village and you will discover how little the official or learned French or German or Italian is used by the peasants, and yet linguistically they will grasp an official text or even a contemporary poem.

Wide vistas and perspectives open up. One of the points which an integrated history will have to tackle at once is the very term of 'Romans', because both the Westerners and the Easterners called themselves Romans. It is a term that looks innocuous enough, but one which admits of two quite different meanings, notably in governmental respects, the one historical in its genesis, the other ecclesiastical, and yet the spoken language of neither Westerner nor Easterner was Latin. Not far removed from this semantic problem stands one that touches the nerve-centre of basic governmental relations. In the West the alienation of those 'below' from those 'above' was very conspicuous from the ninth century onwards; in fact, the alienation was of great help in perpetuating the descending theme of government, yet – and this is only seemingly paradoxical – this alienation was far less marked in Byzantium if I interpret the course of Byzantine history correctly, although at first sight you would have thought that the distance between the emperor as divinity walking on earth, and his subjects was unbridgeable. A whole cluster of problems of profound importance emerges in this very context, and only an integrated kind of history will be able to give satisfactory answers.

You have allowed me to put before you some of the topics, subjects and sources which I would hold are significant enough to be integrated into the framework of a general course on medieval history. Anatomical dissection of individual topics should not be replaced by integrating syntheses but be supplemented, enriched and brought to fruition by integrating what is now autonomous into the whole, so that what formerly led an existence of its own becomes an essential, integral and indispensable part of the totality. If this integration entails the promotion of interdisciplinary studies, for instance, anthropology or medieval literature or medieval art in their manifold variations, all participating branches of learning will derive profit. The mutual fructification cannot fail to be beneficial, and will evidently widen the scope and depth of medieval history in particular. The observer's panoramic view of the several integral elements makes the historical process intelligible and its explanation intellectually satisfying, in a word, this *Zusammenschau* is I think the surest guarantee that the study of the Middle Ages can never degenerate into a sterile branch of learning, but one that because of the multiformity of the component parts is continually posing new problems, demanding new perspectives and pointing towards new horizons. It was the unparalleled richness of the

totality of outlook and the kaleidoscopic character
of the components which in the final resort explains
how and why this long period of some 1200 years
could effortlessly sustain itself and why contemporaries – in this respect assuredly in no wise different
from ourselves – were ever finding new ways and
new methods and new solutions to old problems.
What the medieval world lacked in physical extent,
was amply compensated for by the fertility of mental
resourcefulness and the infinite ingenuity of man's
intellectual capacities matched worthily by the
totality of our ancestors' spiritual vision. By studying
them we can find out what we were before we
have become what we are today.

You may have been wondering whether the time
was propitious for proposing a programme that requires for its successful execution considerable intellectual stamina, discipline and penetration into the
matrix of the sources. It is precisely these requirements which appear to be undervalued if recent
trends are indicative, and this indubitably casts
a shadow on the future of medieval history, at least
locally. I appeal not so much to my colleagues as to
intellectually alert and discriminating members of
the younger generation (because upon them the
future rests), to put aside apathy, prejudice, and pre-
conceived views and to show themselves worthy of
their ancestors – academically and ideologically
– who made it possible for them to pursue within the
precincts of one of the most ancient European seats
of learning the richly rewarding path of history. For
what may be a threat to medieval history today,
will assuredly become a threat to all proper historical

pursuits tomorrow. Although a critical period may well lie ahead for the study of history in general, there is nevertheless sufficient backbone, resilience, vigour and an unquenchable searching spirit in the younger generation to enable them to come through the crisis victoriously and to view the future with justifiable optimism.

INDEX